Upbuilding Black Durham

The John Hope Franklin
Series in African American
History and Culture
Waldo E. Martin Jr. &
Patricia Sullivan, editors

Upbuilding
BLACK
Durham

GENDER, CLASS, AND BLACK

COMMUNITY DEVELOPMENT

IN THE JIM CROW SOUTH

LESLIE BROWN

The University of North Carolina Press   Chapel Hill

Parts of this book have been reprinted with permission in revised form
from the following works: Leslie Brown, "Sisters and Mothers Are Called
to the City: African American Women and an Even Greater Migration,"
in *Stepping Forward: Black Women in Africa and the Americas*, edited by
Catherine Higgs, Barbara A. Moss, and Earline Rae Ferguson (Athens:
Ohio University Press, 2002); Leslie Brown and Anne M. Valk, " 'Our
Territory': Race, Place, Gender, Space, and African American Women in
the Urban South," in *Her Past Around Us: Interpreting Sites for Women's
History*, edited by Polly Welts Kaufman and Katharine T. Corbett
(Malabar, Fla.: Kreiger Press, 2003); Leslie Brown and Anne M. Valk,
"Black Durham Behind the Veil: A Case Study," *OAH Magazine of History*
18 (January 2004); and Leslie Brown, "African American Women and
Migration," in *The Practice of U.S. Women's History: Narratives, Intersections,
and Dialogues*, edited by S. Jay Kleinberg, Eileen Boris, and Vicki L. Ruiz
(New Brunswick, N.J.: Rutgers University Press, 2007).

Library of Congress Cataloging-in-Publication Data

Brown, Leslie, 1954–
Upbuilding Black Durham : gender, class, and Black community
development in the Jim Crow South / Leslie Brown.
p. cm. — (John Hope Franklin series in African American history and
culture)
Includes bibliographical references and index.
ISBN 978-0-8078-3138-0 (cloth : alk. paper)
ISBN 978-0-8078-5835-6 (pbk. : alk. paper)
1. African Americans—North Carolina—Durham—History. 2. African
Americans—North Carolina—Durham—Social conditions. 3. African
American women—North Carolina—Durham—History. 4. Sex role—
North Carolina—Durham—History. 5. African Americans—North
Carolina—Durham—Biography. 6. Community life—North Carolina—
Durham—History. 7. Social change—North Carolina—Durham—
History. 8. Social classes—North Carolina—Durham—History.
9. Durham (N.C.)—Social conditions. 10. Durham (N.C.)—Race
relations. I. Title.
F264.D9B83 2008
305.896'0730756563—dc22   2008008444

cloth   12 11 10 09 08   5 4 3 2 1
paper   12 11 10 09 08   5 4 3 2 1

THIS BOOK WAS DIGITALLY PRINTED

For family and friends,
and Annie

Contents

Acknowledgments ix

Prologue 1

Introduction 9

1 Seek Out a Good Place: Making Decisions in Freedom 27

2 Durham's Narrow Escape: Gendering Race Politics 55

3 Many Important Particulars Are Far from Flattering: The Gender
Dimensions of the "Negro Problem" 81

4 We Have Great Faith in Luck, but Infinitely More in Pluck: Gender
and the Making of a New Black Elite 109

5 We Need to Be as Close Friends as Possible: Gender, Race, and the
Politics of Upbuilding 147

6 Helping to Win This War: Gender and Class on the Home Front 217

7 Every Wise Woman Buildeth Her House: Gender and the Paradox of
the Capital of the Black Middle Class 249

8 There Should Be . . . No Discrimination: Gender, Class, and Activism
in the New Deal Era 285

9 Plenty of Opposition Which Is Growing Daily: Gender, Generation,
and the Long Civil Rights Movement 309

Conclusion 331

Epilogue 343

Notes 345

Bibliography 395

Index 427

A section of photographs follows p. 188.

Acknowledgments

My father grew up in the Jim Crow South and never learned to read or write. But I am finishing a book that discusses the distance between our lives. From then to now, there were countless people who encouraged, pushed, shoved, protested, threatened, cajoled, and enticed me to finish this project, just as there were countless people who did the same thing on behalf of black education in the age of Jim Crow.

Many people have parented, befriended, mentored, and allied with me. It would take another book to mention them all. I begin by thanking my parents, the late James and Louana Brown, who made sure that education was a central part of my life experience. The late Grace and Clifford Knight and the late Ben Wiggins reinforced that priority, and special thanks go to Marjorie J. Wiggins, who reminded me that the elders would be proud. Thanks also to my sister and brothers, Cece, Brian, Martin, and Raymond; to Uncle Jerry and Christine; and to Thomas "Daddy Mack" McLester.

This work would not have been possible without the cooperation and interest of the people who agreed to share their life stories, among them, Addie Marie Faulk, Constance Merrick Moore, Mabel Harris, Johnnie McLester (who turned out to be my aunt), Josephine Dobbs Clement, Theresa Jan Cameron Lyons, and Loretha Parker. Thelma Bailey Lanier and Julia Lucas adopted me, opening their homes (and refrigerators) to me. They provided more wisdom and knowledge than scholarship alone could offer, and they kept me on track when I wandered. Their insights, which came from their years behind the veil, helped me to link the past and the present. They are missed.

In everyone's life there are special groups of people who are the cheerleaders. I met mine at Skidmore College. They include Joanne Zangrando, Mary Lynn, and the members of the Department of American Studies; Tad Kuroda in the Department of History; the staff and students of the Higher Education Opportunity Program; and the Student Affairs staff. I owe special gratitude to Fran Hoffmann, Phyllis Roth, and the Spiders; to Robbie Nayman, Steve Earle, Jon Stein, John Ramsey, Ann Knickerbocker, Sue Layden, and Mimi and Ralph Ciancio; and to Mary Nell Morgan, who told me that I was just crazy enough to do this thing.

I could not have gotten through the fire of writing without the range of people who made the journey as personally fulfilling as it was professionally fulfilling. Tim Tyson (and Perry), Christina Greene (and Jim), Jennifer Morgan and Herman Bennett, Lisa Waller (and Sydney), Deborah Montgomerie (and Simon), Matthew Countryman, Karen Ferguson, Alex Byrd (and Jeannette), Charles McKinney, Celia Naylor, Stephanie Smallwood, Rod Clare, and many others created an interracial community that made scholarship a part of the political struggle. The Center for Documentary Studies provided an intellectual home and framework to understand how scholarship could be useful outside as well as inside the academy. The researchers and staff members of the project "Behind the Veil: Documenting African American Life in the Jim Crow South" made this project seem urgent and important. No one else knows how hard that work really was. In addition, Iris Hill, Paul Ortiz, Darnell Arnoult, and Greta Niu brought cheer and intellectual engagement to the "Behind the Veil" project — they took it seriously and made it fun.

Bill Chafe, Ray Gavins, Nancy Hewitt, Jacquelyn Hall, and Bob Korstad always believed that there was some substance in my work and treated me as a friend and colleague. Each of them read chapter after chapter over ten or more years. Thank you all for never telling me you were bored. Special appreciation goes to Nancy and Ray, whom I admire as model scholars, colleagues, and friends. I send a shout-out to Steven Lawson, who read more than his share of material, and to Anne Firor Scott for saying, "So what if they don't like your work; do it anyway."

Faculty members at Duke University and at the University of North Carolina at Chapel Hill created a welcoming and stimulating environment, including Claudia Koonz, Syd Nathans, Jan Ewald, Kristin Neuschel, Peter Wood, John Thompson, Barry Gaspar, Charles Payne, Monica Greene, and Henry Louis Gates Jr. Judith Bennett, Cynthia Herrup, Jackie Hall, and Suzanne Lebsock hosted and sustained the Feminist Women in History group, an opportunity for graduate and faculty women to engage each others' work and build a scholarly community in a noncompetitive setting where the M&Ms flowed with ease. Beverly Washington Jones, Alice Jones, and Freddie Parker in the Department of History at North Carolina Central University set me on the path to research in Durham and steered me in the right direction.

The professionals who staff research libraries rarely receive the profound recognition they deserve for their guidance and knowledge. At Duke University, Bill Erwin, Linda McCurdy, Zachary Elder, Christina Greene, Alex Byrd, Janie Morris, Virginia Daley, Elizabeth Dunn, Bob Byrd, and Nelda Webb led me to the rich sources in the manuscripts collection, allowed me access to unprocessed papers, and provided critical assistance. Lynn Richardson at the North Carolina Collection at the Durham County Library provided invaluable assistance and made it possible for me to collect wonderful photographs. I thank Doris Terry Williams and Dorothy Phelps Jones at the Hayti Heritage Center at North Carolina Central University for their collegiality and advice and for allowing me to use the collections, and I thank Andre D. Vann for lending me so many useful materials from his rich collection of Durham memorabilia. The staffs of special collections and manuscripts departments at the University of Maryland, the Moorland-Spingarn Research Center at Howard University, the Schomburg Center for Research in Black Culture at the New York Public Library, the Southern Historical Collection at Wilson Library at the University of North Carolina at Chapel Hill, and the North Carolina State Archives provided wonderful research experiences. The interlibrary loan staff at the University of Missouri at St. Louis and Washington University in St. Louis worked miracles.

Along the way, I had the good fortune to be surrounded by great colleagues at the University of Missouri at St. Louis, including Priscila Dowden, Adell Patton, Mark Burkholder, Gerda Ray, Andrew Hurley, and John Wolford. The chairs of the Department of History at Washington University, Derek Hirst and Hillel Kieval, always provided support, and John Baugh, the director of African and African American studies, ran interference when necessary. Henry Berger, Iver Bernstein, Howard Brick, Andrea Friedman, Maggie Garb, Steve Hause, Gerald Izenberg, David Konig, Peter Kastor, Linda Nicholson, Tim Parsons, and other history faculty made my stay at Washington University a worthy effort. Rafia Zafar, Mary Ann Dzubak, Gerald Early, Wayne Fields, and James McLeod made me a part of the campus contingent of political troublemakers. I'll miss the faculty of the Program in African and African American studies at Washington University — namely, Chris Bracey, Rudolph Clay, Jackie Dace, Garrett Duncan, Gerald Early, Ron Himes, Kim Norwood, Lester Spence, Mungai Muntoya, Shanti Parikh, Carl Phillips, Iyabo Osiapem, Priscilla Stone, Joe Thompson, Wilmetta Toliver-Diallo, and Sonia Stevenson — for their camaraderie, their good taste in music, and their faith in me. Robert Vinson and Rafia Zafar I single out for being good listeners. David Rowntree I thank for bringing excitement to the West Campus Library. Raye Riggins, Adele Tuchler, Sheryl Peltz, Molly Shailkewitz, and Margaret Williams, administrative staff and assistants, are forces of nature.

Particular recognition goes to Washington University's dean of Arts and Sciences, Edward Macias, for providing opportunities for leave to work on my book and for finally giving me the boot.

While at Washington University, I was fortunate to have a bright, energetic, and eclectic group of undergraduate and graduate students. Their liveliness, inquisitiveness, intellectual power, and teaching and research skills sustained my own enthusiasm for history. In ways they will never know, they saw me through the final stages of this project. Among them, Keona Ervin, Lorenzo Thompson, Michelle Repice, N'Jai-An Patters, Carmen Brooks, Michelle Purdy, and Dan Scallet kept my spirits up. On the other side of the river, Ellen Nore and Shirley Portwood, aka the Strawberry Ice Cream Gang, created the women's history reading group at Southern Illinois University at Edwardsville and allowed me to participate even when I showed up only for lunch and dessert. Other SIUE faculty extended to me their friendship and unofficial membership in the department of historical studies: Laura Milsk Fowler, Michaela Hoenecke, Michael Moore, Norman Nordhauser, Eric Ruckh, and Allison Thomason. And thank you to Scot Fowler for making things work.

Many people helped me to develop a scholarly voice as I worked on this book. I am grateful to Catherine Higgs, Rae Ferguson, Val Littlefield, and the participants in the "Black Women in the Old World and the New" conference, sponsored by the Ford Foundation at the University of Tennessee, and to Pat Sullivan, Waldo Martin, Emilye Crosby, and the participants in the Summer Institute on Civil Rights at the Du Bois Center at Harvard University. Eileen Boris, Jay Kleinberg, and Vicki Ruiz saw value in my work, as did Kathy Corbett and Polly Welts Kaufman. I owe much gratitude to Kathy Corbett for introducing me to Maine and good writing. I hope my pages provided additional covers through those Maine winters.

An ever-lengthening list of scholars have inspired me and influenced my work, including Tera Hunter, Elsa Barkley Brown, Rosalyn Terborg-Penn, Sharon Harley, Evelyn Brooks Higginbotham, Darlene Clark Hine, Chana Kai Lee, Nell Irvin Painter, Jacqueline Rouse, Paula Giddings, Francille Wilson, Michele Mitchell, Deborah Gray White, Robin D. G. Kelley, Stephanie Shaw, Temma Kaplan, Leon Litwack, Walter B. Weare, Drew Faust, Kevin Gaines, Glenda Gilmore, David Cecelski, Laura Edwards, and Cliff Kuhn.

John Hope Franklin Series editors Pat Sullivan and Waldo E. Martin Jr. and University of North Carolina Press senior editor Chuck Grench believed in this project and that I could do something I never envisioned myself doing. To them, and to David Perry, Paula Wald, Katy O'Brien, and other staff at the press, I owe more than I can ever pay. Thank you also to Elizabeth Kenyon for last-minute research assistance.

This book was made possible by the financial support of grants and fellowships from the National Endowment for the Humanities; the John Hope Franklin Center for African and African American Documentary; the North Caroliniana Society; the Department of Women's Studies, the Department of History, and the Center for Documentary Studies at Duke University; the Missouri Historical Society; and the Office of the Graduate Dean at Washington University and at the University of Missouri at St. Louis.

What do you say about the people who take you in when you feel abandoned? Thank you, Valorie, for walking with me in a green place, and Martha, for asking too many questions.

And then there are the people who sustain you. Pat Totten, Ken and Gretchen Davidian, Jessica Weiderhorn, Stephanie Gilmore, and Betsy Kaminski are friends for life; Kathy, Cathi, Dean, and Carl will always be neighbors; and Anita, Marylyn, Chase, Mary Ann, Emma, Betty, Celeste, and especially Connie are always with me.

Andrea Friedman and Marsha Sanguinette and their sons (my godchildren), Oscar and Corey, made me part of their family. Oscar and Corey brought joy to my life that I had not known before. Thank you for rowdy afternoons, family dinners, video games, and PG-rated movies and for your love, dedication, and embrace. Alex and Jeannette Byrd and the little Byrds, Benja and Jenna, made great allies, friends, and vacation companions. For hours we lolled in the pool, shared books, talked about history and politics, ate some of the best chicken imaginable, saw some of the worst movies ever made, searched for Jonah, and hung out in the parking lot of a Dairy Queen in rural Kentucky. What good times! My out-laws, I mean in-laws, the Valks —Jim and Judy, Eli, Laura, Hayley, Reggie, Heidi, Conrad, Jackson, Bennett, Jean, Hank, and Caroline—welcomed me with good humor to the family.

Last, I want to thank my partner, Annie Valk, who for more years than I can imagine has comforted me and loved me more than I deserved. My best friend, companion, and soul mate, Annie has traveled this long road, walking, running, cheering, and crying with me every step of the way. With humor and grace she has read every word and symbol I have written. She not only has championed, endured, suffered, and tolerated me and this manuscript since graduate school but has done so with an unfailing love and devotion that have sustained me through hard times and lifted me up. Every day she makes me and my life better, fuller, and stronger.

If there are strengths to this work, they are due to all of the persons I mention above and many I have forgotten to list. If there are any weaknesses or errors in this book, they are my fault, each and every one of them.

Upbuilding Black Durham

Prologue

Robert George Fitzgerald met freedwoman Cornelia Smith in Chapel Hill, Orange County, North Carolina, in the fall of 1868. He described her in his journal, using the language of the day, as "a fine-looking octoroon." He was conscious of her color and beauty, but he also was struck by her "modesty" and "spirit." Robert impressed Cornelia, too. A freeborn black from Pennsylvania, he had volunteered for the Union cause and enlisted in the U.S. Navy during the Civil War. Though he had suffered an injury that affected his vision, he returned to his studies at Ashmun Institute (later Lincoln University) in Pennsylvania and then answered the call to teach in the South at emancipation. Robert ran a local freedmen's school and became a leader in the black community. A courageously active member of the Union League, an organization dedicated to politicizing freedpeople, he attended rallies, wrote songs to celebrate Republican victories, and ran for a place on the school board. Cornelia and Robert married in August of 1869. The morning after the wedding, she traveled to the nearby town of Hillsborough. "She is to sew for several ladies," a very pleased Robert wrote in his journal. "She is anxious to do all she can for me. She is to be away three weeks."

Northern philanthropists had withdrawn their support for Robert's school the year he and Cornelia wed. Viewing himself as a "soldier in a second war, this time against ignorance," Robert continued to teach, even though few of his students could pay. So it was Cornelia who cooked, sewed, and borrowed to support herself, Robert, and his school.[1]

Among other aspirations, freedpeople hoped that they might distance themselves from the exploitations of slavery. To do so, they had to redefine black womanhood — for instance, shed the burdens of labor and reproduction that black women had carried in the past and gain the entitlements accorded to white women: the precepts of domesticity and the right to protection and the right of their children to be sheltered and shielded by wage-earning men. Such freedoms assumed a black manhood that could protect and provide for families and, by extension, communities in new ways. The closer a family could come to these ideals, the farther away its members journeyed from the degradations of the past. Robert and Cornelia set out on this road, but from the beginning their progress required more resources than the usual gender roles could provide. In communities across the South, African American women like Cornelia Fitzgerald provided significant resources to make the dreams of freedom come true. To provide for her family and to support the racial cause, Cornelia had to generate income by working outside the home, while at the same time raising her children, and, in traveling from place to place for work, she was exposed to the dangers — sexual insult and assault by white men — that black women always had known. And persistent threats against Robert made them both vulnerable to racial violence.[2]

In marrying and supporting a black activist, Cornelia aligned herself with the cause of racial destiny and mixed among the black social and political circles of Orange County. Yet for all she celebrated, Cornelia knew freedom had a double edge. Cornelia had wed a Union soldier, but she did not relinquish her association with her former owners. Indeed, she took pride in being the "favored" daughter of "Marse" Sidney Smith. Born enslaved, the daughter of a prominent white man, she was a gift to his sister, her aunt, Mary Ruffin Smith. But the unmarried Mary Smith believed that her brother's offspring represented an insult to white southern womanhood, for which she personally suffered. Thus Cornelia grew up in limbo. Mary Smith closely supervised her upbringing, even as she held the child at arm's length. She thought Robert Fitzgerald an acceptable suitor and blessed the marriage. Knowing the South and white southerners, Cornelia might have thought it expedient to maintain a connection to the white side of her past. In an unsettled racial world, an amicable relationship with whites, even former slaveholders, could prove beneficial. It was Cornelia's hope that the patrician status of her father would enhance her own rank in the postwar world, and she embraced her Smith ancestry ambivalently, half proudly and half resentfully—more the first than the second, as the past receded and new struggles emerged. Then, too, the Fitzgeralds told such stories of a free northern lineage that Cornelia clung to what she could in order to measure up.[3]

Optimistic and irrepressible, Robert encouraged his family to join him in North Carolina. His parents, Thomas and Sarah Ann Fitzgerald—respectively, a free black mulatto of Irish ancestry and a woman of Swedish and French descent—sold their Pennsylvania lands and used cash in a cash-poor region to buy an Orange County farm. The enterprising Fitzgeralds found their niche in reconstructing the South as entrepreneurs, educators, and activists. While his neighbor's fields lay fallow, Thomas made several good crops, which he sold at Durham's Station, a railroad crossing on the east side of the county. Richard was the brother with a sharp eye for business; he and brother Billy opened a brickyard in Chapel Hill, the state's university town, taught the trade to freedmen, and did well financially in dealing with whites whose bitterness increased with their need for credit. Robert's sister Mary Jane joined the legions of missionary schoolteachers crisscrossing the state who brought literacy and learning to budding black communities. Protected in the North from the kind of exposure to insult and abuse that Cornelia had known, Mary Jane had come to North Carolina from a different antebellum history than most of the black women she met. Still, she joined them on the front lines in a struggle with ex-planters for control over black childhood, with one side determined to entrap them as laborers and the other working to encourage them as students.[4]

All of the Fitzgerald women worked, but for themselves, their family, and the race, rather than for whites, and from that vantage point, they watched the racial milieu of freedom evolve. Robert's mother, Sarah Ann, and her daughter Agnes opened a restaurant across the street from the courthouse in Hillsborough, where, at the nerve center of Orange County politics, they watched their customers act out a new racial order. As a seamstress, Cornelia Fitzgerald plied a skilled trade, entering the private and semiprivate spaces of the county's prominent white (and black) women. Here, out of the public gaze, clients revealed their most candid temperaments and moods and their secret plans.[5]

Armed with ability and strategically positioned, the Fitzgeralds were public freedom figures who experienced both the perils and the possibilities of emancipation. Ambitious and shrewd, the family was loathed by whites, who viewed the Fitzgeralds' accomplishments as a sign of racial defeat. They were the Ku Klux Klan's worse nightmare: evidence that African Americans could gain the privileges of whiteness, especially of white manhood. Southern whites watched their advantages dissolve, while the Fitzgeralds lived out black liberation with those who had known little more than bondage. As black entrepreneurs, they reversed the racial tradition of economic dependency, earning enough to be autonomous of whites and enough to hold the pecuniary upper hand in negotiations. Any of the Fitzgeralds could pass for white, and they associated with black people, making a lie of any attempt to make race distinctions. It was no secret in small towns like Hillsborough and Chapel Hill that the Smith men had asserted their sexual rights in regard to Cornelia's mother, the enslaved Harriet Smith. That they had raped her belied their images as benevolent white patriarchs, which were constructed to vindicate slavery. That Cornelia had married a black carpetbagger with a passion for radical politics belied her devotion to her master and mistress. Finally, Sarah Ann's marriage to Thomas Fitzgerald, now the family patriarch, reversed the paradigm of antebellum society that took the authority of white men for granted. Sarah Ann, a white woman, had turned away from her race to marry a man of color.[6]

Fixated on reclaiming power, southern whites seized on the premise of racial purity, historicized across generations, to undo black emancipation. Juxtaposed and elevated over black women on whom white men wielded the sexual advantages of power — assault and rape — white women embodied the essence of white purity by virtue of their personae, allegedly chaste and untouchable. Frightened, also, that autonomy could enable black men to seek revenge for whites men's sexual victimization of black women and girls, southern whites made the protection of white women a motivation for fierce resistance to black freedom and a rationale for denigrating African Americans.[7] The men and women of the families Fitzgerald bore witness, as ex-planters and the Klan attempted to regain the upper hand through violence. There had been a hanging in Hillsborough the year Cornelia and Robert had married. Cy Guy was murdered, lynched by a mob "a hundred strong," purportedly for a "scandalous insult" to a white woman. In Chapel Hill, an ex-Confederate colonel, Julian S. Carr Jr., bragged that he had "horse-whipped a negro wench until her skirts hung in sheds" because she supposedly "insulted and maligned a Southern white lady." Both acts bore the markings of sexualized assaults performed in the name of white supremacy. The Fitzgerald brothers armed themselves against night riders and the Ku Klux Klan more than once, and the potential for violence did not wane.[8]

In 1870, the year Mary Pauline Fitzgerald was born to Robert and Cornelia, violence rather than votes determined victories at North Carolina polls. Against that backdrop, Pauline (as she was called) merged the Fitzgerald and the Smith families — northern and southern, immediate and extended, free and freed, black and white, women and men. She represented the first generation of African Americans born into freedom. But she was born into a family under stress. Not only interracial stress, but internal tension about class, caste, color, and status strained family ties as the Fitzgeralds learned about each other. Robert's relatives were appalled at his marriage to Cornelia, in spite of the strength of the partnership, the families' love for Mary Pauline, and the efforts of Cornelia to please the Fitzgeralds. Their daughter-in-law's ambiguous status as the daughter and "favored" slave of a southern white man confused and offended the sensibilities of Robert's family. As to her aristocratic claims, the Fitzgeralds viewed "Marse" Sidney Smith as a drunk, lost to the cause of the Old South, and his sister, Mary Ruffin Smith, as a middle-aged spinster who had allowed Cornelia few freedoms and no education. Cornelia could not read. And she was freed by the Thirteenth Amendment, not by her owner-family. The Fitzgeralds, conversely, were literate, educated, and free for as far back as they knew their family history, and they looked down on Robert's wife.[9]

The almost-white Cornelia passed the color test. But she had remained a slave until emancipation, and she lacked the prestige of the free black lineage the Fitzgeralds had carried south. Robert never quite recovered from this misjudgment in his family's eyes. As far as the Fitzgeralds were concerned, Cornelia carried, if not personified, the obliquity of the black woman's past in slavery. She may well have been modest, as Robert described her when he met her, but her birth within the plantation household attested to slavery's immorality, the experience of sexual insult, abuse, and assault that her mother had known, and the indecorous possibility that Cornelia also had been a victim. They projected onto Cornelia a dissolute legacy, sullied and violated. Inasmuch as Cornelia's virtue might be questioned, so could the Fitzgeralds' respectability for associating with her, or so the in-laws feared. Cornelia maintained only limited ties to her own mother and sisters, but tensions within the family around her ancestry strained ties. Gentility required the aristocratic Fitzgeralds to maintain at least a social distance from their inferiors. A fourth-generation Fitzgerald, Pauli Murray, confirmed in later years that her grandmother "was never accepted by her husband's family and her children were snubbed accordingly."[10]

Cornelia's relationship with her in-laws might have improved if her birthright had carried the value she imagined. In her private writing, Murray suggests that Robert married for the money. But the hundred acres of un-cleared land that Cornelia inherited from her aunt was a pittance compared to the Smith estate left to the University of North Carolina at Chapel Hill. Not just the minimal size of the plot, but the negligible value of the ges-ture damaged Cornelia's claim as a Smith descendant and translated into an income too small to measure against the wealth the Smiths had made on black people's backs. It mattered even less against the Fitzgeralds' claims, as Richard speculated successfully for land on the east side of Orange County. Nonetheless, as Cornelia's secured capital, her land offered her family some stability during the economic downturns in the 1870s. Perhaps the most important capital African Americans could hold, land owned free and clear signified autonomy and distance from whites while providing her family a safety net, a resource, and a refuge that most other black families lacked. Cornelia still had to defend against white neighbors who tried to scare her off, but she and her children stayed on the Chapel Hill property as the tumult of freedom played out.[11]

Despite the familial tensions, a shared desire for safety gave both Fitz-gerald brothers reason to leave the west side of Orange County. Word spread that Durham's Station, the crossroad where Thomas sold his goods, offered expanding opportunities for work and gaining wealth. With a flood of black people arriving for the same reason, Robert and Richard Fitzgerald moved to Durham, where they both established brickyards. But they clung to their inclination to set themselves apart. They built houses apart from each other and away from the black settlement growing by the tracks just south of the center of town.

Their destinies also diverged. Successful brick maker Richard detached himself from his in-laws, as he and his family joined an intimate circle of families who shared Richard's goal of building wealth. Increasingly blind, Robert Fitzgerald depended more and more on his workers and on the women of his family. But he also flailed against the vicissitudes of racism. Like so many black veterans found, the federal government refused him a disability pension for injuries suffered in military service. Then, ignoring Robert's legal rights and his claims to his land, white Durham officials seized a significant part of his property to build a cemetery, a segregated one for whites. So, again, it was Cornelia who stepped in to bridge the gap between income and need. She traveled the road between Chapel Hill and Durham, cooked for her husband's workers, and supervised the children. She rented some of her inheritance to tenants, sold lumber off some acres, and farmed, collected eggs, sewed, and bartered to pay for her children's schooling.[12]

It was a courageous and praiseworthy act for Cornelia to labor on behalf of her family. Because most black families struggled financially, most African American women had to work, if not at a specific job, then in the informal economy, trading and selling their services and goods. One example of the necessary flexibility that African Americans brought to gender roles, women's work—more specifically, their public presence—also violated tenets about women's appropriate place in society: in the home, raising children. Unable to support his family, Robert could not fulfill the role of black manhood, a particular failure for a black aristocrat and one that subjected his wife to the hazards that black women continued to meet on the public roads and streets.[13]

Black people measured their distance from slavery by their autonomy from whites, and Cornelia's labor, however necessary, propelled the Robert Fitzgeralds further down the slippery slope of class. Robert and Cornelia Fitzgerald began married life as members of the black aristocracy from two sides of black society. His failures, her work, and the loss of his business and land doomed the family to a status inferior to the Richard Fitzgeralds. As Murray described it, her grandfather's family fell into the category called "the respectable poor" because of their financial condition, socially positioned "well outside elite circles." The distinctions between the "rich" Fitzgeralds and the "poor" Fitzgeralds grew wider as the next generation came of age. Having grown wealthy, Richard Fitzgerald easily afforded to send his daughters to Fisk University, the prominent black college in Nashville, Tennessee. Cornelia sent whatever she could scrape together—including eggs and chickens—to pay Pauline's tuition at St. Augustine's College in Raleigh, North Carolina, and the child worked for the rest. "There were no other children in school except me, I worked right along with the men and women from 25 to 30 years old," she wrote of her experience.[14]

But, in spite of her academic promise, Pauline Fitzgerald could not finish her education, something the Fitzgeralds valued so highly. In 1885, when Cornelia bore the last of their six children and the government rejected Robert's claims to a pension, their firstborn shouldered the family's financial burden. That year, Pauline Fitzgerald left school, "put up her hair, put on a long grown-up dress, and went to take the county examination for teachers." She received her teaching certification nine days before she turned fifteen and immediately went to work at a Durham school for blacks. Barely an adult herself, Pauline accepted the title of "race woman," charged with nurturing the next generation, in addition to her responsibilities as a daughter supporting her aging parents, her younger siblings, and their families. Her sister Sallie Fitzgerald followed suit. By their occupation and community status,

Pauline and Sallie pulled the Fitzgeralds up into the aspiring class of black strivers, determined to challenge white supremacy but not always able to escape it completely.[15]

The Fitzgeralds came to the postwar South from different directions and carrying dissimilar burdens but sharing ambitions for family and race. They left a set of critical markers on North Carolina's landscape after slavery that attest to the edginess of race politics after emancipation. Drawn together and pulled apart by the challenge, they moved into the maelstrom of the twentieth century with a shared agenda for freedom but along different paths. But the Fitzgerald family history is more than an interesting story about the hopes and fears of freedom. Theirs was a family upbuilt at the moment of emancipation, fashioned in the midst of the racial state of affairs unfolding before them. They created themselves as a unit out of separate pasts, sharing the common experience of slavery and holding common aspirations for freedom. As freedom participants, they also collaboratively upbuilt institutions, founding schools and businesses that lent permanence to black liberation. A microcosm of black community development in process, the families Fitzgerald looked forward to the benefits of freedom, but the mutability of race, gender, and class in the South's political economy created contrasting circumstances for the two families. The gender ideologies of freedom conflicted with the gender realities of freedom to create differential status designations that applauded the "rich" Fitzgeralds and marginalized the "poor" Fitzgeralds.

Upbuilding black communities required African Americans to travel the distance between their nightmares and their dreams. Freedom's people may have hoped for autonomy, but the racial circumstances of emancipation required vigilance against white animosities. They may have wanted to protect African American women and girls, but racism imposed a poverty that required black female labor in order to survive. They may have anticipated participating in politics, but the persistent threat of violence made the polls dangerous terrain. In the end, only half of the Fitzgeralds attained their objectives. Richard Fitzgerald, the entrepreneur, gained national prominence as a successful black businessman; Robert, the teacher and political activist, moved into relative obscurity. Cornelia Fitzgerald, despite her contributions, could not escape her mother's past, nor could she free her daughters from the social and economic burdens that African American women continued to bear well into the twentieth century.

Introduction

"Within and without the sombre veil of color[,] vast social forces have been at work, — efforts for human betterment, movements toward disintegration and despair, tragedies and comedies in social and economic life, and a swaying and lifting and sinking of human hearts which have made this land a land of mingled sorrow and joy, of change and excitement and unrest." So wrote the scholar W. E. B. Du Bois in *The Souls of Black Folk*, his treatise on African American life in the South after emancipation. Using "the veil" as a metaphor for the color line, Du Bois wrote of the racial divide as a fragile, restrictive, translucent barrier between blacks and whites. Impressing the paradigm of racial affairs in the United States and particularly in the South, the veil accounted for black folks' sense of "twoness," Du Bois argued, "an American, a Negro; two souls, two thoughts, two unreconciled strivings; two warring ideals in one dark body."[1]

By the time *The Souls of Black Folk* was published in 1903, a generation of African Americans had come of age with a sense of entitlement to freedom, inheriting their parents' freedom dreams. They expected to manage their own families and demanded to control their own labor; they desired learning and wished to send their children to school; and they wanted to participate in their communities' politics as contributors and citizens. But they encountered the veil, and in this era of Jim Crow, African Americans who sought to rend the veil were captured by webs of rules and rituals, by doublespeak, and by disinformation intended to deny black humanity.[2]

On the black side of the veil lay a place that few white people knew existed and still fewer tried to understand but that all African Americans recognized even if they did not wholly dwell within it. Here, in the chaos of emancipation, black folk survived on mutual aid, wit, and hard work. They embraced themselves as whole beings, not just as citizens — and not just as family, but as community. They founded institutions, wove together a national and international network of association, and fashioned an astute culture of oppositional politics. All the more remarkable, black people of African descent intentionally created a future. Proud that the first generation born in freedom had survived to come of age at the turn of the century, they recognized this as an enormous achievement by people whose freedom was under persistent attack. Subsequently, each generation engaged in the work of racial destiny, not just as a collective act of survival and of thriving in the face of racism but also as the individual and cooperative work of upbuilding for themselves.[3]

Defined by Du Bois as the "social and economic development" of black communities after slavery, upbuilding was the literal and figurative construction of the structures African Americans used to climb out of slavery. Like architects, surveyors, and contractors, black folk upbuilt families, homes, organizations, institutions, and enterprises and erected atop a foundation laid in the past the physical and psychic spaces of black freedom. These efforts required black people to engage in internal discussions about themselves and their expectations of each other as free persons. Upbuilding required their labor and that they contribute diverse resources, keeping common goals in mind. But upbuilding also demanded that African Americans reformulate identity and accordingly that they sort out the meaning of gender and class in determining the roles that each one should play. Thus the institutions they created and the spaces they populated also spoke to distinctions of gender and class as well as the commonalities of race experience and community.[4]

In response to black aspirations, white southerners imposed a racial peace on the region through a troubling set of racial codes known as Jim Crow, which resided but did not remain on the other side of the veil. The jocular term belies the profound abuses perpetrated in the name of white racial supremacy: the lynching of black men, the rape of black women, the burning of black schools and churches, the bombing of black neighborhoods, the destruction of black towns, race riots, and random violence attest that Jim Crow was homegrown oppression and terrorism, an American apartheid sanctioned by all three branches of government. A mockery of black hopes, Jim Crow attempted to appropriate black life and labor by any means necessary. To make the case for black inadequacies, Jim Crow portrayed black people as inhuman, irresponsible, and immoral, diametrically distinct from whites and therefore unable to measure up to their standards of character. Insisting that "the Negro is a Negro and always would be just that and nothing more," whites translated antiblack rhetoric into officially administered discrimination in the arenas of democracy — employment, education, and elections — and sustained it for over a hundred years. Enforced by violence, Jim Crow was purposeful, not only keeping African Americans in a subordinate place in American society but pushing them further down, if not eliminating them altogether.[5]

The system produced a whole list of disparities between blacks and whites, shored up the arbitrariness of white power, and perpetuated injustice and black poverty for most African Americans. Electing to ignore the ambiguities of race to lump all blacks into one disparaged mass, Jim Crow exploited the differences among African Americans as a form of repression. The history of race relations bears this past as an impediment to equality. Racism shaped the contours of the spaces within which black people lived and the context within which they persevered.[6] Pauli Murray wrote from the black side of the line: "We were bottled up and labeled and set aside — sent to the Jim Crow car, the back of the bus, the side door of the theater, the side window of a restaurant. We came to know that whatever we had was always inferior. We came to understand that no matter how neat and clean, how law abiding, submissive or polite, how studious in school, how churchgoing and moral, how scrupulous in paying our bills and taxes we were, it made no essential difference in our place."[7] Insidiously, when Jim Crow battered one black person, it assaulted them all. In turn, the negative act of one reflected on all African Americans, while the positive act of one was viewed as an exception. But it was Jim Crow's duplicity that made for some of its most damning practices. By forcing black people to encounter the color line differently, Jim Crow doubled its effects of vilification: on the one hand, an insult against black womanhood was also an insult against black manhood, and vice versa; on the other hand, by forcing black men and women to encounter the color line differently, Jim Crow caused tension in their relationships with each other. At the turn of the nineteenth century, black female and male leaders, for instance, squared off against each other with regard to race progress. Clubwomen claimed that men did little toward race progress, and the latter blamed the women of the race for not progressing enough. These harsh gender assessments not only reflected anxieties about the meaning of masculinity and femininity but also crossed class lines, with those of the better classes heaping scorn on the less fortunate for holding the race back, and those of the lower classes becoming resentful of how status measured the growing distance among African Americans even within community.[8]

Because Jim Crow presented a confounding adversary, unity against it could emerge in a moment but dissipate just as quickly. In fact, unified action was not necessarily the most effective means of struggle against an amorphous enemy. Even as black folk looked forward together, they had to work collectively and separately on discrete parts of the upbuilding project while facing their own sets of challenges.[9] Disunity represented structural cracks in black communities but also revealed how different contingents of African Americans adapted to racial conditions that expanded and contracted with possibilities. Accordingly, intraracial tensions could operate as creative or complementary forces as well as adversarial ones. Friction might waste energy, but it also generated the sparks that lit new initiatives, new forms of resistance, accommodation, and protest, and new strategies of survival, endurance, and achievement. In this way, upbuilding black communities was the process of internal exchange and dissonance, just as communities themselves were sites of those same dynamics.[10]

In 1912, W. E. B. Du Bois praised the "upbuilding of Black Durham," a small southern city, for its exceptional progress that "characterizes the progress of the Negro American" out of the feudal darkness of the past and into an era of capitalist stability. African Americans in Durham, the town to which the Fitzgeralds had moved, owned and operated several brickyards, a textile mill, a lumber mill, a foundry, a furniture factory, a cigar factory, a library, a hospital, a college, scores of churches, a number of schools, and an astonishing array of retail services, shops, and stores, community organizations, and race institutions. A coterie of entrepreneurs, including Richard Fitzgerald, embraced public political leadership, and their wives and daughters modeled female respectability. Yet, as Du Bois noted, "the significance of the rise of a group of black people to the Durham height and higher, means not a disappearance but, in some respects, an accentuation of the race problem." For the Durham Group, as its notable residents were called, created exactly what southern whites despised: a prosperous black society marked by the elements that whites believed black people could not achieve. Yet Durham's open secret was that, just below the surface of unity and prosperity, class conflicts simmered. Engendered by frustrated expectations, black Durham's internal clashes characterized its development, sometimes stimulating creative initiatives and sometimes stymieing progress.[11]

This book is about a people and a place and the entangled process of making them both and together after emancipation. It is a community study of African Americans that describes how freedpeople and their successive generations in Durham, North Carolina, struggled among themselves and with whites to give meaning to black freedom. The upbuilding of black Durham was one of the most significant black enterprises of the twentieth century. Once a sleepy village, by the end of the nineteenth century Durham was the richest city in North Carolina, one where at least some African Americans, including some among the Fitzgeralds, benefited from the shift from an agricultural economy to one based on manufacturing. With no antebellum foundation, Durham constructed itself into a New South city of industry built on the virtues of hard work, enterprise, and propriety and made out of Fitzgerald bricks.[12]

At least that was the public image presented by the town's boosters. Loosed from Old South hegemony, civic leaders dissociated Durham from the region's unprogressive elements: industrial rather than agricultural, built on free labor instead of slave labor, and not leisurely paced. A local newspaper crowed in 1886: "Nothing stands still. There is very little loafing in Durham. A man who stands on the street corner and gazes at the sky is apt to be run over. The word 'Durham' is synonymous with 'business.' Work is offered to all who desire it."[13] Meanwhile, the state newspaper, the *Raleigh News and Observer*, unfurled the official veil: "It has not been regarded as desirable . . . that the Negro worker should be considered as on the same plane as white men pursuing the same vocations in life. No matter what any calling any white man may choose in the South there is a wide and recognized gulf between him and the Negro workman."[14] Despite the promises the New South might have offered, white leaders determined that the new political economy would differ little from the one that had come before. Defining workers by race and gender in a way that protected white male supremacy, whites ensured that African Americans remained subordinate to them.[15]

If Durham was a "New South wonder," then black Durham was a "New Negro wonder" flourishing in a milieu of racial animosity, its successes positioned at the intersection of W. E. B. Du Bois and Booker T. Washington. In fact, in 1911 Washington, the Tuskeegean, called Durham the "city of cities to look for the prosperity of Negroes," preceding Du Bois's praise written in 1912. Both admired the black community's new "group economy" that Du Bois described, grounded in "teaching and preaching, buying and selling, employing and hiring," and both acknowledged Richard Fitzgerald as a model black businessman.[16] In the nadir of race relations, then, black Durham emerged as a symbol of black nationalism and black pride by the end of the nineteenth century. Modern buildings, owned and occupied by African Americans, rose against a backdrop of repression. Nationally, black Durham was viewed as a symbol of what African Americans could do on their own when left alone by whites.[17]

When, in 1921, whites destroyed Greenwood, the black community of Tulsa, Oklahoma, known as Black Wall Street, African American leaders sought a new beacon of hope. E. Franklin Frazier found a black city on a hill in Durham, a place to exemplify the triumphant climb out of slavery. In 1925, Frazier christened it the "Capital of the Black Middle Class." Durham became home to the North Carolina Mutual Life Insurance Company, the largest black business in the world in its heyday; Mechanics and Farmers Bank (founded by Richard Fitzgerald), strong enough to withstand the 1933 banking crisis; Southern Fidelity Mutual Insurance Company, which bonded the agents of black companies; and the National Negro Finance Company, an innovative investment firm that issued bonds for development projects. Although the finance company failed during the Depression, the black business and professional league could still declare in its promotional film of the 1940s that "Negro Durham marches on."[18]

By then, Hillside High School stood as one of two black public secondary institutions in North Carolina. Mary Pauline and Sallie Fitzgerald were two among the more than 130 African American teachers at eight different schools for black students available in the city in 1938. North Carolina College for Negroes (founded in 1910 as the National Religious Training School, now known as North Carolina Central University) evolved into the state's only publicly supported liberal arts college for African Americans. More than 100 businesses and 600 homes clustered around the intersection of Fayetteville and Pettigrew Streets, the central business district of Hayti, the largest black enclave in town. And North Carolina College for Negroes had attracted men and women academics and students from throughout the country, including historians Helen G. Edmonds and John Hope Franklin, folklorist Zora Neale Hurston, and artist Elizabeth Cattlet. The institution served as a site for critical research and dialogue on topics relevant to black life so much so that Du Bois gave serious thought to joining the faculty.[19]

But Durham, North Carolina, was also a center of industrial racism, where the renowned tobacco factories, notorious for exploiting black female labor, replayed racial slavery in an urban form. Indeed, the tobacco industry drew on its historical roots to forge modernization. As early as 1820, tobacco manufacturers in the Piedmont hired black women — slave and free — to process raw product for cigars and chewing tobacco. Not surprisingly, as the tobacco industry expanded, the city attracted legions of black workers. In fact, it was one of the few industrial jobs available to black women.[20] As rough as it was, working tobacco was preferable to household labor, in which workers had little control of their work space or time. Tobacco-working women — stemmers, sweepers, and feeders — made up the central workforce of the industry that put Durham on the international map for tobacco production and marketing. They also formed a major part of the black working class, the urban proletariat. As such, they were a dialectical force in the racial politics of the urban South. Although black women clung to the lowest rung on the economic ladder, white Durham relied on their labor and black business relied on their dollars.[21]

Set against emancipation and the political economy of race in North Carolina, this book explores upbuilding as gendered praxis, drawing attention to African American women as the central constituency of black migration, urbanization, industrialization, and proletarianization.[22] Using gender to pull apart Durham's remarkable range of black experiences sheds light on the motivations for and the substance of black activism, revealing the reasons African Americans made varying choices: black contingencies faced discrete economic, political, social, and racial challenges that sometimes pulled them in opposing directions.[23]

Parsing the process of upbuilding Durham's black community with a spotlight on women illuminates other divisions among black people, while considering women's discrete position in the project. Critical to their families' endurance and, by extension, the viability of their communities, African American women also possess a collective memory of the most debasing aspects of slavery.[24] Judged in a court where Victorian morals clashed with white patriarchal excesses, African American women carried the shame of a history of their sexual availability to white men, victims of circumstances they did not create, were powerless to stop, and could do little about. As such, positive transformations in black women's lives signified race progress, and their distress was a measure of subjugation.[25] If race progress was measured by how far black people could remove themselves from the degradations of slavery, how do we assess race progress in an industrial community built on the nexus of race and gender oppression with roots in the past? How do we begin to understand black activism in the context of exploitation suffered most egregiously by women in an industrial city with a vibrant black business culture?

Black Durham was home to some of the wealthiest black men in the United States but also some of the poorest African American women in the state of North Carolina. Benefiting least from black or white capitalism, working-class women clustered on the low ground of freedom's terrain. Rather than examine the extremes of accomplishment or oppression, I have elected to look at the space between the two, to see black Durham as a bas-relief, a more complex account than a tale of two cities — one safely affluent and the other severely impoverished. The tension between these disparate lines of inquiry — the work culture of black business dominated by prominent men and the work culture of tobacco dominated by laboring women — reverberates with the burdens and benefits of gender and class as related to the economic, political, and social challenges of the era. I argue here that the protean aspects of identity did not simply link African Americans together as a unified force or divide them into oppositional forces. Rather, the interrelated structures of gender, class, and, over time, generation cast relationships, forged alliances, and fostered alienation among African Americans, creating interconnected, disjointed, and even contradictory relations between women and men and among the black working, middle, and elite classes, migrants and settlers, conservative elders and radical upstarts.[26]

Durham's demographics alone make a compelling case for this book's focus on women as well as men. As it had been from the time of its beginnings as an industrial center of the South, Durham was a city of women. In spite of the uncertain economic picture — and indeed, because of it — Durham's population swelled, with increases among women outpacing the increase among men almost every decade between 1880 and 1950. Drawn by employment in black institutions and in white factories and homes, black women's migration to Durham also increased with the popularity of tobacco products and, consequently, the potential for factory work for women laborers. Those who could not fall back on household labor looked to the women's underground economy that bartered for goods and services. And the consequent in- and out-flow of temporary workers also increased vagrancy and encouraged alternative, illicit forms of wage earning like gambling, entertainments, and prostitution.[27]

Almost everyone who lived in Durham came from someplace else, but intracommunity stress, particularly over gender roles, increased with the in-migration and increase of the black female population. Because often it was based in family struggles, women's migration for work challenged assumptions about men's roles as protectors and providers. Whereas men's migration was culturally sanctioned, anticipated, and even expected as a way to seek employment, women's migration signified social disorder.[28] The ever-shifting population, experienced in commonplace ways, undermined black leaders' sense of community stability as well as their ability to manage their constituencies. The stunning growth of the black population perpetuated the unsettled nature of urban life, strained the infrastructures of the black communities, and challenged the hegemony of the black patriarchs. But women's migration also had important consequences for black institutional life, as new migrants founded their own churches, appointed their own ministers, and turned to their own organizational bases for succor and aid. Durham's black churches, schools, neighborhoods, and streets could barely keep up with the demand for their services; but the multiplication of churches also reflected the ways alienated congregants sought alternative spaces for themselves, where they found their own guidance and promoted their own programs. Small wood-framed and massive brick churches of both prominent and lesser-known black denominations sprang up around the city, signaling an expansion of women's domain.[29]

The skewed sex ratio among African Americans in Durham — specifically the overpopulation of women — also suggests a compelling influence on gender relations, especially with regard to women's adherence to or rejection of traditional roles. Whereas a shortage of partners may have induced black women's strict adherence to gender propriety, the impossibility of marriage encouraged others to throw off gender propriety. Consequently, part of Durham's black culture across all classes was marked by the visible prominence of single women in the city's population. Black leaders feared that single black women were vulnerable to the temptations and dangers of the city, or, worse, that they brought those temptations and dangers to the city. In accordance with the era's social theory, "the preponderance of women in the city," as black mathematician Kelly Miller had called the gendered skew of the black urban population, implied black family disorganization and "dependency, desertion, illegitimacy, and juvenile delinquency," exactly the opposite of a vision of a prosperous, respectable black community. "By the arithmetic of population," a white academic wrote, "hundreds of colored men and women are predestined to remain unmarried. This is a fruitful source of immorality and crime."[30]

Notions of African American women's proper or expected roles, whether held by whites or by black men, translated into control. Racism and misogyny confined black women to those physical spaces deemed appropriate for them. Challenging expectation with obligation, African American women expanded their public roles beyond functional laborer and family member, particularly in urban areas. Their struggle against race and gender indignities demanded that they control the spaces where they cared for their families, led and served their communities, and tended to their own interests. As community agents, friends, lovers, churchwomen, clubwomen, and prostitutes, women from all walks of life created and dominated spaces of their own. They claimed as "our territory" not only female institutions like the YWCA, but also the porches, kitchens, gardens, and walkways of the neighborhood, private gatherings like bridge clubs, and workplaces like the stemming floors. Then they turned their desks, schoolhouses, hospital wards, factory floors, union meetings, and white folk's kitchens into places where they asserted and reaffirmed their politics as black women.[31]

Contributing paid and unpaid labor, time, and vision that ensured community survival, black women in Durham also facilitated the development of the commercial spirit for which black Durham was known. Black-owned enterprises and institutions provided occupational options other than teaching for those who were schooled, and with substantially more pay. The tobacco factories provided a better option than domestic work, more steady employment, and a higher wage. This diverse female workforce bought insurance, saved money, paid rent, invested in real estate, and facilitated the development of other black businesses and services: beauty salons, dress and hat shops, shoe stores, five and dimes, and furniture stores, as well as drugstores, grocery stores, meat and fish markets, movie theaters, cafés and restaurants, all employing and catering to the city's black and female population. In short, that Durham was the "Capital of the Black Middle Class" was due as much to women's substantial labor and buying power as to the genius of their organizational efforts or the talents of its male entrepreneurs. Without them, black Durham could not have upbuilt the society that Du Bois so highly praised.

And yet African American reformers and scholars deliberately cultivated a connection between upbuilding, uplift, and black manhood: pulling men forward as a sign of perseverance against the great odds. Thus, the successful advance of black communities like Durham celebrated the accomplishments of men and in effect negated the contributions of women. Or, more precisely, to specifically value the place of women in black community development undermined the goal of extolling black Durham's progress: to prove that African American men could acquire those qualities that white Americans assumed they could not possess: strong leadership, a middle-class outlook, and a correlating system of values and mores.[32] Viewing the upbuilding of black Durham as a treatise on their manhood, the leading men made community a metaphor for family, anointed themselves patriarchs, and set out to govern a people whose government ignored them at best and repressed them at worst. As race men, they embraced respectability — industry, thrift, and sobriety — as their own uplift project of rising from slavery's degradations and called upon other men to do the same. Once denied the right to their persons and families, they coveted a new manhood, and in the era of self-made men and robber barons, they articulated a masculinist perspective on black freedom.[33]

The fact that black business thrived in a climate that denied black manhood made the upbuilding of black Durham all the more remarkable, or so Durham's black leaders wished to believe. Durham's black male leaders embraced capitalism as a means to black sovereignty in denial of Jim Crow. Yet the Bull City managed to avoid the racial violence of white rioters who destroyed other aspiring black communities, in Atlanta, Tulsa, and Wilmington, where black men also had garnered wealth and influence. Black Durham was a paradox. Particularly for the leaders among Durham's renowned black elite, Jim Crow served as their barrier and their reinforcement. As long as Jim Crow reigned, they could not move into the mainstream of American success. Coming from the encumbrances of white supremacy, its affliction was its asset: the same system that frustrated African American ambitions also created a captive clientele of customers. The absence of other options made these same clients all the more exploitable by black business or led the masses to suspect that such mistreatment occurred. As long as the obstruction of race remained, they reigned within the black community, admired and criticized. Considered conservative for their cautious strategy of civil rights, Durham's black leaders were accused of accommodating segregation. And they did — but not as a capitulation to racism. Rather they viewed upbuilding in the segregated South as a tactic of resistance and as a strategy to outwit Jim Crow.[34]

Durham's black leaders knew southern whites would do anything they could to maintain the color line, including building and supporting black institutions from which freedom movements were launched. For leaders' willingness to control the rest of their communities — or at least seem to — they reaped rewards of white beneficence necessary to community development: schools and educational programs, a hospital, and other institutions that few black communities could claim.

In spite of black leaders' presumptive authority as men, nearly all black women were subject to the injuries of racism and misogyny. Almost unavoidably, then, the interracial politics of black leaders used to maintain the racial peace clashed with those of their constituencies among women and the working class. When racial anxieties rose, black leaders often found themselves trapped between the inclination to mollify whites' hostilities in order to protect their communities and the legitimate complaints of their constituency. Under patriarchal domain, therefore, it was left to black women whose lives did not fit the patriarch's mold of black womanhood to appose and integrate their definitions of freedom with those of the race. For the rise of the race's women signified the rise of the race as a whole, as North Carolinian Anna Julia Cooper explained: "Only the BLACK WOMAN can say 'when and where I enter, in the quiet, undisputed dignity of my womanhood, without violence and without suing or special patronage, then and there the whole *Negro race enters with me.' "*[35]

The compliments that piled onto Durham—for its "fine homes, exquisite churches, and middle class respectability," about which E. Franklin Frazier wrote—related more to women than to men, since women's respectable place was in the protected realm of the home and the church. Furthermore, respectability expressed black people's denial of the troubling black images that whites inserted into public culture. For instance, whites posited black male hypersexuality as a retributive threat to the white race, even though it was white men who posed the sexual hazard for black women. For African Americans, respectability reflected how well they could position themselves away from racism's meanness. Embracing morality—piety and propriety, prudence and enterprise, decorum and restraint—and eschewing vice, black respectability also demonstrated race progress and reform and offered a discourse on self-help and racial uplift. Enacted through gender roles, respectability reflected a collective priority to protect against the intimidations of racism, and virtually all African Americans acknowledged the hegemony of respectability. Against the multifaceted challenges of Jim Crow, black people wore respectability like armor.[36]

And they carried respectability as a sword. Both laboring and upper-class women used respectability as a weapon against personal, sexual, physical, and spiritual assault. Tobacco-working women and household laborers used it to carve dignity onto lives of difficult and often degrading toil. Clubwomen used it as a tool to pry open the hands of white beneficiaries, to support their arguments for woman suffrage, and to make a case to men for building women's institutions. At the same time, respectability marked class divisions within the black community with implications about who had it and who did not. The upper classes used the language of respectability to express their disapproval of lower classes. With gendered undertones, respectability, particularly that of women and girls, linked status and class in a way that highlighted a family's ability to protect if not remove the most vulnerable from public hazards and temptations.[37]

The class dynamic changed with the strengthening of black business. In the twentieth century, the bi-class distinction between the "better class" and "the masses" based on respectability transformed into a scale of distinctions based on distance from the affectations of slavery and, relatedly, autonomy from whites.[38] At one end, a new black elite, substantially urban and focused on financial ventures, emerged to supplant the old black aristocracy. As E. Franklin Frazier wrote to Durham leaders of their position in the class structure, this entrepreneurial elite was "at the top in our civilization," even though the group "retains the name of middle class" as a way to compare it to the dominant society.[39] On the other end, the laboring class confronted white animosity and struggled financially daily. Whereas, among the elite, women remained in the security of the household or worked in the enclaves of black businesspeople and educated professionals, the laboring class could not avoid white animosity, financial struggles, and the persistent threat and presence of abuse. In between, a middle or aspiring class of mid-range professionals, such as teachers and nurses, were not far removed from the constituency with whom they worked, the masses; and they dealt publicly with conditions imposed by racism. Revered by their communities, black teachers and nurses garnered high status, but their authority could be usurped and affronted by white officials. As women willing or expected to remain single, they could not or would not benefit from male providers, and because their incomes shifted with the winds of racial politics, they struggled financially against fluctuating wages and budget cuts.[40]

Thus, women's occupations as a measure of servility—factory and household laborers, nurses and teachers, and the employees, wives, and daughters of the black patriarchs—informed by education and income, determined a family's class status. The new black elite could afford to keep women out of the labor market, but that did not mean that women of the black elite did not work. They labored in the honorable work of the race, on behalf of race enterprise, at community uplift, sometimes as extensions of their husbands and sometimes autonomous of patriarchal influence—all the while preaching the value of respectability. They did not have to encounter the color line *necessarily* or frequently, but as black women they knew its dangers, and as race women they saw it in the eyes of their less fortunate sisters. The working poor among African Americans, mostly women, had no choice but to confront Jim Crow daily. Unable to distance themselves from the typecast of African American female laboring slaves, they were disempowered and subjected to a hostile environment. The middle class, a diverse assemblage of African American aspirants and strivers, represented the mobility, complexity, and elasticity of black urban class stratification, accommodating the children of tobacco workers who became teachers, tobacco workers who by income and thrift managed to purchase property, household and service workers employed by white elites or white leisure facilities (hotels, clubs, restaurants), entertainers, skilled laborers and artisans, beauticians and barbers, leaders among the working class, and a petit bourgeoisie of entrepreneurs who owned small shops and stores.[41]

As it shifted, class distinction proposed a structure that recognized how fortunes could rise and fall under Jim Crow. In a culture of free enterprise, black Durham's social scene effected a fluid paradigm of class, albeit with limits. Manners, morals, and money matched inherited family lines in establishing relational status among Durham African Americans. A coterie of "upstarts," as the aristocratic Fitzgeralds called the new entrepreneurs, rose into the top tier by dint of financial attainments. Education and income, which influenced occupation and quality of life, reinforced but did not entirely define class distinctions; in reality, businessmen struggled with personal finances, and teachers earned less than some women made in service or tobacco. Similarly, respectability did not belong solely to the privileged but also to laboring people who strove to improve their lot. Respectability might lift those who did harsh labor up toward the aspiring class. Without capital, however, respectability alone could not raise the most upright of laborers fully into the middle tier. Women of the working class might rise into the aspiring class by virtue of education, professionalization, or even marriage. Marriage across class lines brought people from disparate circumstances into a similar contingent, but women of the middle class who came originally from the working class rarely married up into the black elite. Nor did women of the black elite marry down into the working class. Similarly, the earnings of those engaged in the underground economy or illegal activities could exceed those of the black elite, but the work itself—related to vices like drinking, prostitution, or gambling—did not carry the respectability to warrant placement into the upper class.

Of course, class differences among African Americans cannot be neatly demarcated, and forging an analysis of class requires a treacherous trek onto theoretical territory.[42] But when differences collide, animosities can emerge at the nexus. By accessing issues related to gender and class, this book seeks to explore these intraracial tensions. The upper classes maliciously criticized the lower classes, holding the latter accountable for barriers remaining in freedom's path; and the lower class could speak of the upper class with contempt and resentment for having been left behind. Some among the Durham elite were notorious for stipulating rules of decorum while using their status to violate the same codes, just as some among the working class (and the elite) freely engaged in the disreputable behavior that encouraged denigrating labels.[43]

Not all divisions and consequent tensions among African Americans fall along obvious fault lines like gender and class. Difference created divisions within a given cohort, defined by any number of factors, including individual personalities, such that even within classes, as within families, among women, and between men, rifts occurred. Black businessmen may have agreed on the role of capitalism in upbuilding and community development, but they disagreed about the importance of electoral politics. Laborers among the working class disagreed about the effectiveness of a strike as a job action, but they acknowledged the value of unions as a collective bargaining body. With the best of intentions, black leaders attempted to quash important initiatives that they believed threatened the racial peace, balking at black labor activism among tobacco workers and hindering National Association for the Advancement of Colored People (NAACP) initiatives toward black educational equality. And, too, into the Jim Crow era, freedom's first generation carried the living memory of slavery, emancipation, and the violent milieu that followed. Their memories informed their relationship to politics on both sides of the color line.[44]

Shaped by the vicissitudes of black life before and after the Civil War, class distinctions were not new to African Americans. Nor were distinctions related to gender a new matter; rather, freedom gave African Americans the opportunity to articulate class and gender ideologies as they related to their experiences.[45] Indeed, race advancement required black people to fashion multifarious strategies of self-assertion and opposition, albeit with common goals in mind. Thus, conflict sometimes (intentionally) reinforced the positions of both sides, and what might seem like divisive politics fractured by gender and class often yielded innovative and effective initiatives, even while producing acrimony. African Americans had to work together and apart to rise from bondage and to find the most effective means of race progress, while also limiting interracial antagonism. They may have shared the desire to eradicate the systemic disadvantages that followed them, but they did not necessarily agree on how — nor could they concur on the reasons Jim Crow continued to block their steps. Captured by American apartheid, which was strengthening at the turn of the century, black folk could neither identify nor forge a singular effective strategy. Rather, multiple lines of attack — forged with harmony or dissonance — were necessary to hack away at Jim Crow's impediments.

How could a people confronting a matrix of oppressions always stand in solidarity across generations? How could gender not matter to a people claiming themselves and their space in a society structured around gendered ideologies about race? How could class not matter to people whose economic fortunes and misfortunes intertwined with the color line? "Life for me / ain't been no crystal stair," begins the Langston Hughes poem "Mother to Son," a poignant comment on what the freedom and Jim Crow generations knew about the lives of those who had come before them. "We were just a generation or two removed from slavery," Julia Lucas pointed out in a moving interview about her life, "and so we knew how far we'd come and how far we had to go." Lucas's generation, the Jim Crow generation — the second one born in freedom — inherited the climb toward freedom's promises but still carried their grandparents' memories of bondage. Lucas's neighbor Josephine Clement similarly recalled: "My father talked to me very frankly about our having been denied our rights, how long it was, and how we should continue to fight." And he gave her a charge: "Your responsibility is to be ready when your time comes. You be ready to go in when I make the opportunity for you to go in." Their lessons indicate that freedom's first generation took an active role in civil rights during their era and that they prepared the next generation to take up the work of racial destiny and freedom, the long civil rights movement.[46]

Consequently, this book also points out that black Durham was a lively and energetic place and that the Jim Crow era was not just a somnolent interval between emancipation and the civil rights movement. Rather, reaching back to emancipation, we can see how African American civil rights activism evolved through the Jim Crow era as black discourse and action on the ground, at the community level, behind the veil. In fact, the part of the Jim Crow era called the nadir, the lowest point in African American history, was also the zenith of the black women's club movement, the black press, and black business. These initiatives, each its own discrete social movement, drew black women and men into organized defiance of white supremacy and demonstrated that black folk had forged a sense of autonomy and distance from whites.

Between emancipation and the high tide of Jim Crow, African Americans gave birth to a remarkable offspring: not only the scholars and intellectuals who brought a New Negro Renaissance to the fore but also the advocates and activists who engineered the approaches used by civil rights activists in the mid-twentieth century. Among them, a number of women — Ella Baker, Septima Clark, and Pauli Murray — articulated an ideology of inclusive participatory democracy that identified gender and class as critical if divisive elements that could be used effectively in the struggle. Murray's pursuits and perspectives — indeed, her feminist insights into race and sex discrimination — were informed by the everyday lives of the African American women she had known growing up in Durham.[47] Writing "The Liberation of Black Women" in the 1970s, this fourth-generation Fitzgerald penned these words: "The historical factors that have fastened the black women's feeling of independence have been the economic necessity to earn a living to help support their families — if indeed they were not the sole breadwinners — and the need for the black community to draw heavily upon the resources of all its members in order to survive."[48]

You and I and all of us had better wait and see what new
form this old monster will assume, in what new skin this
old snake will come forth.
    Frederick Douglass, 1865

1 : Seek Out a Good Place
Making Decisions in Freedom

For a brief moment, emancipation changed everything. Black folk declared freedom, affirmed families, and defied white authorities. Sarah Debro,
who grew up on the Cain plantation just north of Durham's Station, recalled
that with "Yankees all around the place," her mother marched to the "big
house" to reclaim her child. "You took her away from me and didn't pay no
mind to my crying," Debro's mother told their ex-mistress, "so now I'm
taking her back home. We're free now," she claimed, "we ain't going to be
slaves no more to nobody."[1] Surprised and dismayed that he had lost control of the people he had owned, Paul Cameron complained: "At Farintosh
and Stagville all are going to the devil or dogs as fast as they can — wont
work — destroying stock, outhouses, enclosures." The owner of several large
and once well-ordered plantations just north of Durham's Station, Cameron
griped in the fall of 1865 that "just now no one is at work," as the freedpeople celebrated at "a sort of Carnival all at the marble yard and on the
River banks."[2]

Five men from Orange County represented African American interests at the 1865 Freedmen's Convention in Raleigh, which set out three priorities for African Americans: education, self-protection, and civil rights. All five also served on the State Equal Rights League organized at the convention, "to secure, by political and moral means, as far as may be, the repeal of all laws and parts of laws, State and National that make distinctions on account of color" and to "encourage industry, morality, education, temperance, economy, and to promote all things that will elevate us, and build an honorable foundation for our posterity, and to use all legitimate means that are in our power to obtain our rights as citizens of our beloved State."[3] The carnivals were quashed quickly, however, and moments of joy were fleeting as freedpeople realized that freedom posed new kinds of peril and that black folks' paths to aspirations took disparate turns.

In response to black freedom, hostile whites terrorized Orange County blacks. Freedmen's Bureau records provide documentation of numerous cases in which African Americans charged whites with assault and battery, a half dozen in the summer of 1867 alone, including one against a white man for beating a black woman. At least five black people were murdered in the county between 1868 and 1870. When a wood-structured warehouse burned down, whites accused the Union League, an organization that encouraged black political activity, of arson, but more likely the fire was set by white insurgents.[4] Martha Allen had "come free" near Durham's Station because her master had taken his slaves inland to hide them from emancipation by the Union Army troops who controlled eastern North Carolina. Once valued as property, Allen remembered emancipation in Orange County as fearful years, when the Ku Klux Klan terrorized black people, especially "free issue" blacks who had been free before the war and who now stepped into leadership roles. The Klan raided homes to "strip all the family and whip the old folks . . . and then they accosted the pretty yellow gals," making it clear that the old order would not fall easily if at all. Ben Johnson, who was from Hillsborough, recalled several hangings in 1869: Cy Guy's hung over the road for four days "swinging in the wind," when the perpetrators threatened that "any nigger who takes down the body shall be hanged too." "Them was bad days," Sarah Debro remembered. Freedom brought terrible suffering for her: "I'd rather been a slave than to have been hired out like I was." Assessing the difference between emancipation and slavery, Debro pointed out that "I was hungry most of the time." Nor was she any safer: "I had to keep fighting off Yankee men."[5]

Lacking better choices or finding it advantageous, many African Americans elected to stay at the places where they had been enslaved. Assured of the Smiths' support, Cornelia Smith stayed with her aunt and mistress Mary Ruffin Smith and worked as a seamstress in Chapel Hill until she married Robert Fitzgerald. Abner Jordan was born at Paul Cameron's Stagville plantation north of Durham's Station in 1832. He and his family "stayed with Marse Paul for five years after the surrender," before moving on. Cy Hart's family remained at Stagville until Cameron died. Horace Cameron stayed even longer; he worked for Cameron, married Patty Holman, also a freed Cameron slave, and raised his family there. Daughter Janie Cameron (Riley) and granddaughter Theresa (Lyons) were born there. He "never wanted to leave the Cameron place," his daughter explained, and he never did: "He died and was buried there."[6]

African Americans negotiated the best terms they could for their freedom, making decisions that served their economic needs as well as their aspirations. Sometimes that meant following an ex-master, as in the case of John O'Daniel, ex-slave and rumored half brother of the Confederate colonel Julian S. Carr Jr., who moved from Chapel Hill to Durham's Station with Carr and continued to work as his servant. Tempie Herndon and Exter Durham struck out on their own. They had married when they were enslaved but had lived on plantations in different counties. Freedom meant they "could be together all the time, not just Saturday and Sunday." Together they decided that Exter should leave his ex-master and make a try with Tempie's ex-master, whom they concluded was the fairer man. "We rented the land for a fourth of what we made," she recalled. They managed to buy a farm and thus their freedom once more, but surviving and saving required all nine children to work in the fields, "as soon as they could walk good."[7]

Freed with nothing but themselves, black folk hoped to build capital without cash and accepted the crop lien system as one means to accomplish that goal. In a fair arrangement, a family could leverage its labor to produce crops to pay for use of the land, housing, and supplies. Typically, however, landlords — like the planters before them — stole black autonomy by controlling sharecroppers' labor, apportioning returns, and determining the value of both. Collaborating with planters, merchants charged exorbitant interest rates for tools, seed, fertilizer, and goods, with the result that croppers owed more than they could make. The state colluded in passing the Landlord Tenant Act of 1877, which entitled property owners to set the worth of a crop at settling time. The law did not obligate them to put contracts in writing, and many did not. Nor did the act specify that tenants were to have access to ledgers or records. Sharecropping bound black farmers to an economic system that resembled slavery, which, codified in law, assured that African Americans would remain in debt and indebted to landowners. Exter and Tempie Durham made a better-than-average deal, but they were exceptions. Theresa Cameron Lyons recalled that her family was cheated out of most of its earnings. At the end of the year of hard labor, "there'd be nothing left." Still, the black Camerons worked on the white Camerons' land well into the 1930s.[8]

Seeking distance from whites and autonomy for themselves, other blacks elected to leave the farms, plantations, and towns where they had worked as slaves for the places they had heard about. Given the uncertainties of emancipation, it was an adventurous if rational move for African Americans to leave the places where they had lived in slavery, yet thousands of black migrants departed rural districts and small towns in search of family, work, and a safe place to settle. Durham's Station was just such a place, named for the depot built on land donated by the Durham family to the railroad. Barely a settlement, it served as a crossroads on the eastern side of Orange County. It was small but central enough to be a site for official public business, such as tax collecting and voting in 1860. Only a hundred people lived there in 1865, including a wartime community of renegades, refugees, runaways, and others who lived on the margins of southern society. The railroad itself made Durham's Station a destination. It offered a way to leave North Carolina, and plenty of African Americans selected that option. Reflecting on the novelty and persistence of black folk's mobility, Durham's first historian remarked in the 1880s on the "melodic strains" that echoed from "the trains on which they are always moving." Another wrote of blacks' departures, that "a great many have left and gone South and west — so many I believe labor will be scarce."[9]

Those African Americans who decided to come to Durham's Station after the Civil War sought out each other and work, not municipal services, the protection of Union troops, or the safety of numbers. Durham's Station provided none of these, nor any other obvious reason to attract a large population of African Americans. A black journalist once hypothesized that a black community flourished there "because it was neutral ground."[10] The station had witnessed virtually no war activity; indeed, it was nonaligned territory in which Unionists and Confederates began to talk peace. A few black people had lived there before the Civil War as household servants, artisans, smiths, craftspeople, and factory hands residing at their places of employment.[11]

Those African Americans who arrived after the war mostly gathered on the muddy flats, a half-mile south of the depot, well out of the sight of the white majority population. Practicing benign neglect, white civic leaders believed that "they'll be dead in fifty years." Left to its own devices, the black community proved them wrong. In 1877 when John O'Daniel bought land "near the town of Durham in the settlement of colored people near the South East end of the Corporation of said town," it was in "the section called Hayti." Pronounced "hay-tie" and evoking the image of the independent black state Haiti, the settlement represented a flourishing liberation community of homes and institutions. Partly out of caution and partly out of choice, African Americans shaped such postemancipation communities to advance race pride, self-help, and autonomy and to distance black people from the past. Hayti, created out of the complex associational links among free and freed black people, began as a set of connections and collaborations required for mutual survival and celebration. These relationships provided the groundwork for upbuilding but more importantly generated the kind of social capital black people needed to invest in themselves. Built atop a foundation laid in slavery, Hayti signified permanence, not just a representation of freedom but a concrete product of collective decisions made in freedom to find a place where African Americans could assemble and live peaceably without much interference from whites.[12]

"A Natural Extension of My Home"

Durham exemplified the New South movement. Set on the Piedmont, the stretch of sandy farmland cutting diagonally through the state, Durham was built, like any number of pre-urban settlements, out of resources it created, in this case peace and the people and products that came from nearby fields. Three miles north of the railroad stop, at Bennett Place, the Confederate general Joseph Johnston and the Union general William T. Sherman met in April 1865 to begin negotiations to end the war. While celebrating the imminent end of hostilities — or so the legend goes — soldiers from both sides raided John R. Green's little tobacco factory at Durham's Station and shared the stash they stole. Dispersed around the country after the war, veterans sent back for more, making bright-leaf tobacco, the local strain, a wildly popular weed that linked the North and the South.[13]

The demand for Durham tobacco increased so much that the little settlement burst onto the international market. With no critical mass of people, however, the town could grow only by attracting capital and labor. If the tobacco industry had collapsed for lack of one or the other, Durham would have faded away like so many other New South boomtowns. Instead, the population grew. By 1889, some 8,000 people lived in and around the town.

It ranked seventh among the fifteen cities of North Carolina in 1890 (behind Wilmington, Raleigh, Charlotte, Asheville, Winston, and New Bern) and sixth in the size of its black population.[14]

Fashioned out of the ashes of the Civil War, Durham — as the station became known — grew into the richest municipality in North Carolina by the end of the nineteenth century, one where at least some African Americans shared in the city's success. With a steadily increasing population seeking work, black folk hoped that the political economy of freedom would yield new kinds of employment and new relationships to that work. Industries like tobacco manufacturing linked traditional agrarian economies to a modern industrialized world, attracting large numbers of black workers, who moved from rural to urban areas and who supported both white employers and black businesses. The latter, in turn, formed the financial backbone for the development and expansion of black institutions. The institutions — moderately autonomous black facilities — served as vehicles for improving the quality of life. In addition to Hayti, several promising black communities sprouted up around the center of town, including the West End, later called Lyon Park, where the Fitzgeralds built homes, the East End, where a group of black landowners settled, and Pin Hook, later known as Hickstown and more contemporarily as the Crest Street Neighborhood. These spaces provided settlers with opportunities for innovative relationships as black folk gathered legally and for the first time without white interference.

Among those African Americans seeking work, women and children migrants dominated the population, as they did in most southern cities and towns from Atlanta to Memphis. The initial prospects were discouraging. As a correspondent noted in the late 1860s, "A good number of women and children are here yet strolling about — and I don't see any chance for them to live." By 1880, however, industrialization caught up with the African American demand for work. In Durham, black female workers — growing in number along with pounds of tobacco produced and white homes built — produced much of the funds necessary to upbuilding. By the mid-1880s, black women could find plenty of work as hands, servants, cooks, and maids and occasionally as entrepreneurs and teachers. In turn, women provided most of the resources, tangible and intangible, to establish a black institutional life in freedom. Even those who lived in the households of white employers maintained homes in black settlements, made black friends, attended black churches, and joined black associations.

Hayti was the largest and most prosperous of Durham's black neighborhoods, home to thousands of residents and autonomous black institutions in which they worked, worshipped, shopped, and schooled. Here, Margaret Faucette, a widow with thirteen children, started prayer meetings in her rooming house on South Railroad Street. She recruited a minister (whom she married) to start a church, White Rock Baptist, and gave the first dollar for its building. Missionaries Molly and Edian Markham founded Union Bethel African Methodist Episcopal (AME) Zion Church and its free school in 1869. Congregants upbuilt Union Bethel from a mere log cabin into a wood frame structure—and in 1891 into a handsome building renamed St. Joseph AME Zion Church and made of Fitzgerald bricks.[15]

It was hard to tell which came first, a church or the community surrounding that church. Mooring a mobile people to maturing neighborhoods, churches testified to increasing stability. White Rock and St. Joseph anchored Hayti with help from Mt. Vernon Baptist Church, founded in 1885 as a congregational spin-off from White Rock. New Bethel Baptist, also established in the 1880s, provided an anchor for Pin Hook, just northwest of town. The Fitzgerald families founded two different congregations in Durham. Matching the example of philanthropy (and paternalism) of his white contemporaries, Richard Fitzgerald built Emmanuel AME Zion Church on the west side of town, where his workers resided, and donated it to the congregation. Cornelia Fitzgerald's daughters, Pauline and Sallie, convinced the Episcopal Diocese to expand its educational mission to include Durham church services. The diocese formally established St. Titus Chapel, a black Episcopal congregation in Hayti, in 1903. Fourth-generation Fitzgerald Pauli Murray remembered black institutions as "the natural extension of my home life." Advanced by women and furthering the values of uplift and morality, the church was a central gathering place for African Americans, where congregants exchanged information. The church also provided individuals and families with connections to other places through denominational alliances and various organizations.[16]

Centered in the church, women's auxiliaries, missionary societies, prayer groups, and sewing circles supported church initiatives; they also advanced racial self-help by focusing their energies on their communities' needs. Making and collecting food, clothes, and fuel, these groups distributed assistance as lessons of morality and faith. Local women's groups evolved into and emerged out of state and national organizations. Hattie E. Shepard was born in nearby Hillsborough in 1858 and moved to Durham in the late 1890s with her husband, Augustus Shepard, who was the pastor of White Rock Baptist Church. She had served as secretary to the women's Baptist Missionary Circle in Raleigh, the group that in 1884 founded the statewide organization, the Baptist Woman's Home and Foreign Missionary Convention of North Carolina (the Woman's Convention), one of the South's most influential associations of churchwomen. Among its other founders, the Woman's Convention counted Pattie G. Shepard, Hattie Shepard's sister-in-law. The Woman's Convention brought ideas developed by one group of women to a broader constituency. For instance, the organization proposed to "establish and improve Baptist Home Mission Circles in all Baptist Churches and destitute sections of the State." The Durham Baptists established a mission beyond the north edge of the city, near the Stagville plantation. The Woman's Convention also created projects that connected a variety of causes embraced by members — the Colored Orphan Asylum at Oxford, for example, which was founded by Hattie Shepard and headed by her husband. By sending funds to the organization's Chicago-based headquarters in the North, the Woman's Convention also supported programs for education and temperance in other places, representing another way that a mobile people intersected with and connected to each other.[17]

Along with churches, lodges, fraternal organizations, and other associations were groups that black folk called their own, built as they were out of personal connections that crossed sacred, secular, and geographic lines. Among the first was a black chapter of the Order of the Eastern Star, a national secret society founded in the nineteenth century. Originally a women's auxiliary to a fraternal society, the Eastern Star bound its mostly female membership to mutual aid, service, and uplift. Durham's Drusilla Chapter of the Eastern Star included James A. Whitted, a postal carrier, and his wife Tempie Whitted, a Baptist missionary; Minnie Sumner Pearson, a Methodist churchwoman, graduate of Livingstone College, and teacher in the county schools; Caroline Mebane, a washerwoman; John O'Daniel, servant for Julian Carr; and Bertie Boyd, a live-in cook. All were considered among the most prominent black persons in the community. The Drusilla Chapter not only brought people from different neighborhoods and occupational clusters together but also sent delegates to statewide conventions. As the Eastern Star chapters spread at the national level, the organization linked the local to state to nation. In return, Durham families welcomed traveling Eastern Star members, as well as other friends and associates, into their homes.[18]

Although many were founded by whites, the black colleges created another set of crossroads that linked black people from Durham to individuals and communities within and outside of North Carolina. James Whitted's school sat at the entry to Hayti and sent dozens of local students on for higher learning to colleges near and far. Shaw University, in Raleigh, started as regular meetings held by a Baptist minister to teach freedmen to read and interpret the Bible and enrolled five students from Durham in liberal arts, professional, medical, and religious training programs in the 1880s. In that same decade, local students also attended St. Augustine's College in Raleigh, Howard University in Washington, Fisk University in Nashville, and Hampton Institute in Virginia. School-based social groups, fraternities and sororities, and professional organizations strengthened the network of student, family, and alumni connections that provided freedom's first generation with advantages their parents never had. Expected to be models of race progress for people on both sides of the veil, black teachers, missionaries, and professionals moved in widening circles to transmit ideas and initiatives from the schools they attended to the churches they attended and the communities where they lived. To each place they went, churchwomen and educators fueled the emergence of respectability as a hegemonic ideology of black aspirations — an allegiance to temperance, industriousness, thrift, refined manners, and Victorian sexual morals.[19]

Traced through women, moreover, allegiant lines between family, politics, and institutions marked the overlap between individuals, organizations, institutions, and causes. Sarah McCotta "Cottie" Dancy, a sister of John C. Dancy, a well-known AME Zion churchman and black Republican activist in eastern North Carolina, married Aaron M. Moore, a Shaw graduate and Durham's only black doctor. Moore shared John Dancy's penchant for electoral politics, but Cottie Moore was equally visible in black Durham's public life, active in White Rock Church and as a leader of the state Woman's Convention of the black Baptist Church. As a doctor's wife, she was a resource to her community, feeding the hungry who appeared at her door. Her husband's patients who came to their home also benefited from her care, and the community members who called on her in emergencies relied on her wisdom and alliances.[20] Cottie Moore's friend and coworker in local missionary endeavors, Minnie Sumner Pearson, drew another set of connections. A member of the Eastern Star, Minnie Sumner married William G. Pearson, a graduate of Shaw University. Born enslaved in 1858, the son of a freedwoman from Durham, Pearson became a teacher while also sharing business and political interests with Aaron Moore. Hattie Shepard of the Woman's Convention had a son, James E. Shepard, who founded the National Religious Training School and Chautauqua for the Colored Race (later known as North Carolina College for Negroes and now as North Carolina Central University). A graduate of Shaw, he arrived in Durham in the 1890s and lived with the Pearsons. Robert Fitzgerald's oldest daughter, Mary Pauline, joined this group, leaving St. Augustine's College in 1885 to work as a teacher for the principal James Whitted, a prominent minister and proponent of the Woman's Convention in Baptist circles. She later worked for Pearson, who succeeded Whitted as head of the colored school in the 1890s. Among her students, Charles C. Spaulding, who became a prominent businessman, had left rural life "Down East" (the southeast sector of North Carolina) in 1895 to attend the new Whitted School, and he lived with his uncle's family, the Moores.[21]

Spaulding opened a store and became part of an evolving circle of black entrepreneurs who grounded Durham's black society in business and who by the 1880s became the core leadership. Drawn to Durham from the state capital of Raleigh by rumors of prosperity, John Merrick, a barber, partnered with John Wright to open a small shop in Durham. "We struck Durham about the time she was on her boom," Wright recalled; "we went into business and met with success from the opening of our doors." In 1883, Merrick and Wright joined with William Day, the cabinetmaker, to purchase another business, a mutual aid society called the Royal Knights of King David. Merrick, who was freed, and Day, who was free, served as the officers of the Royal Knights. William G. Pearson, the teacher, retained a hand in the venture and took charge as the Supreme Grand Secretary in 1887.[22] Alongside the Royal Knights, the "Colored" Masons, led by John Wright as the Worshipful Master, laid yet another incipient base for mutual aid, self-help, and political organizing. These fraternal societies facilitated coalition building and business partnerships among men. The "three Johns," Wright, Merrick, and O'Daniel, sponsored train excursions, a popular entertainment that gave African Americans a chance to see the state. Merrick and Spaulding also owned a cigar factory, Spaulding & Merrick. But the leading black businessman in town was still Richard Fitzgerald, who also headed the Real Estate, Mercantile, and Manufacturing Company, a general store and tobacco factory that produced "New Durham" and "The 1900" brands of tobacco. He also worked in partnership to create the Durham Drug Company (a pharmacy), and in 1902 he invested with William H. Coleman and became president of Coleman Cotton Mill in Carrabus County, the only cotton mill in the nation owned by African Americans. In 1908, he collaborated with others to found a black bank, Mechanics and Farmers, whose success showed the strengthening of entrepreneurial ventures.[23]

The business and institutional community emerging in Durham generated a buzz about the town as a place where black folk could lift against the drag of the recent past. Most but not all among this core group descended from land-owning families in Columbus County southeast of Durham. Associated with each other before emancipation, they subsumed any status drawn on the past to actively encourage the development of an aspiring class among freedpeople. They were set apart, nonetheless, by the visible material comforts of black progress. Carriages, clothes, and items in homes never owned before suggested that African American professionals, businesspeople, female activists, and church officials could escape the quotidian struggles with poverty that most freed black people confronted. Released from the kind of demands that whites made on sharecroppers and tenants, entrepreneurs achieved autonomy, stabilized their families, and began to realize black aspirations.

Their emergence represented an important transformation within the black community. Unlike most African American families, these families were able to follow the idealized sexual division of labor, with women not having to earn, and those who did holding highly regarded positions as teachers. Referred to by the Fitzgeralds as "upstarts from Down East," their names became the prominent signposts of personal, political, and business networks of the Old North State: Shepard, Merrick, Pearson, Moore, Spaulding. With few aristocratic peers, Richard Fitzgerald linked himself to this group.[24]

In a community creating itself in a rough racial environment, race rather than ancestry fastened black people to each other. Durham's black residents came to know each other as they produced families and constructed institutions. Status differentiation emerged, but because almost everyone came from someplace else the community's social organization initially was fluid. Because Durham lacked an antebellum history, a black aristocracy was nonexistent, except for a handful of "aristocrats of color" who could trace their origins to familial lines of antebellum free blacks and "privileged" slaves. These included the Fitzgeralds, of course, William Day, the cabinetmaker, Miss Ledger, the private school teacher, and John O'Daniel, servant and reputed half-brother of Confederate veteran Julian S. Carr Jr. Light-skinned and educated, artisans or craftsmen, they were clannish, nonetheless, and marked by their sense of superiority in terms of culture and achievement. Yet virtually none among this group were members of the "black four hundred" or among the "best of Negro society," the likes of the Churches of Memphis or the Terrells of Washington, D.C. But the group did include a number of freedpeople, like John Merrick and William G. Pearson, who personally had known the harshness of rural slavery in North Carolina.[25]

But class structure, as such, proved too narrow a term to describe budding status designations among black people in Durham until the 1880s. Known more by dint of hard work than inheritance, Durham's first black families also garnered their status markers through entrepreneurship and property owner-ship, which gradually distinguished one group of blacks from others. Before the end of the nineteenth century, however, anyone who attained gainful and steady employment, including industrial and service workers, and who em-braced the code of morals and public behavior preached by black leaders and institutions shared an elevated status of the aspiring class. Most African Americans depended on whites for their livelihood, in any case, and only a fraction owned property, operated businesses, or worked in the professions.[26] Nevertheless, twenty years after emancipation, rising affluence and comfort testified that some among freedom's first generation did not face the same struggles their parents had faced. An advantaged group, this cohort embraced the responsibility to the communities from which its members came, even as they intermarried. Moving into leadership roles, they assumed guardianship of the black community. Then, too, few African Americans were likely to oppose the goal of building schools, to deny the importance of churches, or to disregard the value of voluntary efforts, especially people with shared memories of slavery. Facing the same opponent of white supremacy, the shared struggle counted more among Durham's black people than fragile differences.[27]

But it is impossible to overlook differentiation created by the new options that freedom made available to some women, however broad or restrained. Pauline Fitzgerald's occupation in teaching reflected one of those opportuni-ties, even though her work reflected the limits of gender after emancipation. As one of a few women enrolled at St. Augustine's College in the early 1880s, she arrived with equal or better preparation — although she was younger — than the men. Formal education had made the Fitzgerald sisters exceptional in that so few African Americans had access to training beyond the three R's. At the same time, the Fitzgerald sisters as women could aspire to few profes-sional occupations other than teaching, missionary work, or service to prom-inent whites. Programs in theology, pharmacy, medicine, or law exclusively enrolled men. Women primarily entered normal schools, usually two-year programs in education.

Status ascribed by schooling derived from the honor of the position rather than the income it provided, given that teachers earned very little and their earnings were subject to political compromises and racial inflexibility. Nor did education excuse its owners from hard work or dedication to racial des-tiny. Pauline and Sallie Fitzgerald grew up inspired by their father's zeal for learning and his demand to excel. "Year after year I went with my father to school every day. He was very strict and would switch me for the smallest thing I'd do," the elder Pauline remembered. As teachers, then, they carried significant responsibility to meet communities' expectations that they not fail, that they strive selflessly on behalf of the race, and that they serve as "a countervailing force against the view that colored people were defined as inferior." Thus, despite their father's inability to provide for his family, teaching provided the Fitzgerald daughters with a venerated occupation, one that granted them influence among their neighbors, if not a living wage, and raised the daughters' family status, albeit not to the level of those of notable names. At the same time, their daily interactions with hundreds of children and families made them integral parts of the communities they served and positioned them at the heart of the movement to build race consciousness.[28]

At first glance, then, Hayti proffered a liberation community where African Americans made decisions for themselves without white manipulation and wove themselves into a rich and complex interior world concerned with its own development. It could be argued, for instance, that black folk shared in configuring Durham's pattern of residential segregation by race through their own actions as much as through their compliance with whites' preferences. Retreating from the direct supervision of whites, most blacks preferred to live among one another, for the sake of their comfort rather than racial custom, with the network of African Americans facilitating a pattern that encouraged migrants to move to places where other blacks already lived. Settling in Hayti, black migrants of the 1880s expanded the residential blueprint developed in the 1860s.[29] The homes, schools, and churches built along the streets of the Hayti district made autonomous space out of the places where blacks lived. Durham passed no segregation laws before the twentieth century, a point of municipal pride. But it did not have to.

Most of Hayti lay outside the boundary lines of the city until 1901, and few black people actually lived within the city limits. Indeed, a broad view of black Durham reveals that the quality of life in black districts reflected a racial order that assigned African Americans to a subservient place, characterized by the white neglect intended to create the inadequate, inferior, or indecent facilities that whites believed blacks could tolerate and deserved. In the end, even without laws, Durham was more segregated than older cities like Charleston and Wilmington.[30] Even while Durham's first history praised African Americans' "growing prosperity," it also noted specifically, "They are a class still distinct from the whites, and for many years they must remain so."[31] Thus, residential segregation may have evolved as the détente of the New South, but it also represented a racial caste system that would prove difficult to alter.

Beneath a skyline of churches and next to the nice houses the more prominent families owned, the masses of African Americans scraped by in the pockets of destitution sprouting on the city's lowlands. Black laborers, factory hands, and household workers spread out along the rutted routes through Hayti, on the slopes beneath Robert Fitzgerald's home in Lyon Park, and between Richard Fitzgerald's mansion and the tobacco warehouses. Near the Fitzgeralds, the Bottoms, as the neighborhood's name suggests, was a basin traversed by ravines. The Bottoms connected to nearby Brookstown by way of a creek along which black washerwomen toiled. Across town, Smoky Hollow, similarly situated and designated, yielded a squalid section of tin-roofed homes and shady activity at the northeast edge of town. In some ways, then, the story of black Durham is one of two cities, one behind the color line that measured a positive distance from slavery. Behind the veil, African Americans created networks of affiliation that developed into community, institutions, and organizations where the philosophy of self-help and judicious initiatives furthered the opportunities black people made for themselves. Using segregation to his benefit, John Merrick expanded his business from one barbershop to six, three for whites and three for blacks. Aaron Moore doctored black patients. Charles C. Spaulding served black customers. Ministers preached to black congregations. Undertakers buried black bodies. This class of entrepreneurs and professionals was able to ward off poverty, find stability, and gain autonomy. In the other one, the racism caused segregation to become one marker of inferiority and of working and living conditions that were deplorable. Nor did racial antagonism fade. Animosities from the past, exacerbated by the present, effected racial conflicts that disadvantaged African Americans in a New South democracy.[32]

"Durham Is the City of the New South"

If relationships provided the groundwork and the community the foundation, labor provided the fuel to upbuild black Durham. Like the Old South, the New South depended upon a steady stream of labor, underpaid, under control, unlikely to openly contest authority, and too racially divided to wield power. Even so, both blacks and whites understood that in this new political economy, the job, the classroom, and the ballot represented instruments of liberation as much as weapons to counter past justifications for planter privileges. Before Reconstruction ended, economics, education, and elections emerged as the arenas of democracy where African Americans pursued freedom, upbuilt community, and staked out citizenship claims. Presenting black folk with a familiar autocracy, whites repeated the Old South in the New South as a paradigm of slave society still based on black labor and gender hierarchy.[33]

Given the name Bull City for Duke's trademark on its tobacco packaging, Durham became a New South center of commerce, distinguishing it from Chapel Hill and Raleigh, the centers of education and government, respectively, in North Carolina. In 1881, the North Carolina legislature chartered Durham County, carved out of Orange and Wake Counties, and named it for the burgeoning city within. By 1887, twelve new tobacco factories had sprung up around town. With orders on hand for two million bricks, Richard Fitzgerald was building a fortune, and prideful Durhamites were building a New South marvel. "Durham invites Capitalists to investigate its growth," *Turner's Directory* boasted in 1889. "Durham exports her bright leaf tobacco to all the principal markets of Europe, and her smoking tobacco and cigarettes to every nation under the sun," promotional materials read. Seasoned with references to its global reach — the Natal, Melbourne, Stockholm, London, Calcutta, Cape Town, Vancouver, and "Tokio [*sic*]" — the story of Durham became a rags-to-riches narrative where the focus on hard work, initiative, ingenuity, and ambition generated a prosperity with the potential to subordinate racial animosities to business and industrial interests. And as though it had no bitter past to turn its back upon, local boosters bragged without ambivalence: "Durham is the city of the New South, an integral part of the United States of America, and as such her motto is 'one country, one flag, one destiny.' "[34]

The absence of an Old South heritage opened the town's power structure enough to let in a range of mavericks, black and white. For a short period of time, ambition could overcome racial restrictions and challenge power wielded historically by planters. Industrial capitalism provided the foundation upon which a new kind of society might be built, and as brick factories replaced log cabins, black and white entrepreneurs built themselves into positions of influence. With the war's end, white yeoman farmer and Confederate veteran Washington Duke returned home, affiliated with the Republican Party, and served as the town's registrar in 1868. Duke and his sons turned their 400 acres and factory barn into American Tobacco Company, a monopoly that grew so large that the government tried to bust it through antitrust legislation. The Dukes found a competitor and political rival in the ex-Confederate colonel, Julian Shakespeare Carr Jr., a white aristocrat who moved to Durham from Chapel Hill seeking wealth in the new environment. A redeemer who took to calling himself General Carr, he proved unable to compete with the Dukes' ingenuity in tobacco. Seizing another New South industry, Carr found a better venture in textiles.[35]

Richard Fitzgerald and John Merrick presented another profile of prosperity, that of wealth, stability, and security among black folk. Rich, influential, and considered "among the most intelligent men" in the city, Fitzgerald sat on a jury in 1880 — probably the first, and, until the mid-twentieth century, the last African American in Durham to do so. And John Merrick, a freed slave, became a prominent property holder on the south side of the tracks just as Fitzgerald had done on the west side of town. Admired by Washington Duke and General Carr — who thought of Merrick as "a born Chesterfield" — the barber represented the self-made man of the 1890s, tending to the most prominent and powerful white men in town with one hand and upbuilding his community with the other. Free and freed, Fitzgerald and Merrick were honored, respected members of Durham's black communities, models of race progress and black manhood. Embracing the cult of domesticity, their wives worked at "keeping house," secure in their sizable homes.[36]

Duke, Carr, Fitzgerald, and Merrick personified Henry Grady's economic vision of the New South, where modern industries might "take root and spread" on southern ground to mark the region's independence from and its incursion into the commercial North. But Durham imagined itself as even more progressive, as its boosters claimed. The "*broad-gauged, Liberal Minded Gentlemen*" among business and civic leaders worked as "an advantage" in creating a spirit of racial cooperation necessary to make the city a success.[37] Widely known by its reputation as a place where ingenuity and energy reaped rewards, Durham attracted a diverse population of workers. When production reached a quarter-billion cigarettes in 1879, all hand rolled, the Dukes recruited from New York a group of Russian and Polish Jews, immigrants skilled in rolling tobacco for cigars. Viewed as peculiar by whites and blacks, they comprised a distinct population and formed the nucleus of the town's Jewish ghetto, a section eventually integrated into the black neighborhood as Hayti spread. They taught the skill of tobacco rolling to young black men but retained the racial advantage of whiteness when it came to wages. When the Dukes' next innovation, a cigarette roller, displaced skilled hands and the smaller smokes overtook cigars in popularity, Jews and blacks vied for the shrinking number of skilled positions, a conflict that undermined their interests as laborers. Similarly, Chinese laundries, established by the 1890s, competed against black washerwomen for work and generated tensions.[38]

Accordingly, when black and white organizers for the Knights of Labor appeared in Durham in the mid-1880s, they found contentious relations not only among workers, owners, and managers, but also among workers themselves. Divided by race and ethnicity despite their common interests as laborers, black and white workers forged separate relationships to the Knights' organizers. To African Americans, the Noble and Holy Order of the Knights of Labor was more than a vehicle to gain higher wages and better working conditions — the organization was a place to represent black people's collective interests as laborers and a way to talk back. Five hundred African Americans — men, women, and children — were employed at Blackwell's tobacco factory in 1884, the year tobacco workers organized into assemblies and engaged in a strike. Organizers also reported that black women household workers desired to bargain collectively for better wages and improved conditions, including protection from sexual harassment by their employers. Still, racially segregated chapters of the Knights signaled factiousness among black and white laborers, with one finding the Knights' strategy expedient and the other increasingly disaffected. "The white people do not take to the Knighthood in these parts," an organizer wrote to the *Journal of United Labor*, the newspaper of the Knights, but the organization was "growing well among the colored folks."[39]

The principles on which the Knights attempted to stand — racial if not social equality, the rights of men to provide for and protect their families, and the dignity of labor — flew in the face of the southern tradition of white hegemony. Black and white workers demanded a living wage, as a matter of freedom and independence, vying for power in an evolving economy. Enraged, local white capitalists harassed a white organizer in Durham who was working with blacks. Unwittingly, the Knights exacerbated racial antagonism, not only by advocating dignity for African American women but also by proposing that black men share the quotidian rights of white men.[40] Open to race baiting, the Knights' internal turmoil disclosed the organization's inability to subordinate racial to class issues, even when black and white workers shared issues. One organizer wrote to Terrence V. Powderly, leader of the Knights of Labor, to complain that a black organizer "will be a useful worker among the *colored*" but "utterly useless to us among *whites*. . . . We feel that to send a *colored* man among the large number of white farmers and mechanics and factory operators who are appealing to us, would be to jeopardize the interests of the order in creating a prejudice against us." Discouraged by the Knights of Labor's ambivalent response to its racial dilemma, African Americans began to lose interest by 1890, and under the pressure of increasingly antagonistic racial politics, the organization lost its strength in the region. Its decline prefigured a series of strained interracial efforts unfolding throughout the late nineteenth century.[41]

As it took shape, Durham promised but rarely delivered freedom dreams for freedpeople who left farms and plantations for a village about which they only had heard. Budding white capitalists and an assemblage of white merchants, managers, and mechanics might have contended with each other for power, but in opposing labor demands and exacerbating labor tensions they quickly found common ground with each other and with white workers on matters of gender and race. Industrialists managed the labor market in ways that sorted whites and blacks hierarchically into skilled, semiskilled, and unskilled positions, creating an employment paradigm that favored whites over blacks and men over women. Ironically, tobacco represented Durham's potential to transform race relations based on free labor, but in the end tobacco mirrored Old South relationships, with the rise of an industrial patriarchy dependent upon the labor of African American women.[42]

Unstable economic conditions had forced both black and white women to enter the public workforce. Black people suffered severe poverty in the years after slavery, but African American women suffered greater poverty, earned lower wages, and encountered greater exploitation than black men or white women and men. It was the stunning and stable increase in tobacco leaf production—Blackwell Tobacco produced some eight million pounds per year in 1889—that shunted black women into the equivocal work of tobacco. Working tobacco paid more and offered significant benefits over household service, even though, as in textiles, the availability of work in tobacco depended on the international economy, product marketing and demand, and the will of the land. Because the work itself was harsh and exhausting, even in the worst economic times African American women did not have to compete with white women for tobacco processing jobs.[43]

As tobacco grew, so did racial segregation. Working leaf was grimy, foul work on the raw products end and considered too rough for white women. But it was available—indeed assigned—to black women. The textile industry, on the other hand, was organized around white women as laborers and, by extension, around white families. Mills mostly excluded black women and men from all positions except cleaning jobs. When tobacco technology shifted to making and marketing cigarettes, white women got the cleaner unskilled jobs of counting and packaging and were paid more than black women. Thus tobacco innovations expanded the job market for women generally but also stretched the racial hierarchy among women that carried beyond the factory. The growing number of white married women gaining employment in tobacco and textiles created a demand for African American women to work as household laborers—in service as cooks, nurses, washerwomen and as maids for whites of all classes.[44]

Excluded from textile mills but preferred by tobacco factories, black women emerged as the central labor constituency in the town's most significant industry, the one for which Durham became internationally known, the one that provided African American women and men with their most likely opportunity to benefit from southern industrial development, and the one that maintained their subservient status in industrial capitalism. White and black men also were segregated by sex and forced to compete for jobs as skilled rollers, positions that held the status of craftsmen. But race relations were such that white men obtained jobs as skilled and semiskilled workers, as well as mechanics and supervisors. Just as African American men began to lose their employment edge in carpentry, ironwork, and smithing, they were limited to the unskilled work of tobacco, doing the dirty work of flavoring and the heavy work of lifting.[45]

Ultimately, the market forces of racial capitalism benefited Piedmont industrialists and not its poorest people. One indicator of all workers' struggles was the astonishing rate at which female employment increased. Leaving farmwork to their families' males, women could find public wage work, day work, and seasonal work more easily than men. For that reason, they dominated the migration stream to Durham. Combined, black and white women accounted for 40 percent of the industrial workforce in the city by the end of the nineteenth century. As race and gender hierarchy played out in Durham's two main industries, women earned less than men, and African American women earned lower wages and found fewer employment options than white women.[46]

Thus, Durham's industry brought men and women, black and white, into the same economic arena, but industrialists consciously organized employment to repeat familiar power relationships — that is, the race and gender hierarchy proved as useful to southern modernization, industrialization, and urbanization as it had to plantation society. Mill work sanctioned white women's labor outside the home but removed them from any contact with blacks of both sexes. Consequently, occupational positions sorted into categories according to the race and sex of the worker, furnishing a form of industrial segregation that not only sustained white males' power over white women and African Americans but also undermined any potential for cross-racial alliances by fostering competition and racial antagonism between workers of both races and engendering a sense of ascendancy and entitlement among laboring whites. With white women entering the public sphere, moreover, African American men who dealt with whites were forced to operate in a very narrow sphere of subservience in jobs as draymen, hacks, janitors, bellmen, servants, and factory hands.[47]

The inequities between black and white tasks were exacerbated by the pay scale. White factory owners and, by extension, white workers believed black workers should be paid less than white workers, because black labor was inferior to white labor. The wage scale also reflected white perceptions that black people and black bodies were worth less than white ones. Another rationalization for substandard "Negro wages" argued that African Americans could and should live on lower incomes than whites. "The Negro is a cheap liver and demands less wages," a white journalist argued in a trade journal. Not only did white owners suppose that African Americans could survive on less money. They also proposed that their living conditions required a lower income.[48]

These urban labor conditions exacerbated the trend toward black poverty, creating situations that required all employable black people — men, women, and children — to work for whatever wages they could obtain in "Negro jobs." According to the 1887 city directory, urban employments had shaken out by race and gender, with whites attaining professional, craft, and clerical positions in numbers that were out of proportion to their population and with black women clinging to the bottom rung of the economic ladder. Almost all African American women worked outside the home — 90 percent among the 478 black women listed in the 1889 directory: 194 as washerwomen, 84 as cooks, and 60 as domestics. Fifty-five worked in some aspect of the tobacco industry, and only eleven held professional employment as teachers, in skilled positions like seamstress, or as proprietors such as boardinghouse owners. For the vast majority of African Americans, Durham provided no magic formula for the race's rise. Black people struggled here as they did everywhere else. The presence of a black aspiring class said more about how the fortunes of capitalism fell to the few than about how modernization changed the South for the many.[49]

"Great Complaint among the Colored People"

A few interracial organizational efforts had begun in the early years of Durham, enough to make it seem like African Americans might participate in the town's political life. The Republican Party, for instance, represented a grassroots coalition of African Americans and whites who shared the objective of seizing power from, not sharing it with, white planters. According to Washington Duke's ledger, blacks composed 40 percent of Durham's electorate in 1868. Moral reform created another venue where white and black interests coincided. In the late 1880s, the Central Prohibition Club of Durham set its Committee on Organizing to work in various parts of the town and the county, "endeavoring to organize clubs in Hayti among the colored people and also at the School House near the cemetery," as the Fitzgerald side of town was known. The temperance group agreed to hold a joint meeting of all of the local clubs, "to which all, white and colored, are invited." In 1888, members of the Colored Prohibition Club presented talks on "the progress of the work among the colored people." Made up of men, these clubs operated as moral arbiters — important in a city where the main street was lined with saloons — and as political organizations that promised support for temperance candidates and whose favor candidates sought in turn. In the temperance movement, African Americans shared some interests with whites but took part in the issue in organizations that were racially separate and a part of black political culture.[50]

Yet politics represented the relationships found in Durham as an emerging municipality, among the city's white civic leaders, the state of North Carolina, and the community of African Americans. And it marked a point where black and white interests conflicted. The tenor of politics in the late nineteenth century suggests that black folk lost ground. When Republicans held power in the township of Durham in 1868, any male twenty-one years or older could vote in the municipality where he had lived for ten days prior, and black Republican influence determined the outcome of municipal elections. In 1874, however, an amendment to the city charter required registrants to prove a ninety-day residency in the township. Alleging that African Americans registered illegally, proponents of the measure used African Americans' mobility as a means to dilute black political potency. In a volatile economic and political milieu, it was difficult for black families to stay in one place for ninety days. Moreover, ninety days provided a wide enough window of opportunity for whites to mount a vigilante crusade against black potential voters.[51]

Richard Fitzgerald, William G. Pearson, John Merrick, and Aaron M. Moore were among the black leaders qualified to vote, and all were resolute about black suffrage. Believing they were free enough to engage in partisan politics, the leading black men became activist Republicans in North Carolina in the 1880s. Their property ownership, influence with a significant constituency of potential voters, and professional ventures represented a potential for black electoral forces to effect change. It was a turning point in Durham's history when in 1888 local Republicans nominated James Whitted and Pearson, both educators, to run for local office. Moving from aspiration to action, their willingness to run invoked the threat of social equality, a challenge to white power represented by the Democratic Party of white supremacy. In response, whites mounted a fiery campaign against "Negro Domination," a euphemism for black power, or more accurately black liberty, autonomy, and citizenship. Social equality, whites believed, allowed black men entrée to a domain to which white men clung dutifully — racial purity, sustained, metaphorically and in fact, by white women's sexuality. Interracial sex not only was taboo but also compromised whiteness and its privilege. Black power exercised in ways that white power had been applied during slavery granted black men the same access to white women that white men had had with black women. To make the case for preventing black empowerment, the language of white supremacy conflated race and gender in ways that made protecting the honor of white women a goal of white power and a task to which all white men must step up.[52] Julian Carr's newspaper, the *Durham Tobacco Plant*, asked its readers: "White men of Durham, those who have any respect for the Anglo-Saxon race, will you fail to do your duty on the 6th of November?" The stark choice — "Will you allow negro rule or a white man's government" — articulated a realization in Durham that whites did not rule completely over African Americans. Measuring the gains of running against the potential losses to violence, Pearson replied to the offer, "I can best serve my race in my chosen profession — teaching," and withdrew. So did Whitted, not that either decision stemmed the tide of racial acrimony their candidacy had raised.[53]

On election day that year, "a number" of black men were "declared ineligible" to vote, according to the local paper, and others were left waiting in line with ballots in hand when the polls closed. In the heat of ensuing accusations of fraud and disfranchisement, the home of the Democratic leader, Caleb Green, burned to the ground. Whites charged the black leadership, specifically a Knights of Labor activist, with arson and armed themselves to "carefully watch" the black community. Then the Colored School burned down not long after the election. The next year, 1889, black leaders fought a state election law that gerrymandered congressional, legislative, and municipal voting districts and broadened the powers of local election officials to deny voting rights to blacks and poor whites. And a black school burned down again. In the context of 1880s heating and fire fighting, buildings commonly burned down, but given the timing of the blazes — during election season — the fires were suspicious, and African Americans believed that whites used arson to retaliate against their demand to vie for power. After the 1889 fire, the "colored Hook and Ladder company" bought a new fire wagon, prompting the *Durham Recorder* to issue an odd and ominous warning to its readers: "When a fire breaks out now, take care, white man." By

1890s, racial antagonism had superseded interracial cooperation in affecting local politics.[54]

Unlike black churches, black public schools — supported by municipal dollars — represented African Americans' literal appropriation of municipal power. From the perspective of white Democrats, blacks had gained too much power. Democrats, as the planter class, controlled Orange County funds between 1865 and 1868 and built no public schools for African Americans. Black educators like Robert Fitzgerald who provided free schools as a part of their missionary efforts either relied on the benevolence of northern organizations or contributed their labor gratis, accepting whatever support the local black community could provide. Most formal learning that Durham blacks acquired before the turn of the century was supported by African American resources as northern support diminished. For their part, African American parents and students demonstrated enthusiasm for educational initiatives. Before it burned down, James Whitted's School enrolled 163 students in a one-room building. The principal wrote to a friend in 1887, "Miss Johnson has more than she can see over and we have had to employ an assistant" — Pauline Fitzgerald. The burning of black schools indicated that the issue of black education was unfolding as a racially politicized matter. With its roots in the Reconstruction legislature where African American lawmakers effectively created it, public education was an extension of municipal and state power exercised postemancipation to confirm and reinforce separate racial worlds. The school issue underscored Durham's race-caste system and demonstrated the lengths to which whites would go to deny African Americans basic entitlements.[55]

That there were black schools to burn down signified the importance of education for teachers, parents, and children and their will to use learning as a means of resistance. One destroyed school reopened in another place, in a sanctuary or lodge hall, and through contributions and labor another school was built. Because it was a struggle to establish and sustain schools, however, few independent efforts stayed in operation long. In his day, Robert Fitzgerald traveled from site to site setting up schools, and his daughters' early teaching careers followed the same pattern. In Durham, where many children worked in the factory and where the impoverished black population was transient, education could reach only a fraction of potential students who lived in and around the city. In 1885, however, the North Carolina legislature authorized local commissioners to issue bonds to build local schools. Subsequently, Durham enacted its first grade-school law, calling for property taxes to underwrite public education with funds from whites supporting white schools and funds from African Americans supporting black schools. The resulting institutions would have reflected the poverty with which African Americans lived, but they were never built. Whites opposed even these minimal efforts to provide education for African Americans. Although the North Carolina Supreme Court declared segregated school funds unconstitutional, Durham whites passed a bond issue to raise funds to construct "suitable grounds and buildings for the Durham grades or public school for white children" and built white schools.[56]

Only with reluctance, then, did Whitted, acting as principal of the Colored School, organize a movement in 1890 to attract to Durham a Negro industrial school based on the Hampton Institute model. Building such a school required white leaders to agree to support the initiative, but Whitted focused on black people's resources. "I should be glad to encourage any effort to bring more money here for school purposes," he wrote to his friend Charles N. Hunter. Aware of his constituents' poverty, however, he believed that "we colored people here are not composed of the kind of material that gets up such enterprises." Assessing the hostility evident in the school battle, he argued a few weeks later, "We are inconveniently located to manipulate successfully with the rings that control all public affairs nowadays." Whitted's letter warned Hunter that any optimism about biracial interest might be premature. Still, the industrial school project built excitement among black people, evidenced by the "series of mass meetings" held by Whitted. The one "on the Fitzgerald side of town" produced "subscriptions of over $1000" from the black community and "a promise of ten acres donated by Richard Fitzgerald." The project garnered enough broad support to generate an interracial meeting at the courthouse. In the end, however, the white residents mounted strong enough opposition to black education in Durham to ensure that the project failed.[57]

A municipality caught in the particular quandary regarding gender, race, and politics, Durham had opened and then quickly closed economic, electoral, and educational avenues, denying black people access to the means to turn a liberation community into the kind of place they had envisioned. Industrialization and the urbanization it fostered, so highly praised by Durham's white capitalists, only briefly threatened to remake the New South into an industrial democracy. Requiring the labor of white women and African American workers of both sexes, industrialization placed the imagined menace of race-mingling right under the noses of white patriarchs. However much they were distanced from whites by race and sex-segregated work cultures and residences, African Americans came too close for comfort in labor, education, and electoral politics. Assertive activity among African Americans in 1888 had incited racial violence, obstruction at the polls, and the burning of black schools, but it also had solidified blacks' determination to make decisions in their own interests.

On an autumn evening during the electoral campaign of 1888, African Americans in Durham held a mass meeting to discuss the question of emigration to Liberia. There is no record of how many — if any — residents actually quit the town to seek a place in an African homeland, but mass meetings and shifting migration patterns sent collective messages of black discontent, restiveness, and willingness to start again. A series of migrations already had ferried black people between geographic locations. Freedwoman Sarah Poindexter had moved to Durham in 1868 from South Carolina with four girlfriends hoping to find work in tobacco. Disenchanted two years later, she had returned home to Columbia, South Carolina. "Durham wasn't as big then," she later said of her decision. The exodus to Kansas and Oklahoma carried thousands of black family groups from the South to the West beginning in 1879, and some 3,000 African Americans from North Carolina moved to Indiana. Meanwhile, the turpentine fields of Georgia, Alabama, and South Carolina lured others farther south during the 1880s. At the same time, ruthless credit practices produced unrelenting debt that drove black people from the surrounding fields to Durham factories. Essentially repression-proof, tobacco production continued to soar, even in difficult economic times. But with more seekers than positions, too few black folk found steady employment or adequate wages in the limited jobs they could get.[58]

"There has been for some time great complaint among the colored people here of scarcity of work," a Durham newspaper assessed in January 1889. "All lines of work have been overcrowded."[59] According to the *Tobacco Plant*, fifty-two black men left Durham to work on the railroad in Tennessee that month, three months after the Liberia meeting and just weeks after the white supremacy campaigned spiked in the 1888 elections. In late January 1889, the *Durham Recorder*, another local paper, reported that "no less than fifty" African American families and a number of individuals had left by train for Louisiana. They filled two coaches. A week later, 100 more families departed. On Friday, 1 February, a train left during the night carrying "nearly a hundred colored people" westward. More than 500 black people had left in the previous three weeks, the *Recorder* reported on 6 February. In late February, another 350 men, women, and children left for the cotton fields of the Mississippi Delta. In April of 1889, the black North Carolina Emigration

Association convened in Raleigh and adopted a resolution denouncing unfair landlord-tenant legislation, unjust treatment before the law, and inequitable distribution of educational funds. A second resolution appointed a committee to "seek out a good place" and to "lay claims to land."[60]

African Americans were reconsidering their decision to move to a town where nothing stood still. Although indicating that the "exodus to Western and Southern states has not taken all the negroes," the *Tobacco Plant* nonetheless was worried: "We are inclined to believe, however, that exodus fever is rather on the increase." Emigration slowed during the summer months of 1889, according to newspapers, during crop time when "work was in demand and wages high." By the end of that summer, however, the *Recorder* sensed new uneasiness: "Now the Exodus is soon to begin again in more alarming proportions than ever, for it is said that seventy-five thousand have registered to i[m]migration to the Southward. We do not believe that so large a number will go, yet there is but little doubt that owing to the general failure of crops in the State, there will be a large exodus." Still, the paper fretted: "We cannot stand this steady drain on our resources." An infrapolitical signal, migration was one tactic African Americans used to express discontent, to control their own destinies, and to affect the production and service systems upon which white power was built. They were effective, judging by the "empty houses" in "black sections of town" noted in the *Tobacco Plant*'s lament.[61]

Withdrawing their labor from tobacco factories and white homes, white Durham's symbols of its growing wealth, African Americans used their mobility to demonstrate how far they had come toward freedom and their willingness to continue the journey. Unable to stem the tide of black migration, whites realized that their control of black people was still powerful but significantly less so than a generation before. The New South depended on black labor as much as the Old South had. "Whites cannot do the work for which the negro seems adapted by nature," lamented one white spokesman. "It would be highly folly to remove the greater proportion of the competent labor and muscle of the South."[62]

Folly or not, enough black folk considered quitting the country, the state, or the city to seek yet another kind of freedom to raise white anxieties. The tensions surrounding emancipation indicated that upbuilding Durham exploited African Americans who in turn learned to exploit new choices. "Most of our capital is invested in muscle," John Merrick argued to a mass meeting of black folk in Hayti. Stressing that their future lay in the South, he strongly recommended that black people not leave for unknown conditions. Many African Americans — individuals, families, and communities — did not agree, evidenced by a northward turn of black migration as the century ended. Black folk were making strategic decisions about how to invest that muscle: to hearten themselves and to frustrate the white vision of the New South.[63]

Momentarily, the end of slavery provided African Americans with the possibility of benefiting from the fluidity — or chaos — of emancipation, but white hostility caught up with the people on freedom road. The next generation, freedom's first, confronted a growing amorphous enemy that could shift and shape oppression as it pleased. Pauline Fitzgerald and her sisters bore witness to escalating segregation and strengthening campaigns for white supremacy. As an example of a white cultural habit of racial inequity and injustice, Jim Crow captured African Americans within the veil and, against their will, assured black disadvantage and white advantage. As hostility transformed into a systemic process of repression, whites circumscribed the route, traced out the paths along which African Americans could progress, and installed hazards along the way. Linked together as "the Negro Problem," successive generations of black folk lived in a society that portrayed them as the cause of their station, required them to alleviate conditions that were imposed upon them, and then demanded that they fall short. In this way, Jim Crow was more a dare than a challenge, one that defied African Americans to compete and, under threat of vengeance, to succeed.[64]

2 : Durham's Narrow Escape
Gendering Race Politics

In 1896, Durham County Republicans again tapped two black leaders to run for office. William G. Pearson and Aaron M. Moore had bitter memories of white violence following the nomination of blacks in the 1888 elections. Faced with the same choices that they confronted eight years before, they made the same decision. Both men declined to run. Moore reasoned in an article in the *Durham Sun* that his patients "demand of me faith and constant performance" and asserted that local black leaders "preferred to encourage . . . the friendly relations that have always existed between the races."[1] Pearson similarly assured whites that the black leaders "would be far better promoted by curbing the disposition to seek official station, and leaving such matters to those of longer experience in that direction . . . and who are better able to allay existing race prejudice and advance our material interests while safely guarding those of our fellow white citizens."[2]

White supremacy campaigns did not turn on what was rational or fair but on sustaining white power by any means possible and in denial of any black political activism. By linking the fate of the white race to that of the nation, white supremacist southerners attempted to strangle African Americans' political aspirations. As the customs and preferences of racial segregation evolved into codified practices of discrimination enforced by violence, Jim Crow became all the more purposeful in keeping African Americans in their subordinate places in American society and in throwing them down even further and attempting to eradicate them.[3]

Setting aside their aspirations for office, Moore and Pearson had seemed willing to relinquish political power to whites, following Booker T. Washington's counsel to downplay claims for equality in electoral politics in exchange for a racial peace that was necessary to upbuild prosperity.[4] This was a logical defensive position as far as black leaders in Durham were concerned and a point made to colleagues by John Merrick. As businessmen, Moore and Pearson saw the value of discouraging white rage and encouraging whites to accept black prosperity, and they knew that even if blacks acquiesced to losing the vote, there was no guarantee of racial harmony. For even while Washingtonians offered conciliation, southern whites escalated their attacks on black liberation. Avoiding political office was not the same as eschewing electoral politics, however, as African Americans in Durham upbuilt political capital by sustaining their political engagement and keeping a focused political agenda.

North Carolina's black men and women shared a deep appreciation for citizenship rights and valued the franchise. Alongside the men, women brought resources to meetings, rallies, and gatherings, contributing their perspectives to debates, building their own organizations, and pressuring male voters to adhere to communities' interests. Thus they fashioned their own interpretations of Washingtonian conservatism and Du Boisian assertiveness. Moore and Pearson and most of Durham's black leaders retained visible roles in Republican circles, attending meetings and conventions, writing letters, and shaping a political agenda that focused on education. Emphasizing their respective roles as physician and teacher — as race men — Moore and Pearson upbuilt black political strength by encouraging men to vote and make alliances with disgruntled whites, well aware that the discourse on black disfranchisement persisted in the background. They also continued to vote, even as white support for black disfranchisement increased.[5]

As a matter of self-preservation, Durham's black leaders paid close attention to the tenor of state and local politics so as to determine their enemies and friends. In the Bull City, the ex-Confederate Julian S. Carr had the most clout as a white Democrat and as Durham's beloved son of the South, although Democrats did not have a stronghold in city politics in the late-

1890s. Washington Duke remained a strong enough Republican that he supported the publication of a black Republican newspaper.[6] Mostly Durham's white residents divided among themselves. The town sustained both a local Republican Party and a contingent of Populist refugees from the Democratic Party and the Farmer's Alliance, no surprise in the Piedmont, where tobacco farmers, white and black, tenants and croppers, commonly feared economic crises due to agriculture. Together, Populists and Republicans made for Fusion politics, a misnomer that suggests political integration. In reality, the races kept separate political organizations. In order to wield enough power to swing the election, African Americans participated in Fusion collaboration, which also offered black people their best chance for a role in North Carolina politics that decade. Several black candidates were elected Down East on the coast, where African Americans were a significant proportion of the population. Fusion also promised political spoils for African Americans, which black leaders in Durham wanted to collect.[7]

Instead of retreating, then, African Americans shifted their forms of activism and launched a movement for human and civil rights, directly challenging whites' determination to dampen black enthusiasm. It was a black civic organization in New Orleans that selected Homer Plessy to challenge segregation on the railroads and to pursue his case all the way to the Supreme Court. In North Carolina, Durham's black Republicans seized on Fusion victories in 1896 to demand political rewards, insisting that several black justices of the peace be appointed. Powerful whites reacted with increased animosity. When the election cycle began in 1898, the *Durham Daily Sun* reminded its white readers that Moore and Pearson had stepped out of their places two years before. "Some Republican leaders [blacks][,] . . . clothed in brief authority," had asked officials to "humiliate the white people of this county" by appointing "four or five negro Justices of the Peace." The *Sun* boasted, "These leaders know full well that no negro could be elected." And in a veiled threat, the paper recalled that the election of 1896 had been "Durham's Narrow Escape," if not from black domination then from the violent white supremacy campaign required to suppress it: all that in response to a demand for minor political office.[8] The 1898 election was the backdrop for one of the most brutal racial confrontations in American history, as whites threatened and destroyed black communities across the state. And yet the black vote returned George W. White to the U.S. Congress for a second time, the last black to serve in Congress until Oscar DePriest's Chicago election thirty years later.

Despite the power blacks might wield, white Republicans realized that black party members provided no electoral advantage to them as whites and that black ascendancy in party ranks actually had weakened the Republican Party among white potential voters. Some black Republicans questioned the wisdom of pressuring the party to nominate black candidates, convinced that stepping back from office might improve the party's position among the white population, with benefits accruing to African Americans for loyalty. White Republican leaders of North Carolina began to speak in support of black disfranchisement as a solution to the race problem.[9]

Faced with a set of quandaries, African American leaders articulated a range of judgments about the political tides and adjusted their positions according to the instability of the moment. Under the pressure of disfranchisement and escalating violence, even the most visible black leaders questioned the relevance of party politics to the daily struggles of black people. At the same time, however, Durham's black politicos came up with a focused political strategy to obtain state and municipal support for specific black demands. Aaron Moore, for example, kept his hand in party affairs that focused on education, writing to white Republican leaders in 1896 that the black electorate was determined "to take some definite action to strengthen our Educational Institutions, to keep our negro schools and negro education . . . out of the clutches of degraded politics and politicians," meaning whites, Democrat and Republican, who betrayed their agenda.

Engaging their neighbors as vested, knowledgeable, and credible recipients of the advantages that should derive from citizenship, Moore and Pearson openly campaigned on behalf of those candidates who responded to their issues and pledged to resist attempts to reverse black gains.[10] In their social and economic circles, Durham leaders probably spoke of politics frequently, promoting the franchise and conveying information. Repeated among the officers in fraternal organizations, professional societies, and church leaders, the names of Moore, Pearson, Shepard, and other Durham leaders kept their positions in state and national political circles. Their bonds evidenced the strengthening political commitments among African Americans and suggested that black folk were acutely aware of how events in one place affected the residents of another. Republican James E. Shepard, for instance, received a political appointment in Raleigh, the state capital, through his multiple connections in black Baptist church associations and fraternal organizations. Durham folk also were linked politically through family ties. Charles C. Spaulding's cousin, George H. White, had held state office and then was elected to the U.S. House of Representatives from North Carolina in 1896. Aaron M. Moore was the brother-in-law of John C. Dancy, black Republican

Party leader and U.S. Collector of Customs at the Port of Wilmington, North Carolina.[11]

Given the electoral strength of African Americans in the southeast sector of the state where blacks made up more than half of the population, the perils of black power loom largest. Black policemen appointed in New Bern, for example, could arrest white offenders, and black revenue officials like John C. Dancy could demand money from whites. To whites, these were intolerable circumstances — blacks with the authority to rule whites. Reaching back, whites drew on a distorted memory of Reconstruction when "they had seen 'Forty Acres and a Mule' buy many a Negro's vote." According to white supremacist logic, "ignorant" black officeholders supplanted presumably intelligent white officials and, worse, exercised power over whites. Thus deeming "Negro Domination" unscrupulous, dishonest, and corrupt, "good government" had to be "white government," according to Democrats.[12] As African Americans accumulated capital and voted the Republican ticket, they threatened the status quo of white patriarchal rule in North Carolina. In fact, freedom's first generation had sent eleven black legislators to the U.S. Congress from the South since emancipation. Their seats in Washington, D.C., proved that blacks could command partisan power at the national level and that they had the attention of the federal government. Black electoral success simultaneously raised white southerners' anxieties that black political influence maintained the Union hand in Confederate politics.[13] Thus, the last election cycles of the nineteenth century provided whites with the opportunity to end black political participation in North Carolina. Coalesced by using race as a unifying force against cross-race alliances, the Democratic Party, led by the state's most powerful whites, laid out an agenda on race in 1898 that tainted the ballot box and sought to make politics about white power over black.

Yet the ballot was only a symbol of deeper, more brutal, animosity. White leaders characterized black political activism as the demise of morality and the ruination of all that the white South stood for. Arguing that African American electoral and economic ambitions masked a demand for "social equality," white conservatives used the phrase as code for their fears that black men desired sexual access to white women. Posing black male/white female relationships as the bane of southern civilization made gender central to the racial power dynamics played out between white and black men.[14]

In the late 1890s, North Carolina African Americans confronted a white supremacist agenda that linked gender to electoral politics as a way to deny black manhood. The election season of 1898 ended the emancipation era with the devastation of North Carolina's most powerful black community, Wilmington, a bustling port city Down East, at the southeastern point of the state. Democrats and those who followed them — white politicians and civic leaders, laborers and farmers — turned a movement against black political power into an honor, a duty, and a virtue, committing a heinous set of crimes in the name of the state. In the view of Julian Carr and North Carolina's most prominent leaders, the second redemption of North Carolina (the first coming after Reconstruction) lay in the successful election of Democrats, the party of white ascendancy. In the spring of 1898, Carr laid out the conditions for racial accord, warning that "if the negro is to continue to make politics his chief aim, there can be but one ending," that being annihilation.[15] Aggravated by blacks' persistent political activities, he built support among whites in Durham and across the state by appealing to race loyalty. "North Carolina is the only State in the Union in which there are more white than colored men, yet the colored men are in authority," overstating the power balance to a friend. Urging him to join the campaign, Carr pleaded, "God, in his infinite mercy only knows what distress will come to North Carolina if the 'black wave' that is about to sweep over the State is not prevented."[16]

"The Harvest Will Come in Due Time"

For days before the 1898 election, a Durham County mob searched for Mrs. Brewer, a white woman and the wife of a white Republican activist. According to the *Daily Sun*, Mrs. Brewer had "eloped" with "negro men." A black man, Wash Atwater, stood accused of the "kidnapping." Mrs. Brewer's father called for retribution against "the negro's hellish designs on innocent women," and, believing that its worst nightmare had come true, the mob rushed to comply. Three days later, Manly McCauley, a day worker on a local farm, paid the ultimate price for black politics. Accused as "the negro who ran away with Mrs. Brewer," his lifeless body hung from a tree three miles outside of town. Mr. Brewer shared the blame for the downfall of his family, the *Durham Daily Sun* lectured its readers: "The husband reaped some of the benefits of Republicanism for mixing up with the negroes, counseling and advising them with their hellish designs on white people and especially pure and innocent young women. . . . It is indeed the strongest object lesson that has been presented anywhere to this part of the country. What could be stronger to induce white men to support the white men's party and vote the Democratic ticket?"[17]

It is not clear if the search for Atwater and the hanging of McCauley were part of the same or of different incidents. In some ways it did not matter

to the Durham mob. Some black male, initially Atwater and finally Mc-
Cauley, would have to (and did) pay for Mrs. Brewer's departure. Furthermore, whether or not Brewer left voluntarily with Atwater, McCauley, or
any other black man and whether or not they fled independently or together
in an attempt to avoid their sure end mattered even less. The two incidents conflated into a singular political meaning.[18] The Atwater-McCauley-
Brewer incident reflected the ways in which race and gender inflamed the
chaos surrounding the elections of 1898. Incidents like Brewer's "kidnapping" provided white Democrats with the opening to make the nexus of race
and gender *the* electoral issue. "Black rapists were attacking Southern girls
and women," one contemporary believed, "and the brutes were committing
this dastardly crime with more frequency."[19] Such episodes, set off by false
allegations and embellished with white supremacist rhetoric, created a racially charged atmosphere. Whites viewed relationships between black men
and white women not only as a threat to their power and control over those
who had been dependent upon them but also as blacks' attempt to dilute
and "mongrelize" the white race by infusing it with black blood. The rhetoric attempted to portray black male citizens as depraved and inhuman
brutes determined to strip the honor of presumably pure and virtuous white
women. As a punishment for black lust, the threat and practice of lynching
etched sexual violence onto the electoral arena. Therefore, McCauley's murder served as punishment for overstepping his bounds and as a form of social
control, a dire warning to African Americans who dared challenge white
dominance.[20]

In the wake of the McCauley affair, North Carolina whites were poised to
give a violent response to any hint of black assertion, and events evolved in
their favor. Prominent white southern reformer Rebecca Felton visited Wilmington, North Carolina, in the summer of 1898. Disgusted by what she
perceived as the inferior moral condition of poor white women, Felton railed
against interracial relations among black men and white women, which she
viewed as the cause of white women's depravity. Counseling white men on
their responsibility, she called upon them to protect their women, and she
advocated lynching as punishment for the crime of rape that she assumed
underlay those relations. Distressed and irate, Alexander Manly, the black
editor of the *Wilmington Daily Record*, a widely read newspaper serving the
state's largest black community, wrote a scathing editorial in response, that
"the morals of the poor white people are on par with their colored neighbors
of like conditions." The fiery editor charged both black and white men to
take responsibility for the decency and propriety of their women. If Wil-

mington's white men were not insulted enough by what they took as a libelous comparison between black and white women, they were outraged that the journalist dared lecture them. Calling white men "careless," Manly accused them of failing to protect white women's virtue and suggested that they keep a tighter rein on the women. "You leave your goods outside the door and then complain because they are taken away," he chided. Finally, laying bare the South's open secret, he lectured: "You set yourselves down as a lot of carping hypocrites; in fact, you cry aloud for the virtue of your women while you seek to destroy the morality of ours. Don't think ever that your women will remain pure while you are debauching ours. You sow the seed—the harvest will come in due time."[21]

Seeds sown deep in the ground of racial slavery would reap social chaos: the loss of control over white women who chose to be involved with black men; the mulatto children of African American female slaves, the product of rape or coercion, who were now free and populating the South; or the reprisals of black men for white intrusions on black slave families and the historical sexual abuse and rape of African American women by white men. When Alexander Manly wrote that the "harvest will come in due time," he implied that white men's transgressions of the past would haunt them, wreaking havoc on the idealized image of the South. No longer under the direct economic, social, or sexual control of white men, African American women could divulge a secret history that disputed the romance of honor that whites imagined for themselves. They now converged on its modern cities as dramatic personifications of the South's barely concealed, convoluted, racial-sexual history.[22]

Articulating his sense of moral—and, by extension, racial—superiority, Manly committed the worst of racial offenses, not only challenging white men's ability to manage their dependents, but also doubting white women's virtue and sexual purity; not only implying that interracial relations were voluntary, but also suggesting that white women preferred black men. Even worse, Manly implied that black men might make retributive violence.[23] The editor's words might have raised African Americans' spirit, but to whites it was menacing and galling. Clearly aware of the racial line in the sand, Manly had stepped over it. Like fellow journalist Ida B. Wells, Manly exposed the sham of southern male honor and chivalry upon which white supremacist ideologies were based. In Memphis, Tennessee, whites burned down Wells's press in response to her editorial against lynching and her suggestion that white women were voluntarily complicit in sexual relations with black men and that white men had lost the base of their authority. And if Durham whites did not believe this was true, the Atwater-Brewer-McCauley affair provided a timely reminder that the problem was not limited to the ideas of a singular writer in Wilmington. Such perceived threat to their political and sexual dominance provided the clarion call for white supremacy to take action through state politics. Manly's press would suffer a similar fate.[24]

As elections approached in the fall of 1898, white Democrats across the state had turned Manly's editorial into a bludgeon to denigrate African Americans' integrity, a foil to whip up race frenzy, and a rationale to deny black men the vote. For two weeks before election day, the *Wilmington Messenger*, the white newspaper, and the *Raleigh News and Observer*, the state newspaper, reprinted Manly's words (highlighting the most offensive in capital letters). Openly Democratic partisan newspapers timed their publication of Manly's editorial to coincide with — and legitimize — the racial hysteria building around the election. And if Manly's message, enhanced by editorial emphases, was not sufficiently inflammatory, the *Messenger* also ran the story of the Atwater-Brewer-McCauley affair. White Durhamites saw evidence of their worst fears in Mrs. Brewer's willingness to leave her husband in favor of an African American companion and heard their most dreaded threat voiced by Alexander Manly.[25]

Beyond Wilmington, Manley's editorial provoked multiple responses from blacks. When he planned a tour of North Carolina, black leader Booker T. Washington knew that Wilmington was "agog and excited" because of Manly's statement. According to Frank Safford, a Washington adviser, whites were "making political capital out of it." Safford hoped that a visit by the most prominent African American in the United States might deflect white attention from white people's obsession with Manly's remarks. Suggesting that the situation presented the Tuskegeean with an opportunity to "bring about a fine feeling between the races," he wrote to Washington, "Many have referred to your Atlanta speech as being just the thing to help defeat the force of these Democratic denunciations of the whole race." Accordingly, on his trip across the state, Washington preached his doctrine of "material growth among colored people." Although he did not overtly denounce black electoral activity, he did minimize its importance. Regarding Manly's editorial, Washington said nothing.[26]

A number of Carolina's black leaders, however, praised the editor's courage. The Sunday School Convention, of which Republican activist James E. Shepard was a leader, wrote to the *Daily Record*: "After seeing the bold yet manly stand that you have taken for our people, yes, our race, especially our ladies . . . you have our approval and endorsement and [we] pledge ourselves to ever stand by you to the hazarding of our lives." The convention's statement so enraged Wilmington's white supremacist leadership that white editors published it alongside Manly's words.[27] Two weeks before election day, Henry P. Cheatham and John C. Dancy, black Republican activists from Down East, spoke at a rally in Durham. A former congressional candidate, Cheatham publicly warned the "large crowd of colored people" gathered at the courthouse that "when the Democrats get into power your liberties and your rights will be cut off." He accused white Democrats of cheating on elections by putting Republican votes "in the hole in the table" instead of the hole in the ballot box. Alerting his audience to impending violence, he urged blacks to "show [whites] that you want your party rights."[28] Guilty by association with Manly and his Wilmington allies, Cheatham and Dancy personified the anxieties of Durham's white Democrats and raised them another notch. The next day, in the column next to the story of Cheatham and Dancy's visit to Durham, the *Daily Sun* offered a parallel response: "Democrat Speaking Tonight" on "good government and white supremacy." The paper encouraged its readers to "be sure and be present and bring everybody with you to the speaking that you can."[29]

Tensions were bound to snap. The Durham papers never called specifically for violence, insisting that lynching disfigured the town's best face. The Bull City could distance itself from the McCauley hanging because it had occurred three miles outside of town, but newspaper accounts of other incidents barely disguised white Democrats' intention to vilify blacks and their white potential allies. The *Daily Sun* reported, for example, that in Red Springs, North Carolina, a resolution had passed "to ostracize and treat as negroes all [whites] who work and vote for negro domination in this campaign," with employment "preferences" given to those "who uphold and vote for white supremacy," an action intended to draw all whites into the white supremacy fold. African Americans reportedly armed themselves for an impending assault. In Lumberton, according to the *Sun*, "negroes to the number of forty or fifty, all armed," appeared at a meeting of whites, "threatening to kill the white people and burn down the town."[30] Truth or rumor, these incidents evidenced whites' fear that African Americans were preparing for a racial war.

During the week before the election, the Durham papers joined the *Wilmington Messenger* and the *Raleigh News and Observer* in urging whites to retaliate against displays of black insolence. They called upon white men to "stand by" their race, and summoned them to "vote the white man's ticket." The day before the 1898 elections, Julian Carr stepped down from his chairmanship of the Durham Democratic Executive Committee with this appeal:

"Be fair, be honest, deceive, defraud, debauch no man, but see that everyone, white or colored, who desires to vote the *Democratic* ticket, exercises that privilege." That same day the paper reported for the third time that Manly McCauley "was found hanging to a tree, near the public road, three miles from here." Summoning what might be called family values to the Democratic platform, short notices asked *Sun* readers: "Do you love your wife, your children, your mother? Vote the Democratic ticket tomorrow." And white women, though disfranchised, also entered the fray: "The white womanhood of the State appeals to the fathers, husbands, sons, and brothers to do their whole duty at the polls tomorrow. Will this appeal be in vain? It must not."[31]

African American women did not have the franchise, but that did not mean that they were absent from electoral politics. In fact, the ballot was a point of contention between the sexes, with women applying the pressure to ensure that men remained loyal to black interests. Serving as "complements in one necessary and symmetric whole," Anna Julia Cooper wrote, women's activities reinforced those of men. It was "a woman's privilege from her peculiar coigne of vantage as quiet observer, to whisper just the needed suggestion or the almost forgotten truth." As the moral anchors of families and communities, African American women believed in their right to publicly represent and articulate their positions and to argue against men's temptation to sell their votes to the detriment of black communities. "You do not find the colored woman selling her birthright for a mess of pottage," Cooper wrote. "Black women in the South have actually left their husbands' homes and repudiated their support" for men who were disloyal by " 'voting away' the privileges of herself and her little ones." Indeed, "it is largely our women in the South to-day who keep the black men solid in the Republican party," Cooper maintained. "There are not many men, I can tell you, who would dare face a wife quivering in every fiber with the consciousness that her husband is a coward who could be paid to desert her deepest and dearest interests."[32]

Although written records of their activities have not been preserved, it is unlikely that Durham's black women kept silent. The "large crowd of colored people" who attended the Cheatham and Dancy meeting probably included African American women from Durham and its environs. Among them, black washerwomen, tobacco hands, teachers, and homemakers would have expressed their own perspectives on southern racial politics. Communities of women belonging to choirs, local missionary circles, delegations, and conventions probably used the church as a political forum where moral and spiritual sensibilities blended. Women put their family ties and organizational networks into operation: Minnie Pearson and her husband, William G. Pearson, at St. Joseph Church; Hattie Shepard and her son, James E. Shepard, in their network of Baptist missions and Sunday schools; Cottie Dancy Moore with her brother, John C. Dancy, and her husband, Aaron M. Moore, in Republican circles; Mary Pauline and Sallie Fitzgerald with their father, Robert, and the parents of their students in their neighborhoods. Within secret societies like the Eastern Star, in literary societies, and in church circles, men and women engaged in the debate as well. Black columnist Sarah Pettey Dudley of the *Star of Zion*, a national newspaper published in North Carolina by the African Methodist Episcopal (AME) Zion Church, advised women church activists to "carry important issues before the wives, sisters and mothers" of voting men and to talk to other women to "urge them to influence their husbands, brothers, and sons."[33]

Moreover, black women were positioned to serve as mediators or spies in passing sentiments overheard among whites to their networks of kith and kin. Those who worked as household laborers would have overheard discussions among their employers. In fact, the peculiar etiquette of race enabled African American domestics to acquire information, because whites in close proximity to a black in the household pretended to ignore the other's presence. Therefore cooks, maids, laundresses, and nurses heard as much if not more than John Merrick learned eavesdropping on white men in his barbershop.[34] And like African American women in other places, they brought pressure to bear on black men to represent their families as Republicans. And they did not always whisper, as plans that appeared in newspapers revealed. According to the *Raleigh News and Observer*, the "Colored Ladies Association" of Wilmington issued the following statement:

> Resolved that every negro who refuses to register his name next Saturday that he may vote, we shall make it our business to deal with him in a way that will not be pleasant. He shall be branded a white-livered coward who would sell his liberty and the liberty of our whole race to the demons who are even now seeking to take away the most sacred rights vouchsafed to any people. We are further
>
> Resolved to teach our children to love the party of manhood's rights and liberties, trusting in God to restore order out of the present confusion. Be it
>
> Resolved Further, That we have these resolutions published in our *Daily Record*, the one medium that has stood up for our rights when others have forsaken us. Respectfully submitted,
>
> An Organization of Colored Ladies[35]

Similarly, the *Durham Daily Sun* reported that, according to the *Searchlight*, a black Republican newspaper, African American women in Kinston, North Carolina, planned to "compel their husbands and male relatives and friends to vote the Republican ticket." The Kinston women warned men: "Adhere to the preaching of the Republican and Fusion parties. If you don't hell will catch you to the delight of the devil." Whether these proposals represented actual threats, unsubstantiated myths, or white fictions, their publication increased white anxiety about black women's ability to influence their families and communities. At least some Durham whites took these warnings seriously. The *Sun* informed its readers: "You can look for the 'burley negro' on the 8th day of November at the ballot box in a solid phalanx animated by the negresses."[36]

"A Live and Let Live Philosophy"

"A strict watch has been kept on a number of negroes" who allegedly "illegally registered," the *Durham Daily Sun* reported on the afternoon of election day, and on Wednesday the newspaper concluded that 8 November had been "Beautiful Weather on White Supremacy." The paper reported a few "problems" among African Americans who attempted to vote. Durham remained peaceful, but Down East, where white Democrats planned to win the bid for supremacy, if not by votes then by "clogging the Cape Fear River with the bodies of negroes," black political activists faced their worst fears. The actual electoral outcome did not matter, because on the day after elections, in an astonishing coup d'état, white Democrats seized the government of Wilmington. Directed by the "victors," a white mob stormed Manly's *Daily Record*, destroyed the press, gutted the offices, burned the building, and then devastated businesses, housing, and life in the major black neighborhood. "The Rebellion was organized resistance," a participant later explained, "on the part of the white citizens of this community to the established government, which had long irked them because it was dominated by 'Carpet Baggers' and Negroes." The goal of the massacre, he explained, was "to establish 'White Supremacy' in the city, the state, and throughout the South, and thereby remove the then stupid and ignorant Negroes from their numerically dominating position in government." In order to do so, "the white people of Wilmington overthrew the constituted municipal authority overnight and substituted a reform rule . . . with some needless bloodshed."[37]

News of the Wilmington Riot traveled by newspaper, and the *Durham Daily Sun* did its part: "exciting time in the city of WILMINGTON," screamed the front page headline. African American networks carried the details. Armed whites banished black leaders, literally marching them out of the city.

Fear for black life and livelihood compelled hundreds of African Americans to flee Wilmington for the Piedmont. Thomas Rivera, an undertaker, feared that his wife was in danger, having heard that whites were stopping and stripping black women on the street. And he believed hundreds lay dead in the street. A tide of refugees made their way across the state, carrying the horror of what they had seen in Wilmington and rumors of what they had heard. Rivera surfaced in Durham with his wife and children and settled among his friends, including the Moores, the Pearsons, and the Shepards.[38]

Very little is known about election night or its immediate aftermath in Durham. According to Durham news sources, a few blacks were arrested for rowdiness, but the papers offered little else. Did black Durhamites go to the polls on election day 1898, or did they elect to stay home? Did Durham whites make any attempt to stop them or instigate an attack on Hayti? Perhaps whites and blacks confronted each other from their separate sides of the railroad tracks, armed with either weapons or words. The *Sun* reported no violence, but the silence about the day is deafening. A curious set of connected events suggests that Bull City whites and blacks negotiated a truce. Within days of the election, the city announced plans to build a black public school, the Durham Colored Graded School. Julian Carr, the new chair of the school board, appointed William G. Pearson to be principal. Building a public school for blacks in the very places where black schools mysteriously had burned down during political tensions intimates that white and black Durhamites had come to a political peace: one that traded ballots for books.[39]

Other factors explain the absence of widespread racial animosity in Durham in 1898. First, subtle punitive measures had been used to send clear messages and castigate resisters. Whites may have wanted their servants to carry the threat back to black communities. Local newspapers clearly had warned that the possibility of violence was real. Vicarious threats of violence may have held Durham's black community in check. The discourse of white supremacy, dominating the state's newspapers, may well have dampened enthusiasm among black members of the Republican Party with messages that black desires for public office would be extinguished. Indeed, Durham blacks, even when nominated for public office, refused to run. It is equally likely that without an antebellum tradition to defend, Durham's white capitalists lacked the historical sentiment to sanction the destruction of Hayti, Durham's prominent black district. Furthermore, in defining itself as a New South phenomenon—a place that turned Fitzgerald's bricks into buildings and where distinct patterns of residential segregation occurred without the need for laws—Durham had to live up to its reputation. Its promotional materials boasted that race cooperation rather than race conflict lay at the foundation of the city's goals for economic expansion, making Durham "an excellent opportunity for the safe investment of capital."[40] In addition to capital, the city needed an abundant supply of black labor to depress wages and to frustrate labor's organizing power among whites. Whites' tolerance of a black elite had encouraged continued in-migration by sending the promise of peace and prosperity along African American networks.

Conceivably, too, white civic leaders—those like Washington Duke and Julian S. Carr who preached at black churches and donated to black causes—took a moral stance and refused to sanction the destruction of black homes and institutions that day. Duke, the most powerful among Durham's white capitalists, had helped to build St. Joseph AME Zion. The stained glass window of Duke that the congregation installed in the front wall of the church hung like a shield of protection. Thus, the relationship between white benefactor and black institution bound one of the most impressive black churches in Durham to one of the richest men in America in a protective and paternalistic relationship. The affiliation represented white elites' perception of modern, urban industrial progress: racial cooperation sustained by paternalism. The belief that white Durham held to its progressive promise captured the attention of other black leaders. In 1912, W. E. B. Du Bois credited Trinity College (later renamed Duke University) with nurturing an enlightened perspective among Durham whites. Similarly, Booker T. Washington wrote that Durham's white leaders abided by a "live and let live" philosophy.[41]

More likely, however, black Durham was too politically weak to matter in Durham's electoral politics. Few and ineffective though they were, and probably for that reason, the leading black men of Durham—Moore, Pearson, Merrick, Fitzgerald, Whitted, Shepard, and a few others—continued to vote, even as most African Americans statewide were disfranchised. In Durham, the black vote—especially of a select few entrepreneurs—represented the link between property rights and citizenship rights, acknowledging the argument that excluded ignorant voters of both races from the process. Moreover, African Americans in Durham lacked the numerical threat of "Negro Domination," accounting for only one-third of Durham's population, itself comprised of mostly the nonvoting women and children who made up the core workforce in white-owned factories and homes. African Americans held pluralities and majorities in North Carolina's northern rural corridor and along the coastal plain where Wilmington and New Bern were located. But in the Piedmont surrounding Durham and in the mountain regions to the west, African Americans lacked numbers sufficient to influence an election outcome in which all the whites took the same side, as they did in the white supremacy campaigns of the late nineteenth century. The black male elite vote may have been an important symbol, but it offered no real political clout. Like most North Carolina counties, Durham had neither elected nor appointed African Americans to municipal, state, or national office after Reconstruction. Even when tapped for office, Durham blacks had chosen not to run, establishing black Durham's tradition of leaving political office to whites. Although few blacks realized it at the time, they created their black political culture under a set of exigencies that fortified the racial status quo.[42]

Meanwhile, if liberal white Durham's "live and let live" philosophy disallowed the destruction of black Durham in 1898, it was because black Durham had little to destroy. African American leaders recognized this, too. Black folk in Wilmington were more affluent than those in Durham. Indeed, those few symbols of progress — a handful of black businesses, a smattering of political leaders, two wooden ungraded schools, and several churches — represented both the distance African Americans in Durham had come since emancipation and the limits of their community growth. Most black Durhamites were poor, employed as factory hands and household servants. In the short term, African Americans had much to gain and little to lose in trading ballots for books and racial peace. In the end, the brutality in Wilmington allowed Durham whites to strengthen their progressive, "liberal-minded" position. The repeated and suspicious burnings of black schools, the murder of Manly McCauley, and the persistence of racial hostility reminded African Americans of their vulnerable position and underlined white disregard for both black life and black property. Yet, for racial capitalism to succeed in Durham, its proponents recognized the value of tolerating at least some black progress to maintain order on both sides of the veil. At this moment, too, another Durham myth was born: "It can't happen here." For the next generation, whenever racial tensions erupted elsewhere into mass violence, rioting, or mob action, Durham's black and white leaders resurrected the slogan to encourage racial calm. When violence swept Atlanta in 1906 and Winston-Salem and Greensboro in 1919, the phrase "It can't happen here" echoed in Durham.[43] "It," meaning racial bloodshed, could not happen because of the peace Durham blacks had negotiated with whites.

Insidiously, white supremacy as articulated in Durham agreed not to hinder the ambition of some African Americans as long as they did not demand social equality, meaning that black leaders should keep to themselves and control their community. In the meantime, white Durham used the growing wealth of a few African Americans to fashion the city's reputation for black prosperity and perpetuate the myth of racial accord. The pretense, for the reality was quite different, proved useful to whites in encouraging streams of black people willing to do the grueling work of industry. In truth, the facade of racial cooperation reinforced a caste society where some African Americans were allowed enough latitude to create symbols of progress but insufficient flexibility or power to forge significant change. Visible black wealth in Durham, then, was tolerated, even protected, by local leading whites who accepted the aspirations of the black elite as long as those ambitions could be contained within limits. Richard Fitzgerald, John O'Daniel, John Merrick, Aaron Moore, and a handful of other black men grew wealthy, and the masses of black folk did find work. And, certainly, white affluence in Durham depended on black labor for sustenance. Powerful whites allowed some black wealth, at least conceptually, knowing they would never permit an African American to acquire capital equal to theirs.

On this strategy of race relations and at this moment, Durham constructed its reputation for "racial cooperation," a term that suggests blacks and whites worked collaboratively. In reality, the term signified an accord wherein African Americans did not challenge whites' claims to power—that is, they accommodated white supremacy—and white folk did not summon violence to maintain the racial order. Ironically, the more the local economy depended on black labor, the more publicly Durham whites embraced black prosperity. And the more enthusiastically the black elite praised local race relations, the more easily industrialists exploited black laborers.

"A Cancer Gnawing at the Heart of This Republic"
In 1898, Booker T. Washington had to admit,

We [Americans] have succeeded in every conflict, except in the effort to conquer ourselves in the blotting out of prejudice. . . . Until we thus conquer ourselves I make no empty statement when I say that, we shall have, especially in the Southern part of our country, a cancer gnawing at the heart of this Republic, that shall one day prove as dangerous as an attack from an army without or within.[44]

That cancer of prejudice was killing blacks. The Wilmington Riot, some have called it a massacre, broke out less than two months after Washington had received a warm Carolina reception. Thirty lynchings occurred in the state between 1889 and 1900, twenty-one of them African American men accused of rape or murder. More often than not, the charges were used to justify white contempt for black political and economic aspirations. Although Durham boosters claimed that no lynchings occurred in Durham per se — Manly McCauley was hanged three miles outside of town — several happened in alarming proximity. Two blacks were lynched in Concord the year that Richard Fitzgerald joined with other African Americans to open the black-owned Coleman Cotton Mill in that town.[45]

As an overblown allegory of the perils of "Negro Rule," the Wilmington saga served as a barrier to black political participation for more than half a century in Durham, evoked by whites as an admonition and by blacks as a reminder of the need for caution. At the place where history and memory intersected, the Wilmington incident informed future actions, including the seemingly conservative choices that blacks made. Invoked as a warning in times of political indecision or critical change, it shaped individuals' and leaders' debates and decisions.[46] Over time, evoking Wilmington became a way for Durham's black leaders to retain their influence in a community that was in a state of perpetual change. Having experienced a narrow escape, they donned memory like a symbolic robe of experience to calm white enmity and to validate their local authority in steering black politics through the mid-twentieth century. Conrad Odell Pearson, William G. Pearson's nephew and later an attorney-activist in Durham, believed that his uncle and James E. Shepard "capitalized on it" to prevent changes they could not dictate. Others were truly frightened, believing that Durham blacks might suffer "repercussions like they had in Wilmington and different places in the state, where people were shot down at the polls and told to run, [get] out of town, and so forth." In time, a younger generation challenged both that memory and its power. But for the time being, the younger Pearson explained, Durham leaders "were naturally very cautious."[47]

Durham's black leaders continued to vote, albeit in small numbers, a testament to a racial accord that conferred black citizenship rights but prevented the growth of black influence. Nevertheless, the state's worsening racial climate shaped the town's politics well into the twentieth century. Events unfolding in North Carolina in 1899 confirmed that racial repression would continue until black freedom was undone. As if the horrors of November 1898 were not enough, two days into 1899, whites lynched a black man accused of assaulting "a most excellent widow lady" in nearby Chatham County. Four days later, a suspicious fire almost destroyed the new Durham

Colored Graded School. The North Carolina legislature, its newest members elected in 1898, opened the session in January with talk of segregated railroad cars. Over the objections of both blacks and white railroad officials, the joint committee on railroads submitted a segregation bill and anticipated its passage by the end of January. Democrats also introduced legislation making black and white cohabitation a felony. By early February, an amendment to the North Carolina Constitution that was intended to eliminate black suffrage had passed in the House and was on its way to the Senate. Across the state, whites rallied behind the banner of white supremacy, and black disfranchisement was approved by popular vote within a year. North Carolina imposed literacy tests, the poll tax, and the grandfather clause, effectively barring most African Americans from the polls. The *Durham Daily Sun* heralded the outcome, reprinting Democrats' assurances that black disfranchisement would "resolve the negro problem," at least in the electoral arena, as it had in other states. "It is a matter of understanding and capacity," Senator Furnifold Simmons claimed. "The white man has more sense and capacity than the negro and inherently understands the duties of suffrage and citizenship. . . . The uneducated white man can be trusted to cast a more intelligent vote than can an educated negro."[48]

As their public political life contracted, African Americans grasped at those few opportunities to protect their diminishing rights. Segregation on public transportation quickly followed black disfranchisement. "The latest abuse of power and profanation of justice by the dominant race is the Jim-Crow street car," the *Voice of the Negro* complained, remarking on the "startling celerity [with which] the craze for separate street cars is spreading all over the South."[49] In Durham, the "colored" Hook and Ladder Co. No. 1 joined with the city's white firemen to endorse James McNeil as commissioner of railroads. President of the North Carolina Volunteer Firemen's Association, McNeil had helped to organize black fire companies, including the one in Durham, and he supported their continuation. With the legislature debating segregation on railroad cars, African Americans hoped their white allies would oppose the proposal. But more immediate concerns soon took precedence as another arson incident caused $8,000 damage to the Durham Colored Graded School, a building insured for only $3,500.[50]

"Christian Men, and Not Cowards"

When African American delegates arrived at the Republican state convention in 1902, they were jeered out of the hall by whites who sang and cheered as a band played the popular song:

Coon, coon, coon,
I wish my color would fade,
Coon, coon, coon,
Quite a lighter shade,
Coon, coon, coon,
Morning, night or noon,
It's better to be a white man
Than a coon, coon, coon.[51]

Insulted, African American political activists, like Durham Republican James E. Shepard, had to reconsider their sense of politics and place. With the recent riot in Wilmington fresh in their memories and the derision of "lily-white" Republicans ringing in their ears, black Durhamites vanished from partisan politics. Records from the black North Carolina Republican Executive Committee in 1908 and 1916 list no Durhamites among the leadership, a turnabout from two decades earlier. As the fury and frequency of white violence increased, their retreat must have seemed wise.[52]

To say that Durham's African Americans closed ranks and accommodated white supremacy, however, assumes that electoral politics were uppermost among black concerns and that voting was the only form of influence they could exercise. It also oversimplifies a racial milieu that was terribly complex and ignores the differences among Durham's leading black men. They did concur on some matters. They agreed that if coon songs mocked African American men and if losing the vote robbed them of manhood rights, if the threat of lynching denied them sexuality and the threat of rape denied them control of their families, then African American men would have to define manhood in new ways. They agreed that the Wilmington Riot was indeed the "very beginning of Negro disfranchisement in the South," as one participant later assessed, and "an important step in the establishment of White Supremacy in the Southland."[53] Thus, in the context of Wilmington, Durham's black leaders agreed to forge a shrewd inward-looking strategy of community, fully cognizant of white prerogatives and concerns.

"With the New South the New Negro must arise and modestly, manfully, courageously, take his place in the march of progress," Washington asserted at the turn of the century. "The old order of things has truly passed away, and side by side, white men and black men must determine to work out their destiny to a successful issue."[54] What the Durham group understood was that whites would do anything they could to sustain segregation, including supporting black institutions. It would be the job of African Americans to make those institutions the best they could be. Durham black leaders and entrepreneurs seized on these opportunities of racism to shape their own strategies and to advance the nationalist agenda at the center of Booker T. Washington's message. Black schools, however segregated and unequal, promised a path to progress for black youth that meant more to the mass of black folk than the vote. And schools were the way to protect and nurture the next generation. Durham's leading black men agreed to turn education into a political cause.

But they disagreed on the exigencies of electoral politics. Modifying their political agendas, some Durham black leaders chose to distance themselves from the proponents of partisanship. John Merrick recognized in a speech he made immediately after the Wilmington massacre that "we are allowed to own homes and farms, run farms, do banking, business, insurance, real estate business, and other minor business that is done in this Commonwealth. . . . It's time for us to protect ourselves." Merrick and his supporters among Durham black leaders encouraged and engaged themselves in building black institutions and organizations to serve black people's needs, black businesses to serve black people, black banks to hold black money. As to politics, Merrick declared, "We ought to leave them alone."[55] It was Merrick's preference to keep his distance. Merrick argued that African Americans had gained little from electoral challenges. Whereas whites in the post–Civil War South had "turned their attention to making money," he claimed, African Americans had turned theirs to "politics and paying a debt of gratitude." Asserting that the "debt to the Republican party has been paid," Merrick counseled, "let us think more of our employment and what it takes to make peace and stop trying to think we are the whole Republican Party." Believing that politics "corrupted good men" who "have to stick to it for protection," Merrick was angered that the masses in Wilmington "did not even surmise the extent of the growing trouble" and "never in their lives report[ed] any benefits of office." As far as he was concerned, the ambitions of the few had done "a great disservice" to "the masses."[56]

Freedman turned statesman, Merrick sought to allay black fears of a rising tide of race hatred. "So many of my people think slavery is not something of the past" and fear that it "may return at any time." Thoroughly conscious that freed labor benefited Durham's white industrialists, he assured his neighbors, "I want to say that the 'white folks,' as we call them, have not got time any more to own Negroes when they can pay us less than it takes to own us." For most African Americans, "employment to sustain our families" should be their priority. To those who lived and worked in poverty, who lacked the protection or stability that affluence bought, and who confronted the degradation of racism daily, political parties were interchangeable. "We have got to labor, or rather the masses of us, for our support . . . for those who have it for us to do. And that, I need not hesitate to say, is the white people of North Carolina, both Republicans and Democrats." Urging caution, he continued: "Now the thing for us to do is to do like other men. They do what is best to protect [their] land, railroad, mill, factory, and real estate interests." Preaching racial harmony, he also recommended: "Let us protect what we have. . . . Let us now make our bed[s] as soft as possible; the softer we make them the better they lie."[57]

Merrick had always proved taciturn on electoral politics. For years, the sagacious barber had listened intently but with rare reply to his white male customers, Durham's most prominent leaders among them, as they pontificated on matters of race. Still, as his friend and biographer R. McCants Andrews pointed out, Merrick offered the black community neither "a retreat from manhood" nor compromises with white supremacy. "I know we ought to have our share of representation," Merrick contended, but he also added: "We ought to have our share of responsibility, so as to make us manifest the proper interest." Thus, he advocated the acquisition of property and wealth as a tactic for "manifesting proper interest." Future electoral strength might reside therein. Understanding the capitalist imperative, Merrick counseled the importance of thrift and capital accumulation: "That is what makes people representative, is having something to represent."[58]

At the other end of the spectrum stood James E. Shepard, born in the hopes of emancipation and educated at Shaw University in Raleigh. Like Merrick, he firmly held that it was the duty of African American men to represent the black community, but he believed that duty required the franchise. In the mid-1890s, the Republican Shepard had reminded the party's recalcitrant whites of the strength of the state's black vote. He argued during the 1900 debates on black suffrage that disfranchisement left "no middle ground" between slavery and freedom. Linking voting rights to manhood rights, he held that the best way to make a good man was not to "unman him."[59] Moreover, to flee from southern white hostility was "unmanly" under the terms Shepard set forth at the 1902 Emancipation Day celebration at White Rock Baptist, one of Durham's most prominent black churches. Such ceremonies, marking political holidays on the African American calendar, brought African Americans together to recall and renew the promises of freedom. Using the black church as a political space and the pulpit as a podium, Shepard exhorted his audience to "be Christian men and not cowards," calling upon the gathering to remain in the South to struggle. "I know the prejudices," he maintained, "but we must first work out our salvation in the land where our fathers died and which they loved."[60]

Much of what Shepard had to say echoed the counsel of every leader's call for morality and responsibility, thrift and temperance, protection of and provision for families, particularly for wives and daughters. He put faith in the development of young people as leaders to guide their communities into the future. In addition, he proclaimed to the hometown crowd that "to advise the negroes as a unit to eschew politics would be unwise and contrary to the spirit of free institutions." Refusing to relinquish black rights, Shepard advised: "Those that are fitted should, if possible, exercise the right of the franchise, and those that are not should fit themselves to meet the requirements of the law." African Americans who met the requirements of citizenship were entitled to vote, and, according to Shepard, African Americans owed it to themselves to prepare to use the franchise.[61]

By 1903, however, after the insulting incident at the 1902 Republican convention, Shepard seemed to concede that the message of disfranchisement was a "lesson in manhood." In a post–election day speech he gave in Charlotte, he seemed to acquiesce to black disfranchisement: "A black man must serve his years of bondage, as all races had before him had to do. . . . When these are acquired he will stand forth in power and glory." His words would have sounded like a giving in to white supremacy had he known how long the struggle would take, had he not carried such a strong penchant for politics, or if he had not descended from a family of renowned race men and women. In his speech, Shepard reminded his audience that "the further responsibility is upon us as a race to rear families with the thoughts of citizenship ever before them." Drawing from a biblical text, Shepard suggested that African Americans might "wander forty long years in the wilderness for chastisement and training" but would be led "safely to the promised land" by one who "can be trusted as a guard and guide." Like a candidate, he set out a platform he believed could bring the "power and glory" he desired for the race: "The negro must learn this lesson, and the sooner the better it will be for his peace of mind[:] if he desires power for the future he must be educated or own something." Whereas Merrick led by identifying with one group, "the laboring classes, like myself," Shepard defined himself as a torchbearer who stood above the masses lighting the way to "the final success."[62]

While the political discourse continued, many black Carolinians still considered Durham a city of "magnificent possibilities." Charles N. Hunter described black Durhamites less than a year after the Wilmington massacre: "They are united in their persistent efforts to that end." Amid the bleakness, there were reasons for hope. Once a teacher in Durham and now editor of the *Raleigh Blade*, Hunter praised a new generation. "Boys and girls [who were here] when I was here teaching school have grown into manhood and womanhood, many of them heads of families." He paid special attention to the continued growth of churches. White Rock Baptist Church had just called a new pastor to serve and the North Durham Mission had organized into a formal congregation. The unfolding Durham story was not altogether exceptional but was characteristic of black urban development in sites across the region, as migrants created neighborhoods and communities in the midst of white racial hostility and violence.[63]

To Hunter's generation, born in slavery, these were not simple demographic shifts but phenomenal transformations, if not yet milestones, that marked racial progress: the first generation born in freedom had survived to come of age. Among its achievements, Hunter documented the individual young people from Durham who were able to attend the black schools and colleges that opened after the Civil War. Two of Richard Fitzgerald's daughters attended Hampton Institute, in Virginia, and another had graduated from Fisk, the celebrated university in Nashville, Tennessee. A new teacher arrived in Durham to teach domestic science at the new Durham Colored Graded School. Julia McCauley, from Washington, D.C., had attended the college program at Howard University. As a new member of the small black aspiring class, she was welcomed among the expanding networks of association, including the three literary clubs that met weekly, one at White Rock Baptist, one at St. Joseph AME Zion, and the third at the nondenominational Volkamenia Literary Club, started by Sallie Fitzgerald when she returned from summer school in Virginia. These networks of association continued to expand among the small but growing educated class of black Durhamites.[64]

As an entrepreneur, Hunter knew that Durham's small-town elites were pleased to see their accomplishments in print; he therefore served the city he frequented and saluted Durham's lively social world. Unquestionably, the Wilmington Riot had been destructive to black political aspirations, but black folk knew life went on, and accordingly they planned a future. Just before year's end in 1898, Richard Fitzgerald's daughter Lillian, the Fisk graduate, married one of her father's business partners, the pharmacist J. A. Dodson. The couple honeymooned in Washington, D.C., and planned to move into a large new house on Lee Street in Hayti when they returned. That fall, two other daughters had returned to Hampton to continue their studies. And Richard's niece, Mary Pauline Fitzgerald, Robert's oldest child, an experienced teacher at age twenty-nine, married Charles Morton Dame, appropriate to the Fitzgeralds' class and color consciousness, a red-haired, blue-eyed graduate of Howard Law School.[65]

It is unlikely, however, that Hunter could write about some of the personal disappointments known by freedom's first generation, some too deep and hidden to make it into the historical record. With race restrictions increasing, Charles Dame was barred from practicing the profession for which he had trained at Howard Law School. He accomplished little as a legal footman for white attorneys, and he prospered even less. Searching for a place where Charles might practice law, the Dames left North Carolina, first for Virginia and then for West Virginia. Along the way, the couple lost two infants to death. Deeply discouraged, Charles Dame seized what seemed to be his only option: "As white as any white man," he decided to cross the color line and pass into the white world. He asked his wife to join him. Despite her family's color complex, and with her own skin "the color of strawberry cream," Mary Pauline Fitzgerald Dame chose not to pass. Having inherited her father's dedication to racial uplift, she believed her destiny was linked inexorably to the people her husband had decided to flee. Unable to reconcile such opposing survival strategies, the Dames separated. Charles disappeared, and Mary Pauline moved to Baltimore to live with a sister. She eventually returned to Durham, deserted and disillusioned.[66]

The Dames, like virtually all African Americans, came to understand that the "separate but equal" doctrine of the Supreme Court decision in *Plessy v. Ferguson* not only sustained discrimination but allowed it to expand. The decision also signaled the federal government's withdrawal from the southern race war, unleashing decades of white supremacist violence, legal segregation, and black disfranchisement. The Wilmington Riot revealed not only whites' determination to forge disorder and to deny African Americans rights, but also their willingness to compromise democracy by violence. Spilling over into occupational restrictions, *Plessy* assured that Mary Pauline Fitzgerald Dame's husband, Charles, was excluded from a career he had so desired. Given white opposition to African Americans among the professions, Dame could not practice law unless he became white. One historian contended of the period: "Faced with the certainty of failure blacks over the years lost heart for the fight." Charles Dame certainly seemed to concede defeat.[67]

Yet, even as white Southerners solidified Jim Crow, African Americans shaped effective resistance through a wide variety of tactics, some publicly organized, others more subtle and spontaneous. Some of the most determined acts of resistance were personal. Charles and Mary Pauline Dame, for instance, chose divergent strategies. Charles Dame elected admirably or not to outwit the race problem by passing. He became a colleague at the bar of people who believed they had used the law to distance themselves from him and his ilk. Heir of the man who called himself a soldier in the second war against ignorance, Mary Pauline Fitzgerald Dame made a different decision, more commendable, perhaps, but no less subversive. She returned to teach at Durham's West End School, where racial uplift and respectability became her weapons of choice against racism. Here, she imparted a sense of dignity and race pride to two generations of students.

It is unfortunate, but it is true, that the dominant race in
this country insists upon gauging the Negro's worth by his
most illiterate and vicious representatives rather than by
the more intelligent and worthy classes. Colored women
of education and culture know that they cannot escape
altogether the consequences of the acts of their most
depraved sisters. They see that even if they were wicked
enough to turn a deaf ear to the call of duty, both policy
and self-preservation demand that they go down among
the lowly, the illiterate and even the vicious, to whom they
are bound by the ties of race and sex, and put forth every
possible effort to reclaim them. By coming into close
touch with the masses of our women it is possible to cor-
rect many of the evils which militate so seriously against us
and inaugurate the reforms, without which, as a race, we
cannot hope to succeed.
    Mary Church Terrell, 1896

3 : Many Important Particulars
Are Far from Flattering
The Gender Dimensions of
the "Negro Problem"

When they left their protective circle of family, community, and institutions, Charles and Mary Pauline Dame encountered aspects of Jim Crow
they had not predicted. Members of freedom's first generation, the newly
married couple shared similar experiences, including privileged access to
education far beyond what most African Americans could attain. Their communities accorded them admiration and respect for their achievements and
anticipated their emergence among the ranks of race men and race women
who lived and worked as models of the best of all things black, who engaged in uplift and activism directed toward improving conditions of the less
fortunate, and who presented themselves in ways that denied the negative
traits that whites assigned to black people. The communities also hoped that
Charles could shoulder his responsibility as a race man at the bar, and that

Mary Pauline would carry hers as a race woman in the classroom. It probably was dispiriting for African Americans that, when he confronted the bitter disappointments of racial exclusion, Charles chose to pass. They probably realized that being refused admittance to his profession had "unmanned" him, stolen from him the opportunity to prove that blacks were not an inferior people and also that he could stand up against the gendered racial structures determined to weaken black masculinity.[1]

For her part, Mary Pauline Fitzgerald Dame came to the color line with expectations shaped by her family and community. The daughter of a freed slave and a race activist, she had grown up under the pressure of these demands: that she would strive to achieve freedom's promises wholly dedicated to her family, community, and race. In addition, she faced expectations set out for her as a woman by the particular demands of female respectability that sustained her middle-class status: that she live a life beyond reproach, that she exercise the strictest sense of morality, accepting Victorian codes of propriety and decorum, that she adhere to mainstream conventions of sexuality, and that she dedicate herself to racial uplift by direct action and example. In the mold of the black women's club movement, Mary Pauline lifted as she climbed, accomplishing an acrobatic feat worthy of high praise: pulling herself upward with one hand and her less fortunate sisters with the other.[2]

The gendered code of respectability was ambiguous, though, and not always fair. On the one hand, expectations for respectability positioned black women with resources above reproach to counter verbal offensive. These tenets had shaped Mary Pauline Fitzgerald Dame into a model of black womanhood. On the other hand, the code also relegated black women to places considered appropriate for them, limiting their authority, autonomy, and opportunities. Black educational institutions, for example, were no more likely than white institutions to open the door to legal, medical, or religious training for women, viewing these public occupations as an unsuitable domain. Thus, Charles could access professional opportunities that were closed to Mary Pauline. Missionary work or teaching — and teaching children at that — were just about the only suitable professions black women could pursue at the turn of the nineteenth century. Once Charles left her, furthermore, propriety required Mary Pauline to eschew the kind of freedom that might allow her to explore nontraditional options; indeed, the dictates of decorum prohibited her moving about as a single woman alone. Instead, Mary Pauline was relegated to the duties that fell to her as the oldest daughter in the family. As Pauli Murray wrote of her aunt, she had no choice but to return home to Durham, where she "slipped into her accustomed harness, and it was taken for granted that she would have no further life of her own."[3]

Respectability could not protect Mary Pauline or any other black woman from personal hurts imposed by fellow race men. Respectability was supposed to shield her from insults, unpleasant encounters, and sexual harassment and sexual assault, the persistent difficulties that plagued African American women's lives. But, by affecting African American women and men in different ways, the doctrine of Jim Crow forced them to come at the problem of racism from distinct positions that obviated gender and class disparities among black folk. Gendered Jim Crow increased the ways that whites could vilify black folk but also created fissures. The one between Charles and Pauline forced them to make contradictory decisions and destroyed their family.[4]

In her classroom, Mary Pauline fought against the effects of oppression and degradation, not just by fashioning herself as a model of race progress, but by instilling self-respect, building self-esteem, and impressing a sense of dignity on the children of Jim Crow in ways that highlighted black humanity. Hers was challenging work that required her to look back as well as forward. Yet many in the better class of African Americans felt the need to distance themselves from their less fortunate neighbors. Jim Crow's ability to frustrate initiative compelled members of the better class to distinguish themselves from black folk whom they believed lived down to white expectations, even as they worked to raise black folk's awareness of their potential as a race. Doing so, they calculated, exemplified a race becoming modern: hard work garnered success; individual achievement signified group accomplishment; self-actualization symbolized the rise of the race; and perfection denoted progress.[5]

But the stereotype of the iniquitous black woman served as an impediment to African Americans' economic advancement. Ruling whites demanded that black women work but limited black women's employment options on the basis of their alleged character flaws. Devaluing black women as workers depressed wages such that African American workers struggled to survive, but the strategy also reasoned that as per their condition, black people did not require what might be thought of as a living wage. Moreover, believing it reasonable to presume black women's degradation, whites used erroneous perceptions to rationalize racial restrictions. Denying virtue to black women laborers, white employers excluded them from all except those roles to which they had been assigned historically: the heavy work of agriculture, the dirty work of manufacturing, and the subservient work of household labor.[6]

Finally, the tactics of Jim Crow depended upon illogical conclusions about gender and respectability as justifications for oppression. Jerome Dowd, of Durham's distinguished Trinity College (now Duke University), for example, believed that African American women should be limited to certain kinds of work. Alleging that "from the standpoint of the interests of both the operatives and the capitalist, the Negro has not been altogether satisfactory," Dowd warned local factory owners against using black labor. "What is the defect? [Black people's] constitutional and hereditary physical and moral unfitness for the extraction of manufacturing product."[7] In Durham, Dowd's analysis meant that, unless absolutely desperate for laborers, white factory owners — who stressed morality to their workers — barred African American women from positions other than cleaning in southern textile mills where white women dominated the labor force.

Such comments infuriated black women leaders, especially those of the aspiring classes. "Out of the ever vexing and mysterious hydra-headed evil we name the race problem," black woman activist Addie Hunton wrote, "there seems to have grown of late a sentiment, if you will, whose particular function is to magnify the moral weakness of Negro womanhood." Hunton continued: "To her is charged every weakness of the race. . . . Everywhere her moral defects are being portrayed by her enemies; sometimes, veiled in hypocritical pity, and again, in language bitter and unrelenting."[8]

Combating Jim Crow required multifaceted approaches to undo the worst of its damages. Against a rising tide of black ambition and achievement among freedom's first generation, southern whites wielded the power to discriminate. Loosed by the Wilmington Riot, disfranchisement, and the apathy of the federal government, apartheid in the American South became a ruthless enemy, shifting and shaping oppression as it pleased, on one hand ignoring the ambiguities and contradictions of race in order to sustain white domination and, on the other, recognizing differences in order to mount its strongest offense against specific targets. And for that reason, African Americans were powerless to prevent the profound abuses of Jim Crow and the forms of enforcement employed in the name of white supremacy. At best, those who had resources might limit the extent to which racial repression circumscribed their form of black freedom. Segregation was only half the story, and the least of the affronts. The obvious inequities meant little to white public officials in charge of administering the law.[9]

The pressure of segregation caused African Americans to assess their own roles in the so-called Negro Problem. Black leaders like W. E. B. Du Bois spoke passionately for unity and action to prevent the race from becoming a casualty of racism but also engaged in a harsh critique of those black people who, they believed, impeded racial progress: whoremongers, ward heelers, youthful loafers, gamblers, criminals, and the women who were in the "vast army of black prostitutes that is today marching to hell," as Du Bois penned. These criticisms, he insisted, were necessary internal analyses of the problems that thwarted race progress. But these views reflected the kinds of condemnation that black male and female leaders publicly engaged in, well-meaning but callous criticisms of the disadvantaged, the unemployed, and, most unforgivably, black working-class people damned for their straits. African American efforts to lecture the race on its shortcomings amounted to derisions that echoed the views of whites, despite the best intentions.[10]

And yet, in the same ways that Du Bois's comments reiterated the disparagements that southern whites used to rationalize black inferiority, deny black humanity, sustain white supremacy, and maintain black denigration, his words reflected a harsh critique mounted by African American men against women of the race. A traitorous stance, this willingness among black men to defame black women echoed in the sharp divide created at the intersection of gender and class. African American women could not shake loose the humiliation imposed by their history, and even the race's "best women" suffered the humiliations of gendered Jim Crow. It fell to women, then, to take up the gendered banner of race in defense of themselves. "It remained for a Judas Iscariot," Addie Hunton wrote of the way black male leaders betrayed the race, "to make the assertion that 'not only are ninety percent of the Negro women of America unchaste, but the social degradation of our freedwomen is without parallel in all modern civilization.'"[11]

Black women activists protested the way Jim Crow's strategies denied their aspirations and at the same time challenged the kind of surly scolding that leading black men let loose on them and their working sisters. They looked on their poorer sisters with pity, but it was no secret that they also shared the sentiments expressed by black men of their class and of white people generally.[12]

The gendered aspect of the Negro Problem affected men and women differently. Disfranchisement eliminated a critical manhood right but also silenced the political voice of the whole black community. Lynching and mob violence acted as mechanisms to control black men, while signaling their inability to protect their own families and leaving white men "free to seduce all the colored girls" they could, as Ida B. Wells-Barnett maintained. "But it is death to the colored man who yields to the force and advance of a similar attraction in white women."[13] Inasmuch as the obstacles constructed to deny black manhood enabled whites to impose themselves on African American women's public and private lives, black women had plenty of reason for alarm regarding their own security, as well as that of black men. Caricatured as licentious and wicked Jezebels who lured virtuous men to the sin of inappropriate sexuality, black women stood accused — by white men, white women, and black men — of bringing about their own shame.

Whites who required black workers for their homes could not reconcile their beliefs in black immorality and hypersexuality with their personal needs to have African American women as household laborers in intimate contact with their families. An alternate, equally false, and similarly degrading image solved the dilemma. The "Mammy," a stout and officious domestic, offered a desexualized and innocuous black woman.[14] Evocative of devoted, submissive, and tolerably efficient workers, representations of mammies, pickaninnies, and uncles mocked black people while feeding "old negro" plantation myths that diminished threat. Along with characters like the "Jim Crow" and "Zip Coon" of minstrelsy, these and other farcical portrayals injected these figures of black people into public culture through advertising, film, and theatrical performances. Appearing endearingly dim-witted or slick and deceitful, these images shaped the national perception of black people. Southern whites found these icons oddly comforting because they looked back to the historical aspects of black temperament that they believed they had known and certainly preferred.[15]

In Durham, local white leaders and capitalists celebrated these horrific images of black people, using them for their pleasure and prosperity. White fraternal orders paraded down Main Street in mocking blackface, passing John Merrick's barbershop and the tobacco factories where black people toiled. One local white-cast minstrel show, "The Power of Fun and Frolic," showed whites' freedom to ridicule black people. These displays of racist themes used public space to assault African Americans and commercialism to express white contempt of blackness. Advertisements for North Carolina tobacco products like "Nigger Head Tobacco," "Marburg Brothers Smoking Tobacco," and "Bull Durham" used degrading depictions of African Americans in national and international markets. An entire series of W. Duke & Sons advertisements caricatured African American women, children, and men, reminding the Dukes' black workers of how their employers truly viewed them. Other depictions featured nostalgic images with demeaning, crude humor, one more vituperative than the next. Photographs and postcards of lynchings for which the participants posed celebrated the destruction of the black body politic, with the spectators posed for effect. One 1908 postcard pictured a gruesome hanging, adding the lines: "The negro, now, by eternal grace, Must learn to stay in the negro's place."[16]

Coupling antithetical perceptions, white constructions of black people linked these menacing and nonsensical portrayals in bewildering ways. Emancipation and citizenship had unleashed the subliminal beast of black sexuality that had to be destroyed lest it endanger the white race. At the same time, docile, malleable, laughable characters were too ignorant, too readily swayed, and too easily controlled to warrant their participation in politics. As they crowded into cities like Durham, African Americans confronted perplexing myths. The trusted male slave turned assertive rapist and political threat, but the "bad" black woman remained immoral or turned loving and obliging. In any case, black folk were deemed incompetent workers, whose shortcomings reinforced whites' justification for Jim Crow and disfranchisement. Thwarting attempts at direct responses, whites also claimed that blacks who resisted categorization simply reiterated the feared racial menace; those who protested too much risked physical peril.[17]

But African Americans were crucial to the southern economy, which presented whites with a quandary of their own making. On the one hand, the southern farms and factories, indeed, southern life and comfort, could not survive without them. African Americans provided the bodies required to perform the harshest and most subservient labor. On the other hand, southern whites could not envision amending their perspectives to accommodate or incorporate African Americans into southern society on an equal basis. Thus, the Negro Problem portrayed black folk as a drag on southern civilization and as the cause of its troubles but at the same time required African Americans to alleviate the horrid conditions with which they lived under segregation. In this way, sociologist Gunnar Myrdal pointed out in his treatise on American race relations, the Negro Problem was really "the white man's problem," inasmuch as white people as a collective were responsible for trapping black Americans in disadvantaged circumstances.[18]

Apartheid drew both common and dissimilar obstacles for black women and men to surmount. The tumult in southern race dogma also caused both unity and disunity among African Americans who were assailed by unyielding and pervasive bigotry in its multiple forms. The internal discourse among African Americans articulated and interconnected gender and class frictions, generating both frustration and force. But these contentions stimulated the multiple strategies that black folk employed to seize the promises of freedom. Even as white southerners recast Jim Crow into the gendered forms with which they assailed black women, African American women invented forms of resistance to the ruthless ploys of racial degradation that affected the race as a whole and them as women specifically. The arduous task of overcoming and undermining the problematic images of women made them all the more cognizant of the dilemma facing black Americans. If whites judged the race by its women, then only through its women could the race rise. The task of racial destiny demanded that black women lend energy, resources, and labor in the home and outside: that they embrace the cult of domesticity and violate its protocols simultaneously.[19]

"The Sisters and Mothers Are Called to the City"

Just as Jim Crow nurtured its gendered elements to maintain power over African Americans, gender also facilitated the ways that black folk leveraged their resources for their own protection and benefit. Linking their economic needs with their personal ones, black families considered gender as well as the risks faced differently by men and women in making decisions about their lives. Accordingly, women and men migrated to different places for distinct reasons and under disparate circumstances. African American women came to Durham fleeing the dangers of sexual assault as well as to escape the poverty of rural life and to seek employment. As Annie Mack Barbee explained about rural South Carolina, "It got so dangerous." Her father, Charlie Neconda Mack, brought his family to Durham not only because he failed as a cotton farmer, or because whites burned down the black school his children attended, but also because his daughters faced the threat of sexual assault and exploitation.[20]

African American women left families in rural areas to find ways to increase family incomes. They moved to Durham seeking employment as household laborers in the growing number of white homes in the city and as factory workers in tobacco, an industry dominated by African American women. But they also migrated out of the South. Albeit ephemeral and difficult to track, patterns of black women's migration reveal that they were more likely than men to leave the farm for an urban area. Consequently, African American women outnumbered men in most cities, in Durham by more than 15 percent by 1890, a population shift that outpaced those of white males and females and black males, and, conversely, men predominated among black rural residents.[21] Economic circumstances warranted women's rather than men's migration off the farms. Du Bois once argued that "the Negroes are put in a peculiarly difficult position, because the wage of the male breadwinner is below the standard, while the openings for colored women in certain lines of domestic work, and now in industries, are many. Thus while toil holds the

Table 3.1. Black Population of Durham, 1880–1950

Year	Men	Women	Number of Men per 100 Women		
			Durham	Rural Durham	North Carolina
1890	860	999	86.1	98.1	96.3
1900	1,024	1,217	84.1	96.4	94.6
	(+19.1%)	(+21.8%)			
1910	3,106	3,763	82.5	90.8	94.8
	(+203.3%)	(+209.2%)			
1920	3,637	4,017	90.5	100.1	96.0
	(+17.1%)	(+6.8%)			
1930	8,616	10,101	85.3	108.3	94.6
	(+136.9%)	(+151.5%)			
1940	10,401	12,946	80.3	103.1	95.7
	(+20.7%)	(+28.2%)			
1950	11,967	14,154	84.5	101.6	95.4
	(+15.1%)	(+9.3%)			

father and the brother in the country and town at low wages, the sisters and mothers are called to the city."[22]

Confronting persistent poverty, a farm family functioned as an economic unit to sustain self-sufficiency but also operated as an age- and gender-segregated enterprise. That is, farming traditions assigned men, women, and children to separate work. Ideally, men did the heaviest and most public work of plowing the fields, settling up, and taking the product to the market. Among African Americans, however, women could and sometimes did do any of these tasks. In tobacco farming, men also hung and cured leaf, graded it for market, and traveled to the city to sell the crop at auction. Gender roles assigned women and children lighter tasks such as making seedbeds, weeding, and transplanting. In addition, women performed double duty in the household work of laundry, food preparation, and child care. And farming followed the agricultural calendar, planting in early spring, maintaining crops through the late spring, and harvesting in the fall. As the cost of farm materials — seed, tools, fertilizer — exceeded the value of women's labor on the farm, it was a better economic investment to dispatch women to other forms of income. By shifting assignments and allowing males to take up some work once considered female labor, families released women to seek other ways to contribute to the household income. Many aspects of women's farm labor — child care and cooking, for instance — translated to urban household labor. Women and girls, therefore, could be sent to cities more easily than men. Seeking jobs as domestics, black women accepted live-in and day jobs that separated them from their families.[23]

Second, the industrial calendar of tobacco labor meshed with the agricultural calendar to favor the transient nature of women's employment. Mostly seasonal, tobacco employment ran highest during "green season," the time of the year when the industry "worked up" new tobacco. Beginning in early May and lasting through mid-July, green season fell in the period between planting and harvesting. Once the fields were plowed and planted, female kin could be released to the factories. For those families who remained tethered to the land, the proximity of urban centers like Durham provided flexibility to sustain both rural and urban labor, allowing women to travel back and forth, working in town during the processing season and on the farm during planting and harvesting. Urban labor supplemented work on the farm. Hastie Price recalled that her mother divided her time between the tobacco factory in Durham and the family's rural farm. On the farm, Price, her brothers, and her father remained to raise cotton, fruits, and vegetables while her mother traveled between urban and rural homes following the seasonal rhythms of agriculture and industrial production.[24]

Adding paid work did not exempt women from their usual household tasks. Instead, it doubled their duties or shifted the burden of household labor onto children during the period when one parent worked in Durham and a daughter stayed home. While her mother was away, Price assumed the role of housekeeper and farmer, working "like one of the boys." Those women fortunate enough to find permanent work might establish one home in Durham while maintaining another in the country. Children then often joined the mother and settled in town. Not only women, but also girls, searched for work. Described as "near trained" by age seven, they were expected to work in white homes alongside a parent or older kin.[25]

Southern cities presented more viable, flexible, and familiar options than did northern locales for many black families, who could increase their earnings through multiple forms of work. Migration to a nearby city enabled families to stay connected as members moved back and forth between sites. If one family migrated, extended kin could follow. Mabel Harris's grandparents sent their three daughters to Durham in the 1910s to live with relatives so that they could go to school.[26] As the Harris family's decisions illustrate, work was only one reason black women migrated off the land; they also searched for educational opportunities for their children. Reginald Mitchner's mother moved to the city determined to earn enough to keep her children in school. The Mitchners had sharecropped in Franklinton County, and when Reginald's father died in 1916, his mother finished out the crop. "She decided that she just couldn't operate the farm and get the children the schooling they should have. . . . So we moved to Raleigh." Several months later, they moved to Greensboro. Reginald's oldest sister, then age seventeen, and oldest brother, age fourteen, "heard about the tobacco plants in Durham. They wanted to come to Durham so she [his mother] picks us up and moves us to Durham." The Mitchners' kinship networks made moves possible. While Mitchner and his siblings cared for each other, his mother moved back and forth between Durham and New York where she worked in "garment factories and hat factories to make extra money," a pattern she continued into the 1940s.[27]

Because few rural landlords would rent to single women or to families who lacked adult male kin, the city provided the only option for black women on their own. Family disasters — death, disablement, divorce, or desertion — left women without economic possibility in the country. Female-headed households and families with mostly girls were especially likely to migrate off the farm. Widowhood presented particularly difficult economic circumstances, and black women had consistently higher rates of widowhood than black men or white women. Not surprisingly, Durham's black population included a high concentration of African American widows. But even extended families of women struggled. Theresa Jan Cameron Lyons explained that when the sheriff arrested her two uncles, "the landlord made us move because we didn't have anyone to help us plow [with] the mules." Her family, consisting of all women — her grandmother, mother, aunts, and cousins — moved from farm to farm, before eventually moving to Durham.[28]

"Laboring under False Impressions"

The multiple migrations of African American women put the black population into a swirl of motion from the South to the North and from rural to urban. In North Carolina, and especially in Durham's home plants of Liggett and Myers and American Tobacco (both formerly of the Duke Trust), factories thirsted for workers. White households found it difficult to maintain domestic workers. "The exodus of Negro labor is beginning to affect the people in the city," the *Charlotte Observer* remarked about the labor situation in North Carolina in July 1903. Employers were required to pay "more for labor now than they have in many years," the article claimed. Emigration — and the resulting loss of black (cheap) labor — combined with black agitation and resistance in the early 1900s to unlock factory doors.[29]

In fact, a "distinct shortage of white workers" had forced Julian S. Carr to violate his own employment practices and hire black women as textile workers when he opened Durham Hosiery Mill #2. The "advisory spirits," including Jerome Dowd, the Trinity College professor, warned Carr that "the rhythm of the machines would put them [African Americans] to sleep." No doubt Carr, a strident racist, shared these views, but he built his experiment on examples that Dowd ignored. Black women had worked "satisfactorily" in selected mills in the South, including at Fayetteville, Concord, and Charleston, and, given the choice between black workers or no mill, Carr proceeded with his unconventional plan. The Carr mill opened in 1902, employing a few white supervisors and fifty African Americans, mostly women. Black female mill workers elicited an outcry from whites. Arguing that Carr was "taking the bread out of their mouths," whites variously threatened to blow up and burn down the mill. Because white women mill workers in town believed African American women were morally blemished, they refused to speak to the white foreman hired to supervise blacks.[30]

The African American women who went to work in the mill expressed a different form of remonstrance; they acceded to the offer of employment with tacit obstinacy. Julian S. Carr III, the general's son, described the situation in later years: "The negroes had no idea of machinery; they could trace no connection between the knitting machines and the finished product. . . . Rules meant nothing to them." Black mill workers, he claimed, ignored regulations about the use of the restroom and disregarded the discipline of a regular work schedule, arriving late, leaving early, and, just as often, failing to appear at all. Blacks most likely understood the work and their responsibilities but simply refused to comply with Carr's factory dictates. They were aware that past exclusion from the mills had been based on judgments about their presumed inadequacies, particularly the standards of morality Carr believed black women lacked. Knowing that they had been accused of stupidity, slovenliness, and laziness, they now refused to join in the owners' version of a docile black labor force. They accepted the jobs and then refused to comply with employers' demands. Julian Carr III tellingly observed in talking about the mill: "I think they regarded themselves as attending some sort of an exhibition in which they were expected to be interested but hardly to participate."[31]

Black employees eventually consented to work, but only after they named the terms of their cooperation and manipulated the situation to their specific, if muted, demands. For example, when the Carrs placed "Aunt Martha" and "Uncle Paul" in supervisory positions, order commenced. African Americans in "posts that had authority had a distinct appeal to the negroes," Carr conceded, and he admitted that "we gave up trying to prevent absences for weddings, funerals, or the circus. . . . We took it as fact that every one of them would take a solid week off to join in the annual yearly meeting of his or her particular church." Contrary to predictions, the mill turned a profit within eighteen months of its opening. Black hosiery mill workers did not gain all of the benefits offered to white workers at the other mills in town — educational facilities, for instance, and improved working conditions — but they won other contests of wills.[32]

Contemporary white observers referred to the South as a "country without strikes," where laborers were unlikely to challenge white authority. "Unsystematic, and not being an organizer himself, the negro is a free lance in the labor field," a 1903 article in the *Literary Digest* suggested.[33] Yet those same observers ignored, or refused to recognize, when and how black laborers expressed dissatisfaction with working conditions and wages. An absence of labor organizations, moreover, did not necessarily indicate an absence of organized labor activity among workers. The black women who agreed to work for the Carrs, for example, engaged in a collective act of resistance and oppositional politics through slowdowns and absenteeism that turned white presumptions of black ineptitude and immorality into forms of protest. In a variety of situations, African American women refused to work as a strategy for gaining some control over their space and their labor. These everyday forms of resistance disputed white notions that black workers lacked ingenuity and resourcefulness.[34]

But black workers' and women's formal organizing efforts were occurring across the state. In 1904, Samuel Gompers, head of the American Federation of Labor, advised the Brown and Williamson Tobacco Company, in Winston-Salem, to concede to the unionization of black workers as a way to manage their employees: "A well-ordered union seeks to establish the highest satisfactory relations between a firm and its employees." A union, he argued, "restrains employees from precipitous action and assures the firm against strikes." From Windsor, North Carolina, educator Rhoden Mitchell wrote to Charles Hunter: "The women here want to regulate their work,

cooking, washing, and general house work, at a reasonable and living price."
Mitchell organized the Working Woman's Society to represent household
workers. "The working women in town and cities must submit to the subject—*What I do, the amount I get, and what it costs to live?*" Mitchell's flyer
read. Connecting women's labor rights to community development, the organization promised "the opportunity to exercise and exert them for the
general good of women and the advance of civilization."[35] As the news of
labor activities passed along state and local networks, Durham could not
remain immune from the labor activism occurring elsewhere among blacks.

In addition to gaining the liberty of setting their own priorities and naming
the terms of their cooperation, black women workers at Carr's mill gained
more jobs. The "colored mill" expanded its workforce to 400 female workers
over the next two decades, and increased to 700 by the late 1920s. Tobacco
factories, facing similar labor straits, also began to hire black laborers, especially women. Between 1902 and 1904, the number of black workers reported
in city directories doubled; by 1908, wages also had increased.[36]

Still, as expanding employment opportunities drew black women to industry, leading whites grumbled about the shortage of domestic workers, even as
they criticized the quality of work among this class of employees. White
newspapers, journals, and magazines consistently complained about theft,
scams, insolence, and disappearances. In one Durham case, a group of white
men complained that five times they had paid one "old timey negro" to find
black women household laborers, but each time, the women left within a
week. "Housekeepers in Durham as well as elsewhere complain of the diffi-
culty in getting servants and keeping them after secured," the *Morning Herald* complained. "It is a pity that our class of servants should be to such a large
extent without moral sense." Black workers' discontent fueled white employers' dissatisfaction even as the latter depended more and more on the
former. "They have their schools and churches in which they study and
worship," the paper asserted about the black community. In exchange, the
paper implied, "the colored people in this town as everywhere are depended
upon for house and kitchen work." It is not surprising, then, that individual
workers who resented these expectations found ways to express their disgruntlement. Martha Evans, a Durham cook, allegedly furnished dinner for a
group of black prisoners from her white employers' pantry. Covered with
linens and served on china, the meal was carried to the jail on a silver tray.
Although the *Durham Morning Herald* noted that Evans "broke the law" and
undermined "her employer's faith and good nature," she seemed "not at all
discontent to go to jail."[37]

"Our Greatest Desideratum Is Good Character"

Seeking protection from aggravated white employers and from guilt by association with recalcitrant black workers, many more affluent African Americans distanced but could not insulate themselves from the "inferior" members of the race. They held the less fortunate culpable for the ways that whites' animosity affected them. Black leaders like Charles N. Hunter joined the harangues of the urban progressive reformers. Hunter used a column in a white newspaper, the *Raleigh Morning Post*, to chastise black workers. "I have collected some opinions of employers of negroes labor as to its character. These in many important particulars are far from flattering." He pointed out that a majority of both black and white employers complained that "we are unreliable, inefficient, and thriftless."[38] Hunter repeated the mantras of morality, thrift, and industry. "Our greatest desideratum is good character," he wrote to the editor of the *Independent*. "We must undergo the discipline [of] work, moral restraint, self-sacrifice, Christian living. We need a great Century movement along the line here indicated."[39]

Hunter targeted working-class women specifically. "A lady occupying a very responsible position in one of our business houses had to remain away from her duties . . . because her cook took a notion to 'go fishing.' " Railing against "the indifferent character, inefficiency and irresponsibility of a large proportion of the servant class of our people," he wrote in another editorial: "This servant problem is as much a condition in the town as the labor problem is on the farm; there is not only scarcity, but unreliability in both instances." Seeming to attack directly the workers at Carr's mill, he penned: "Many of them are laboring under the false impression that since they are inadequately remunerated for their service they will make that service nearly commensurate with pay received as possible. They seem to think that poor pay and poor work will tend to an enhancement of labor values. They argue too that since their wages are so low they are justified in quitting one job for another just as soon as there is the slightest promise of work. . . . These views are erroneous."[40]

Hunter further argued: "The best and speediest means of advancing wages is to advance the quality of the labor performed." Taking up the Carrs' grievance, he contended: "In case of a circus, or an excursion, or a picnic, or a society parade, or a big funeral, that they wished to attend or take part in," black laborers "drop work and leave."[41] The black women who worked for the Carrs clearly disagreed with Hunter, believing that in the face of labor demands, their reluctance to work yielded more gains than losses. Hunter either ignored their success, defined success in different ways, or believed women should not make demands. The aspiring class suffered, Hunter complained, from "the embarrassment of having to adjust themselves to the senseless whims of every ignoramus of the race in the community."[42]

Another correspondent feebly attempted to defend the elite of black womanhood, asking the *Raleigh News and Observer* editor "why should it be charged that the wives and daughters of our best negro men seek the companionship with the most degraded whites?" Having disengaged men and women of the aspiring class from "the most degraded negroes," he ranked his class as deserving of better treatment from whites. He defined the "Negro Problem" as whites' inability to recognize the difference: "We ask that the aspiring class of white people . . . allow the aspiring class of negroes to retain their social distinction, build up their social circles, and that instead of trying to degrade them, they say a word to encourage them."[43] By engaging in these disparaging discourses, the black aspiring classes attempted to distinguish themselves from their inferior neighbors. Those neighbors, increasingly, were women. Black leaders like Hunter interpreted black working-class women's strategies of resistance as "the indifferent character, inefficiency and irresponsibility of a large proportion of the servant class of our people"[44] and rejected them. Coupled with the mark of degeneracy, the women's actions brought down the wrath of the aspiring class who, like whites, could not or would not hear the veiled demands of black women workers.

After the turn of the century, then, leaders of the aspiring class voiced their response to the Negro Problem with claims of material progress and moral purity among the few. But in turn, they blamed the victim for continued white prejudice, a situation they did not create and could not control. Male and female leaders kept up a persistent lecture that preached to the masses about their shortcomings: demanding thrift from people who had no money, hard work from people already engaged in harsh labor, and high morality from people who suffered daily abuse and exploitation from whites. Piercing the surface of racial solidarity and exacerbated by the recriminations of whites, the tirades of black community leaders fostered divisions among African Americans. Distancing from white fury, members of the aspiring class insulted the black folk among whom they were forced to live as a way to address the race problem their own way. The correspondent to the *Raleigh News and Observer* spoke of his frustration: "I do not understand why it should be charged that all negroes are seeking social intercourse with the most degraded whites, when it is only the most degraded negroes who seek such intercourse, and the whole negro race regret[s] this very much."[45]

"Lifting as We Climb"

Attempting to change the perceptions of the race that whites held, the aspiring class presented itself as the prototype of black respectability, models of black manhood and womanhood who offered themselves as paragons of morality to whites and as examples of race progress and potential to the masses. Charles Dame, before he passed over the color line, and Mary Pauline Dame were trained as archetypes of the race, charged with challenging insulting images through their respectable public personae in order to overturn the conceptions held by whites. The image of the black man as "savage" and "Sambo" and the black woman as wicked "wench" and bossy "Mammy" could be replaced, the aspiring class hoped, with portraits of respectability: black Americans uplifted through education, refinement, culture, and affluence. Blacks might therefore join "southern civilization" by presenting themselves as civilized. To accomplish this feat, leaders believed, blacks would have to display personal qualities that overrode accusations of immorality and ineptness with high moral ideals. Members of the aspiring class hoped furthermore that by distinguishing themselves from those who lived down to white expectations, they could also raise blacks' awareness of their potential as a race. Because whites' character assaults invoked the degradation of bondage, the aspiring class represented progress, defined as distance from slavery-like conditions. Nothing less than a full face-lift and a complete break with the enslaved past could ameliorate the social conditions of the modern black person.[46]

Women in particular, although not exclusively, took up this arduous task. Through organizations like the National Association of Colored Women (NACW) and its hundreds of local affiliates, black women attempted to rise above reproach to address issues specific to them as women. Reinforced by the club movement's unified voice, women activists took it upon themselves to represent the silenced and, at the same time, to defend themselves in ways that male leaders could not. Indeed, clubwomen concluded that men were ineffective in dealing with the gender complexity of the Negro Problem. Fannie Barrier Williams and others involved in women's clubs throughout the United States believed that "at the very time when race interests seem at such a low ebb [and] when our race leaders seem tongue-tied and stupidly inactive in the presence of unchecked violent resistance to Negro advancement, it is especially fortunate and reassuring to see and feel the rallying spirit of our women."[47]

But the centerpiece of the black women's club movement was its dedication to an uplift that connected them to their less fortunate sisters and those sisters to the fate of the race. "The National Association has chosen as its motto: Lifting as We Climb," Mary Church Terrell wrote, and "both policy and self-preservation demand that [women of education and culture] go down among the lowly, the illiterate and even the vicious, to whom they are bound by the ties of race and sex, and put forth every possible effort to reclaim them."[48]

The black women's club movement, with its emphasis on female moral superiority and its public critique of African American male leaders' short-comings, carried both a national and a state profile. A few North Carolina women attended national meetings. At the 1896 organizing meeting of the National Federation of Afro-American Women, a precursor of the NACW, a "Miss Jones" from Raleigh represented the North Carolina delegation and presented Mrs. Booker T. Washington with a bouquet of white roses "in appreciation of the wisdom and kindness she has shown as chairman of the Convention." Branches of the NACW, like the Biddle University Club of Charlotte, sprang up in select areas of the state, and individual women, like entrepreneur Lula Spaulding and educator Charlotte Hawkins Brown, brought North Carolina perspectives to the national scene and national initiatives to the state.[49] In national, state, and local meetings and in the pages of their own publications, clubwomen refined their arguments and carried them to the public through civic appearances and articles for black news-papers and periodicals, forums to carry on their work as "earnest, intelligent, progressive colored women," repeatedly comparing themselves to white per-ceptions of "ignorant and immoral" black women. When clubwomen looked upon their less fortunate neighbors, they saw situations that caused them to wonder whether whites' perceptions might be valid. The mass of African Americans did live in squalid conditions that the aspiring class had managed to escape; they did lack the education and refinements that the aspiring class valued; and they did exhibit insolent behaviors that the aspiring class criti-cized (but sometimes committed). Accordingly, women among the aspiring class charged themselves with responsibility for "the moral education of the race with which we are identified," as Josephine St. Pierre Ruffin wrote in calling for a national meeting.[50]

For the cause of race development, clubwomen clothed themselves with authority as vital and influential women, as members of their communities, and as mothers, homemakers, and workers charged with the social and moral uplift of their people. Wearing the badge of respectability, embellished with the language of "domestic virtue," "moral impulses," and "standards of fam-ily and social life," they set themselves apart from the masses. "Among colored women the club effort is the effort of the few competent in behalf of the many incompetent," Fannie Barrier Williams explained. Secret societies, she elucidated, "demand a higher order of intelligence than is required of church work." Williams also claimed that inasmuch as patterns of differentiation symbolized the advancement of a society, they also reflected the progress of African Americans: "It ought to be born in mind that such social differentiations as women's interests, children's interests, and men's interests that are so finely worked out in the social development of the more favored races are but recent recognitions in the progressive life of the negro race." By extension, the development of distinct social classes, reinforced by attendant gender roles, represented social progress.[51]

In short, clubwomen defined themselves as "superior" to others. Their duty, in Williams's interpretation, was to "exercise a more helpful sympathy with the many of the race who are without guides and enlightenment in the ways of social righteousness." A clubwoman was, according to Williams, "the real new woman in American life" who "succeeded in lifting herself as completely from the stain and meanness of slavery as if a century had elapsed since the day of emancipation." A mere generation away from slavery, clubwomen intentionally distanced themselves from their constituents. "We have organized with a hope of lifting the masses beneath us and thus lifting ourselves," Mrs. Booker T. Washington once wrote to a colleague regarding the NACW. The NACW motto, "Lifting as We Climb," acknowledged that those who were to be lifted were beneath those who were to do the lifting.[52] From a self-elevated position, clubwomen defended black women's moral integrity and promoted their own competence and intelligence while emphasizing class distinctions. Only by demonstrating their distance from the people with whom they were associated, they believed, could they publicly address the issues of rape, immorality, and caricatures and at the same time stake a claim to their own respectability.

"The Colored woman has awakened to her responsibility and realizes that she is a factor in the world's civilization and in the race's progress," North Carolinian Mary A. Lynch proclaimed to the Negro Young People's Christian and Educational Congress in 1902. "The reform movements among women to-day," she continued, "are doing powerful work to make the state, the church and the home more happy and more holy." Clubwomen and activists like Lynch viewed the vote as a weapon that black women might use to undercut the vices of the streets and to shield children and themselves "against the saloon, the gambling house, the den of vice and all the corruptions of politics." The reality of the vote, however, was distant. Black leaders therefore focused on remaking themselves into model "race men" and "race women," shouldering the burden of race as an act of "uplift" and claiming that efforts to better themselves also benefited the masses.[53]

"In the Hands of the Missionary Women"

In Durham, the work of uplift among women took on a variety of forms. Although women's secular associations existed in Durham, none affiliated with the NACW at this time. The North Carolina Federation of Colored Women's Clubs was not organized officially until 1909, by Charlotte Hawkins Brown and others, including Durham clubwomen Julia McCauley Warren, Minnie Pearson, and Cottie Moore. But affiliated and federated clubs were slow in forming. In fact, the oldest black women's club in Durham, the Daughters of Dorcas, did not form officially until 1917, although its members earlier engaged in activities as friends calling themselves the Busy Women's Club. For the most part, Durham women mostly practiced their activism through religion. Fannie Barrier Williams may have believed that club work demanded a higher order of intelligence than church work, but the church, as an extension of the home, provided Durham's African American women a place to set their agenda and direct their initiatives. The church, furthermore, afforded a readymade pulpit from which they could articulate and act on urgent concerns. Church work, moreover, brought together diverse sets of hands and accomplished more than any secular organization because the church dominated black institutional life.[54]

Sustained by few resources, "race work" required enormous personal energy, significant organizational innovation, large numbers of volunteers, and a broad imperative for change. Minnie S. Pearson and Hattie E. Shepard led the respective Methodist and Baptist missionary societies; others directed Sunday schools and joined Pastor's Aid to take up short-term projects designated by the minister. Still others worked with the Ladies' Aid in raising funds for churches' physical needs: a new organ, instruments for the church band, or furnishings for Sunday schools.[55] Church organizations linked women's needs and efforts in multiple ways. Shepard, for example, served as a board member of the Women's Home and Foreign Mission Convention. She also presided over the Senior Missionary Society at White Rock Baptist Church, which organized auxiliaries in other areas of the city. The Grant Street Mission and the East End Mission sat within poorer neighborhoods, and the City Missionary Society joined these efforts under a citywide Baptist umbrella. The local mission also supported another of White Rock's oldest traditions, the Sunday school orchestra. Thus, churchwomen preached not only the gospel of salvation but also the gospel of cooperation, community, and coordinated effort.[56]

Whereas the black women's club movement focused on refuting negative perceptions about African American women, churchwomen made civic work central to missionary work, engendering a strategy of resistance to Jim Crow that operated behind the veil. Women's missionary circles associated with individual churches, and their broader governing societies, like the Women's Home and Foreign Mission Convention, provided spaces where black female leaders could speak with a respectable public voice and gain the support of a broader public. Black churchwomen deflected negative images and built positive ones by embracing the national clubwomen's more politicized program through missionary work. Through religious organizations, women preached and enlightened their flocks on the connection between the political position of African Americans in society and perceptions about black morality. From her post as the head of the Baptist Home Missionary Society in North Carolina, Pattie G. Shepard (Hattie Shepard's sister-in-law) conceded that "church and state" matters affected all African Americans but claimed that the central issue for the race was its "standards of morality." Moreover, in her call for a higher moral touchstone among African Americans, she held both men and women responsible, but criticized mainly the former. "Men do not respect their women," she asserted, and thus they shared the blame for young women "becoming mothers before they are wives" and consequently suffering "shame and disgrace." These problems, she argued, were "destroying us as a race."[57]

While the club movement articulated principles of responsibility and respectability to move other women to activism, women's church work concentrated on action itself. At the annual Interdenominational Sunday School Convention held in Durham in 1905, for example, messages of moral uplift fused with those of heavenly reward. "When they turned away from God, dishonored their women, gave themselves up to sensuality and licentiousness, they crumbled and fell," Professor John R. Hawkins preached. "Let us raise our standards, brighten our ideals, and trust in God." Accordingly, the crowd received Annie D. Shepard's "thoughtful paper on moral beauty" with "fervor." But the participants transformed lectures on morality into other kinds of lessons. The Bible served as the text for both the teachings of the church and for teaching literacy. Because church leaders knew that future enfranchisement required literacy, the session on "Primary Sunday School Work" encouraged a class of children to make "liberal use of their pencils and notebooks."[58]

Also unlike club work, church work cut across class lines and brought women from different institutions and occupations together as equals in common enterprises like missionary circles and delegations to women's church organizations. Nonetheless, the individual and local endeavors of a cross-class contingent of women disappeared in larger assemblies, as women who hailed from the aspiring class came to the forefront. Still, because black churches depended on the already-strained resources of their congregations, the small group of women leaders who hailed from the aspiring class could not have done the work alone. Rather, they had to call on willing workers to "redouble" their efforts: "Only whole souled, heart-work counted," they advised. To accomplish their goals, women must wield "prayer and self-sacrifice." North Carolinian Sarah Dudley Pettey wrote for the *Star of Zion* on the work of the Woman's Home and Foreign Missionary Society of the AME church (WHFMS): "All around us we have missions struggling for existence, and, too, some of our largest churches have weighty mortgages hanging over their heads." This burden, which churchwomen bore, "could be averted if our missionary department was on a solid basis and in good working order."[59]

Holy contemplation proved insufficient. "Loyalty to the church" demanded that women "unite with enthusiasm and work together in harmony," not only among themselves but also with male leaders. To answer these many needs, the WHFMS, founded in 1900, united local and state organizations to initiate a "Women's Day" theme for Sunday services. Despite their concerted efforts, they encountered clergymen who "have never taken it very seriously." Like clubwomen, churchwomen held opinions on the black male leadership, specifically of the black clergy, who interfered with the implementation of their programs and whom they viewed as a hindrance to their activities. Churchwomen also generated suggestions about how to deal with recalcitrant ministers. Annie Walker Blackwell, the corresponding secretary of the WHFMS, entreated ministers directly to put church work "in the hands of the missionary women." If no such organization exists, she suggested, lend the endeavor "to the best workers." Blackwell believed these to be the church's women.[60]

WHFMS officers stood between their women followers and male ministers who, interpreting women's enthusiasm as a criticism, felt threatened. Blackwell advised a quiet strategy to soothe fragile egos. "Take him [the minister] aside," she advised; "seek cooperation with the pastor in a way that he can't say no." Such a strategy included rather than excluded men in resolving the gendered aspects of the race problem. "If he is a man that wants to be considered *the leader* in everything done in his church, suggest to him in private certain things to be done," Blackwell recommended, "or better [,] ask if he doesn't think it well to do certain things for the advancement of the work." She continued: "The other kind of pastor will lay his plans and give them to the women to work out, knowing that whatever success comes to any part of the church under his pastorate, he will get a large part of the honors."[61]

Substantive blessings for women's missionary work came not only through pastors' recognition but also through the financial support offered by local congregations. Hence, the WHFMS created a special collection for its causes. Suspecting that funds were being "pinched," particularly by ministers, "especially where the collections has been large," officers discovered ways to appease pastors while encouraging women's groups to form in individual churches. Thus, Mrs. K. P. Hood, wife of the AME bishop, recommended that where an "auxiliary society" existed, one-third of the funds be kept for local purposes. And to assure that women were acknowledged for whatever efforts they lent, women leaders asked that whatever funds women raised, including those solely for local purposes, also get reported to the WHFMS.[62] Finally, realizing that ministers were partial to the church's hierarchical structure because it maintained their status, AME women called on the bishops to use their influence in securing pastors' cooperation with missionary women.[63]

The Baptist Woman's Home and Foreign Mission Convention of North Carolina (the Woman's Convention or the WC) made a charge similar to that of their Methodist sisters, and it faced similar difficulties. The fact that Pattie G. Shepard, Hattie E. Shepard, and Sally Mial — among the WC's founders — all married prominent ministers facilitated their independence as activists because the role of "minister's wife" made them "helpmeets" to their husbands. But Pattie Shepard, known for her "choice flow of language and her great executive ability," also "swayed great audiences wherever she appeared not only of the gentler sex, but of the opposite as well." When the men did not listen, the WC's women appeared "on the floor of associations and Convention as well as at the churches."[64] The WC, founded in 1884, insisted on autonomy. This position created an independent women's movement within the black Baptist church that combined race, gender, and church politics in one association. Sally Mial and Lizzie Neily, two WC leaders in North Carolina, wrote the male-led Baptist Convention: "We, sisters of our denomination, have organized ourselves . . . for the purpose of aiding you in the work of the Missions, especially among women." Durham principal James A. Whitted, a historian of North Carolina black Baptists, noted that despite "strenuous efforts" to transform the wc into "an auxiliary of the men's Convention," women resisted. They "would never consent to the changes" and accomplished more by "existing separate and apart."[65]

Fund-raising was one of black women's most important functions in church work and illustrated how they tested limits, their own and those of male church leaders. As a women's movement, the Baptist wc set its own agenda and put the moral, social, and economic needs of women and their families at center stage. It endeavored to establish missionary circles in "all Baptist churches" in impoverished sections of the state. Stretching its scope, the wc promoted Sunday schools, Bible reading, and church going in their communities, supported the Oxford Orphan's Asylum, and cooperated with the northern-based Baptist Home Mission Society. The wc also created and sustained a Women's Training School (for missionaries) at Shaw University. Its work reached beyond the shores of the United States as well. Through the Lott-Carey Convention, a separate foreign mission that sent representatives to Africa, the wc wholly funded the work of Cora Ann Pair and sent her to Liberia in the 1900s to establish a mission school.[66]

Locally, the wc's missionary circles divided their work between home visitation, Bible instruction, and charity distribution. Women church activists not only understood the role of education in uplift and preparation for voting but also grasped the importance of property ownership in providing protection from exploitation. As Whitted wrote, however, the wc focused on "the greatest need of this people emerged from slavery with all of its stains": home training and guiding and instructing family members on values, mores, and behavior. The wc did more than help the poor and spread the gospel. Indeed, such an interpretation misses the ways that its objectives centered on other uplift. Rather, the wc applied a biblical interpretation of black women's place in communities that rid them of the negative stains of slavery: "Negro Baptist Women as soon as they were free to work and earn wages for themselves followed the example of the women Jesus had trained for the first Missionary Society." Poverty required women's employment, black Baptists understood, and forgave or overlooked employment as a transgression of traditional gender roles. More important, some women blemished with past immorality were chosen to "spread the gospel message." Thus, whatever their pasts, women uplifted themselves through both their employment and their church work; membership required only that women currently be "of good moral character."[67]

Church-based organizations granted women leadership roles, recognizing that women provided a necessary component to racial uplift, community building, and racial destiny, and connected women's issues to race issues directly. Because churchwomen often experienced resistance from male leadership, as the WC and the WHFMS efforts illustrated, they had to negotiate within church structures. But even mixed-sex, female-dominated, secular associations embraced certain gender conventions in defining women's role in the community. Sallie Fitzgerald, considered a "silver tongued orator," founded the Volkamenia Literary Club as an organization to bring Durham's coterie of educated young adults together for cultural and social interaction. But the group elected C. F. Rich, a young black male lawyer, to serve as president; Sallie served as the organization's secretary. Similarly, within secret societies, women's groups functioned as auxiliaries to men's assemblies. The Eastern Star, the Household of Ruth, the Lady Knights of King David, and others accordingly included male officers.[68]

Nonetheless, Durham's secular organizations created intellectual spaces where women debated race matters on an equal footing with men. Intended to encourage their members to shape informed opinions, literary clubs enlarged the number of "public" places where women spoke across gender lines. Julia McCauley, the new domestic science teacher at the Durham Colored Graded School, joined Volkamenia soon after its start. So did Hattie E. Shepard's son and daughter in-law, Annie D. and James E. Shepard. For the Volkamenia's weekly meetings, one member prepared a paper on an assigned topic for discussion, and all brought newspaper clippings about current events. In addition to art, music, and literature, the subjects of migration, segregation, and images of blacks were likely topics, and the role of women in a dynamic black community held the attention of club members. Although women served as the nucleus of the membership, the Volkamenia Club was not exclusively a women's club, nor do extant records reveal any focus on specifically women's issues. But certainly race issues dominated discussions. Clubs with similar memberships — the Twentieth Century Club, a literary society, and the Schubert Shakespeare Club, with an emphasis on the arts — also were founded in the 1900s. The Volkamenia Club retained its focus on current events and intellectual pursuits and maintained a membership roster from among the elite and middle classes of Durham. Its programs expanded over the years and became central to black Durham's intellectual life, sponsoring speakers, developing scholarship and award programs, and initiating voter education and literacy programs.[69]

At the beginning of the twentieth century, women's clubs and female-dominated secular organizations linked with the church, the workplace, and the family as places where black Durham planned for its future. With more sites where they could deliberate and represent themselves, women joined the chorus debating the issues most relevant to black people of the day: the so-called Negro Problem, politics, community building, and migration. Positioned to participate in community decision making, African American women elected alternately to avoid and confront their white neighbors. The black women's club movement was never intended to function as a place where women of various classes intersected, except through uplift. The churchwomen's movement, however, embraced African American women of all classes who themselves embraced the demands of respectability.[70]

Migration out of the South provided one way for black people to escape the harsh economic effects of repression. Between 1880 and 1910, African American women left the South in greater numbers than men, but they could not avoid discrimination or the unforgiving rhetoric that followed them. Others organized into sacred and secular organizations designed to uplift the race through self-help and mutual aid and to respond to the ruthless ploys of racial degradation — the women's clubs, auxiliaries, and missionary circles that shouldered the "too heavy a load" of elevating the race. African American women laborers employed their own forms of protest, often subtle and spontaneous actions that spoke to their discontent and their refusal to cooperate with systems designed to humiliate them. And while some masked their contempt for whites by donning stereotypes and pretending to accept the perceptions of whites, they did so as a necessary strategy of survival. Among the better class of Negroes, some attempted to distance themselves from Jim Crow and those blacks who offended the sensibilities of the black elite. Passing provided an out, but this was available only to those light skinned enough to vanish into the white population. And many who could have taken that route chose to stay and fight.[71]

Assessing their circumstances from contending perspectives, African Americans articulated their struggle in ways that clashed and even contradicted their common goal of facing the Negro Problem. Consequent fissures in black solidarity brought people other than the leading black men to prominent roles as activists on behalf of the race. Thus, although weaknesses appeared along the wall of unity, as might be expected from a people under the stress of racism, the barrier that kept out the destructive powers of racism strengthened with more people pushing against it. In increasing numbers, African Americans from diverse constituencies recast respectability, making it a specific duty to work for on behalf of the race, each other, and themselves individually. In doing so, they used connections forged from individual relationships and local networks to create an impressive range of associations and strategies. In the process, women in particular emerged as agents for change.

Clubwomen and women missionaries, for example, used the links they forged among national, state, and local organizations to develop race work that spoke specifically to African American women, while also offering a gendered critique of leadership. They also defended the sisterhood. "Immorality and thrift do not mate very well," Hunton argued, "and in spite of all the accusations, the Negro woman has been the motive power in whatever has been accomplished by the race."[72] Accepting the responsibility to provide for their families while defending themselves, African American women led the migration out of rural areas in search of better-paying jobs. They moved off southern farms in ever-greater numbers, and often against male leaders' wishes. Just as whites exploited their labor — and for that reason — black women workers exploited their circumstances and found creative ways to express discontent. Others fought for unity, but it eluded them. These divergent approaches also represented the multiple modes of resistance that African Americans designed to avert and deflect repressive schemes. Taken together, they illustrated blacks' varying quests for improved qualities of life.

Black Durham continued to mature as a community, but not without obstacles. Segregation created a world where the city's African Americans had to unite in self-protection and self-interest, but as their differing needs and perspectives emerged, they formed into groups ever more clearly demarcated by class and gender norms. Those who toiled in the factories and in domestic service, while sharing common spaces, lived increasingly separate lives from the aspiring class. Few, especially among women and workers, left conventional records to tell of their thoughts, actions, or perspectives, but many left the imprint of their lives on both black and white leaders who responded to their presence with a combination of pity and scorn. Their actions were part and parcel of the larger movements around them.

It is questionable, in the end, whether divisions among blacks impeded or enhanced community growth, but it is clear that multiple forms of activism, defined by gender and class, expanded African Americans' efforts to upbuild black Durham. The "whole souled, heart-work" of churchwomen — in maintaining links with kin, in building and sustaining institutions, and in facilitating settlement for newcomers — helped African Americans preserve and promote the unity Charles N. Hunter had praised about Durham. Even as working women's migration inspired class-based anxieties among black leaders, their movement represented one way that black people attempted to meet their needs. The leading black men may have disapproved of the ways that working-class women resisted Jim Crow, but they did not have to confront the forms of exploitation and abuse the masses faced. The upbuilding of black Durham required capital, both economic and social, and folk on every corner contributed in their own ways. To realize its aspirations for growth and success, black Durham would have to struggle with the fortunes of both the prosperous and the poor.

Today, there is a singular group in Durham where a
black man may get up in the morning from a mattress
made by black men, in a house which a black man built
out of lumber which black men cut and planed; he may
put on a suit which he bought at a colored haberdashery
and socks knit at a colored mill; he may cook victuals
from a colored grocery on a stove which black men fashioned; he may earn his living working for colored men,
be sick in a colored hospital, and buried from a colored
church; and the Negro insurance company will pay
his widow enough to keep his children in the colored
school. This is surely progress.
  W. E. B. Du Bois, "The Upbuilding of Black
  Durham" (1912)

4: We Have Great Faith in Luck, but Infinitely More in Pluck

Gender and the Making of a New Black Elite

Susie V. Gille stepped off the train in late January 1906 and created a
sensation in Durham. She wore a white, high-collar, puff-sleeved blouse and
layers of black skirts. She had arrived on the Jim Crow car and probably was
covered in soot. She pulled her railroad trunk with straight-backed dignity,
asked directions in schoolmarm English, and made her way through the
muck. She had come to work for the North Carolina Mutual and Provident
Association, the colored insurance company, and she was prepared to stay. A
graduate of Wilberforce College, classically educated, professionally skilled,
and single, Gille was a southbound black woman migrant whose skills were
unappreciated in the North and a Yankee outsider who, ironically, found
work in the Jim Crow South. In a town where the most visible African
American women were the ones whose alleged offenses the *Morning Herald*

delighted to report, Gille provided, for whites and for blacks, a different image of African American womanhood.[1]

Gille's arrival was a part of the shaping of a new black elite, urban-based and southern and less concerned with lineage and color than the old black aristocracy. Whether up from slavery like the Merricks or coming out of freedom like the Moores, the members of this new elite focused on generating and accumulating wealth — cash, capital, and assets — to set themselves apart from the masses. Children of both freedpeople and the first generation born into freedom, they projected a vision of autonomy lit by its distance from Jim Crow's shadows. And because of their own struggles and those of their parents, elites were in intimate contact with members of the middle and working classes who sometimes were family members. While providing a substantial pecuniary basis for institution building — which sometimes led them to view community institutions as their own — their wealth also could buy protection, which they valued most highly. Thus these men measured manliness by their ability to create an environment where women could be respectable, indeed, could be expected to be respectable. And they measured womanhood by this achievement, and by contributions to the community over which men presided. Part Washingtonian, part Du Boisian, part Terrellian, they tread the racial world carefully. As the Talented Tenth (although the elite and middle class together made up less that 5 percent of Durham's black population), they dedicated themselves to uplift; and as members of organizations, they attached the ladder they climbed to the wall used by the rest of the race.

In the same way that the respectability of women reflected on the status of the family, Gille personified the respectability of her employer, North Carolina Mutual and Provident Association, later named North Carolina Mutual Life Insurance Company. Well dressed, polished, and genteel, Susie Gille was the personification of respectability and of the best attributes of African Americans. By extension, she also presented a discernible affirmation of the Mutual's uprightness as a business. As a visible representative of the company and as a woman, she was to model a public expression of a private life above reproach and in repudiation of any hint of impropriety, just like North Carolina Mutual. Together the Mutual and Susie Gille provided evidence of race advancement and the ability of African Americans to attain what whites believed they could not: an effective black patriarchy that could protect and provide for its charges — respectable, well-mannered, and educated women and children. Thus Susie Gille's opportunities — to graduate from college, to find good work, and to engage in an active social life that led to marriage — spoke directly to Mutual men's sense of their success, shaped as it was in a society that sought to deny black men their station and black women their virtue.

The new arrival might have been surprised by what she saw on her initial venture from the train station to Hayti. Main Street, running through downtown and parallel to the railroad tracks that separated whites from blacks, was lined with more saloons, factories, and warehouses than the stores and banks that would have characterized a truly prosperous business district. So at least in appearance, Durham was not all it claimed. But newly built warehouses and factories, including a mill Gille's employers owned, signaled an expanding economy and wage-earning prospects for women laborers. Across the tracks to the black side, new brick buildings indicated a fledgling business district taking shape at the intersection of Fayetteville and Pettigrew Streets. Churches announced the institutional foundations of growing African American communities, with White Rock Baptist and St. Joseph AME Zion standing like the twin sentries of faith and respectability and observing the procession of African Americans as they passed up and down the hill. The Victorian homes of Gille's employers, adorned with polygonal bay windows and wraparound porches, graced either side of Fayetteville Street, the main thoroughfare through Hayti. All this illustrated the possibilities awaiting the chosen. But there were few other impressive sites. Fayetteville Street was a muddy rutted road where ragged shops and stores and houses leaned against the Victorian elegance. Side by side, they gave an incongruous sense of community. The ramshackle houses of Mexico on the northwest edge of Hayti were constructed of salvage lumber and revealed the dreadful poverty in which most African Americans lived. Even the place where Susie Gille worked, the new brick office complex housing North Carolina Mutual and Provident Association, sat on Parrish Street, a narrow unpaved alley behind a row of white-owned buildings. Thus segregated from Durham's other financial institutions, the Mutual, for all its importance to the black community, remained outside of the city's central business district.[2]

Reportedly, Gille brought "culture and class" to a generally unrefined town, and she was quite an attraction. Stories tell of adults and children descending on her office just to watch "the flying fingers of the colored girl from the North who typed without even looking at the keys." Her burnished Royal typewriter and her shorthand notebook distinguished her from the Mutual's other clerks, though they, too, were among the most prominent young black women in town. A stenographer, Miss Sue, as she was called, represented technology and speed, skill and professionalism, progress and modernization. Perhaps in other settings she would have been no more than a low-level professional on a scale that put lawyers, doctors, and businessmen on top. But for an African American woman, her job was an extraordinary opening, for few if any other fields of employment could grant her more respectability, more protection, or more pay.[3] Black Durham expected exemplary conduct from its professional women workers, and as a new arrival Gille probably endured extensive scrutiny. Rigid codes of behavior and constant surveillance shielded her and her peers from the dangers black women faced: hostile encounters with whites, sexual insult, harassment or abuse, inappropriate explorations of sexuality, and bad examples among the lower classes. After her initial trip to Durham, she rarely traveled alone. Rather, her employers, friends, and colleagues provided protective company. Propriety further dictated that she not live by herself. As a single woman, she boarded with a family headed by a prominent man who could provide protection and supervision. The daughters of her employers, her most likely friends, introduced her to Durham's social and cultural black world and instructed her as to where she should and should not go.[4]

She joined the older of the two most prominent churches, White Rock Baptist. Here, one of North Carolina's most notable churchwomen, Hattie Shepard, led the missionary circle, and Aaron M. Moore, Durham's only black physician and her supervisor, led the Sunday school. Her occupational skills increased her social capital as a contributor to community uplift. Appropriate to her station, she participated in (and later led) the choir and taught a Sunday school class. Gille joined the Volkamenia Literary Club, founded by Mary Pauline Fitzgerald Dame and her sister, Sallie Fitzgerald, which brought young African American professionals together to debate the issues of the day. More than likely, Susie Gille favored private, appropriately chaperoned, social affairs. For these, she was expected to secure a gentleman escort, one who came from her generation and class in business or the professions. In addition to her superior intellectual acumen and her flair for style, she honed her domestic skills so that when she married — as she was expected to do — she could keep a proper house, raise proper children, and properly host guests.[5]

Gille settled into the city's routine. The morning whistle screeched from the bull atop the Duke tobacco factory and could be heard for miles around calling hundreds of African Americans, mostly women, to work in the industry for which Durham was best known. They followed the route trod hours earlier by the hundreds of black household workers who crossed the city to get the white folk ready for the day. Gille counted herself among the fortunate — the dozens of black professionals who arrived downtown at 7:45

to prepare for an 8 o'clock start. From her workspace at the front of the building, she could see the people passing by, and she probably reflected on all the insurance company hoped to be: an autonomous black institution providing highly regarded employment for talented black professionals, an influential black business that symbolized race pride and enterprise, and a resolute challenge to whites' perceptions about black folk.[6]

As extensions of their employers, the people who worked for the Mutual took on the work of invalidating racist stereotypes as part of their jobs. Gille's position obliged her to exhibit élan, efficiency, and expertise for public viewing. Yet she also was expected to be deferential, particularly to men, who, in the gendered world of race, granted her very little autonomy and who presumed that as a respectable woman she would demand little on her own. She represented the conjunction of Jim Crow and gender, fully aware of the irony inherent thereto: inasmuch as Mutual men had negotiated with whites the meaning of racial prosperity, Mutual women would have to negotiate with black men the meaning of racial respectability. The conventions of black business in Durham translated morality into an obsession with acceptable public (and private) decorum. Improper conduct, secular recreation, gaudy clothes, drinking alcohol, or loud talk tagged African Americans as reprobates who demonstrated a lack of self-respect and who reflected poorly on the rest of the race. For young women professionals whose interests in popular culture and fashion grew with the Mutual, these demands must have seemed like unreasonable restrictions.

Instead, Mutual employees were expected to show piety, cleanliness, thrift, hard work, intelligence, good manners, high morals, and adherence to appropriate sexual mores, all to illustrate that African Americans were capable of being what whites believed they were not: worthy citizens who could uphold the ethical imperatives of the American mainstream. When it came to the rest of black America, the Mutual's rhetoric could offer the same harsh criticisms that other black leaders spoke, but Mutual leaders also believed that respectability was something poorer African Americans could achieve. "When we began, we didn't have a thing," C. C. Spaulding, the Mutual president explained. "We had no money, no knowledge. But we had sense enough to put up a big front of respectability."[7] Part of the work of a Mutual agent was to investigate the "habits, manner of living, financial standing, and family history" of prospective customers. Thus intimately knowledgeable about personal as well as public circumstances of members of their communities, the Mutual's insurance agents were distinguished, prominent figures in black communities.[8]

At the same time, the Mutual seemed to represent exactly what southern white racists wanted to destroy: black people who achieved in defiance of Jim Crow. Susie Gille must have grasped the fragile position of the Mutual. Race relations were especially tense the year she settled in Durham. The company had barely settled into a new building on Parrish Street in 1906 when whites attacked black Atlanta and destroyed another flourishing black community possessing a similar emerging black elite like the one growing in Durham. The well-remembered Wilmington episode had demonstrated that economic progress and political engagement incurred the rancor of racists, and most of the building's employees remembered the massacre and heard its echoes in the hall. Recurring assaults on southern blacks who accumulated property showed that Mutual founders held ambitions that many white North Carolinians opposed. Mutual colleague James B. Dudley, president of the North Carolina A&T College in Greensboro, argued as much to Booker T. Washington. In a 1903 letter, Dudley wrote of lynching: "It is the success of the intelligent and progressive negro which seems to be widening the breach between the races . . . because of his success." The reverberations of these attacks on successful African American communities alarmed black Durhamites, reminding them that they also lived in the fragile state of racial calm. In fact, forgetting was impossible. In 1921, just as the Mutual planned to move its offices to another new structure, whites destroyed the Greenwood section of Tulsa, Oklahoma, a thriving black community of businesses and professionals, called the Black Wall Street because of the wealth and capital accumulation among African Americans.[9]

Still, the Mutual and its employees portended a New Negro in the urban South, who embraced black capitalism as a means of survival and as a nationalist struggle. When Alain Locke penned the phrase in the 1920s, he defined the New Negro by achievement and self-determination, a reverse of the tradition of black subjugation to white control. Black business in the New South excelled in the first criteria; the second was impossible to meet. Freedom's first generation experienced firsthand the codified severity of Jim Crow, which touched the lives of virtually every African American regardless of status or class. Durham's black elite emerged within an apartheid system enforced routinely by violence and learned to use segregation to its advantage, believing it could provide a route to autonomy otherwise denied by Jim Crow. Whereas the Harlem-based literary movement promoted the distinctiveness of black culture and praised its contributions in broadening the concept of American arts, the New Negro in Durham embraced the economic opportunities enabled by racism, one of the few ways that African

Americans could thrive in the South.[10] The employees of North Carolina Mutual exemplified the New Negro of Booker T. Washington's era: "With the New South the New Negro must arise and modestly, manfully, courageously, take his place in the march of progress." "The old order of things has truly passed away, and side by side, white men and black men must determine to work out their destiny to a successful issue."[11] But Durham leaders also exemplified the Du Bois model of the Talented Tenth—"the educated and intelligent of the Negro people that have led and elevated the mass[es], . . . Negro leadership [that] sought from the first to rid the race of this awful incubus."[12]

Putting into effect Washington's emphasis on economic development, they made their bricks of money and climbed them past the masses of black workers and past the middle class to make a new status group, an urban black elite autonomous of whites on the basis of wealth. Their assets provided the resources to accomplish two objectives: first, to protect their families—and by extension their communities—from Jim Crow's worst offenses; and, second, to take their places as active, informed, and qualified citizens who contributed to and held a justifiable stake in the governance of the wider society. In doing so, they reconstructed themselves as public exemplars of a southern nouveau riche, a new black elite, and an answer to the Negro Problem. The Mutual understood that the race rose with its women, thus the importance assigned to women like Susie Gille in making this New Negro image. In business and politics, the race's success was measured by male value and achievement. Coon songs at political conventions had mocked her employers as African American men and losing the vote had robbed them of manhood rights. The threat of lynching had denied them sexuality and the threat of rape had denied them control of their families. And thus African American men would have to redefine manhood, in this case through upbuilding black business.

"The Company with a Soul and a Service"

North Carolina Mutual and Provident Association, Susie V. Gille's employer, held its first organizational meeting just weeks before the Wilmington massacre. It was chartered by the North Carolina legislature a year later, in 1899, following a fight led by the last among North Carolina's African American elected representatives. The Mutual was born of the drive for self-sufficiency and financial independence that spurred the black business movement. It was not the first black business in Durham—indeed, it was but one of a series of enterprises. The successful brick maker Richard

Fitzgerald was the centrifugal force in several early ventures, but here John Merrick, the barber and entrepreneur, played the role of organizer. Joining him were his friend Dr. Aaron Moore; William G. Pearson and Pinkney Dawkins, educators; James E. Shepard, the pharmacist and Republican activist; Dock Watson, a tinsmith; and Edward A. Johnson, dean of the law school at Shaw University in Raleigh. According to legend, the first claim broke the bank and the investors split, leaving Merrick and Moore as the central players in the North Carolina Mutual and Provident Association as the others went off to other ventures. James Shepard formed his own company, a real estate and investment firm; and in 1903, with William G. Pearson, J. A. Dodson, and John C. Dancy, he organized Carolina Mutual Life Insurance Company, the result of which is unrecorded. Meanwhile, Merrick continued to barber and Moore continued to see patients, but they hired the energetic Charles Clinton (C. C.) Spaulding, Moore's nephew and a Merrick business partner, to manage the business and sell insurance.[13]

As the ties among the founders revealed, the trend toward entrepreneurial collaboration was well grounded by the time the Mutual emerged, coinciding with the founding of the National Negro Business League (NNBL) in 1900 by Booker T. Washington. Speaking at the 1915 meeting of the NNBL, C. C. Spaulding publicly attributed the "first inspiring cause" of their organization to Booker T. Washington, although there is no evidence that the Tuskegeean communicated with the founders before 1910. Washington may have encouraged the venture philosophically when he toured North Carolina in 1896. During that trip, he preached his gospel of economic self-help as an answer to white supremacy: "When it comes to business pure and simple, the black man is put on the same footing with the white man . . . and here it seems to me is our great opportunity."[14] Another account of the Mutual's start credits the white tobacco magnate Washington Duke with impressing the idea upon Merrick. As the family barber, Merrick had traveled extensively with the Dukes and had no doubt developed a strong business sense as he developed his talent for listening. Neither scenario of the Mutual's founding is really certain, but both narratives were useful. Crediting Booker T. Washington, Washington Duke, or anyone but themselves with their endeavor placed the Mutual associates in a favorable light with the Tuskegee Machine, Booker T. Washington's network of influence, and with white industrialists like Duke. It also aligned them publicly with a conservative stance on the race question and provided further political insurance against a potential white backlash. In either case, the public story symbolically deemphasized the more threatening specter of independent black initiative.[15]

The emergence of North Carolina Mutual and Provident Association around the time of the Wilmington bloodbath, its public affiliation with Booker T. Washington, and its founders' willingness to suggest that a white man participated in its creation all suggest that Durham black leaders turned inward at least partly out of caution. And, indeed, the Mutual might have represented a post-Wilmington move away from politics and toward community uplift as a way of countering racial fears and anxieties. In any case, the spirit of black enterprise and the practice of commercial investment existed in Durham long before Washington considered the city worthy of notice, and the project took off as North Carolina's battles over black politics intensified. Indeed, in later years, C. C. Spaulding acknowledged that the idea for the Mutual grew out of an Atlanta University conference held in 1898, titled Efforts of Negro Betterment and organized by W. E. B. Du Bois. North Carolina Mutual, then, can be seen as an outgrowth of entrepreneurial efforts inherent to the urban South where racial segregation created a critical mass of customers and a captive clientele to be served.[16]

The Mutual's goal was to make financial capital out of social capital and in so doing to garner political capital. Built on the themes of progress, thrift, and uplift, the Mutual was not a corporation. Rather, the buyers of insurance policies became part owners of the company and partly responsible for its success. Mutual representative George W. Powell told the audience gathered at the 1910 meeting of the NNBL: "We are much interested in benefiting the masses of our race in every way we can, especially in the way of saving a bit of their earnings for the unexpected, by making investments of a small amount of their income into Insurance Companies." And, of course, the profit motive was never far from investors' minds. The need for insurance in a high-risk world, the increasing black population of customers, and the fact that white insurance companies refused service to black customers fueled the Mutual's success. The Mutual also reflected its founders' philanthropic interests. In addition to providing for "the sick and those injured by accident, and the burial of the dead," the charter specified that "a certain percent per annum of the proceeds . . . shall be turned over to the Colored Asylum at Oxford, North Carolina." With its motto, "the Company with a Soul and a Service," the Mutual offered — and continues to offer — itself as a center for community-oriented projects. Virtually any initiative that Durham blacks undertook during the Jim Crow years occurred with the Mutual's knowledge, if not always its sanction or support. In this way the Mutual operated as the municipal government of black Durham.[17]

More important than seeing themselves as part of a movement, the triumvirate of Merrick, Moore, and Spaulding as the Mutual's leaders recognized that communities were based on individuals held together by a common inherited vision of emancipation. At its heart, the Mutual responded to basic community concerns of the urban working class in the twentieth century: the eventuality of sickness, accident, and death given the work it did and the poverty with which it lived. A doctor, Moore was particularly aware that everyday factors could negate a lifetime of work. A spouse's death denied the black family a crucial second income; family sickness called children out of schools. Most African Americans, particularly women who labored in low-paying service and industrial work, could ill afford luxuries. But insurance was not a luxury, the Mutual preached; it was a necessity. Counseling fathers on their family roles, the company's newspaper advertised its services: "Death is pursuing you at this moment. Don't let your departing words be 'Good-bye darling. I bequeath you my troubles and debts. Give me a decent burial.'"[18]

Mutual founders believed that their race-centered efforts could transform a city of black settlers and refugees into an autonomous African American community. With the Mutual — the company and the consciousness — at the center, a black leadership cluster emerged in Durham, which was destined to become nationally renowned. Covering the generational span across free, freed, and freeborn, the members represented a broad spectrum of political ideologies and social perspectives. They shared a memory of racial violence and consequently united under a singular goal: security. A distinguished, complicated, even enigmatic circle, their differences made them thrive, stimulating new initiatives and fueling businesses and institutions that complemented rather than competed with each other. At heart, they shared the conviction that the solution to the Negro Problem lay not only in free enterprise, hard work, and wealth but also in community and in garnering esteem and consideration from each other as well as from whites.

The fact that Durham's African American leaders did not challenge segregation — in fact, they embraced it — does not mean that they discouraged black aspirations, accommodated racism, or lacked a sense of pride. Although an important motive for the severity of Jim Crow was to depress blacks' expectations, to make them less secure, and, "to lead them with minimal resistance down the inevitable path of racial extinction," as one historian argued, that plan failed with the Durham elite. In upbuilding the company and then using it to upbuild other institutions, the black elite determined to keep their most important resources — their money and their families — out of the hands of whites. To them, this was an even more radical stance than protest, for it was carried out like a stealth operation behind the veil. "Every colored man who succeeds in business brings his wife and daughter a little nearer that sphere of chivalry and protection in which every white woman finds shelter and vindication," said educator William G. Pearson in praise of black entrepreneurship. In the face of disfranchisement, sexual violence, and scientific racism, the Mutual symbolized the southern New Negro's determination not only to beat the racial Darwinists at their own game but also to create a secure environment for African American women and girls in which to achieve respectability.[19]

Neither a repudiation of electoral aspirations nor a surrender to white supremacy, the founding of the North Carolina Mutual and Provident Association served also as a strategy of gathering strength for future political participation. By publicly advancing the accumulation of capital, the Mutual founders resolved to restore African Americans' citizenship rights. They did not intend to abdicate their roles in electoral politics, even if they chose briefly to defer the ballot to dodge the bullet. Rather, they proposed distinctly political initiatives — economics and education — even as they downplayed partisan activities. They retained their civic vision, masked as it was by guarded rhetoric. In the aftermath of Wilmington, Mutual associates kept the ballot box in view, and, articulating ideologies of black manhood through their doctrine of economic uplift, they sought other means to control their communities.

Merrick, Shepard, Spaulding, and their colleagues encrypted these politics in local institution building. In accomplishing what they set out for themselves, Durham's black leadership cohort founded some of the most important black businesses in the nation. With a $5,000 contribution from the Mutual, for instance, a group of entrepreneurs started a hosiery mill in Durham, encroaching on the textile manufacturing domain of white entitlement. Challenging outright the way that white employers disparaged black women, black mill owners employed African American women in positions typically held by white women. Mutual leaders also organized a black hospital, a Boy's Club, and several educational initiatives, including school construction and teacher training programs. Nor were they necessarily understated. Handsome horse and buggies, fancy cars, and fine clothing revealed a taste for material goods.[20]

In 1906, just after Susie Gille arrived, North Carolina Mutual and Provident Association opened the Parrish Street office, a two-story brick structure that housed the Mutual on the second floor. In other parts of the building, the Royal Knights of King David, a clothing store, a shoe store, a barbershop, a drugstore, and a newspaper rented offices. The next year, Richard Fitzgerald, James E. Shepard, and William G. Pearson (who was also the principal of the black public school) founded Mechanics and Farmers Bank as a sibling institution to North Carolina Mutual, with offices on the first floor of the Parrish Street building. Fitzgerald served as president; Merrick succeeded him upon the brick maker's death in 1910; and Pearson in turn succeeded Merrick when the latter passed away in 1919.

These institutions in insurance, manufacturing, retail, and banking laid the groundwork, and similar businesses expanded the financial base of the black elite. Bankers Fire Insurance Company was founded in 1920, and W. G. Pearson was installed as president. When Pearson started the Fraternal Bank and Trust Company later that same year, Mutual officers, including C. C. Spaulding, served on its board and Pearson continued on the board of Mechanics and Farmers Bank. Another company, the Merrick-Moore-Spaulding Land Company, combined a real estate agency with a demolition firm and a construction business. Originally formed in 1911, it evolved into the Merrick-McDougal-Wilson Company managed by John Merrick's oldest son, Ed, and two of the younger Mutual executives. Originally it bought, sold, rented, and managed properties, but it eventually sold liability insurance, becoming the Union Insurance and Realty Company. Simultaneously, Richard L. McDougal founded the Mutual Building and Loan Association in 1921. Promoting "thrift and property," the Mutual Building and Loan Association (MB&LA) encouraged home ownership by selling twenty-five-cent "shares" that matured into savings certificates to provide a down payment on a house, the mortgage to which the MB&LA held. Bankers Fire Insurance Company then insured those homeowners. Finally, the founding of the National Negro Finance Corporation (NNFC) in 1924 with its headquarters in the city confirmed Durham's place as a regional and national financial center for African Americans. Originally named the Durham Commercial Security Company, the NNFC pledged social uplift by marketing securities, selling investments, purchasing bonds, and making loans to fund development projects, black schools, and recreation facilities, programs that whites refused to support. Robert R. Moton, who succeeded Booker T. Washington as head of Tuskegee in 1915, sanctioned the project and served as its first president.[21]

Despite the racial divisions that had fueled the growth of the Mutual and its sibling institutions, whites found that doing business with black entrepreneurs was a good investment and not simply a matter of beneficence. In 1908, for example, Merrick took out one of the company's first loans, $6,000 from the Duke-owned Fidelity Bank, and paid it back in a year. A black-owned bank also was useful to whites. Among the Mutual legends, one tells of whites who hid money—or money problems—by using Mechanics and Farmers Bank. Nonetheless, to white Durham, and to African Americans in other places, the stunning growth of black business seemed incongruous within a racial milieu structured by Jim Crow and obsessed with depressing blacks' dreams. Even more surprising was the pride (albeit condescending) with which whites allowed a black business culture to grow. Within two years of the opening of the new Mutual offices, a business complex, including a movie house and a café, spread along Parrish Street; this "North Carolina Mutual block" was praised by the *Durham Morning Herald* as "a Colony of the Colored."[22]

Some of those colonists were bold, given the race riots destroying black business in Atlanta the year the Parrish Street complex opened. With a cigar factory, a tobacco factory, a lumber mill, a textile mill, a foundry, a drug company, an insurance company, a bank, and a range of affiliated retail and service establishments, black business culture in Durham was made out of moxie and motivation and earned praise in the black press. This public success of black men might also have raised questions among white North Carolinians, particularly after W. E. B. Du Bois's 1912 statement that black Durhamites' "social and economic development is more striking than that of any similar group in the nation." Instead, white Durham's promotional materials invariably extolled African American achievement. A 1904 brochure of Greater Durham applauded black businesses like the "colored rug establishment" and the Fitzgerald Drug Company, which was "centrally located" on Main Street and carried "stock of the finest quality only, and well selected." The store provided the "best attention[,] and the highest satisfaction is guaranteed to everybody."[23] Indeed, the Chamber of Commerce defined racial accord as its formula for success: "Durham's rapid rise to industrial and educational power is the result of a spirit of cooperation between the white and colored population," a 1926 brochure boasted in self-admiration, ironically echoing Du Bois's claim.[24]

Black Durham was unique in not being destroyed by white rage, but that did not mean that black residents felt safe from white attack. In fact, the danger was such that to survive and thrive, Durham's black leaders had to carry the Mutual's message of affluence with enough finesse to assuage white resentment with one hand and upbuild with the other. During the planning stages of the black mill, for example, C. C. Amey, a teacher and a mechanical genius, had asked to learn about the knitting machines in one of Durham's white-owned mills. Because he was refused, he went north to learn the technology. His knowledge was central to the startup of the mill, but at his 1910 presentation to the NNBL convention, co-owner Aaron Moore made a point to acknowledge not Amey's ingenuity but General Julian Carr's willingness to send "a few trained helpers" as start-up assistance. After the doctor's presentation, Booker T. Washington asked Dr. Moore to hold up samples of socks so that attendees could see "what our people are able to do in this direction." Not allowing pride to impede opportunity, Moore displayed "goods made at the only mill of its kind in the United States which employs Negro labor and Negro capital." Then, assigning responsibility for the company's success to the business leaders of the race, Moore appealed to his audience: "We expect that you, representatives of the 10,000,000 of Negroes in this country, will subscribe for some of our stock, or at least place orders with us for these goods."[25]

As curiosity grew into interest, Durham emerged as a southern center of black life, host to major conventions and tours each year. Once the National Religious Training School and Chautauqua for the Colored Race (later known as North Carolina College for Negroes and now as North Carolina Central University) opened in 1910, black Durham hosted conferences on the critical issues of black politics and education. The *Norfolk Journal and Guide*, a prominent black newspaper, praised a 1916 three-day interracial conference on secondary and higher education at the college as "the first of its kind held under the auspices of a single institution among our people." Organized by James E. Shepard, the meeting drew hundreds of participants and over thirty speakers from around the nation, among them W. E. B. Du Bois, Dean Kelly Miller of Howard University, and Joel Spingarn, the head of the NAACP. The Mutual held its own two-day conference on insurance in 1918; and in 1919, the North Carolina Medical, Dental, and Pharmaceutical Association, an organization of African American doctors, dentists, and pharmacists, convened in the city.[26]

By the 1920s, the Mutual, its sibling institutions, its subsidiaries, and black Durham itself had made enough of an impact on African American culture to generate a designation and an essay by E. Franklin Frazier in Alain Locke's collection, *The New Negro*. Formally recognized as a part of the "Negro Renaissance," black Durham expressed racial pride, not through a celebration of African American arts and letters like its northern counterpart in Harlem, but through the elite's embrace of capitalism. Harlem may have been the hub of black creative and cultural life, but Durham was the center of its business life. And if Harlem shed the past to experiment with new forms of expression, black Durham reached into the past to reshape freedom's dream of black autonomy by embracing the gospel of wealth and work. Dubbing Durham the "Capital of the Black Middle Class," sociologist Frazier praised the city's black "middle class" as an achievement that modeled mainstream society. But Frazier went a step further in comparing the Durham scene to black America. He separated out Durham's black elite as distinct and elevated over the black bourgeoisie, the middle class of whom he became critical.[27]

Like all of Durham's advocates, and like black leaders generally, Frazier intentionally used the masculine pronoun "he" and referenced "men" in extolling the virtues of Durham. Booker T. Washington hailed Durham as a place where black men provided "shining examples of what a colored man may become when he is proficient and industrious." The *St. Luke Herald* urged its Richmond, Virginia, readers to "go to Durham" to see "the industrious Negro at his best. Go to Durham and see the cooperative spirit among Negroes at its best. Go to Durham and see Negro business with an aggregate capital of millions. Go to Durham and see twenty-one Negro men whose honesty and business sagacity are making modern history."[28] Conceptually, the business of black capitalism was a male enterprise. That is, men were supposed to preside, provide, and protect, responsibilities that Mutual men took seriously. John Merrick, its organizer, the older of two sons born to a slave and her white owner, knew the vulnerabilities his mother had faced and imbued each of his business ventures with a sense of male accountability. Consequently, the Mutual marketed its business as a way for black men to act out a significant role in a society that offered them none. "As long as it is God's will," Merrick stated in his last public appearance, "I want this institution to move, for men to support their families."[29]

Founded by men, the Mutual initially hired only men as agents to represent the business in public and employed so many male teachers/principals of black schools in small communities that it feared creating a shortage. "Professors," as such educators were known, carried authority in their communities along with the message of the Mutual into the private homes of potential customers, their students' parents. In turn, the Mutual name offered a reciprocal benefit in that an association with the company gave agents credibility as local leaders who could use the company name in race work. Representing himself as a Mutual agent, for example, Charles N. Hunter coordinated North Carolina's efforts in the exposition movement, garnering participants for various fairs and expositions to commemorate black history. Hunter then used the Mutual's contacts and the name to create interest in the project from other black institutions and organizations. Working independently, such agents could earn more money and recognition than they could teaching, but with one foot in education and one in business, race men like Hunter and Pearson used the Mutual and its affiliates to create the independence necessary to do race work.[30]

"Women Were Not Supposed to Be in the Forethought"

With its patriarchal sweep, the Mutual's rhetoric of race pride and enterprise carried a subtext: women should not have to bear the family's burdens, and men should step up to the responsibilities of black manhood. As husbands, Mutual men disapproved of wives' employment. They expected wives to work, but at home raising children, keeping house, and hosting parties and in the community at missionary and club work. Constance Merrick Moore Watts, granddaughter of both Aaron Moore and John Merrick, recalled that her grandfathers never wanted her grandmothers to hold jobs outside the home.[31] Even with its male-centered vision, however, North Carolina Mutual recognized the financially untenable position of African American families and understood that black communities required the labor of women to prosper. But as businessmen, they realized that educated women provided a coterie of professionals that their companies desperately needed; and as race men, they encouraged single educated women to pursue employment in professions, specifically in race work. They also believed that male authorities should carefully safeguard single women before releasing them to the shelter of marriage.

Accordingly, as affluent fathers, Mutual men educated their daughters and encouraged them to seek professional employment at the financial and educational institutions they founded and led. Constance Watts's aunts, Geneva and Mabel Merrick, still single in 1906, worked at the Mutual but left the company when they married. Likewise, Fannie Jones, John Merrick's half-sister, worked as the Mutual's first clerk but left her employment when she married Aaron Moore's nephew, C. C. Spaulding. Constance Watts's mother, Lyda Moore (Aaron Moore's daughter), taught music until she married Ed Merrick, John Merrick's son. She then curtailed her teaching career. Following the family pattern, when Watts graduated from Talladega College, she, too, went to work at the Mutual until deciding to pursue an MBA at Columbia University. But when she married, she gave up career aspirations, despite her advanced degree. To achieve these idealized gender roles, elite African Americans needed to garner resources that ensured that married women did not have to work for wages, that children could be attended to full-time, and that young people would have educational opportunities.[32]

Notwithstanding its male focus, black business in the New South developed in cities where the number of women significantly exceeded the number of men. As primary customers for basic insurance and as a core workforce of the company, women played a fundamental role as prospective clients and as promoters. "Often, the wife is the one who starts her hubby on the road to success by leading the way in matters of thrift," William G. Pearson pointed out in one bank publication. The loss of either parent to sickness or death exacerbated a family's financial hardship and necessitated female labor; and the loss of male kin placed a particular burden on women. The company's business tactics, therefore, not only reflected the patriarchs' perspectives on the role of men but also their realistic assessments of women's needs and their roles in their families. Its charter specifically listed "relief of widows and orphans" before all other categories of philanthropic work.[33]

Women figured prominently as customers and therefore proved crucial to the company's success. Initially, the Mutual offered "industrial insurance," minimum protection policies designed for people who could afford only small weekly premiums. A nickel-a-week policy paid $1.60 in sick benefits and a $20 death benefit. In its early years, these policies accounted for 90 percent of the company's premium income, and agents sold them mostly to women. At the 1915 meeting of the NNBL, C. C. Spaulding noted that three-quarters of Durham's black residents held insurance with the Mutual. "As a rule," he added, "the majority of colored women in our section carry industrial insurance. . . . The men do not. . . . Many of our men are woefully neglect about providing for their families as they should do in the matter of insurance." And he noted, "We have to help more widows, whose husbands died leaving no insurance, more than any other class."[34] Of 104 Durhamites who received sick benefits in 1903, 68 were women. At the same time, the centrality of women to this particular race enterprise occasionally made Mutual managers anxious, not just because of "too much sick benefit insurance on women"—which was true—but because, as directors pointed out, "men are the breadwinner and should be carrying the bulk of insurance." Thus training instructed agents to "house to house canvass when men are at home."[35]

The Mutual founders viewed the company as one of their race responsibilities. Connecting the themes of enterprise, race pride, and family values, the company and the race merged into one and the same. Merrick, Moore, and Spaulding preached that what "the Mutual"—the triumvirate and the company—could do, the race could do, and attempted to convince African Americans that "it"—the race and the company—could not fail. Company materials promoted the point. The Mutual published its own newspaper, the

North Carolina Mutual, an internal organ sent to clients and made available to the public. Here the company preached its message of responsibility. "People who do not carry insurance," one article reprimanded, "do not help churches." The company listed the dollar values of assets in its advertisements and on its letterhead, offered rewards for information about fraud, and warned people away from apathetic and unscrupulous businesses, white or black. The back piece in the *North Carolina Mutual,* a booklet, for example, listed "Figures That 'Talk,'" in the form of company assets, insurance in force, and profits from 1904 to 1921. Similarly, a full-page advertisement in the *Durham Morning Herald* provided financial figures from the Mutual's twenty-fifth annual statement. Recognizing that it — and the race — suffered when smaller companies failed, the Mutual chose to absorb several that were about to go under. Both an altruistic and a business decision, buyouts negated the perception that black business was weak. For example, in its first expansion in 1906, the Mutual bought out People's Benevolent and Relief Association, a small faltering company in Charlotte, North Carolina.[36]

Ultimately, however, the Mutual held the African American community responsible for making race enterprise successful. Responding to the notion that "the white man's ice is colder" or that black enterprises were untrustworthy, Merrick wrote to the *North Carolina Mutual* readers: "You must . . . offset such impressions." The Mutual asserted that rewards lay in the future. "Redouble your efforts," the company urged its clients, "and cooperate with us for a generation yet unborn." An investment in the Mutual made for a triple investment in the race: life insurance to protect and provide for the family, to expand the community's economic worth, and to provide employment for other African Americans.[37]

Because women, the Mutual's primary customers, were most likely to read the company's advertisements, the Mutual put out a message that women wanted to hear, as well as the one the patriarchs believed. "Our people should see to it that their boys are put to work," the *Durham Negro Observer,* another company-sponsored newspaper, preached: "Begin upon your boys when they are young. . . . Keep them off the street . . . from such a class who hang around the poolroom . . . and keeping out of the way of jobs."[38] A column in the *North Carolina Mutual* harped on men's responsibilities, decrying "the man who dies expecting to go to heaven and leaves his sorrowing wife and hungry children to face the cold charities of the world. . . . He deserves a seat away back behind the thief." In a major promotional brochure, dated 1921, published letters from beneficiaries testified to the Mutual's reliability and the importance of insurance coverage so that "some other poor mother and wife may be benefited." Detailing the "untimely death" of husbands and thanking "such able men of our race" for their prompt payment of claims, the letters' authors noted that their husbands had been reluctant to buy and often careless about maintaining their policies. "Had my husband not been persuaded to hold his insurance, I don't know what I would have done," one woman wrote. "Think," the publication responded. "We sell protection that protects. Give us your application today. Keep your premiums in full for you cannot tell when your summons will come."[39]

North Carolina Mutual was especially responsive to black women as customers, looking to them to help "in breaking down prejudice [among blacks] against Negro business ventures." Spaulding demanded that his agents treat black women customers with deference and instilled that policy during agents' training. Whereas a white agent would "walk right into a negro [household] without even knocking on the door or without even taking off his hat after he has entered the house," Mutual agents engaged in courteous interactions with women and therefore created an even stronger reputation for professionalism in business. Volume rather than profit margin, Spaulding was convinced, would increase the company's income; and women passed along the company's reputation for honest, courteous, and respectful customer relations through their diverse networks.[40] Similarly, Mechanics and Farmers Bank translated the ideology of gendered respectability into practical application on site. The bank offered an escort from the train station if requested by out-of-town depositors and also set aside a Ladies' Deposit Room where "female depositors who come a great distance with their moneys in their attire may be free to unearth their treasure." The room, provided so that "any woman or child will be free and willing to go to the bank," signaled a private, protective space for "the ladies who often show hesitancy in entering the main banking room which is filled with men." Its brochure quickly added that the room was only an option "and does not prohibit ladies from entering the main banking area."[41]

In the same ways that the Mutual used gender, family, and community to sell insurance, the company also used its women workers to project respectability. From the beginning, the Mutual employed a significant number of women, like Susie V. Gille, to do clerical work. In the early years, for example, Moore's half-sister, Fannie Jones, staffed the office operation while Spaulding hawked insurance, Aaron Moore practiced medicine, and John Merrick continued to barber. In the office, women were the most conspicuous personnel associated with the company. Dore Whitted's desk, positioned opposite Spaulding's, could be seen through the front window of the Mutual's 1902 office. She was the person passersby would have identified with the company on the other side of the glass. In later years, women were the gatekeepers, the first line that greeted customers who came to the office.[42]

Because they served as the company's formal face, it was incumbent upon them to be model black women and model race women. Mutual women were distinguished by gender and occupational status, but they were often better educated than the businessmen for whom they worked. They hailed from the nation's historically black colleges and universities — Wilberforce, Howard, Fisk, Lincoln, Morris Brown, Talledega — and from the Ivy League. Sadie T. Mossell Alexander, the first African American woman to earn a doctorate in economics (University of Pennsylvania), went to work at the Mutual in 1921. Responding to a query from the NNBL audience about employing women agents, C. C. Spaulding, the Mutual's manager and later president, boasted that he hired "anyone who could deliver the goods." Most of its agents were men, who were able to leave family behind as they traveled to sell insurance and recruit new staff. Nonetheless, by 1915, women held one-quarter of the positions as agents, with many directing their own offices in the field. Women also claimed the vast majority of the positions among the home office staff, which, in that year, outnumbered agents. And like Susie Gille, they were visible. Gille attracted so much attention that within a few months of her arrival, she was offering a course in shorthand and typing to "an enthusiastic class of young men and women who are taking lessons three times a week."[43]

In addition to excellent business acumen, Mutual women were expected to have an aptitude for domestic skills. Women owned the few boardinghouses that functioned as hotels before black investors built the Biltmore Hotel in 1926, a landmark of the Hayti business district. Mostly, however, women among the elite — workers and wives — hosted, housed, and made arrangements for visitors to the Mutual and the city. Some continued to host eminent black visitors even after the Biltmore opened because the facility could not accommodate all of the attendees who came to black Durham's conferences and meetings. Furthermore, as an entertainment hot spot, the Biltmore was considered inappropriate for prominent guests like Mary McLeod Bethune, president of Bethune-Cookman College (and later Franklin D. Roosevelt's appointee to the National Youth Association), who visited the city regularly. Although the North Carolina College for Negroes (originally the National Training School) accommodated some, most out-of-towners looked to private homes for respite, as when the mother of a nursing student graduate assumed that Mrs. William J. Kennedy would welcome her as a guest during graduation weekend.[44]

Inasmuch as the Mutual was a public institution among African Americans, the private lives of its female associates, wives, and workers were public as well. Portrayed as manifestations of Mutual men's success, Mutual women were models of racial aspirations and affluence, privileged enough to occupy a private sphere but elevated so that all could see. Through them, the Mutual presented itself as a principled race entity and its founders and managers as principled race men. Essentially, Mutual women were on display, like exhibits to be visited by touring travelers. Large photographs of Durham's leading women accompanied articles in national publications about meetings in the city. In 1929, Eula Lee Wade, secretary to the vice president of North Carolina Mutual, graced the right corner above the fold of the front page of the *Pittsburgh Courier*. Her "duty," according to the newspaper, was "to show visitors through the famous Mutual Building." The *Courier* also pictured Mrs. Clyde Donnell, wife of the medical director and daughter of John Merrick, under the heading "Durham Beauty." The caption referred to her "most lavish" home in Durham and gave her address. Under the photograph of Mrs. A. Moore Shearin, daughter of Dr. Aaron M. Moore, the *Courier* described her house, enumerated the rooms, and listed its appliances and amenities.[45]

Durham's distinction as a travel destination for African Americans and conference site subjected women employees and wives to exhausting inspection. While attending the 1927 "Fact Finding and Stock Taking" conference, for example, W. E. B. Du Bois joined journalist Alice Dunbar-Nelson and artist Georgia Douglass in boarding at the Fayetteville Street mansion of Clydie Fullwood Scarborough. In her diary, Dunbar-Nelson derisively called her hostess, newly wed to undertaker John Scarborough, "the scared bride," clearly intimidated by guests of such renown. Dunbar-Nelson also complained that she served "cold funeral meals," despite her "very palatial home, a most gorgeous place."[46] In retrospect, the very idea of public exhibition seems exploitative of women's work both inside and outside the home, and it would be interesting to know if the women themselves felt insulted, denigrated, or imposed upon by their display. Mrs. Kennedy was cordial but brusque in a note informing the mother of the nursing graduate that she had found the woman one place to sleep and another to take her meals. It was said that Spaulding's wife refused to host the procession of visitors he brought home. Still, trained as race women, they realized that the barrier between public and private was as transparent as the veil between the races, and most carried out their husbands' and supervisors' expectations.[47]

Then, too, they may well have been stunned by their own affluence. Although many of the Mutual women of Gille's cohort were the upwardly mobile daughters of freedpeople, they were still in touch with grandparents and knew elders who had been enslaved. Eva Whitted (Goins), daughter of James A. Whitted, freedman and educator in early black Durham, worked with daughters of John Merrick. Educated at Claflin College, Whitted and her women colleagues were raised to believe that as race women they made personal sacrifices for the cause of racial uplift. Even if they despised the tedium of housework, maintaining a proper household evinced their — if not their household laborers' — respectability. Those honored were pleased that the newspapers made their hard labor seem effortless; after all, this was the sign of a good hostess. Still, they also must have felt that such detailed attention was intrusive and that some references were particularly inappropriate. Enumerating the modern amenities of Shearin's house, for instance, the *Courier* divulged that she owned a baby grand piano, an Orthophonic Victrola, an automatic hot water system, and an ornate four-poster bed, revelations that stepped beyond the bounds of decorum.[48]

When she arrived in Durham, Gille joined an assembly of young women who seized the expanded opportunities for professional women to work for black businesses and institutions, especially those headed by prominent men. Bess Johnson (Whitted) joined the Mutual the same year Gille arrived, transferring to the Durham home office when the company bought out her employer, People's Benevolent. A 1905 graduate of Barber Scotia Seminary, Whitted handled all of the Mutual's money and occupied the dual position of cashier and head bookkeeper at the company for over forty years. The Mutual also hired trained nurses to staff its medical facilities, and the Mutual supplemented the salaries of black public health nurses in every major city where it maintained an office, facilitating the transition of nursing from household labor to skilled work. Ironically, C. C. Spaulding claimed not to value higher education. As he explained to the audience at the 1915 NNBL convention, "We put more stress on the practical than the theoretical." Among the staff, however, women were consistently better educated than the men, almost always having a college education, which neither Spaulding nor Merrick had. Indeed, the Mutual expected its clerks, stenographers, and secretaries, even those on the summer staff, to be college students or graduates, women with a "definite plan," dedicated to a set of goals and accomplishments.[49]

Spaulding's comment seems an easy trivialization of higher education and suggests that, within company walls, women struggled for recognition as something other than ornaments. The Mutual's convictions about the place of women certainly frustrated Sadie T. Mossell Alexander. Despite her qualifications, education, and aspirations, Alexander was appointed assistant actuary—to her the equivalent of a clerical job—although she did the work of an actuary, which was the equivalent of a management position. Discontented at the Mutual, she happily accepted an offer to marry and return to Philadelphia where she entered the University of Pennsylvania law school. Bess Johnson Whitted was eminently prepared when in the late 1920s a consultant suggested that the Mutual create the position of comptroller. A "whiz at mathematics and English," Whitted kept records consistently accurate "to the penny." Unable to perceive of women in a management capacity, however, Mutual men simply ignored the consultant's recommendation, and Whitted waited until 1949 for a promotion. That year the board of directors elected her assistant treasurer. Viola Turner's career followed a similar pattern. A 1919 graduate of Morris Brown College in Atlanta, she accepted a position at the home office in 1924, having worked for the Mutual in several other states. As secretary to the treasurer, she built the Mutual's stock portfolio, doing the research, making contacts, and presenting her recommendations to the executive committee members who made the decisions. Yet she gained neither ownership nor autonomy; rather she had to get permission to take every step and tolerated her supervisor's condescension of what he termed her "little project." Turner's work not only added significantly to the twenty-million-dollar increase in assets the Mutual enjoyed in the 1940s but also encouraged a shift in the culture of the business. In 1957, Turner finally was appointed treasurer of the Mutual. She was elected to the board of directors three years later, the same year she was promoted to vice president of the organization.[50]

Whitted's and Turner's promotions made them pioneer businesswomen, not only at the Mutual but also in corporate culture. Such recognition was long overdue, given Turner's accomplishments, but was characteristic of women's place, generally, in the Mutual's scheme of gender dynamics. Reflecting on her life with the Mutual, Turner observed: "Our men were not too happy about your being too intelligent. . . . Sometimes I was a whole lot smarter than they were. But I was also smart enough not to have acted like I was smarter than they were."[51] Margaret Kennedy Goodwin, daughter of William J. Kennedy Jr., Spaulding's right-hand man and the company's official historian, remembered women's dilemma: "Women were not supposed to be in the forethought, they were supposed to be in the kitchen." But women like Viola Turner and Bess Whitted "had the brain power, the same drive, and the same will to make things happen that men had. . . . [They] sort of dressed it up in ruffles and bows, [and] were smart enough not to let their drive and vision irritate the gentlemen."[52] Women were passed over for promotion by men whom they had trained; they made less money than men who did similar work; and they embarked on their Mutual careers at different points than men within the company ranks. Men started off "geared for top management," Turner complained. Women were "geared to be somebody's secretary." The first African American woman elected to a seat on the New York Stock Exchange, Turner did not accept the rationale that men, because they supported families, should be accorded higher ranks or salaries. Instead, she saw her position in a hierarchical paradigm of gender playing out unjustly. Still, she loved her job and had few other options; in the Jim Crow era, working for the Mutual was still one of the best employment options available to African American women or men.[53]

"Our Territory"

Having joined the Mutual in its early years, women employees became integral to the company's business practices and culture, providing both social and financial capital toward the upbuilding of black Durham. North Carolina Mutual had invented itself around individuals' talents and skills, and executives were loath to lose those who proved crucial to their success. By making themselves indispensable to the company and mentoring each other, Mutual women appropriated a place for themselves as they brought their capabilities and education to bear on the largest black business in the United States. Creatively they used company space and needs to shape arenas where they challenged both patriarchal restrictions and Jim Crow. In doing so, they also reshaped the culture of propriety and respectability as it applied to women of their class.

Women's space within the company reflected protections which the women accepted on some levels and chafed against on others. As the Mutual prospered, each new home office building elevated women's work space up from street level, removing them from the public life of the street. In the 1906 building, the company offices were located on the second floor. In the six-story structure built in 1921, the Mutual operated on floors three and above. Within the male-dominated Mutual, women used their female-dominated spaces as arenas of communal relations with each other and as sites of contestation with both black and white men. Here women redefined the meaning of black womanhood and respectability while shaping an effective site to protect from Jim Crow's offenses. Actually, few whites came to the Mutual, meaning that Mutual women did not regularly experience the vicious abuses with which most other African American women workers had to deal. Those whites who did come to the office, however, were usually authority figures: insurance examiners and state officials who held the racial ground in the outside world. The women employees of the Mutual were expected — by their supervisors and their guests — to show deference to white bureaucrats, although no matter how well or how accurately they kept records, the outlanders' working assumption presumed otherwise.

Not surprisingly, Spaulding cultivated a patriarchal relationship with the women who worked for the company. They referred to him as "Poppa" and to the management as "our official family." Like a sentinel, Spaulding watched over them, wary of the hazards of public life and sensitive to criticisms of impropriety. To advance its reputation of female virtue, the company's 1921 brochure trumpeted the splendid working conditions for female employees. The new offices provided women with "a modern healthful building in which to work." That same year, with so many women joining the company and with an acute shortage of appropriate housing, the Mutual opened the Clerks' Home, "a comfortable place of abode for the lady clerks" where they could find "clean, warm lodging, wholesome food, and a refined atmosphere." In this way, the Mutual provided another form of protection and a way to "care for its employees."[54] For their part, Mutual women, single and distant from their families, viewed the Clerks' Home as a thoughtful, convenient, and even necessary gesture, but they also saw its location — across the street from C. C. Spaulding's house — as an intrusion on their private lives. And that was its intent. From his house, Spaulding could and did spy on their activities. "He'd run your life if he could," Viola Turner remembered.[55]

Despite the inconvenience and annoyances caused by continuous surveillance, working for the Mutual yielded many advantages, not the least of which was income. Black women just starting to work in tobacco in 1915 earned $2.50 per week; North Carolina Mutual started its assistant bookkeepers, an entry level clerical position, at thirty dollars per month and promised regular increases thereafter. Women who worked for the Mutual also took lunch, the main meal of the day, in the Mutual cafeteria, free of charge, and, if single, they enjoyed free housing or boarded inexpensively enough to afford the other amenities of Mutual life: clothes, travel, and entertainment. They also worked fewer hours under much better conditions than most black women workers. Steady income, coupled with their intimate knowledge of investments and finance, facilitated their purchasing properties and investments and their escape from persistent supervision. Home owning furthered women's autonomy in their private lives by moving them out from under the scrutiny they endured. Fannie Rosser, employed by the Mutual in 1914, had invested in real estate, stocks, bonds, and utilities by the 1920s. She held private mortgages, made extensive loans to individuals, and had a four-room brick house built for herself at the depth of the Great Depression.[56]

Upward—though limited—mobility also was possible as women engaged in professional development activities through mechanisms like the Mutual Forum, a weekly meeting at which employees contributed to company problem solving, learned about other departments, became skilled at handling personal finances, and engaged in discussions about contemporary issues. Because well-known visitors to the Mutual often appeared at the Forum, employees came into contact with prominent American figures. On the travel itinerary of virtually every white liberal and black leader, scholar, or activist, the Mutual hosted numerous important guests over the years: Eleanor Roosevelt, Norman Thomas, and Mary White Ovington, among whites; Emmet J. Scott, James Weldon Johnson, A. Philip Randolph, Adam Clayton Powell Jr., and Mary McLeod Bethune, among blacks. There were also international visitors from Europe and Africa. These meetings expanded Mutual women's world beyond the home and the office and connected them to black political culture. These experiences and their social roles in them increased women's importance to the company and proffered a response to the race problem.[57]

In keeping with the motto, "the Company with a Soul and a Service," Spaulding expected Mutual employees to share their talents and resources with the larger community. They were required to attend church every Sunday, and many held prominent positions, men in church leadership and management and women as Sunday school teachers and choir members. The younger generation of women, the second born in freedom, joined the Durham chapter of the NAACP during the 1920s. Intermeshing their occupational work with their club work, Mutual women joined the YWCA and founded their own chapter of Iota Phi Lambda (a sorority of black businesswomen). Bess Whitted founded the Mutual Glee Club and the Mutual Quartet, which performed for black and white audiences as "singing ambassadors of good will." Susie Gille taught Sunday school and directed the choir at White Rock Baptist Church. Through Iota Phi Lambda, Viola Turner and Eula Wade brought programs on banking, investment, education, and employment to young women at the YWCA. Wade also served as membership secretary for the local NAACP. Fannie Rosser served on the Junior Ladies' Board for Lincoln Hospital. All of them used Mutual resources—time, telephone, stationery, equipment, and space—to advance their projects.[58]

These adaptations of women's voluntary associations blended business and race pride with public relations and fun. It was well known that Spaulding demanded temperance from his employees. A community patriarch, he wielded influence in the church as well as in finance. It was rumored that he was behind an attempt to expel Bess Whitted from White Rock Baptist Church for drinking, dancing, and playing cards. Adept at turning business into pleasure, Whitted sponsored much of the revelry for which black Durham became known. She founded the Algonquin Tennis Club, a private lodge for the black elite, and subsequently established regular tennis tournaments for the new black elite's young people. Arranging concerts and dances as both fund-raisers and entertainments and throwing some of the best parties in town — including an infamous daylong celebration every year on New Year's Day — Whitted was the center of social attention during almost every conference sponsored by the male elite, regularly violating the expectations for decorum and temperance. Notwithstanding her displeasure with Clydie Scarborough's deficiencies as a hostess, Alice Dunbar-Nelson enjoyed "a dutch supper, plenty of liquor, and dance by the Orthophonic at Martha Merrick Donnell's with Bess Whitted," returning to the Scarboroughs' home to wake Clydie's husband, the undertaker, at two o'clock in the morning.[59]

In this peculiar melding of personal and private lives experienced by single black female employees, the Mutual's demands extended to daily life outside the company walls. Infractions brought censure and admonition. C. C. Spaulding once threatened to fire Viola Turner for wearing pants outside the Clerks' Home on a Saturday afternoon (she was not working), and she almost quit when he reprimanded her for wearing a red dress to work, a color he considered inappropriate for a business setting.[60]

The culture of North Carolina Mutual advanced women's efforts to meet men socially. Numerous dinners, conferences, and soirees encouraged coupling, but the company expected couples to marry. Yet Mutual women increasingly defied Victorian propriety regarding their private lives. Whereas the patriarchs assumed that, once they married, women would leave their positions as employees for positions as full-time housewives, Mutual women expanded their sphere by demanding to continue working even after they married. Susie V. Gille wed Moses T. Norfleet in 1915 and retained her position. Bess Johnson married Orin Amey Whitted in 1917 and also remained. Cultural conventions still required that women employees clear their personal decisions — to marry, divorce, or change residence — with their employers, but over time few women tolerated their employers' intervention and ignored their advice. When Viola Turner divorced her second husband, she did have to ask her supervisor for permission to stay on the job, and he agreed. A few years later, she married for a third time. Bess Whitted also married and divorced several times, a decision that once made front-page news in the *Carolina Times*, Durham's local black newspaper. Her personal decisions had no affect on her job, her professionalism, or her reputation for accuracy and acumen, although she was threatened with expulsion from the church for exercising her personal freedoms. Eventually, the issue of women's marital status became an out-of-bounds topic as far as their employment was concerned, and divorce lost the dishonorable taint that came with the voluntary ending of a marriage at the time. By the 1940s, at least informally, the company had no official policy regarding the marriages of its staff members, and it was not unusual for spouses to be employed at the same enterprise or at one of the sibling institutions — in different departments, however, and with husbands outranking wives.[61]

Company publications also encouraged women to develop "pretty snares," as Susie Gille Norfleet, editor of the *Whetstone* newsletter for Mutual employees, wrote in her column, "Strictly for the Girls." In it she provided information on dressing well: "Put your best foot forward, morning-noon-and-night, with the right shoes for every ensemble and a shoe wardrobe to fit your tastes." She also counseled on men and marriage. "Marriage by mutual consent with no thought of financial gain is the traditional American way," Norfleet penned in one of her last columns in the 1940s. "However, if a girl hustles the proposal along a bit by turning up her natural charms . . . well, what's the harm in that? She'd be foolish if she didn't use every wile at her command to captivate the man of her choice."[62]

Within the Mutual's social world, yet another gender dynamic unfolded. For all of their rhetoric about respectability and protection of women and their self-congratulatory concern for women's hardships, male executives sometimes exhibited unseemly behavior toward the women who worked for them. As in most cases of sexual harassment among African American women, few who shared the experience went on record about specific incidents or specific men. Most commented only in passing that "everybody" knew and expected that sexual favors would be asked of women who worked at one of these businesses, or that at some point a married male executive would ask a female employee to "go with him." Longtime Mutual employee Viola Turner agreed: "These rascals were having all sorts of love affairs, from what I've heard. . . . That sort of living." Indeed, male executives referred to their intricate network of enterprises as a "honey hole," a term rife with sexual allusion, where they could burrow in and enjoy the good life that was not only distanced from hardship but pierced with pleasure. Among their pleasures, Mutual men found an abundance of women.⁶³ In the workplace the line between voluntary and coerced relationships blurred when it came to sex with supervisors who were married. Women considered those experiences part of the cultural and social world of the new black elite, part of the personal freedom bought with financial independence and employment security, and part of the conditions they accepted given the gender imbalance among Mutual employees. One woman recalled: "I did some things that I am not very proud of now; but I don't think I had a reputation. That's how life was in Durham at that time. . . . Men thought they should have wife, girlfriend, whatever."⁶⁴

Mutual women remade the internal culture of the company in other ways, using their space to forge strategies of resistance to Jim Crow. "The third floor," Viola Turner claimed, "was our territory." Upon arrival, visitors encountered a waist-high counter, behind which sat well-dressed African American women at work with the focused concentration of a diorama. It was a virtual guarantee that white male visitors would commit some offense by making inappropriate gestures or violating fundamental etiquette, refusing to use "Mrs." or "Miss," for instance, and refusing to remove their hats. White men's actions were intended to undermine Mutual women's carefully constructed respectability, which they were equally determined to maintain. On the other side of the counter, Viola Turner and her associates expected white visitors' insults and responded with a practiced charade of racial etiquette. Springing to life, they acted out a script that reversed the terms of interactions and embarrassed the ill-mannered.

Turner, for instance, was cued to the race of the visitor by the way she was addressed. Identified by her nickname "Brownie" in the office, Turner turned a deaf ear to those who called her anything else. She refused to answer to "Viola" unless preceded by "Miss." On one occasion, she took a white insurance inspector to task for expecting her to do so. When whites who came to the office asked for "Charlie" or the "preacher," referring to C. C. Spaulding or any other black man of authority, Turner turned to her women colleagues and asked, facetiously: "Have you seen a preacher here this morning?" Or she asked the other women: "Charlie? We don't have a Charlie working here do we, ladies?" After several moments of mocking banter she feigned understanding: "Oh! You must mean Mr. Spaulding. I'll tell him that you are waiting. And may I take your hat while you wait?" To punish the offender for his rudeness, she hung the hat, returned to her desk, and, without passing on the message, resumed her pose in the tableau.⁶⁵

Delighted to convert incivility into politeness, the compatriots referred to the improved manners among regular white visitors as their "getting religion." Having a good laugh at Jim Crow's expense, they tamed its intemperance, limited the extent of injury to themselves, and struck back. On one occasion, a white woman visitor, dissatisfied with Turner's manner, threatened to report her to the Ku Klux Klan. Turner encouraged the woman to bring on the Klan if she wanted and sent a white woman who had never before been challenged by a black person into the lobby in tears. Equally bold, Bess Whitted refused to look up from her work when debt collectors from department stores arrived at the office to demand from her a payment on the expensive clothing she had bought. Pencil in hand and ledger open, she would say, "Just go on back downstairs, you know I don't have any money to give you today."[66]

With its circle of women employees, North Carolina Mutual Life Insurance Company could proclaim itself to be "The Greatest Negro Insurance Company in the World," not simply by dint of its wealth but by linking the ideological themes of race pride, enterprise, respectability, and thrift, each shaped by gender. Even as it held that business was a man's world to be led by male providers, the Mutual patriarchs acknowledged the active role of women, both as its core workforce and as its customer base. At the same time, women challenged the patriarchs' interpretation of public and private respectability, at least as far as the elite was concerned. And they brought a lively spirit to the tedium of the gospel of work, even as they strengthened the southern New Negro's resolve to rise above the cheerless aspects of Jim Crow.

"The Negroes Gather Capital by Pennies"

Of course, the black business clique, as Du Bois pointed out, was a "closed circle of social intercourse," and it was a very small group. None of their enterprises provided extensive employment for Durham's 5,000 African Americans in 1910. Impressively, the hosiery mill employed 500 women in 1912 when Du Bois toured, but even this barely made a dent in the employment picture. Nor were the ventures always successful. The mill closed in 1916 due to a slump in the textile industry that it might have overcome if it could have held on for one more year for the war economy to boom. The National Negro Finance Company faltered after a successful start, embarrassingly so, when its manager disappeared. Though it struggled to stay afloat through the late 1920s, the National Negro Finance Corporation finally collapsed during the Great Depression, as black business felt the acute effects of economic decline. Solidarity, too, proved difficult to maintain, even if most who left the Mutual retained common interests with the triumvirate, sat alongside them on boards of directors, and served as the trustees of other companies and institutions. Even the programs directed to the masses did little to alleviate the poverty that overwhelmed most African Americans. Despite the appeal of McDougal's ideas to make property owner-ship more accessible to the less affluent, not many black folk were able to purchase homes through the program. Too many tobacco workers struggled against quotidian demands. In the end, Durham ranked extremely low, near the bottom, in black home ownership compared to other North Carolina cities.[67]

The series of subsidiaries and independent organizations associated with the Mutual and with Mechanics and Farmers Bank hoped to provide a range of financial services to the black public for the purposes of upbuilding, but, in fact, these enterprises with their overlapping management structures and boards of directors allowed the elite to keep the money within their own cir-cle and to reinvest in themselves. For instance, Pearson founded the South-ern Fidelity and Surety Company specifically to ensure that funds black businesses otherwise paid to white firms for bonding purposes remained in black hands. Thus the financial benefits of black business—political, eco-nomic, and social—accrued to an elite who, not coincidentally, encouraged their children to intermarry and their sons and sons-in-law to follow their fathers' and fathers-in-law's footsteps.[68]

Consequently, the community development project forged by Merrick, Moore, and Spaulding fostered an urban-based class system built on a frame-work that made financial capital the most crucial determinant of social capi-tal. Increasingly, elite, middle-class, and working-class identities each carried clear gendered overtones where status could be determined by the elite's distance from the masses, but also by their independence from whites or, more correctly, by their ability to avoid the racial or gendered insults of daily life. If class is measurable, then, one variable that separated one class from another among African Americans in Durham was women's occupations. That is, a family's class was determined by whether or not the women of the family had to work, and if so at what kind of employment and in what proximity to whites, especially males, or to the black masses. "The best Negroes are withdrawing their sons and daughters from house service just as quickly as they can," the *Crisis* pointed out, because those positions offered "the worst" and most vulnerable conditions in the "civilized world."[69] If a family could adhere to prescribed gender roles, even the expanded ones engendered by Mutual women, its women and children were being sheltered. Men could engage in the public sphere as guardians, protectors, and custodians of their families, and by extension their communities, as black men with their manhood — if not manhood rights — intact.

Those who worked for the Mutual and its subsidiaries therefore rose above the middle class to become not only the employers of other professionals but also of black household laborers. And those who struggled financially and who worked directly for whites fell below. Pauli Murray's family considered themselves the black aristocracy, descendants of freeborn black Yankees. They resented their displacement in the local hierarchy by "upstarts" from Down East, as rural southeast North Carolina was known. The Moores, the Spauldings, and the Merricks forged family dynasties in Durham, wounding the Fitzgeralds' pride. The Robert Fitzgeralds' precarious financial condition meant that the abandoned Pauline Fitzgerald Dame always had to work and that she bore the responsibility to support three generations of family in her household. Their position was further diminished by residence. The descendants of Robert Fitzgerald, who had gone blind and was unable to work, lived in the West End, rather than in Hayti where the black elite built new modern homes. Pauli Murray wrote: "Our distance from the hub of the cultural life and our lack of mobility made me acutely conscious of living outside the elite circle."[70]

Still, with so many people not far removed from slavery, black Durhamites recognized that for most African Americans the struggle against financial odds did not necessarily yield gender propriety. The needs of black families often required women to work outside the home in conditions much less attractive than the Mutual offices. Whites grouped African Americans into one undifferentiated mass, but the urban black elite defined and defended themselves through hard work, religiosity, cleanliness, and a respect for the dominant moral codes, enhanced by an income that separated and protected them from harsh scrutiny. Domestic workers, cooks, and tobacco workers who provided social capital through church and community work could thus stand alongside teachers, clerical workers, and entrepreneurs as models of racial respectability. For African American women, opportunities to enhance social status existed outside of the labor market through organizational and church work. Prior to 1900, then, Durham's black better class had included many who, like Mary Pauline Fitzgerald Dame, later were isolated from the elite by the community's evolving stratification.[71] As African Americans moved into the maelstrom of the twentieth century, church and civic work could still enhance the status of working-class blacks but did not lift them to parity with the new black elite that was able to make the best of Jim Crow's opportunities.

Beginning in the 1910s, the most affluent of Durham's black families built a set of stately homes that guarded both sides of a tumbledown Fayetteville Street. John Scarborough, the undertaker, owned the most elaborate dwelling on the street, which was constructed with Doric columns and Palladian windows salvaged from old plantation houses. Large multi-bedroom Victorians constructed near the homes of the patriarchs housed unmarried teachers and women clerks who boarded with prominent families. Viola Turner resided with a Mutual executive's family when she arrived in Durham in 1920. Johnnie Blount McLester, a social worker, lived with the family of a minister, and Marie Faulk, a teacher, rented a room in the home of a senior teacher, a widow who accepted her younger colleagues as tenants. Crowded out by the masses but affluent enough to move, married Mutualites established other residential developments. One, south of the boundaries of Hayti in a section known as "College View," contained bungalows, cottages, and Sears & Roebuck mail order houses set along quiet winding streets.[72]

Neighborhoods reflected a widening material gap between affluence and poverty among African Americans in Durham, although the dichotomy between the two created room for upward mobility, at least in the early twentieth century. Through social and employment networks, African Americans who arrived in Durham with few resources could rise into the upper class. Thelma Bailey's grandmother had migrated to Durham to work in the tobacco factories just before the turn of the century. Bailey's father, who worked in the factories as a young man, was hired by the Mutual to sell insurance to his coworkers. His association and success assured that his daughter, Thelma, could enjoy higher education at Virginia State University. She worked at one of the Mutual's associated businesses, Mechanics and Farmers Bank, during her summer vacations. When she married Clarence Lanier, a graduate of Howard and a barber with a shop for white trade, Bailey withdrew from the workforce to become a stay-at-home wife as a matter of preference. As a part of the new black elite, she moved in its social circles, enjoying a life of bridge clubs, private parties, and extensive travel.[73] Similarly, Theresa Jan Cameron Lyons, the daughter of rural sharecroppers, found a rare opportunity as a Mutual employee in the 1940s that allowed her to leave the farming life behind.[74]

With the growth of black business, however, definitions of class became all the more refined, and while some archaic factors fell away, it became more difficult over time to move from the status of laborer to one of professional. Surprisingly, the new class configuration de-emphasized color, a concern central to the members of the old aristocracy, like the Fitzgeralds. This is not to suggest that individuals did not maintain color consciousness; they did. In fact, Bess Whitted, who was herself dark skinned, rebuked others whose skin was equally dark as somehow less than her. But, in its early years as in its later ones, the Mutual and its sibling institutions separated color from ability in hiring. Photographs of Mutual office personnel and agents record a range of skin tones and hues; company materials emphasized instead the staff's uniformly professional appearance.[75] In addition, the Durham elite shared their advantages with relatives and friends, encouraging them to migrate from Down East to Durham to be housed, educated, and employed. Here, kinship and friendship ties expedited employment, education, and institutional affiliation while multiplying links among members of Durham's black elite. "We always had someone from 'down in the country' staying at our house and going to school," Constance Watts remembered. Most came to go to school and continued on to college and other careers, she noted, "but their jumping off space was Durham."[76]

Nor did class position completely demarcate associations among community institutions or groups. That is, men, women, and children of the elite valued their relationships with people from other classes, but the extent of contact between them followed a clear set of guidelines. Because Durham had few black schools at the time, young people regularly associated across class lines at grade level. Nevertheless, because African American girls and women in public were frequently subject to sexual threat, status also signified a family's ability to protect daughters. Beyond the home lay contact with the unknown and unknowable, the uncontrolled and uncontrollable. Affluent parents sought to restrict their children to the places they knew and to contact with people with whom they were comfortable. Constance Watts grew up in the 1920s with children whose parents worked in service and the factories as well as in business. "I was crazy about my classmates," Watts emphasized. But although Watts's childhood home was always open to all of her friends, her parents restricted her travels. "Off of Fayetteville and Umstead and all, they lived in real poverty. Whereas at school they were fine," Watts carefully explained. "[But my mother] did not know them. She just didn't know their morals and all that. So I didn't do a lot of visiting. We saw kids at church."[77]

Affluence provided children of the black elite with benefits that protected them from racism but that also gradually closed their social circle as they grew up. As one informant explained, "Unlike many other people our parents were able to do for us . . . so we didn't have it quite so bad as the others." The number and class affiliation of students also constricted as their educations advanced. It was mostly the children of the elite or the aspiring middle class who attended school beyond the sixth or eighth grade. Alternative education was another marker of class. Watts's parents sent her and her sister to Palmer Memorial Institute, a private school near Greensboro headed by clubwoman Charlotte Hawkins Brown, fifty miles to the east, and their contact with childhood friends diminished. Watts acknowledged: "I guess that's where you could draw the line. . . . [My parents] could afford to send us to a private school."[78] Private school provided another gateway, another mechanism that protected students from the crudeness of the racial world and provided another entrée into a broader circle of middle-class and elite families throughout the United States. Through Palmer, the elite guided its children into appropriate behavior, training in manner and morals, and, not least, intellectual engagement, preparation for higher education, and preparation for roles as race men and women.[79]

Whether founded to serve urgent needs, to provide a route to the professions for black men and women, or as a strategy of self-help, capital accumulation, and autonomy, North Carolina Mutual and its affiliated institutions exemplified a tactic used by Durham's black leaders to create an insular world. Within that world, the urban elite maneuvered to position succeeding generations for their rightful claims on citizenship. Distanced from whites and from the masses, these elites presided over their people. Capitalizing on African Americans' search for economic strength, improved opportunities for their children, and independence from white control, they challenged white perceptions about blacks while winning praise as the embodiment of race progress.[80] At the same time, within the African American community, class lines deepened, because of the development of a black elite and by an expansion of the laboring class. The process was shaped in part by the continued in-migration of women coming from rural districts to work in white households and in factories where they met Jim Crow's ugliest face. The urban class structure, therefore, was marked out in distinctly gendered ways, bottom-heavy with black female laborers and top-heavy with the women of the black elite.

"The Negro gathers capital by pennies from people unused to investing," Du Bois had written about black Durham in 1912. "He has no experts whom he may hire and small chance to train experts; and he must literally grope for success through repeated failure."[81] North Carolina Mutual and Provident Association, renamed North Carolina Mutual and Life Insurance Company in 1919, worked its way into becoming the largest black business in the world by 1925. It was produced, promoted, and buttressed by Jim Crow on one side and reconstructed manhood and womanhood on the other. Made of Durham bricks, men's vision, and women's creativity, the Mutual and its subsidiaries provided an economic foundation for building African American communities both within and beyond Durham. A model of race possibilities, the company achieved Booker T. Washington's dream while meeting Du Bois's call for assertive leadership that challenged the South's precarious race politics. "We have great faith in luck, but infinitely more in pluck," Aaron Moore had told the NNBL audience in 1910.[82] In Durham, the new urban black elite had managed to transcend the regular insult of Jim Crow and distance itself from the humiliations that most blacks suffered.

Durham's leading black men had emerged by the mid-1920s — as they had hoped and planned — as public agents for the black community, poised to enlarge their roles as political players in the effort to transform the southern political landscape. The Mutual benefited from the war economy in the 1910s, as the company and its subsidiaries followed their clients north in the Great Migration, establishing offices in places where migrants settled. With the passing of Richard Fitzgerald in 1910, John Merrick in 1919, and Aaron Moore in 1923, leadership passed to the younger cohort of businessmen and to women. Cottie Moore, for example, succeeded her husband on numerous trustee boards of religious and civic institutions.[83] The energetic C. C. Spaulding became president of North Carolina Mutual Life Insurance Company, the ostensible head of state for black Durham, and the leader of the black business movement in America.[84]

E. Franklin Frazier put black Durham's star on the New Negro map in 1925. In his contribution to Alain Locke's anthology on the cultural mission of modern black people, *The New Negro*, Frazier asserted: "In the composite portrait of the New Negro must be put the sharp and forceful features of the Negro man of business." In Durham, he claimed, an "outstanding group of colored capitalists" had "entered the second generation of business enterprise," deserving of a place in the manifesto of black arts and letters because "they worked hard, not because of necessity, but to expand their businesses and invade new fields." A sharp critic of his race, the black sociologist was known to carp on "the Negro's love of leisure and sensuous enjoyment." Of Durham's leading black men, he wrote: "Their pleasures are the pleasures of the tired business man who does not know how to enjoy life." Nonetheless, he admired that "the Negro in Durham" could "maintain fine homes and expensive cars," obtained, as they were, through "faith in the acquisition of wealth by thrift and the sweat of his brow." Thus, according to Frazier, the black men of Durham had made a black town as remarkable as Harlem — and more respectable: "Durham offers none of the color and creative life we find among Negroes in New York City. It is a city of fine homes and middle-class respectability. It is not the place where men write and dream; but a place where black men calculate and work. No longer can men say that the Negro is lazy and shiftless and is a consumer. He has gone to work. He is a producer. He is respectable. He has a middle class." "Durham," Frazier extolled, "is promise of a transformed Negro," uplifted and modernized into a model of race progress, the elite of the race, possessing a "very important and conspicuous place" in black society.[85]

Black Durhamites might have reacted to the characterization of "conspicuous" with some ambivalence, having been chilled by the destruction of Greenwood, the black business district known as Black Wall Street, in the Tulsa race riot of 1921. The Mutual had just expanded into Tulsa and Oklahoma City in 1920, while at home in Durham the company had started construction on its modern office complex, to be built in its Parrish Street enclave downtown. The building was slated to open in 1921 when whites obliterated the Tulsa neighborhood. Set off by a rumor that a black man had raped a white woman in downtown Tulsa, the injustice was covered in the black press and by word of mouth on the networks of agents and black organizations. The Tulsa destruction must have conveyed an important lesson back to Durham, one that echoed the Wilmington era: obvious success among blacks still incurred the wrath of whites. As they did so well, the leading men of Durham used the appropriate racial protocol to diffuse any tension, animosity, resentment, or spite. The directors checked the measurement of the tallest building in town, and made sure that theirs did not exceed it. In the end, the Mutual structure rose above all others in town, except one. "The building and the company are things that every citizen of Durham . . . can justly be proud of," exclaimed the *Durham Morning Herald*, "an example of what can be done by the negro if he goes about it in the right way." Another paper praised the Mutual for "lifting its race from the quagmires of careless spendthrifts" in denial of "the bogie man they themselves have created in their own minds."[86]

Still, when it opened in late summer 1921, quietly, in the months after the riot, the Mutual's six-story, marble-trimmed, fireproof building made a robust statement of race pride, resiliency, and security. To blacks, this was an inspiring stronghold, rising like a phoenix in defiance of Jim Crow, which just recently had destroyed one Black Wall Street. The new Mutual building marked the establishment of another. To whites, the building said that, in Durham, African American men were safely installed in their space, making black money, not political hay or passes at white women. To both sides, North Carolina Mutual's success reflected white Durham's tradition of racial tolerance and forbearance, and consequently its position as a progressive city, a model for the rest of the South. Perhaps the shock of the Tulsa race riot had worn off by the time the Mutual celebrated the building's grand opening in December of 1921. A thousand African Americans gathered for the event, a third of them from out of town. In celebration, the Durham Business and Professional League produced a commemorative pamphlet, *Milestones along the Color Line*, depicting "property owned and controlled exclusively by Negroes," a world the elite claimed to have made. Photographs of trimmed lawns, ivy-covered churches, stately office buildings, enormous houses, and orderly vistas honored black advancement and the world the elite had made, a triumph over the kind of denigration the Tulsa riot had brought.[87] North Carolina Mutual may have represented the height of black progress, making money from money, but it did not represent the whole picture of black life in the South, not even in Durham.

We wear the mask that grins and lies,
It hides our cheeks and shades our eyes, —
This debt we pay to human guile;
With torn and bleeding hearts we smile,
And mouth with myriad subtleties.

Why should the world be otherwise,
In counting all our tears and sighs?
Nay, let them only see us, while
We wear the mask.

We smile, but, O great Christ, our cries
To thee from tortured souls arise.
We sing, but oh the clay is vile
Beneath our feet, and long the mile;
But let the world dream otherwise,
We wear the mask!

Paul Laurence Dunbar, "We Wear the Mask,"
in *Lyrics of a Lowly Life* (1896)

5 : We Need to Be as Close Friends as Possible
Gender, Race, and the Politics of Upbuilding

North Carolina Mutual Life Insurance Company built its business on image—respectability, race pride, and responsibility—while creating the new black elite of Durham. The company's expansion assured its success. Charles C. Spaulding, manager, urged Mutual agents to find new customers while attempting to hold on to their old ones. Given the high attrition rates among its insurance policyholders, the Mutual had to cultivate a broad clientele. Because its customer base was severely disadvantaged by urban poverty, the Mutual counted on the quantity of policyholders, not the quality of their lives. Stuck in low-wage positions, barred from little more than rudimentary educations, and suffering terrible health, most clients barely managed the few cents per week that insurance cost.

And, in truth, the high-risk urban populations that bought Mutual policies were more likely to die than to see their policies mature. Few black families accumulated enough wealth to live in comfort, as compared to Durham's white elites or even the white middle class. Most African Americans lived in dreadful poverty, exacerbated by the institutional aspects of Jim Crow. More-over, black financial institutions tested and reshaped the boundaries of Afri-can Americans' designated place in the racial order, but their successes held little more than symbolic meaning for most black laborers. Still, that symbol-ism was important. The Mutual stood for the future in that its mission was to save the race by encouraging black people to plan ahead and to invest in themselves. The company's success depended upon it being concerned with basic quality of life issues for black people in the South — improving health and increasing life expectancy — but so did the survival of the race. Health care, however, required more capital than African Americans could afford. Building a hospital also required a change in policy if not attitude on the part of white elites. Sustaining one required the social capital of dedicated volun-teers and professionals, mostly women, trained to do the hands-on labor of race work.

Death and disease took an enormous toll on African American residents of the urban South, and Durham was no exception. Excluding stillbirths, the death rate among Durham's African Americans in 1910 was 26.0 per thou-sand, compared to 16.6 per thousand for whites. The death rates among whites in Durham declined to 10.0 per thousand by 1920 but increased to 29.9 for blacks during the same period. Infant mortality ranged even higher: an astonishing 411.0 deaths per thousand live births among black children aged 0 to 1, excluding miscarriages and stillbirths, versus 137.5 for whites in 1910. According to a 1920 U.S. Public Health study, urban blacks were subject to higher disease and death rates than those who lived in rural areas or white city dwellers.[1] With life expectancy among southern blacks averag-ing only thirty-six years in 1910, the Mutual might have profited more by allowing a policy to lapse than by persisting to collect weekly premiums. Compelled to focus on health problems and realizing that white health care workers neglected black patients, North Carolina Mutual established a pub-lic health program that included a medical department in the home office to conduct studies, disseminate information, organize campaigns, and treat the illnesses of policyholders, and a coterie of public health nurses to work in cities where the Mutual had offices.[2]

The poorest among Durham's residents and the Mutual's primary cus-tomers, African American women suffered most intensely. Although black women had slightly longer life expectancies than black men, between 1900 and 1914 disproportionately more women than men died in Durham, a trend that slowed but did not reverse before 1930. Due to a combination of factors surrounding poverty, and according to a 1926 Children's Bureau report, "the high mortality rates among negro mothers exists in spite of an unusually favorable age composition." For example, in the age bracket ten to forty-four, when mortality should have been lowest, black women suffered higher death rates than black men, white women, or white men. The difference was even greater in the narrower age bracket fifteen to thirty, peak childbearing years. Of course, males suffered as well; among adults over age forty-five, for example, men demonstrated higher mortality than women. Contaminated surface wells, miserable working conditions, and poor public sanitation, the usual results of industrialization and urbanization, affected black women of childbearing and working age more so than they did white women or black men. Disparate mortality rates exposed the connections among race, gender, class, and death with African American women and men experiencing heightened vulnerabilities at different stages of their life cycles that directly affected the next generation. Not only were black infants far less likely than white babies to survive their first year, but those who survived were less likely to grow up under the care and guidance of healthy mothers.[3]

Turn-of-the-century Durham was a dirty, disease-ridden place where "Durham fever," any of several undiagnosed maladies, ravaged the city's population. The air, infused with fine brown dust, reeked of tobacco. African American women worked and lived in the unsanitary conditions of a Jim Crow municipality. Like virtually all of her neighbors, Annie Mack Barbee's family lived in a two-room house on Poplar Street in Hayti that had no private bathroom. "The street was not paved," she remembered, "and when it rained it got muddy and in the fall, the wind blew all of the dust in your eyes and face."[4] Unpaved streets and a lack of indoor plumbing made housekeeping an endless and seemingly futile task. Worse, inadequate housing, insufficient heat, poor ventilation, inadequate diet, and overwork contributed to malnutrition, tuberculosis, typhoid, pneumonia, diphtheria, and a heightened susceptibility to influenza, measles, and other contagious diseases. Exacerbated by the physical stress of pregnancy, their proximity to school-children, their work in steamy factories, and their intimate contact with white families as well as their own, adult black women were exposed to virtually every epidemic that spread among the local population.

The unhealthy situation knew few barriers. Constance Merrick Moore Watts, granddaughter of Dr. Aaron M. Moore, recalled that one of her aunts was so ill for so long that she rarely left her room. "They had a lot of tuberculosis in Durham at the time; we called it the catarrh."[5] Catarrh should have been treated with bed rest, healthy diet, and fresh air — prescriptions that few African Americans could fill. Because the care for patients fell to the women of the household, African American women endured the pain of sickness and death three times over: as sufferers, as healers, and as mourners.

If death and disease were consequences of urban life, especially the result of black impoverishment combined with municipal neglect, limited educational opportunities exacerbated the problems. Freedom's first generation of teachers, women like Mary Pauline Dame, worked to expand literacy and increase school attendance. These improvements brightened a bleak picture, as the Jim Crow generation, freedom's second cohort, proved to be as enthusiastic about education as freedom's first generation had been. Despite the barely tolerable condition of black schools statewide, attendance figures for African American children ages ten to fourteen years surged, from 46 percent in 1890 to 73 percent in 1910, higher in urban than in rural areas. Inadequate transportation contributed to the fact that only two-thirds of the potential black student population enrolled in Durham County schools in 1900, and barely 40 percent of the registered students appeared each day. By 1910, however, overall enrollment had increased by 20 percent, but the number of teachers for those students remained the same. Literacy among African Americans also increased significantly. In North Carolina, black illiteracy declined from 61 percent of the population in 1900 to 37 percent by 1910. Although daily school attendance remained poor, illiteracy among African Americans in Durham County dropped from 46 percent of the population in 1900 to 21 percent a decade later.[6] Still, in 1920, only three schools served the educational needs of the thousands of black children residing in Durham: Whitted School, which had replaced the Durham Colored Grade School; West End School, where Mary Pauline Dame taught; and East End School.

African Americans, even among the elite, did not command the material means to build from scratch community institutions like hospitals and schools. Critical demands for better health care and schooling compelled black leaders to call on white philanthropists for support. The black patriarchs might have preferred to go it alone, but as Margaret Kennedy Goodwin culled from stories of white altruism, black leaders already had learned that "even with vision and drive you need some capital."[7] Yet, whereas education and schooling remained contentious issues through much of the twentieth century for African Americans, health initiatives offered blacks and whites a cooperative space in the name of public service. Ironically, health care also played out on the dangerous turf of Jim Crow and gender relations. The quirks of Jim Crow forged effective tools that the black elite used to garner positive responses to requests for funds and other considerations from a coalition of ruling whites, including reformers, philanthropists, politicians, and officials. Inasmuch as racial magnanimity signified the success of industrial capitalists — at least those who were too wealthy and powerful to care about the color line — it also turned on the tap through which the public funds trickled. Influenced by southern reformers and northern philanthropists, and following the lead of its own industrialists, white state and civic officials made extraordinary decisions to provide public support for institutions African Americans demanded. Compared to other states and cities, North Carolina and Durham provided several progressive initiatives in black health and education. As far as black folk were concerned, public institutions should have been entitlements. After all, propertied African Americans paid taxes several times over as a direct cost of segregation. They contributed disproportionately to the public funds that built white schools and provided disproportionate resources for building black schools. Blacks who took the lead in health and educational initiatives shaped their strategy to the necessities of Jim Crow, but what they demanded, they demanded as rights, not favors.[8]

Durham's black leaders were very much aware that white authorities would do almost anything to maintain racial segregation, and they used this knowledge to negotiate with ruling whites for the building of public institutions for the African American community. The black patriarchs' ability to deliver private and public funds to black causes illustrated their engagement in state and local politics, despite their disfranchisement, even as the resulting programs and projects demonstrated the limits of their political power. They procured from white civic leaders a set of institutions that were partly supported by public funds by assuring ruling whites that black facilities benefited both their causes. The institutions they founded served as sites from which challenges to Jim Crow were launched. Whether that leadership involved guiding or overseeing depended on the amount of autonomy any given leader could negotiate for his or her institution. In the context of the period, in 1898, with race relations souring, this kind of institution building charmed the snakes of Jim Crow.

This is not to say that black leaders simply accepted racial segregation as a better option than racial exclusion, or that the task of founding and sustaining these institutions was accomplished easily, or even that the institutions themselves were successful. When they were presented with a set of requests, white benefactors often were unconvinced by claims of just plain justice and required blacks to present an alternate rationale for their largesse. Then, too, African Americans had to nurture a workable consensus among local white officials, white southern reformers, white northern philanthropists, and moneyed whites. They had to induce goodwill and appeal to whites' humanitarianism, and even then, they could never be grateful enough. They could ill afford for whites to infer discontent or insult on their part, so easily done with a single indelicate step. Importantly, however, as citizens and taxpayers "having something to represent," the black patriarchs believed they had a right to facilities that would attend to community needs.[9]

Appearing compliant, African Americans wore the mask of acquiescence and, working from a disadvantaged position, acted out the peculiar rituals of Jim Crow race relations. Exploiting whites' sense of superiority, black leaders used obsequious and disingenuous tactics of race protocol to undermine the intent of Jim Crow by turning segregation into an advantage when possible, making for effective politics.[10] For instance, the barber John Merrick understood that the etiquette of Jim Crow race relations required favored African Americans like him to look to white patrons like Washington Duke for assistance. And William G. Pearson, whose education was paid for by Julian S. Carr Jr., owed at least some of his achievement to the general, and he had no choice but to tolerate the racism of the man whose help he sought. Once questioned about the elites' amiable relationship with the ex-Confederate, one black leader responded, "We prefer to think of General Carr in terms of his benefactions, not his politics." Thus the Durham black elite opted to cite "the friendly feeling" between the races in Durham, well aware that the assertion mostly was not true. At the 1907 Emancipation Day celebration, for example, a committee led by James E. Shepard laid out numerous examples of injustice and unfair treatment — segregation, disfranchisement, violence — but closed by thanking the white community for "extending a helping hand" through donations to churches and institutions and by employing black people.[11] Such absurd pronouncements eased the way for black elites to elicit demands as favors. "We need to be as close friends as possible so as to demand more for our different services," Merrick advised, especially with "the best white people of the South," as benevolent whites were known.[12]

In publicly downplaying their misgivings about whites, the black elite of Durham exhibited an impressive dexterity at racial etiquette. In reality, most black leaders held whites in contempt. Known to tip his hat to a white man while calling him a "son of a bitch" under his breath, Merrick knew that elections were not the only political principles of importance to African Americans. As Robert E. Park, a contemporary white sociologist, pointed out, "It seems that there are no racial antipathies that cannot be overcome by a scrupulous adherence to etiquette." By etiquette he meant adhering to the rules governing appropriate social behavior. The black elite of Durham excelled at navigating racial minefields by attending to such protocols.[13] In this way, black leaders in Durham faced the fight instead of fleeing and held onto a place in North Carolina politics.

Black leaders sought out both private and public support for a hospital and for schools by manipulating the contradictory imperatives of Jim Crow. In order for the racial order to sustain itself, whites had to perform the opposite of Jim Crow's impulse and grant rather than deny African Americans access to health care, education, and training. Black health care required black nurses, doctors, and technicians; black schools required black teachers; and both fields needed training programs. Individually and as a group these professionals provided support, inspiration, and guidance to strengthen the black community as best it could. And they staffed the institutions where antiapartheid activism was planned and started. The irony must have made black southerners wonder if they truly could dismantle the master's house with the master's tools. Certainly, the strategy required unspoken goals and tactics. For while Jim Crow demanded dependency, African Americans desired autonomy, and black leaders of the Jim Crow era faced the ambiguous task of playing up one to attain the other.

Upbuilding black institutions required social capital as well as financial capital and the work of many hands, especially for the struggle to gain white support. Turning the paternalism of race on its head, black leaders joined interests and enlisted the support of their respective white benefactors, the Dukes and the Carrs. Washington Duke and Julian S. Carr Jr. hailed from diametrically opposed white positions in the Old South. Duke, the tobacco farmer cum magnate, was born on the poorer eastern side of Orange County. Carr, the tobacco magnate cum textile industrialist, was born on the more affluent west side to a prominent Chapel Hill family. Duke had little more than a rudimentary education. Carr had been educated at Harvard. Duke, a Republican, believed that the future of the New South lay in the peaceful reconciliation of black and white interests. Carr, although he discouraged mob violence and was affectionate and generous toward individual blacks, was nonetheless a prominent Democrat and a vociferous proponent of white supremacy. Moreover, the Dukes jostled Carr out of the tobacco manufacturing market by overpowering him financially, raising the latter's ire. Playing one family off the other, fashioning intricate alliances with one while trying not to offend the other, and culling verbal if not financial support from the Dukes' and the Carrs' respective allies must have proved exhausting and sometimes futile, especially when whites expressed resolute opposition to black demands. But the hospital and schools that resulted, albeit too small, overcrowded, and underfunded to meet community needs fully, still alleviated tragic circumstances, established sites for further activism, and created important symbols of race pride and progress.[14]

Shaping and transforming these institutions exposed the extent and the limitations of both interracial cooperation and collaborative activism. African Americans had to concede some control over their institutions to whites, and then fractured lines like gender and class set up competing expectations. Thus black folk fashioned disparate relationships with the institutions they created collectively. Nonetheless, the hospital and schools were an example of how black men and women and people of different classes collaborated to assure institutional success. In this way, their funding served as counterexamples of class and gender conflict, although some contention did arise, inasmuch as it was the labor of men that founded these institutions and it was women who assumed the challenge of sustaining them. Health care and education provided expanded professional venues for African American women, including those from the laboring classes.

Thus, institution building also provided a view of the gender dimensions of the urban class structure. Teachers and nurses, virtually all women, were employed in institutions founded by black male leaders, which afforded a somewhat protected environment. Gender protocol, like race protocol, also demanded that teachers and nurses defer to black males and all whites but elevated their status compared to the working class, even though these professionals might earn less income. Yet teachers and nurses went between the elites for whom they worked and the black masses among whom they worked. Their daily contact with the masses made them an integral part of the communities where they worked. On the one hand, they were mediators for their working-class charges, informing black elites about their needs and protecting them from the scorn of the upper class. On the other hand, they were subject to the gendered insults of racism. Nothing reminded them more of their positions than the regular visits by white officials who, with no hesitation, humiliated teachers and nurses before their charges. Pauline Dame and Sallie Fitzgerald Small walked this fine line between the elites and the masses. "Grown folks regarded them with deep respect," Pauli Murray wrote about her aunts' standing in their neighborhood. "The children looked upon them with a mixture of fear and awe, not unlike that accorded to a policeman."[15] Marie Faulk, who followed her mother into the teaching profession, explained: "The teacher was, at that time, one of the most prominent people in all these sections," referring to the black neighborhoods dispersed around the city.[16] Moreover, some of the women who took up nursing or teaching came from middle-class backgrounds, the children of teachers, ministers, and landowners whose families supported their college or normal school education. But many were able to rise from the working class into the professions through contributions of their local associations and churches and by working for their tuition. Still others, like the abandoned Pauline Dame and her now-widowed sister, Sallie, descended from the aristocracy, but economic circumstances required that they work to support their families, which reduced their class status. By virtue of their educations, however attained, and their vital positions in communities, women teachers and nurses were accorded middle-class status, setting them apart from the rank and file of black wage earners.

Education and health care were important women's issues during the Jim Crow era. Women made up the majority of the teachers, students, health care workers, and patients. They also were the "willing workers," the volunteers, who supported programs in both areas. Although the male elite assumed their subordination, they welcomed women's contributions. In this way, women's labor in education and health care presented black Durham with an iteration of secular club work. As a part of their education, women teachers and nurses grasped the imperatives of racial uplift. Josephine Clement, a native of Atlanta who migrated to Durham, recalled the imperatives instilled by her parents, her teachers, and her church: that certain expectations "to achieve, to teach, and to work across class lines" accompanied the privilege of advanced education.[17] Like the women who worked for the Mutual, nurses and teachers were instilled with high moral principles that in turn they preached to their flocks. Bearing responsibility for "moving the race forward," their work in many ways epitomized the schizophrenic character of uplift. They proselytized on manners, morals, character, and culture in ways that often echoed the disparaging sentiments of black elites. At the same time, they emphasized success, self-esteem, and race pride.[18]

"Not One Act of Disloyalty Was Recorded among Them"

The building of the black hospital testified to the intricate patterns of inter- and intraracial cooperation and conflict necessary for the development of public institutions. Lincoln Hospital, the first nondenominational hospital for African Americans in North Carolina, was also one of the earliest black health facilities in the nation. Opened in 1901, it served its community loyally until it closed in 1976. It continues to serve as a public clinic. Its founding also represents the intersection of gender, class, and Jim Crow, emerging from the entangled history of race relations.[19]

The hospital movement in Durham began when George W. Watts, a white investor, civic leader, and business partner in Duke Tobacco Company, donated the funds to establish a hospital for whites in 1895. Aaron M. Moore, still the town's only black doctor, proposed that a hospital be built to serve Durham's black residents as well. Agitation for his project continued in the late 1890s and through the peaking of race tensions in North Carolina. Moore persisted, even though Durham's white community refused extensive philanthropy. With the aid of John Merrick, he targeted the Dukes as potential benefactors, writing to James B. Duke in 1899: "I pray that you grant me a few minutes of your time in the interest of the suffering sick of our city." At the same time, different persons brought multiple pressures to bear. The Duke family doctor, who was white, joined with John Merrick, the family barber; W. H. Armstrong, the Dukes' black butler; and Addie Evans, their black cook, to convince the Dukes of the idea's merit. As Moore later explained about their collective pressure, together they "had a fairly good opportunity to see that the matter did not grow cold." Finally, Watts announced that he intended to add a "colored ward" to the white hospital.[20]

Dissatisfied, Moore objected to a racially segregated ward, stating that the provision would "lead to practical difficulties." Those "practical difficulties" provided the doctor with the rationale to argue for a facility that would serve Durham's African Americans over the short and the long term. A segregated ward would not give black physicians "sufficient opportunity to develop," Moore maintained, and a single ward would prove "insufficient" for the growing black population.[21] There was more to Moore's reasoning than these conditions, but tactful allusion advanced his cause more quickly than simple truth. Black doctors could not adequately attend black patients in a white hospital. They would be banned as blacks from using instruments, equipment, or services. These were reserved for white patients. Shared medical facilities raised the specter of a real or imagined blood mixing, a topic the black physician dared not broach. Race etiquette, furthermore, stipulated that Moore could not suggest that white doctors would not willingly provide care for blacks or that African Americans distrusted whites to offer adequate medical services. Nor could he as a black man hint at another critical issue — hospitals were female spaces. Women provided much of the patient care in hospitals at the turn of the century. Thus, any care for black men would have to be done (unacceptably) by white women.

At Watts Hospital, the board of trustees, comprised of prominent male civic leaders, designated white elite women — their wives and single women in the professional community — as the voluntary association to supply hospital needs, to furnish rooms and secure donations of clothing, gowns, linens, and food. Another contingent of white clubwomen tracked the hospital's quality of care, supervised nurses and nursing students, and joined the institution to the community. Black patient care would have demanded that women of the white elite serve black men. Even as nursing professionalized, the code of Jim Crow demanded that white nurses not care for black patients, especially men. Finally, despite these real dilemmas, any candid discussion of these racial barriers might have implied — or whites might have inferred — insult, ingratitude, or threat on Moore's part. Assuring that his efforts would be undermined at best or his person injured at worst, Moore's influence as a medical proselytizer should not be understated. More missionary than businessman, he energized the black community to demand health care facilities and mobilized blacks on their own behalf. But gender and class issues reinforced the motivations for white support as much as benevolence. Whites' perception that African American women were dirty, debauched carriers of disease enabled black leaders to introduce their idea another way, framing a discourse that blamed sufferers for the illness, while also outlining a set of rationales for assisting them. Diseases that ran unchecked in one community crossed into another, Moore argued, without having to point out that African American women household laborers like the Dukes' cook Addie Evans worked for whites in intimate circumstances. "It will be well to remember," white philanthropist Julius Rosenwald averred, "that germs recognize no color lines and the disease in one group threatens the health of all."[22] Domestics had access to most areas of whites' homes; cooks handled food; washerwomen laundered clothes near groundwater streams or in open ravines or drew water from stagnant pools that likely were polluted. Black women handled all of the raw products in the tobacco plants. The most powerful argument to be made for white support of black health care initiatives, then, may have referred to Addie Evans.

Working closely with Moore, John Merrick was the person credited with turning the idea into reality. As the family barber, he, like Addie Evans and W. H. Armstrong, was positioned intimately within the Duke household. Although not necessarily a benefit, this proximity meant they knew the minds and moods of their employers. They could nudge Duke by raising the topic directly, for instance, with the advantage of knowing when Duke might be open to a hearing. Merrick used this entrée to gauge when and how to broach the matter with the Dukes. When the prideful Washington Duke announced a plan to erect a monument on the new Trinity College campus dedicated to the faithful slaves who protected white women during the Civil War, Merrick gently suggested an alternative memorial. Entreating Duke to "do something for those slaves' descendants" — the people who grew the tobacco, worked in his factories, and served in his homes — Merrick urged the family to redirect its memorial to something the black community truly needed. He elicited a donation of $8,500 to erect a black hospital in Hayti.[23]

Lincoln Hospital opened in 1901 at the corner of Proctor and Corzet Streets, three years after the peak of race hatred and the year disfranchisement went into effect. The Dukes' dedication was inscribed on a marble tablet at the entrance to the hospital: "With grateful appreciation and loving remembrance of the fidelity and faithfulness of the Negro slaves to the Mothers and Daughters of the Confederacy, during the Civil War, this institution was founded by one of the Fathers and Sons. Not one act of disloyalty was recorded against them."[24] Named for Abraham Lincoln, a Republican president whom African Americans revered, Lincoln Hospital presented a set of symmetries too elegant to be coincidental. Beyond the juxtaposition of slavery and freedom in a southern city, the institution signified peaceful reconciliation between the Confederate soldier, Duke, and the ex-slave, Merrick, and evidence that they, too, had found common political ground. In honoring those who cared for the women and children of Confederate soldiers, Lincoln Hospital also acknowledged Duke's responsibility to the children of slaves, including his own. His biographer notes that Washington Duke briefly owned one slave, a woman named Caroline. According to legend, he purchased her to take care of his children and household when his wife died but freed her before the Civil War. She returned to his household to take care of his children when the Confederate Army drafted him. In appreciation, Duke reportedly later gave her two houses — one to live in and one to rent out — and remembered her in his will. Another account connects Duke and African American slaves through Dr. Stanford L. Warren, allegedly a son of Washington Duke and a slave woman named Anne Warren. The second black physician to live and work in Durham, Stanford Warren was also considered a cofounder of Lincoln Hospital, although his role is not recounted in African American sources.[25]

Perhaps, too, Lincoln Hospital offered a nudge to the aristocratic Julian S. Carr, the unyielding Democrat, from the yeoman farmer and Republican Duke, now secure enough in his power to sanction such an exceptional initiative. Ironically, and most relevantly, this monument to southern slaves who protected Confederate women was born out of the mores that prohibited white women nurses from caring for black male patients, even as it acknowledged black women's health issues and reflected black leaders' sense of responsibility to black women and their intent to care for their own community. The building of Lincoln Hospital stood as evidence that the same cadre of men who were expelled as Republican activists were still able to procure public funds from public coffers and share trusteeship with whites. Built with philanthropy and supported by additional public funds, the institution linked black capitalism, black institutions, and black communities. Finally, the hospital offered a site for secular women's activism to emerge; for, although men founded the hospital, women played the most integral roles in its programs.

"A Power in the Uplift of the Race"

Following the model at North Carolina Mutual, black women emerged as the core workforce, patrons, and patients of Lincoln Hospital. And, as at the Mutual, the women employees of Lincoln Hospital worked in an all-black environment, mostly protected from the more sexually precarious positions of laborers and elevated to the sainted position of nurse. Modeled after the philanthropy of Julius Rosenwald and the Rockefeller Foundation, funds to underwrite a nursing school at Lincoln Hospital were donated by B. N. Duke and Mary Duke Biddle, Washington Duke's children. They viewed their support as an investment in the training of black health and education professionals to modernize the South. Formalized nurses' training programs— founded when "the servant class no longer furnished nurses"— transformed nursing from a household worker's job into a respectable career position for young African American women. Lincoln Hospital's nursing school opened in 1903. The school's graduates provided skilled medical support for Lincoln's staff and public health nurses for the black community. Such schools proved profitable in terms of labor resources. In return for their training, students filled several roles for the hospital that were necessary to the daily operation.[26]

Nonetheless, nursing, like clerical work, perpetuated women's lower status. In both cases, the worker served at the whim of the employer. Women in nursing were subordinate to doctors in the same way that clerical workers were beneath managers. Like business, nursing required skill, efficiency, and assertiveness, and as the brochure for the Lincoln Hospital Nursing School detailed, doctors expected "a cheerful, willing obedience to authority" and "dignity, decorum, and quietness of manner" as part of women's "professional spirit." These themes echoed the expectations of the Mutual. But there were important differences regarding women's personal autonomy. Nurses at Lincoln were expected to "rise and remain standing when physicians" or other authority figures "approach[ed] them or enter[ed] a room or ward." Viola Turner at the Mutual would hardly have tolerated this practice. Nurses' clean, white, starched and pressed uniforms, blouses, and caps signified their professionalism and their virtue. They wore only regulation attire, a full uniform with white stockings and shoes and blue cape whenever they were in public, including in church. For many, the hospital was their residence and house rules limited social contact with the opposite sex. Thus, even as nursing opened a career path that promised the prestige of teaching, it subordinated women to men, limited their mobility, and restricted their independence.[27]

But the hospital did offer new options for African American women who could not count on support from their families. They worked in exchange for tuition. Admission was competitive, with evidence of respectability required. Due to the strenuous nature of the work, the Lincoln Hospital School of Nursing limited admission to "young women, aged 18 to 35 . . . of average height (over 5 feet) and weight, of good physique, with teeth well cared for." Beyond the physical requirements, prospective students faced a battery of other specifications. All applicants submitted two "testimonials," one from their pastor "stating that they are morally fit" for nursing and one from a recent teacher or employer regarding academic ability. Hospital regulations also dictated personal behavior, establishing guidelines for public propriety regarding appearance, visiting, and outings beyond the campus. Student nurses had to ask permission to leave the grounds and could not move about alone. In addition to stimulating a young woman's interest in the field of medicine, the nursing program at Lincoln hoped to "fit" its students for the middle class, "to lead her to a useful and noble womanhood." Accordingly, the program sought out those "not only fitted for nursing, but also to be a power in the uplift of the race."[28]

A small, perpetually understaffed and overburdened institution, Lincoln leaned heavily on its students and nursing staff. In his 1918 report to the board of aldermen, Moore noted that the hospital had only three paid staff people (he took no salary). Patricia Carter, who replaced Julia Latta as director of nursing in 1911, simultaneously managed the positions of hospital superintendent and public health administrator. Considered the "breath and life of Lincoln Hospital," she served as assistant director, as well as head nurse, anesthetist, bookkeeper, and stewardess, and she was known to refuse a salary when finances demanded budget cuts. The janitor and the washerwoman were the only other paid employees in these early years. Once its nursing curriculum was extended to three years in 1910, the hospital could combine its need for inexpensive labor with its ability to provide excellent training. The student nurses provided the central workforce, including hospital staff and public health nurses for the community. They also generated income for the hospital. According to a 1924 report, in addition to providing service without cost to the institution, student nurses were instrumental "in earning $350 for services rendered in private homes in the city."[29]

People in the early twentieth century generally feared hospitals. Considered a last resort for medical care, they were sites of death. To carry the health message to the masses, nurses' work extended beyond the hospital walls to churches, organizations, schools, and private homes. Julia Latta, director of nursing from 1903 to 1910, oversaw the graduation of fourteen nurses into the Durham black community and then left Lincoln for public health work. Hired by the Durham County Department of Health as its first black nurse, she took health care into the community and led the effort to eradicate disease and other health problems that plagued African Americans. When black people refused to go to either facility, the hospital or the county health offices, Latta set up headquarters outside of both. For instance, she led an antityphoid campaign at the library in Hayti in 1918. In addition to making home visits, organizing antituberculosis campaigns, and leading health education programs, public health nurses performed dental and medical examinations and provided treatment at clinics, churches, and schools.[30]

Latta also organized the black community's response to the disastrous flu pandemic of 1918 that swept through Durham (and the United States and the world), closing public entertainment, churches, and schools. To serve a desperate community, Lincoln sent its trained nurses to assist Latta in the community and substituted untrained staff at the hospital. During March and April of 1918 alone, Latta and Carter organized nurses, teachers, and volunteers and coordinated 470 visits to "colored" homes, compared to 395 such visits reportedly made by whites. According to Latta's summary, their work ranged from giving baths and changing dressings, to cleaning and fumigating homes, to teaching nutrition and better health strategies. The black nurses provided similar assistance for whites and procured assistance for the needy of both races in the form of funds, medicines, and linens.[31] Of course, African American women had taken care of ailing whites for ages, so it was no concession to race or gender propriety for black nurses to provide services to local whites. As women, and specifically as African American women acting in a service capacity, the combination of gender, race, and subservience eased their way. Uniformed black nurses provided a soothing image of black domestics. As further evidence of the paradox of Jim Crow, in the face of biology and death, race mattered little, although this particular path across the color line ran only one way—white nurses did not provide services to African Americans.

Health crises brought Durham's black women's club movement to the forefront of community activity, deeply engaging the urban black elite, who used their substantive resources and energies to procure donations. One of the most active groups, the Daughters of Dorcas, Durham's first federated black women's club, included among its members Maggie Moore Lennon, Dr. Moore's niece; Cottie Dancy Moore, his wife; and Lyda Moore Merrick, his daughter. Dorcas evolved from the Busy Women's Club, which had bought milk for needy tuberculosis patients as one of its earliest initiatives, and it continued those efforts. Dorcas women and Iota Phi Lambda, the businesswomen's sorority, also furnished two private hospital rooms, supplied linens annually, donated reading material, and collected money. The hospital's Junior Lady Board purchased the cribs for the maternity ward; the Senior Lady Board equipped the kitchen, raised funds for food, and oversaw the dietary department. The local chapter of the national black sorority Alpha Kappa Alpha bought a warming table for meals. Upon Aaron Moore's death in 1923, Cottie Moore and Lyda Moore Merrick donated a house and furnishings for a nurses' residence in his honor.[32]

Clubwomen organized around health issues in other ways. In 1912, black women founded the Negro Civic League, which took up the issues of home ownership, better education, and public health. Among its activities, the league generated initiatives such as cleanup days and health campaigns that focused on homes and neighborhoods. As a cross-racial/cross-class concern, public health united white and black women in common activities, although they worked in separate realms. In cleanup campaigns, for example, black and white women focused mostly on their own neighborhoods. More permanent activities similarly followed the color line. White women appealed to Brodie Duke, son of Washington Duke, for a tuberculosis hospital and got a site. Moore led an unsuccessful drive to have the tuberculosis hospital opened to black people, too, but, instead, with donations from the white women's civic league, Lincoln was able to add a wing for tuberculosis patients. In his 1918 report to the city aldermen, Moore thanked the "ladies of the Durham Civic League," who provided "guidance and help in securing and equipping a tubercular annex which has been a blessing to the entire community."[33]

Other black women's groups formed as a part of Lincoln Hospital itself. Variously, Boards of Lady Managers, Senior and Junior Boards, and Ladies' Auxiliaries (wives of doctors and dentists) provided volunteers, managed the hospital's daily operations, did the clerical work, and held fund-raising drives. In 1906, the *Negro Observer* reported that the Lincoln Board of Lady Managers and Auxiliary Committee bore the entire expense of hospital charity. To be asked to serve on behalf of the hospital was considered recognition of an individual woman's status, as well as her contribution to the community. The 1938 Senior Lady Board, for example, included notable clubwomen who were also the relatives of Durham's black leaders: Minnie Pearson (then president of the North Carolina Federation of Colored Women's Clubs), Maggie Lennon (Aaron Moore's niece and a founding member of the Daughters of Dorcas), and Cottie Moore (also of Dorcas) all served as officers. The list of members included the deceased Mrs. Martha Merrick, a gesture that recognized her and John Merrick's standing in the community. The Junior Lady Board was comprised of the wives and daughters of the second generation of black business leaders and managers and thus recognized a younger generation of willing workers and clubwomen. Fannie Rosser, a bookkeeper at North Carolina Mutual, unmarried and older than most of her fellow board members, wrote to a friend that she felt doubly honored by her appointment to the *Junior* Lady Board.[34]

When in 1924 a fire ravaged the twenty-three-year-old hospital building, James B. Duke and Benjamin N. Duke, Washington Duke's sons, pledged $75,000 for a new facility if the people of Durham would match their gift. The city and county governments each promised $12,500, white citizens contributed $25,000, and black citizens raised the rest. The modern building, a three-story brick structure, was built on the old Stokes Plantation, a location that further extended the hospital's ironic legacies. The plantation house, donated by the Dukes and two business allies, served as the nurses' residence. From the top of the hill, African American women nurses, guarded by their male employers, watched over their community's health.[35]

Built to accommodate a total of eighty patients, the new Lincoln Hospital was already overcrowded the day it opened in 1925. Of eighty-five patients accommodated on moving day, eighteen came from other towns where no health facilities existed.[36] The city, the county, the state, and several philanthropies regularly allocated or donated funds to cover some of the costs of care. Promised an annual appropriation from Durham County, Lincoln became a publicly supported institution, albeit with limited funding. Because the city's other hospitals allowed very limited access to black patients, Lincoln bore virtually all of the responsibility for all medical charity cases among African Americans. According to its 1938 report, two-thirds of Lincoln Hospital's 1,827 patients were partial pay or charity cases. Some of these costs were covered by the Duke Endowment, a philanthropic initiative established by James B. Duke, and by the county and state funds intended specifically for crippled children. In addition, the Chicago-based Julius Rosenwald Fund provided $3,800 per year for training purposes. The remainder of the cost of medical care for the indigent came from the hospital's operating budget and from funds raised by black organizations on behalf of the Hospital.[37]

Although black leaders, freedom's first generation and the men who followed them, always had to negotiate for financial support, Lincoln Hospital remained mostly a labor of love by Aaron Moore, who never gave up his vision of an institutional initiative sustained by black people on their own behalf. As it grew in size and reputation, the hospital expanded educational goals for black people. A postgraduate clinic for black physicians began in 1933. Lincoln also offered training for black medical technicians at its laboratory and X-ray facilities in the 1930s. In this way, Moore's work and the hospital produced a range of black pioneers in the medical field, including Margaret Kennedy Goodwin, one of the first black X-ray and lab specialists in the United States. The *Durham Morning Herald*, marveling at Lincoln, praised the facility as "a masterpiece of work . . . as fine a hospital as will be found in the South." The black elite claimed it was "a striking example of what can be accomplished in a community where both races work together."[38]

But Lincoln Hospital was also a striking example of what the black community could accomplish. Women's organizations raised desperately needed money, supplies, and equipment, and volunteers donated energy and time that the payroll could not buy. Visiting and reading to patients, providing holiday food and cheer, and hosting visitors, African Americans manifested race pride through their control of and attention to the institution. Until his death in 1923, Aaron Moore served as Lincoln's superintendent without compensation; he also bequeathed three of his rental properties to the Lincoln Hospital Nursing School. With rent from these houses paying for "worthy girls who are desirous of taking nursing training," Moore's gesture made it possible for poorer women to pursue professional careers and for ordinary people to be their supporters.[39]

The hospital clearly served multiple purposes in accordance with its place as part of the segregated racial structure necessitated by a Jim Crow society. Before the opening of the new building, it provided the only emergency care, surgery, lab tests, and other medical services available to Durham's black folk. Over the years, it added wards, including one for disabled children. As a black-controlled facility, the hospital served as a base from which health initiatives were launched and represented increased professional opportunities for black men and women. Collaborating with the Mutual, the hospital supported the annual Negro Health Week, using nurses, teachers, and students in a series of educational programs, clinics, and parades that disseminated information, provided health care, and generated race pride. With obstetrics and pediatrics among its finest programs, Lincoln Hospital became a center for change.

The twentieth-century health movement improved life expectancy among southern African Americans, from an average of 36 years in 1910 to 41.4 years in 1920 and 47.5 years by 1930. The death rate showed a similar pattern, dropping from 26.1 to 22.3 per thousand in the 1920s.[40] The death rate among African Americans in Durham similarly improved, dropping from 29.9 to 22.4 per thousand during the same decade. Significantly, Lincoln's focus on women and children's health, through prenatal guidance, mothers' classes, nutrition programs, well-baby clinics, and midwives' training, all led by nurses, dramatically decreased deaths among women and their infants. Durham County reported that black infant mortality, at over 400 deaths per thousand live births in 1910, fell to 196.0 per thousand by 1923 and to 173.5 per thousand by 1924. In the end, individual and organized efforts between doctors and nurses, teachers and students, clubwomen and volunteers, and white donors and black administrators combined to ameliorate health problems and mortality among Durham's black population, especially among women and children.[41]

"Education Will Best Fit Them for Service to God and Their State"

The ravages of disease struck African Americans and whites alike; thus the threat of death motivated important collaborative efforts. Durham's black elite could effectively exercise their skill at racial diplomacy in the matter of health care because those gains benefited both races. The drive to expand educational opportunities for black children was a far more contentious matter. For the most part, whites preferred that blacks receive no education at all. When in 1902 the North Carolina Bureau of Labor surveyed farmers about a compulsory education law, all but a few white respondents objected because the law would apply to African Americans as well as whites. "When you educate a negro it ruins them for labor," one complained. Another concluded, "We can't raise cotton and tobacco with a compulsory education law."[42]

For their part, African Americans demanded more and better education. Rev. J. F. Jordan answered the same survey from the perspective of African American parents and teachers: "I think compulsory education is an absolute necessity," he argued. "You may think this statement very strong, coming from a negro preacher and editor, but this is my honest conviction. I am in [a] position to know, to some extent, the conditions of my people in this state. I know an education will best fit them for service to God and their State." African Americans like Jordan championed education for the potential it held for black youngsters, promising principled guidance as well as literacy and learning that could raise standards of living and yield democratic citizenship. Whites defined that citizenship as second-class and used blacks' illiteracy as an argument for disfranchisement. African Americans' enthusiasm for education, some whites feared, might increase their demands for the vote, for if the larger purpose of public education was to train youth for the responsibilities of citizenship in a democracy, it would certainly prepare African Americans for that goal. Once they became a part of the electoral arena, whites dreaded, ideas of social equality might follow, or worse, black domination. Literacy readied African Americans to meet a requirement to vote. But whites also opposed compulsory education because it drew black child laborers out of the fields and the factories and into the classroom. Indeed, a compulsory school law "would put two negro children in school every time it put one white child," as one white farmer charged. Whites also framed their opposition in terms of taxation, fearing that white funds might be used to educate black people. As another farmer warned the Bureau of Labor, "The burden will be on the white race to partly educate a lot of worthless negroes, who are too independent already."[43]

Confronted with these obstacles, African Americans — the elite and the folk — experienced congested, inadequate schools that white officials had set aside for them. But they sought better. Educator William G. Pearson, whom C. C. Spaulding described as "identified with every phase of negro progress and uplift in Durham," served as principal of Whitted School and by extension as the unofficial superintendent of all public black schools in Durham, city and county. Positioned directly between white administrators and black people, Pearson always took a conservative approach to public politics, although he had been active as a Republican. He lacked the autonomy that he had in his business ventures and in black-controlled institutions like Lincoln Hospital. Pearson, born a slave in Durham, had witnessed persistent school burnings in the last third of the nineteenth century, and thus he defined progress as acquiring something whites did not want African Americans to have. Beloved despite — or perhaps because of — his difficult position, "Prof Pearson," as he was known among Durham blacks, persevered with "race cooperation" to obtain almost every benefit available to African Americans in elementary and secondary education.[44]

A man of few public speeches, Pearson allowed his race politics to be defined by his reputation and his actions. He had been outspoken on the matter of black education since his days as a Republican activist in the 1880s. One of the group that abandoned the early North Carolina Mutual venture, Pearson played a supportive rather than leading role in the multiple enterprises of the black elite. His name always appeared as a board member or executive of local black institutions as each was founded in the early twentieth century. In 1920, he founded the Fraternal Bank and Trust Company, serving as president, and its forerunner, the People's Building and Loan Association. Locating these institutions in the Hayti business district, Pearson intended the banks to attract and serve customers who refused to go to the Mechanics and Farmers Bank downtown near the Mutual. Eventually, Fraternal and People's both merged with Mechanics and Farmers, which opened a branch in Hayti. Pearson also owned extensive real estate and a number of tenements that he rented to migrants. He continued to serve as well as the Supreme Grand Scribe of the Royal Knights of King David, as head cashier for Mechanics and Farmers Bank, and as trustee of Lincoln Hospital. Pearson was more devoted to education than to business, but his business income allowed him to live comfortably despite his small salary as a school principal. Pearson's wealth also freed his wife, Minnie Sumner Pearson, from work. When they married, she left her job as a teacher and gave her time to community efforts through her missionary work at St. Joseph AME Zion Church and through civic organizations, including the North Carolina Federation of Colored Women's Clubs.[45]

Lest whites believe that Pearson was too uppity, the *Durham Morning Herald* assured its readers in an editorial that the principal placed himself squarely on the conservative side of the public education debates among black leaders. Praising Pearson, the newspaper wrote: "It has been said by some that negroes, given a slight taste of liberal arts, learn to look with disgust upon the industrial arts, but the teachings of Professor Pearson [have] neither encouraged nor tolerated such thoughts, as he holds that the moral effect of industry is that it promotes self-respect and self-reliance."[46] Often powerless to do more than sustain his school, Pearson was accountable directly to his patrons, including school board president Julian S. Carr Jr., who appointed him principal, and to Carr's colleagues and successors on the local board of education. For that reason, he may have leaned toward a publicly conservative position in order to obtain those programs that whites were willing to support.

Other black leaders, such as Aaron Moore, whose autonomy as a physician gave him more leeway, demanded what Pearson could not. Moore remained as adamant about education in the twentieth century as he had been as a Republican, complaining to state officials that African Americans "in the main have not had enough schooling to either fit them for the demands of urban life or to make them content in the rural districts." As a consequence, he pointed out, "the criminal class" remained "discouraged and nonproductive constituents." The inequities in education also disturbed him. "The Durham County Board gave twice as much for each white child enrolled as for each colored child," he protested to the state's educational administration.[47] If the doctor needed an opening to publicly advocate for African Americans' educational needs, he found two: southern whites' ambivalence about public education and their uneasy alliance with northern philanthropists.

Public education presented white southerners with an intrinsic dilemma, especially as African American claims increased. On the one hand, universal education could effect economic progress by creating better workers and improving the external image of a region perceived by the North as backward and unlearned. Thus white liberals and reformers supported an educational renaissance in North Carolina in the early 1900s. On the other hand, southern white officials also feared that any movement toward compulsory education might have to incorporate blacks and that their white constituencies might resist. The decision to support public education rested on political priorities rather than racial ideologies or educational thought. Because the disfranchisement amendment limited suffrage to literate voters (unless they had registered under the grandfather clause), thousands of illiterate white voters could fail the required reading test unless compulsory education was required of whites. "The warning of the Amendment to those who cannot read and write after 1908 is all the spur that the law can give the people," white Durhamite C. K. Robinson wrote the Bureau of Labor. One solution to the white voting problem was to provide public education to white children so as to sustain white supremacy into the next generation.[48]

Some whites opposed compulsory education under any circumstances, but the threat of federal intervention loomed largely enough as an issue for white politicians to make public education for blacks a way to avoid that possibility. Charles D. McIver, a white education reformer, feared that rejecting universal education outright in North Carolina would "arouse hostility among people outside of the state who are now silent in the [suffrage] amendment." He spoke with authority as secretary and field agent of the Southern Education Board (an umbrella organization of northern philanthropies interested in southern education), as a member of the governor's Central Campaign

Committee, and as president of the State Normal and Industrial College at Greensboro. If the suffrage amendment that had disfranchised blacks went to the Supreme Court, McIver worried, "it may be declared unconstitutional." In order to maintain that racial barrier to voting and to avoid a court decision unfavorable to white southerners' political hegemony, McIver concluded, it was useful for southern politicians to include blacks in their plans to extend at least limited public education to all.[49]

North Carolina's superintendent of public instruction, J. A. Joyner, responded to other white concerns. Admitting that he preferred not to deal with "this most perplexing problem of the education of the Negro, about which there are so many conflicting and divergent positions among my people," Joyner laid to rest the question of taxation. "The Constitution," he wrote, "directs that in the distribution of funds no discrimination shall be made in favor of either race." The black population made up 32 percent of the state's population, but they received "less than seventeen percent of the school money." Joyner correctly assessed that compared to "taxes, fines, forfeitures, penalties," and the other monies that blacks "constitutionally" contributed to public coffers, whites actually "contributed" very little to black education. In addition to noting the issue of a double tax burden on blacks, Joyner gave one other reason to assure access for blacks to schools. "If the Negroes become convinced that they are to be deprived of their schools and of the opportunities for an education," he argued, "most of the wisest and most self-respecting negroes will leave the state," leaving behind "only the indolent, worthless, criminal part of the Negro population."[50]

Using out-migration and federal intervention as risk factors and armed with their own sense of rightness, southern education reformers like McIver, Joyner, and Nathan C. Newbold, the State Agent for (Negro) Rural Schools, developed a plan of action. The "people outside of the state" to whom McIver referred strengthened the position of white officials at home. To further their goal of converting the South to northern standards of social welfare and economic efficiency, northern donors took an interest in southern education and figured prominently in educational schemes for the state. The Peabody Fund, established in 1867, for example, provided funds to be administered "for the welfare of the suffering South" and supported the Hampton-Tuskegee model of industrial education. The Slater Fund, founded in 1887, provided "support of furthering Negro education," underwriting, for example, the Slater Industrial and Normal School at Winston-Salem, renamed Winston-Salem Teachers College. The General Education Board (GEB), through the John D. Rockefeller Foundation, "promoted education in the

United States without regard to race, sex, or creed." The Julius Rosenwald Fund supported the building of a number of black public schools in North Carolina, including some in Durham County. Finally, the Anna T. Jeanes Fund established the Jeanes Supervising Industrial Teacher program in 1907. These and other northern trusts granted money to support education for southern blacks and pressured southern whites to cooperate in improving the region economically.[51]

Through the various programs, northern whites collaborated with at least some white southern reformers to liberalize southern educational policy. Thirsting for money, white southerners, promoters and detractors of black education alike, accepted northern benefaction. Money helped foster compatible perspectives and gave southern educators a way to justify their work, at least administratively, regarding black education. Philanthropists and their officers arbitrated the ideological conflict between intransigent white southerners who insisted on exclusion and their reform-minded counterparts who perceived black education as a form of functional supervision, mollifying both with the assurance that industrial training reinforced African Americans' subordinate position. Strongly influenced by Booker T. Washington and believing they understood African American needs better than blacks themselves, philanthropists proved reluctant to underwrite classical education offered at the private and denominational institutions like Fisk University in Nashville, Tennessee. Established by African Americans and northern missionaries right after the Civil War, Fisk, Howard, Talledega, and other black elite schools prepared the Talented Tenth for leadership. Rather, white philanthropists promoted the Hampton-Tuskegee model where black teachers trained black children in agricultural, industrial, and domestic arts and sciences.[52]

Beneficent whites argued that industrial education prepared African Americans for the jobs they would most likely — and should, in their judgment — perform: occupations that placed them under whites' authority. Furthermore, they asserted, industrial education, imbued with moral dictates, served as a form of social control. Industrial education did not mean training for work in industry, factories, or other mechanized fields. Instead, industrial training entailed teaching black students to shed those characteristics they were assumed to possess: irresponsibility, unreliability, idleness, and ineptness. Under the guise of providing correctives to social problems, the "gospel of work," as shared by white reformers and some black elites, amounted to behavior modification, intended to inculcate aptitude and attitude. In the name of uplift, this strategy actually worked to confine the black masses to subservient positions like household labor. These attitudes combined to undermine African American self-determination. Black educators who sought support from one of the funds got money only by offering programs consistent with reformers' ideals. Approval from Tuskegee went a long way as well. The institution's extension department, for example, administered the Rosenwald funds used to build county schools for blacks. Thus African Americans who dissented from Washingtonian ideas either failed or struggled against enormous odds to succeed.[53]

In 1909, James E. Shepard faced just such a problem when he founded the National Religious Training School and Chautauqua for the Colored Race in Durham (later known as North Carolina College for Negroes and presently as North Carolina Central University). Like his colleagues among the capitalists, Shepard embraced a nationalist sentiment that exploited segregation to further racial destiny. But when Shepard applied for funds from the GEB, one evaluator wrote: "The plan of the institution as set forth in the prospectus embrace[s] a college or university on the one hand and a Chautauqua or training school on the other. . . . Three departments are operating: a literary department[,] a theological department, and a commercial department." Modeling his school on Northfield Academy in Massachusetts, Shepard intended to train students to be missionaries, ministers, businesspeople, and teachers, exceptional but representational. According to Shepard's vision of black education as he articulated it to whites, industrial training and academic training went "hand in hand" with moral training. His language evoked the Booker T. Washington spirit: "It awakens the sluggish, dormant energies and turns them into channels of usefulness and service."[54]

But Shepard's intellectual ambitions for students were beyond what whites would tolerate. Philanthropists, who preferred the Hampton-Tuskegee model, gave his proposed academic program little attention. In fact, the GEB criticized the leader's "largely one-man enterprise," his refusal to affiliate with any denomination, and his "perfectly free hand." The GEB inspectors reported, "It is difficult to see what place this institution could fill that other institutions do not." The correspondence between Shepard and the GEB illuminates the ideological conflict between black educators and independent white administrators. Although the National Religious Training School produced teachers, conducted summer institutes for ministers and educators, and sponsored conferences on education, the GEB refused all of Shepard's applications precisely because he attempted to set his own agenda. The GEB offered "no objections" formally to the plan, but it also offered no money. Consequently, the institution struggled to stay afloat and floundered between 1909 and 1924, closing briefly in 1915 due to lack of funds.[55]

But Shepard did not give up easily. Before it closed that year, the National

Religious Training School had offered summer schools for black teachers, conducted conferences for ministers, and brought speakers to town, among them W. E. B. Du Bois and clubwoman Mary Church Terrell.[56] It took Shepard all those years to shore up the institution, and as in the case of the hospital, doing so required resources, policy shifts on the part of southern whites, and compromises on the part of African Americans. Northern philanthropists and southern reformers controlled black education, philosophically and financially, and they defined the type of schooling African Americans should design and offer. Benefactors believed they wielded power to determine who among African Americans should preside over the institutions: those who had proven credible, that is, those who had aligned themselves with the industrial educational agenda. Thus, for the most part, black educational initiatives underwritten by one of the funds employed doctrines and practices consistent with overseers' ideologies. Filtered through white administrators — state agents, fund directors, school boards, and supervisors — these philanthropies rarely assisted independent efforts by blacks.

Education in settings outside the public schools made more effective community initiatives possible. African Americans used a range of public spaces to gain access to learning. Churches, barbershops, beauty parlors, and other arenas controlled by black people also served as places for reading, discussion, and analysis. A library could have served community interests well, but African Americans were prohibited from using the Durham County Public Library. Durham County had used Rosenwald funds to set up libraries in rural black schools, but black city schools were ineligible and thus went without. Unable to draw on philanthropic bequests for this purpose, African Americans amassed their own resources. In 1913, Aaron Moore organized the Durham Colored Library for the purpose of "placing good wholesome reading matter in the reach of our Negro boys and girls," seeking specifically to "help those who are not able to select and purchase books for themselves." Initially located in a basement room of the White Rock Baptist Church, the collection moved in 1916 to a small brick building on Fayetteville Street, the main street in Hayti, built on property purchased from John Merrick. James B. Duke contributed $1,000, but Durham's black citizens, the Sunday schools of White Rock Baptist and St. Joseph AME Zion Church, and women's organizations raised the remainder and maintained the library over the years.[57]

Just as women supported Lincoln Hospital's work, they sustained the library's programs. Hattie Wooten, the first librarian, managed the institution, assisted patrons, and developed programs in reading for both children and adults. In 1932, Selena Warren, daughter of Dr. Stanford L. Warren, who became superintendent of Lincoln Hospital when Aaron Moore died, succeeded Wooten and expanded the library's services. Under Warren's direction, the library offered literacy and reading programs, distributed books in neighborhoods, the hospital, and schools, and enlarged its collection by nearly 11,000 books. The library served as a center for adult education in particular. The Volkamenia Literary Club established a newspaper reading circle that taught literacy as a step toward voter registration. Reading groups, discussion groups, and book signings enhanced community intellectual life. For children, the library offered summer programs and showed movies as an alternative to the segregated theaters of downtown. Hence, like the hospital, the library joined men's public involvement and women's organizing abilities to enhance community life.[58]

As the case of the Stanford L. Warren Library illustrates, African Americans initiated most of the education programs that benefited their community, including requests for philanthropic or public funds. For instance, to support a field worker on behalf of the North Carolina Teachers Association, Aaron Moore raised $325 through the Masonic Lodge. An autonomous and assertive leader who answered to no one but his conscience and community, Moore was positioned to make demands of whites. He appealed directly to Nathan C. Newbold for attention to the state's "colored" rural school facilities. Moore's request, strengthened by pressure from black leaders, teachers, and communities, convinced Newbold to gather applications to the Anna T. Jeanes Fund in 1915 from ten North Carolina counties. The Jeanes Supervising Industrial Teachers, chosen from among the best of experienced black public schoolteachers, augmented the work of the rural one-room schoolteachers with training, assistance, and demonstrations at little cost to the county. Dissatisfied with the lack of response from his local board of education, Moore circumvented board members and personally visited Newbold's office in 1916 to request a Jeanes teacher for Durham County.[59]

Moore initiated the Jeanes program locally, but women delivered education throughout the state, a pattern that operated to African Americans' advantage. In accordance with the program's doctrines, "they taught cooking, sewing, gardening, basketry, chair caning, rug making, paper cutting, millinery, carpentry," and other manual labor successfully, as Newbold reported to the Jeanes Fund in 1917.[60] But because the Jeanes program entrusted African American teachers with the hands-on part of the school programs, it also facilitated their independence. A virtual army of community organizers, Jeanes teachers visited homes, classrooms, and churches. According to

Newbold's report, thirty-five North Carolina Jeanes teachers visited 1,145 county schools in 1917 alone. "Teachers have been quick to see that the public gathering is a good place to promote their work," Newbold wrote. "They organiz[ed] 483 Improvement Leagues, 788 community meetings, 135 county meetings." Because they called their own meetings, they created forums where parents, teachers, and local leaders assembled, strategized, and mounted challenges to what the state offered African Americans educationally. According to Newbold, in the name of promoting "better health, better homes, and better school conditions," Jeanes teachers organized local communities to achieve several other outcomes, including "extended school terms, 62 new schools erected, 39 repaired." African Americans themselves provided most of "the labor, materials and cost of the improvements."[61]

Beyond organizing school building and improvement programs, however, African Americans exerted little control over educational reform. Matching grants projects, like Jeanes and Rosenwald programs, "presumed cooperation" among the agencies, the state and county boards of education, white supervisors, Jeanes teachers, and the black community. "Presumed cooperation" still translated into white control. To allay the Durham school board's fears that Jeanes teachers acted too independently — all the more suspect in light of Moore's end run around local authorities — Newbold assured the Durham County Board of Education that their Jeanes teacher worked as a "regular employee" of the county and was "subject to the supervision and direction of the county superintendent."[62]

These complex cooperative ventures presented African Americans with compound problems. First, philanthropy did not necessarily encourage the development of new projects but often supported projects African Americans were already doing on their own. Funders viewed preexisting projects like Mothers' Clubs, Civic Leagues, Homemakers Clubs, and literacy programs as worthy of their investments. In Durham in 1916, for example, $100 from the GEB supported a Homemakers Club, previously a canning club. Similarly, Moonlight Schools, another Jeanes assignment, provided adult literacy classes at night and evening schools. In 1916, Pauline Dame taught in one of seven such schools that operated in Durham County. Her class enrolled sixty-five people, aged thirty-five to sixty. But these, too, were already set up in churches and at the Warren Library.[63]

Second, white school officials forced African Americans to bear most of the costs not covered by philanthropy. Durham's Frank Husbands, one of the few male Jeanes supervisors, earned a salary of thirty-five dollars per month for six months' work in 1916, only fifteen dollars of which was paid by the county, with the remainder coming from the Jeanes Fund. W. H. Wanna-maker of the Durham County School Board, opposed to spending public funds on African American education, took advantage of Husbands's services and admitted that the county benefited from the Jeanes program. But he balked at a request to increase Husbands's salary the next year, writing to Newbold: "It is a little harder to get the public—white, especially—to see the wisdom of paying out more."[64]

When Mattie Daye became the Jeanes supervisor for Durham County in 1917, the school board reluctantly agreed to increase its contribution to her salary by five dollars. But the personnel change also gave the board an op-portunity to ask Newbold for additional Jeanes funds to support her ex-penses. A potentially better program, Wannamaker understood, would "se-cure[e] considerable help for it from our progressive and well-to-do colored folk." Aaron Moore, hoping to maintain the county's interest, already had arranged a subsidy of an additional $2.50 per month for Daye's work. New-bold rejected the Durham board's request, but he did agree to offset the county's contribution to Jeanes with GEB funds for equipment and agreed to apply for a Rosenwald school for one of the county districts. In short, by trading one set of private subsidies for another, the state and county used mostly private funds to provide black public education. For the additional thirty dollars per year that Durham County paid Daye, the county got one hundred dollars from the GEB and a recommendation for a Rosenwald school that further relieved white taxpayers of responsibility.[65]

Third, such compromises among whites still cost African Americans money. The Rosenwald Fund matched contributions from the county for constructing new buildings, with African Americans making up the differ-ence. African Americans raised the funds to build the East Durham colored school.[66] The Rosenwald program also controlled all aspects of construction; the county school boards selected plans from a series of precise designs Rosenwald required. The title of the program led to the popular belief that the Rosenwald Fund paid for the schools, but the diversion of public tax funds resulted in African Americans paying taxes both directly to the public treasury and for black public education. African Americans therefore bore the major cost of building Rosenwald schools, with Jeanes teachers doing most of the organizing and collecting and black farmers donating the land. For example, each school required a minimum of two, and preferably three to five, acres of land, and black landowners usually donated the property.

Furthermore, although the county could draw on a state loan program to supply its share of the money, African Americans contributed as taxpayers to the public treasuries from which that loan was drawn and from which the county paid its part. In addition to raising their part of the necessary cash for construction, African Americans often provided the labor, supplies, and materials. With school taxes largely diverted to pay for white schools and blacks putting up private funds to finance their own public schools, African Americans paid more than the cost of their own education. And because black people provided so many of the resources necessary for school construction and Jeanes programs, white school officials had to allocate very little, not even praise.[67]

Despite their initial misgivings, southern white bureaucrats learned to accept and even negotiate for northerners' altruism. Chair of the Durham County school board W. H. Wannamaker wrote to Nathan Newbold for suggestions regarding programs to improve the county schools. "I would like to see one or two good negro schools here," he wrote, "in which girls and boys are taught the fundamental trades and occupations." Newbold recommended that the board build a county training school, "offering the industrial work which they [African Americans] ought to have." Such schools, Newbold explained, "would receive $500 from Slater Board toward teachers' salaries and also some assistance from the General Education Board for equipment." For a program focused on "vocational agriculture" for teenaged boys, the county could count on money from the Smith-Hughes Fund. Thus, county officials could design the programs to attract white philanthropy, but "in every case," Newbold added, "the Colored people ought to do everything they can in furnishing cash, labor, land, or material."[68]

Northern philanthropy made it possible to build schools in places where none had existed before and to improve some school facilities. The Durham County school system consolidated its multiple one-room schools into nineteen "colored districts" by 1919, employing two or three teachers in each. African Americans amassed enough resources to build eight of these schools as Rosenwald schools, some with libraries. Better facilities subsequently encouraged school attendance. Serving a growing number of children, teachers effected greatly improved literacy. Mattie Daye's 1919 school census noted only forty-two illiterate young people among African Americans, aged twelve to twenty-one, in the county.[69]

"The Harvest Is Great, but the Laborers Are Few"

As they did in black health care, African American women emerged as the fulcrum of black education, providing the labor, generating the primary force behind improving the schools, and increasing the number of black children who obtained a formal education. Pauli Murray's aunts, Pauline Fitzgerald Dame and Sallie Fitzgerald Small, had gone to work as teachers on the cusp of two significant educational changes for African Americans in North Carolina: the establishment of publicly supported schools and the shift in the teaching profession from a male- to a female-dominated occupation. They joined the legions of young women who entered college and took up careers in education; in 1890, the numbers for black men teachers and for black women teachers were virtually even in North Carolina, but within a decade, women outnumbered men.[70]

The black teaching force in Durham city schools was composed of two men and thirteen women in 1901. At the county level, where men traditionally had held positions as teachers and principals of one-room schools, black women held thirteen of eighteen positions in 1902. By 1910, the teaching force had doubled and the number of women teachers had tripled, with women outnumbering men in the field by more than three to one. In 1915, there were five male and twenty-nine female African American teachers in the city of Durham. As rural schools consolidated and the gender balance of teaching shifted even further, women held almost all of the appointments in the county schools, including three of the six new principalships in 1919.[71]

But in spite of all the efforts to build schools, African Americans could hope for little more than rudimentary schooling provided by an overworked and underpaid teaching staff. A county superintendent's report stated that, in 1900, twenty-six "colored schools" were scattered throughout the area, all "of the one-room type, of crude design, poorly furnished, ventilated and lighted."[72] Teachers' salaries also bore the mark of racial discrimination. Dora Barbee, a black county teacher, earned $17.50 per month in 1904 while a white teacher in the same district earned $40.75. The county appropriated another black school only $125 for the 1904–5 academic year, $67.50 for the fall and $57.50 for the spring — half the sum spent on the district's white school. This appropriation paid the teacher's salary, expenditures for equipment, books, and fuel, and the census taker. Increases gained one semester did not last into the next, when funds ran low. Sadie Husband earned a surprising $26.25 per month for the fall of 1905 but only $17.50 per month in the spring, and the entire school year lasted only a few months.[73]

A similar situation existed in the city, where black teachers routinely earned less than white teachers. Black teachers may have had less education than their white counterparts, but they carried a heavier load in terms of enrollments, facilities, and responsibilities. According to a 1915 report by the superintendent, two-thirds of the white teachers had college diplomas, but only one-tenth of black teachers were similarly educated. The remaining 90 percent — including all of the women — had received normal school educations, the equivalent of eighth grade.[74] But black schools presented teachers and their students with appalling working conditions. West End School, where Pauline Dame returned to work in 1910, and where her niece Pauli Murray attended school, served an impoverished community of black working-class migrants. A remote facility called "the school in the woods," West End sat just outside the edge of town. The "dilapidated, rickety, two-story, wooden structure" that Murray remembered sat on a clay yard across the road from Liggett and Myers tobacco warehouses.[75]

Looking more like one of the warehouses than a school, West End was built so haphazardly that it creaked and swayed in the wind. "When there was a windstorm you could just hear the wind blowing through," Murray recalled. Carried in the wind, tobacco dust, "brown silt, like fine snuff," came through the cracks. On the outside, West End was covered with peeling paint and paint blisters; on the inside, bare splintery floors, leaky plumbing, and broken drinking fountains evidenced disrepair. Students "wade[d] through pools of foul water" to get to restrooms that were always out of order. Murray remembered the closest white school for equally poor white children as "a beautiful red and white brick building on a wide paved street," replete with lawns and flower gardens, equipped with playgrounds, and surrounded by an eight-foot fence topped with barbed wire. She and her classmates used the "greasy, torn, dog-eared" books handed down by the white students who attended these better-equipped schools. With too few books for too many users, West End students learned mostly by recitation, progressing through several levels of first grade before continuing to the second grade. Pauli Murray wrote of her elementary school experience: "Our seedy run down school told us that if we had any place at all in the scheme of things it was this separate place, marked off, proscribed and unwanted by white people. . . . We came to know that whatever we had was always inferior."[76] Nonetheless, whites complained about providing black education. A white farmer from Durham County wrote to the Bureau of Labor: "I think the negroes are making more rapid strides along educational lines than the whites."[77]

County programs generated interest in education on the part of African American parents and teachers, but rural programs did little to improve urban education. Dependent on a school board that lacked the altruism of philanthropists, city facilities decayed. In 1885, Pauline Dame had taught seventy students aged six to twenty in grades one through eight at Durham's single "colored school," a one-room structure.[78] West End, where she taught in 1910, was little better than the old school had been, no more than the flimsy shell Pauli Murray described. Little had changed in the years in between. In 1911, the city claimed three black public schools: Whitted, West End, and East End.[79] The only school for African Americans in all of Durham County with grades above the third or fourth, Whitted attracted students from Rougemont, West End, East End, Hickstown, Walltown, and beyond. Citing enrollment pressures and increased interest among African Americans, the city expanded Whitted School to eight grades in 1912 and called it a "high school." Whitted had ten grades by 1917, but more grades did not necessarily translate into more advanced academic work for Whitted students. At the turn of the century, the white high school offered all four secondary grades and a range of subjects, including mathematics, sciences, history, English, Greek, Latin, drawing, and mechanical training. To the rudimentary skills students learned in county schools, in contrast, Whitted added little more than domestic sciences and manual training.[80]

Although W. G. Pearson acquired for his schools whatever white officials might offer, Whitted's expansion represented little more than further preparation for traditional black employment in low-paid vocations or, worse, occupations that were rapidly disappearing. In the fall of 1912, as steam laundries replaced washerwomen, Whitted added laundry to the cooking and sewing classes already in place. In the manual trades, Whitted offered woodworking and furniture making, even as mechanization transformed these vocations from crafts to manufacturing jobs reserved for white men.[81]

But even these small steps in public education were enormous accomplishments for Durham blacks. According to a 1916 Phelps-Stokes report, Durham and Raleigh were the only two cities in North Carolina to offer "some high school work." Southern schools lagged behind those in other parts of the country. Consequently, graduates from the Durham public school system discovered that their program did not meet the criteria for the completion of a "high school" education outside of the South. Most high schools for southern blacks did not provide an accredited four-year program or a high school diploma adequate for admission to a northern college. African American students who reached secondary education did so by attending one of North Carolina's eleven denominational schools that maintained four-year programs or one of the handful of privately funded institutions like Charlotte Hawkins Brown's Palmer Institute. Otherwise, only by admission to the State Technical and Agricultural College at Greensboro or to one of the three normal schools or by leaving the South altogether could a student attain an acceptable high school education. To qualify for "open admission" at New York's Hunter College in 1926, for example, Pauli Murray had to earn two and a half more years of high school credits.[82]

Like their counterparts in the county, then, African Americans in the city depended on a poorly paid, overworked force of teachers who were allowed to train students in little more than basics. Advanced teacher training, provided through state- and agency-funded summer institutes, offered black educators minor improvements in their own instructional skills. For example, the state's 1919 summer school program for black teachers, as outlined by Superintendent Newbold, consisted of a few sessions in pedagogy, "reading, spelling, number work, writing and nature work." But the guidelines emphasized domestic arts, specifically "cooking, breads, meats, desserts, canning, preserving, [and] drying, sewing, basketry, shuck mats, chair caning and repair," manual instruction in "keeping fences, gates, door steps, etc. in repair," and "learning to make simple things, axe handles, hoe handles, brooms, fly screens, fly traps, foot stools, box furniture, and any thing that is needed around the home or barnyard." Lastly, teachers were encouraged to learn school management, school law, and gardening, especially in response to the shortages that occurred during World War I. The state recommended that white local superintendents be invited to lecture at black teachers' summer institutes on such subjects as patriotism and the food supply.[83]

Summer institutes for African American teachers differed from training provided for white teachers. The Durham summer institute for white teachers, held at Trinity College, went further than demonstration classes, to focus on "reading, phonetics, spelling, arithmetic, geography, and grammar besides professional subjects."[84] But the program for black teachers followed the basic state outline. Receiving minimal instruction on academic subjects, their institute offered "very constructive" work in rug making, weaving, and canning. Principal Pearson himself, in what the *Durham Morning Herald* called "the real methods in teaching," demonstrated soap making and basket making. Praising his technique, the *Herald* concluded: "Pearson is doing things that will fit the teachers for the places they will have to hold." Following the state's suggestions, Durham superintendent C. W. Massey lectured teachers on "moral power," and John Sprunt Hill, a local white businessman, spoke on conservation for the war effort. The Durham program did add black speakers. James E. Shepard lectured the teachers: "You are to teach love, thrift, patriotism, and loyalty." And Pearson himself lectured on the importance of morning opening exercises, including music, prayer, and scripture lessons. Whatever the curricular shortcomings of the program, summer school provided black teachers with the opportunity to network, organize, and improve their skills. Of the 4,000 black teachers in North Carolina, 2,500 registered for summer school in 1924.[85]

Translated into classroom work and reinforced by Jeanes teachers and public health nurses, summer school offerings facilitated improvements in students' quality of life, even if they did not provide significant change in their academic attainment. Students learned to make minor improvements on the homes where they lived. Sewing classes taught those who owned little clothing to make their own. Cooking classes encouraged better nutrition and diet. Gardening helped families who survived on cash crops to increase the yield from their plots. And instructions on cleanliness and sanitation served to improve health and increase life spans. In addition to the standard curriculum, black teachers certainly instilled race pride and self-esteem in their students. Theresa Jan Cameron Lyons fondly recalled the role that teachers played in her life. A descendant of slaves on the Cameron plantation north of Durham, Lyons grew up very poor. Because her family of tenant sharecroppers relocated from farm to farm in search of fairer landlords and better land, she moved from school to school. Motivated by her teachers and compelled by her poverty, Lyons worked hard to catch up. If nothing more, the presence of black teachers suggested possibilities beyond the drudgery of farm labor. "When I'd go to school and I would see the teachers and they had cars and they were dressed nice, I would say, 'there *is* another world.' "[86]

Most students, including Lyons's cousins, did not continue into the upper grades. Many lived lives divided between school, the farm, and the household, and, among the three, school came last. Called to work or home by family need, the vast majority of Durham's black students went to work in the tobacco factories or in white homes as soon as they reached their teens. Whitted School enrolled only fifty high school students in 1917, including twenty-five in the eighth grade, eleven in the ninth grade, and fourteen in the tenth grade.[87] For the most part, Whitted aimed to prepare students for hard work in perpetually low-paid employment and for good citizenship, defined by whites as good behavior. Only a few might continue on to higher education or to a prominent position in the community. These were held up as examples of Whitted's achievement and consequently the success of the educational philosophy under which they were trained.

For example, a 1918 editorial in the *Durham Morning Herald* called for "more and better education for the colored population." Citing a survey of graduates of the Whitted School, including "the manager of the North Carolina Mutual and Provident Association [Charles C. Spaulding] as an example of the school's good work," the *Herald* argued that education had "tended to eliminate crime among the colored people" and had produced "a body of men and women who are highly desirable citizens, people who are working for the betterment of the race and the community."[88] Such praise meant little in terms of benefits. When the city school board refused to spend $100 from its budget to finance the 1919 summer school in Durham, Pearson paid the money out of his own pocket. Newbold visited the program and, pleased with what he saw, arranged for a $100 contribution from the Jeanes Fund toward expenses.[89]

Teachers passed their heavy burdens on to students; those who attained an advanced education inherited the charge to advance the race. But success in some ways wrought its own dilemmas. Commencements, exhibits, speakers, and school programs brought the African American community together to admire and celebrate students' accomplishments, stressing achievements over defeats, instilling pride in the student and their parents and friends, and winning prizes. But these events also put children, teachers, and principals on display for the purposes of whites' self-congratulation. Open to the white public, black public schools, teacher training sessions, and school programs exposed African American students and educators to scrutiny. Ironically, high accolades brought more visitors, not fewer, as whites felt free to slight, offend, and insult students and teachers. At the same time, parents, teachers, and students yearned to display their progress to the public, despite white criticisms. To black families, student exhibitions of arts and crafts, music recitals and recitations, and annual graduations represented race pride or achievement. The *Herald* assured the public that Principal Pearson was simply keeping his students and teachers under control and in line with white expectations.[90]

African American women did much of the hands-on work for schooling in a system where whites were disinclined to allow African Americans to exercise control. They were vulnerable, therefore, to pressure from whites who, as administrators, had license to interrupt and encroach upon their classrooms and their spaces. The sponsors upon whom black administrators depended — from superintendents to philanthropists — reserved the right to influence and critique students and teachers. Such "unavoidable contact" with white people built up "silent resentment," Pauli Murray penned. "There was the school superintendent who came to our annual exercises, stood on the rostrum beaming with affability, and made a speech praising us for our progress. We children sat taut waiting for the chilling moment when he smiled condescendingly and said, 'You people,' or 'You're a credit to your race.' We knew without turning our head that our teachers had also stiffened." Without restraint, white visitors censured what they disliked and saw no need to justify their intervention. African Americans, dependent on whites' goodwill, often were forced to stifle their objections. The insults took on gender connotations because women teachers suffered affronts more often than men. Pearson, for example, was referred to as "Professor," not always derisively among whites and always respectfully by blacks. But white observers consistently found opportunities to undermine women teachers' authority and insult or embarrass them by addressing black teachers only by their first names, even in front of their classes.[91]

Other than providing minimal assistance to improve school facilities, whites left African Americans to address their own concerns, within limits. The superintendents of public welfare enforced the compulsory attendance law when it finally was adopted in 1913, for example, but made the measure a low priority regarding black students. The State Board of Charities and Public Welfare, which supervised county welfare officials, gave little attention to African Americans before 1925, when it established the Division of Work among Negroes.[92] Even with new buildings, there were not enough classrooms to accommodate all of the students in the district. Annie W. Holland, head of North Carolina's Jeanes supervisors program, reported in a 1924 survey: "If the school attendance law was enforced there would be no place to take care of the children."[93] Furthermore, the work of educating black youngsters extended beyond the classroom and beyond the students themselves. A teacher in a small town, Pauli Murray explained, combined the roles of "instructor, social worker, truant officer, psychiatrist, adult education specialist, and community leader." After instructing their students during the day, her aunts taught parents and grandparents at night school. Maintaining a visible presence in the community where they taught required additional effort. On Sunday mornings, Pauline Dame and Sallie Fitzgerald taught Sunday school and went to services at St. Titus Episcopal Chapel. They then attended Second Baptist, their students' church, in the evening.[94]

Contact with students' communities was important because often the children themselves were reluctant to come to school and had to be encouraged. After taking attendance each morning, Durham teacher Marie Faulk left the classroom to locate her absent students and bring them to school. Here, too, individual teachers placed themselves between administrators and students and focused on the immediate problems to be solved. Teachers used their ties with missionary circles and women's clubs in attempting to address students' distress. Each year, Volkamenia club members, for example, asked city schoolteachers to submit a list of things their students needed. The

Volkamenia women then collected the items, sorted clothing by size and sex, and distributed the items to teachers.[95] Mabel Harris kept a closet in her classroom stocked with toiletries and extra clothing, and she often bathed students. These actions, of course, required teachers' sensitivities to students' pride. Harris explained: "We would take children to the bathroom, where other children couldn't know what was going on, because we wanted those children to feel wanted and not feel inferior to others . . . and the children, well, they would just cry." Despite the responsibilities poor youngsters carried, Harris said, "Children are just children."[96]

Annie Holland's Jeanes report highlighted economic hardships that the children faced. Poverty kept families from buying clothes, books, and supplies; sickness in the family required children to stay at home to assist; and the demand for child labor and, in particular, tenancy kept many youngsters out of school and in the fields, if not because of family need then because the landlord demanded their labor.[97] Theresa Jan Cameron Lyons struggled to stay in school. She recalled: "I went to school with shoes with holes in the bottom, where I had to put cardboard. Even though we could go sell tobacco and the stuff that we planted, after he [the landlord] took his share, there would be nothing left. And I would be so excited, I was thinking that I was going to get some new clothes, [but] there was nothing left." Lyons was dedicated to staying in school, but this came at a cost to her family who did without her labor: "I never wanted to live the kind of life my family was living. I wanted to learn to count money and to be able to say, 'no, not half.' "[98]

One issue of concern for black educators, especially teachers, was that of black parents, particularly those of the working class, whom teachers often perceived as unenlightened, uninformed, and uncooperative. To better understand their pupils' needs and to keep parents informed of students' progress, teachers called on students' homes regularly. Working-class parents perceived these visits as presumptuous intrusions, much the same way teachers viewed white supervisors' impertinent incursions on their classes. Teachers visited, parents believed, to judge their homes and ridicule their poverty.[99] For their part, however, teachers justified the means by the ends. In particular, black families who migrated from rural to urban areas were not in the practice of sending their children to school every day and needed persuasion. "They had to be trained," recalled Marie Faulk.[100] Teachers sometimes intervened between students and parents, pressuring the latter to allow children like Lyons to stay in school. Having the attention of white administrators, Annie Holland argued for better school facilities, transportation, and teacher training. But she also saw problems that the community could solve itself. "Lack of cooperation between teachers and parents," according to Holland, impeded teachers' work and children's education. Contending that "parents should be taught the value of an education and its importance in the life of the child," the Jeanes supervisor proposed that each school establish a Parent-Teacher Association (PTA).[101]

Through PTAS, in addition to home visits, teachers conveyed the importance of school to reluctant families. The otherwise publicly shy Pauline Dame gave a speech to an organizing meeting of the PTA at West End School. "Truly the harvest is great, but the laborers are few," she lamented. For too many African Americans, short-term family needs outweighed long-term investments in education. Black parents, lacking time, knowledge, and resources, proved reluctant to appear at school functions, meet with teachers, or get otherwise involved. Realistically, parents needed to turn the supervision of their children over to teachers while they worked. Parents and teachers thus shared the guidance of children, Dame reasoned. "It is our duty to train the young mind and make it strong and fully developed for future usefulness." Holding "mothers especially" accountable for children's upbringing, she asked, "Let us get together, come out to the meetings, and reason together."[102]

Educators like Pauline Dame, Marie Faulk, and Mattie Daye successfully rallied black parents around school causes. Once organized, African Americans found other ways to make their voices heard. At the teachers' institute in 1919, for example, county superintendent Massey held a session with the PTAS from the black county schools to hear from "the patrons regarding school conditions." Seizing the opportunity granted them — and seizing on the rhetoric of democracy used to rouse American efforts in World War I — black parents pointed out that the county spent eleven dollars per child on white schools but only four dollars per student on black schools. Massey, however, denied "discrimination on the part of the board in dealing with white and colored schools" and argued that poor facilities in some districts were "due to lack of cooperation of the part of the patrons with school authorities. . . . Whenever patrons manifest the proper interest, and took steps to better conditions," Massey insisted, the board of education "would meet them more than half way." In response, the parents suggested that "such interest could be aroused by giving negroes representation on the district school board."[103]

Forty years would pass in Durham before that suggestion gained serious attention from whites, although the thought, the desire, and the plan remained strong among blacks. In 1919, primary and secondary education problems seemed to have no resolution other than spending even more money and expending even more of teachers' energy. That year, the Durham school board promised to build two new high schools for the city, one for whites and one for blacks. Characteristically, a prideful city planned to spend on the black school "as much as half the amount expended on the white high school." When by 1920 the black high school still had not been built, African Americans expressed their frustrations another way. Whitted High School "burned mysteriously" to the ground, according to Pauli Murray. Not long after, East End and West End Schools also burned down.[104]

Previous school burnings in Durham had been instigated by whites who resented and resisted black gains. Durham's black educational facilities went up in flames whenever the political fires burned too hot. This time the burnings signaled the same problem from a different point of view. "It was rumored," Pauli Murray elucidated in her family history, "that the fires were not accidental but rather that the only way to get decent education for colored children was to burn down the old buildings." African Americans, it was rumored in the black community, had set the fire.[105] If so, then the fires represented a form of black agency but also revealed the limits of black leaders' abilities to satisfy community needs and the willingness of at least some African Americans to step beyond their leaders' strategies to try new and more forceful tactics. Unequivocally, students like Theresa Lyons respected teachers' work, and Pauline Dame and Mattie Daye surely gave their best. Aaron Moore and W. G. Pearson, did, too. But whites' resistance to black demands made the black leaders' and teachers' Herculean efforts seem paltry when compared to what the black community needed, wanted, and had earned.

Whatever facilities African Americans acquired proved "inadequate and inferior," as Pauli Murray wrote. Yet they were centers of community pride and dignity, and for that reason, black men and women often could transcend the inequities and tensions among themselves to concentrate on the task of improving a given institution. Even with the benefit of solidarity, however, change required more than what black teachers and black leaders, parents, and students could give and necessitated more voices than those of nurses, teachers, and male leaders. The black patriarchs' ability to deliver private and public funds to black causes illustrated their ability to wield influence in political matters beyond the vote, even as black public institutions demonstrated the limits of their political clout. But the covert action of burning schools spoke volumes about other blacks' frustration, which ran deeper than health care and educational issues. For Theresa Lyons's family, economic racism forced them to move from place to place trying to escape the poverty, debt, and unfairness that plagued them as sharecroppers. They rarely settled in one place long enough for Lyons to catch up with her class. Whether or not blacks actually burned down Whitted School in 1920 or whether the rumors represented wishful thinking, they still signified Lyons's sentiments. In the fiery language that leaders and teachers could not use, the torching of Whitted School and the idea of torching the school reflected African Americans' desire to say, "No, not half." African Americans were rethinking Merrick's advice: the time "to be as close friends as possible" had passed.

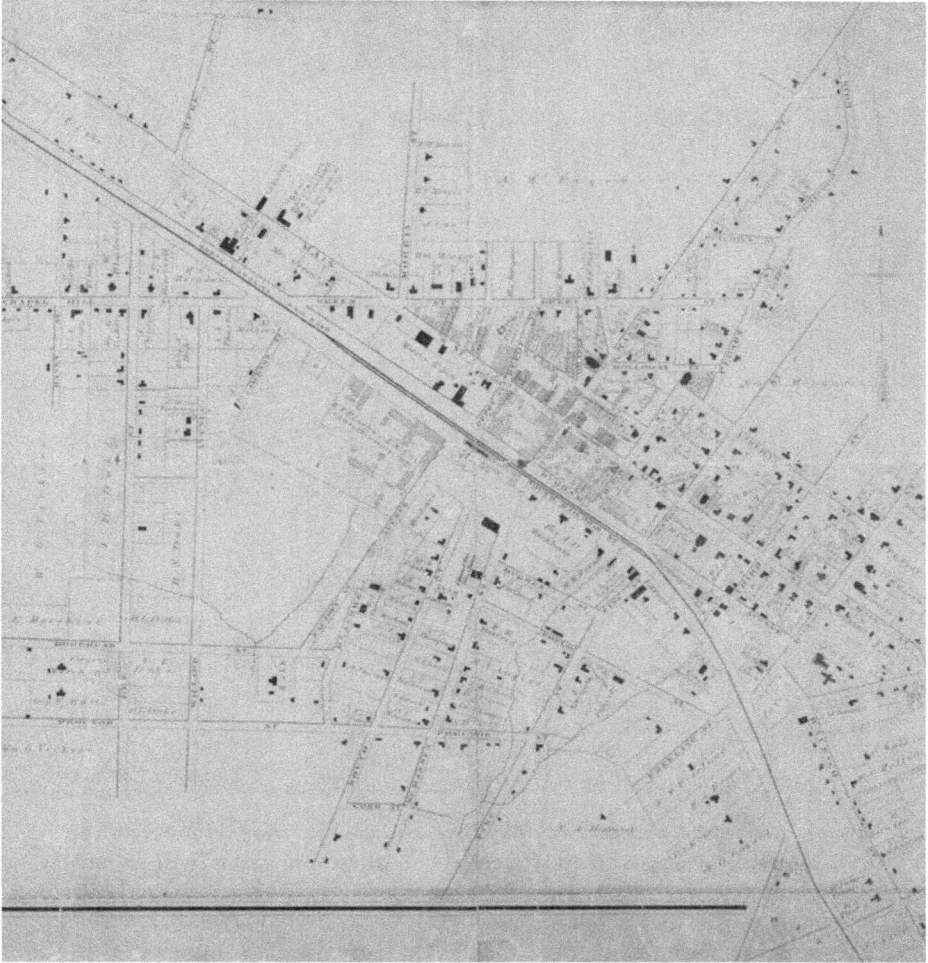

Gray's New Map of Durham, 1881. This is the first map of Durham to name streets and property owners. In the center, south of the railroad tracks, sits the "colored school." The Red Cross School marks the entrance to Hayti, which lies outside the official boundary of Durham proper. (Rare Book, Manuscript, and Special Collections Library, Duke University)

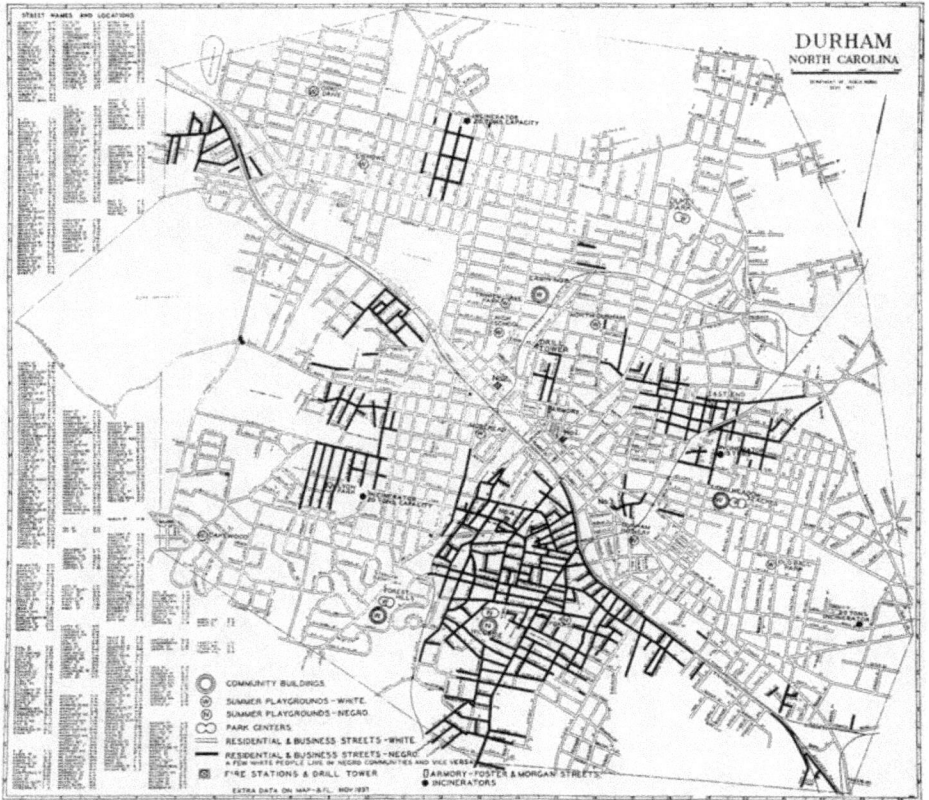

This map was created as part of a Works Progress Administration study of Durham in 1937. The dark lines marking the streets where African Americans lived reveal how racial segregation was inscribed into the landscape. The five black neighborhoods of Durham were, from the bottom and moving clockwise, Hayti, West End (Lyon Park), Hickstown, Walltown, and East End.

Freed in 1865 by the Thirteenth Amendment, Tempie Herndon Durham is pictured here at age 103, when she was interviewed for the Federal Writers' Project, sometime between 1936 and 1938. Tempie and her husband, Exter, had married when they were enslaved but had lived on plantations in different counties. Freedom meant they "could be together all the time, not just Saturday and Sunday." Together they decided that Exter should leave his ex-master and work for Tempie's ex-master, who they concluded was the fairer man. "We rented the land for a fourth of what we made," she recalled, and buying their freedom once more, they managed to buy a farm. (From *Born in Slavery: Slave Narratives from the Federal Writers' Project, 1936–1938*, North Carolina Narratives, vol. 11 [Washington, D.C.: Library of Congress, American Memory], <http://memory.loc.gov/cgi-bin/query/D?mesnbib:198:./temp/ammem_70Zo>)

Black family working tobacco. (Durham Historic Photographic Archives, North Carolina Collection, Durham County Library)

This photograph of the Durham County Home Prison Farm, ca. 1880, shows members of the white superintendent's family to the right and armed guards overseeing a work crew of black men and women. Prison farms, like the sharecropping system, became a means by which whites stole black labor. (Donated by Mrs. E. V. Leigh; Durham Historic Photographic Archives, North Carolina Collection, Durham County Library)

This drawing from *Frank Leslie's Illustrated Newspaper* depicts African Americans at a railroad station in preparation for departure from North Carolina. African Americans from the Tar Heel State joined the exodus of black folk from the South to Kansas, Oklahoma, and Indiana. They also left North Carolina for the North and further south seeking employment. Dissatisfied with working conditions, discrimination, violence, and politics, black people withdrew their labor from the factories and homes that made Durham a New South city. When families moved, they removed men, women, and children from the local labor force. Women also migrated out of the South alone to other areas where they might improve their living conditions. (From *Frank Leslie's Illustrated Newspaper*, 15 February 1890, 35; Library of Congress, Prints and Photographs Division)

Some families elected to stay on the land they had worked as slaves. This group, which includes three generations of family members, still lived at the Occoneechee plantation in the 1920s. (From the family album of Rufus Carr, Durham Historic Photographic Archives, North Carolina Collection, Durham County Library)

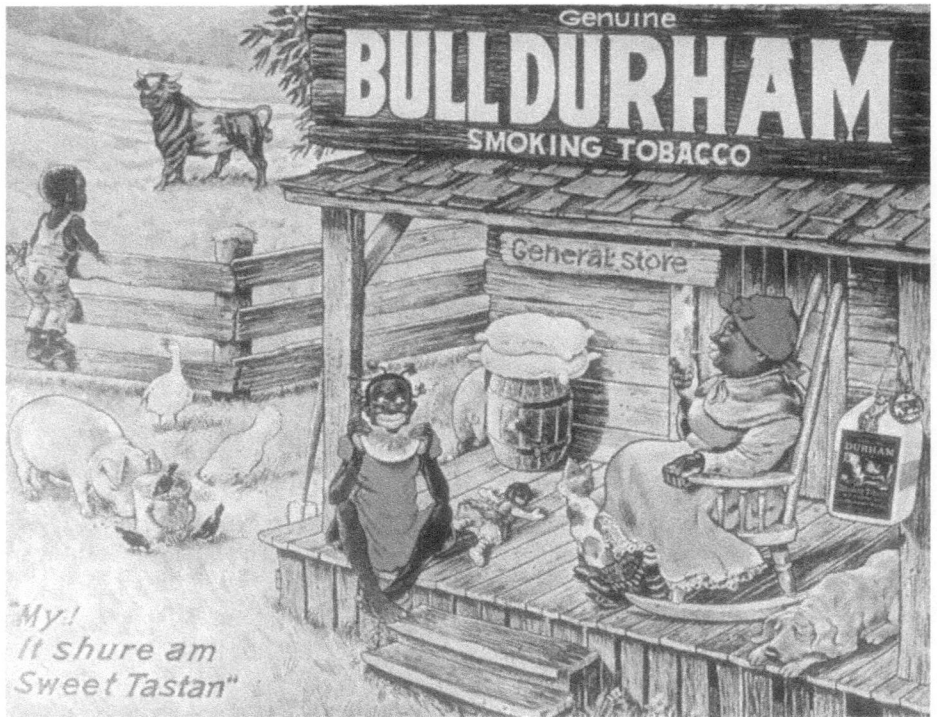

This advertisement for Bull Durham Tobacco was one in a series created by W. Duke & Sons that caricatured African American women, men, and children and let them know how their employers thought of them. (W. Duke & Sons Tobacco Collection, Rare Books, Manuscripts, and Special Collections Library, Duke University)

Graduating class of the Whitted School, ca. 1890. Education was one of the primary objectives of black folk in obtaining freedom's promises. After the Civil War, African Americans of all ages sought learning wherever they could, but the first phase in the struggle for black education was the campaign for universal education for children. The Whitted School in Durham was established as part of this movement. Few African American children could attend school, and fewer still could stay enrolled until graduation. Among those who could were the children of the aspiring class, who accumulated the resources to keep their children from having to work. Originally a free school, Whitted graduated some of Durham's most esteemed black citizens among freedom's first generation, including Charles C. Spaulding, president of the North Carolina Mutual Life Insurance Company. The next step in formal education was to attend normal school, and only the most fortunate could obtain professional training. (Durham Historic Photographic Archives, North Carolina Collection, Durham County Library)

West End School, 1906. Mary Pauline Fitzgerald Dame, who imparted a sense of dignity and race pride to two generations of students at the school, is pictured second from the right in a black dress. (Durham Historic Photographic Archives, North Carolina Collection, Durham County Library)

John Merrick, Charles C. Spaulding, and Aaron M. Moore, the North Carolina Mutual triumvirate. According to legend, after the first insurance settlement broke the bank, the other investors quit, leaving Merrick, Spaulding, and Moore to carry on the business. All three were nationally known as successful businessmen. (C. C. Spaulding Papers, Rare Books, Manuscripts, and Special Collections Library, Duke University; Durham Historic Photographic Archives, North Carolina Collection, Durham County Library)

Officers of North Carolina Mutual, 1911. *From left to right*: Aaron M. Moore, John M. Avery, John Merrick, Ed Merrick, and Charles C. Spaulding. (C. C. Spaulding Papers, Rare Books, Manuscripts, and Special Collections Library, Duke University; Durham Historic Photographic Archives, North Carolina Collection, Durham County Library)

North Carolina Mutual office staff, 1909. Mutual managers preferred that women not work but realized that young, educated African American women—including their daughters—provided a necessary workforce. The face of the company, Mutual women were known for their fashionable attire. Susie V. Gille, who arrived in Durham from the North in 1906 to work at the Mutual, is pictured at left in the second row. (C. C. Spaulding Papers, Rare Books, Manuscripts, and Special Collections Library, Duke University; Durham Historic Photographic Archives, North Carolina Collection, Durham County Library)

North Carolina Mutual office staff, 1940. Visitors to the company found black women at work, posed as though in a diorama. The third floor was "our territory," recalled Viola Turner, pictured here at left. Turner would become vice president of the Mutual in 1960. Bess Whitted, who was promoted to assistant treasurer in 1949, is second from right. (C. C. Spaulding Papers, Rare Books, Manuscripts, and Special Collections Library, Duke University; Durham Historic Photographic Archives, North Carolina Collection, Durham County Library)

Pictured here with director Bess Whitted (far right), the North Carolina Mutual Quartet thought of themselves as "singing ambassadors of goodwill." They performed for both black and white audiences. (C. C. Spaulding Papers, Rare Books, Manuscripts, and Special Collections Library, Duke University; Durham Historic Photographic Archives, North Carolina Collection, Durham County Library)

In 1910, during a tour of North Carolina, Booker T. Washington (middle row, sixth from right) visited Durham, where he preached at St. Joseph AME Zion Church and toured Hayti. He later wrote that Durham was "the city of cities to look for progress of Negroes." The Tuskeegean's praise shielded the assertiveness of black Durham's business community, allying it with his conservative politics. (Durham Historic Photographic Archives, North Carolina Collection, Durham County Library)

The North Carolina Mutual block. By 1921, black businesses including North Carolina Mutual, Mechanics and Farmers Bank, a clothing store, a shoe store, and a café spread along Parrish Street in downtown Durham. (C. C. Spaulding Papers, Rare Books, Manuscripts, and Special Collections Library, Duke University; Durham Historic Photographic Archives, North Carolina Collection, Durham County Library)

Jones Hotel, ca. 1921. Before Durham's Biltmore Hotel was built, black travelers to the city had to stay in boarding houses, rooming establishments, and small hotels. Managing these establishments was one of the few business opportunities available to black women. (From *Milestones along the Color Line* [1921])

Situated at the corner of Pettigrew and Fayetteville Streets, the Wonderland Theater was one of a number of prosperous businesses located in the center of black Durham's business district. This modern moviehouse was owned by Frederick K. Watkins, known as the Movie King. It offered the latest films and other entertainment for Durham African Americans. In this photograph from 1926, a poster advertises *The Barrier*, starring Lionel Barrymore. The auditorium at the Wonderland also served as a meeting place for the black members of the Tobacco Workers Union International during the 1920s and 1930s and other black organizations. A multipurpose building, the Wonderland also housed Watkins's real estate office and a beauty parlor. (Durham Chamber of Commerce Papers, Rare Book, Manuscript, and Special Collections Library, Duke University)

The first men called up to serve in World War I from Durham were African Americans. (Durham Historic Photographic Archives, North Carolina Collection, Durham County Library)

Gleaners Class homecoming, St. Mark's AME Zion Church, ca. 1930. The development of churches in Durham marked the expansion of the black community. Founded as part of the early Durham community, St. Mark's remained an important community institution well into the twentieth century. Sunday school class homecomings brought current members of the church together with people who were once affiliated with the church but had moved away. (From Elizabeth Holman, photograph by Willie T. Jones; Durham Historic Photographic Archives, North Carolina Collection, Durham County Library; reprinted with the permission of Rev. Dr. G. Ray Coleman)

Children enrolled in Scarborough Nursery, ca. 1935. (Clydie Fullwood Scarborough Papers, Rare Book, Manuscript, and Special Collections Library, Duke University)

Students at North Carolina College for Negroes, ca. 1920. (Durham Historic Photographic Archives, North Carolina Collection, Durham County Library)

Lincoln Hospital Nursing School graduation, 1930s. (Donated by the Lincoln Hospital Nursing School Alumni Association, Carolyn Henderson; Durham Historic Photographic Archives, North Carolina Collection, Durham County Library)

A woman doing laundry in Durham's Brookstown neighborhood. Household laborers like washerwomen preferred to take their work home where they could also watch their children. (Donated by Georgia Taylor; Durham Historic Photographic Archives, North Carolina Collection, Durham County Library)

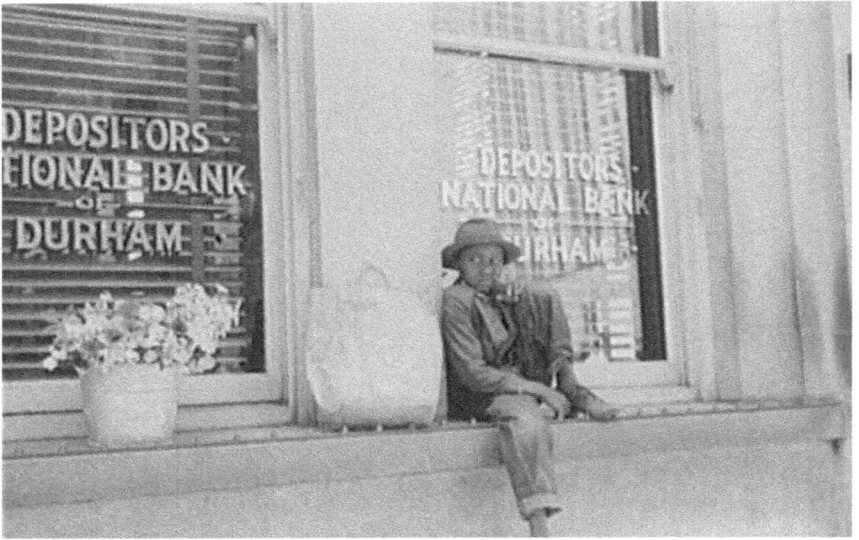

Young boy selling flowers in downtown Durham to farmers who have sold their crops. (Photograph by Jack Delano for the Farm Security Administration, Library of Congress, Prints and Photographs Division)

Shift change at the Liggett & Myers tobacco factory on Morgan Street, ca. 1930. Black workers emerge from the factory wearing aprons. Black and white women worked at different jobs in different buildings. (Donated by Dr. Louise Hall; Durham Historic Photographic Archives, North Carolina Collection, Durham County Library)

Fayetteville Street bus, ca. 1936. The Fayetteville Street bus ran from the rural suburbs to downtown Durham by way of the main thoroughfare in Hayti, Durham's largest black neighborhood. Because public transportation was racially segregated, requiring African Americans to sit in the back, many black women chose not to ride the bus. (Alvin T. Parnell Photograph Collection, Rare Book, Manuscript, and Special Collections Library, Duke University)

The immediate program of the American Negro means nothing unless it is mediate to his great ideal and the ultimate ends of his development. We need not waste time by seeking to deceive our enemies into thinking that we are going to be content with a half loaf, or by being willing to lull our friends into a false sense of our indifference and present satisfaction.

W. E. B. Du Bois, "The Immediate Program of the Negro" (1915)

6 : Helping to Win This War
Gender and Class on the Home Front

On Saturday, 30 March 1918, thousands of black folk gathered at the county courthouse to send off the first men from Durham called up to serve in World War I. They numbered ninety-four, all African American draftees for the new national army. The Sunday School Orchestra from White Rock Baptist Church played patriotic music for the crowd jamming the courtroom, the corridors, the stairs, and the streets. Members of the fraternal order, the Royal Knights of King David, all of them leading race men and a generation too old to serve, honored the inductees and lined them up for the march to Union Station where they entrained for Fort Jackson, South Carolina. When the recruits departed the courthouse, parading in squads of ten, a few spectators broke down in tears, but most beamed, waved, and cheered. "Durham didn't know it had such a colored population," the *Durham Morning Herald* reported, "until it watched the colored people gather at the court house and later at Union Station." It is unclear whether the crowd's number, spirit, or allegiance surprised the *Herald*, but the turnout was clear evidence of black dignity and pride. "When the colored soldiers went off to war," Pauli Murray penned, "Grandmother took me down to Union Station to see them go, and I was very excited over the parade of hundreds of colored men smartly dressed in new khaki uniforms and broad brimmed hats." Someone gave Murray one of those hats and she wore it constantly during the war years.[1]

According to the *Herald*, additional black registrants "begged" to replace the disqualified and the "slackers" who failed to show. "The spirit of the colored men was about the finest I have EVER seen," one army officer commented — "all that any patriotic American could wish to see in the men who are going to training." Indeed, black soldiers from the Durham area gave more than their share to the effort. They accounted for almost half of the men sent up by the Durham draft board, although they made up less than a third of the county's male population. The greater the number of black men called up by the Durham County board, the *Herald* asserted initially, the fewer the number of white men that would be needed to fill the county's quota, a claim it later had to retract as an insult to white patriotism. Service in the war was an honor, whites later said in the weeks after the draft began, complaining that only black men were receiving public tribute.[2] In any case, Durham's black leadership could not have hoped for a finer show of patriotism and unanimity.

The United States had entered World War I in 1917, and by the end of that year the national emergency had created a situation in which Durham's African Americans turned the race struggle in a new direction. The soldiers' send-off demonstrated not only that African Americans rallied in support of black servicemen but that black leaders could deliver the black community's resources. "The colored citizens of Durham and Durham County will go over the top," C. C. Spaulding declared, taking charge as the chair of the local colored committee on war work, "just as they have done in all previous campaigns in which they have been enlisted for furtherance of the government's war program." If black leaders could deliver fighting men and black labor, they could leverage those resources to ask more of white elites. African Americans may have been accepting W. E. B. Du Bois's call in July 1918 to "close ranks" with "our white fellow citizens" in support of the American side of the international conflict.[3]

Needing black labor and thus with no choice but to recognize the wisdom of garnering black support for World War I, white leaders assessed black perspectives and fretted. "At present, except for Durham, our Council has no regular system of communicating with the Negroes," the head of the state's

Council on Defense admitted to the county chairmen. "We have no way to know as to their feeling about the war." The national emergency, therefore, presented Durham black leaders with occasions to expand their leadership roles beyond the African American community and to present black concerns directly to federal, state, and municipal officials. John Merrick, Aaron Moore, William Pearson, and James Shepard, familiar figures to white officials and powerful whites with whom they negotiated for resources, took their places in preparing the black community for hardship and in acting as emissaries between African Americans and whites, a position they sustained through the rest of the Jim Crow era.[4]

The exigencies of a national emergency drew black leaders from behind the veil to serve as public agents for the local, state, and federal government, charged with building support for the war among black people. Calling for discipline and cooperation, at the same time, Durham's black leaders rejected the conciliatory part of Du Bois's message to "forget our special grievances." Rather they used the American entry into an international conflict as the judicious moment to articulate obvious inconsistencies between ideologies of freedom and practices of racial repression and to make clear the duplicities of American values. African Americans had to fight in a Jim Crow unit and sacrifice on a Jim Crow home front.[5] At the same time, the rhetoric of the war — to make the world safe for democracy — armed African Americans with a weapon to make demands to the benefit of black folk, especially after they contributed disproportionate resources to the cause. Leaders embraced their responsibility to deliver the black community's loyalty to local, state, and national authorities, but they also used the crisis to highlight the hypocrisies of black life in an America fighting for freedom.

The ironies were startling. Abroad, black and white soldiers fought a common enemy in racially segregated ranks, while on the home front blacks and whites battled each other on the factory floor and the public street. Blind to the most glaring disparities, white officials wielded patriotic duty as a tool to control discontented black communities, to quell quotidian unrest, and to tighten white supremacist rule. In their separate ways, then, black people used the pressures of war demands as openings for their expressions of anger, frustration, and protest. Tactics of protest among workers, conflicting in style and substance with the plans of the black elite, also placed factions of African Americans at odds with each other. These tensions challenged the idea of community cohesiveness. And yet, despite increased intraracial tensions, Durham's black folk united behind the cause of war as it benefited the cause of the race. "The American Negro demands equality — political equality, industrial equality, and social equality," Du Bois had proclaimed in the wake of Booker T. Washington's death in 1915, "and he is never going to rest satisfied with anything less." World War I provided the occasion to make this claim forcefully.[6]

The demand for manufactured goods increased the number and kind of factory jobs available to black women. As tobacco factories shifted into high gear and black women were hired by the hundreds, African American women workers forged their own culture of resistance and mobility. As more positions opened on the line, women who could moved from white homes to the factory floor, and newly arrived migrants filled these positions in household labor. The availability of work increased women's migration from rural areas to Durham, but seemingly new employment options in the North encouraged their migration out of the city. The most visible change came for women of the black elite and middle class. Before the war, there had been no active black women's club movement linked to the national associations, although there were clubwomen organizations in other cities in the state. Because of men's leadership in Durham, women's club work was overshadowed. In any case, men of the black elite preferred that the women of their families not engage in secular forums that gave women a public presence in black politics. But between the hospital and various women's war efforts, a black women's club movement affiliated with national organizations finally emerged in the 1910s. Stepping out from male leaders' shadows, Durham's black women cooperated with elite white women, strengthening their organizations for a postwar launch of uplift initiatives and demands for woman suffrage. In addition, during World War I, black workers increased their agitation. On the streets and in factories, a persistent buzz of discontent indicated a working-class drift away from the patriarchs' politics of racial adjustment. Employers complained that they were losing black workers to migration, and tensions in the factories surrounding labor issues brought black women tobacco workers into direct conflict with white male supervisors.

Behind genuine unity, African Americans experienced the war's opportunities and exploitations in ways that exposed class and gender discord and played out increasingly assertive tactics on the part of black constituencies. Much to the dismay of black leaders, talk of unionization became loudest around 1919, just as the war came to an end. The end of the war fueled the fire of citizenship rights that had smoldered in Durham's black communities since 1898, especially since African Americans had contributed more than their part. Finally, the aging and death of freedom's first generation of leading black men — John Merrick in 1919 and Aaron Moore in 1923 — brought forth a younger cohort of male leaders emboldened to press for substantive change in politics and willing to let their wives do the same.

As a strategy of strengthening the bond between the races, demonstrations of allegiance and concern brought African American leaders into dialogue with powerful whites. Motivated especially by the national need for black support, white leaders included black leaders in discussions on the war effort. The U.S. Department of Labor was aware that black workers were necessary to the nation's ability to meet the industrial challenges of the era. The agency established a Division of Negro Economics and appointed the first black graduate of the Chicago School of Social Work, George E. Haynes, to head the division. In turn, Haynes set up a state-level network, and Durham's black leaders rallied to his cause. Dr. Aaron M. Moore accepted an appointment to serve as the special agent and State Supervisor of Negro Economics in North Carolina. In this role, he frequently met with state and local white government and business figures to articulate the perspectives of black workers and with workers to gain their support for wartime priorities as expressed by whites. It was at Moore's urging, for instance, that Governor Thomas Bickett set up a Negro Advisory Committee, its members selected from among the state's black leaders.[7]

Moore faced a daunting task. Not all black citizens were enthusiastic about the war or even desired to serve in the military. Eight "slackers" in Durham declined to report for the first draft and were detained. One, found at the Bull Factory "complacently working his job," was arrested. Another refused to register because "King Jesus" told him "to have nothing to do with this war." He was jailed and faced federal charges. Yet another left the county to escape military service; authorities apprehended him in Arizona. Dozens of men — divided equally among blacks and whites — failed to respond to subsequent calls. The local draft board offered a reward of fifty dollars for the arrest of loafers, idlers, and vagrants and promised that delinquents would be "forced" to work, or, worse, "hunted down," a term that provided enough motivation for a reluctant few to respond.[8]

Far-flung neighborhoods and institutions made Durham a difficult black community to organize. Still, black people separated their frustrations and discontent with Jim Crow from their support for African American men and women in uniform. Thus they could arrange and participate in a range of patriotic demonstrations, even when whites excluded them from "community" events. The Durham Red Cross (white) made no arrangements to accommodate African Americans at the Park Fete, a one-day fund-raising affair at the segregated Lakewood Amusement Park. The black Masons followed that festivity by marking St. John's Day, a Masonic holiday, with a patriotic program of music and speeches. They included no fraternal rituals that might suggest exclusivity. Keeping black interests at heart, the Masons allocated the proceeds from the fund-raiser to Lincoln Hospital.[9]

Durham whites did include African Americans in several efforts to coordinate local war work. Black women, as well as white, participated in voluntary organizations for war-related programs and knew of each other's efforts. When a woman representative of the Fourth Liberty Loan drive arrived in Durham, the local white coordinator informed her that "Mrs. Martha Merrick and Mrs. Minnie Pearson" had already begun to "work up a big public meeting with a musical program" in the black community. John Merrick, president of North Carolina Mutual and Provident Association, as it was still called, and C. C. Spaulding, Mutual manager, pledged the company's support for war savings stamps programs. While Governor Thomas Bickett called upon Aaron Moore to lead the project of monitoring the labor situation among African Americans, the white chairman of the local Liberty Loan drive appointed John Merrick to head up the black community's efforts. In the factories, workers ran their own campaigns. Many tobacco hands pledged a day's pay to the United War Work Campaign, and almost every black person employed by the Bull Factory donated. In the first week alone, black workers had raised $1,000.[10]

White leaders tapped into black Durham's network for advocates of patriotism. James E. Shepard and William G. Pearson, among the state college presidents and school principals whose institutions depended upon public monies, were called upon to get black cooperation. From their platforms, they pontificated on the race's responsibility and attempted to dissuade the masses from resistance and migration. Shepard, president of the National Religious Training School in Durham, spoke in Hillsboro on behalf of the Red Cross fund in 1918. He warned his African American audience that, notwithstanding their oppression, "this is not time to rock the [boat], but a time for obeying the government's orders and helping to win this war." Educator and editor Charles N. Hunter promoted food conservation and increased efforts to use home production as a means of gathering food supplies to survive anticipated shortages. "This is our war. We are in it; it is our country and our cause," Hunter lectured students, parents, and teachers at the opening exercises at Whitted School. S. G. Atkins, president of Slater State Normal School, was appointed state secretary for "colored work" for the National War Savings Committee. Addressing an audience at White Rock Church, Atkins contended: "We, as colored people are not satisfied with the injustices and prejudice heaped upon us, but this is no time for that. Do your duty first."[11]

Duty meant participating in all home front aspects of the war. For Pauli Murray, whose family had no men in uniform, duty still involved sacrifice. The Fitzgeralds, like most others, substituted blackstrap molasses for sugar and used salt pork for leaner meats. Food shortages required people to rely on produce grown in their own gardens and to share scarce resources with neighbors. Jeanes teachers managed to get local and state support for canning clubs and community gardens that African Americans established as a part of the food conservation movement. Teachers also promoted programs like the War Work Campaign, the war savings plan, and Liberty Bonds that supported the war financially while encouraging individuals to save for the future. Because these initiatives matched the gospel of wealth preached by the Mutual and bank officers, black businessmen endorsed them as beneficial to the community. Among the strongest contributors to the drive, Mutual employees of all stripes invested thousands of dollars in Liberty Bonds sold by the firm.

Duty also included engaging race issues, although not necessarily pursuing change. Black folk followed news about black troops, the work of black Red Cross nurses, and the travels of black government administrators. Pauli Murray read to her grandfather from the local *Herald*, the weekly *Norfolk Journal and Guide*, a regional black paper published in Norfolk, Virginia, and the *Crisis*, the Du Bois–edited journal of the NAACP.[12] Black periodicals helped to foster a sense of urgency among African Americans in their debates about how they related to the military and the war, the trends in migration, and organized labor. In Durham, duty also meant not upsetting the delicate balance between tolerance and need that black leaders had urged. "Not rocking the boat" did not require putting aside racial disgruntlement or agitating for rights but did mean that blacks were to avoid antagonizing white authorities. Black workers found this last directive hard to follow.

The World War I boom in tobacco and textiles brought expanded employment for African Americans in towns like Durham. The production of small cigarettes, popular because soldiers could carry them easily and women preferred them, generated enormous industrial growth. Between 1912 and 1920, tobacco production increased by 22 percent and earned Durham its nickname as the Bull City. Antitrust legislation busted the behemoth American Tobacco, but the split yielded new sets of corporations, warehouses, plant facilities, and factories, from large ventures like Liggett and Myers to small dealers like Imperial Tobacco and Export Leaf. All of them hired black women workers by the thousands. These developments facilitated heightened racial tensions as expanding production called for more race and gender segregation. Black and white workers, women and men, worked at different tasks and in different buildings and for different companies. At Liggett and Myers, for example, black women worked on the stemming floors in the new Flowers Warehouse on Morgan Street, built during the war, while white women worked on the "cigarette side," across the street. Imperial and Export hired only black women, by the hundreds, who were supervised only by white men.[13]

Factories, then, served as one of the places where workers, in this case black women tobacco workers, initiated confrontations with Jim Crow, especially issues of economic racism. They unsteadied the waters by stirring labor activism, spontaneous and organized, disrupting labor supplies, and resisting the prerogatives of white owners, managers, and foremen and government and union officials.

"You Have to Put Dignity On"

By 1918, most African American tobacco-working families in Durham had come from elsewhere. Blanche Scott's family, for instance, had come from Winston-Salem, another North Carolina tobacco town. Her grandmother, Minnie Roxy, had moved from rural Virginia to Winston-Salem during the late nineteenth century, seeking work in the R. J. Reynolds Tobacco plant. Scott's mother, also named Minnie, was born there. Her father, Richard Scott, had moved from Virginia to Winston and found work as a skilled tobacco roller at the Reynolds factory. The Roxys and the Scotts moved to the Bull City, drawn by the promise of better pay. Richard Scott found work as a skilled roller at American Tobacco; the Roxys and Minnie Scott found work at Liggett and Myers. By the time the Roxys and Scotts moved to Durham, it was the richest town in the state, and at least some African Americans had found ways to share in the wealth. Scott's parents and grandparents hoped to join the momentum of upward mobility for which black Durham was known.[14]

Scott was probably one of Pauline Dame's students. Born in Durham in 1906, she attended West End School for the primary grades. Like most children in the neighborhood, she grew up in an extended family, comprising three generations and multiple relations. And like most black folk in Durham, they faced challenges that Pauline Dame's teaching could not meet. The Roxy/Scott family settled into a black neighborhood on the west side of town where the Robert Fitzgeralds also lived and came to suffer some of their same ills. Municipal neglect, multiplied by overcrowding, had turned the neighborhood into "the Bottoms," an "odorous conglomeration of trash piles, garbage dumps, cow stalls, pig pens and crowded humanity." Labor disputes coupled with mechanization to eliminate the skilled positions held by African American men like Richard Scott. Although he found a job easily at Liggett and Myers, it was heavy, dirty work with less prestige and lower pay than the one he had held at American.[15]

Because all of the adults had to work, the responsibilities of running the household fell to Blanche Scott, the oldest of five children. When the 6:30 bull whistle called the elders to the factory in the morning, she was left at home to care for the younger children. Due to illness, Minnie Scott could work only sporadically; and even when she could, her earnings failed to close the gap between family wages and the rising cost of living. Thus, each child, in turn, became a wage earner. At age nine, Blanche Scott got her first job as a household worker, caring for a white family's child for fifty cents per week. In the summer of 1918, with tobacco production stimulated by World War I, twelve-year-old Blanche Scott was hired at Imperial Tobacco, which had opened in 1916. A small firm, Imperial specialized in processing raw tobacco and initially employed 300 people, mostly African American women and girls, including several of Scott's school friends. They worked as stemmers, paid by the pound of tobacco they handled, nine cents for every hundred pounds of leaf processed. She gave her first week's wages, $2.50, to her mother. In 1919, child labor legislation raised the legal working age to fourteen, and Scott and her young coworkers were "cut off" at Imperial. Talking her way into one of the vacancies at Liggett and Myers, she took a position at a bench next to her grandmother, a place left by someone gone north. Now working throughout the year, she divided her days between the factory floor and the classroom, earning five dollars a week in tobacco while still contributing her labor at home. "When I drew $6.50, I got to feeling I was rich."[16]

African American women tobacco workers made up an urban proletariat, conscious of their shared position and a common struggle. More work was the only benefit they obtained from factors that swelled the demand for tobacco, encouraged the growth of industry, or stimulated the economy. Just as easily as they might find a job, however, they could lose it. Their children, especially the girls, were pulled into the public labor force at an early age and kept there for most of their lives. Blanche Scott's family history could be repeated with few modifications by thousands of African American women who worked tobacco during the Jim Crow era. Reginald Mitchner's family had left its farm in Franklin County in 1916 after his father died. The family moved to Raleigh, then to Greensboro, and finally to Durham, where the factories paid "better than average."[17] Mabel Harris's aunts had been sent by their parents to Durham in the 1910s to live with relatives so that they could go to school, but the immediate needs of the Durham branch of the family pushed the girls into the factory instead.[18] These stories echo themes of labor's mobility but also demonstrate the limited effect of industrial expansion for African American women. Some young women from tobacco-working families did advance from West End's elementary grades to Whitted School's upper grades, but they balanced school, factory work, and domestic work. In 1922, at age sixteen, with eight partial years of schooling, the experienced Blanche Scott went to work full time at Liggett and Myers and worked there until 1946.[19]

Economic downturns slowed production as readily as labor disputes or bad weather. Gradual structural changes in tobacco manufacturing eventually made stemming a seasonal job, providing most of the black women who worked tobacco with employment only a few months a year. Some hands managed to stay working the same job in the same factory for decades, but for the most part, black women workers were the last hired and the first fired. Tobacco work was not as unstable as the next worst option, household labor. When she could find no factory work, for instance, Scott "would just go to school and get another service job until they start[ed] back hiring at my age, and I'd go back again."[20]

When she did work in the factory, Scott recalled long hours, 7:00 A.M. until 5:00 P.M., with barely a half-hour break all day. She endured rude and lecherous foremen who cursed and abused women workers and smelling the burley tobacco, a stench so strong "I'd take an orange peeling and hold it in my mouth, and that would keep me from getting sick." The abuses of industrial labor — especially tobacco work — encouraged workers to move on when they could, and African American women had good reason for their dissatisfaction. Black laborers performed the dirtiest, heaviest labor and the foulest tasks in any industry, and tobacco was no exception. Black men transferred tobacco from the warehouse to the factory where they worked the large flavoring vats. They rolled wet leaves onto hogsheads, large barrel-shaped bundles of tobacco each weighing as much as 500 pounds. From the flavoring rooms they carried the hogsheads on their shoulders onto the factory floor. There, black women and a handful of black men did the work of "rehandling," sorting and hanging the leaves. They divided the hogsheads into individual plants, separated and tied the plant ends together, and hung them to dry. Once the leaves dried, the process of stemming began. Stemming was the lowest-paying and one of the harshest jobs in the industry. Lines of women ripped leaves from the plant stems by hand and fed them into machines that chopped the tobacco into small pieces for packing into cigarettes. Stripping made women's palms sore, and feeding the machine was dangerous. Despite the hazards, children who were old enough to work labored on the line alongside experienced stemmers, and youngsters were hired to sweep the floors.[21]

Stemming required dexterity and speed. Bright-leaf tobacco, easily stripped, could be handled quickly, but its lighter weight required women to work faster in order to earn the same money. Burley tobacco was heavier but more difficult to work with. The loads of burley tobacco brought in from Virginia were filled with sand, chicken feathers, and manure, making it nasty to handle. The stemming area was a hot, steamy, unventilated room. Black workers toiled drenched with sweat and covered with dust. Many complained of nausea and coughing, symptoms of respiratory diseases that raced through the factory at epidemic proportions. Their loss of appetite exacerbated malnutrition. African American women suffered horrible working conditions and a number of health risks, evidenced by the regularity of difficult pregnancies, stillbirths, deaths from tuberculosis, and episodes of fainting from heat exhaustion.[22]

The well-documented hardships of working tobacco went beyond dealing with raw product. In 1915, the YWCA took its investigation into working conditions for women to the South. Addie Hunton, national activist, traveled south on behalf of the YWCA to survey working conditions for African American women and found them dreadful. A decade later, the situation was little better than what Hunton had reported. A 1922 study published by the Women's Bureau, a division of the U.S. Department of Labor, documented the harshness of black women's labor: they worked longer for less pay under worse circumstances than white women did. A survey of thirty-nine tobacco establishments, including those in Durham, found that the standard workday for black women averaged ten hours, compared to nine for white women. Management "permitted" as much overtime as desired, the study recorded, but in fact it was mandatory. African American women accepted the additional hours out of necessity. Paid by the pound rather than by the hour as white women were compensated, black women knew that the longer they worked, the more tobacco they stemmed and the greater income they earned. In addition to segregation, long hours, and short-lived employment, women workers suffered from foremen and managers who held the absolute power and who were determined to retain and restrain African Americans in their traditionally subservient positions.[23]

In fact, if there was a job that represented Jim Crow's intent to debase African American women, it was working tobacco. Tobacco work duplicated slavery in many ways. Women were selected for positions as though they were on the auction block. On the first day of green season, when the factories began to hire seasonal stemmers, hundreds of black women gathered in groups at the front steps of the factory. Foremen appeared periodically to select the workers they wanted, choosing the ones who presented the physical characteristics of strength and youth. "I rate them by their muscles," one foreman informed an investigator. "The stronger they are the better they are." Putting women to work at tables fashioned like troughs, furnishing drinking water from a barrel, and in some cases providing no washroom, employers criticized black workers for untidiness, yet provided no facilities for them. While workers focused on their families' needs, observers chose other interpretations for African American women's seeming acquiescence to harsh conditions. One Women's Bureau investigator characterized black women workers' relationships with their employers as "childlike obedience, loyalty and allegiance," as a sign of "faith and confidence" on the one hand and "servile fear and suspicion" on the other. Employers considered black women laborers property, not far removed from legal servitude. One remarked, "We keep our Negro labor as bound and subservient as possible because it doesn't pay to do otherwise." Most notoriously, foremen subjected black women to degrading treatment. "Negroes have no intelligence," the foreman quoted above continued. "Only brute treatment appeals to them."[24]

Brute treatment entailed verbal, physical, and sexual abuse, a situation that outraged women who had little choice but to endure their foremen's appalling behavior. Dora Scott Miller distinctly remembered "a one-eyed fella named George Hill" from South Carolina. "He was tight. He'd get on top of the machines and watch you to see if you were working alright and holler down and curse. Curse and we working. That's what we had to undergo. . . . You didn't say anything. You said anything, you went out." Sexual harassment and abuse occurred frequently, and many women complained that foremen "fumbled their behinds" and told "nasty jokes." Terminations happened just as frequently. "Just like you come up there to get a job, they could hire you, if they didn't like the way you do, they could fire you," Blanche Scott stated flatly. "I always tried to do my work right so they wouldn't have to just get on me."[25] Annie Mack Barbee reiterated this point and knew the reason: "Lord, they'd fire them all the time. . . . There [was] a lot of prejudice up there among the foremen." Black men suffered, too, from insults and abuse, and they responded in similar ways. One young man, whom a foreman called "boy," threatened to throw the boss out a fourth-story window and was stopped only through the intervention of other workers seeking to protect the worker. Charlie Mack remembered that white foremen "loved to put their foot in your tail and laugh." Mack also warned his boss, "You put your foot in my tail again ever I'll break your leg."[26]

Sometimes the factory hummed with the rhythm of women at work; other times that factory floor carried a tenor of madness. Some women worked in a frenzy to avoid contact with the foreman; one worked in loud deliberate motions and intentionally ignored the "big boss" when he appeared; another talked to herself to discourage unwanted advances; yet another screamed when the foreman approached. Annie Mack Barbee took a more direct approach and physically threatened her supervisor. Just speaking about the factory evoked Barbee's bitterness years later: "I know white folks is mean and nasty. I know that. I don't have to ask anybody. But if you don't stand up and demand respect they won't give you nothing; you have to demand it and let them know that you are willing to pay the price for it. . . . I don't care how low your job is, regardless, it's honest work. You have to put dignity on."[27]

Dignity was exactly what foremen tried to deny and what women demanded through their challenges to the foremen's authority. What supervisors sometimes interpreted as poor work habits were actually protests acted out through slowdowns, absenteeism, and negligence. Foremen complained about black workers: "They give so much trouble in being unreliable and irregular. . . . They are terribly indolent, careless, and stubborn," offering a stark contrast to workers' description of diligence. Rarely satisfied, foremen justified their condescension with fulsome pride. "Whenever they give trouble," one remarked, "we give them rough treatment and that quells them for a while. Rough treatment is the only thing that will reach them."[28]

The calm that foremen demanded often came in the form of song. Supervisors eager to exceed production quotas encouraged the melodious strains and reveled in the sight of women stemming in rhythm. On the other side of the wall, the sound of music was not as soothing. One longtime Durham resident, hearing women's voices outside of the factory, described the tone as "eerie . . . sounds that I shall never forget." Coming closer to describing the meaning of work songs, she explained, "They were not singing from joy, but to ease the monotony of long hours going through the same motions day in and day out."[29]

Women workers' songs were not intended to entertain listeners. "Our head man . . . loved to hear us sing. We wouldn't stop working to sing," stated Mary Bailey. She fondly recalled the sound of song in the factory setting, but she considered singing a form of collective expression. Bailey described music as an aspect of camaraderie. "Everywhere we worked at the factory, we would just have a spell of singing." Song also reflected candor. What women could not say outright, they could say in music. "They would let you sing, but you couldn't do much talking unless you talked low. You had to work!" Bailey recalled. With each woman bringing her particular voice, expression, and pitch into the performance, their lives evoked the complex affecting harmonies for which gospels and spirituals are known. When supervisors forbade talking on the factory floor, for example, women raised their voices together in song.[30] Song captured allegiances forged in the factory and played out in friendship circles, working teams, and clubs. Experienced women recommended and then trained new workers, but inexperienced workers caught the brunt of foremen's temper. Singing helped a new worker to work at a pace that would bring good earnings and relief from the boss. Through the voices of women workers, song spoke in solidarity against the abuses of Jim Crow and their work, of hard times and injustice. Work songs like "The Hamlet Wreck," composed by black workers at Liggett and Myers, recalled a railroad accident that crushed a segregated wooden car carrying dozens of St. Joseph AME Zion Church Sunday school members. And spirituals like "By an' By" and "Lay My Burden Down" were not simply "soulful chants" that hypnotized white listeners but were prayers for better days and threats to quit.[31]

The alliances created among workers made it possible for people to survive under difficult conditions. Annie Mack Barbee recalled, "When you're working, there's got to be some harmony there to make the work easier for you." Women covered for each other when necessary, stemming extra to help someone who "felt low" on a given day. They also used their alliances as forms of protection and protest. Bailey remembered colluding with another worker to avoid tasks they disliked and hiding when they learned their foreman planned to move them to another area. Workers refused to inform on others when asked. "You didn't hire me to tell you who was working and who weren't working," as Bailey described one confrontation. "You hired me to work. Now if you want to know about them people not working, you look and see for yourself, cause I ain't telling you nothing."[32]

Pushed to the limit, "putting dignity on" and "laying my burden down" could also mean leaving, exacting a cost that women sometimes were willing to pay. Tobacco work offered better than average wages, if only for a few months a year. Quitting a factory, the strongest form of protest, sometimes resulted in work at another plant, particularly with a recommendation from a friend or family member. But resigning could also lead to less desirable options: domestic work or unemployment. When better alternatives presented themselves, women accepted them with enthusiasm. Blanche Scott tired of working tobacco, took the night shift, attended beautician school during the day, and eventually opened her own shop. There she gained the dignity and autonomy that came with self-employment and working with a black clientele.[33]

Household labor offered an alternative for those forced by anger, disgust, health, or supervisors to leave the factory. For example, Maude Brown left American Tobacco at age thirty-two because of illness and took a position as a domestic. Although only one-third of black women workers in Durham were employed as household laborers, 95 percent of such positions were held by black women. But "out of work" and out of the tobacco factory for the rest of the year, black women took in wash, performed day labor, returned to the family farm or to school — or, in the constant search for better employment and wages, they left one position or one city for the next.[34] Domestic service and tobacco work shared many characteristics. Referrals, for example, often came through friends, neighbors, and kin. Heavily supervised, household laborers were subject to the whims and abuses of white employers. The racial hierarchy played out similarly when a black woman entered a white home through the back door in a subservient position. While there, she was expected to honor all other social and racial taboos, including never challenging her employer's decisions. Racial etiquette dictated that whites deny their employees common courtesy. Refusing to use her name, Maude Brown's employers called her "Nita," while she called them "Mr. and Mrs. Daniels."[35]

There were, however, clear differences between the two occupations. "Working out" paid less than working tobacco, and, because domestic service was arranged on an individual basis, it offered less flexibility than factory work and the hours were unpredictable. Household laborers worked on demand, from early morning, before the white family rose, until late evenings after the family's dinner. Full-time positions provided little time off, perhaps only Thursdays and every other Sunday. Day work, temporary household employment accepted by those who could find no permanent position, posed an even more precarious situation. All black domestics encountered greater risk of sexual abuse from white men in the isolated private setting of white homes. One option for household laborers, however, was to leave one private home for another or to find work in the factory.[36]

Still, as insecure and as awful as working tobacco might be, "it was the best you could do, and the most money you could make," Dora Scott Miller remembered, and those who could get themselves employed at the factory were glad to "get on." And get on, they did. A 1918 census of West Durham, where new black migrants settled in Hickstown and Walltown, found that of 664 working African Americans living in that section, only 11 hired out as cooks, 22 took in washing, and 23 did odd jobs. The remainder found employment in factories and mills.[37]

African American women filled positions in Durham factories as quickly as they opened. But they also left white households for the warehouses as soon as green season began, and left the South for northern opportunities when they could. The North Carolina report to the Division on Negro Economics noted that "crowds of workers leave year-round industries as soon as the warehouses opened." A Women's Bureau study similarly detailed the ways that black female workers moved from position to position to increase their small incomes. But the Women's Bureau report highlighted the effects of these transitions on black women: "The substitution revolves itself into work of a makeshift type, such as housework, laundering, day's work house cleaning and other kinds of uncertain employment."[38]

An Even-Greater Migration

Workers still rallied to the cause of the war, but daily they rallied to the cause of their own lives. The war spurred economic growth and strengthened demands for more and cheaper labor, a resource that white leaders expected black leaders to deliver. For its part, labor saw opportunities elsewhere. The black working class, those who experienced Jim Crow's abuses in the most personal ways, used the opportunity of war to step beyond southern racism's reach. With World War I slowing immigration from Europe and with northern factories, mills, and households seeking new sources of workers, black laborers pondered migrating out of the South. When they did, they captured the interest and imagination of leaders, awestruck by the willingness of so many to trade their southern roots for northern chances. At the same time, southern industrial expansion quickened the usual trends of localized female migration that had characterized the making of Durham as a city. Thus the even-greater migration unfolding in the South provided the backdrop to the Great Migration drama on the main stage.

While black America turned its attention to men — those who were fighting, working, and leading — African American women joined their male counterparts in migrating north, expanding and accelerating a migration process that had begun a generation before. Moving from the country to the city, they responded to family demands for their income with the pay envelope from the factories. Migration by working-class women set in motion a dynamic process of displacement, one that destabilized labor on the local level. Black workers withdrew themselves as a resource at a critical moment. Those who remained behind turned factory floors and white homes into spaces where black workers — mostly women — and white managers — mostly males — played out struggles of will and frustration. With their sights set on race and not necessarily gender, black male leaders were surprised at the willingness of the race's most vulnerable constituency to align itself independently of them.

As with the Negro Problem, migration as an issue demanded that black leaders, scholars, and theorists respond to a question that had no clear answer. Black migration itself was nonlinear and, in the minds of many leaders, illogical. In 1917, W. T. B. Williams, black educational adviser to white philanthropic organizations, admitted that "the abnormal movement among the colored people is striking in many ways. It seems to be a general response to the call of better economic and social opportunities. The movement is without organization or leadership. The negroes just quietly move away without taking their recognized leaders into their confidence any more than they do the white people about them. . . . They rarely consult the white people, and never those who may exercise some control over their actions. They will not allow their own leaders to advise them against going North."[39]

African American women produced the most dramatic changes in Durham's black population. Until the Great Migration of World War I, the population shifts for black women had outpaced all other groups. When Durham's population rose significantly, black women accounted for the greatest change. During World War I (and again during World War II), that trend reversed. Durham's population increased only slightly, and black women demonstrated the least growth. Between 1910 and 1920, the black male population increased by 17 percent but the black female population increased by only 6 percent. At first glance, these figures might seem to represent greater migration to the city on the part of men, and this may well have been true. But given that the population increase of black women failed to keep pace with natural increase (2 percent per year, or 20 percent for the decade), it is just as likely that Durham was losing its black female population.[40]

Distracted by the movement of men, most black leaders ignored women's mobility. Contemporary studies that did look specifically at the demographic trends among women still failed to capture the complexity of women's lives. In his analysis of black migration during World War I, for example, economist George E. Haynes indicated that black women's employment had declined and argued that "thousands of Negro men for the first time found it possible to secure sufficient wages to provide for their families so that their wives remained at home, free from the necessity of having to earn the daily bread in addition to performing the duties of housekeeper, wife, and mother." Using census data in a later study, statistician Joseph A. Hill also found that the gainfully employed segment among all black women in the United States declined from 58 percent in 1910 to 44 percent by 1920, the World War I decade. Thus Hill proposed tentatively that "in a time of high wages, and despite high costs of living, it is not improbable that the Negroes may have experienced some improvement in their economic position, making it less imperative for the women to contribute to the support of the family."[41]

Yet, as industrial expansion translated into increased employment for men, it also translated into increased employment options for women. Given the economic circumstances of most black families, the improved employment situation for men and increases in male incomes did not dramatically change the economic demands on women's lives. African American women continued to engage in multiple kinds of work because poverty ran too deep for one paycheck to relieve it. Women continued to perform paid work outside the home to supplement family earnings, and, as they had done historically, they looked to the city.

The reported downward trends in women's employment can be attributed to changes in methods of census enumeration that undercounted women's labor (and probably men's) by tallying individuals and not their jobs. Little real change in women's employment patterns occurred, but two significant changes in the manner of data collection account for how African American women's work was discounted. First, the census of 1910 was taken as of 15 April, during the planting season. Women who worked in agriculture thus were included in the 1910 count. The 1920 census was taken in January, however, during a lull in farming. Women who worked in agriculture were less likely to be counted that year. Also, January, the off-season for temporary employment in industrial tobacco, caught women who worked as seasonal laborers out of work. Therefore, they too would have been missed in the census count. Second, in 1910, enumerators were instructed to count as farmworkers women who worked on the home farm for the family; however, they were instructed in 1920 not to include women who did farmwork "only occasionally" or "for a short time each day" but to count only those who worked "regularly." Farmwomen who engaged in multiple, season-based tasks or employment, worked periodically, or for periods of each day, as many black women did, would not have been considered "gainfully employed." Moreover, whereas the 1910 census enumerators were instructed specifically *not* to assume that a woman had no occupation, the 1920 instructions omitted this direction. Census takers easily could speculate that when male heads of household worked, women held no employment; consequently, they asked no questions. Lastly, because Hill's analysis focused on workers aged sixteen and older, he neglected crucial segments of African American laborers by omitting those aged fourteen and fifteen (or younger) who, like Blanche Scott, were gainfully — if illegally — employed. This strategy also missed girls who at ages younger than fourteen worked unofficially as household workers.[42]

Finally, it is likely that women's transience and the types of work they accepted made accurate enumeration impossible. As seen in earlier years, African American women had been making the trek from the country to the city since Reconstruction and from the South to the North since the 1880s. They dominated the black populations of northern and southern cities until the 1910s (and continued to after 1920). Living in groups of friends and families or as workers in white households and traveling between county and city and between the North and South, they were as itinerant as men and just as difficult to count. Distrustful of white authorities who came to their homes, they were no more likely to fully answer a census taker's questions.

In any case, few African American women actually fit the statistical profile Haynes and Hill described. Rather, men and women welcomed the occasion for work, and women's ephemeral labor in fields, factories, and homes continued during all economic times, the prosperous and the poor. For all of its flaws — among them the assumption that people held only one occupation at a time or resided in only one place — the census does reveal unmistakable trends of increase in urban employment for women (by 42 percent between 1910 and 1930), with much of that increase coming in industry. The sharp rise in employment figures for those particular fields also verifies significant shifts. Between 1910 and 1920, the number of factory workers in North Carolina climbed by over 200 percent and the number of mill workers rose by over 500 percent. Additionally, black institution building had expanded the number of teachers and nurses among professional women workers by almost 50 percent.[43] Rural employment may not have decreased as much as the census indicated. According to the census, the number of black women farmworkers fell from 27 to 15 percent nationally between 1910 and 1930 (from 60 to 32 percent in North Carolina).[44] But if women's employment did demonstrate a significant transformation in job patterns, it came in the transition from rural to urban occupations. With factories in desperate need of hands during the war, African American women in Durham found employment in the textile mills as well as in its tobacco factories. In truth, one of the most important changes for African American women that occurred in the twentieth century was the rural-to-urban shift of the black population. According to the 1930 census, 48 percent of employed black women in Durham worked in factories. Except for the few dozen in professional, semiprofessional, and clerical work, the remainder worked in service. But unlike black women's employment in other places, domestic work employed less than half of the population of black women in Durham. By 1930, the number of women exceeded that of men employed as clerical workers, servants, factory operatives, and teachers and equaled the number of men employed in insurance and real estate and in professional and semiprofessional service.[45]

"Workers Whose Lives Are So Haphazard"

The face of black Durham's workforce changed quickly. As leaders shared concerns over this development with colleagues and acquaintances, their anxieties fueled their sense of the instability in black communities. Migration transformed black communities by bringing unfamiliar people to Durham's doorsteps desperately seeking work. Aaron Moore noted in his final report on the Tar Heel State: "Many North Carolina laborers had been recruited through employment agencies" in an "indiscriminating" way. As a result, he argued, the "shiftless" and "unstable" were "imported into North Carolina cities."[46] Black officials were no more able than white ones to grasp these changes. As they had before, working-class African Americans ignored the counsel of opponents to migration and chose their own paths, leaving leaders to puzzle. In their new advisory roles to local, state, and federal agencies and to foundations and philanthropic organizations, black leaders searched that much harder for answers to frustrating questions about where their constituencies had gone.

The general sense of flux generated an anxiety among civic officials, who laid the blame for instability on African American women. Their migration, resettlement, and impermanent work habits exasperated white and black leaders alike. North Carolina governor Thomas W. Bickett called an emergency meeting of black and white advisers in 1917. Among its first concerns, the group emphasized the "scarcity" of black laborers for the "silk mill" in Fayetteville, which had closed due to a shortage of labor. African American women performed the labor in that mill. During the summer of 1918, white businessmen complained of a "vagrancy problem," a term they applied to the general sense that African Americans appeared to be "out of work." The Chamber of Commerce executive committee assumed that when Imperial Tobacco opened, the "green season" would draw workers — black women — back to the plant and that the problem would be solved. After the factory opened, local newspapers reported white residents' grumblings about the "servant problem," more accurately, the shortage of household workers caused when domestics chose to work at Imperial instead of in white homes. The county health department expressed concerns, stepping up its warnings regarding typhoid. The director blamed the "curtailment of sanitary efforts" on the "shortage of labor," again referring to either the departure or the lax attitude of black women household workers. Lastly, the city council endorsed measures to halt the work of labor agents, even as newspapers carried paid advertisements that recruited maids and other service workers to other locales. Exasperated southern white businessmen in Durham joined their counterparts in the region, with some reluctance, to ask for federal intervention "to put a stop to this movement of laborers on the grounds that it was handicapping the south not only in its manufacturing industries" but also in "the raising of food crops."[47]

To assure the nation a workforce dedicated to "necessary" employment, Provost Marshal General Crowder issued a "Work or Fight Order," remanding every able-bodied male of draft age to a job or military service. In the South, "Work or Fight" laws operated to restrict the mobility of African American women and to force them (if they were not employed) into assigned jobs. Like their colleagues in other cities, Durham's white civic leaders endorsed "Work or Fight" measures and applied them directly to black women. Although arrests for noncompliance in Durham seemed not as blatant as those in Atlanta or Memphis (where women of the black elite who did not have to work were arrested for vagrancy), the local war advisory board categorized domestic work as essential, making the black women who did these jobs subject to reassignment from one position to another at the whim of the board and its members, curtailing women's autonomy that might have come from increased wages.[48]

Local attempts to enforce the ordinance in absurd ways signaled a breakdown of white leaders' authority and their inability to control the restive black workforce. Yet the ebb and flow of women workers into and out of the city of Durham, and in and out of job categories, continued to erode the reliability of the workforce whites depended on. Black women made their worlds safer by asserting their rights and defying white authority on the streets as well as on the job. The *Herald* reported on belligerent activities, as a rash of "Negro crimes" occurred in crisis numbers, with African American women as well as men accused of "assault." In one instance, a black woman, determined to exit a streetcar ahead of a white woman, supposedly "shoved her roughly to one side." Both she and her companion were arrested. In another incident, two women, considered drunk and disorderly, attacked the police chief when he tried to arrest them. The policeman also arrested a black man who refused to assist with the women's apprehension and charged him with "neglecting and refusing to aid an officer." Of the group that assailed the police chief, all were fined ten dollars, but the women were sentenced additionally to sixty days in the county workhouse.[49]

Other arrests came as a result of local police subjecting the black community to greater than usual surveillance. The *Herald* reported frequent closings of bawdy and disorderly houses. Visible prostitution, historically evident in Durham, resulted from any combination of factors at play: a good wartime economy gave men — white and black — resources to buy sex. At the same time, expanded populations of women in want or need of money provided casual liaisons and more business for sex workers. Disorderly houses offered opportunities for a range of diversions, including drinking, carousing, and reveling. Complaints came in response to the crime and violence that resulted from such activities. Through the local police, authorities attempted to control these independent underground enterprises and to compel the women who worked in them to accept "productive" positions in white homes and factories. Accordingly, black women prisoners served on chain gangs (illegally), and they also cooked and laundered for white prisoners in the jail, for black prisoners in the convict camps, for white authorities such as the sheriff and deputies, and for the white people who resided at the county home.[50]

The opportunity to moderate between black and white residents led black representatives to approach civic leaders in May 1917. C. C. Spaulding and Aaron Moore met with the Durham Chamber of Commerce to warn that black labor was leaving the city. Moore used meetings like these to recount his community's grievances. At one chamber meeting these representatives argued that wage increases might stem the migration. The average wage for black men was eight dollars per week, according to Moore, "$2.00 too little" to meet a family's basic expenses. For that reason, "1,500–2,000 colored people" had left Durham in the previous ninety days.[51] At the governor's meeting on labor, black leaders noted that their constituents had few reasons to cooperate. Municipalities had ignored the demands and needs of black neighborhoods. Workers' houses sat on unpaved, unlit streets where the resulting lack of drainage exacerbated the poor sanitation about which white civic leaders complained. Embarking on an educational campaign to "preserve morale and competency of Negro workers," Moore, as the official spokesperson for the state, asked employers for "greater consideration of their workers." Among his recommendations were urgent requests for increased wages, improved working conditions, better race relations, and "appreciation" of the value of blacks to the state. "Since the great majority of Negroes are working class," he noted in defense of his poorer neighbors, "their permanent interests are as laborers, and these interests are in the maintenance of living wages and good working conditions." Few white employers responded, however, and the frustrated Moore wrote in his final report: "Until more interest is taken in these meetings by the white leaders, and until they are followed by constructive programs for better law enforcement and education[,] they cannot measurably influence the tendency of the Negro to move."[52]

Forced to draw from a transient pool, whites criticized recalcitrant black workers and made black leaders responsible for keeping the race in line. Holding both worker and employer accountable for the labor crisis, African American advisers enumerated industrial abuses and suggested solutions. But they also held the black working class responsible for its solution. Speaking at schools, churches, and workplaces, Moore and his committee members listened to workers' questions, considered matters of public health, and promoted "ideals of efficiency and recreational activities." But the Negro Advisory Committee also criticized black workers' characters, cleanliness, and transience, linked their work to their deficiencies, and emphasized limits over aspirations. At times, black leaders' rhetorical chastisement overshadowed calls for better pay and working conditions. "Tobacco work is seasonal; the wages are high and no great intelligence is required for much of the work," the committee noted. "The work of the industries is dirty and does not invite workers of particular skill. It is hard to promote cleanliness, efficiency and thrift among workers whose lives are so haphazard, who come and go through the streets in their working clothes and who are not generally considered as advanced workers." Despite its arguments for improved workers' conditions, the committee could do little to compel white employers to act. Indeed, what white employers and supervisors heard was evidence that supported their perceptions about black employees: no great intelligence among people not generally considered advanced and whose lives were haphazard. These key phrases reinforced whites' impressions rather than bringing about change. Thus, the advisory group's efforts led to no significant changes in working conditions for the poor.[53]

"If the Colored People Can Be Moved"

Few black workers heard or were moved by committees and reports; instead, they took matters into their own hands. The Durham newspapers hinted that organized labor activity had begun even as the United States entered the war. But the paper rarely mentioned any specific activities among blacks. For example, the *Herald* reported on "rumors and general talk" about unions among "comparatively skilled men" on the "cigarette side," where whites worked. Other newspapers reported on labor activism in Norfolk, Richmond, Petersburg, and Winston-Salem, sites where tobacco factories existed and where extensive in-migration of black women had occurred during the World War I era. The Durham paper only made a passing reference to troubles that had occurred "in some of the departments" at Blackwell Tobacco, a leaf-processing plant that employed mostly black women stemmers. Whenever labor activity surfaced, white civic leaders issued reminders about "loafers" and the "labor supply," and black leaders moved into action to discourage labor organizing.[54]

Aaron Moore brought George Haynes to speak in Durham shortly after cryptic reports of labor unrest appeared in the local paper. Haynes met with "representative white employers and some representative colored leaders" and with blacks at a mass meeting at St. Joseph AME Zion Church. At these sessions he emphasized efficiency in "the pressing days of war production." In his report on black labor in North Carolina, however, Haynes noted that in "one North Carolina city it was reported that a Negro union had been organized to which the white workers objected." In fact, African American women workers engaged in labor activity in virtually all of the tobacco towns where they clustered, including Durham. And the American Tobacco Company, a branch of which was located in each of these cities, was among the central targets by 1918.[55]

Durham black workers had begun to organize themselves by the time the Tobacco Workers International Union (TWIU) arrived in the last year of the decade. Affiliated with the American Federation of Labor, the TWIU built on black labor activism to launch a forceful organizing campaign among Durham white tobacco workers in 1919. The union had been operating in Durham on and off since the late nineteenth century. Although the organization adopted resolutions friendly to black laborers in 1897, 1902, and 1917, its racism excluded black laborers from its ranks, for the most part. Black leaders questioned the value of labor organizations for black workers, not only as exclusive organizations but also as threats to the racial peace between the black and the white elites. During the war, however, black laborers moved into industry in larger numbers. Pressured by African American labor advocates like George E. Haynes, the American Federation of Labor was convinced that black workers strengthened rather than weakened labor's hand.[56]

Arthur Vance Cole, a white tobacco worker from Durham who had been fired for his organizing activities, represented the TWIU locally. He held weekly meetings for three months in the spring of 1919, recruiting both black and white workers to segregated associations. The black local proved more enthusiastic than the white one, Cole complained to E. Lewis Evans, secretary of the TWIU: "We are enlisting but few new [white] members, only one or two at meetings." Intimidated by city and county officials, whites rarely attended meetings, and their Local 153 struggled to sustain itself. But black Local 154, whose members gathered at various churches around the city, started to press its demands.[57] Pleased with black organizing, TWIU president Anthony McAndrew noted that "the colored people realize probably what organization means to the work in the tobacco industry." Writing to Cole he noted, "It appears to me peculiar that these corporations make no pretense to discourage the colored workers."[58]

McAndrew got to the heart of the TWIU and black union activity. Tobacco companies forestalled unionization by keeping workers apart and fueling competition between them. Whites who unionized risked termination and replacement by African Americans who would accept the jobs willingly, even with lower pay. "If they could get cheap colored labor in all departments they [factory owners] undoubtedly would do so," E. Lewis Evans griped to Cole. Thus, in some ways, whites had more to lose than blacks through labor agitation. The TWIU, however, stood to gain from the racial conflict. Union officials understood that black labor organizing and labor concessions generated passion among whites, who resented any gains that black workers might make. The TWIU, sharing corporate perceptions of black workers and viewing white labor as its more critical element, stimulated rivalries between the black and white locals. Arguing that blacks were getting "ahead," the union encouraged white workers to organize in response.[59]

The TWIU encouraged the antiblack sentiment among white workers, who resented the fact that African Americans dared make labor demands and who begrudged any progress they made, even though whites neither desired nor had sufficient numbers to take the positions black people held in tobacco work. "If the colored people can be moved to any kind of large motive, the White people will take greater heart and a revival of their own movement will be automatic," Evans explained to Cole. The "motive" that Evans sought came in the spring of 1920 when another boom began in tobacco and factories increased the working hours in processing plants. Evans reported "some spirit of discontent over the fact that the colored are getting more time than the Whites," because "the Whites are of the opinion that it is because of the union. If this is so, it seems that it is an opportune time to get on the job and make a weld while the iron is hot."[60] Mixed metaphors aside, Evans instructed Cole to continue working with blacks but to put the majority of his energies into the white local. Needing black unions — and disagreeing with secretary Evans — McAndrew sent Cora Hogan, a white woman organizer, to help Cole with both groups. Hogan attended black meetings safely as a white woman because the majority of tobacco hands who participated in the black union were women. But she shared Evans's interest in white workers. "He [McAndrew] will have to learn that the employers are not half as interested when they form a Colored union as when the White is organized, for they know the colored cannot do anything without the Whites."[61]

Still, white locals spread slowly in Piedmont factories. In Durham, Winston-Salem, and Reidsville, North Carolina, and South Boston, Petersburg, and Richmond, Virginia, white locals affiliated with tobacco factories drifted along, requiring additional energy from organizers. Black locals, suffering from lack of attention, became even harder to sustain. Fearing the loss of its base, white union officials for "the colored local" stepped up their efforts. Neglecting the strongest element among black tobacco workers, union officials turned to black male workers to assist in organizing and ignored the rank and file of black women. But African American women were effective organizers, as demonstrated in their church work, networks of family and friends, and camaraderie on the factory floor, and they also suffered the most abuse. The nature of their work, however, ran counter to the goals of unionization. African American women provided a transient workforce, comprising a massive body of workers during green season but not necessarily during the winter months when the TWIU efforts peaked. Ignoring or rejecting the women as facilitators, TWIU union officials sought to make black male leaders "the working instrument."[62]

In response to the union effort, black leaders among the elite hedged. They refused to allow themselves to be used as a "working instrument" by working-class whites, the union leaders whom they believed were of a lower class than they. Nor would they ally with an initiative that had the potential to cause racial animosity. Black leaders may have agreed that workers deserved better wages and conditions, but they were reluctant to support any efforts that raised the ire of whites. Moreover, they shared a distrust of unions with other black leaders, knowing that only when it was to white workers' advantage did labor unions pay any attention to black workers' problems. The elite eschewed tobacco workers' activism in any case, believing it smacked of Bolshevism, or even worse, the racial disquiet they sought to allay. Rather, anxious about deteriorating race relations following the armistice, members of the black elite responded to rumblings about labor action with a series of mass meetings in Durham black communities, where they preached "good feelings between the white and colored races" and blamed "outsiders" for the unrest among blacks.[63]

Union activity faded by the mid-1920s, but not because of black leaders' intervention or efforts to discourage it. Instead, as the postwar economy slowed tobacco production, all workers faced reductions in hours and pay and layoffs. Neglected, disregarded, and trumped, its membership facing unemployment, black unions dissolved in Durham. Ironically, another upswing in tobacco production was about to occur, and with it migration tides brought another surge of black working women into the city. In the meantime, economic and demographic trends had combined in one way to provoke agitation among tobacco workers and in another to suppress any momentum for labor activism. For fleeting moments through the 1920s, unionizing efforts were renewed. But, failing to work with black women workers, the TWIU did not get a firm hold on Durham until 1943. And even then, the interracial struggle and the disregard for the power of black women as organizers made it difficult for either side to negotiate from a position of strength.

"The Universal Mother"

"The colored women are valuable members of the women's army of America," proclaimed the *Star of Zion*, the North Carolina–based newspaper of the AME Zion church in 1918, quoting the famous black writer, journalist, and activist Alice Dunbar-Nelson. During World War I, Dunbar-Nelson served as a member of the Woman's Division for the National Defense Council, made up of civilian advisers charged with encouraging Americans to support the war effort. Traveling throughout the South as the field representative for "colored work," she toured North Carolina in February 1918 to assess African American women's participation in local and state programs. In Charlotte, she found black women "simply aching to be put in touch in an official way with the situation," but in Durham, African American women already were mobilized. There, Martha Merrick (wife of barber and entrepreneur John Merrick) and Minnie Pearson (wife of principal William G. Pearson) had gathered their friends and colleagues; teachers like Pauline Dame and Sallie Fitzgerald had assembled their students; and nurses Julia Latta and Patricia Carter had turned their volunteers into an army of activity.[64]

Encouraged by black men and sought out by white women, women of the elite and middle class emerged as visible community organizers for the Red Cross, for savings and Liberty Loans programs, and for local initiatives to support men in uniform during wartime. Aspects of these activities were called "interracial," although black women and white women were mostly engaged in projects under the same banner but in separate fields. The Durham County chapter of the American Red Cross incorporated black women from its start. According to its history, the Durham chapter was founded in the spring of 1917. African American women operated as an auxiliary chapter that met apart and on matters relevant to black soldiers. For the most part, the black Red Cross leadership was drawn from black elite women, who had the time and resources to do significant volunteer work. Among them, Julia McCauley Warren, who had moved to Durham in 1899 to teach domestic science at Whitted School and later married Dr. Stanford L. Warren, chaired the executive committee. Lillian Dodson, wife of pharmacist J. A. Dodson and daughter of Richard Fitzgerald, participated as one of the rotating chairs of the auxiliary. Other officers mixed Red Cross work and their employment in race work. Public health nurse Julia Latta served as the organization's vice chair, and librarian Hattie Wooten was the secretary.[65] Notwithstanding, the black Red Cross represented a sizable contingent of African American women, some 480 strong in 1918. Two additional auxiliaries, one in Rougemont and the other at Lincoln Hospital, increased those numbers.

Because no troop trains passed through Durham, most projects involved send-off and welcome-home festivities, fund-raising, the production of comfort items, and the delivery of local services. Even this required more hands than clubwomen alone could provide. The black auxiliary furnished shaving kits and lunches for the black soldiers who entrained for camp; produced clothing, operating gowns, and items for use on the front; collected $600 in donations from the black community; and contributed $200 more to the soldiers' homecoming celebration. African American women's Red Cross work also linked race relations with fund-raising and the larger community. Two public concerts raised another $500. One held at the Academy of Music featured "old plantation melodies and other fine musical numbers" to attract a white audience, for whom the Red Cross women reserved all first floor

seating.[66] In addition, the Lincoln auxiliary organized the missionary societies of various churches to host a Red Cross Room at the hospital. From
there they provided aid and information to black soldiers and their families.
Offering additional war support, black teachers organized public school students to march in the Red Cross parade. For the welcome-home celebration,
Durham housekeepers baked 250 cakes, work actually done by black cooks
and domestics. On top of all this, women took up collections in churches to
establish "hostess houses" that offered wholesome, supervised, mixed-sex
entertainment at the various military camps and canteens where black soldiers were stationed.[67]

Red Cross initiatives crossed the lines of race and class, drawing on the
energies of women willing to participate in drives that focused on home front
and battlefront needs. Donating and distributing milk, food, and nursing
assistance brought volunteers into contact with strangers among the activists
and the needy. In 1918, the global flu epidemic struck Durham. According to
Pauli Murray, her aunt, Sallie Fitzgerald, worked on behalf of the Red Cross
at Whitted School, transformed temporarily into a hospital to care for the
sick. In a nod to the breadth of black Red Cross contributors, the *Herald*
published an article about Luetta Haskins, a laundress from the Walltown
section, who volunteered two hours per day at the Trinity College Red
Cross, pressing bandages for shipment.[68]

Home front efforts not only advanced black women's organized activities
but also brought them into not-so-unfriendly contact with whites, especially
women, although it is not clear if black women sought out whites or if white
women sought out blacks. Either way, local white women activists were
proud to inform national and state representatives of Liberty Loan programs
that African American women were engaged in the work as well, with "Mrs.
Martha Merrick and Mrs. Minnie Pearson already working up programs
among the colored." Surprisingly, too, white women acknowledged black
women's contributions in ways that subsumed race to the larger cause. In an
unusual gesture that recognized Durham's black female leaders as respectable
women, references to African American women activists, such as those appearing in *Everywoman's Magazine*, used courtesy titles, Mrs. and Miss, for
every woman identified, white and black. In this way, if no other, the Red
Cross reaffirmed its self-characterization as "the Universal Mother, knowing
no race, nor creed, nor color, in its ministry of service to mankind."[69]

But whatever fairness African Americans hoped to achieve, whatever recognition they thought they deserved, whatever brief expressions of appreciation whites extended during the national emergency, black people still expe-

rienced as much if not more Jim Crow during and after the war as they had faced before. Because it was to their advantage, the members of the executive committee of the Durham Chamber of Commerce took note of Dr. Moore's perspective regarding labor and migration when he met with them in 1917. Toward the end of the war, however, the committee returned to its old ways. Moore presaged postwar tensions, sending a letter to the board in the spring of 1919 inquiring about the organization's plans "in the matter of seeing to [the needs of] returned soldiers and sailors, as well as other unemployed [persons]." But neither the executive committee nor the Chamber of Commerce itself engaged in any discussion or offered Moore a response.[70]

The War to Make the World Safe for Democracy briefly shifted the ground on which leaders and laborers, women and men, white and black, met. At variance with demands for black resources — money, labor, and spirit — white authorities could not prevent African Americans from tearing holes in the veil. Black leaders leveraged their influence in restive black communities and emboldened their strategies of race relations. Using the moment to reposition themselves in interracial politics, they stepped forward to request considerations for Durham's African American residents. But they accomplished little for their constituencies. Indeed, whites used law and law enforcement to hold the civic and industrial fabric together, drafting the bodies of African American men and remanding the labor of African American women. Yet, between white capitalists' needs for their labor and organized labor's need for their membership, black workers found space to insert their demands for wage increases. Although black labor interests advantaged union efforts to build a movement on the Piedmont, organized labor did not broaden its sight line beyond the place where Jim Crow and gender intersected. If there was a place of common ground, it was the Red Cross, where white and black elite women realized their common support for military sons.

As soon as World War I ended, southern patriotism reverted to previous form. In August 1917, a parade intended to raise enthusiasm for the war included a "Colored People's Section," albeit at the end of the parade. The welcome-home celebration for soldiers in 1919 incorporated a "Colored Committee," made up of Durham's leading black men among its planners, a formal recognition that would not have occurred before the war. Nonetheless, the parade program designated no place for African Americans to march among — or behind — the contingents of white military companies, bands, floats, fraternities, schoolchildren, war workers, and businesses. Nor were black businesses, institutions, and organizations represented in the parade. And black soldiers, if they marched at all, came behind the unnamed "unattached soldiers and sailors" at the end of the line.[71] Politics as usual had returned by the early summer of 1919, when white Durham welcomed Texas B. Ritchie to town to "perfect the organization of a local branch of the Loyal Order of the Klansmen." And at a meeting where Durham black citizens decided to build a war memorial to those lost in battle, the speaker, a white military chaplain, warned them to "stop thinking about social equality since it was a vain and foolish thought." Whites expected business as usual and welcomed the resurgence of the Ku Klux Klan.[72]

For the black working class, little had changed at all. Sharply improved economic conditions sparked as much transience as ever. Earnings rose, but so did costs. By the end of the war, and despite the development of new organizing tactics, racial discrimination and abuse by white authorities persisted and in some places escalated. Racial tensions turned into white-on-black assaults and rioting that swept through American towns and cities. More often the victims and not the perpetrators, the black masses frequently were accused of making trouble. During the 1918 riot in Winston-Salem, whites reportedly killed five black people (and probably more). Fearing the same events in Durham given the same circumstances, African American leaders did what they always did: publicly lectured the race on public conduct and soothed the white folk's anxieties. C. C. Spaulding wrote to the *Herald* in reference to the Winston-Salem assault: "I am convinced that the demoralizing actions of our shiftless, worthless element are as revolting to us as a whole as they are to the better element of the white race." Spaulding's letter to the editor reprimanded insolent blacks, as though they brought racial attacks upon themselves, and he addressed the issue most dear to him. He closed by thanking the *Herald* for reminding Durham residents that "no such violence could occur here."[73]

7 : Every Wise Woman Buildeth Her House

Gender and the Paradox of the Capital of
the Black Middle Class

Little more than a settlement of freedpeople two generations earlier,
by the mid-1920s, black Durham was the "Capital of the Black Middle
Class." As black sociologist E. Franklin Frazier wrote in 1925: "We have in
Durham today the outstanding group of colored capitalists who have entered
the second generation of business. This is significant as few Negro enterprises have survived the personal direction of its founders."[1] Recruited by
Frazier to the New Negro movement, Durham's leadership had shifted gen-
erationally with the passing of John Merrick, Aaron Moore, and Richard
Fitzgerald. As president of the Mutual, C. C. Spaulding became the titular
head of black Durham and the dean of black business in the United States.
Meanwhile, Dr. Charles Shepard stepped into Moore's shoes as a public
spokesperson on black health and superintendent of Lincoln Hospital. His
older brother, James E. Shepard, like Spaulding, had been born on the cusp
between slavery's last generation and freedom's first generation. Presiding

over the struggling National Religious Training School and Chautauqua, James Shepard transformed the institution into a state-supported center for higher education in the liberal arts, business, and education for African Americans. Among the younger generation, Louis Austin moved to Durham from Wilmington, bought the black Durham newspaper, and renamed it the *Carolina Times*. William G. Pearson's nephew, Conrad O. Pearson, graduated from Howard Law School and returned home to Durham to practice law. Not only did the number of prominent male leaders increase, but they presided over larger and more influential institutions and the economic trends of the 1920s continued to strengthen their financial bases.

They were beneficiaries of the New South political economy, the financial condition of which allowed them to embrace an ideology of black nationalism and black manhood that viewed patriarchy as an appropriately traditional gender role for men. John Merrick's dying wish for the Mutual was that it endure "for men to support their families," a theme that inscribed Durham's black business culture.[2] Just as the men of the elite community extolled their embrace of manhood, women of the elite began to articulate a similar message about womanhood. In fact, as male expectations eased with the generational shift, their community work shifted from the sacred stage of the church to the secular arena of public politics. Julia Warren and Minnie Pearson, prominent women in their own right, stepped into significant leadership roles, establishing new venues of women's activism. They were joined by widows Cottie Moore and Martha Merrick and followed by their daughters and their peers. The established group was joined in the 1920s by a younger generation who had attained elite or middle-class status through their education and employment. Ever-growing, North Carolina Mutual increased the size of its staff, especially in the clerical and accounting divisions, drawing to the city young African American women trained in business at the historically black colleges around the nation and at North Carolina College for Negroes. It was this wave of employees that brought Viola Turner and Eula Wade to the Mutual. With the opening of Hillside High School, William G. Pearson recruited young women teachers, including Clydie Fullwood Scarborough and Marie Faulk. Trained in education, social theory, and club work, they proffered new ideas and organizing strategies for racial uplift. And the generational shift among male leaders created space for women to emerge as activists.

If men in leadership exemplified the southern New Negro, what of the role of the New Negro woman? Like her hypothetical partners among men, "the most determined women forge ahead to results other than mere survival," penned Elise Johnson McDougald in her essay for *The New Negro* tome. "The task of Negro womanhood," she argued, was to reclaim her "finest spirit." Calling upon her sisters to take their places in the public sphere, McDougald charged, "To the gifted the zest of meeting a challenge is a compensating factor which often brings success." Turning her attention to her community and "obsessed with difficulties which might well compel individualism, the Negro woman has engaged in a considerable amount of organized action to meet group needs," McDougald pointed out. This she accomplished "through her intricate network" of local clubs, state federations, and national associations.[3] African American women historically shared a place on the participatory agenda of uplift. Yet representing the intersection of the New Negro woman — concerned with personal autonomy and public usefulness — and the New Negro — who no longer accommodated racism — young women refused to abide by the dictates of traditional womanhood, even as they worked as women for the advancement of the race. Good wages made the New Negro woman possible, as Mutual women demonstrated by wearing the latest fashions, listening to the latest music, and enjoying an animated social life of card playing, dances, and dinners.

The Durham they occupied in the 1920s was a lively place. Indeed, black Durham could claim two black mainstreets, one located downtown on Parrish Street and the other in Hayti. With the Mutual, the bank, and other black financial institutions providing the backing, small businesses sprouted along Pettigrew Street on the black side of the railroad tracks and up the hill for several blocks on Fayetteville Street. A filling station, a plumbing store, a restaurant, a dance hall, a print shop, and seventeen other storefronts filled in the two blocks between the White Rock Baptist Church and St. Joseph AME Zion Church. In between the businesses, grand homes mixed with squat bungalows and apartment buildings competed for attention architecturally with the fraternity hall. Along Pettigrew Street, the Biltmore Hotel and F. J. Watkins's Wonderland Theater anchored a string of shops. The Biltmore and the theater also housed small service enterprises on their upper levels. The newspaper office, the undertaker, and the library also clustered at Pettigrew and Fayetteville Streets, making the intersection the informational center of black Durham, the place where African Americans of all classes crossed paths.

The setting, with its mythical reputation for moneymaking, brought black Durham national notice and thrust it onto the national stage as a virtual black town. In reality, daily life behind the veil and within the black community had little to do with white folks. Except for occasional interlopers or clients, interracial relations took place on the white side of the color line. Inasmuch as laboring black folk embraced the goals of self-determination and racial advancement, they also were dedicated to protecting and supporting their families as the most important of black institutions. Black people especially among the laboring class lacked control over the economic conditions of their lives and were often forced to transcend gender roles whether they embraced them ideologically or not in order to survive.[4] Paradoxically, though, in the context of the postwar economy, just as the success of black business allowed women's gender roles to expand among the middle class and elite, the same elements made it possible for some families among the working class to realize traditional gender roles. Among those who in the past had had to send multiple family members out to work, for instance, good employment for some black men meant that their wives could choose to not work for whites. In 1920s Durham, therefore, some African American men of the working class could enact conventional manhood and some women could embrace traditional womanhood, at least as long as money flowed and personal disasters did not interrupt the course of family life.

In the meantime, the veil was like a fort, shored up by black families and institutions, providing a protective shield against the quotidian affronts of racism. Thus, despite its shortcomings — like the fact that it had no twelfth grade — Hillside High School was a center of pride: a vast brick building staffed by new teachers promising to expand the educational opportunities available to Durham's black youth. Flush with money from steady paychecks earned by Durham's black laborers, black business thrived. *Milestones along the Color Line: A Souvenir of Durham, North Carolina, Showing the Progress of the Race*, published in 1922, contained photographs of the result — "property owned and controlled exclusively by Negroes" — depicting the banks, businesses, fraternal societies, office buildings, homes, schools, and churches that marked the elites' status. Compiled by the black entrepreneurs who comprised the Durham Business and Professional League, *Milestones* provided "evidence of the progress being made by our race group in this section of the South," proof that at least the black elite had attained their aspirations to leave slavery and its memory behind.[5]

But *Milestones* portrayed only one Durham. The trimmed lawns, stately office buildings, enormous houses, and orderly vistas shown in *Milestones* contradicted the images of the other Durham populated by workers who "come and go through the streets in their work clothes," as described by Aaron M. Moore during World War I.[6] From the bay windows of the black elite homes, the music of Schubert and readings of Shakespeare competed with the sounds of street culture that swelled to create another more shadowy reputation for black Durham. Piedmont country blues were played on the street, and the latest movies were screened at the Wonderland, drawing African Americans toward the profane and away from the sacred, contradicting the message of respectability preached by the upper classes. Tobacco workers formed vocal quartets that impressed church audiences, but like blues musicians, they also earned extra money at house parties around town. The open sexuality of women blues singers embarrassed respectable folks even more than workers who raised their voices on the factory floor with their messages of defiance. The refrains of popular singers such as Ma Rainey, Bessie Smith, and Ethel Waters celebrated freedom from men.[7] As one singer boasted, "I'm no man's mamma now."[8]

Indeed, the booming times of the 1920s relieved some of the burden of the laboring poor and translated into good spirits and perhaps some relief from the decades-long tensions that followed freedom. In a good economy, the mills and factories ran two or three shifts, providing steady employment, flexible hours, and plenty of work. Rising incomes made it possible not only for African Americans to concentrate on themselves and their communities but also for Durham residents white and black to allay racial tensions. Racial segregation actually strengthened in workplaces, education, and residences, now codified into the architecture and the landscape, as well as the law and the culture. But separately and without interference from whites, African Americans had upbuilt their own spaces in Durham — privately owned public spaces for African Americans of all genders.

Still, not all of black Durham prospered, even though industrial expansion in the mid-1920s indicated strong economic conditions. The benefits of the good economy were short-lived, at best, and translated into few substantial changes for most African Americans given the realities of urban employment in the South. There was always a possibility that a reversal of upward trends could slow the factories and mills, close others, and cut the hours and pay of many workers, and if that happened, African Americans would lose their jobs first.[9] In fact, for most African Americans, hardship quickly followed brief gains. And family decisions about the urban and rural trek continued to rest on familiar gendered terms: women and men, but still mostly women, sought urban employment. Tobacco workers and household laborers struggled to keep their jobs in any climate, and many black families still relied on women's ability to obtain and maintain their employment. This gendered economic distress of the black masses projected an image of neediness, not security, and exacerbated concerns that race scholars, observers, and champions might have preferred to submerge.

Black Durham's bright veneer failed to obscure the feminization of urban poverty. Indeed, black Durham epitomized the unmistakable link between gender and poverty, now handed off to the Jim Crow generation. "Through-out the years of history," McDougald wrote, "woman has been the weather-vane, the indicator, showing in which direction the wind of destiny blows."[10] Women's poverty demonstrated just how permeable the black community remained to the hardships of Jim Crow, despite the significance of notable entities like the Mutual. In Durham, the mass of women among the working class reflected privation and worse, a stagnation if not a reversal of black progress. Side by side, the thriving Durham of the black elite and middle class and the dire straits of the working poor represented the ways that black American life had changed since emancipation. Although she was no better off than most of her working-class neighbors, Cornelia Fitzgerald, Pauli Murray's grandmother, patrolled the fence along the property line of her Durham homestead and dared her neighbors to cross the line. Murray viv-idly recalled the denigration that her grandmother heaped on the changing cast of residents in the Bottoms. Shouting across her barricade, the Fitz-gerald matriarch called one neighbor out as a "blaspheming South Carolina darky" and roared that others "come pushing in here lately, crowding out respectable folks with but a shoe box and the rags on your back."[11] Class conflict ran deep.

At the National Negro Business League meeting in 1926, C. C. Spaulding called upon his colleagues to cooperate in strengthening the economic base of their communities toward "the extermination of unrest. . . . We find one of the greatest handicaps to our group has been their unsettled condition, which has caused them to move from place to place, seeking to better their financial condition."[12] The persistence of black migration weighed heavily on Spaulding's mind, and women continued to do most of the migrating. Within the patriarchal structure the elite had built, women's migration, un-settledness, and quality of life in the city reflected family chaos, which so-ciologists like Frazier measured by "dependency, desertion, illegitimacy, and juvenile delinquency." In addition, vagrancy, prostitution, and an increase in crime and violence, the elite assumed, accompanied the poverty experienced by the female masses who moved to the city.[13]

In short, black Durham actually experienced more of what Frazier deni-grated than of what he praised. Hayti witnessed an extensive crime spree — bootlegging, prostitution, and a series of shootings and stabbings — during the summer of 1924 when unemployment ran high during the mid-decade depression, and the welfare department placed some thirty-five abandoned black children in orphanages, foster homes, and training schools. "The test of the strength of a community," Spaulding had noted in a 1921 speech, "is the strength of the weakest element of the population."[14] Whatever the black elite accomplished in Durham, it was rendered inadequate by the lives that black people had to live in the hollows and alleys of Durham's black neighborhoods.

"An Ordinary Man"

The prominence of poverty among black women does not imply that black men of the working class did not work. They, too, could access only a narrow range of employments. Apart from the hundred or so men employed in business and education and the few hundred who farmed, most African American males worked as laborers in the factories and mills or in service as janitors, dishwashers, bellhops, gardeners, and draymen. About one-quarter of Durham's black working men found gainful employment doing the heavy lifting of tobacco processing. Boys did the work of sweeping floors, collecting coal, shining shoes, and doing odd jobs and errands to earn money. Like women, many men also traveled back and forth between the country and the city, balancing family responsibilities with employment opportunities. For instance, George Scarborough, a Durham blues musician, recalled that his brother was the first in the family to leave the South Carolina plantation where the family sharecropped. He worked in the shipyards in Wilmington and then moved to New York. When he married, he moved to Durham, where his wife could find work, but he traveled back to South Carolina, where he "worked and helped out with the family" while his wife continued to reside in the Bull City.[15] Julius Davis's father, traveling from New York homeward to South Carolina, stopped in Durham and stayed because he found work.[16] Reginald Mitchner, also a blues musician, explained that men came to Durham because "it was a place that you could make money":

One of the biggest drawing cards for Durham was Liggett and Myers and American Tobacco Company — what used to be the Bull Durham Factory. That was the biggest incentive to come to Durham. The average man, he could get a job — a job that paid a salary. You know when a person is used to living and trying to raise a family on sporadic work, you know, where sometimes you got it and sometimes you ain't — well at least you come to these places and get these jobs. Whatever they're paying you was usually the average or sometimes better than the average, but you could look forward to it every week. And that way you could predict your future.[17]

Charlie Mack came to Durham in the 1920s with firm ideas about the roles of women and men from his father. He dedicated his life and work to making sure that neither his wife nor his children were disrespected, whether by white supervisors at the factory or white men in private homes. He demanded, as long as he could work, that his family abide by his rules, but he also knew that economic conditions might weaken his resolve.

The youngest of seven children, Charlie Neconda Mack was born in 1890 in Darlington, South Carolina, and grew up in a farming family, successful enough that they rented their land. Because they did not sharecrop, they sold their own crops at harvest and managed their financial affairs without the encumbrance of whites. Mack's father was a minister as well as a farmer and earned enough to educate his children. Mack briefly attended a training school but returned home to farm with his father and stayed there until he married in 1911. The daughter of a landowning man, Annie Miller, Mack's wife, did not have to work outside the home, although she helped on the farm. As the Mack family grew, it prospered in farming until 1920, when the farm produced only nine bales of cotton. In 1921, the boll weevil infestation swept through the Carolinas like a nor'easter out of the lower South, eating crops and profits. Mack harvested only one bale of cotton that year. With no income, no prospects, and a family, Mack shouldered his responsibility as a father and husband and borrowed money to leave South Carolina. "I couldn't stay," he recalled; "I had six children and I know: no jobs available."[18]

By the time he arrived in Durham in 1922, "that name [had] been out there for years." Some of his friends from South Carolina already had come to Durham, following the stream of migrants who sought employment in the factories, and they found a job for him drying tobacco. "I had the job before I came on, walk[ed] right into the job." It was work that would "whip an ordinary man," but six-foot-six Mack handled it easily and got a raise early on to thirty-five cents per hour. Working forty hours, he made fourteen dollars per week. With that pay, he recalled, "you could buy everything," including groceries, rent, light bill, and water bill, and "then have some left." By Christmas, a proud Charlie Mack bragged, "I had all my children with shoes, clothes, and everything on them." The Macks had no problem finding a house on the black side of the railroad tracks; there were "plenty of big houses . . . run down, some of them, but nobody living in them." They found a house large enough for a family of eight on Poplar Street, off Fayetteville Street, between Hayti and Mexico.[19]

The children found Durham "exciting," oldest daughter Annie Mack Barbee recalled, especially compared to the "very dull" life on a South Carolina farm. Poplar Street was "very friendly" but also a place of frequent public violence. The Macks lived about a block from Murder Alley, a narrow strip along a section known for frequent street fights. "It was very exciting" for the children "to see somebody lay somebody out" on the street. Some neighbors fought, others "weren't so nice, using them kinds of words [cursing]." But there was a lot to do in Hayti for youngsters who explored the city; the "movies house, bakery, barbershop, and all that, right there in Hayti," kept the children occupied. "If we wanted anything, we'd go around there to the bakery and get it. Wanted to go to the show, go right down to the corner." Hayti was a lively place with "people passing by, going back and forth to work. . . . We were really right in the center." Raised by a "strict" father and "loving" mother, Annie and her sisters learned life lessons through spirit and action. Deeply religious, both parents were active in Mount Vernon, where tobacco workers comprised the congregation.[20]

An imposing patriarch, Charlie Mack was made in the same mold as the businessmen and leaders who lived on the upper end of Fayetteville Street, the black elite. Mack's sense of family extended to his neighbors, friends, and colleagues. He was elected treasurer of the community fund among black tobacco workers at Liggett and Myers, an informal mutual aid society. They entrusted him with hard-earned resources, cash that came back to workers when they fell on hard times. A man of strong race pride, Mack spent his money in Hayti's black business district and banked at Mechanics and Farmers Bank. His wife "didn't work," Annie Mack Barbee reminisced about her mother. She may not have worked in the factory, but she was part of the extended family of tobacco workers, bound on one hand by the shared benefits and detriments of factory work and on the other by being a helpful neighbor and staunch churchwoman. When she took sick, it was the women of that community who came to her aid. According to Charlie Mack, "Somebody [was] in my house all the time. I had to work, [but] folks at the factory could work all day at the factory, [then] someone stay[ed] all night in my house. . . . Women would come with laundry baskets of clothes and put them down." They offered gentle, meticulous care for his ailing wife; "they['d] strip her, give her a bath, comb her hair and carry the clothes back home [to] wash and iron them." Women from Mount Vernon came by every evening to "take over everything," managing the household and doing the labor of housekeeping and child rearing. Mack was thankful for the assistance and support and grateful that his wife "died like a queen."[21]

When her death left Charlie Mack to raise six children alone, word of his distress traveled to Durham's voluntary circles of women activists. Enlarging their roles, building secular networks, and affiliating finally with the state and national women's secular organizations to address urban problems, especially those that affected young women, the clubwomen wanted to prevent young women like Charlie Mack's daughters from falling prey to the dangers of the city. The girls were vulnerable to such influences, they thought, without maternal supervision. The reformers also wished to prevent them from having to work under the cruel conditions of the factory. Lastly, they were anxious to exercise new influence with whites, in this case to compel the municipality to pay attention to its black residents. They informed the city welfare department of Mack's predicament, and the bureau acted on the call.

Mack agreed with the clubwomen that black girls should be closely supervised for their own protection and that they should grow up to be responsible and respectable. He shared their concerns about the hazards of their neighborhoods and knew that vices of the street such as drinking, cursing, and violence occurred too regularly there. But Mack did not appreciate the intervention of the middle class and the elite, however well intentioned the efforts to find assistance for his family. "A gang of white niggers over on Fayetteville Street," as he called the agents of reform, "wanted my children. They went to [the director of public welfare] and told him a man 'round on Poplar Street got a gang of little ones and he can't take care of them. [Their] mama is dead. We want you to step in there and get them out from him and we'll take them." An angry Mack refused. "Well, they ain't going to get none of them." Mack viewed the reformers as adversaries who interfered with his autonomy and his role as a family man and patriarch. He resented their confidence that they knew more than he did about managing his family affairs because they were of a different class. As far as Mack was concerned, he was raising his children in a "Christian home" with the same high moral values to which the elite and middle class clung, and his success or failure could not be judged fairly by those who did not experience the same circumstances.[22]

The welfare department responded to the reformers' request and agreed to pay the expense of sending the sisters back to South Carolina. Mack accepted the offer but still feared for his daughters' safety. In rural areas, outside the kind of protections an urban community could provide, young African American women were vulnerable to the menace of white men, subject perpetually to sexual assault and harassment inherent to rural life. There were other dangers as well. Although the girls lived in Manning with their grandparents and attended a Rosenwald School across the street from their grandparents' home, the school itself was not out of harm's way. In fact, "because [the school] was black . . . it burnt to the ground," Annie Mack

Barbee remembered. In addition, "old white men riding down the high-
way . . . picking up girls" made them vulnerable to the same elements that
Mack had wanted them to escape. He refused to leave the girls in South
Carolina for long and, when he remarried, brought his daughters back to
Durham.[23]

By then, the economic boom of the 1920s had begun to fade as the Great
Depression set its weight on black people well before 1929. With his hours
cut, his overtime limited, and his youngest children needing clothing and
food, Charlie Mack sent his three oldest daughters to work at the Liggett and
Myers factory. In 1928, Annie went to work at the age of fifteen, Mae at
fourteen, and Pansy at thirteen. Mack preferred tobacco work over household labor because for all its hazardous features — encounters with foremen,
harsh toil, and unsanitary conditions — the factory was a place of camaraderie, populated mostly by familiar black faces, many of them neighbors and
family. In any case, neither Annie nor her sisters tolerated mistreatment by
whites. For protection from the insult of Jim Crow, they looked to their coworkers and their community, institutions, and friends. They lived in their
father's house as he required and turned their pay over to him until they
turned eighteen. Then, if they remained in Mack's household, they paid for
room and board.[24]

The core of clubwomen's efforts to improve the lives of young women
among the laboring class reflected the tenets of respectability that had survived the turn of the century, and according to these tenets, tobacco was not
respectable work. Indeed, it resembled the conditions of bondage in that
foremen — like masters — disrespected, intimidated, and sexually harassed
black women workers. Women subjected to these conditions did not meet
the demands of female respectability. Once employed in tobacco, women
rarely could leave and thus could not rise in class, status, or condition. Annie
Mack Barbee might have agreed with the clubwomen. Thinking back, she
explained, "Going in a place like that [the factory] to work, you never get
anywhere in your goals. . . . You don't go anywhere."[25]

Still, the Macks sought autonomy, not another form of dependency. Perceived as meddlers, activist women incurred resentment from people whose
goals were to reduce the restrictions of Jim Crow and gender. Besides, Mack
and his family did embrace the tenets of respectability as they applied to
gender roles. As long as Mack could farm successfully, he could support his
family in South Carolina on the land, and as long as he could make good
money, he did not let his wife work for anyone else. Once he began to
struggle, he believed it was his responsibility as the male head of household

to hold his family together. They moved to Durham because Mack could find work there, and as long as his earnings allowed, his wife stayed home, his children attended school, and the family enjoyed the good life of the city. The church and the community served as an extended family of guardians and shields. After his wife passed away, however, Mack could not manage work and the care of his daughters well. A concerned father, he sent his daughters away because they were girls, but he sent them to family and brought them back as soon as he could provide them with a mother figure in the household. Had his children been boys, Mack might have considered returning to farming because each child would have contributed to work on the farm. Then, too, if they had been boys, the agents of reform might not have intervened.

"Emphasizing Virtue in Our Early Girlhood"

Upbuilding new institutions, women activists stepped into leadership roles after the deaths of John Merrick in 1919 and Aaron Moore in 1923 to expand programs for uplift. World War I had opened venues for action and activism that had not existed before. African American women historically committed to community work, but, as one woman explained, "it was the men who did things. We didn't have to, because the men did it."[26] The black women's club movement had not reached Durham by the end of the nineteenth century, most likely because such efforts had been the purview of the city's leading black men. A few organizations, like the Volkamenia Literary Club, brought the black community's intellectual elite together, and, of course, Eastern Star as a mutual aid society had been formed in the early days of the black community. But surprisingly few female voluntary associations had extensive operations in Durham outside of the church. The black women's club movement of the turn of the century with its articulated critique of black men's leadership had not emerged as part of the internal politics of upbuilding black Durham. Nor had local women's organizations been particularly visible, even during the heyday of the National Association of Colored Women's Clubs — although after Lincoln Hospital was built existing women's organizations supported public health initiatives and created a project around which new women's groups organized. The Daughters of Dorcas, founded officially in 1917, and the sororities expanded their presence in Durham in the 1920s. In this endeavor, Durham's most prominent black women demonstrated an impressive ability to sustain race work. Lincoln Hospital and public health issues like the flu epidemic of 1918 also had brought the women of the black elite into the public arena and into contact, albeit limited, with white women who shared these priorities. But not until World War I did Durham's elite and middle-class women make a substantial organizational impact on the urban milieu, and even then their work focused on the war effort—selling Liberty Bonds, joining the Red Cross, and seeing to the needs of black soldiers.

During World War I, problems associated with urbanization worsened with the wartime explosion of the population, exacerbating the difficulties that young women faced when they moved to the city to seek employment. A growing female population put pressure on the housing market, for instance, as single women searched for suitable places to live. If they did not have family or contacts, they found it almost impossible to find decent housing at a reasonable cost. Durham postmistress and realtor Bernice Ingram rented houses and apartments to couples but found "three or four other women" living there, too.[27]

Middle-class women could find places in the homes of the black elite or in facilities provided for them. Teachers, for instance, could find housing at teacherages, or group housing, as assigned by William G. Pearson, principal of Hillside High School (built after World War I) and unofficial superintendent of black education. Young single women, like those who came to work for North Carolina Mutual and Provident Association in the 1910s, mostly lived with the families of Mutual officers until Clerks' Home was built in the early 1920s. Some new arrivals sought assistance from the Red Cross, and church groups provided some resources. Not surprisingly, prominent black women like Julia Warren, who lived in large homes, took young women into their households, but individual efforts failed to meet the larger needs of young women who desired more flexibility than was possible under the roofs of Durham's black patriarchs. And, too, the elite were not likely to take in the farm girls and transients who sought work in the factories.[28]

Durham's black clubwomen turned to the theme of character to address feminized poverty. Barely removed from the outrages committed against female slaves, black women and girls of freedom's second and third generations, they feared, had lost the momentum generated by their foremothers in protecting and projecting a positive image of African American women. Although "the laws of evolution are at work and turning our once 'black wenches' into an admired womanhood," one editor of the *Star of Zion*, newspaper of the AME Zion Church, claimed, there remained "the imperative need of emphasizing virtue in our early girlhood in the homes and pure sociology in our society aside from that secured through the school career and contact with the higher social influences." Complaining that "thousands of girls have but ordinary school training which does not lift them out of the vociferous street conduct and [that] behind this is a loose home training or none at all," the editor called upon mothers to "get together, organize and formulate plans and devise schemes" to gather young women "to be lectured to and instructed in morals, hygiene, social conduct, self-care, and the rudiments which make for ladyship."[29]

These efforts carried civil rights overtones in that the abuse and harassment suffered by African American women at the hands of whites resulted from prejudice. Promoting black respectability, the elite believed, created a route to better race relations and, by extension, better conditions for black workers — specifically, household training programs were needed to emphasize morality and appropriate gender roles, to make the laborer less vulnerable to advances from the men of the household. The elites believed that whites would never recognize African Americans as citizens as long as some women among the race exhibited aberrant behaviors. In addition, women leaders hoped to help young women take their places as race leaders and models of womanhood who could speak not only to the injustices and inequality mandated by southern law but to the unfairness of prejudice and its effect on black people generally. In the South, the *Zion* editor continued, there was no law "to compel a white man to legally honor a Negro woman he has wronged." Both men and women of color had taken to openly resisting "designing white men," who finally were "meeting with the scorn and womanly disdain they so richly deserve in their dastardly, unmanly and illogical assumptions that there is no virtue among Negro women." Still, "the strength and progress of the race" depended upon "the character of its women." Accordingly, it was the responsibility of clubwomen to address these issues through uplifting women in particular. "Negro men respect their women when convinced that they are ladies of honor," the writer posed, and "the women of the race have much yet to accomplish in bringing their less fortunate element up to the required standard."[30]

Addie Hunton (who would soon travel with the American Expeditionary Forces in Europe in World War I) must have been surprised at the minimal public activism among black women in Durham. Touring as the secretary for city work for the ywca, Hunton came to Durham in 1912 to survey working conditions in southern industry for black women and girls. She visited North Carolina in the spring of that year, just after the journal *World's Work* published Du Bois's article, "The Upbuilding of Black Durham," which praised the city's black social and economic development as an answer to the race problem. Looking more broadly at a different side of African American life,

Hunton presented a different picture: "The life of the colored people in these towns [Winston-Salem, Durham, and Fayetteville] [was] a picture full of shadows." Hunton found tobacco work "too dark, too depressing," a story "too long to be unfolded" in her written report to the board.[31] Hunton and Du Bois wrote tales of two cities, one affluent and dominated by men, the other impoverished and dominated by women, one imbued with respectability, the other permeated with immorality. The strength of Durham's black business community did lead social worker Hunton to conclude that in Durham the shadows were "not so deep." The women employed by "the colored mill," for example, were considered "of a superior type," meaning they demonstrated the respectability that she did not find among other women laborers. For them, the situation was "more hopeful." As to what might be done to improve the degrading work conditions at Liggett and Myers or American Tobacco, Hunton believed that "people who are interested in the welfare of the factory hands" might act on their behalf. That role, she believed, fell to the clubwomen of Durham.[32]

As a pioneer in race relations and women's labor, the YWCA and its interracial efforts looked southward where it proposed to establish programs in cities and at historically black colleges and universities. Originally, the YWCA was founded in response to the growing numbers of young women moving to the cities, to take up issues relevant to female education, labor, and empowerment. With the building of its programs for African American women, the YWCA initially supported segregated local chapters, which operated as subsidiaries to the main local (white) YWCA. The result of Hunton's work in Durham was the establishing of a YWCA at the National Religious Training School (North Carolina Central University). An active college chapter, the National Religious Training School's YWCA hosted a conference in December 1912 that attracted 118 students, who were "very quietly dressed and earnest in manner." The meeting marked "an epoch" in the work of the YWCA, argued Hunton, but she had an even greater hope that the student group could spark efforts among adult women to devise programs to meet young women's needs.[33]

The racial politics of Durham — and of the YWCA itself — did not allow a "colored Y" facility to exist without a white one, and not until after World War I did white women in Durham take up the project of establishing a YWCA. Julia Warren, wife of Dr. Stanford L. Warren, joined by Minnie Pearson, wife of principal William G. Pearson, and Janie Spaulding, cousin of C. C. Spaulding, took up the task of establishing a branch of the YWCA in Hayti. They hoped this YWCA would respond to the social needs of single working women and bring them under the guidance of the association's Christian values.[34] Because the YWCA was an interracial organization, Warren, Pearson, and Spaulding sought the cooperation of local white women they knew through the public health, Liberty Loan, and Red Cross programs. Like most interracial efforts, theirs failed initially. For a variety of reasons, including personality clashes, conflicting goals, and race prejudice, interracial YWCA work proceeded very slowly. Conversations began again in 1919, and once again failed.

In 1920, the local Women's Defense Committee (white) used funds left over in its treasury from war work to finance a YWCA for white women. Many YWCAs had come about as an extension of war work to accommodate working women's needs — to provide residential housing and hostess houses and to pass on information about the war to families. In Durham, the YWCA movement began with different issues in mind.[35] Because industrialists, the husbands of Durham's white clubwomen, feared that unionization might result from gatherings of young working-class women, the city YWCA work did not focus on them. Instead, the original program set up rooms in one of the buildings downtown where white clerical workers could gather for discussion and appropriate activities. Local white YWCA interests sought to provide a healthful place for young businesswomen rather than mill workers to gather for lunch, rest, meetings, and entertainment. The Central YWCA (as the white YWCA was known) opened in an office building downtown, but not until it grew out of its space and was offered the Durham Hosiery Annex in West Durham did the white YWCA include an "industrial program" geared toward white women who worked in the factories and mills.[36]

Warren, Pearson, and Spaulding, a female activist triumvirate, restarted negotiations in 1921, this time with the Central YWCA, to found a black YWCA. Such a facility, they believed, would provide healthful recreation and education and a residential space for young black women while reinforcing clubwomen's embrace of the idealized role of womanhood. Thus, in many ways, black clubwomen shared the philosophical underpinnings of the project with their white counterparts. In moving toward building a black YWCA, however, activists met resistance. Few, if any, efforts had been made to forge institutional connections between blacks and whites in Durham since the days of Fusion politics, and joint secular institutions essentially were unknown. Local negotiations required intervention by the YWCA's national secretary, Eva Bowles, who came to Durham to shine the light of national perspectives on local circumstances.

Establishing the black YWCA, then, set another precedent in women's interracial work, but not, apparently, a successful one. White women activists did not accept Bowles's position, that black women should be able to "help make policies." Holding the opinion that black women could "think from actual knowledge of facts," Bowles was discouraged that "colored secretaries from headquarters [were] excluded from Southern soil." She disagreed with the policy that "the YWCA can never in any place or in any part of its work go faster than the people of the community will permit." Bowles was impatient that African American women had to wait "for the white women to have a change of heart." As Bowles wrote in her annual report in 1922, "This year has proven the futility of an understanding [because] white people interpret colored people to white people."[37]

In 1922, Warren, Spaulding, and Pearson tried again, asking that a different representative from the national YWCA headquarters come to Durham with a "view to establish a colored branch." That July, Adele Ruffin, another national secretary for "work with the colored," requested an individual interview with the all-white board of directors of the Durham Central YWCA. According to the minutes of the meeting, Ruffin assured the white women that "leaders among the colored people of Durham were ready and anxious for this work to be started and were prepared to bear their share of the expense." She added, however, that in accordance with national policy, "such a step would never be taken unless the Central YWCA had a part in financing the movement and the salary of the Secretary." After a "thorough and conscious discussion," during which Ruffin was asked to leave the room, a motion passed to let the Central YWCA administration cooperate. By December 1922, the "colored YWCA," a branch named for Harriet Tubman, had rented a building, hired an executive secretary, and selected a board of management. By February 1923, the "colored Y" had enrolled 200 members and begun a study on "the trends of the races" and was offering classes to young women in "millinery and current events."[38]

The YWCA became a way for black women activists to work out relationships with white women, but the Tubman Y had to struggle for autonomy. In accordance with national guidelines, the Central Y supervised the Tubman branch through a Committee on Colored Work — and in accordance with southern tradition, that committee was completely white. The Tubman branch operated separately regarding its finances and programs, but technically the Central YWCA approved any programs, as well as the budget, and refused to recognize that the Tubman YWCA might have a different mission. The Community Chest, a municipal funding agency, denied the Tubman YWCA's direct request for funding, demanding that it be routed through the

Central YWCA board.[39] And most interracial events lacked substance. An "interested group" of white women toured the offices of North Carolina Mutual, the Royal Knights of King David, and the Bankers Fire Insurance Company in 1925, but the Central YWCA did little else toward improving race relations.[40]

Not until 1934 did the secretary of the Tubman branch attend a Central executive board meeting, and then only "after dinner had been served and cleared," a point made in the YWCA minutes to assure others that racial propriety had been observed. Unable to transcend Jim Crow for the sake of sisterhood, the white women mostly avoided social contact, under the guise of not wanting to embarrass or offend the African American women with whom they could not break bread, despite the teachings of Christianity. Minutes of executive committee meetings, moreover, made only references to reports offered on "the colored situation" rather than to any specific initiative taken on behalf of the Tubman YWCA. In 1934, the Central board did decide to "back up" the Association for Southern Women for the Prevention of Lynching in their appeal regarding "an Alabama case," in which nine young black men (the so-called Scottsboro Boys) were falsely accused of raping two white women. Finally, in late 1934, the executive board replaced the Committee on Colored Work, an ineffectual group, with an Interracial Committee, chaired by a white woman, who served as an ex-officio — that is, nonvoting and powerless — member of the Central board. Thus the Tubman YWCA could claim only a symbolic presence on the Central board, in the form of a white woman representative.[41]

Still the YWCA initiative marked a turning point in interracial work among women in Durham. After 1934, the YWCA project began to reflect "bi-racial" concerns, which in reality managed the connections and served as a buffer between black and white women leaders. White board members attended meetings at the Tubman branch; in 1936, Durham hosted a state interracial conference on YWCA administration and leadership; and in 1938, the board allowed an interracial group of students interested in industrial workers to use the main building, "provided they have no meals together there, or elsewhere."[42] Beyond these polite interactions, black and white women struggled to find a way to work together productively. Christian convictions rarely traversed the color line; indeed, the church remained the most segregated institution of all, despite a common faith. Against a strong tradition of segregation and wary of the "peculiar circumstances attending the work of the colored," white members of the Central board took very small steps.[43]

Still, war work and the YWCA brought Durham's African American women into some contact with white individuals who were associated with other female activist networks. Once interracial meetings began, local white and black leaders found common ground in three places. They agreed, first of all, that "the race problem can only be solved through cooperation and understanding between the races." Second, black and white women agreed to coordinate efforts around issues regarding women's and children's health — prenatal care, the life expectancy of babies, and the health of mothers. To that end, the YWCA Interracial Committee cosponsored immunization programs and children's health clinics in black neighborhoods, although not until the late 1930s and the 1940s.[44] As social service agents, then, black and white clubwomen learned to coordinate their efforts and collaborated to introduce other programs. In 1928, for instance, at an interracial meeting in Durham, black clubwomen endorsed initiatives to train and license midwives, which was promoted by white women. To encourage black clubwomen to support the program, Mrs. Thomas Bickett, director of the North Carolina State Board of Public Charities and Public Welfare, pointed out that almost three-quarters of the births among African Americans were presided over by midwives.[45]

The third matter — the problem of "idleness" among black working-class women, as Bickett put the matter, or "the untrained negro servant," as North Carolina clubwoman Charlotte Hawkins Brown stated the issue — proved more problematic. Returning to the themes echoed at many an interracial meeting, the question of domestic service "from the viewpoint of the employer and employee" provided the elite of both sides with the most productive area of collaboration. Household laborers, exploited and harassed, would likely have disagreed. For their part, white women recommended programs to "prepare the Negro servant for more honest, intelligent, and efficient service to her employer," while black clubwomen desired to "secure from the employer more and better protection for the servant including a living wage." As a result, the project emerging out of interracial efforts focused on training working-class women for what both black and white reformers regarded as appropriate employment, despite the fact that those who held such positions deplored the job.[46]

Through the YWCA, sororities, and other initiatives, black clubwomen promoted household labor as a viable and reputable employment option. Such training, they believed, offered a means to calm the racial waters by improving the relationship between black and white women at their most intimate point of contact. Better workers who met the standards of respectability, furthermore, better represented the race and race progress, black clubwomen thought. Finally, they hoped, trained domestic workers would gain deeper respect from employers in the form of better pay, better hours, better conditions, and, most important, personal safety. For this, black women activists held white women activists accountable. At an interracial meeting in Atlanta, forthright Charlotte Hawkins Brown, a leader in the national black women's club movement, spoke as clearly as she could in this touchy setting to the problem of white sexual assault on black women: "We have for a long time been painfully conscious of the many unjust and humiliating practices of which colored women in the South have been the victims. There is no one of us who has not at various times and places been called upon to face experiences which are common to the women of our race. We, therefore, take this opportunity to call to the attention of white women certain conditions which affect colored women in the relations with white people, and which, if corrected, will go far toward decreasing friction, removing distrusts and suspicion, and creating a better atmosphere in which to adjust the difficulties which always accompany human contact."[47]

Ultimately, interracial work put the onus for improving the circumstances of domestic work back onto those who suffered its exploitations the most, the household laborers themselves. Judgments based in respectability, then, preserved rather than challenged the race and gender paradigm of appropriate place. Professionalizing domestic labor, a project promoted by the YWCA, women's organizations, and educational institutions, in reality reinforced the subservience of the job and reified the idea that black working-class women were supposed to serve others. Annie Mack Barbee and her tobacco-working sisters preferred to escape such work, seeing household labor as an option only when factory employment was scarce, and then only as temporary work. Sponsors furthermore misunderstood, if not disregarded, black working-class women's knowledge: that domestic workers were not only exploited but were paid without regard for ability. The worker, furthermore, did not control the work environment; rather, the employer prevailed. Thus household labor offered none of the autonomy the women of the elite expected for themselves.[48]

Nonetheless, black women's organizations took up the program with enthusiasm. Notices in the *Carolina Times*, Durham's black newspaper, and the *Durham Herald-Sun* announced training classes "open and free to all employed girls and young women who wish to become trained domestic workers." Providing a certificate and recommendation upon completion, the programs suggested that graduates might find employment among Durham's best white families.[49] During the 1930s, Alpha Kappa Alpha, a sorority of black college-educated women, cosponsored such training programs with the National Youth Administration, a New Deal agency where Mary Mc-Leod Bethune directed the Division for Negro Youth. For "Negro women who have received no definite training in household duties," the program offered "a better understanding of the work," including "thorough training in individual health and personal appearance [and] of suitable clothing for work," in addition to "planning and marketing; how to prepare and serve all types of foods; housecleaning; laundrying; and other worthwhile things" necessary "to become more valuable to employers and to receive higher wages."[50]

Perpetuating the idea of training for domestic work illustrated one manifestation of uplift's equivocal thrust: a misguided sense of working-class women's needs and black elitism. On the one hand, Alpha Kappa Alpha conducted scholarship drives for young women of sorority caliber. On the other hand, the group sponsored domestic training programs that sent a message reserving higher education for the privileged like themselves and assigning manual labor to their social inferiors not of college "caliber." Furthermore, such training also acknowledged that upward mobility was not appropriate for all. Equally important, the training of domestic workers benefited not only white women but also women of the black elite. Members of Durham's Alpha Kappa Alpha, a premier sorority, and Durham's black women reformers hired domestic workers themselves. "They hired these women in their homes," asserted Johnnie McLester, secretary of the Tubman YWCA. Simultaneously, black elite women's ability to hire black maids represented a way to exhibit the status differential between themselves and their lesser sisters: the women they hired to work in their homes were the women they perceived to be outside their social circle.[51]

While Durham's black women reformers looked to the YWCA movement to exercise their perspectives, another organization looked to them for the resources and influence they might bring to a wider circle. The North Carolina Federation of Colored Women's Clubs (NCFCWC) provided another venue where black women built onto the fragile relationships established with white women during the war. Charlotte Hawkins Brown, head of the Palmer Memorial Institute, a private black high school near Greensboro, founded the NCFCWC in 1909. The organization took up the call of the National Association of Colored Women (NACW) to lift as they climbed. While "encouraging Negro women to venture into all lines of human endeavor," the NCFCWC also set out to "raise the status of Negro women through clubs" and "to envision the gradual ending of discriminatory practices."[52] Although Brown herself was prominent in the NACW, she had limited success in encouraging participation back home. "The women of N.C. are not enthusiastic in their interest [in] the National," Brown wrote to Mary McLeod Bethune, NACW president in 1924. Even among those active in state work, none hailed from Durham, where men historically led. Nor, perhaps, had Brown paid much attention to Durham. The town's black leaders had concentrated on the local scene for its upbuilding efforts. Bethune herself recruited Minnie Pearson to the work of the NACW. Writing in 1927, Bethune encouraged Pearson, "I know that you will do all you possibly can to help put over the program of our National Association of Colored Women," and asked that Durham women "keep closely in touch with me and my work."[53]

In any case, the NCFCWC remained a struggling, loosely affiliated group of local women's clubs without much force in the national picture. As late as 1929 an embarrassed Brown could gather only thirteen representatives from North Carolina to attend the NACW's national convention.[54] In Durham, additionally, where church work gained more attention than club work, only a few secular service groups of women were active, although social and literary circles thrived. For these, Charlotte Hawkins Brown had little patience. Invited to speak at a meeting of the Volkamenia Club, Durham's foremost literary society, she commented, "You know me surely as a very busy woman, and while I scorn not the delights of literature in all of its beauty and art, my utilitarian program has deprived me of that recent research and study sufficient to meet the demands of a literary organization."[55] Still, the NCFCWC got a small foothold in Durham with the Woman's Home and Foreign Missionary Society, Eastern Star, Household of Ruth, and Kings Daughters, whose national structures affiliated with the NACW. The state federation's motto, "Every wise woman buildeth her house," already informed Durham women's local work. One Durham service organization, the Daughters of Dorcas, joined the NCFCWC in 1919, keeping Lincoln Hospital as its primary project. Its affiliation with the state organization directly introduced the clubwomen's imperatives to local community work and linked Durham women to the state and national club movement that they had overlooked before.[56]

Already familiar with similar efforts through the NACW and through funding her school, Brown led North Carolina's African American women into the newly forged arena of interracial work in the South. Judging that "frankness, patience, and intelligent listening between the leaders on both sides" operated to the benefit of both communities, Brown represented African American women's perspectives at several conferences, including a ground-breaking meeting in Memphis of southern white women with "upright women of the colored race."[57] A moving gathering, the meeting laid the foundation for future endeavors, as white women accepted "a deep sense of responsibility to the womanhood and childhood of the Negro race" as well as a "great desire for Christian settlement of the problems that overshadow the homes of both races." Among a long list of "recommendations" presented, issues relevant to the health and welfare of children proved the easiest to address, and specific action items emerged surrounding these issues. White and black women wrestled most with "the servant problem," the point where the lives of black and white women intersected most closely.[58]

The complaints of white women were familiar: the lack of reliability, responsibility, and honesty on the part of domestics. African American women seized the opportunity to point out that black household laborers were overworked, underpaid, and lacking in protection, that is, they remained the sexual prey of the men in the household. Although holding white women accountable for the supervision of their households, black women reminded their counterparts that both groups shared responsibility to address the problem. For all the positive outcomes — shared rejection of lynching and sexual violence, the need for a "fair attitude" in the press toward African Americans, and an agreement in principle to work cooperatively — black and white women elites laid common ground on the subject of morals, especially those of the black working class.[59]

"Not Criminal Always, but Untrained"

In 1919, Charlotte Hawkins Brown presented the second initiative that the NCFCWC engaged: a facility for "the class of negro children now who have nobody's attention . . . the little boys and girls who find their way into the courts. Not criminals always, but untrained; for it is positively true . . . that while the average colored mother watches over the children of the white race, her own children are growing up in the streets neglected and uncared for."[60] The project, to build the North Carolina Industrial Home for Colored Girls at Efland, sought to provide a residential facility for "girls who stand on the brink of ruin." Specifically, the home would protect, supervise, and educate young women who engaged in disreputable behaviors and illicit sexuality and who seemed destined for pregnancy, prostitution, or prison. In the eyes of NCFCWC members, the Efland Home gave such young women "a chance to learn how to make an honest living, to be self-respecting and conscience free."[61]

The Efland Home built on the heritage of several institutional services that dated back to the nineteenth century: the Colored Orphan's Asylum at Oxford, Foulk's Reformatory for Negro Youth, and other facilities that had received support from black churches, women's and fraternal organizations, and white philanthropy. Perpetually overburdened, these places accepted children with no parents and those considered too young to enter the prison system. The NCFCWC viewed the Efland Home as a preventive and corrective measure to stem the social problems inherent to poverty as they applied to young women. Espousing the similar purpose of uplift as its predecessor, the Efland facility differed significantly from orphanages in targeting delinquent girls or girls considered sexually at risk. Clubwomen—black and white— also believed that among the working class, at least, adolescents should be segregated by sex, and that girls' homes should be distinct from boys' homes in preparing the sexes for their separate roles in society: women as wives, mothers, and caretakers, and men as husbands, breadwinners, and providers. Moreover, whereas boys who "landed in training schools had already fallen," a white clubwomen explained, a school for girls sought to "to strengthen [girls'] character so they may resist temptation." On this basis, Samarcand Manor, a facility for white girls, had received public funds.[62]

Once established, Efland Home depended on private donations, and NCFCWC members turned to churches and to women's clubs like the Twentieth Century Club in Durham for support.[63] The facility's clientele and its purpose also required delicate solicitations of both white philanthropists and black male civic leaders. For that reason, and others, the home struggled to survive. Brown sought patronage from the white North Carolina Federation of Women's Clubs and the approval of Nathan C. Newbold, head of the state Division of Negro Education and a white education reformer whose influence among state officials could prove valuable. White women's support gave the Efland project credibility. Brown pointed out to Newbold, for example, that the black women's federation planned to undertake this effort "just as the white women did in the organization of the Stonewall Jackson Training School."[64] Newbold responded, "There is a movement on foot led by Dr. Moore to establish just such a school as you have in mind." In addition to potential competition from Durham's esteemed doctor, Aaron Moore, Brown faced a financial hurdle. She wanted the energies of Jeanes teachers directed to raising funds in a December campaign, because "our people . . . spend a great deal of money at Christmas time." Newbold dissuaded Brown from this move, too, noting that a health drive and Red Cross campaign would occur simultaneously and that Jeanes teachers would lead those programs.[65]

Despite Newbold's caution, Minnie Pearson, Julia Warren, and the NCFCWC mobilized existing networks, influenced their husbands and black businesses, and launched a fund-raising campaign. Subsequent to Pearson's intervention with Durham businessmen, Brown assured Newbold of the Durham elites' support. With all of the pieces in place, she announced the NCFCWC's plans to raise funds in 1921. White women backed the Efland program and joined with black women (including Julia Warren and Minnie Pearson) in serving on the board of directors and on the executive committee overseeing the operation. William G. Pearson functioned as the sole male representative. The Women's Home and Foreign Mission Society of the AME Zion Church added Efland to its list of charities, as did the North Carolina Teachers Association. Minnie Pearson led regular fund-raising drives and took up collections in churches to help finance the effort as well. When the money ran out, the staff and individual women like Julia Warren made personal donations. Beyond that support, Efland survived on the farming, sewing, canning, and other work performed by the residents.[66]

Efland held the NCFCWC's attention throughout the early years of the organization. Each annual state convention included sessions on fund-raising, the needs of the home, and the worthiness of the project. Meetings held close to the facility included field trips to the school; selected students attended those further away. At its 1925 meeting, the NCFCWC raised $2,000. With that guarantee, Minnie Pearson and Julia Warren convinced North Carolina Mutual to hold a mortgage on Efland Home in 1926, with Pearson, Warren, Charlotte Hawkins Brown, and two others as trustees. These women, representing NCFCWC, therefore owned and controlled the property. When the state legislature finally appropriated $2,000 in 1927, the NCFCWC set a goal to pay off the mortgage and to present Efland Home to the state, free from all encumbrances. At its 1929 meeting in Charlotte, the North Carolina Federation of Women's Clubs (white) passed a resolution to support black women's efforts to gain state control of the Efland Home. Shortly thereafter, the North Carolina Council for Social Service, a group of white progressive reformers to which white suffragist Gertrude Weil belonged, added their endorsement. That year, the black federation paid off the monies owed to the Mutual. Notwithstanding, the NCFCWC must have incurred other substantial encumbrances over the years, because it was not until 1943 that the organization announced that Julia Warren, the Efland's first donor, had burned the mortgage. The NCFCWC planned to "give" the Efland Home to the state.[67]

But the state did not accept it until a few years later. And Efland floundered for reasons other than financial ones. Much of its work proved irrelevant to the needs of young working-class women. In large part, the home, like similar facilities, reflected the biases of the women who founded it. Classes in sewing and cooking prepared already-struggling young women for positions as exploitable household laborers, positions that working-class women preferred to avoid. Although black businesses like the Mutual hired women as office workers, Efland offered no programs in bookkeeping, secretarial skills, or clerical work. Nor did it prepare young women for college, where they could get training for professional work in nursing and teaching. In any case, the Mutual was unlikely to hire women who had been sent to a facility for delinquents. A few Efland graduates did go on to teach in rural schools, where an eighth grade education provided work for several months of the year. And some residents found positions as dressmakers and seamstresses. But, as the state raised the qualifications for teachers and as mechanization and standardization displaced handiwork, Efland students were hard-pressed to find jobs.

Probably few of the young women sent to Efland wanted to admit to their time there, and their impressions of the home went unrecorded. The extant reports from 1947 suggest mixed reviews. A survey of thirty-one young women who left what was by that time called the State Training School for Negro Girls rated their experiences as "fair" or "poor." Seventeen of the students released that year had not fared well in finding employment, but fourteen apparently did find work and success, at least by the standards applied by the facility's supporters.[68] Thus the legacy of Efland Home and the State Training School for Negro Girls reveals more about the intersections of interracial club work and the state than it does about cross-class successes or failures. Efland Home itself reflected the limited effectiveness of clubwomen's institutional efforts, even interracial ones, in dealing with black poverty and its consequences. Its transition from a private to a state-controlled institution represented official recognition that such institutions and domestic training programs provided ways to address urban problems, and that black leaders supported those schemes.

In the 1930s, the North Carolina Board of Public Charities considered taking the issue of miscreant young women a step further by establishing a maternity home. John R. Larkins, head of the North Carolina Division for Work among Negroes, following Lawrence Oxley, met with various black leaders statewide to consider the proposal. "I take the opportunity to call your attention to the fact that the Negro girl is still neglected and our men still asleep," Larkins reminded C. C. Spaulding in 1937.[69] When Ruth Rush, dean of women at North Carolina College for Negroes, succeeded Minnie

Pearson as president of the NCFCWC, Larkin entreated: "Your endorsement and recommendation will give impetus to the establishment of this institution." Rush balked, believing that a maternity home implied even less respectability than an industrial home like Efland. She responded that she was "hesitant to attack the problem because I know so well the attitudes which many people have."[70] Rush counted her employer among the staunchest opponents. In fact, James E. Shepard told Larkins flatly, "this type of thing will only give them an incentive to continue this undesirable practice." Once again respectability trumped need.[71]

Despite their elitism and their caution, or perhaps because of it, clubwomen emerged as cross-class, cross-sex, and cross-generational arbiters. They were caught, after all, between the masses who, in forging their own urban culture, rejected the leadership of prominent men and elite men who floundered in search of mechanisms of social control. Still, in order to assert their public prerogatives, clubwomen had to cooperate rather than compete with men, ask men's advice whether they needed it or not, and make gentle suggestions to cajole the stubborn or apathetic. At the same time, the work reinforced negative stereotypes in order to enlist white women's cooperation and extended those perceptions to inform state initiatives that dealt with African Americans' tribulations.

The female-focused institutions the clubwomen founded operated in multiple ways. On one level, many were voluntary and social reform efforts that reflected a middle-class impulse to inculcate respectability and thereby "uplift" the race. Just as often, this constituted efforts to socially control the behavior of the less-privileged classes. For example, the Efland Home, later called the State Training School for Negro Girls and then the State Industrial Home for Colored Girls, aimed to save adolescent girls from delinquency by offering them housing, literacy, and occupational training, though mostly in household labor. Similarly, the Tubman YWCA offered job-training programs to black women, but again mostly for jobs in domestic service. The Tubman YWCA program appeased the white female board of the main branch, but under the leadership of a younger woman, Johnnie McLester, who took over in 1937, the YWCA took up more constructive programs. Calling on women from North Carolina Mutual and Mechanics and Farmers Bank, McLester held discussion groups at which young people could speak their minds. She also saw to it that the YWCA program disseminated information on banking, insurance, beauty culture, literacy, and voting. Finally, McLester's guidance provided recreational options, opportunities for travel, and interracial contact with young women from other YWCAs, each of which were otherwise closed or limited in its constituency. On another level, then, the YWCA and such institutions provided support and programs to educate and empower African American women.

"A Much Needed Service"

One particular initiative, established by black Durhamites, approached the dilemma facing urban black women in a different way. The Scarborough Nursery served as another kind of center, focusing on women and their children. Managed by another of Durham's prominent clubwomen, the Scarborough Nursery, founded in 1918 and originally called the Scarborough Home, functioned as an emergency shelter for families made homeless by fire or other misfortune. The Scarborough Home later expanded to include a preschool and kindergarten for children and daytime and evening classes in parenting, nutrition, literacy, and politics for mothers. A versatile institution, it provided services to people whose needs were ignored or denied in the culture of Jim Crow by whites and by most black elites.

When Clydie Fullwood married John Scarborough, the undertaker, the couple established the nursery as an institutional solution to the problem of abandoned children. Originally, John Scarborough founded Scarborough Home as a childcare center and shelter for destitute families. Scarborough's work brought him into intimate contact with all classes of African Americans, and he witnessed not only the problems of poverty but the limited means that people had to address them. Familiar with death as an outcome of sickness, fire, and accidents, he knew of the inability of poor families to deal with the expected and unexpected. Clydie Fullwood, the high school Spanish and chemistry teacher at Hillside, lost talented students to the factories and similarly understood these problems. Together, the two recognized that juvenile delinquency, furthermore, was symptomatic of the poverty that forced mothers without other options to leave children unsupervised when they worked.[72]

Clydie Scarborough enlarged the program in 1932 to include a kindergarten and classes for mothers. When the Scarborough Nursery moved to a new site on Pettigrew Street in 1938, it opened "as a new phase . . . offering to the Negro community a much needed service, the supervision and instruction of pre-school children from ages two to five. In order that the school may serve those who need it most, only 5 cents per day will be charged each child attending."[73] The nursery provided a direct service for black working mothers, but the program also taught black children responsibility and self-reliance. Viewing children's health and nutrition as urgent priorities, the nursery gave each entering student a full physical examination and appropriate immunizations; an assistant inspected each child for cleanliness daily; a nurse provided biweekly physicals; and the children received a hot meal every day. Clydie Scarborough knew that these children needed care beyond the nursery school and extended her project to include an educational component for mothers and frequent evening seminars for parents on preventive health, nutrition, and education. With support from the undertaker and the state and donations from local women's clubs, the nursery initiated another innovation: a sliding fee scale. Because of this, and the fact that the program's ideals resonated with parents from all walks of life, the Scarborough Nursery counted the children of factory workers, nurses, teachers, businesswomen, secretaries, and domestics among its students.[74]

Of course, the projects that clubwomen in Durham engaged in came about in accordance with a perception that "too many women" populated the black communities. The numbers themselves were neither known nor relevant. Rather, their activism was based on a sense of anxiety, inherent, perhaps, to a modernized, urbanized society. In increasing numbers, African Americans left farming as a way of life and means of survival, in search of the steady paycheck that urban employment offered. Many African Americans who moved to the city preferred the overcrowded conditions and the lively culture of the street to the frustrations of rural life. As a way to address specific community problems inherent to poverty, building institutions for women symbolized the upper classes' desire to supervise the rank and file and to police their children. In conflating the racial relations agenda with the rights agenda, clubwomen provided municipal services for residents whom state and city agencies historically had neglected. Those residents were looking for autonomy, however, not another form of dependency. Their fists tightened by class tensions, African Americans remained determined to fight their own battles of Jim Crow and gender conventions.

"Votes for Mothers, Votes for Children, Votes for Teachers"

Suffrage provided another arena where black women might find common ground across their class differences but where women and men, and white women and black women, sometimes divided. By 1920, African American women in the Bull City had organized into a maze of local organizations that brought women together over national, state, and local women's issues. But their efforts often brought contempt instead of public approval. The war provided the opportunity for both black men and women to reassert voting rights, and African American women had been discussing suffrage among themselves at the Mutual, at schools and hospitals, in their homes, at church, and through their organizations. Suffragists, white and black, had increased agitation for the vote during the 1910s, and the movement surged between 1917 and 1919. As the war ended, President Woodrow Wilson argued for and Congress passed the Nineteenth Amendment, granting women the right to vote by removing sex as a barrier to the ballot.

Through the black women's club movement, Durham's African American women joined with white suffragists to argue for passage of the Nineteenth Amendment as a civil right for themselves and for the race. But they did not necessarily support the legislative agenda of white women activists after suffrage was achieved, and the battle put a strain on race relations. Far more than women's voluntary work had, woman suffrage raised the ire of white southerners, because giving African American women the vote would double the electoral strength of black people. Thus the debate over woman suffrage offered white legislators a powerful opportunity to raise racial fears and put the question of race and suffrage back on the political table. In the worst-case scenario, woman suffrage offered the most substantial challenge to white power since Fusion politics. Congress had relented on suffrage as a means of acknowledging white women's home front contributions. Yet, as the Equal Suffrage Amendment made its way to the floor of the North Carolina legislature for ratification, white politicians raised familiar objections. Even a prosuffrage senator had to concede that "the most powerful reason [to oppose the Equal Suffrage Amendment] is that it would bring on race troubles, which we should not inflict upon ourselves."[75]

The North Carolina Federation of Women's Clubs, the umbrella of white women's civic and social organizations in the state, came out in support of woman suffrage at its 1918 meeting. Among those organizations, the Durham Civic Club and Durham white suffragists argued that the war effort had demonstrated that the nation had needed its women to contribute and that their role had demonstrated the advantages of women's participation in public affairs. Although some of North Carolina's white suffragists tried to isolate the issue of race from the question of the ballot, that separation proved impossible. White suffrage groups from several counties petitioned the General Assembly of North Carolina in support of "An Act for the Extension of Suffrage in Certain Cases," those certain cases being white women. Mattie Southgate Jones, wife of a prominent Durham businessman, expressed her resentment about the direction of woman suffrage: "After the civil war . . . the men with whom Miss [Susan B.] Anthony and Mrs. [Elizabeth Cady] Stanton had worked for reforms, turned their backs upon the women saying

'This is the Negro's Hour.' " But North Carolina's white suffragists argued their case using the progressive ideology of public welfare. "We believe that enlisting the active support and cooperation of our women will result in greater progress and efficiency in many of our public undertakings such as the development of our public school system; protection of town and rural sanitation; beautification of towns and rural districts; and the general promotion of the public good," penned Gertrude Weil, North Carolina's leading white suffragist. As to the race problem, Weil argued, the woman question subsumed the race question. Writing for *Everywoman's Magazine*, Weil noted that "the political relations between the white and negro races is already fixed by the United State[s] Constitution; the promised 19th Amendment will affect only the political relations between the sexes." Rather than promote black domination or empowerment, Weil contended, woman suffrage "provides that white women shall be on terms of political equality with the white man, and that the negro woman shall be on terms of political equality with the negro man." Indeed, contrary to legislators' fears, woman suffrage actually strengthened the white vote.[76]

African American women immersed themselves in the debate about woman suffrage. Men did as well. William G. Pearson, a staunch conservative who was accountable to the school board, might have opposed woman suffrage, at least publicly, but his wife, Minnie Pearson, was chair of the executive committee of the NCFCWC, which made woman suffrage its most important effort. In any case, "Miss Minnie" as she was known, "always did as she pleased."[77] She would have facilitated deliberations on suffrage for the Schubert-Shakespeare and Twentieth Century Clubs, the literary organization and social club to which she belonged. Similarly, Susie Gille Norfleet would have discussed suffrage with Mary Pauline Dame, Sallie Fitzgerald, and Annie D. Shepard at Volkamenia Club meetings. Annie D. Shepard's husband, James E. Shepard, was a Republican activist in the 1890s who always believed in the elite's responsibility to vote. He supported woman suffrage and welcomed women to the small circle of Durham voters. Members of St. Joseph and St. Mark AME Zion Churches read the *Star of Zion*'s call: "Let every mentally sound woman with a vision and a soul who hears about it, present herself for registration," and the topic was covered, undoubtedly, in the local black papers, the *Negro Observer* and North Carolina Mutual's publications, as it was in *Crisis*, the NAACP journal to which dozens of black Durhamites subscribed.[78] The discourse on woman suffrage in the South gave elite women an opportunity to support their male counterparts' political strategies. But as far as North Carolina legislators were concerned, the race question provided the rationale to vote against woman suffrage: in pockets like Durham, where some black men continued to exercise the franchise, "political equality" translated into votes for black women, at least those from the upper classes, who would then be the equals of white women.

The woman suffrage amendment was ratified in August 1920, despite the opposition of North Carolina and other southern states. In the fall, Durham women went to the polls to register for the first time. On 15 October 1920, the first day that women could register to vote, over fifty African American women from Durham successfully registered: fifteen on the west side of Hayti at the courthouse, twenty-nine on the east side of Hayti at Perry's Lumber Yard, and a handful at other sites.[79] Most likely many more tried and were turned away. This the NCFCWC anticipated and so created another plan. Durham's own Minnie Pearson, presiding over the NCFCWC, participated in shaping and promoting the strategy black clubwomen planned to use throughout the state in achieving registration: to wait until the last two Saturdays of registration, 22 and 29 October, and then appear en masse at the polls. If women in Durham followed through on that plan—and very likely they did, for there were certainly many more than fifty black women interested in voting—the newspaper did not report it. The *Durham Morning Herald* reported only registrations up to 17 October, including the ones on 15 October, and remained silent on black registration activities thereafter.[80]

In whatever ways women in Durham organized themselves to seize the ballot, and however many women attempted to register to vote, those who participated clearly remembered their first official trek to the polls. Among her personal effects, Mutual bookkeeper Fannie Rosser kept the list of Republican candidates who ran for election on "November 2, 1920," a date she noted in her bold script on the side of the long strip of paper. She might have retained the document to remember her first vote, or to remember being turned away. In either case, preserving the memento showed her sense of its importance.[81]

Women determined to vote still needed men's support, because getting to the courthouse was easier than getting on the registration books. It was a white registrar's job to allow as few black voters as possible to slip through the regulations. Among women's civic responsibilities, however, C. C. Spaulding especially counted voting. With the passage of the Nineteenth Amendment, the voting strength of the black elite, limited and ineffective though it was, more than doubled. Viola Turner recalled in detail one of her first ventures beyond the black world. Spaulding, now the company president, took her and two other women, as he did all new employees, to the Durham courthouse to register. "Only somebody like Mr. Spaulding probably could get you registered," Turner explained. "If I walked down there to be registered, I never would have gotten registered." Conrad O. Pearson, an attorney and W. G. Pearson's nephew, concurred: "Shepard or Spaulding could get you registered." With woman suffrage, Mutual men and women sought to increase black Durham's political voice. In this way, women embraced the quest of the Mutual founders to reestablish black citizenship rights in the electoral arena by making the regular journey to the registrar and gathering a few voters at a time.[82]

On the day that Spaulding took Viola Turner to register, however, only two of the three women passed the literacy test. The barely literate registrar refused the third woman, who could read as well as her colleagues. Challenging the decision, Spaulding inquired when she could return and accompanied her on a successful second attempt. His emphasis on employees' acquiring the opportunity to vote tied respectable class behavior to civic participation for women and men. His regular trips to the courthouse with potential voters and his challenges to the reluctant registrars dispute notions that his focus on business necessarily left out political participation.[83]

African American women presented an important new category of potential voters. North Carolina Mutual women like Susie Gille Norfleet and Fannie Rosser, nurses and teachers like Julia Latta and Mary Pauline Dame, and clubwomen like Julia Warren and Minnie Pearson strengthened the black community as activists. Now suffrage presented a chance to add their voices in politics as well. Accounting for over half of the black population in Durham in 1920, women also made up the majority of professionals, including 90 percent of the black teachers and 60 percent of the home office staffs of black financial institutions, and thus more than half of Durham's black potential voters with their own agenda to promote.[84] Working in black-dominated settings, like the schools, the hospital, and the library, politicized black women represented more than the elite. For black women voters, as for white women, the franchise translated into "votes for mothers," "votes for children," "votes for teachers," and "votes for housewives," in short, into social reform.[85]

Nevertheless, they may have been ambivalent about the perceived benefits of the suffragists' legislative platform. Among the priorities of the League of Women Voters, for example, child labor laws and legislation to protect women workers by limiting their hours were priorities. North Carolina's white suffragists debated whether or not they should support a child labor law to restrict the employment of children under the age of sixteen. Gertrude Weil, who moved on to become state president of the league, personally embraced such measures, but publicly the league opposed any labor prohibitions. Under pressure by their husbands, often business owners, the state league did not mention child labor in its resolutions. Resisting federal intervention, they planned instead to "push a state measure for child labor restriction as the more desirable alternative to federal regulation," that is, to argue that the state should move positively on the issue to prevent the federal government imposing its will on the South once again.

Durham's black elite and middle-class women certainly agreed that children should stay in school, that black working women deserved better conditions, and that shorter hours helped mothers spend more time with their children. But black voting women also knew that African American families depended on children's and women's wages to survive. In fact, black women tobacco workers often preferred to work as many hours as they could manage, and Annie Mack Barbee and her sisters preferred earning money in tobacco work to attending school, where their training focused on household labor.[86]

With women added to the registration rolls, and with the recent war rhetoric of making the world safe for democracy as their support, Durham blacks amassed enough strength to establish a nonpartisan Colored Voters League in 1922, still a daring move.[87] As a letter from "one of the most prominent colored men in this city" to the *Durham Morning Herald* explained, the organization was "formed to promote better citizenship among the colored citizens," to get "a number of negroes to place their names on the registration books of the county," and to serve as a "channel of public information." The *Herald*, however, reflected whites' revised sense of fear. The newspaper conceded that the members of the Colored Voters League "theoretically . . . have the right idea" but cautioned that "there is danger of the colored voters arousing antagonism if they become too vigorous in their use of the ballot." Black women's electoral participation, then, had aroused precisely the old threat. "There are many memories of years gone by still lingering," the editorial pointed out in reference to the Wilmington Riot. "Those memories are disappearing, but they should be permitted to pass away entirely before taking steps that have the possibilities of recalling former conditions. . . . Continuous activity on the part of any class, set, or organization has a tendency to consolidate opposition[;] in that case, [their efforts] will prove futile."[88] Futile or not, African Americans expressed their intent to lay claim to what was rightfully theirs, and not always in genteel ways like voting.

The success of the Scarborough Nursery and the failures of the Efland Home demonstrate that female-dominated institutions could reach across the divide of class but that their effectiveness linked directly to their abilities to address working-class interests and needs. One area of success came in encouraging the working class, the rank and file of African Americans, to participate in electoral politics. The Volkamenia Club's reading circles at the library had always encouraged the illiterate to learn to read, but with the passage of the Nineteenth Amendment and the imperative to increase black voter strength, Volkamenia used its literacy programs to encourage the working class to vote. Under Minnie Pearson's leadership in the mid-1930s, the NCFCWC carried that initiative further through a campaign to encourage "Negro women to register and vote intelligently in the Tar Heel State for men, women and principles, rather than parties." Night school programs, attended by "more women than men," like one taught by Pauline Dame at West End School, offered classes in literacy, citizenship, and American history. With these emphases, clubwomen and teachers facilitated discussions of woman suffrage and politics. These efforts laid the groundwork for clubwomen to connect gender politics and the needs of black neighborhoods to partisan politics. In this way — and with the election of Franklin D. Roosevelt — clubwomen helped lead African Americans away from the Republican Party of Lincoln toward New Deal Democrats.[89] But voting alone offered only a limited solution to urban problems. Persistent poverty generated continual unrest and a demand for radical measures.

8 : There Should Be . . . No Discrimination
Gender, Class, and Activism in the New Deal Era

In 1933, African Americans in Durham took 2 January, the first workday of the year, off to celebrate Emancipation Day. The observance com-
memorating the day Abraham Lincoln issued the Emancipation Proclama-
tion in 1863 usually fell on 1 January, marked by Midnight Watch on New
Year's Eve. For respectable folks, parents, and kin, religious services and
history programs featuring local schoolchildren followed during the day at
one of the prominent churches. There, on the community platform, youth
renewed the hopes of the past in reciting words of faith and freedom —
readings from the Bible, the Declaration of Independence, and the Procla-
mation itself. The annual tradition provided African Americans with self-
sanctioned space to honor themselves, but the observances had changed over
time. Midnight Watch had transformed from a moment to anticipate the
promises of freedom into an occasion for meditation — from a triumphant
event that marked a sanctified moment in black history to a secular holiday
that noted the passage of time. Public events still provided the platform for

the leading black men to preach the psalms of respectability, but more and more people opted to skip the solemn ceremonies and the prospect of hearing leaders pontificate on morality, thrift, and toil, preferring to share in the festive occasion by visiting, feasting, and resting. Private gatherings of friends and family strengthened bonds and uplifted spirits. Josephine Clement remembered that Bess Whitted threw the biggest bash in town: "All day New Year's Day, you could drop in any time during the day, and depending on what time you went you would eat whatever they were serving, all day."[1]

But, after fifty years, the celebratory aspects of emancipation had worn thin. Two generations after freedom, the everyday circumstances of black life left little to cheer about for most folk, especially during the Great Depression. In accepting the charge to conduct an "intelligent study of Negro life with its social problems," the Division of Work among Negroes, a newly established branch of the State Department of Welfare, found plenty. In 1926, division head Lawrence Oxley enumerated the lack of wholesome recreation and worse: "questionable dance halls, gambling clubs, and even more vicious resorts." "The apathy of the Negro lower class is probably an even worse situation," he appraised. Migration had wrought "a more fundamental social disorder," especially in the large industrial centers like Durham. "The native Negro population in itself present many social health and economic problems which tax the facilities of the State's social agencies and institutions," Oxley complained. "Add to these problems the social ills and human weaknesses of a large group of ignorant and socially sick Negroes from other states, and we have a situation that abounds with many complexities." As far as Oxley was concerned, African Americans should assume "in large degree responsibility in solving their own problems."[2] In his biennial report for the division in 1932, Oxley noted that the severity of the Great Depression had challenged the ideological underpinnings of public social welfare. His work had shifted from encouraging African Americans' self-help initiatives to representing the state's "conscientious efforts to alleviate the effects of the deepening economic depression" on the race. "The Negro as a group in our state has had the largest proportion of unemployed," Oxley penned. "Nineteen thirty-one–thirty-two have been years of financial losses, of mental and physical suffering disproportionately shared."[3] Self-help was not enough—it had never been and never would be as long as Jim Crow maintained its stranglehold. Autonomy, except for a few, was not possible. The stress of a deepening economic depression prompted Durham freedpeople and their descendants to reassess freedom's dreams. Two generations later, postslavery struggles had not receded, and, for too many black folk, 1933 did not look much better than 1863.

This was a special year, however. It was the sixtieth anniversary of Emancipation Day and a very special occasion. So, in fact, Emancipation Day was a major celebration in 1933. On 2 January, thousands of people gathered along the streets of Hayti to watch the commemorative parade. The spectacle stepped off from the William G. Pearson Elementary School, a newly built facility named in honor of the community elder. Heading the procession, youngsters represented the student bodies of Hillside High and each of the black elementary schools, Pearson, Lyon Park, and East End. The Royal Knights of King David, the time-honored fraternal society started by John Merrick, had thrived under the guiding hand of Pearson as the Grand Treasurer. Its float led the parade. North Carolina Mutual's entry came next, linking the black tradition of mutual aid and self-help to black business. Next, displays and marchers from the Durham black chapters of national fraternal organizations — American Legion, the Elks, and the Odd Fellows — signified a claim to citizenship, their members riding horseback. Heirs to that responsibility, the Boy Scout Troop #55 from White Rock Baptist Church walked behind. Toward the end of the parade, a special float carried "the mothers and fathers of pre–Civil War Days," personifying the memories of slavery and the reason for the day. An assembly followed at Pearson School, opening with the men's chorus of the Second Baptist Church singing James Weldon Johnson's tribute to black struggle, known as the Negro National Anthem — "Lift Ev'ry Voice and Sing." Woven throughout, "expressions by pre-war parents" were punctuated by comments from Pearson himself.[4]

But the Emancipation Day ceremonies reflected a moment of intraracial harmony only at first glance and marked a shift in community relations. Rather than the usual processions of elites, the various neighborhood churches shared the stage at Pearson Elementary in 1933. Rev. A. Croom, from the Union Baptist Church, an activist center in the East End neighborhood, read the scriptures; Rev. W. C. Williamson, from Mt. Vernon AME Zion, a central institution for black tobacco and mill workers, served as the master of ceremonies; and Charles E. Steward, president of Kittrel College, near Raleigh, delivered the principal address. A chorus from the Second Baptist Church, instead of the formal choirs of White Rock Baptist or St. Joseph AME Zion Churches, provided the main musical features of the program.[5] With the audience offering up its voices in "a song full of the hope that the dark days have brought us," the 1933 celebration acknowledged a shared past and the community's diverse constituencies.

Two generations removed in 1933, many of the celebrants of the day's events recalled slavery and emancipation, the disappointments of Reconstruction, and the terror of bitter struggles that followed. Their children, the first generation born in freedom—Mary Pauline Fitzgerald Dame and her cohort of colleagues and friends—founded the institutions and organizations that prepared the next generation to battle against Jim Crow. Pearson had engaged that battle across three generations. A vociferous opponent of the Confederate colonel Julian S. Carr Jr. on the issue of black education, Pearson ended up the de facto superintendent of black schools in Durham. Pearson had survived by acting as a moderating force among blacks and between blacks and whites.

Adjusting the public face of public education to the demands of Jim Crow, he had succeeded in establishing one of the few public high schools in the state for African Americans. Its core curriculum trained most black students for household labor or industrial arts, the jobs that whites believed most appropriate for them. Admired and feared by his students, parents, and teachers, he became the community spokesperson for resources that strengthened programs that, on principle, Carr opposed. Pearson's method assured that at least some of his students were trained to open another front on the color line. But Hillside's academic program also furthered dreams of college and graduate school. Out of the forty students in Pauli Murray's class of 1926, seventeen had gone on to college. Murray herself graduated from Hunter College in January 1933, eager to take on the challenges of Jim Crow and gender.

In praising his older colleague, C. C. Spaulding noted that Pearson "had a hand in every phase of Negro Progress and uplift in Durham." He kept the other in the lion's mouth. Despite, indeed because of, his conservatism, William G. Pearson was the wealthiest black man in Durham—his shining Pierce Arrow automobile said discerningly so. But when it came to politics, "he didn't lead." So claimed his nephew, Conrad O. Pearson.

The younger Pearson made his name that year, 1933, opposing his uncle. Trained at Howard Law School, C. O. Pearson returned to his hometown, Durham, to begin the work of civil rights lawyering. His career represented a turn away from the tradition of moderation that had brought his uncle acclaim on both sides of the color line. Thus, the ceremonies that year paid tribute to the energetic seventy-four-year-old Prof Pearson and called upon others, including his nephew, attorney Pearson, to step up and serve.[6]

The Pearsons' divergent positions—conservative and radical—marked off the generational breadth reflected in the prism of black activist strategies and the challenges mounted against the traditional black leadership in the Jim Crow era. An emphasis on upbuilding, a sense of manhood and womanhood, and a strategy of stable race relations comprised the ideological pieces related to black elite leadership. Their ideology did little to ease either daily oppression or the broader structural framework that upheld apartheid. Accordingly, most African Americans remained vulnerable to the unstable economy of the Great Depression era. And yet, as the national institutions — federal government, race organizations, labor unions — pondered solutions to obvious problems, it was the members of the black elite who were positioned to mount the most direct challenges to Jim Crow during the New Deal era and the least likely to do so.

Most clearly, three distinct factions intersected and clashed in the 1930s: first, the old guard of patriarchs, male leaders who were the founders and heads of Durham's most significant black institutions; second, contingents of tobacco workers and middle-class teachers, mostly women hard hit by the Depression; and third, a younger generation of professionals, who termed themselves the Radical Young Negroes. The interactions among these groups demonstrate how race work in the 1930s transformed from a focus on the internal black community to a broadened civil rights agenda that demanded equal protection and fair implementation of government policy at the federal level. The strategy reflected a renewed demand for political space within the black community on the part of women and, now, on the part of a new generation. Conrad O. Pearson's Jim Crow generation took up new arms.

Two national agendas — one in economics and one in civil rights — put the political economy of the South at the center of African American discourse on the problem of Jim Crow. Thus, while black Durham dealt with its internal unrest, institutionalized struggles against Jim Crow crowded out the reform movement. Efforts based on personal interracial relationships also changed into tactics of collective protest and direct confrontation. African Americans looked to reenter what were once the new arenas of democracy in the South — the school, the labor market, and the ballot box. African American spokespeople had hoped they might nudge along changes in race relations that could emerge organically from the national rhetoric of New Deal politics, a rhetoric that linked economics, fairness, rights, and government responsibility. They were disappointed, but not surprised, that New Deal programs, the new president's collaborative solutions to the problem of economic recovery, maintained, and indeed codified, inequality.

"Back on the Breadlines Again"

Durham black leaders found the usual self-help strategies collapsing. They ended 1932 dedicated to raising contributions toward the general relief fund of the city welfare department. The money was to be used for school lunches "for undernourished and underprivileged school children," black and white. Initiated by Lawrence Oxley, the drive recognized that, although African Americans accounted for a numerical minority of the population, they received the "largest portion of relief" in the city. Speaking to a mass meeting at Hillside High School, Oxley stipulated, "Negroes should assume some responsibility for relief efforts." Following up, teachers, principals, and members of the Parent-Teacher Association conducted a door-to-door canvas, but the need, made even worse by the Great Depression, was greater than the community could provide. Leaders had hoped to raise $5,000, but soon lowered the goal to $1,000, and finally raised a disappointing $700.[7]

African Americans had been able to donate thousands of dollars to war work and savings campaigns fifteen years before. Now, this few hundred dollars paled against the depth of need. Black occupational spheres had shrunk as factories and private homes curtailed their demands for their labor. Tobacco-working black women did the labor white women did not do but still had to cling to these terrible jobs. Nonetheless, hiring freezes, cuts in hours, and speedups on the line combined to create more and harder work for declining wages for many. Household laborers existed even more precariously, with weekly positions cut to days and pay reduced to what private employers were willing to pay, which was sometimes nothing at all or only clothes and leftovers in lieu of cash. And children who had been able to attend school now hung around looking for ways to earn money.[8]

The working class did not suffer alone through the Depression, which actually exposed, at least to each other, the financial fragility of the black elite. Fannie Rosser, the frugal Mutual clerk, called in the various personal loans that she had made to friends. "We are back on the breadline again," she wrote to a couple having trouble paying her back. "If I had a husband, it would not look so frightful."[9] Others from the Mutual were unable to pay their bills. Job inquiries at the Mutual increased, although the company did virtually no hiring. One woman wrote to manager William J. Kennedy on behalf of her husband but also expressed the hope that, "if there are no vacancies for an agent or an inspector, there possibly will be a vacancy for an office lady to do clerical and typing. I am qualified to do both."[10]

The middle class faced declining incomes. For example, teachers' salaries fell. Whereas Mary Pauline Dame's teacher contract called for a salary of $945 in 1926, it paid only $726 in 1932 for a longer school term and teaching more students. Seven schools in the city and county handled some 7,000 students. Walltown School, in the neighborhood near Duke University, was so overcrowded that students attended schools for half days in two shifts. Hickstown School, at the edge of town, had doubled its enrollment, but the city hired only one additional teacher for the facility and made up the remaining costs of Negro education by cutting the industrial arts program at Hillside High School. The situation worsened as the Depression wore on. School funding did not expand with the needs of black schools, and in the fall of 1938 Pauline Dame was asked to teach two sections of the fourth grade at Lyon Park School, a total of eighty-six students each day, "for not very much more money." In the fall of 1940, the overload had not been relieved, and she managed seventy-four students in her class and still struggled financially, "for it is water, light, phone, insurance, taxes and car and last but not least my church money *every* week the year round," she wrote to her niece, Pauli Murray. "So where is it all to come from?"[11]

Black businesses thrived, however. When newly elected president Franklin D. Roosevelt closed the nation's banks to assess the strength of each as a first step of the early New Deal recovery program, Mechanics and Farmers Bank passed inspection, even as other local banks failed. Not only did Mechanics and Farmers surpass others in soundness, but rumors flew that the bank let customers in through the back door, benefiting both black and white business.[12] North Carolina Mutual Life Insurance Company also did well. During the month of August 1933, applications for insurance increased 28 percent; the increase was 56 percent in December and 48 percent for January, over the previous year.[13] The surge did not reflect improved economic conditions among its clientele. The financial instability its customers felt caused a need for a sense of security. A small investment in a Mutual policy assured some resources for the family in case of illness or death, a necessity in tough economic times. But even with an increase in sales, the Mutual looked to cut costs, conducting an efficiency study and testing clerks on accuracy, speed, and thoroughness as well as neatness, regularity, interest, cooperation, and ability to handle personal affairs, all with an eye to letting some personnel go.[14]

Black people found some hope in New Deal agencies' willingness to consider black perspectives, especially as, one by one, agencies and departments hired African American professionals as advisers, assistants, and directors of Negro affairs. Well known and well respected in black circles, Mary McLeod Bethune, educator and head of Bethune-Cookman College, former president of the National Association of Colored Women, and founder of her own umbrella association, the National Council of Negro Women, led the way into the administration as the Director of Negro Affairs for the National Youth Administration. Robert C. Weaver, a Harvard graduate with a Ph.D. in economics and a professor at North Carolina A&T University, held a similar position as the Associate Advisor on the Economic Status of Negroes for the Department of the Interior. Lawrence Oxley, plucked from the North Carolina Board of Public Charities, also joined the "black cabinet," as the group of African American administrators was known, at the Department of Labor. These black activists and intellectuals who entered the administration understood that as the purview of the federal government expanded, so did the opportunities to affect conditions for African Americans.[15]

C. C. Spaulding knew them all and proved influential in black cabinet circles, advising agencies on black affairs, smoothing over disputes, and recommending appointees.[16] Among those he mentored, Robert C. Weaver was at home in Washington, D.C., when Congress opened hearings on the National Industrial Recovery Act in the summer of 1933. A centerpiece of New Deal legislation, the act proposed to set standards for wages and hours, which were called National Recovery Administration (NRA) codes, to be negotiated by manufacturers and labor advocates and moderated by New Deal officials. Realizing that no African American groups had prepared to submit testimony, Weaver and a colleague, John P. Davis, a graduate of Harvard Law School, determined to inform the political process. Young and buoyant, Weaver and Davis made up the Negro Industrial League, essentially an ad hoc committee of two, to represent black perspectives. They monitored press releases, wrote hearing testimony, and contacted leaders throughout the nation to solicit data, funds, and support. They gained the support of several national organizations, including the NAACP and the National Urban League, which came together to form the Joint Committee on Economic Recovery. Most of the affiliated organizations and individuals promised financial support, but few came through. C. C. Spaulding was among those who did contribute, funding Weaver's travel and research.[17]

Spaulding positioned himself to take advantage of the New Deal on behalf of the race, and he succeeded, using conservative tactics. Against the preference of other national black leaders, he supported the appointment of Clark Foreman, a white southerner, as the Director of Negro Affairs at the Department of the Interior. Then he recommended Weaver as Foreman's assistant, over Davis's objections. Also against the wishes of black leaders across the country, Spaulding supported the establishment of an Industrial Commission on Negro Affairs, an initiative that other African American leaders saw as an implicit act of government codification and thus a sanctioning of racial segregation. According to Spaulding, writing to Weaver, because "Negroes especially in the Southern States do not receive anything like equal consideration from relief agencies," a department specifically dedicated to race relations and specifically African Americans' issues would render at least "some benefit." Despite pressure from his leadership colleagues, who "quite naturally . . . will be opposed to the creation of a Commission which should deal only with Negro problems on the theory that the activity of such a commission would be in support of segregation in Government supervision," Spaulding pointed out that, "if the Government is justified in the creation and maintenance of a special commission for the purpose of looking after the welfare of the American Indians, it is also necessary that a somewhat similar commission be created and maintained for [Negroes]." In taking this stance, Spaulding resurrected the Booker T. Washington philosophy, accommodating segregation, because he believed that the other choice was exclusion and also because his position eased the racial anxieties of white southerners who controlled New Deal funding and programs.[18]

In the view of a younger generation and of many other national black leaders, however, the political milieu of the 1930s offered the potential to transform the race question, from one that focused on African Americans' shortcomings to a focus on racial inequity as the cause of black poverty and its effects. At the same time, worsening economic conditions kindled a general rethinking of the traditional role of government. Laissez-faire tendencies had failed, compelling the newly elected president to speak of his administration as a vehicle of change and as a mechanism to improve people's lives. As issues of poverty and rights conflated in the 1930s, heightened political consciousness encouraged African Americans to increase their expectations regarding the protective and supervisory role of the government. For his willingness to speak to the fate of the masses, Roosevelt garnered political capital among African Americans in the North. For his affiliation with the party of white supremacy, he garnered political capital in the white South. Southern blacks watched carefully for signs that Roosevelt and his administration was sending messages that they had a place in his recovery plan. In fact, through its hearings on legislation, its appointments of women and African Americans to advisory posts, and its proposed programs of work and relief, the New Deal produced opportunities to inject black perspectives into the national discourse on economic rights.[19]

Arguably, the New Deal held the potential to change the South in terms of the region's economic relations based on racial exploitation. Through its rhetoric, if not always its actions, the federal government inspired demands for inclusion among constituencies used to being excluded. In fact, most New Deal programs excluded black people and/or targeted whites only. Given that African Americans, including the conservatives, recognized the need for economic relief as a means of achieving freedom, the New Deal's economic recovery plan gave black folk a target to critique. In a first step to demonstrate their support for Roosevelt's legislation, Durham's black leaders launched a campaign to encourage their colleagues to display the blue eagle, the symbol of support for the NRA. A further campaign by the local chapter of the National Negro Housewives' League, an auxiliary to the National Negro Business League (NNBL), asked women to sign the "Consumers Statement of Coopera- tion," pledging to "cooperate in re-employment by supporting and patroniz- ing employers and workers who are members of the NRA."[20]

By then it was clear, however, that the New Deal would not live up to its propaganda. The NRA encouraged businesses to cooperate in managing pro- duction and setting wage and hour scales for workers. With limited par- ticipation from labor and virtually none from African Americans up to that point, the emerging proposals for wage codes recommended racial discrimi- nation. Testifying at congressional hearings, John Davis pointed out that industries put forward measures that discriminated against black workers and boosted the potential for abuse. He argued further that, "in view of the human misery at this time and the purpose of the Industrial Recovery Act . . . [and] in view of the fact that the Negro has suffered more during this time, than any other racial groups, provisions be made to pledge employers to practice no discrimination by virtue of race, color, or creed."[21] Most black leaders agreed. Editor Fred Moore, of the *New York Age*, a northern black newspaper, wrote of the 1933 meeting of the NNBL, "We are loyal citizens only asking fair play and an equal chance to participate in the fruits of our labor and of our constitutional rights."[22] Robert Moton, heir to Tuskegee and Booker T. Washington's role, spoke at the annual convention of the NNBL that year. Taking a position that Washington might have opposed, Moton stressed that he did not support the outcomes being negotiated in Washington, D.C. "It would be suicidal," he declared, "for Negroes to take the position that they should receive less pay than is given other people for the same service." Moton affirmed, "There should be, in my opinion, no discrimination regarding wages of Negroes."[23]

For African Americans, gender discrimination exacerbated racial discrimi- nation. Southern white manufacturers, landowners, and politicians insisted that the wage and hour code reflect local and regional customs, that is, black workers earned less than white workers and women earned less than men. Factory owners argued the case on several points. First, they alleged — with proof to the contrary — that the inefficiency of southern black workers demanded their lower compensation, and, second, that offering black and white workers equal pay would result in racial tensions that would disrupt production. Third, they maintained that they could not afford to pay black workers equal wages, and that to do so would cause the plants to become unprofitable and to shut down, resulting in still higher unemployment for both whites and blacks. Or, worse, as they perceived it, higher wages in the factories would draw people from the rural areas, who would fill the relief rolls. Finally, they contended, the short-term consequences of black under-employment paled against the prospect of massive unemployment in an already impoverished region. This position gained support among conserva-tive black leaders like C. C. Spaulding, who worried publicly about the state of the race in the present. The goal of whites, however, was to sustain the racial caste system that not only segregated black and white workers but also kept the former subservient. In maintaining disparities in the wage and oc-cupation structure, they hoped to keep black workers "cheap and amenable." If such were not the case, they threatened to hire white workers as replace-ments in those positions where African Americans clustered.[24]

"The progress of Negroes has not been at an equal rate to that of whites," Eugene Kinckle Jones of the National Urban League pointed out in a memo to Roosevelt. "The disparity between white and Negro living standards, which is already far too great, may become considerably increased if present trends proceed unchecked."[25] The NRA codes, moreover, did not cover fields with high concentrations of African American workers, excluding whole classes of black workers from the minimum wage provision: office boys and girls, learners, apprentices, watchmen, junior employees, and "other" cate-gories. Of the 12,000 black laborers in textiles across the South, 9,000 — charwomen, truck hands, and unclassified workmen and -women — were excluded from the minimum wage guidelines and the guaranteed forty-hour week. The codes and other New Deal program legislation also ignored household laborers, farmhands, pieceworkers, and children (still widely used although labor laws prohibited their employment). Nor did the codes protect African Americans from being displaced by whites. According to the Na-tional Urban League and John P. Davis, proportionately more African Amer-icans than whites received relief benefits, and the number increased steadily between 1933 and 1935. In 1933, 26.7 percent of black urban dwellers were on relief (compared to 9.7 percent among whites); in 1935, that number had increased to 39.5 percent for blacks, compared to 14.6 percent for whites.[26]

In setting out a wage structure based on industrial racism and a political economy intended to disadvantage blacks, white executives of manufacturing firms constructed the minimum wage floor as a staircase, with whites on the upper levels receiving the highest end of the scale, and African Americans on the lower steps earning the lower wage. The tobacco industry dragged its feet on creating a scale at all; in the meantime the Supreme Court declared the NRA codes unconstitutional.[27] Still, a study of tobacco workers in Durham revealed that white males earned on average $15.17 per week; white females earned on average $14.58 per week; black males earned on average $12.63 per week; and black females earned on average $11.14 per week. And black laborers worked longer hours for that much less pay. A 1935 study of black families on relief in tobacco cities, including Durham, revealed that their incomes were "tragically small." Of 477 families surveyed, 108 had two or more members working full-time and still earned less than $300 per year. Although one or more members of each family interviewed remained employed full-time, the total family incomes among tobacco workers ranged so low that many qualified for federal relief.[28]

African American laborers were affected in other ways. On her trip through North Carolina, journalist Lorena Hickok, serving as the eyes and ears of Washington's New Dealers, found that blacks accounted for three-quarters of the people moving from the country to town in search of work. Finding no jobs, they applied for relief, which also paid benefits based on a racial differential. Although industries actually boomed in 1933, managers anticipated a decline in employment during 1934 because of acreage reductions in tobacco and cotton. Recommended by the Agricultural Adjustment Administration, another New Deal agency, the program called for landowners to reduce their crops to control overproduction and declining prices. The strategy left southern tenant farmers and sharecroppers without land to work, wandering the state homeless. The Civil Works Administration (CWA), a subdivision of the Federal Emergency Relief Administration, offered little better. Providing relief jobs during the winter of 1933/1934 on infrastructure and agricultural projects, the CWA paid African American and white workers different salaries.[29] Finally, as white workers displaced African Americans, even in those jobs that black people previously had been restricted to, black unemployment soared. Almost half of the African Americans on unemployment relief were domestic workers, who, because of race, found it more difficult than whites to find new positions. With white families shifting the work of the household to the women of the family, black domestics were laid off. But they received less attention from municipal employment services than whites and were less likely to have their needs addressed. Repeatedly, Hickok heard whites say that "if two men are hungry, a white man and a black man, and one of them must go on being hungry, it must be the black man," or, "if the black man has a job, and the white man hasn't, the black man must give it up to the white man . . . if he wants it." But once again, it was women, the critical contributors to family economies, who suffered most from the Depression's effects and the New Deal's response.[30]

Missing this critical element of women's contribution, black leaders' position did little to change the situation. In an awkward meeting in Durham at the North Carolina Mutual offices, Hickok tried to determine Durham black leaders' perspectives on how African Americans managed under the New Deal. Some of their views came as no surprise. "Expressed as politely as their bitterness would permit," they complained about "white discrimination against blacks" and about worker displacement that was likely to result in "permanent unemployment" for African Americans. Domestic service, they reported, remained "the only field of employment still left entirely to Negroes in the South," but they feared that "white people would invade that field too," given the pressure for higher wages. Pearson protested, "White people threaten employers if they don't let Negroes go and hire white help." In this way, Pearson and many other leaders believed that the New Deal was "just forcing us Negroes out of our jobs, that's all." In questioning southern traditions of discrimination and putting on the table discussions that southern race relations had disallowed, New Deal programs fanned the cinders of racism, Durham conservatives believed. Thus Spaulding, to Hickok's surprise, supported the wage disparity paid by the CWA. Equal wages, he said, "created problems." The "Negro case work supervisor" suggested further "that Negro women working in the sewing rooms be given an opportunity to enroll in classes under teachers who would train them as house servants." Hickok was not enthusiastic, but the group disagreed. In fact training working-class women in household labor had become a standard uplift program in Durham. Because many domestics worked "for nothing at all now, save their board," the supervisor argued, training programs provided "the only way to get their wages up." "Train them. Make better servants out of them," he contended. A "trained maid" made six dollars per week, compared to "$2 paid [on] the average."[31]

A discouraged Hickok realized what Spaulding's cohort did not: "Negro labor, by accepting lower wages, can break the whole thing down here in the South." Put another way, the race question revealed how ideology and implementation failed to mesh, given the lack of oversight and the limits of federal influence on local and regional politics. But what Hickok did not realize and the Durham cohort did was the value of their conservative position. For although the New Deal programs were created at the national level, they were implemented at the local level, and local politics benefited black Durham more than national politics. A series of New Deal programs put together funding for a new apartment complex, new buildings at the college, including an auditorium, along with a Federal Theater Project and National Youth Administration monies to support student workers and provide student financial aid. These projects benefited the middle class, including college students and young couples. Toward assistance for the working class, they managed to get money to support the Scarborough Nursery and a child care facility at White Rock Baptist Church and a National Youth Administration project at the YWCA to train black women in domestic work.

Whatever sense of fairness Washington New Dealers might have wanted to articulate, the political realities translated into greater power for white southerners in Congress, a bloc necessary for the Roosevelt administration to sustain its support for programs. Neither Congress nor the president proved likely to support legislation calling for nondiscriminatory practices in the codes or in the distribution of resources. White southern politicians were unlikely to accept any form of racial equality that New Dealers might desire to impose. In his congressional testimony in 1935, John P. Davis concluded that "the effect of the labor provisions of the NRA codes result in a lessening of [Negro] wages." He also claimed that "compliance has broken down completely in the South." Among those affected most, black mill workers and factory hands, mostly black women, "felt let down, especially as the tobacco industry dragged its feet in setting a code."[32]

Under pressure from labor activists, the tobacco industry set out a wage scale that affected black workers in mixed ways. American Tobacco and Liggett and Myers in Durham both prepared to adjust workers' wages and hours in compliance. For most black laborers, however, these new standards translated into higher hourly wages but shorter working hours, speedups, stretch-outs, layoffs, and increased living costs, so that many did not get ahead. One woman explained to Charles S. Johnson, surveying the Durham scene, "They raised me once . . . and I didn't have speed-up, but they laid off one-fourth of the people in my room after the last raise we got." Another noted, "They cut off a lot [of people] downstairs," although the scale improved her condition slightly. Whereas she had worked eleven hours a day and fifty-five hours per week, under the new adjustments, she worked fewer hours for the same income after three raises. Still another pointed out that before the NRA "the hours were so long that when night came you were nearly dead." A fourth pointed out: "We're working less and making more. But I still can hardly get enough to live on. . . . If you got bills to pay, it takes more now to pay them. It takes more for house rent, more for food, more for everything." Because the wage scale shifted pay rates from piece wages to hourly wages, factory hands felt they had less control over the amount they could make than they had had before.[33]

"The Colored People Have Been Treated So Dirty"

The Roosevelt administration may have preferred that industries regulate themselves in consultation with representatives of labor. In the South, this appeared unlikely, given the weakness of labor organizations. Concerned mostly with skilled labor, the American Federation of Labor (AFL) had hesitated to expand into those fields where semiskilled and unskilled labor dominated and therefore avoided working with African Americans. But the AFL had managed to keep a foothold in tobacco in Durham since the late nineteenth century, when it had organized the rollers. Due to mechanization, those jobs had changed over time, but through the Tobacco Workers International Union (TWIU), the AFL had attempted to retain a role in labor matters related to the industry. During World War I, the TWIU focused on white and black workers, with mixed results. Without consistent attention, then and throughout the 1920s, local unions fell apart. In the 1930s, the AFL continued to demonstrate a preference for supporting and defending the rights of white workers, who, like their bosses, favored their interests over blacks, and ignored the benefits that interracial unionism might offer. Liberal whites, like Lucy Randolph Mason, a Virginian and head of the National Consumers League, pointed out that treating the races differently undercut labor's strength by feeding whites' fears of competition from African American workers. As long as manufacturers could sustain racial divisions, black laborers posed a threat to workers overall. In desperate need, and willing to accept lower wages, or worse, to function as scabs and strikebreakers in the case of any organized activity, the surplus of black labor maintained a downward pressure on wages and allowed industry to profit unfairly on labor's backs.[34]

If there was a place for black workers to find a voice in New Deal discourses, it was through Section 7a of the NRA legislation. Section 7a allowed laborers to organize, to bargain collectively with managers and company officials, and to participate in setting the wage and hours scale for the code. Bolstered by the legislation, organizing efforts in the tobacco industries resumed. Organizers from the TWIU returned to those sites where they had shown strength before: Durham, Winston-Salem, and Reidsville, North Carolina, and to the big factories of Virginia. In these places, they attempted to revive dormant locals and start new ones. But there were problems, none-theless, including an essentially apathetic union, white workers who opposed black demands, black leaders who opposed unionization, and Section 7a itself, which lacked any assurances for implementation or oversight.

And the TWIU showed a conflict between rhetoric and action. In its philos-ophy, the TWIU viewed black workers as critical to maintaining a united front of labor as a national resource, worthy of equal attention. In reality, the TWIU placed an emphasis on white workers and neglected black perspectives. In this way, the union repeated its history. It ignored African American women as an important contingent of black laborers and relied upon whites who neither cared about nor supported the interests of black workers. In hoping to garner black support, the TWIU did propose a wage increase for African Americans, but the plan caused white unionists to retreat because it offered something to blacks that it did not offer whites, even though the latter maintained a significant income advantage over the former. W. B. Culbreth, president of Local 176 (white) in Durham, opposed the TWIU proposal, argu-ing that it benefited his constituents "absolutely none." "I cannot ask a white man to join our organization," he wrote, having backed "such a thing." Although union officials proposed that whites could demand a raise at a later date, Culbreth balked, reasoning that "the negroes will want additional pay, as much as the white operators." If the union failed to recommend a blanket raise — meaning the same percent across the board — he argued, "there will be dissension later on."[35] And there was. Two years later, as union efforts continued to move slowly, a white worker grumbled: "The Code, according to the ratio of pay, hurt me. I was making 39¢ and it raised me to 42¢. But the darkies that were making only 25¢ or 28¢ have been raised to 40¢[;] I should have got the same ratio."[36]

Digging in, the TWIU struggled to enroll black members, hoping to gain strength in numbers, which might motivate the tobacco industry to submit a code proposal in preparation for contract negotiations. But "the colored are lots more obstinate than I thought they would be," one organizer communi-cated to E. Lewis Evans, the TWIU president. He offered his usual crass response: "I see you find the NIGS are not easy." A flood of black workers joined the TWIU in the spring of 1934, but after an initial surge, the organizer complained, "The colored people are coming in slow." Working only two or three days per week after the crop reduction, workers struggled to pay union dues — a dollar to join and twenty-five cents per week dues seemed an ex-orbitant price to pay for scorn. Moreover, the union considered itself the domain of men, as representatives of family needs through the organization.

Women, who were the majority of tobacco workers, also managed the work of the household and had children to be fed and supervised, and few found time to spare for nightly union meetings, a point the TWIU failed to acknowledge. Judging sparse attendance as apathy, local organizers complained: "We have a lot of colored people who are interested. But as you know they are not reliable."[37]

The fact that some African American laborers even considered unionizing prompted black leaders to intervene. Some black ministers started denouncing the union from the pulpit. Fearing that congregants might listen, union representatives met with the Durham Ministerial Alliance but "could not get any satisfactory agreement." Reportedly, an official at Liggett and Myers had bribed local black ministers to talk down the union and to prevent tobacco hands from organizing. Local organizers complained that they were "in the midst of a hornet's nest in Durham," stuck between white workers and black resistance, and unable to discover "who is pushing the buttons on this case." Still, local officials rejected Evans's offer to send "a good colored man . . . to dig a garden you cannot get over the fence to,"[38] or, more clearly, to do the work that white men could not do. In 1935, John Davis, referred to by white unionists as "that colored man from Washington," had communicated with local black leaders and businessmen, explaining that the TWIU backed a discriminatory wage scale for blacks — one more point that supported their opposition to unions, in addition to the possibility that unionization would ignite racial problems that they wished to avoid. The union interpreted Davis's message to mean that he did not want workers to become members of the union, but that was not the case. Rather, Davis proposed that black workers hold back their affiliation with the union until the organization supported and secured equal wages for both races. A new organizer, sent by Evans to work in Durham, assessed: "I do not think that we will get much out of either the colored Preachers or the businessmen in the way of getting the people to come into the union; it is not in their make up."[39]

The limited interracial efforts of organized labor had failed in Durham by 1935, the year Congress passed the Wagner Act, which legalized labor's ability to organize and collectively bargain. The TWIU maintained segregated unions, and even then refused to allow the black local to operate independently of whites. As a result, African Americans remained ambivalent about the efficacy of belonging. Distrusting whites, unionists, and corporations, they saw no benefit to organizing, especially given the likelihood that participation would lead to unemployment. They remained suspicious, as well, that as blacks they only served to further the demands of whites, and mostly this was true. Evans, still the head of the TWIU, realized that effective collective bargaining required black cooperation. He attempted to force his organizers to work across the color line. "The colored people of Durham do not seem to feel the need of organization," Evans complained. He interpreted their reluctance as "yielding to the dictation" of black leaders and white management. "The boss, you know, does not want the Negroes organized[;] they want to use them to lick the Whites with when the storm comes." Realizing that tobacco interests "do not like to have to pay the Colored man a decent wage," he also recognized that the same sentiments held among "a large number of people who like to see the negro kept down."[40]

Replacing one organizer after another in Durham, Evans directed local representatives in 1934 "to make a special effort to get the colored people in. . . . As I understand it, there are some 10,000 of them in the two shops [Liggett and Myers and American Tobacco], so you see there is some job to be done."[41] But organizing efforts continued to falter. One local organizer realized that black women as well as men should be recruited. But he wrote of his frustration with his assistants: "They are sincere," he defended, but "just don't know how to approach the colored sisters and brothers." Although the TWIU finally brought in a black organizer, it continued to make the same mistakes. For a meeting of local presidents in Washington, for instance, "no colored worker was invited." The organizer worried that "they might take offence." Organizers furthermore tended to "leave the impression that we are trying to help you," he wrote to Evans, but "that won't go here." Although he tried to facilitate a changed approach, he noted that "the local boys [white] . . . seem to think they know it all."[42]

For their part, potential black unionists might have been of two minds about labor organizations, and in any case they made their decisions based on their own needs and observations, refusing to yield to the pressure or advice of white organizers. Because the TWIU intended to preserve a wage differential, signing on signified accepting inequality and unfairness from groups that had historically excluded, segregated, and denigrated African Americans, in spite of any claims of justice. Black workers were not convinced that unions looked after their best interests. When strikes raged in the textile mills across the South in 1934, TWIU Local 183 (white) in Durham pledged to support mill strikers, and, briefly, union membership surged. But the example did not encourage black initiative; rather, it dampened interest. Annie Peterson, a black mill worker, felt that African Americans had been caught in the middle between management and whites before. She worried that black mill workers who "fool[ed] around with white folks striking" would find that "white people [could] strike them out of a job." Instead, she suggested that her coworkers take advantage of the opportunity to secure more work for themselves. She convinced Julian S. Carr III, owner of the mill, to let black workers in "through the side door."[43] Knowing their precarious position in the labor market, black tobacco hands also hesitated to get behind an organization that might take an action that would put them out of work. Nor did they feel secure in receiving the kind of reciprocal support white tobacco workers offered their mill-working friends, who also historically had denied them access to employment.

Not until they were assured that the AFL planned no job action did a significant number of African American laborers join the TWIU. A thousand people apparently signed up at a meeting at the Wonderland Theater in Hayti in 1934. They, too, voted to contribute toward a fund to support textile workers but were appalled when the textile strike incurred the wrath of mill owners.[44] Ending in violence and loss of life in many places, the textile strike ended in Durham with the loss of jobs. The experience produced skepticism among African Americans, fearful of losing the limited employment options they had. When Charles Johnson interviewed Durham workers about their opinions regarding unions, one woman remarked that, in the aftermath of the 1934 strike, "we were scared to mess with it." Another claimed that she did not believe in unions. "I didn't see where it did the hosiery mill no good. . . . I don't believe the union done nothing. We got that raise because the white man give it to us."[45]

Conscious of who held the real power over their hours and wages, African American workers hesitated to join an organization that challenged those who controlled their ability to earn, but there were more reasons that made blacks reluctant. Only when seeking strength in numbers and stimulated by the labor-friendly legislation had the TWIU sought them out. Snubbed initially, and generally ignored, many black workers also felt they had been deceived by union promises and methods, particularly after a white union official stole hundreds of dollars in dues. As one worker commented to Charles Johnson, "It would be pretty hard to get up a union in this town because colored people have been treated so dirty."[46] And, too, African Americans knew that the hand of whites' retribution extended beyond a given factory. In Winston-Salem, for instance, a group of factory workers regularly used the black YWCA for meetings of their "pool association," a mutual benefit group. One Sunday, they found themselves locked out of a meeting at which Louis Austin, firebrand editor of the Durham black newspaper *Carolina Times*, had planned to speak in support of unions. A damning leaflet exclaiming, "Organize and raise wages and standard of living," had found its way into the hands of town Community Chest officials. Central YWCA officials, a Community Chest agency, ordered the black YWCA secretary to "call off" the meeting. The staff called the secretary into the YWCA office to berate, humiliate, and threaten her with unemployment if she could not "prove that she was not associated with the movement."[47]

In pursuing improved wages and conditions, African American laborers saw little value in the white local as a mediator on their behalf. As late as the 1930s, the national TWIU still regarded black locals as a way to strengthen whites' negotiations, much as it had in the 1910s. Otherwise, the black local posed a competitive threat to whites' positions in the industrial hierarchy. For their part, African Americans viewed the union as one vehicle through which they might promote their own agenda, making an end run around local union leadership and whites and then going to management as a black collective. African American members of locals in Durham and Reidsville directly contacted E. Lewis Evans, president of the TWIU, considering him "clothed with the authority to negotiate a joint, mutual agreement between American Tobacco Company and the colored employees" of the corporation. Representing potentially tens of thousands of union members in Piedmont factories, the plan garnered Evans's support.[48]

In working with other black locals, organizers were surprised to find that the strength of Reidsville and Richmond unions concentrated among women stemmers: "Some of the DURHAMITES were very BASHFUL when they saw a house full of 'GIRLS' at the meeting," Evans ribbed a local official. "It is good that they [are] so interested."[49] With black women stemmers outnumbering male workers at the plant, the union had much to gain by paying attention to gender as well as race. Under pressure, Evans eventually appointed several black organizers, all male, and men remained the leaders of locals. Women held secondary offices, such as secretary and treasurer. Membership drives were launched through the churches and through door-to-door campaigns, targeting potential allies, where and when they were found. Unionists also established their own places to meet, in black churches and at the Stanford L. Warren Library, and conducted their discussions in the barbershops, beauty parlors, and pool halls in black neighborhoods.[50]

Black unionists were disappointed once again that raises offered in the 1937 tobacco contract were not as large as those for the whites, but the small raise that did come about due to union efforts fueled increased interest among African American workers. They took matters into their own hands: "The negroes at the stemming plant," mostly women, "did gather and pray that their burden of work would be lessened," an organizer reported. Several weeks later, they threatened to stop work if they were not given chairs to sit

in while they worked.[51] Labor activism potentially raised the level of antagonism between blacks and whites and exposed black leaders' inability to influence their constituents. When "the big negroes stepped into it in a big way,"
African Americans laborers ignored them. The members of one church, for
instance, threatened to withhold the salary of a minister who opposed their
joining the union. At another church, black workers walked out on a leader
who spoke against the union at a church service. Yet another group left a
church to start another "when their minister refused to support them."[52]

The black leadership community itself split over the issue of workers'
unionization according to generation. James E. Shepard, president of North
Carolina College for Negroes, and C. C. Spaulding, head of North Carolina
Mutual, opposed it; Louis Austin, editor of the *Carolina Times*, supported it.
Rev. Miles Mark Fisher, proponent of the social gospel and a minister called
to lead White Rock Baptist Church in the mid-1930s, offered the church as a
meeting place, in direct opposition to the preferences of C. C. Spaulding.
Representing the church establishment and his preference, Spaulding in-
sisted to Fisher: "Those who are in authority and who are giving employment to our people are watching every move we make. It might be well for
the Union to meet elsewhere." F. K. Watkins, owner of the Wonderland
Theater, offered his business at the corner of Pettigrew and Fayetteville
Streets in the center of the black business district as a meeting place. Julia
Lucas, owner of a barbershop located near the factory, backed the union
drive and encouraged her customers to talk in her shop. Positioned between
workers and the elite, these younger supporters shared close ties with tobacco hands. Fisher counted hundreds of them among his congregants and
hoped to bring them into more activist circles in the church to challenge the
power the elite held over the institution. To Julia Lucas and F. K. Watkins,
tobacco workers were their main customers.[53]

Still, the old guard of black leaders held back their support. Ever the
moderate, Spaulding kept his reservations about unions. They "have not
benefited Negro members as much as white members," he maintained in a
speech in 1938. "As a race we should be more concerned about making good
with the opportunities we already have, and strive to improve our efficiency."
Six years into the New Deal and Spaulding had seen little more than frustrated dreams. New strategies proved no better than old ones, in his mind.
The NRA codes and voluntary wage scales had left black incomes stagnant
and had incited racial tensions. "The sooner we come to understand and
adjust ourselves to conditions as they are, the sooner we will rid ourselves of
the myth that is causing so many of us to lose our grasp on the opportunities

that once were ours," he offered as advice. "We again counsel our people everywhere to turn their eyes within and lay more stress on efficiency and thrift. The possibilities of our group are unlimited could we but visualize our opportunities and work together constructively, cooperatively, and mutually in a common cause."[54]

The persistent murmur of unionizing presaged the future direction of black political activism, while also reflecting a broader impatience among Durham residents. And the 1930s milieu continued to shake up a range of political, economic, and social issues, bringing the leadership under fire from all directions. Laboring black folk were frustrated and tired of hearing the refrain from leaders that "this is not the time."[55] Florida Fisher Parker, Rev. Miles Mark Fisher's daughter, recalled: "The people at North Carolina Mutual wanted to control what black folks were doing."[56] Conrad Odell Pearson maintained that, as long as Spaulding remained black Durham's figurehead, James E. Shepard remained in his office and "pulled the strings."[57]

But those strings were to be tested. In bringing their activism out from behind the veil, African Americans in Durham had entered an era of political optimism, if not significant political success. Whereas they once had viewed the law, legislation, and electoral politics as of little help, a series of transformations combined to make their tactics more assertive. World War I and woman suffrage had combined to put voting back onto the black political agenda in the 1920s, providing another means of change. Women's organizations like the North Carolina Federation of Colored Women's Clubs (NCFCWC) and local clubs like the Volkamenia Literary Club encouraged African Americans to increase their voting activities. And the NCFCWC encouraged women's efforts to make the shift among black voters from the Republican Party of Lincoln to the Democratic Party of Roosevelt. Both parties could find black Americans in their camps, but not for long. By the 1938 election, a significant number of blacks had switched from Republican to Democrat, among them C. C. Spaulding and his younger colleagues. "The Negro deserted the Republican Party beginning in 1932," Dean James T. Taylor explained at a district meeting of black Democrats, ostensibly "because they realized that the GOP was at sea and heading the country toward ruin and disaster."[58] A fundamental shift had occurred. That year, 1932, North Carolina black leaders had met in Durham to form an Independent Voters League, the first organization of its kind in the South. Its purpose, according to members, was to "demand that Negroes be given an opportunity to exercise their political rights as guaranteed by the Constitution, and to further promote the Negro's participation in politics and government by way of the ballot box." As of April 1933, the organization had registered a thousand black voters in Durham, about a tenth of the town's black population of voting age, enough political intensity to get the city's attention.[59]

Agitation put Durham's black leadership in a position to make political demands on white leaders. Guided by C. C. Spaulding, black Durhamites began a series of campaigns, or, more accurately, appeals to local white officials through a citizens' committee. Among their requests, black citizen leaders called on white registrars to cease denying the rights of African Americans who went to the polls that fall. With youngsters wandering the streets, many of them unemployed, the citizens' committee asked that the school board appoint an attendance officer for the black schools and install telephone service. Committee members also sought a number of municipal improvements to African American neighborhoods, including street paving and lighting for the side streets of Hayti. Aggravated by unemployment and a growing population, crime had increased sharply in the 1930s. To deal with a range of offenses that occurred regularly in black neighborhoods, leaders asked the city commissioner to appoint black patrolmen to work the streets. Louis Austin, the newspaper editor, demanded that political parties appoint black magistrates and justices of the peace, and he pressed to have Hayti redistricted into a single voting ward and for African Americans to be designated to watch the polls on election day. Finally, the citizen committee raised the issue of jury duty, from which African Americans were excluded. Four years later, only some of the requests had been granted, and neither the police nor the jury duty issues had been addressed. These represented extensions of white authority and of the law — and a hegemony that whites refused to relinquish. Still, African Americans held a Negro Democratic Convention in Durham in 1938, a most daring act. For white Democrats locally and statewide still held on to white supremacy and advocated the use of violence to sustain it.[60]

Partisan politics divided Durham's black community by class again, but for different reasons. African Americans who worked as household and industrial workers clearly supported Democrats, not only for the New Deal programs but also because white Democrats were their employers. Among the most active, mill worker Annie Peterson organized black voters among textile and tobacco hands in the mid-1930s to support several campaigns by Julian S. Carr III, owner of the mill. During Carr's first campaign for mayor, she made calls to people she knew, and, during his second run, she stated, she "got out and worked myself to death for him. I went around and I got all the [blacks] to register. When Election Day came, I hauled them to the polls in my car." Pleased that Carr had won, Peterson explained, "If he hadn't I would have had to leave town."[61]

Peterson asserted that she also supported Carr in order to obtain from this powerful politician the things the community needed. Given her contact with him, she accomplished more through her electioneering for the black community than black elites could achieve with compliance. After Carr was elected, she explained: "I got all these lights down here on Fayetteville for colored people." She also said that she convinced Carr to set up sewing machines in the homes of black women who, having young children, could not go back to work, and to put knitting machines in the schools so that young women could learn the work. "I know a lot of girls that worked under me that worked their way through college by working in the mills. I had no education myself, but I pat myself on the back. . . . I did pretty good." Minnie Simms, formerly an office clerk for the Mutual who left for employment in one of the tobacco factories, also did political work in the 1930s. What began as helping two colleagues who asked her to teach them to recite the Preamble to the Constitution expanded to sessions with others. "When I started working in politics we had about eighteen Negroes registered in my precinct. Now [mid-1940s] we have five hundred and seventeen," she reported to a researcher.[62]

The elites made the same claims to progress, but they referred to political workers like Peterson and Simms as "ward heelers," a derogatory term for working-class people, who, by upstaging elites' authority in electoral politics, disrupted the order of black affairs. Accused of being bribed for their votes, Peterson and Simms responded that they never took money. They believed that any cracks in the elite's influence resulted from their lack of compassion and understanding of the circumstances confronted by the masses and not from inappropriate acts by those blacks who worked at the precinct level.

The Great Depression exacerbated economic racism but it also illuminated the differences among cohorts of African Americans. "The gap between our professional group and our laboring, domestic, and agricultural groups is entirely too wide," Tuskegee head Robert R. Moton reported, continuing the theme of internal friction at the 1933 meeting of the NNBL.[63] Moton proposed a strengthened middle class to bridge the gap between the top and bottom of the black class structure. A potential cross-class alliance did exist at the nexus of gender and labor issues. Numerous tobacco-working women had lost their jobs, and, with their salaries slashed, teachers earned less than those tobacco hands who managed to hold on. Divisions deepened as the economic situation deteriorated and interest groups searched for strategies to break apartheid's grip.

9 : Plenty of Opposition Which Is Growing Daily

Gender, Generation, and the Long Civil
Rights Movement

In the 1930s, the NAACP launched a civil rights campaign that used the courts to dismantle Jim Crow. Conditions specific to Durham, including the importance of C. C. Spaulding himself, persuaded national organizations to view the city as a brilliant location to press a new strategy, one that moved from requesting only a small share of resources to demanding an equal share. In the political milieu of the 1930s, with its range of competing ideologies, the NAACP grasped the imperative to rebuild the nation and fashion a participatory democracy. Focusing on public education as a common, necessary experience in American society, the NAACP began the steps that led to the Supreme Court decision that dismantled Jim Crow, *Brown v. Board of Education*.

Where better to launch a campaign against racial inequities than where black leaders were unlikely to suffer economic repercussions for their activism? To its external boosters, black Durham always had stood as a symbol of positive racial attributes, mutual aid, self-help, race pride and enterprise, ingenuity, initiative, and autonomy. And it helped this radical cause that black Durham had a reputation for caution and vigilance in racial affairs. "The Durham Group," as NAACP officials called local black leadership, was known to support the organization — Spaulding and his managers had donated money. Second, the Durham Group knew how to manipulate the racial status quo to its benefit. Knowing that southern whites would do anything to maintain segregation, for instance, black Durham had gotten some of the best public education facilities for African Americans in the South, including the only high school for black students in the state and one of the few in the region, seven elementary schools and an eighth in the planning stages, and North Carolina College for Negroes. Within the local educational community, teachers were the NAACP's strongest supporters, and over a hundred black women teachers staffed the Durham black schools. Durham's Jim Crow generation had followed the path as instructed, but now they were prepared to step into their new roles as social engineers who would launch the next phase of the battle against segregation and discrimination.[1] They would lead the following generation into the streets in the 1950s and 1960s. For now, they represented a generational shift in leadership on the local stage. The national race agenda turned the spotlight on Durham.

In 1933, two campaigns based in North Carolina marked the NAACP's first efforts to equalize black and white education. In February 1933, Cecil McCoy and Conrad O. Pearson, William G. Pearson's nephew, working independently of the NAACP, proposed to challenge the practice of excluding black students from the University of North Carolina at Chapel Hill. The political differences between the younger and the older Pearson alarmed local whites immediately. An editorial in the *Durham Morning Herald* tagged McCoy and Pearson as "younger and more assertive members of the Negro race," charging that the black attorneys were "playing with fire." The paper agreed that African Americans might present "a strong case with the constitution forming the vital part of their brief." But "all things that are just are not expedient," the editor warned. "To our way of thinking, they will find in the end that they have won not a victory but a costly defeat." The suit had gone forward, the newspaper claimed, over the "mild protest of more tolerant and conservative group[s]," meaning Spaulding, the senior Pearson, and James E. Shepard, president of North Carolina College for Negroes. "Members of the Negro race, certainly its leaders, do not object to segregation," the newspaper claimed, "and the white race insists upon it." Not surprisingly, the paper issued a veiled threat: a win in the courts would "rob" African Americans of "many rights now enjoyed."[2]

Those rights, of course, were limited. Even if the city agreed to make the improvements that Durham leaders had requested, none of them changed the status of Jim Crow, expanded African Americans' access to advanced education, or increased their entrée to power. For that reason, and many more, the young lawyers pressed their case. Conrad O. Pearson filed suit against Thomas Wilson, registrar of the University of North Carolina at Chapel Hill, who had refused admission to Thomas Hocutt, graduate of the North Carolina College for Negroes, to the university's school of pharmacy. Behind the scenes, black leaders and white officials negotiated two possible courses of action: the state would pay the tuition for Hocutt, the plaintiff, and for any other African Americans who desired to attend graduate school out- side of the state, or the state would "make provisions" at "one of the Negro institutions now operating" for the creation of new graduate programs. The Durham paper preferred the second option, that Hocutt "be educated at home," in North Carolina, a place the *Herald* considered a "more acceptable environment."[3] In that way, Hocutt would remain within the framework of Jim Crow, compliant with segregation and hopefully inclined to serve the population of blacks in a similar vein.

The NAACP regarded Hocutt's case as precisely the circumstances it needed to attack segregation at its most vulnerable point. African Americans in most states, and especially in the South, could not attend the schools where pro- grams led to professional fields that required licensing and specialized train- ing. In order to practice law or pharmacy, which were regulated by the state, the legal team argued, students should be able to train in the state where they intended to practice. None of the North Carolina black colleges offered law or pharmacy training and therefore did not fulfill the mission of public education. It would be a costly endeavor to pay tuition for black southern graduate students to attend programs in the North. This prospect also irked white southerners because such education implied a liberal outlook that they hoped to keep outside the region. Segregated graduate training, which older black leaders and liberal whites might have preferred, also required that black facilities be equal to those offered at white institutions. In pharmacy and law, this would require the enormous expense of building facilities, hir- ing faculty, and furnishing libraries and laboratories equal to those of the prestigious University of North Carolina at Chapel Hill. Either choice, as far as the Durham lawyers and the NAACP were concerned, would financially break the Jim Crow system by bankrupting the state. Finally, a decision that admitted black students to white-only schools theoretically reversed *Plessy v. Ferguson*, the constitutional underpinning of Jim Crow in the southern polit-

ical economy and in race relations. Overturning *Plessy* on the basis of graduate education not only carried implications for K–12 education but also
foreshadowed revolutionary transformations in other southern institutions
like unions and in spaces like public accommodations. The Hocutt case
served the NAACP legal agenda well in beginning its effort to dismantle the
structural underpinnings of Jim Crow.[4]

African Americans in Durham split over the appropriateness of the suit. In-
deed, black leaders, reportedly through the local branch of the NAACP, backed
a proposed bill to authorize out-of-state tuition as a "cooling off" strategy.
Still, the "militant Negroes voted to demand a showdown on the case," in the
Herald's language. In contrast to the local branch, the NAACP supported the
suit, sending William Hastie, its premier attorney, to assist Pearson and
McCoy.[5] Filed in Durham County Superior Court, the case was moved to
Raleigh and into the state judicial system where Wilson, the university regis-
trar, argued that Hocutt lacked sufficient preparation to enter the institution.
Hastie made a strong argument, which, with the Constitution on its side, the
NAACP possibly could have won. But Hocutt's apparent failure to follow all
application procedures doomed his case. Unable to produce a transcript
certified by his graduating institution, Hocutt lost on a technicality that was
engineered by James E. Shepard, president of North Carolina College for
Negroes, which intentionally withheld Hocutt's transcript. Holding this last
card, Shepard acted to protect his institution and reinforce his position; he
declared that Hocutt would not graduate in the spring, as the plaintiff had
claimed. Shepard worried, appropriately so, that the state would retaliate, to
the detriment of black education, potentially cutting funds or denying any
future expansion. Furthermore, Conrad Pearson maintained, Shepard had
grown powerful in black educational circles as a warrior and negotiator. The
NAACP's intervention usurped his local power and influence. Head of the
strongest of the state's black colleges, Shepard was positioned to demand
more for his constituency. The Hocutt case, in his view, threatened to end his
reign and to undermine the progressive stance that whites had been willing to
take in expanding educational options for the race.[6] Thomas Hocutt's suit,
although a defeat on the way to *Brown v. Board of Education*, inspired the
NAACP legal team by highlighting the strength of direct challenge. But for
Shepard, the case was won.

In the fall of 1933, the NAACP took up a different campaign that tested clear
educational inequities, a campaign to equalize black and white teachers'
salaries. Here too Durham's black community divided. As with the Hocutt
case, as this movement unfolded, discrete and often contradictory voices

(and silences) revealed African Americans' competing agendas, demands for influence, and leadership. And, once again, NAACP lawyers viewed Durham in 1933 as the appropriate time and place for a fight. The NAACP still believed that Durham could be the stage for this battle, anticipating support from the educational and business communities, which historically had fought the degradations of the Jim Crow South. As Roy Wilkins, then assistant secretary of the NAACP, wrote to C. C. Spaulding at the Mutual in the fall of 1933, "We are counting on you as always, to advise and aid us in this important matter." Spaulding fell silent.[7]

Durham had maintained a local branch of the organization since 1919, but as Conrad O. Pearson described typical membership procedures, "You pay your money and then say nothing."[8] But neither Spaulding nor Shepard nor the senior Pearson paid dues. The triumvirate wielded influence in North Carolina black politics and in white progressive circles. Spaulding, for example, served as treasurer of the Commission on Interracial Cooperation, an association of liberal whites and black spokespersons. All three men also believed that their leadership, the welfare of their community, and the survival of their institutions depended on not vexing whites. Frustrated by the Durham elite's hold on state black politics and angered by Spaulding's reticence, a younger cohort of activists — including Cecil McCoy, Conrad Pearson, and Louis Austin — determined to test the old guard. George Streator, a self-referenced "radical" and college professor for North Carolina A&T at Greensboro and now editor of the *Crisis*, wrote to Walter White: "Calling Spaulding when the radicals are on the warpath" was a "Durham racket," he warned. "Spaulding . . . frequently capitalizes on his ability to swing things out of reach of radical Negroes."[9]

Once again, black Durham's constituencies disagreed with each other. This time, three different factions entered the fray, each from different standpoints. Teachers, virtually all women, supported the NAACP effort; the old guard of male leaders publicly contested the NAACP; and the younger generation of self-styled radicals, also male, supported the NAACP but mostly declined to defy the leadership of the old guard. As the various perspectives unfolded, African Americans operated at cross-purposes, agreeing ideologically perhaps but disagreeing in their approach to — or retreat from — the tactics of the NAACP. A proposed suit to end discrimination in teachers' pay appealed to educators and young radicals. Both viewed salary equalization as a race issue in that black and white teachers earned very different salaries for similar work. Not only did the state of North Carolina spend less on black students than on white pupils, but also, according to the 1933 school law, the state paid black teachers 30 percent less than it paid white teachers.[10] "The bulk of teachers in public schools in North Carolina are paid between $45.00 and $56.00 per month for eight months out of the year," the NAACP pointed out. "When figured on a weekly basis this amounts to a wage of between $7.50 and $9.50 per week." By comparison, unskilled tobacco workers made $10.00 per week.[11]

Teachers also viewed salary equalization as a labor issue, uniting workers of a particular occupational group to organize for improved wages and working conditions. Moreover, the matter linked gender issues with class and race. Schoolteachers worked in a feminized field, doing a job that was considered women's work. The profession required respectability, and respectable married women did not work in public. Thus, the vast majority of Durham black teachers were single and financially responsible for themselves. But still they earned significantly less than the clerks at the Mutual or its sister institutions, and some teachers earned less than laborers in Durham tobacco factories, as the NAACP's 1933 study of wages illuminated. Although their occupation represented both uplift and upward mobility for African Americans, teachers were underpaid and overworked.

Women educators bore an additional expense: their public image as role models required the accouterments of female respectability. As one teacher stated, respectability and race pride cost money. Addie Marie Faulk, a Durham teacher, could not afford to buy a car but refused to ride on the segregated bus. She lived in a teacherage, a boardinghouse for single teachers across town from her assigned school, West End, and therefore used taxies, shared the cost of rides, or walked to get to work. Because they could not count on the city, black public schoolteachers bought materials for classroom use out of their own pockets. Already struggling financially with rent and expenses, Faulk and many of her colleagues took on summer employment in factories or in service in northern cities, away from the eyes of their students and parents. One teacher who had elected to work at a Durham factory found herself ostracized by her coworkers, who resented a middle-class person taking a job that might have gone to a friend or kin. Faulk went to New York to work as a waitress; another summer she worked in a factory loading gunpowder into bullets. Summer employment still proved insufficient, however, and she could barely support herself in the months when she received no pay for teaching. She explained: "By the time you travel there and back, and pay your rent and everything, and then you had to buy a new outfit for school, you had so little left."[12]

Matters worsened in the 1930s. When the Depression set in, all North

Carolina teachers received a pay cut. Black teachers, already on the financial margins, lost even more. Many bore the additional cost of tuition, as the state demanded increased qualifications for teaching. Faulk and her colleague Mary Pauline Dame had entered teaching when it required less than a secondary education. Under the new guidelines, both had to enroll in summer school and take extension courses during the year to meet new standards for certification. Even then, as an informational flyer pointed out, according to salary guidelines for the 1933–34 school year, "the very lowest paid and lowest trained white teacher is to receive as much as the best trained and highest paid Negro teacher with the same experience. This is an insult to this group which represents one of our leading professions [and] an affront to the entire Negro citizenry of the State."[13]

Of course, teachers also understood that salary represented only one of a number of equity issues in education that needed attention. East End and West End schools remained dilapidated buildings where students studied in unacceptable conditions from ragged books and with no supplies. The gap between black and white student/teacher ratios widened, even as the school year lengthened and school populations increased. And the racial salary gap grew.[14] One last galling matter was teachers' status as middle-class female workers. Although their positions set them apart from the working class, the demands of respectability required their subservience to the black male authorities for whom they worked, in this case, their school principals and the de facto superintendent, William G. Pearson. Teachers also faced the insulting intrusions of white supervisors, who entered their classrooms at will, called them by their first names, and criticized them in front of their students. Joining the NAACP gave a public voice to women who had none otherwise. As the tensions built over the salary equalization drive, though, women teachers found themselves silenced, caught between the NAACP and local black leadership, with their own perspectives falling into the generation gap between the younger and older leaders.

The NAACP opened the fight in 1933 by contacting teachers directly. George Cox, the director of agents at the Mutual, agreed to have his employees draw up a list of teachers in the state, and, after a "nice and encouraging meeting in Durham" — as he called a session with Shepard — Cox believed that a statewide meeting in Raleigh "will come out all okay."[15] In the meantime, hoping to avoid a showdown, a "delegation of Negroes" contacted the state Commission on Interracial Cooperation (to which Nathan Newbold, Director of Negro Education for North Carolina, also belonged) "and almost begged them" to recommend that teachers' salaries not be reduced.

The commission refused. The Executive Committee of the North Carolina Teachers Association (black), headed by S. G. Atkins of Winston-Salem State and James E. Shepard of North Carolina College for Negroes, submitted letters of resolutions to the governor, asking him to intervene, but also to no avail. "There seems to be but one remain[ing] course that can be taken," an NAACP leaflet explained, "to take the case to Court and follow it through even up to the United States Supreme Court if necessary." This recommendation was sure to antagonize white state officials, and it also alarmed those African American leaders, like Shepard and Pearson, who depended on public funds for their schools. To allay their concerns, the NAACP proposed making the dispute a state issue, that is, presenting the case as an initiative coming from North Carolina folks, rather than have it appear as though New Yorkers or Washingtonians were elbowing in on local territory, and hiding Durham behind the guise of a state association. Walter White, head of the NAACP, recommended that local branches organize themselves into a "State Federated branch of the NAACP. This State-Wide branch will in turn push the case in court."[16]

For their part, the old guard did everything it could to hobble the NAACP efforts, acting out of freedom's first generation's memories of the white supremacy campaigns of the turn of the century that brought racial fury down upon those who fought to have a role in American society. For Spaulding, who had been badly beaten by a drugstore clerk in Raleigh in 1931, the memory of violence was painfully fresh. Now the old guard balked at the idea of direct confrontation with white authorities, after *Hocutt* and at the same time as challenges were being mounted in Washington, D.C., over the NRA differentials for black and white workers. Spaulding, Pearson, and Shepard now took a public stance in opposition to the NAACP in the hope of demonstrating to influential whites their disapproval of a campaign that looked like protest or, worse, that advocated social equality.[17] In response to the NAACP proposal, the triumvirate allowed neither a planning meeting nor a rally in support of the salary equalization campaign to be held in Durham. Spaulding and Shepard would not communicate with NAACP officials throughout the campaign.[18]

Still, some 2,500 African Americans attended the Raleigh meeting in the fall of 1933, including 100 from Durham. "They made history," George Streator penned as the *Crisis* editor, "because they came to give lie to the oft-quoted libel that Southern Negroes are satisfied with their lot, and as an oppressed people are content to be led and advised . . . by those who hold for them the narrow vision of submerged status." As to those who had warned them away, Streator wrote, "the ruling class in North Carolina was stirred by their coming." Missing, however, were the "old-line leaders," Streator claimed. "It is amusing to note that the forces of reaction," as he called the old guard, "are attempting to spread the propaganda that the National Association for the Advancement of Colored People has a standing sneer for the teachers." Encouraging the North Carolina Teachers Association to "take the organization out of the hands of the weasel-worded, petty school politicians," meaning Atkins, Shepard, and Pearson, Streator hoped they would "throw the organization into State politics." Calling on North Carolina's African Americans to join the State Federation of Branches, he promised that "old and young will serve" and that "women will receive splendid recognition." But at the core, Streator noted, "here was a task for strong men, and it appears that strong men have accepted the challenge."[19]

To sustain teacher interest, Walter White sent Daisy Lampkin, an outstanding organizer for the NAACP, to North Carolina to meet with teachers in each major city. To circumvent the Durham Group, White called upon other state activists to lead the campaign, among them Dr. George E. Nightengale of High Point, H. C. Miller from Greensboro, and W. Avery Jones from Winston-Salem. Lampkin arrived in December 1933 to promote the program by talking to teachers "without publicity."[20] She found a range of opinions. A hearty welcome greeted her at the first stop, where she met "courage teachers" who attended a large membership rally, and she garnered almost "100% membership from teachers" in Charlotte, followed by a similar enthusiasm in Salisbury. She found some support in Greensboro. But about Winston-Salem she wrote, "Teachers are afraid to be identified with the NAACP . . . and Prof. Atkins of State Teachers Association is keeping quiet." After a visit to Asheville in the western mountains of the state, she reported that the situation was "absolutely hopeless." By the time she reached Durham, she found "plenty of opposition which is growing daily, from certain leaders."[21] Most appalling to Lampkin, someone started a campaign to raise money from the community to cover the salary differential. "The State Interracial Commission through Newbold has sent out an appeal for funds to fight for an increase in teachers' salary," she informed Walter White, "and the children of the schools are giving 2 cents each in some cities. The money is being sent to Mr. Spaulding, Treas. Some of the teachers thought it was for the NAACP," she claimed. More likely the teachers were cooperating as they were instructed.[22]

The teachers were certainly afraid. George Streator pointed out, "The teachers themselves had just fear of the Philistines who are put in the influential places." James Taylor, another young voice at the North Carolina College for Negroes, asserted that teachers feared "the stigma of taking a position in such affairs [as] might endanger their jobs."[23] Just before Lampkin's tour, Shepard had attempted to intimidate the campaign's supporters by summoning state and local black leaders to Durham for a supposed conference of educators. Holding the closed-door meeting at the Mutual, he locked out the staunchest NAACP supporters, the group calling themselves the "radical young Negroes," which included Louis Austin, the editor of the *Carolina Times*, Durham's black newspaper, as well as Hocutt's lawyers McCoy and Pearson, who now worked directly with the NAACP. Shepard had hoped to rid himself of opponents.[24] George Nightengale admitted that he hesitated to attend. "Some of the 'leaders' might be playing politics at the expense of the NAACP," he noted to Walter White at the national office. In this way, they hoped "to cultivate the good will of the legislature and thereby secure for their institutions larger appropriations for next year."[25]

After the meeting, William Trent, president of Livingstone College in Salisbury, called the session "useless and futile" and said that "Shepard is again playing his usual 'Uncle Tom.' "[26] As usual, Shepard proposed a compromise strategy to circumvent the NAACP and appeal to local whites. Suggesting that the group go on record as acting independently of any other organization, he pressured the conference attendees to organize into an association to work as an alternative to the NAACP. And he nominated his father, Augustus Shepard, now elderly, to serve as the president. As its critics predicted, this "conference of educators," as Shepard had billed it, accomplished little more than adopting a statement that looked no further forward than any set of resolutions issued previously. The group embraced "most of the NAACP philosophy." It "condemned" lynching and mob violence, "scorned" the barring of Negroes from jury service, "hit" on disfranchisement, and argued that the teachers' wage scale reduced educators "to the level of janitors." Finally, the document called for "scrupulous observance of the law as it is written."[27]

Once Lampkin returned to New York, the old guard intensified its public opposition to the NAACP's efforts and continued to pressure teachers to do the same. A letter to the editor of a state newspaper from an anonymous black leader — rumored to be William G. Pearson — claimed that the NAACP was more interested "in money it hoped to get from North Carolina Negro teachers than it was in their welfare." The writer further assured white state officials "of our determination to support our schools and to avoid social equality." Similar articles appeared in other papers, provoking an NAACP defensive response in the press. "The NAACP program is not one of violence; it seeks equality and justice under the law," the article asserted. "The propaganda in the daily papers has only served to unite colored people more. . . . In this crusade, colored people are a unit."[28] But the memories of the Wilmington Riot overrode any pledge the NAACP could make, the anonymous letter writer had explained. Disclosing exactly what the "older Negro men" thought, the author wrote: "I have seen upheavals before, in 1898. It began with Negro editors and young lawyers."[29] The description fit the NAACP coterie, as well as Conrad Pearson, Cecil McCoy, and Louis Austin. Here, then, Wilmington was brandished like a sword, wielded this time by blacks to evoke the threat of racial terrorism. In exchange for white forbearance, the old guard offered assurances that African Americans would never make the same mistake.[30] C. C. Spaulding was said to be truly frightened, according to Conrad Pearson, believing that Durham blacks might suffer "repercussions like they had in Wilmington and different places in the state, where people were shot down at the polls and told to run, [get] out of town, and so forth." In time, a younger generation challenged both that memory and its power. In the meantime, and throughout the first half of the twentieth century until all of the old guard had passed away, black Durhamites "were naturally very cautious."[31]

For their part, then, the young Negro Radicals, businessmen and professionals themselves, supported the NAACP. Impatient for changes in the racial status quo, they had facilitated Thomas Hocutt's attempt to enter the University of North Carolina at Chapel Hill and supported tobacco workers' efforts to unionize. They also tended to mount vociferous challenges to Jim Crow. Then, too, the black institutions over which the old guard reigned employed or supported many of these contingents. Louis Austin at the *Carolina Times* depended on advertising from the Mutual and from Mechanics and Farmers Bank. James Taylor, another NAACP supporter, was a dean at North Carolina College for Negroes, under James E. Shepard. M. Hugh Thompson, Cecil McCoy, and Conrad O. Pearson, local attorneys, relied on the Mutual and its subsidiaries for a steady flow of work. Ministers and their churches depended on the elites for salaries, housing, and support.[32] Thus, the younger generation may have resented the old guard's power and influence, but they respected it. As one told a researcher, "These white people in town think that Shepard has a lot of influence among Negroes here, and if we oppose him, it will destroy his influence with the white people. It doesn't make any difference whether Shepard has any influence or not, the white people think he does. I have learned not to fight him."[33]

Learning not to fight the elder elite meant learning to work around them, a difficult task when Spaulding, Pearson, and Shepard had their hands in every public program that black folk in Durham initiated. Any activity that challenged their position had to circumvent or outmaneuver all three. Formidable men, Durham's race leaders historically demonstrated admirable and successful shrewdness in negotiating with whites. They had managed to keep a set of significant financial institutions from being destroyed, while also negotiating to establish a set of black public institutions — the hospital, the college, the high school — that made Durham an exceptional place. Like most black male leaders of their era, this group articulated a masculinist vision of black achievement. They endowed their vision of racial progress with economic accomplishments, extended the concept of family to their community, and anointed themselves as patriarchs to rule over a people whose government ignored them at best and oppressed them at worse. In thwarting the NAACP, the Durham leadership acted on its patriarchal privilege (as they defined it) to decide on the best course of action and the best position for its constituency, even though the constituency disagreed. In doing so, they turned their backs on a contingent upon whom they had called for help many times, betraying the teachers who had taught their students the Mutual way to save. "We must build institutions for employment. And if that be true, then we must support Negro financial institutions," one businessman had told teachers at a local meeting. "Impress these facts upon the minds of your pupils and the people of our communities in which you teach." The teachers had encouraged their students to join savings clubs and their parents to buy insurance, but the institutional leaders fell silent when it came to their case with the NAACP.[34]

The battle over teacher salary equalization transformed into a generational power struggle and an insider/outsider contest for authority in internal black politics but devalued teachers' perspectives. Bickering about process instead of outcome frustrated the NAACP and the teachers by making the unequal-salary issue moot. But the elite manipulated circumstances to acquire more of the trappings that made Durham the "Capital of the Black Middle Class." In the years after the NAACP teachers' wage campaign, James E. Shepard exploited the opportunities to remind state officials of his stance during the fray. Also in those years, North Carolina College for Negroes obtained a law school, a graduate school, a public health school, and a black version of virtually every new higher education program established in the state. C. C. Spaulding, Mutual president, was rewarded with a place on several New Deal advisory boards. From this position, he garnered for Durham a Civilian Conservation Corps camp, National Youth Administration programs, and several Works Progress Administration projects, including job training (in household labor), child care (at White Rock Baptist Church), and construction programs and a Federal Theater Project for North Carolina College for Negroes.[35] In 1937, the Federal Emergency Administration of Public Works announced that it had allotted a grant of $126,000 for the construction of a fire-resistant 409,000-square-foot auditorium and library, a three-story 275,000-square-foot dormitory, and seven brick-faced, two-story, six-room cottages for teachers at the North Carolina College for Negroes in Durham.[36]

More assertive activism did not pass away. Whatever threats they may have perceived, almost all of Durham's black teachers joined the NAACP in 1934, an act of defiant resistance to Jim Crow and to black male authority.[37] Their reluctance in regard to Lampkin aside, the salary campaign engaged teachers, according to NAACP membership lists. They added their names to branch lists by the hundreds that fall. The Durham branch membership grew from 22 names, divided equally between women and men, at the end of 1918, to 198 at the beginning of 1934, six weeks after Lampkin's visit. Of those 198, 119 were women, teachers, clubwomen, and Mutual employees. Furthermore, other African Americans spoke what conservative black leaders might have believed but could not say openly. Although William Pearson thought he could not lend his name to the cause, his wife, Minnie Pearson, could. A forgiving interpretation of Pearson's perspective suggests that, through NAACP membership, clubwomen like Minnie Pearson represented their families' private political perspectives. For instance, C. C. Spaulding did not belong to the NAACP, but some of his officers and staff did; James E. Shepard joined in 1927, the year he ran for president of the North Carolina Teachers Association. (He was reelected several times between 1919 and 1945.) His brother, Charles H. Shepard, director of Lincoln Hospital in the 1930s, paid dues to the organization every year.[38]

And therein lies the key to the interactions among African Americans in Durham. In the 1930s, at the depth of the Depression and the height of the Jim Crow era, it was highly unlikely that any initiative to equalize black and white education — whether pushing for desegregation or salary equalization — could have succeeded in North Carolina. Durham's black leaders did not oppose salary equalization — indeed, a cynical interpretation of their position would say that their businesses benefited from teachers' increased incomes. Nor did black leaders oppose the NAACP, although they would have preferred that it take its campaign elsewhere. In fact, Spaulding often quietly gave money to various causes to support the good fight. In 1935, he gave $50 for the NAACP's Gold Medal Award.[39] There were benefits, however, to positioning the NAACP as an "outside agitator."

The NAACP gave up the teacher salary campaign in North Carolina after 1934. But teachers neither withdrew their support for the NAACP nor abandoned the education equalization effort. NAACP memberships might have fluctuated every year, but many teachers sustained their interest in the NAACP. Mary Pauline Dame insisted on contributing her dollar each year for membership and loved to read and discuss the *Crisis*. Marie Faulk put her energies into fund-raising and door-to-door campaigns to raise awareness of the NAACP's mission and to collect dues and donations. Moreover, even when they did not join as individual members, Durhamites joined the NAACP as members of churches and organizations that took out institutional subscriptions. At the same time, teachers turned to their own organization, the North Carolina Teachers Association, which actually strengthened with the demise of the NAACP drive. This group can be credited with expanding the length of the school year, obtaining transportation to school for rural pupils, and increasing the number and quality of black schools in the state.[40]

"No Action of Any Sort until 'Pussyfooting' Has Been Exhausted"

The NAACP, nevertheless, had overestimated its ability to move the old guard and underestimated the power of the Durham elite. In the spring of 1937, Austin and his young cohort launched a movement to start legal proceedings against the city and the local board of education for "discrimination in the public schools," calling upon the NAACP once more. "The white people here have twelve grades in their public school system while the colored have only eleven," Austin wrote.[41] The NAACP was "more than interested in the proposed case in Durham." The NAACP legal team had just won *University of Maryland v. Murray* in that state's Supreme Court, which gained admission to the state law school for black students. Simultaneously, *Missouri ex rel. Gaines v. Canada*, a suit to demand that Missouri admit a black resident to its state university law school at Columbia, was making its way through the courts. And at the same time, the NAACP was planning to argue a similar case in Baltimore County, Maryland, this one with the objective of establishing high school facilities for African Americans.[42]

"If the time is ripe for investigation," Charles Hamilton Houston, the NAACP's main legal strategist, answered Austin, "arrange a mass meeting of the Durham branch." Thurgood Marshall, another member of the NAACP's legal team, also directed Austin to "start raising a general defense fund for this case."[43] Houston excitedly contacted Dr. J. M. Mills, one of Durham's young doctors: "There have been very striking developments recently in our educational campaign and I think it would be very helpful to the citizens of Durham and to our Durham Branch if a good mass meeting could be arranged." And he encouraged Hugh Thompson, another activist attorney, to "start pushing this matter along."[44] Spaulding, Shepard, and Pearson, already ahead of the drive, contacted the members of the board of education, "one of whom we know very well and he is very liberal in his relationship with our inter-racial affairs (as liberal as southerners are)." Thompson responded, "We are of the opinion that it would be best to let this Committee exhaust every effort at their disposal, then call on the NAACP, after we have exhausted all of the ingenuity and efforts at our command."[45]

Among those efforts was a Citizen's Committee formed by African American leaders in Durham. Coming out of Shepard's counsel at the closed-door meeting, it was later called the Durham Committee on Negro Affairs (DCNA) and proposed taking up NAACP-like initiatives at the local level. A wary Houston warned that citizens' committees might better "protect" themselves "by building as strong an NAACP Branch in Durham as possible" to make it an "effective fighting organization."[46] The DCNA took up discussion of the teacher salary issue but proposed to turn the battle over to a state umbrella organization. The head of the Raleigh branch of the NAACP made clear his opinion of these negotiations after a discussion with Hugh Thompson: "I gather from his discussion that it is his hope to have the action started by the North Carolina Committee on Negro Affairs." Black Durham's network of committees and catalog of declarations led no further than studies or requests. The NAACP representative gave his take on Durham race leadership: "No action of any sort until 'pussyfooting' has been exhausted."[47] Thompson wearily responded: "Very little, if anything, can be accomplished" by either the committee or white allies, but the latter "at least have their opportunity to do something and this can not hinder our future and present plans."[48] With the matter at rest, the NAACP abandoned its work through the Durham branch.

Thus, the DCNA supplanted the NAACP as the organization charged with working on behalf of the black community's issues. Its executive committee was made up of only men, but women leaders emerged from the DCNA's subcommittee structures, where they did the legwork of change. Julia Lucas, chair of the education committee, regularly attended meetings of the school board and spoke on behalf of the black community, demanding sidewalks, paved streets, and a crossing guard program for the black schools. Mostly, she worked one-on-one with whites who owned the small businesses that surrounded her barbershop. Sweeping the sidewalk and chatting, Lucas made the DCNA seem nonthreatening, and she built up white support.[49] In other ways, women usurped the DCNA's work. Minnie Pearson, elected president of the North Carolina Federation of Colored Women's Clubs in 1935, took up voter registration as the second project of her organization. Locally, her club colleagues expanded their literacy classes and reading groups at the library, the hospital, and the night schools.

Common cause did not sustain unity, however. When the DCNA, the North Carolina Federation of Colored Women's Clubs, and the Volkamenia Club began a voter registration drive in the early 1930s, they did so in a nonpartisan way, throwing support behind the candidates who backed their causes and backed black voter registration. Often that meant supporting whatever candidate agreed to appear before the DCNA to state his position.[50] In the mid-1930s, with local white interests split between Roosevelt's Democratic Party and the fiscally conservative Republicans, the DCNA believed that with enough voters, blacks held the balance of power. Louis Austin, editor of the *Carolina Times*, appeared before the Durham County Republican Executive Committee to ask for a precinct and black poll handlers in Hayti. Wanting the growing black vote, the Republicans agreed, as long as African Americans promised to stay out of the political arena otherwise. Lucas and her female cohort then took up the work of transporting voters, sitting at the polls, and certifying registrants.[51]

That voting slowly increased meant that some changes had occurred in electoral procedures, but mostly the status quo of enforced Jim Crow, segregation, racial discrimination, and exploitation remained. Women, workers, and radicals continued to pressure the old guard by developing — and using — their own tactics of social, political, and economic advancement. Salary equalization for North Carolina teachers, however, was achieved because of NAACP cases won in Virginia and Maryland. Similarly, wage increases granted to tobacco workers in the early 1930s emerged from the persistent pressure of black and white laborers, despite their tensions, but were rooted in the political environment of the New Deal era. Consequently, many black Durhamites — workers, women, and the younger generation — viewed the old guard as a barrier to change and their sovereignty as an impediment to civil rights efforts. They put their energy into outside organizations, the NAACP and unions, because they had no choice but to look elsewhere for initiatives of change.

NAACP membership, which had been seen as a militant stance at the high tide of Jim Crow, had grown by fits throughout the 1930s in Durham. None-theless, three years after the salary campaign, an NAACP organizer found "an unusual amount of the 'leave-it-to-us-and-our-white-folks' sentiment; that 'outsiders' cannot help 'us' much, etc." He also found that "Shepard, et al., have some organization in Durham 'to do the same thing as the NAACP is doing.'" Still, the president of the local NAACP branch "seemed very apa-thetic."[52] Madison Jones, NAACP youth director, found a similar situation when he visited Durham in 1941. The local branch president told him that people in Durham "pay their dollar but do not touch the status quo." As to the DCNA, Jones wrote: "They have a Committee on Negro affairs which has been handling the things in the tenor of their way of thinking. It does not function much because it is a smoothing over proposition. A high school was burned to the ground recently. Arson on the part of whites is suspected. . . . Several other attempts were unsuccessful but this time it really burned to the ground. As yet the colored folks have done nothing about investigating it. They say, 'you cannot prove anything.'"[53] The burning of schools stirred up memories of the past, when black educational institutions went up in flames whenever racial tensions ran high. For their part, Durham leaders probably felt vindicated for their hesitation to move to the fore in creating structural changes in the racial caste system of the South. The old guard would not directly confront Jim Crow or promote equality.

"The Upper-Crust Negroes Have Failed to Take Any Steps"

In 1936, the Mutual opposed NAACP intervention again. Oscar King, a white man and a son of a Durham County commissioner, was accused of rap-ing a thirteen-year-old black girl, the daughter of his family's cook. Preferring that her adolescent daughter not remain at home unsupervised after school, her mother had insisted, against the girl's wishes, that the girl care for King's children. One evening when King was driving the girl home, he attempted to assault her. She escaped the vehicle and sought shelter at the home of a white family, who called the police. Officers took her into custody. Both the *Dur-ham Morning Herald* and the *Carolina Times* chastised the police for their inaction, because King was not arrested and no warrant was issued, although the matter was taken to a grand jury. For a variety of reasons, and probably out of fear and confusion, the girl changed her story. She was, according to prosecutors, unable to account for the time between fleeing King and arriv-ing at the house to which she went for protection. Her mother's version also showed inconsistencies. She hesitated to support her daughter's charges, she admitted, because she was influenced by her employer. Fearing loss of her job in the depths of the Depression, she also refused to swear out a warrant for King's arrest, as demanded by the police. In the end, white jurors struck down the girl's claim, stating that the evidence was conflicting.[54]

Conrad O. Pearson wrote to Charles Hamilton Houston: "The upper-crust Negroes have failed to take any steps" on the matter. Complaining about the local chapter's apathy, he wrote: "As you know, the Durham branch does not function and the well-to-do Negroes have very little sympathy for the workers. The working class people are very much disturbed over this matter and . . . [are] willing to organize . . . in a struggle to force the peace officers in Durham County to do something."[55] To attorney Pearson, the case provided an opportunity for the NAACP to move into Durham. For its part, the NAACP recommended that, before proceeding, the branch president "thorough[ly] check . . . on the girl's reputation, habits, and friends. . . . If we can prove she is a virgin, the offence becomes all the more terrible." And in a side memorandum to Walter White and Roy Wilkins, Houston added that White "has wanted action in North Carolina. Perhaps this . . . will answer his prayers."[56] M. Hugh Thompson, Pearson's partner, was willing to intervene, but only "if his association with the case does not conflict with the property interests of the uppercrust negroes of Durham." Thompson also proved unable to convince the mother to stand by her original story. "We believe, due to the fact that the mother of this child works for Oscar King, that she has been subsidized," Thompson wrote to Roy Wilkins, and suggested that "this matter will have to be left in its present status."[57]

Leaders of both generations questioned the respectability of women from the laboring class, and, rather than cross the old guard, even the radical young lawyers let go of a case that embodied the circumstances still facing black women in the city. Southern racism had changed very little, and the majority of African American women still were unsafe on the streets of the city or at their places of employment. Opting for calm race relations rather than a common racial struggle, Durham's black leadership group once again disappointed — indeed infuriated — their constituency. Louis Austin took the old guard to task in 1937, writing in the *Carolina Times*: "Negro leaders are still a bunch of spineless, gutless, bed-ridden near humans who don't give a tinker's damn about the masses of the race so long as they are well kept and well thought of by the oppressor."[58]

Any militant legacy in the long civil rights movement in the "Capital of the Black Middle Class" rested on the shoulders of the Thomas Hocutt case. Frustrated, the NAACP essentially abandoned all activism through the Durham branch. Spaulding, Pearson, and Shepard continued until their deaths

in subscribing to the idea that southern whites would continue to do everything they could to sustain segregation and that the best strategy to improving black life was to take advantage of that position. This, for the old guard,
was the answer to their freedom dreams — build black institutions that benefited African Americans.

On the heels of the Supreme Court decision in *Missouri ex rel. Gaines v.
Canada*, the state of North Carolina agreed to open a law school at North Carolina College for Negroes. According to the *Gaines* decision, any state that
provided legal education had to provide it to all its qualified residents in order
to satisfy the equal protection clause of the Fourteenth Amendment. It was no
longer acceptable to pay the expenses of graduate education out of state for
African Americans, as the state of North Carolina had done since the 1930s;
nor could the state refuse to create a separate law school. Pauline Dame,
knowing Murray's ambition, wrote to her niece: "The law school will open in
full in Sept. How I wish you could enter then and take law."[59] But Murray had
her own opinion of the school and of racial politics in Durham. Writing to
Thurgood Marshall of her "sleuthing" in Durham, she expounded on the
inadequacies of graduate work as it was unfolding at the North Carolina
College for Negroes. The faculty "does not approve of the idea of a Negro
graduate school in the campus," and the "library facilities are very much
below par. . . . There are a few individual students who wish to apply to the
University [of North Carolina at Chapel Hill]," she continued, "but [they]
have no encouragement from their President or the local community."[60]

Employed by the Workers Defense League, a left-leaning organization
that advocated for laborers' concerns, Murray was working on the case of
Odell Waller, a sharecropper convicted of murdering a white landlord who
faced the death penalty. Referring to the conservatism of the black leadership
in Durham, she wrote to a colleague: "Durham needs a Workers Defense
League Branch here. There are a gang of Negro lawyers who have plenty of
work but no money." Of the Tobacco Workers International Union's policy
of segregated locals, she wrote: "The Negroes seem to be the backbone of
the industry in the stemming departments of the factories, but the existence
of separate locals keeps the Negroes suspicious of the white workers and of
the leadership of their own 'jim-crow' local." She noted the need for "a white
radical organization to join hands with the local NAACP and push for some
needed reforms and change."[61] Her aunt Pauline worried about her niece:
"There are strange things happening every day," she warned. "I do hope that
from now on you will be *very* careful of everything that you do. Keep out of
these radical things."[62]

Meanwhile upbuilding continued in Durham. By the late 1930s, African American women in Durham had established numerous organizations—local chapters of the National Council of Negro Women, LINKS Incorporated, the sororities Alpha Kappa Alpha and Delta Sigma Theta, a Housewives' League, and literary and cultural societies, in addition to the Tubman YWCA. Durham women were active in the North Carolina Federation of Colored Women's Clubs, which shifted its emphasis from the problems of female delinquency to voter registration and black participation. In addition to these citadels of middle-class respectability, a range of organizations sprouted in the working-class neighborhoods of Walltown, Hickstown, East End, and Lyon Park. The Pearsontown Community Club and the Walltown Community Council demanded of white politicians the same for their neighborhoods that Hayti residents demanded for theirs. Women finally joined the Tobacco Workers International Union, but they refused to support a strike in 1939 when the male-dominated union joined with white workers and disregarded the women's demands. The Southern Negro Youth Congress, founded in Richmond, Virginia, in 1937, had taken up organizing tobacco workers there and in the tobacco towns of North Carolina. The Durham Negro Youth Federation canvassed door-to-door for a voter registration drive. These activities reflected impatience with the traditional conservatism of black leaders and a gender and generational divide that had widened since the turn of the century. C. C. Spaulding, James E. Shepard, and William G. Pearson felt the pressure but still were more interested in keeping the friendly relations between the races than in pressing for substantial change in conditions for Durham's African American residents.[63]

Tensions increased in the South as the world war against Nazism, fascism, and racism abroad magnified the hypocrisy of American racial politics in the 1940s. At a 1942 meeting in Durham at North Carolina College for Negroes, a mostly southern collective of black leaders and intellectuals met to speak, without the critique of northern race activists, on the course of race relations in their region. All but five of the fifty-nine attendees were men. The statement, known as the Durham Manifesto, exposed the chasm between the radical thought of the younger set of the group and the caution of the old guard. Yet, charged with writing a declaration that brought together the differing viewpoints among the attendees, Charles S. Johnson wrote a surprisingly candid interpretation: "A racial caste system and a democratic society were not only incompatible but impossible." While calling for equal education, equal pay, and equal opportunity, the statement was a laundry list of specific economic and social reforms needed: voting rights, equalization of teacher salaries, desegregation of unions, for example. Conferees came to a consensus as "fundamentally opposed to the principle and practice of segregation," but their statement did not call for an end to segregation, either immediately or in the future. In fact, the more cautious members of the group, including the Durham contingent, viewed a direct battle against Jim Crow as sabotage of their own goals. Southern white liberals could accept the declaration as a workable device for future change, but most southern whites viewed the statement as extremist because it did not endorse segregation.[64]

The persistent focus on race relations meant little to most African Americans, because their encounters with the evil of Jim Crow varied so much from the experiences of the black elite who held the reins of power. Only a direct challenge to the facets of racial segregation and discrimination could improve working conditions for women on the line in the tobacco factories or increase the wages of domestic workers. Only a direct confrontation — whether in the courts or on the streets — would bring about voting rights in a way that would manifest black political power. Only a paradigm shift could bring an end to racial and sexual abuse for black families. Only these measures could create the conditions necessary for black folk to live out their aspirations.

Although she never responded directly to the Durham Manifesto, Pauli Murray would have believed that the statement did not go far enough. Segregation of any kind was unacceptable as far as she was concerned, on the black or white side. "Over more than two centuries, enough criss-crossing of racial lines and recirculation of genes within designated races has occurred to make the notion of racial purity a highly questionable biological concept for many future Americans," she penned for the second edition of *Proud Shoes* in 1978, coming to terms with her "mixed ancestry linked with an immediate slave heritage."[65] To her mind, integration — and the struggle for it — were the only strategies that could dismantle the American caste system. When she started law school at Howard University in the fall of 1940, she launched a career that not only built on the Fitzgerald tradition of race pride but also recognized the forces of gender and class. In her seminal article, "The Liberation of Black Women," she began, "Black Women, historically, have been doubly victimized by the twin immoralities of Jim Crow and Jane Crow."[66]

Her aunt Pauline Dame might have grasped a kernel of that idea when she and her sister Sallie wrote: "During these long and sometimes discouraging years of segregation, the Negro teacher had carried a double burden. She has had to impart knowledge and civic pride to the Negro child under conditions which have been difficult at best. More importantly she has had to give the child a sense of self confidence and a feeling of worth against almost overwhelming odds and disparagement on many sides."[67] Pauline Dame inherited her dedication to education from her father, Robert G. Fitzgerald. When he died in 1919, she became the head of the family, a position that she held from when she was fifteen years old. The year 1940 marked her fifty-fifth year in teaching, and except for the year or so in which she moved around with her husband, Charles Dame, who had forsaken the race to enter the profession of law, all of those years were spent in Durham and all of them at the same school. Having drawn on her father's faith in education as a tool of uplift, she carried out her charge as a race woman to lay the building blocks of the struggle for the youngsters she taught.

Pauli Murray also absorbed the Fitzgerald expectations, "stern devotion to duty, capacity for hard work, industry and thrift, and above all honor and courage in all things." Murray inherited her aunts' race pride, but she chafed against racial segregation. "The hatred of segregation was not hatred of community life among Negroes," Murray explained in an interview. Indeed, she agreed that there were many "positives" about an exclusively black social and community life. "These were comfortable. The point at which life became unbearable was in the contact with the white world . . . and being made to feel inferior by all the signs and symbols and the etiquette."[68] Murray had graduated from the renowned Hillside High School, and it had been her hope to go to Columbia University in New York City, only to discover the two forms of discrimination that shaped her later activism around civil rights. First, Columbia did not accept women, and, second, although she had graduated at the top of her class at Hillside High School, she had attained merely a Negro education, up to the eleventh grade. No accredited college or university would accept her until she met the requirements of secondary education as defined in the North. This required almost two more years of classes, which she completed in one year before she enrolled at Hunter College.

In 1938, Murray applied to the law school at the University of North Carolina at Chapel Hill. She was certainly qualified, having graduated with honors from Hunter. But also, as a descendant of the Smiths, her grandmother's people and the landowners who had donated land and money to the institution, she had the advantage of legacy. The legacy of race meant more than the legacy of heritage, however, and Murray was denied admission. That year she became a rebel. On a trip home to Durham from New York City, she was arrested in Virginia for refusing to sit in a broken seat at the back of the bus. Aunt Pauline was furious, but that was only the beginning of the generational tensions building between them. The fourth-generation Fitzgerald, Pauli Murray, had begun a career in civil rights — to dismantle the apartheid under which her ancestors had suffered.

The law of life is the law of cooperation, and unless we learn thoroughly this fundamental tenet of social organization I fear that the historian of the future, when he attempts to record the history of the black man in America, will write [of] "a people possessed of tremendous possibilities, potentialities and resources, mental and physical, but a people unable to capitalize [on] them because of their racial non-cohesiveness."

Mary McLeod Bethune,
NAACP Spingarn Medal recipient, 1935

Conclusion

Charged with depicting local American history and life, scholars and documentarians of the 1930s captured the distressing depths of poverty and despair caused by the Great Depression. An overview of African American life during that era reveals a range of familiar images, especially of the hypocrisies of racial segregation, still-living memories of slavery, and the unevenness of government assistance. Static and disheartening, these portraits depict the misery and anxiety of black poverty. Mary McLeod Bethune's assessment reflects the range of the different African American constituencies and identified this conflict as an impediment to progress. Even an alternate portrait of the era that highlights the achievements of black professionals and success among the black elite misses the liveliness of intraracial black politics in the New Deal era. None of these representations alone are definitive, of course — they must be considered in relation to each other, just as their subjects lived, together and apart, behind the veil.

It is important to recognize that clashes, or, more gently, disagreements, among African Americans account for the rich and creative forms of resistance and protest that black folk had to use to beat back everyday racism.

In fact, it seems almost impossible to really show the multiplicity of black opposition movements of the 1930s or capture their vigor. Moreover, dissent among African Americans provides evidence of the range of outward-focused energies marshaled against the true enemy, Jim Crow, not necessarily against each other. For in ignoring apartheid's nebulousness, we have weighed too lightly the substance of its repressive structure and nullified the true impact of Jim Crow's persistent outrages committed for the purpose of denying black freedom. Whites segregated, exploited, and abused African Americans and used Jim Crow to drive wedges among black constituencies in the hope of weakening black forces. African Americans used that wedge to push their activism in new directions.

Still, even as we honor the activism of the past, we should also remember the reason that activists mounted the challenges that they did. African Americans of the Jim Crow era would have preferred to direct their efforts toward building a quality of life that matched their aspirations. The renowned black Durham was formed as a strategy of self-protection: "The acquisition of money and securities is the source by which we reach the condition of genuine man- and womanhood," a brochure for "the Durham Group" proclaimed in 1937. "For without money or securities there can be no leisure; without leisure there can be no thought; without thought, there can be no constructive achievement."[1] However true this statement, there also could be no freedom without an end to oppression and the tyranny of white supremacy.

That Durham emerged in the 1920s as the "Capital of the Black Middle Class," as E. Franklin Frazier called the African American community, was not a miracle; it was the outcome of the phase of resistance that took shape after emancipation. One ex-resident argued in 1928 that Durham became the "Capital of the Black Middle Class" as "the climax of a dramatic half century in the development of a Southern city in which the Negroes were incidental figures upon the stage." In other words, black Durham's growth was immaterial rather than intrinsic to postbellum developments: capitalism, industrialization, and urbanization. Others have argued that Durham lacked an established white aristocracy clinging to Old South expectations or barring the way, and therefore a prosperous black community could form in such a New South city, given enough tolerance or leeway. Booker T. Washington credited "the friendly feeling between races" and "the sanest attitude of white people toward the black" for the upbuilding of black Durham. W. E. B. Du Bois acknowledged the "high ideals of Trinity College" (Duke University) and whites who were "sympathetic and helpful." The *Durham Morning*

Herald, often quick to criticize the city's African Americans, gave its own backhanded analysis: "If the Negro is going down," the editor once wrote, "for God's sake let it be because of his own fault and not because of our pushing him." White patriarchs celebrated black Durham's prosperity, feeling, as Washington recognized, "disabused long ago of the 'social equality' bugbear."[2]

A close analysis of black Durham reveals that core financial institutions and a small coterie of black entrepreneurs emerged in the quiet eye of the nineteenth-century racial storm and at the center of the southern black business movement. As a strategy to reclaim a public life for disfranchised African Americans, the North Carolina Mutual Life Insurance Company and its sibling institutions served as the public face for black Durham. These represented African Americans' postemancipation ideologies about mutual aid, self-help, and autonomy. Their founders and leaders, self-anointed patriarchs, articulated a masculinist vision of black achievement. Yet most of those who praised black Durham curiously looked past the fact that the vast majority of African Americans lived in neighborhoods blighted by poverty, lacked extensive education, suffered the ravages of disease and early death, endured precarious employment cycles, and encountered appalling treatment at the hands and in the minds of southern whites. And the leadership of black Durham, like those who sung its praises, slighted the fact that those who missed out on the Mutual's vision for the race were, for the most part, the women who filled the ranks of the working class. Theirs was the usual experience of African Americans in the urban South, but this experience was overshadowed by the towering presence of a culture of black business, shunted aside by a public display of black respectability.

Out of the scenarios heralded by Du Bois, Washington, Frazier, and others, the black male elite in Durham built a financial and racial sanctuary to protect themselves and their families — especially women — from whites. Over time, their dominion expanded. In addition to serving on the boards of directors of each other's companies and in advisory capacities to numerous African American organizations and institutions, company executives were called upon to sit on a variety of interracial committees, commissions, and boards. Dr. Aaron M. Moore served as special agent and Supervisor of Negro Economics for North Carolina as a part of the federal Division of Negro Economics during World War I. Charles C. Spaulding, who succeeded Moore as president of the Mutual in 1923, served on the board of the North Carolina Commission on Interracial Cooperation and later as an influential personality in African American New Deal circles.[3] Two decades after disfranchisement, Durham's leading black men did emerge — as they had hoped and planned — as public agents for the black community, speakers in a variety of settings, and political players in the effort to transform the southern political landscape.

That landscape, however, offered very little flexibility for most African Americans. Indeed, because the politics of respectability and caution sought to escape white prejudice, it offered limited defense against racism. Respectability, the central theme in making black Durham, could not overcome white power. For that reason, the 1930s found black Durham in the throes of controversy over a range of political, economic, and social issues. Race leaders realized that the prosperous side of black Durham existed because African Americans were bound together under Jim Crow. They acknowledged that African Americans shared a belief in the merits of race pride and enterprise and recognized that women and workers had contributed to building the city's renowned institutions. At the same time, other groups of African Americans had to launch initiatives to benefit themselves. Whenever black workers organized, as they did periodically from the 1880s to the 1930s, black leaders disapproved. In public they hailed the "friendly feeling between races" and blamed "outsiders" for internal dissent, even as they privately recognized the fallacy of those perspectives. Likewise, in 1933, when the NAACP began a drive to equalize black and white teachers' salaries in North Carolina, black male leaders retreated. But working women viewed the issues raised by the NAACP and even the Tobacco Workers International Union as critical. As the core workforce in education and industry, women considered race issues and workers' issues as inextricably linked to women's issues. Hundreds of teachers from throughout the state appeared at the NAACP rally in Raleigh in 1933; and, despite their employers' objections, Durham's black women teachers joined the NAACP in record numbers immediately after the meeting.[4] When the NAACP withdrew from its North Carolina drive, teachers continued to wage their campaign through the North Carolina Teachers Association. Similarly, African American women workers placed themselves at the center of the Tobacco Workers International Union's program in the 1930s. Union organizers realized subsequently that for unionization to succeed among black workers in Durham, they had to organize the women stemmers.[5] Thus, in taking up the issues of wages and work conditions, women not only put forth efforts on behalf of other African Americans but also acted as arbiters on their own behalf.

As women workers and the black laboring class looked for new ways of resisting exploitation, the black male elite turned away. The elite did not necessarily object to campaigns for access to America's promises. Shepard, elected president of the North Carolina Teachers Association in 1938, supported increasing teachers' salaries, but "such a movement," he wrote, "should not be directed by an outside agency."[6] The black male elite, moreover, did view militant organizations as useful in one way: "The white man will do things for us to keep the NAACP out," one leader explained to Ralph J. Bunche, who examined the Durham Committee on Negro Affairs (DCNA) for his study of black leadership.[7] Still, black leaders believed that national race and labor organizations could disrupt the local racial peace, which was so critical to sustaining the ongoing development of the internal black community. Remembering Wilmington, the old guard remained wary of efforts that directly challenged white power and instead favored working matters out quietly. Representatives of North Carolina Mutual and its sibling institutions — the banks and other financial businesses, the college, the fraternal organizations — had forged judicious reputations among whites; thus the members of the male elite were happy to support national groups' efforts elsewhere but not at home.[8] Good race relations, they hoped — naively, it seems now — would ease the pains of racism.

Furthermore, Durham leadership wanted to protect the power base it had created. Initiatives by less-privileged African Americans challenged the elite's prerogative to lead black Durham in its own way. "When people get to the point that they are in control, they don't like to share that control, even with a kinsman," recalled attorney Conrad O. Pearson, William G. Pearson's nephew and an activist in his own right.[9] Florida Fisher Parker, a minister's daughter who grew up in Durham in the 1930s, stated flatly: "The people at North Carolina Mutual wanted to control what black folks were doing."[10] Many viewed the Mutual and the power of its president, C. C. Spaulding, as an impediment to change rather than as a benefit. One state NAACP organizer observed about the association's drive to equalize black and white teachers' salaries: "It is useless unless we swing the center of this thing away from Durham."[11] Durham's black male leaders, at least the old guard, believed in racial cooperation, but by that they really meant that black folk should step back and allow its leadership to guide the direction of race progress.

The meaning of "progress," however, varied among community constituents. Mutual president C. C. Spaulding and his cohort drew on their past experiences to inform the present, and, out of fear, they were determined to keep a lid on any aggressive activities to destroy Jim Crow, not because they did not want segregation to end, but because, once angered, whites could turn their laissez-faire stance into violent rage so quickly. And if they did, all of black Durham could be destroyed. But with pressure building from below, that lid could not be forced shut forever. Pushing against the patriarchs as well as against whites, the rest of the black community divided over a number of issues in the 1930s, with class, gender, and, finally, generation as the partitions. Overlapping activisms, through the NAACP, union organizing, and even the expanding voter base, presented the male elite of Durham with a continuous crisis in leadership, even as each initiative opened the door to further protest and potential change. Black leaders founded their own response that could function in lieu of consistent public affiliation with the major national associations. The DCNA, established in 1935 as a forum, an outlet, and an action organization, dedicated itself to "the educational, economic, social-civic, and political welfare of the Negro" but provided little more than a place where African Americans could air their frustrations. But its existence impressed those seeking the means to forge societal change. Analysts of black political culture, like Ralph Bunche, applauded the DCNA as a model of strong political consciousness and cooperation.[12]

But beneath the philosophy of cooperation lay a vision of the future, not an immediate action plan. And the race loyalty required to sustain the black elite, nevertheless, could not translate into race unity. Seen from the inside, the DCNA and the perspectives of the leaders operated as an extension of the vision of the black male elite, one that often looked past its constituents' priorities and needs. Although African Americans from all occupations were welcome to speak at meetings, leaders made all decisions behind closed doors in the boardroom of the Mutual.[13]

In sum, African Americans in Durham distinguished between the "welfare of the Negro" and black freedom. Finding the former insufficient, many tired of hearing leaders respond to their initiatives by saying, "This is not the time." Consequently, Louis Austin, editor of the *Carolina Times*, the black community newspaper, took the DCNA and the "Fayetteville Street gang" (as he called the Spaulding leadership contingent) to task. It was after listing the problems that Durham's African Americans faced in 1937 — another year in which black teachers remained underpaid, black rural schoolchildren still walked to school, city schools remained overcrowded and dangerous, and the unionization of tobacco workers faltered — that Austin had decried that "Negro leaders are still a bunch of spineless, gutless, bed-ridden near humans who don't give a tinker's damn about the masses of the race so long as they are well kept and well thought of by the oppressor."[14]

Self-styled young radicals like Austin, and even some among the second generation of Mutual officers, supported the NAACP, unions, and political action. But they also faced a dilemma: their influence in the community or with the elite often was based on the ability to balance their personal perspectives with those of conservative leaders. The Mutual, for example, was the largest advertiser in Austin's *Carolina Times*. Others feared losing their jobs. Viola Turner, a Mutual employee, once chastised a white insurance auditor for the way he treated her and was sure that Spaulding's wrath would end her career. The patriarch, surprisingly, simply told the inspector, "You can't treat these young ones the way you have treated us older ones."[15] Thus, Spaulding did allow some flexibility; indeed, the radical side of black Durham could say publicly what Spaulding and his cohort could not. At the same time, the younger generation feared that their open opposition to the old guard might undermine the old guard's influence with whites.

In the final analysis, however, the ones who suffered most directly from Jim Crow also effected enormous change, in spite of black leaders' interference. Spaulding's cohort may have objected to many initiatives, but it is unclear whether their reservations undermined black activism. Rather, their obstructionism enhanced others' activism by pushing alternative contingents to seek different avenues toward change. Although elite men attempted to control the place of women within their community, women simply did not accept the subservient places assigned to them. They used their numbers and their understanding of how gender and race intersected to put their talents and expertise at their jobs and at organizing to work for themselves. They staked out places in the companies, industries, and communities they claimed as their own. Teachers and nurses, caught in the middle as the politics of education and health care played out between white and black men, managed to bring about significant change in the quality of life in the communities where they worked. They organized themselves and their neighbors to build and run facilities, lengthen school years, extend health care, prolong life, and provide services otherwise denied.

Although Durham's leading black men opposed interference by the NAACP, teachers' willingness to join strengthened the organization and, in some ways, sustained it in North Carolina. Through the North Carolina Teachers Association, educators enlarged their protests against wage inequities and working conditions by taking their case directly to state authorities, linking the teachers' salary issue to the problem of broader inequities in black education.[16] Likewise, while black civic leaders' objections to unions shored up their position among whites, workers found other ways to articulate their point of view, directly challenging ministers as well as white unionists, managers, and owners and founding their own institutions when established ones proved inattentive. Thus, even as employed African American women shared concerns for wages and working conditions, they also defined uplift in different ways from each other, with the professional classes developing strategies geared to issues of respectability, access to education, and career opportunities. Their working-class sisters employed tactics that focused on alleviating the immediate causes and effects of poverty and challenging those who subjugated them.

The politics of respectability, the cornerstone of elite- and middle-class black women's movements to uplift the race, generated such disparate reactions as animosity and admiration, contempt and respect. Because Jim Crow refused to acknowledge individual ability or potential and sought to push all blacks further down in society, those who made gains clung to the symbols of their achievement and distanced themselves from the masses. The elite and middle classes clung to the symbols of progress — their businesses, clubs, homes, moral codes — to shore up their prestige. In this way, they also shielded themselves from the reality of poverty, despair, and discrimination, which threatened all blacks in the Jim Crow South and widened the chasm between the classes.

Although segregation created places where African Americans could retreat from the hostility of whites and upbuild for the future, it also hid divergent qualities of life behind the veil. Accordingly, segregation created a paradoxical world of elaborate and often ambiguous relationships among the black working, middle, and elite classes and between women and men. Race leaders demonstrated admirable shrewdness, but they also erected barricades that other African Americans had to hurdle. The male elite intended to protect black people, especially women, from the insults of Jim Crow, just as clubwomen intended to uplift them. Finding these gender and class prerogatives too constraining, many African American women, from those who worked for the Mutual to those who worked at the factories, asserted their own kind of agency, managed to defend and shield themselves, challenged their male counterparts, and countered Jim Crow. In this way, women and workers defined their own versions of freedom.

World War I, a watershed in black Durham, presented another paradoxical situation. Black women and men joined in patriotic efforts to secure the promises of a war to make the world safe for democracy, to support their fighting men, and to withstand the trauma of the home front. Elite men seized the opportunity to position themselves favorably with whites and to reemerge in public light. Meanwhile, elite women came out of the shadows and joined war initiatives by working in interracial and cross-class circles. At the same time, however, home front conditions moved the various factions of the black community in different directions. Leaders asked their constituencies not to "rock the boat" and, acting on Du Bois's advice, encouraged their constituents to "close ranks" and unite behind the war effort. Simultaneously, the masses devised their own forms of protest. Women retreated from white homes and advanced toward the factory, left the South for the North, migrated against the wishes of black and white civic leaders, and thereby vexed both.

From their beginnings, the forms of cooperation and conflicts that played out between blacks and whites and among African Americans themselves centered on the fact that Durham's core working population, black women, remained transient, despite the demands of white leaders and the opposition of black ones. Indeed, gender and class contestation always lay beneath the surface of racial solidarity, precisely because women of all classes broke out of assigned gender roles while elite black men tried to contain them. With persistent migration, with the numbers of women growing faster than the numbers of men, with working-class African Americans far outnumbering the elite and middle class, who — to use the phrase of the day — spoke for the Negro? The answer is, everyone.

From its beginnings, then, black Durham experienced persistent tension, which accounted for both its transformation and its stagnation. The history of black Durham signified the cacophony of black folk's giving voice to their different visions of freedom and acting on their own behalf. Their disparate circumstances heightened the dissonance, revealing that racial harmony was as much a myth behind the veil as in front of it. Nonetheless, inasmuch as the African American elite may have wanted to build an insulated community united under the banner of race progress, black Durham did not exist in a vacuum of time and space. Most African Americans, particularly migrant women, lacked the protection or stability that could be bought with elite assets. And most, therefore, experienced the degradation of white racism daily. The demands of respectability, still in play in the interwar years, did little to change this. Although the working class could view the elite as role models and could take pride in the latter's accomplishments, the rank and file also came to resent their leaders' distance, self-proclaimed authority, and misunderstanding of the needs of others.

Still, class and gender conflict produced more sites of activity than unity would have generated. The number of black churches in Durham expanded precisely because migrants felt excluded from the old ones. And as transitional black neighborhoods matured throughout the city, they came up with their own organizations. The DCNA may have wanted to address the issues of black people in Durham, but throughout the city, beyond Hayti, associations like the Price Street Neighborhood Club, the East End Betterment Society, and the Walltown Community Council, founded in the 1940s, demanded white leaders' attention to their blocks, as well as to Fayetteville Street. African American women who dominated these institutions and organizations were "the sisters behind the brothers" and served as critical players in the direct-action civil rights movement after World War II.[17]

Yet, in viewing the divisions and the resulting discord among African Americans in 1930s Durham, one can see no guarantee that such a movement would begin. And it did not. Rather, the black freedom movement of the 1960s extended the discordant activism of the eras that had gone before. Class and gender friction generated energy and sparked a multiplicity of initiatives on behalf of the black community during the Jim Crow era and yet again during the civil rights era.[18] That is, black Durham accomplished more by operating several fronts simultaneously than by moving in one single direction. The DCNA, for instance, often conflicted ideologically with other black groups, but the separate efforts of tobacco workers, teachers, clubwomen, the union locals, the NAACP, the North Carolina Teachers Association, and the DCNA, taken together, actually expanded the range of black activism, and all of their tactics were necessary to generate change. Class and gender divisions might have imposed limits on the desire and ability of black constituents to work *together* to change the South's racial structure and improve the lives of African Americans. But those differences did not prevent progress or advancement. Instead, they inspired a myriad of agendas and, subsequently, a range of effective means of resistance and protest. Intraracial alliances could temporarily — and only temporarily — bridge the class, gender, or generational divide, especially given the power of Jim Crow, but the internal conflict of black activism also set the divided trajectory into the civil rights movement and beyond.

As a result, the outcomes of black struggles for freedom and equality held varying degrees of significance and relevance for different groups in the community. Durham, North Carolina, like most southern cities, was a place where gender and class conflict among African Americans could and did surface with regularity. Between 1869, when Cornelia and Robert Fitzgerald married, and 1954, when their daughter, Mary Pauline, left to join her niece, Pauli Murray, in New York, conditions of oppression and want persisted for African Americans in Durham, but not because black Durham had failed. As African American women and men of the various classes moved back and forth within their multiple roles, their values intersected in many ways; blacks of both genders and of all ages and social classes respected and understood the concept of mutual support in the face of racial oppression; and the community was strengthened within by a shared consciousness of their condition as African Americans in an oppressive society. They did not always successfully bridge the distances between each other, but in their separate ways they resisted and reshaped the pervasive constraints of Jim Crow, making important gains for various segments of the community at various moments.

Of what relevance is it, then, that Durham was the "Capital of the Black Middle Class"? Were its visions of or its reputation for prosperity, growth, and mutual struggle a reality or an apparition? Perhaps, like the civil rights movement itself, it was both, and therein lies Durham's significance and its lessons. The legacies of the "Capital of the Black Middle Class," like those of the civil rights movement, are ambiguous, paradoxical, and contradictory. C. C. Spaulding opposed A. Philip Randolph's March on Washington, proposed in 1941 to pressure President Franklin D. Roosevelt to prohibit racial segregation in industries that obtained federal contracts. This came to be a strategy of modern civil rights activism and a fundamental principle of equal protection under the law, a principle that emerged out of civil rights activism itself.[19] Spaulding pleased powerful whites but sealed the place of the black elite — as behind its followers, taciturn and in the back rather than vocal and at the forefront of the coming revolution.

In 1948, Daniel Byrd traveled south on behalf of the NAACP, seeking places where African Americans might be willing to file court cases to challenge racial inequalities in education. The previous year, in Clarendon County, South Carolina, a small group of parents had brought in the NAACP to take up just such a tactic. There, the local school board refused to provide buses to carry black students to school, although it provided transportation for white students. The Clarendon County case had attracted attention in black circles. Byrd hoped to drum up support for the Clarendon case, and he hoped to encourage the prominent community of black Durham to reconsider its decision to abandon the case against inequality that had been discussed in the 1930s. At the same time, the more radical contingent of Durham blacks was considering whether to bring suit against the school board for offering twelve grades for white students but only eleven grades for African Americans.

The attendance at a mass meeting was good, Byrd reported. But, otherwise, the practice of "pussyfooting" continued. J. H. Wheeler, president of Mechanics and Farmers Bank, served as the secretary of the local branch of the NAACP and chairman of the DCNA. Off-the-record, he expressed the desire to support a Durham case through the NAACP. But as a banker beholden to the head of his sibling institution, Wheeler was "not desirous of opposing Mr. Spaulding." The DCNA, albeit considered a forward move on the civil rights front, "does not move" on any initiative "unless Mr. Spaulding approves it," Byrd discovered. As to the local interracial organization, it too was ineffective. In Byrd's admittedly cynical view, the interracial committee existed to "channel Negro thought and activity in the direction whites [designated]" and "to discover in advance any ideas for proposed legal agitation on the part of Negroes and compromise the issue before it get to the filing state." In any case, southern white liberals' idea of a progressive racial platform did not end segregation or make any significant move toward equality.[20]

That said, Daniel Byrd's report also noted that the youth council of the NAACP thrived. By 1947 it had a very active membership of 973 young people, who met to discuss, formally and informally, their plans for the race struggle.[21] Like their parents, grandparents, and great-grandparents, this fourth generation born in freedom understood that racial peace required good race relations, defined as "good Negroes" accommodating segregation and its philosophical underpinnings of uplift. But the civil rights generation rejected that role even more assertively than freedom's first generation had done before. Similarly, the younger activists used critical race institutions, the ones upbuilt in freedom and expanded in Jim Crow, as the places to shape their plans. And like their ancestors, the activists of the 1950s and 1960s embraced, rejected, and expanded on each others' vision and approach, even as they chafed against strategies used by the generation before.

Hope is a crushed stalk
Between clenched fingers.
Hope is a bird's wing
Broken by a stone.
Hope is a word in a tuneless ditty —
A word whispered with the wind,
A dream of forty acres and a mule,
A cabin of one's own and a moment to rest,
A name and place for one's children
And children's children at last . . .
Hope is a song in a weary throat.
    Pauli Murray, "Dark Testament," 1970

Epilogue

When Pauline Fitzgerald Dame and her sister Sallie Fitzgerald Small left Durham in the 1950s, they undoubtedly believed that significant change had occurred. Dame had begun her teaching career in a tumbledown structure with few material resources and a lot of energy. She had seized on one of the few wage-earning careers available to her as a woman among the "better class of Negroes." She took part, alongside her parents, in the community's fight to get the Rosenwald School that replaced West End School. But she also kept her niece, Pauli Murray, away from her less-fortunate schoolmates, Dame's students. Yet the same class sensibilities that positioned her between the elites and the masses also had broken the ties among the Fitzgeralds in the 1870s.

Dame probably did not approve of the black arsonists who torched West End School, but she loved the modern brick structure that replaced it. The Lyon Park School, where the Fitzgerald sisters worked in their final years of teaching, contained a library, a cafeteria, a nurse's office, audiovisual and playground equipment, and conveniences that they never could have imagined when they began their careers. Her work there was, on one hand, part and parcel of black Durham's continuing story of pride and progress in the face of poverty. Recognizing her part in the movement to create these changes, Pauline Dame wrote, "I feel that my life as a teacher had not been in vain."[1] The Supreme Court decision in *Brown v. Board of Education* (1954) specifically overturned *Plessy v. Ferguson* (1896), the "separate but equal" mandate that had helped to break up the marriage between Mary Pauline Fitzgerald and Charles Morton Dame. In response to *Brown*, which declared segregated schools unequal, the Fitzgerald sisters wrote to the editor of the *New York Times*: "We have rejoiced to see this day come at last."[2] But they did not trust that desegregation would improve the lives of the poor African American children they had worked with all of their lives. The old idea of social equality came up again as the battle to admit black students to adequate public schools began. The Fitzgerald sisters wondered if but hoped that "the citizens of the South will find that they may well trust the welfare of the South's children to Negro teachers in cooperation with their white colleagues."[3]

Notes

Abbreviations

ADVC — Andre D. Vann Collection of Durham Memorabilia, privately held by Andre D. Vann, Durham

AVCP — Arthur Vance Cole Papers, Rare Book, Manuscript, and Special Collections Library, Duke University, Durham

Born in Slavery — *Born in Slavery: Slave Narratives from the Federal Writers' Project, 1936–1938*, North Carolina Narratives, vol. 11 (Washington, D.C.: Library of Congress, American Memory) <http://memory.loc.gov/ammem/snhtml/snhome.html> (22 January 2006)

BTWP — Louis R. Harlan, ed., *The Booker T. Washington Papers*, 14 vols. (Urbana: University of Illinois Press, 1972–89)

CCSP — Charles C. Spaulding Papers, Rare Book, Manuscript, and Special Collections Library, Duke University, Durham

CFSP — Clydie Fullwood Scarborough Papers, Rare Book, Manuscript, and Special Collections Library, Duke University, Durham

CHBP — *Charlotte Hawkins Brown Papers* (Cambridge, Mass.: Schlesinger Library, Radcliffe College, 1992)

CNHP — Charles N. Hunter Papers, Rare Book, Manuscript, and Special Collections Library, Duke University, Durham

DCCP — Durham Chamber of Commerce Papers, Rare Book, Manuscript, and Special Collections Library, Duke University, Durham

DNE — North Carolina State Department of Public Instruction Records, Division of Negro Education, North Carolina State Archives, Archives and Records Section, North Carolina Division of Historical Resources, Raleigh

DWN — Division of Work among Negroes, North Carolina State Board of Charities and Public Welfare Records, Social Services Record Group, North Carolina State Archives, Archives and Records Section, North Carolina Division of Historical Resources, Raleigh

EFFP — E. Franklin Frazier Papers, Moorland-Spingarn Research Center, Howard University, Washington, D.C.

ESAC — Equal Suffrage Amendment Collection, North Carolina State Archives, Archives and Records Section, North Carolina Division of Historical Resources, Raleigh

FRP	Fannie Rosser Papers, Rare Book, Manuscript, and Special Collections Library, Duke University, Durham
GPTWB	Governors' Papers: Thomas W. Bickett, North Carolina State Archives, Archives and Records Section, North Carolina Division of Historical Resources, Raleigh
GWP	Gertrude Weil Papers, North Carolina State Archives, Archives and Records Section, North Carolina Division of Historical Resources, Raleigh
HFP	Howerton Family Papers, Rare Book, Manuscript, and Special Collections Library, Duke University, Durham
HHC	North Carolina Center for the Study of Black History, Hayti Heritage Center, North Carolina Central University, Durham
JBDP	James Buchanan Duke Papers, Rare Book, Manuscript, and Special Collections Library, Duke University, Durham
JLP	Julia Lucas Papers, privately held by Julia Lucas, Durham
LHP	Lorena Hickock Papers, box 15, Harry L. Hopkins Collection, Franklin Delano Roosevelt Presidential Library and Museum, Hyde Park, N.Y.
MBP	Marion Butler Papers, Southern Historical Collection, Manuscripts Department, Wilson Library, University of North Carolina at Chapel Hill
MC	Military Collection, North Carolina State Archives, Archives and Records Section, North Carolina Division of Historical Resources, Raleigh
NAACPP	*Papers of the NAACP*, microfilm (Frederick, Md.: University Publications of America, 1986–)
NACWCR	*Records of the National Association of Colored Women's Clubs, 1895–1992*, microfilm (Bethesda, Md.: University Publications of America, 1993)
NACWP	Papers of the National Association of Colored Women, Mary McLeod Bethune Archives, National Council of Negro Women Office, Washington, D.C.
NCCC	North Carolina Counties Collection: Durham County, Rare Book, Manuscript, and Special Collections Library, Duke University, Durham
NCCICP	North Carolina Commission on Interracial Cooperation Papers, Southern Historical Collection, Manuscripts Department, Wilson Library, University of North Carolina at Chapel Hill
NNBLR	*Records of the National Negro Business League* (Bethesda, Md.: University Publications of America, 1994)
PMP	Pauli Murray Papers, Arthur and Elizabeth Schlesinger Library on the History of Women in America, Radcliffe Institute for Advanced Study, Harvard University, Cambridge, Mass.

PNCF	*Hampton University Peabody Newspaper Clipping File* (Alexandria, Va.: Chadwick-Healey, 1982)
RBP	Ralph Bunche Papers, Schomburg Center for Research in Black Culture, New York Public Library, New York, N.Y.
RBRP	R. B. Russell Papers, Southern Historical Collection, Manuscripts Department, Wilson Library, University of North Carolina at Chapel Hill
RCWP	Robert C. Weaver Papers, Schomburg Center for Research in Black Culture, New York Public Library, New York, N.Y.
SJFP	Southgate-Jones Family Papers, Rare Book, Manuscript, and Special Collections Library, Duke University, Durham
TC	W. Duke & Sons Tobacco Collection, Rare Book, Manuscript, and Special Collections Library, Duke University, Durham
TWIUA	Archives of the Tobacco Workers' International Union, Special Collections, University of Maryland Libraries, College Park
WDP	Washington Duke Papers, Rare Book, Manuscript, and Special Collections Library, Duke University, Durham
WGPP	William G. Pearson Papers, Rare Book, Manuscript, and Special Collections Library, Duke University, Durham
WJKP	William Jesse Kennedy Jr. Papers, North Carolina Center for the Study of Black History, Hayti Heritage Center, North Carolina Central University, Durham, now in Southern Historical Collection, Manuscripts Department, Wilson Library, University of North Carolina at Chapel Hill
WKPP	W. K. Parrish Papers, Rare Book, Manuscript, and Special Collections Library, Duke University, Durham
YWCAP	Durham YWCA Papers, Rare Book, Manuscript, and Special Collections Library, Duke University, Durham

Prologue

1. Murray, *Proud Shoes*, xv, 34–37, 45–54, 203–28, 241–43; Robert George Fitzgerald diary, typescript, 6 October 1868, 9 August 1869, folder 325, box 12, PMP.
2. Carby, *Reconstructing Womanhood*; Carby, "Policing the Black Woman's Body," 738–55; Mitchell, "Silences Broken, Silences Kept," 433–44; Mitchell, *Righteous Propagation*, 3–15; Marable, *How Capitalism Underdeveloped Black America*, 70–78. See also Brown, "Negotiating and Transforming Public Space"; Brown, "Womanist Consciousness"; Shaw, *What a Woman Ought to Be and to Do*; Giddings, *When and Where I Enter*; White, *Ar'n't I a Woman*; White, *Too Heavy a Load*; hooks, "Ain't I a Woman"; Davis, *Women, Race, and Class*; Davis, *Blues Legacies and Black Feminism*; and Painter, *Southern History across the Color Line*.
3. Murray, *Proud Shoes*, 45–56; 216–18.
4. Ibid., 217–19; Murray, "Proposal to the City Council of Durham," folder 327, box 12, PMP.

5. Murray, *Proud Shoes*, 230.
6. Ibid., 56–66.
7. Hall, *Revolt against Chivalry*, 137–57; White, *Ar'n't I a Woman*, 62–90. See also Bynum, *Unruly Women*; Edwards, *Gendered Strife and Confusion*; and Gilmore, *Gender and Jim Crow*.
8. Ben Johnson, in *Born in Slavery*, pt. 2, 8–13. See also Weare, *Black Business in the New South*; and Hall, "The Mind That Burns in Each Body."
9. Murray, *Proud Shoes*, xv, 34–37, 45–54, 203–28, 241–43; Murray, *The Autobiography*; Journal of Pauli Murray, 18 July 1933, folder 1352, box 76, PMP. There had been no mention of slavery in the Fitzgerald family's oral history, but Pauli Murray, Mary Pauline's niece, discovered that the Fitzgeralds indeed were descendants of a runaway slave and that their prideful assumptions were untrue.
10. Journal of Pauli Murray, 18 July 1933, folder 1352, box 76, PMP.
11. Murray, *Proud Shoes*, 242–43; Harris, *The Harder We Run*, 8–10.
12. Murray, *Proud Shoes*, 203–28.
13. Jones, *Labor of Love, Labor of Sorrow*, 51–59.
14. Clippings, *Raleigh Blade*, 8, 13 July 1899, scrapbooks, box 13, CHN; Pauline F. Dame, "Autobiography of My Life," typescript, folder 273, box 11, PMP; White, "The Slippery Slope of Class in Black America," 80–95.
15. Journal of Pauli Murray, 18 July 1933, folder 1352, box 76, PMP; Murray, "Proposal to City Council of Durham," folder 327, box 12, PMP; Pauli Murray to Alma Louise Fitzgerald Biggers, 24 June 1975, folder 331, box 12, PMP; Pauline F. Dame, "Autobiography of My Life," typescript, folder 273, box 11, PMP; Murray, *Proud Shoes*, xv, 34–37, 45–54, 203–28, 241–43; Murray, *The Autobiography*, 29–30; Lillian Fitzgerald to Charles N. Hunter, 3 October 1890, and Maggie Fitzgerald to Charles N. Hunter, folder 1, box 2, CNHP; Jones, *Labor of Love, Labor of Sorrow*, 51–59; Shaw, *What a Woman Ought to Be and to Do*.

Introduction

1. Du Bois, *Souls of Black Folk*, 181, xxix.
2. Litwack, *Trouble in Mind*, xiv; Hahn, *A Nation under Our Feet*, 1–20; Kelley, *Freedom Dreams*, ix.
3. Mitchell, *Righteous Propagation*, 4; Brown, "Womanist Consciousness," 610–33.
4. Brown, "Negotiating and Transforming Public Space," 107–46; Gaines, *Uplifting the Race*, 2–3; Hahn, *A Nation under Our Feet*, 163–65.
5. Odum, *Race and Rumors of Race*, 19; Woodward, *Strange Career of Jim Crow*, 97–109. See also Foner, *Reconstruction*; Litwack, *Trouble in Mind*; McMillen, *Dark Journey*; Williamson, *The Crucible of Race*; Anderson, *Education of Blacks in the South*; Shapiro, *White Violence and Black Response*; Massey and Denton, *American Apartheid*, x, 2, 15–16; Chafe, "The Gods Bring Threads to Webs Begun," 1531–50; Higginbotham, "African-American Women's History and the Metalanguage of Race"; Gilmore, *Gender and Jim Crow*; Dailey et al., *Jumpin' Jim Crow*; and Brundage, *Under Sentence of Death*.

6. See, for example, Franklin and Moss, *From Slavery to Freedom*; Higginbotham, *Shades of Freedom*; Chafe et al., *Remembering Jim Crow*; Packard, *American Nightmare*; Meier, *Negro Thought in America*; McMillen, *Dark Journey*; Litwack, *Trouble in Mind*; Gilmore, *Gender and Jim Crow*; Ortiz, *Emancipation Betrayed*; Ferguson, *Black Politics in New Deal Atlanta*; Cecelski and Tyson, *Democracy Betrayed*; and Sullivan, *Days of Hope*.

7. Murray, *Proud Shoes*, 270.

8. White, *Too Heavy a Load*, 56–86.

9. I differ slightly with my good friend Michele Mitchell, who argues that "people of African descent acted upon the assumption that the race was unified, institution building was possible, and that progress was imminent." I argue that divisions among African Americans were not new in slavery and that unity was something African Americans strived for as a part of the freedom struggle. I further argue that they could not achieve such an ideal status because activists, reformers, and everyday folk were so conscious of their differences. Mitchell, *Righteous Propagation*, 5–7.

10. Kelley, "We Are Not What We Seem"; Kelley, *Hammer and Hoe*; Kelley, *Race Rebels*; Hunter, "Domination and Resistance," 205–20; Higginbotham, *Righteous Discontent*, 2; Higginbotham, "African-American Women's History and the Metalanguage of Race," 251–74.

11. Du Bois, "The Upbuilding of Black Durham," 334–38.

12. Durham Chamber of Commerce, *Durham: Queen of the Golden Belt*, box 1890s, NCCC; Turner, *Turner's Durham City Directory*, 21; Anderson, *Durham County*; Ayers, *The Promise of the New South*, 55–80; Department of the Interior, Census Office, *Eleventh Census of the United States: 1890*, pt. 1, *Population*, 546.

13. *Durham Tobacco Plant*, 1886, cited in Hall et al., *Like a Family*, 24.

14. *Raleigh News and Observer*, 6 October 1886, in Logan, *The Negro in North Carolina*, 86.

15. Haley, *Charles N. Hunter*, 88–92. See also Edmonds, *The Negro and Fusion Politics*; Anderson, *Race and Politics in North Carolina*; Gilmore, *Gender and Jim Crow*; Greenwood, *Bittersweet Legacy*; Anderson, *Durham County*; Crow, "Fusion, Confusion, and Negroism," 364–84; Escott, *Many Excellent People*; Goodwyn, *Democratic Promise*; Woodward, *Origins of the New South*; Ayers, *The Promise of the New South*; and Logan, *The Negro in North Carolina*, 186.

16. Washington, "Durham, North Carolina, a City of Negro Enterprise," 642–50; Du Bois, "The Upbuilding of Black Durham," 334–38.

17. Du Bois, "The Upbuilding of Black Durham," 334–38.

18. J. M. Avery to E. Franklin Frazier, 2 June 1925, E. Franklin Frazier to J. M. Avery, 6 June 1925, folder 10, box 131-6, and E. Franklin Frazier to C. C. Spaulding, 24 August 1925, folder 18, box 131-15, ser. B, EFFP; Du Bois, "The Upbuilding of Black Durham"; Frazier, "Durham: The Capital of the Black Middle Class," 333–41; Holsey, "Pearson—The Brown Duke of Durham," 116–17; Bunche, *The Political Status of the Negro*; Weare, *Black Business in the New*

South; Parisher and Hennessey, "Negro Durham Marches On." On black business, see Butler, *Entrepreneurship and Self-Help among Black Americans*; Kenzer, *Enterprising Southerners*; and Holt, *Making Freedom Pay*.

19. "Hayti, Former Hub of the Black Community," *Durham Herald*, 21 April 1989; Parisher and Hennessey, "Negro Durham Marches On"; Durham City Schools, *Directory of Officers and Teachers*, 1938–39; Franklin, *Mirror to America*, 99, 111–12, 116; Allen, *Black Awakening in Capitalist America*, 94–95.

20. On the development of the tobacco industry and female labor, see Durden, *The Dukes of Durham*; Boyd, *The Story of Durham*; Anderson, *Durham County*; Tilley, *The Bright-Tobacco Industry*; Cox, *Competition in the American Tobacco Industry*; Janiewski, *Sisterhood Denied*, 80–81, 85, 97; Manning and Byrne, *The Effects on Women of Changing Conditions in the Cigar and Cigarette Industries*; Shields, "A Half-Century in the Tobacco Industry," 419–25; Department of Labor, Women's Bureau, *Negro Women in Industry*, 28–30; Hall et al., *Like a Family*; and Lebsock, *Free Women of Petersburg*.

21. Indeed, Tera Hunter, in *To 'Joy My Freedom*, suggests that African American women were critical to the development of the urban centers of the New South as well as to the development of black communities. See also Jones, *Labor of Love, Labor of Sorrow*; Janiewski, *Sisterhood Denied*; Korstad, *Civil Rights Unionism*; Trotter, *Black Milwaukee*; and Lewis, *In Their Own Interests*, 32–33.

22. Hunter, *To 'Joy My Freedom*, viii; Robinson, "The Difference Freedom Made," 51–74; Robinson, "Plans Dat Comed from God," 71–102. On North Carolina, see Edmonds, *The Negro and Fusion Politics*; Logan, *The Negro in North Carolina*; Anderson, *Race and Politics in North Carolina*; Haley, *Charles N. Hunter*, 10; Crow et al., *Race, Class, and Politics in Southern History*; Gavins, *The Meaning of Freedom*; and Gilmore, *Gender and Jim Crow*.

23. Hewitt, *Southern Discomfort*; Schwalm, *A Hard Fight for We*; Ferguson, *Black Politics in New Deal Atlanta*; Lewis, *In Their Own Interests*.

24. Nora, "Between Memory and History," 284–300. See also Fabre and O'Meally, "Introduction," 6–8; and Gavins, *The Meaning of Freedom*.

25. Mitchell, "Silences Broken, Silences Kept," 433–44; Mitchell, *Righteous Propagation*, 13–15; Marable, *How Capitalism Underdeveloped Black America*, 70–78. See also Brown, "Negotiating and Transforming Public Space"; Brown, "Womanist Consciousness"; Carby, *Reconstructing Womanhood*; Carby, "Policing the Black Woman's Body," 738–55; Giddings, *When and Where I Enter*; White, *Ar'n't I a Woman*; White, *Too Heavy a Load*; Davis, *Women, Race, and Class*; Davis, *Blues Legacies and Black Feminism*; and Painter, *Southern History across the Color Line*.

26. As a survey of gender and class and the relationship between the two, this book draws upon but differs significantly from previous scholarship on black Durham. For instance, Walter B. Weare's book on the North Carolina Mutual Life Insurance Company focused specifically on the contingent of renowned black businessmen. Dolores Janiewski has written on the dynamics of female labor as experienced by white and black women factory workers. In a similar vein, Beverly

Washington Jones has detailed the work and community lives of black women tobacco workers, the central industrial labor force. These two last works describe the Durham milieu within a shorter scope of time, Janiewski for the years 1890 to 1920 and Jones for the interwar years. *Upbuilding Black Durham* surveys a longer time line, from emancipation through the interwar years and into the early 1940s, and considers the complex relationships of race, gender, and class not only as a matter of race relations but more importantly as a centerpiece of internal community dynamics. More recently, Christina Greene has written about the gender and class dynamics of civil rights activism in Durham from the 1940s to the 1970s. See Weare, *Black Business in the New South*; Janiewski, *Sisterhood Denied*; Jones, "Race, Sex, and Class," 441–51; and Greene, *Our Separate Ways*.

27. Brown, "The Sisters and Mothers Are Called to the City," 129–40.
28. Hunter, *To 'Joy My Freedom*; Carby, "Policing the Black Woman's Body"; Frazier, "Family Disorganization among Negroes," 204–7; Hine, "Black Migration to the Middle West."
29. Gaines, *Uplifting the Race*, 2–5; Grossman, *Land of Hope*; Sernett, *Bound for the Promised Land*.
30. Carby, "Policing the Black Woman's Body"; Cha-Jua, *America's First Black Town*, 3; Miller, "Surplus Negro Women," 182–92. A professor of mathematics at Howard University, Miller traveled widely and wrote extensively about African American life in the South and in the North. For this study of migration, he analyzed the populations of fifteen cities with black populations numbering over 20,000, eleven of them in the South. Woofter, "The Negro on a Strike," 84–88. On the sex ratio, see Guttentag and Secord, *Too Many Women*.
31. The scholarship on African American women's community activism is voluminous. See Hine et al., *We Specialize in the Wholly Impossible*; and the sixteen-volume series edited by Hine et al., *Black Women in United States History*, which includes Lash-Jones, *Jane Edna Hunter*; Guy-Sheftall, *Daughters of Sorrow*; Salem, *To Better Our World*; Jones, *Quest for Equality*; and Thompson, *Ida B. Wells-Barnett*, all of which focus on the era. See also Hine and Thompson, *A Shining Thread of Hope*; Brown, "Womanist Consciousness"; Jones, "Race, Sex, and Class"; White, *Too Heavy a Load*; Higginbotham; *Righteous Discontent*; Mitchell, *Righteous Propagation*; Shaw, *What a Woman Ought to Be and to Do*; Shaw, "Black Club Women," 10–25; Jacobs, "Give a Thought to Africa," 209–13; Littlefield, "Agency and Constructions of Professional Identity," 17–29; Ferguson, "African American Clubwomen and the Indianapolis NAACP"; Greene, *Our Separate Ways*; Rouse, *Lugenia Burns Hope*; Taylor, *The Veiled Garvey*; Hewitt, *Southern Discomfort*; Gilmore, *Gender and Jim Crow*; Giddings, *When and Where I Enter*; Hunter, *To 'Joy My Freedom*; Schwalm, *A Hard Fight for We*; Wolcott, *Remaking Respectability*; Stansell, *City of Women*; and Deutsch, *Women and the City*.
32. Frazier, "Durham: The Capital of the Black Middle Class"; Brown and Valk, "Our Territory," 207–33; Gaines, *Uplifting the Race*, 12.
33. Summers, *Manliness and Its Discontents*, 2–3. See also Carby, *Race Men*; Ross,

Manning the Race; Bederman, *Manliness and Civilization*; Mitchell, "The Black Man's Burden," 77–99; and Gaines, *Uplifting the Race*, 112–16.

34. Gavins, *Perils and Prospects of Southern Black Leadership*, xiii; Myrdal, *An American Dilemma*, 207.

35. Carby, *Race Men*; Meier, *Negro Thought in America*; Higginbotham, "African-American Women's History and the Metalanguage of Race"; Higginbotham, *Righteous Discontent*; Cooper, *A Voice from the South*, 31; Giddings, *When and Where I Enter*; Brown, "Womanist Consciousness."

36. Gaines, *Uplifting the Race*, 15.

37. Higginbotham, *Righteous Discontent*, 185–229; Wolcott, *Remaking Respectability*, 3–9; Gaines, *Uplifting the Race*, 3–6.

38. In tracing out the complicated and changing patterns of class and gender relations in Durham's African American community, I have sketched out categories that do not always follow the definitions given by the era's social theorists, black or white. Such studies, however, proved helpful in understanding how scholars of the period thought about their subjects and in grasping the possible motivations behind their conclusions. Closely examined, their work often provides equivocal analyses. On the one hand, most contemporary social theory, attempting to provide credibility for African American leadership, modeled the black class structure after the white class structure and associated class and status with influence and relationships with whites. For the most part, these models failed to take into account gender (except to link marriage and respectability) or the role of leadership among the working class. On the other hand, some analyses of class, Charles S. Johnson's in particular, provided instructive clues on the ways that African Americans themselves thought about class. Likewise, Elise Johnson McDougald's analysis proved helpful because she considered women's roles. See Warner, "American Caste and Class" and "Introduction," in Davis et al., *Deep South*; Myrdal, *An American Dilemma*, vol. 2, *The Negro Social Structure*, 689–705; and Cox, *Caste, Class, and Race*, 489–508. Charles S. Johnson's model delineated five distinct categories of class (elite, upper-middle, middle, working, and fringe laborers) based on work: the type of labor, perception of the work, required education, and contact with whites at the work site. Johnson's analysis proves helpful but unwieldy in discussing a specific site like Durham where the numbers of people who fell within some of his categories were insignificant. For example, very few traditional "upper class" elites or aristocrats of color lived in Durham. Johnson, *Patterns of Negro Segregation*. Elise Johnson McDougald defined the elite as a small leisure group of wives and daughters of black businessmen, followed by women in business and the professions, the many women in the trades and industry, and, last, "a group weighty in numbers struggling on in domestic service, with an even less fortunate fringe of casual workers, fluctuating with the economic temper of the times." McDougald, "Task of Negro Womanhood," 370. My study collapses categories identified by Johnson and McDougald into

three groups. The wives of black businessmen and the women who worked in black business shared consanguine status, supervised and protected in a woman's sphere, so to speak. And I combine the women in industry with those who worked in household labor because, due to economic cycles and the seasonal nature of southern industrial employment, working-class women often alternated between the two. Indeed, most of these women were in "the less fortunate fringe of casual workers" that McDougald describes.

39. E. Franklin Frazier to C. C. Spaulding, 24 August 1925, folder 18, box 131-15, ser. B, EFFP.

40. On the economic lives of black nurses and teachers, see Hine, *Black Women in White*; and Shaw, *What a Woman Ought to Be and to Do*.

41. Mitchell, *Righteous Propagation*, xx. I use class and status here interchangeably, building the framework on internal black community dynamics rather than on relative caste, a status position that is relative to whites. Borrowing Mitchell's term, "aspiring class," as a substitute for "middle class," I argue here for a social structure in flux.

42. White, "The Slippery Slope of Class in Black America"; Brown, "What Has Happened Here"; Hewitt, "Compounding Differences."

43. Gaines, *Uplifting the Race*, 160; Kelley, "We Are Not What We Seem"; Hunter, *To 'Joy My Freedom*.

44. Nora, "Between Memory and History," 284–300; Fabre and O'Meally, "Introduction," 6–8; Gavins, *The Meaning of Freedom*.

45. Du Bois, *Souls of Black Folk*, 181–83; Harris, *In the Shadow of Slavery*; Sidbury, *Ploughshares into Swords*; Hahn, *A Nation under Our Feet*; Kelley, *Race Rebels*; Kelley, "We Are Not What We Seem"; Kelley, *Hammer and Hoe*.

46. Lucas interview; Clement interview; Hughes, "Mother to Son," 7; Hall, "The Long Civil Rights Movement."

47. Shaw, *What a Woman Ought to Be and to Do*, 209–10; Hall, "The Long Civil Rights Movement," 233–55; Ransby, *Ella Baker and the Black Freedom Movement*; Clark, *Echo in My Soul*; Murray, *The Autobiography*; Olson, *Freedom's Daughters*; Nasstrom, "Down to Now"; Chafe, *Civilities and Civil Rights*; Greene, *Our Separate Ways*.

48. Murray, "The Liberation of Black Women," 185–97.

Chapter One

1. Sarah Debro, in *Born in Slavery*, pt. 1, 247–53.

2. Paul C. Cameron, quoted in Anderson, *Durham County*, 153.

3. "Minutes of the Freedmen's Convention in Raleigh, NC on 2nd, 3rd, and 4th of October 1866."

4. Ibid.; "Freedmen's Bureau Report of Outrages in North Carolina, February 1867–December 1867," Records of the Assistant Commissioner for the State of North Carolina, Records of the Bureau of Refugees, Freedmen, and Abandoned

Lands, Record Group 105, Publication Number M843, Roll 33, National Archives, Washington, D.C.; Haley, *Charles N. Hunter*, 10; Du Bois, *Black Reconstruction in America*, 532–34; Anderson, *Durham County*, 129.

5. Martha Allen, in *Born in Slavery*, pt. 1, 14–15; Ben Johnson, in ibid., pt. 2, 9–13; Sarah Debro, in ibid., pt. 1, 253.

6. Murray, *Proud Shoes*, 208–9; Abner Jordan, in *Born in Slavery*, pt. 2, 381; Riley and Phillips interview; Lyons interview.

7. Tempie Herndon Durham, in *Born in Slavery*, pt. 1, 283–90; Penningroth, *Claims of Kinfolk*; Foner, *Story of American Freedom*, 100–113; Foner, *Reconstruction*, 77–87; Litwack, *Been in the Storm So Long*.

8. Lyons interview; Escott, *Slavery Remembered*; Litwack, *Been in the Storm So Long*; Logan, "The Economic Status of the Town Negro," 448–90; Ransom and Sutch, *One Kind of Freedom*; Stanley, *From Bondage to Contract*; Schwalm, *A Hard Fight for We*.

9. Correspondent, quoted in Anderson, *Durham County*, 155; Paul, *The History of the Town of Durham*, 25–26; Jones, *End of an Era*, 5;

10. Holsey, "Pearson — The Brown Duke of Durham," 116–17.

11. See Rabinowitz, *Race Relations in the Urban South*; Holsey, "Pearson — The Brown Duke of Durham"; and Jones, *End of an Era*.

12. Anderson, *Durham County*, 152–57; *Gray's New Map of Durham, 1881*; Boyd, *The Story of Durham*, 278; Hunter, *To 'Joy My Freedom*, 22–26; Robinson, "The Difference Freedom Made," 51–74. See also Holt, *Making Freedom Pay*; and Schwalm, *A Hard Fight for We*.

13. Paul, *The History of the Town of Durham*, 25–26; Boyd, *The Story of Durham*, 59–60; Anderson, *Durham County*, 126.

14. Department of the Interior, Census Office, *Eleventh Census of the United States: 1890*, pt. 1, *Population*, 546.

15. Paul, *The History of the Town of Durham*, 49–50, 235; Branson, *Directory of the Businesses and Citizens of Durham City*, 52–59, 191–92; Anderson, *Durham County*, 152–57, 258; Rev. S. L. McDowell, "Historical Sketch of White Rock Baptist Church," folder 4, box 1, WJKP; reprint of E. D. Markham Papers, in Bailey, *Dedication of the Ediam D. Markham Memorial Building*; Murray, *Proud Shoes*, 237.

16. Fisher, *Friends*; Valentine, "History of St. Joseph's AME Church," and Rev. S. L. McDowell, "Historical Sketch of White Rock Baptist Church," box 1, folders 111–12, WJKP; Roberts, *Durham Architectural and Historical Inventory*, 113, 132, 163; Weaver, "The Development of the Black Durham Community," 297–98; "St. Titus Church, Durham, N.C.," Notes of Pauli Murray re: "Durham Mission" (colored), from *Dioceses of North Carolina Journals*, 1880–1911, folder 326, box 12, PMP; "A Proposal to the City Council of Durham, 23 March 1978, folder 327, box 12, PMP; Journal of Pauli Murray, 18 May 1933, folder 1352, box 76, PMP; Murray, *Proud Shoes*, 245.

17. "An Appeal for Help to the People of the State in Behalf of the Colored Orphan

Children of North Carolina: Colored Orphan Asylum" (1890); "Colored Orphan Asylum of North Carolina, Oxford, NC" (1900), in *Documenting the American South*; Board of Public Charities, *Annual Reports of the Board of Public Charities*, 1884–1925; *Centennial Year: Women's Baptist Home and Foreign Missionary Convention of North Carolina*, 5, 78, 95; Gavins, "The Meaning of Freedom," 199–200; Whitted, *A History of the Negro Baptists*, 114, 282–85; "Obituary of Hattie E. Shepard," folder 135, WJKP; *Proceedings of the Fortieth Annual Session of the Women's Home and Foreign Mission Convention of North Carolina*, 13; *Proceedings of the Forty-fourth Annual Session of the Women's Home and Foreign Mission Convention*, 27–28. The *Forty-fourth Proceedings* give the founding date of the first circle as 1878; Higginbotham, *Righteous Discontent*, 257n22; Gilmore, *Gender and Jim Crow*, 154–55.

18. *Twentieth Session of the Supreme Grand Chapter of the Eastern Star, North Carolina Jurisdiction*, 64; Mangum, *Mangum's Directory*; "Obituary of James Anderson Whitted," folder 135, WJKP; *Proceedings of the Fortieth Annual Session of the Women's Home and Foreign Mission Convention of North Carolina*, 4; "Obituary of Minnie Sumner Pearson," programs and clipping, WGPP.

19. On education and uplift, see Anderson, *Education of Blacks in the South*; Shaw, *What a Woman Ought to Be and to Do*; Gaines, *Uplifting the Race*; and Higginbotham, *Righteous Discontent*.

20. Constance Merrick Moore Watts interview; Dancy, *Sands against the Wind*, 70; "Obituary of Cottie Moore," ADVC.

21. Andrews, *John Merrick*, 26; Holsey, "Pearson — The Brown Duke of Durham"; Weare, *Black Business in the New South*, 59.

22. *Forty-one Years of Insurance Service*, WGPP.

23. Andrews, *John Merrick*; *Forty-one Years of Insurance Service*, WGPP.

24. Branson, *Directory of the Businesses and Citizens of Durham City*, 200; Andrews, *John Merrick*, 24–26, 41–45, 135. The real estate arrangement was formalized with the founding of the Merrick-Moore-Spaulding Land Company in 1910. Goodwin interview, ca. 1992; Constance Merrick Moore Watts interview (Watts is the great-grandchild of John Merrick and Aaron Moore); W. J. Gaines to Washington Duke, 17 November 1893, WDP; Boyd, *The Story of Durham*, 279–81, 286–87; Upchurch and Fowler, *Durham County, Economic and Social*, 10; Branson, *Directory of the Businesses and Citizens of Durham City*; Paul, *The History of the Town of Durham*, 241–42; Al Spaulding, interview by E. Franklin Frazier, 11, 12 September 1934, Columbus, N.C., Notes, box 131-92, folder 7m, EFFP; Weare, *Black Business in the New South*, chaps. 1 and 2; Greenwood, *Bittersweet Legacy*, 77–112. See also Hahn, *A Nation under Our Feet*.

25. Murray, *Proud Shoes*, 56–70; Gatewood, *Aristocrats of Color*, 7–29.

26. Michele Mitchell uses the term "aspiring class" to describe those who strived for both economic security and bourgeois respectability. Mitchell, *Righteous Propagation*, 5.

27. Higginbotham, *Righteous Discontent*, 204–6; Higginbotham, "Beyond the Sounds of Silence," 58.

28. Murray, *Proud Shoes*, 270; Pauline F. Dame, "Autobiography of My Life," typescript, folder 273, box 11, PMP; Branson, *Directory of the Businesses and Citizens of Durham City*; Ramsey, *Ramsey's Durham Directory for the Year 1892*; Mangum, *Mangum's Directory*.

29. Department of the Interior, Census Office, *Eleventh Census of the United States*, 1890, pt. 1, *Population*, 546; Department of the Interior, Census Office, *Twelfth Census of the United States, Taken in the Year 1900, Census Reports*, vol. 1, *Population*, pt. 1, 671; Ramsey, *Ramsey's Durham Directory for the Year 1892*; Mangum, *Mangum's Directory*; Kiser, "Occupational Changes among Negroes in Durham," 22a.

30. Schnore and Evenson, "Segregation in Southern Cities," 58–67; Demerath and Gilmore, "The Ecology of Southern Cities," 135–64; Rice, "Residential Segregation by Law," 79–99. See also Murray, *States' Laws on Race and Color*; Durham Chamber of Commerce, *Durham: Queen of the Golden Belt*; and Woodward, *Strange Career of Jim Crow*.

31. Paul, *The History of the Town of Durham*, 26.

32. Gatewood, *Aristocrats of Color*, x; Bynum, *Unruly Women*, 103; Weare, *Black Business in the New South*, 43; Greenwood, *Bittersweet Legacy*, 4–5, 81–85.

33. Korstad, *Civil Rights Unionism*, 112.

34. Durham Chamber of Commerce, *Durham: Queen of the Golden Belt*; Branson, *Directory of the Businesses and Citizens of Durham City*; Turner, *Turner's Durham City Directory*, 19; Guldbrandsen, "Entrepreneurial Governance in the Transnational South," 83–98.

35. Dula and Simpson, *Durham and Her People*, 9–11.

36. Boyd, *The Story of Durham*; *Population Schedules of the Tenth Census of the United States, 1880, Orange County, Durham Township*.

37. Durden, *The Dukes of Durham*; Boyd, *The Story of Durham*; Tilley, *The Bright-Tobacco Industry*; Cox, *Competition in the American Tobacco Industry*; "Henry Grady Speech to the New England Club in New York," 1886, in Harris, *The Life of Henry W. Grady*; Janiewski, *Sisterhood Denied*, 80–81, 85, 97; Durham Chamber of Commerce, *Durham: Queen of the Golden Belt*.

38. The story of Duke and Durham, Carr's competition, and tobacco workers is retold in virtually every history of tobacco and of Durham. Durden, *The Dukes of Durham*; Boyd, *The Story of Durham*; Tilley, *The Bright-Tobacco Industry*; Tilley, *The R. J. Reynolds Tobacco Company*; Cox, *Competition in the American Tobacco Industry*; Durham Chamber of Commerce, *Durham: Queen of the Golden Belt*; Smith, *Durham Station: A Play in One Act*; Winkler, *Tobacco Tycoon*, 47–53; Branson, *Directory of the Businesses and Citizens of Durham City*, 161; Seeman, *American Gold*; Janiewski, *Sisterhood Denied*; Manning and Byrne, *The Effects on Women of Changing Conditions in the Cigar and Cigarette Industries*.

39. "R.J.C.M.W., L.A. 7478" to "Editor," 11 June 1887, *Journal of the United Labor*, in Foner and Lewis, *The Black Worker*, 3:274–76; Paul, *The History of the Town of Durham*, 49.

40. Glickman, *A Living Wage*; Logan, *The Negro in North Carolina*, 102–4.

41. H. G. Ellis to T. V. Powderly, 17 August 1886, John R. Ray to T. V. Powderly, 19 May 1885, T. V. Powderly to J. M. Broughton, 12 June 1885, John R. Ray to T. V. Powderly, 22 June 1885, John R. Ray to T. V. Powderly, 19 January 1885, J. M. Broughton to T. V. Powderly, 8 February 1887, Frank Johnson to T. V. Powderly, 14 February 1887, in Foner and Lewis, *The Black Worker*, 3:251–58.

42. Durden, *The Dukes of Durham*; Boyd, *The Story of Durham*; Anderson, *Durham County*; Tilley, *The Bright-Tobacco Industry*; Cox, *Competition in the American Tobacco Industry*; Janiewski, *Sisterhood Denied*, 80–81, 85, 97; Manning and Byrne, *The Effects on Women of Changing Conditions in the Cigar and Cigarette Industries*; Shields, "A Half-Century in the Tobacco Industry"; Department of Labor, Women's Bureau, *Negro Women in Industry*, 28–30; Hall et al., *Like a Family*.

43. Turner, *Turner's Durham City Directory*, 25; Upchurch and Fowler, *Durham County, Economic and Social*; Janiewski, *Sisterhood Denied*, 100–102; Lebsock, *Free Women of Petersburg*, 10, 182–85; Jones, *Labor of Love, Labor of Sorrow*, 134–41; Roediger, *Wages of Whiteness*; Jacobson, *Whiteness of a Different Color*; Nelson, *Divided We Stand*.

44. Korstad, *Civil Rights Unionism*; Boyd, *The Story of Durham*, 278; Anderson, *Durham County*, 159; Tilley, *The Bright-Tobacco Industry*; Shields, "A Half-Century in the Tobacco Industry"; Janiewski, *Sisterhood Denied*, 100–102; Lebsock, *Free Women of Petersburg*, 10, 182–85; Jacqueline Jones, *Labor of Love, Labor of Sorrow*, 134–41.

45. Manning and Byrne, *The Effects on Women of Changing Conditions in the Cigar and Cigarette Industries*; Shields, "A Half-Century in the Tobacco Industry"; Department of Labor, Women's Bureau, *Negro Women in Industry*.

46. Goldin, "Female Labor Force Participation," 87–112; Johnson, "The Tobacco Worker"; Department of the Interior, Census Office, *Eleventh Census of the United States: 1890*, pt. 1, *Population*, 546; Department of the Interior, Census Office, *Twelfth Census of the United States, 1900*, pt. 1, *Population*, 671; Department of Commerce, Bureau of the Census, *Thirteenth Census of the United States, 1910*, vol. 3, *Population*, 294–313; Hunter, *To 'Joy My Freedom*; Korstad, *Civil Rights Unionism*.

47. Janiewski, *Sisterhood Denied*, 4–5; Glenn, *Unequal Freedom*; Roedegier, *Wages of Whiteness*; Jacobson, *Whiteness of a Different Color*; Nelson, *Divided We Stand*.

48. Collins, "The Negro Must Remain in the South," *North Carolina University Magazine* (1890): 147, quoted in Logan, *The Negro in North Carolina*, 77.

49. Branson, *Directory of the Businesses and Citizens of Durham City*, passim; Turner, *Turner's Durham City Directory*, 99–129; Kiser, "Occupational Changes among

Negroes in Durham," 22a–b, 39–40, 50–51, 68–69, 76–77, 96–99, 113–14, 122–23, 127–28; Logan, "The Economic Status of the Town Negro."

50. "Record of the Proceedings of the Central Prohibition Club of Durham, North Carolina, 1886–1892," NCCC, box 1890s.

51. "Duplicate Copy of the Registry of Voters in the Durham Election Precinct in the County of Orange, North Carolina," 3 November 1868, NCCC, box 1860s; Boyd, *The Story of Durham*, 103; Logan, *The Negro in North Carolina*, 77–82; Kousser, *The Shaping of Southern Politics*, 183.

52. Gilmore, *Gender and Jim Crow*, 91–118.

53. *Durham Recorder*, 3 October 1888; *Durham Tobacco Plant*, 5 October 1888.

54. *Durham Recorder*, 13 November 1889.

55. James A. Whitted to Charles N. Hunter, 17 November 1887, James A. Whitted to Charles N. Hunter, 30 October 1890, folder 3, box 1, CNHP; Pauline F. Dame, "Autobiography of My Life," typescript, folder 273, box 11, PMP.

56. *Law and Resolutions of North Carolina, 1885*, 87, sec. 1 and 2, Act of 11 March 1885; *Riggsbee v. Town of Durham*, 96 N.C. 800 (1886); *Duke v. Brown*, 96 N.C. 127 (1887), cited in Logan, "The Legal Status of Public School Education for Negroes," 355–56; Coon, "The Beginning of the North Carolina City Schools," 235–47.

57. James A. Whitted to Charles N. Hunter, 24 November, 20 October, 30 October, 26 December 1890, 20 January, 21 February 1891, folder 1, box 2, CNHP; Logan, "The Movement in North Carolina to Establish a State Supported College for Negroes," 172–73; *Law and Resolutions of North Carolina, 1885*, 87, sec. 1 and 2, Act of 11 March 1885; *Riggsbee v. Town of Durham*, 96 N.C. 800 (1886); *Duke v. Brown*, 96 N.C. 127 (1887); Logan, "The Legal Status of Public School Education for Negroes," 346–57; Coon, "The Beginning of the North Carolina City Schools," 235–47; Westin, "A History of the Durham School System," 14.

58. Logan, "The Movement of Negroes from North Carolina," 54–55. See also Painter, *Exodusters*; and Hahn, *A Nation under Our Feet*.

59. *Durham Recorder*, 23 January, 6, 27 February 1889; Kousser, *The Shaping of Southern Politics*, 183. See also Mabry, *The Negro in North Carolina Politics since Reconstruction*; and Logan, *The Negro in North Carolina*.

60. Logan, "The Economic Status of the Town Negro," 448–60; Du Bois, *Economic Cooperation among Negro Americans*, 51–52; Gavins, "The Meaning of Freedom," 177–78; "Proceedings of the [North Carolina] State Emigration Convention, 27–28 April 1889," cited in Logan, "The Movement of Negroes from North Carolina," 51–56; *Durham Tobacco Plant*, 1886, cited in Hall et al., *Like a Family*; *Durham Recorder*, 23 January, 6 February 1889.

61. *Durham Recorder*, 28 August 1889; Branson, *Directory of the Businesses and Citizens of Durham City*; Ramsey, *Ramsey's Durham Directory for the Year 1892*; *Durham Tobacco Plant*, 4 January, 2 February 1889.

62. Collins, "The Negro Must Remain in the South," quoted in Logan, "The Movement of Negroes from North Carolina," 65.

63. John Merrick, quoted in Boyd, *The Story of Durham*, 281–83.
64. Odum, *Race and Rumors of Race*, 17–26; Woodward, *Strange Career of Jim Crow*, 97–109. See also Litwack, *Trouble in Mind*; McMillen, *Dark Journey*; Williamson, *The Crucible of Race*; Chafe, "The Gods Bring Threads to Webs Begun"; Higginbotham, "African-American Women's History and the Metalanguage of Race"; and Gilmore, *Gender and Jim Crow*.

Chapter Two

1. R. B. Russell, L. S. Scruggs, A. M. Moore, R. B. Fitzgerald, et al., "To the People of North Carolina," enclosure with letter to Marion Butler, and clipping, 7 June 1896, folder 20, box 2, MBP.
2. *Durham Daily Sun*, 7 October 1896.
3. Edmonds, *The Negro and Fusion Politics*, 218–22. See also Woodward, *Strange Career of Jim Crow*; Williamson, *The Crucible of Race*; Woodward, *Origins of the New South*; Ayers, *The Promise of the New South*; McMillen, *Dark Journey*; and Litwack, *Trouble in Mind*.
4. Washington, "The Atlanta Exposition Address," in *Up from Slavery*, 223–24.
5. Brown, "Negotiating and Transforming Public Space." See also Hahn, *A Nation under Our Feet*.
6. L. G. Flagg to Washington Duke, 24 March 1896, and Jas. E. Shepard to Washington Duke, 17 April 1896, WDP.
7. Edmonds, *The Negro and Fusion Politics*, 3–4; Woodward, *Origins of the New South*, 277–78; Anderson, *Race and Politics in North Carolina*, 37–38.
8. *Durham Daily Sun*, 4 November 1898; Edmonds, *The Negro and Fusion Politics*, 129.
9. Haley, *Charles N. Hunter*, 88–92. See also Edmonds, *The Negro and Fusion Politics*; Anderson, *Race and Politics in North Carolina*; Gilmore, *Gender and Jim Crow*; Greenwood, *Bittersweet Legacy*; Anderson, *Durham County*; Crow, "Fusion, Confusion, and Negroism," 364–84; Escott, *Many Excellent People*; Goodwyn, *Democratic Promise*; Woodward, *Origins of the New South*; and Ayers, *The Promise of the New South*.
10. Brown, "To Catch the Vision of Freedom," 66–99; A. M. Moore to R. B. Russell et al., "To the People of North Carolina," RBRP.
11. Al Spaulding, interview by E. Franklin Frazier, 11, 12 September 1934, Columbus, N.C., and Research Field Notes, folder 7, box 131-92, EFFP; Edmonds, *The Negro and Fusion Politics*, 92.
12. Hayden, *Story of the Wilmington Rebellion*, 31.
13. Edmonds, *The Negro and Fusion Politics*, 158. See also Litwack, *Been in the Storm So Long*; Litwack, *Trouble in Mind*; Foner, *Reconstruction*.
14. Gilmore, *Gender and Jim Crow*, 71–89, especially 77; Hall, "The Mind That Burns in Each Body," 328–48.
15. Julian S. Carr Speech, 8 February 1898, cited in Weare, *Black Business in the New South*, 40. On the events in Wilmington, see Edmonds, *The Negro and Fusion*

Politics, 136–57; Cecelski and Tyson, *Democracy Betrayed*; Wilmington Race Riot Commission, *Draft Report on the Wilmington Riot*.

16. General Julian S. Carr Sr. to Captain W. K. Parrish, 7 September 1898, WKPP.

17. *Durham Daily Sun*, 4, 7 November 1898; Gilmore, *Gender and Jim Crow*, 114.

18. Gilmore, *Gender and Jim Crow*, 114.

19. Hayden, *Story of the Wilmington Rebellion*, 31.

20. Hall, *Revolt against Chivalry*, 139–42; Gilmore, *Gender and Jim Crow*, 114.

21. Manly, "Mrs. Felton's Speech." According to Josephus Daniels, editor of the *Raleigh News and Observer*, William L. Jeffries, associate editor of the *Wilmington Daily Record*, later claimed to be the author of the article; Daniels, *The Editor in Politics*, 297, cited in Edmonds, *The Negro and Fusion Politics*, 147.

22. Manly, "Mrs. Felton's Speech."

23. Hall, "The Mind That Burns in Each Body," 328–49.

24. Manly, "Mrs. Felton's Speech"; Wells, *Memphis Free Speech*, 21 May 1892, reprinted in "A Red Record," in Wells-Barnett, *Selected Works of Ida B. Wells-Barnett*, 145–46; Hall, *Revolt against Chivalry*, 145.

25. Edmonds, *The Negro and Fusion Politics*, 173; Gilmore, *Gender and Jim Crow*.

26. Frank E. Safford to Booker T. Washington, 30 August 1898, in *BTWP*, 4:459.

27. Manly, "Mrs. Felton's Speech."

28. Hayden, *Story of the Wilmington Rebellion*; *Durham Daily Sun*, 21 October 1898.

29. *Durham Daily Sun*, 21 October 1898.

30. Ibid., 20, 28 October 1898.

31. *Durham Daily Sun*, 28 October 1898; "Col. Carr's Farewell Address to Durham County Democrats," *Durham Daily Sun*, 7 November 1898.

32. Cooper, *A Voice from the South*, 138–40.

33. Dudley, *Star of Zion*, 18 October 1896, quoted in Gilmore, *Gender and Jim Crow*, 102.

34. Doyle, *The Etiquette of Race Relations in the South*, 136–59.

35. *Raleigh News and Observer*, 22 October 1898.

36. *Durham Daily Sun*, 25 October 1898.

37. Cheatham, quoted in *Durham Daily Sun*, 21 October 1898; *Durham Daily Sun*, 8, 10 November 1898; Cecelski and Tyson, *Democracy Betrayed*; Wilmington Race Riot Commission, *Draft Report on the Wilmington Riot*.

38. Edmonds, *The Negro and Fusion Politics*, 168–69; Rivera interview.

39. Glenda Gilmore argues this point about North Carolina politics after the Wilmington Riot. Gilmore, *Gender and Jim Crow*, 87.

40. Durham Chamber of Commerce, *Durham: Queen of the Golden Belt*.

41. Du Bois, "The Upbuilding of Black Durham"; Washington, "Durham, North Carolina, a City of Negro Enterprise"; Merrick speech, quoted in Andrews, *John Merrick*, 33; Merrick, quoted in Boyd, *The Story of Durham*, 279.

42. Crow et al., *History of African Americans in North Carolina*, 209–11.

43. *Durham Morning Herald*, 21 November 1918.

44. Frank E. Safford to Booker T. Washington, 30 August 1898, in *BTWP*, 4:459; Booker T. Washington, speech at the Peace Jubilee, Chicago, ca. 6 November 1898, quoted in *Star of Zion*, 10 November 1898.

45. NAACP, *Thirty Years of Lynching in the United States, 1889–1918*, 84.

46. Nora, "Between Memory and History"; Prather, *We Have Taken a City*.

47. Pearson interview.

48. Kousser, *The Shaping of Southern Politics*, 239; *Durham Daily Sun*, 2, 6, 26 January, 2, 20, 22 February 1899. The disfranchisement amendment was to go into effect in 1902. *Durham Daily Sun*, 24 April 1899.

49. Barber, "The Aggressiveness of Jim-Crowism."

50. *Durham Daily Sun*, 8, 12 February 1899.

51. Haley, *Charles N. Hunter*, 142.

52. North Carolina Republican Executive Committee, H. H. Taylor to C. N. Hunter, 25 October 1908, folder 3, box 3, CNHP; North Carolina Republican Executive Committee (Colored) to the Colored Republicans of North Carolina, 11 March 1916, Scrapbooks, box 13, CNHP.

53. Blake, "Narrative of the Wilmington 'Rebellion' of 1898."

54. Washington, "The Story of My Life and Work," in *BTWP*, 1:89–91.

55. John Merrick, 1898 speech, quoted in Andrews, *John Merrick*, 155–61.

56. Ibid.

57. Ibid.

58. Ibid.; Pearson interview.

59. James E. Shepard speech, clipping from the *Raleigh Morning Post*, 2 January 1900, Scrapbooks, box 13, CNHP.

60. Shepard speech reported in *Durham Daily Sun*, 2 January 1902.

61. Shepard, "The Negro as an American Citizen," *Raleigh Morning Post*, 6 November 1903, *PNCF*, frame 103.

62. Ibid.; Shepard speech reported in *Durham Daily Sun*, 2 January 1902.

63. Clippings, *Raleigh Blade*, 8, 13 July 1899, Scrapbooks, box 13, CNHP.

64. Ibid.

65. Clippings, *Raleigh Blade*, 13 July 1899, Scrapbooks, box 13, CNHP; *Durham Daily Sun*, 28 December 1898; Pauline F. Dame, "Autobiography of My Life," typescript, folder 273, box 11, PMP; Journal of Pauli Murray, 18 June 1933, folder 1352, box 76, PMP; Murray, *The Autobiography*, 14–15.

66. Pauline F. Dame, "Autobiography of My Life," typescript, folder 273, box 11, PMP; Journal of Pauli Murray, 18 July 1933, folder 1352, box 76, PMP; Murray, *The Autobiography*, 14–15; Murray, "The Fourth Generation of Proud Shoes," 4–5.

67. Woodward, *Strange Career of Jim Crow*, 97–109; Kousser, *The Shaping of Southern Politics*, 239; Litwack, *Trouble in Mind*, xiv, 105–6; Du Bois, *The College Bred Negro*, 87; Williamson, *The Crucible of Race*, 224, 248.

Chapter Three

1. Ross, *Manning the Race*, 13.
2. Giddings, *When and Where I Enter*, 31; White, *Too Heavy a Load*, 43–44; Hine, "Black Migration to the Middle West"; Shaw, "Black Club Women"; Shaw, *What a Woman Ought to Be and to Do*.
3. Murray, *The Autobiography*, 15.
4. Dunbar, "We Wear the Mask," in Dunbar, *Complete Poems*; Pauline F. Dame, "Autobiography of My Life," typescript, folder 273, box 11, PMP.
5. Gates, "Trope of the New Negro," 143.
6. Jones, *Labor of Love, Labor of Sorrow*, 110–12; Goldin, "Female Labor Force Participation," 87–108; Hunter, "Domination and Resistance," 205–55; Department of Commerce, Bureau of the Census, *Negroes in the United States*, 85; Hamilton, "Recent Changes in the Social and Economic Status of North Carolina Farm Families," 42, 81.
7. Hall, *Like a Family*, 66–67, 157; Dowd, "Negro Labor in Factories."
8. Hunton, "Negro Womanhood Defended," 280.
9. Woodward, *Strange Career of Jim Crow*, 34.
10. Gaines, *Uplifting the Race*, 2.
11. Hunton, "Negro Womanhood Defended," 280.
12. Terrell, "What Role Is the Educated Negro Woman to Play in the Uplifting of Her Race?" 176.
13. Wells-Barnett, "Southern Horrors," in Wells-Barnett, *Selected Works of Ida B. Wells-Barnett*, 19.
14. Mitchell, "Silences Broken, Silences Kept," 433–44; Mitchell, *Righteous Propagation*, 13–15; Marable, *How Capitalism Underdeveloped Black America*, 70–78; Brown, "Negotiating and Transforming Public Space"; Brown, "Womanist Consciousness"; Carby, *Reconstructing Womanhood*, 3–19; Carby, "Policing the Black Woman's Body," 738–55; Shaw, *What a Woman Ought to Be and to Do*; Giddings, *When and Where I Enter*; White, *Ar'n't I a Woman*; White, *Too Heavy a Load*; Davis, *Women, Race, and Class*; Davis, *Blues Legacies and Black Feminism*; Painter, *Southern History across the Color Line*; Gilmore, *Gender and Jim Crow*; M. M. Manning, *Slave in a Box*, 21–25.
15. Gates, "The Face and Voice of Blackness," xvi–xx.
16. Ibid.; McElroy, *Facing History*, xvi–xx; Atwan et al., *Edsels, Luckies, and Frigidaires*, 89–94; Kern-Foxworth, *Aunt Jemima, Uncle Ben, and Rastus*, 270–71; Manning, *Slave in a Box*; Bull Durham advertisement, TC; *Durham Daily Sun*, 28 March 1899; *Durham Morning Herald*, 10 February 1918; postcard from Henry Louis Gates Jr.'s collection of black ephemeral materials, reproduced in Gates, "The Face and Voice of Blackness"; Allen, *Without Sanctuary*; Litwack, *Trouble in Mind*.
17. Giddings, *When and Where I Enter*; White, *Ar'n't I a Woman*; White, *Too Heavy a Load*; Shaw, *What a Woman Ought to Be and to Do*.

18. Myrdal, *An American Dilemma*, vol. 1. See also Odum, *Race and Rumors of Race*, 17–26; Woodward, *Strange Career of Jim Crow*, 97–109; Litwack, *Trouble in Mind*; McMillen, *Dark Journey*; Williamson, *The Crucible of Race*; Chafe, "The Gods Bring Threads to Webs Begun," 1531–50; Higginbotham, "African-American Women's History and the Metalanguage of Race," 251–73; and Gilmore, *Gender and Jim Crow*, 2.

19. Giddings, *When and Where I Enter*, 31; White, *Too Heavy a Load*, 43–44; Hine, "Black Migration to the Middle West," 127–46; Shaw, "Black Club Women," 24–35; Shaw, *What a Woman Ought to Be and to Do*, 4–5.

20. White, *Ar'n't I a Woman*; Hine, "Rape and the Inner Lives of Black Women"; Hine, "Black Migration to the Middle West," 130; Barbee interview; Mack interview.

21. Jones, *Labor of Love, Labor of Sorrow*, 110–12; Goldin, "Female Labor Force Participation," 87–108; Hunter, "Domination and Resistance," 205–55; Reiff et al., "Rural Push and Urban Pull," 39–48; Department of Commerce, Bureau of the Census, *Negro Population*; Department of Commerce, Bureau of the Census, *Negroes in the United States*, 85; Hamilton, "Recent Changes in the Social and Economic Status of North Carolina Farm Families."

22. Du Bois, "The Damnation of Negro Women," 105.

23. Riley and Phillips interview; anonymous Behind the Veil interview; Page interview; Pedraza, "Women and Migration," 303–25; Byrne, *Child Labor in Representative Tobacco-Growing Areas*. The Children's Bureau study focused on Florence County, South Carolina, and Halifax County, Virginia, tobacco-growing areas in the Piedmont.

24. Mebane, *Mary*, 165; Price interview.

25. Riley and Phillips interview; anonymous Behind the Veil interview; Clark-Lewis, *Living In, Living Out*, 56–57; Janiewski, *Sisterhood Denied*, 28–32.

26. Clark-Lewis, *Living In, Living Out*, 56–57; Mitchner interview; Harris interview; Riley and Phillips interview; Jones and Eglehoff, *Working in Tobacco*, 35, 27; Janiewski, *Sisterhood Denied*, 27–32.

27. Mitchner interview.

28. In Durham in 1930, for example, 15 percent of black women were widowed, compared to 5 percent of black men and 11 percent of white women. Department of Commerce, Bureau of the Census, *Negroes in the United States*, 183; Goldin, "Female Labor Force Participation," 110; Reiff et al., "Rural Push and Urban Pull," 39–48; Lyons interview.

29. Johnson, "The Tobacco Worker," 114; *Durham Morning Herald*, 2 September 1906; "Negroes Still Leaving," *Charlotte Observer*, reprinted in *Star of Zion*, 10 July 1903; Wesley, *Negro Labor in the United States*, 241–42.

30. Carr, "Building a Business on the Family Plan," reprinted in Boyd, *The Story of Durham*, 125; Dowd, "Negro Labor in Factories," 588; "After All the Causes," in Foner and Lewis, *The Black Worker*, 5:4.

31. Carr, "Building a Business on the Family Plan," reprinted in Boyd, *The Story of Durham*, 126.

32. Ibid.

33. "The South—A Country without Strikes," in Foner and Lewis, *The Black Worker*, 5:100–102.

34. Hunter, "Domination and Resistance," 205–20; Kelley, "We Are Not What We Seem," 94; Scott, *Domination and the Arts of Resistance*; Levine, *Black Culture and Black Consciousness*, 239–70, 300–320. Scott refers to this strategy as infrapolitics.

35. Samuel Gompers to Brown and Williamson, Co., in Foner and Lewis, *The Black Worker*, 5:123–24; Rhoden Mitchell to Charles N. Hunter, 5 September 1905, broadside, "The Working Woman's Society: Reasons Women Should Organize," folder 4, box 2, CNHP.

36. Carr, "Building a Business on the Family Plan," reprinted in Boyd, *The Story of Durham*, 126; Kiser, "Occupational Changes among Negroes in Durham," 22a.

37. *Durham Morning Herald*, 8, 22, 25 August 1906.

38. Hunter, "The Negro's Opportunity: Involvement in Quality Services Will Advance Standard of Wages," *Raleigh Morning Post*, 15 January 1904, clipping, Scrapbooks, box 14, CNHP.

39. Charles N. Hunter to "Dear Sir," 20 January 1904, folder 5, box 2, CNHP.

40. Hunter, "The Negro Servant Problem," *Raleigh Morning Post*, n.d., ca. 1903, Scrapbooks, box 14, CNHP.

41. Ibid.

42. Ibid.; "The Negro's Opportunity," *Raleigh Morning Post*, n.d., ca. April 1902, Scrapbooks, box 13, CNHP.

43. Stewart, "Negro Side of the Negro Problem," *Raleigh News and Observer*, n.d., ca. April 1902, Scrapbooks, box 14, CNHP.

44. Hunter, "The Negro Servant Problem," *Raleigh Morning Post*, n.d., ca. 1903, Scrapbooks, box 14, CNHP.

45. Stewart, "Negro Side of the Negro Problem," *Raleigh News and Observer*, n.d., ca. April 1902, Scrapbooks, box 14, CNHP.

46. Gates, "Trope of the New Negro," 143.

47. Shaw, "Black Club Women," 20; White, *Too Heavy a Load*; Williams, quoted in Giddings, *When and Where I Enter*, 83.

48. Mary Church Terrell, "What Role Is the Educated Negro Woman to Play in the Uplifting of Her Race?" in Lerner, *Black Women in White America*, 176.

49. "History of the Club Movement among the Colored Women of the United States of America, 1902," *NACWCR*, reel 5.

50. Ruffin, "Address to the First National Conference of Colored Women," 14, in Lerner, *Black Women in White America*, 441–43.

51. Williams, "The Club Movement among Colored Women," 379–82; Gaines, *Uplifting the Race*, 67–99.

52. Williams, "The Club Movement among Colored Women," 379–80; Mrs.

Booker T. Washington to Mrs. H. R. Holloway, 6 December 1895, *NACWCR*, reel 5.

53. Lynch, "Social Status and the Needs of the Colored Woman," 185–88. On race and womanhood, see Giddings, *When and Where I Enter*, 82–88; Gilmore, *Gender and Jim Crow*, 31–60; and White, *Too Heavy a Load*, 21–142. See also Shaw, *What a Woman Ought to Be and to Do*; Higginbotham, *Righteous Discontent*; Gaines, *Uplifting the Race*; and Rouse, *Lugenia Burns Hope*.

54. Daughters of Dorcas affiliated with the NACW in the early 1920s. Wesley, *History of the National Association of Colored Women's Clubs*, 311–27; Gilmore, *Gender and Jim Crow*, 177–202.

55. Faulk interview. See also Higginbotham, *Righteous Discontent*.

56. Fisher, *Friends*, 12, 19.

57. Pattie G. Shepard, quoted in Gilmore, "Gender and Jim Crow," 314.

58. *Durham Morning Herald*, 4 August 1905, clipping, Scrapbooks, box 14, CNHP.

59. Mrs. A. W. Blackwell, "The General Convention: Of the Woman's Home and Foreign Missionary Society"; *Star of Zion*, 22 October 1903; Mrs. C. C. Dudley, "Our Missionary Convention," *Star of Zion*, 13 August 1903; Higginbotham, *Righteous Discontent*, 207–8.

60. Annie W. Blackwell, "Woman's Day," *Star of Zion*, 27 August 1903.

61. Annie Walker Blackwell, "W. H. and F. M. Society," *Star of Zion*, 8 August 1903.

62. Mrs. K. P. Hood, "An Appeal," *Star of Zion*, 13 August 1903.

63. Blackwell, "The General Convention," *Star of Zion*, 29 October 1903.

64. Whitted, *A History of the Negro Baptists*, 112–13.

65. Sallie Mial, quoted in Higginbotham, *Righteous Discontent*, 94, 257n22; Whitted, *A History of the Negro Baptists*, 117–18.

66. Whitted, *A History of the Negro Baptists*, 113–14, 62; McLester, *Brief History of the Woman's Auxiliary*.

67. *Proceedings of the Forty-fourth Annual Session of the Women's Home and Foreign Mission Convention*, 11; *Proceedings of the Fortieth Annual Session of the Women's Home and Foreign Mission Convention*, 26–27.

68. Pauline F. Dame to Mrs. Merrick, 31 January 1955, folder 266, box 11, PMP; Pearson, *Rituals of the Lady Knights of King David*; Garrett interview; Brown, "Womanist Consciousness," 618–21.

69. Volkamenia Club Minutes, JLP.

70. White, "Slippery Slope of Class."

71. White, *Too Heavy a Load*, 13–20; Gaines, *Uplifting the Race*, 11.

72. Hunton, "Negro Womanhood Defended," 282.

Chapter Four

1. Kennedy, *The North Carolina Mutual Story*, 27, 72, 77, 87; *Whetstone* 4 (September 1949): 43; Reid, *The Urban Negro Worker in the United States*, 1:7; *Durham Morning Herald*, 21, 23, 26 June, 22 August 1906.

2. Roberts, *Durham Architectural and Historical Inventory*.

3. Kennedy, quoted in Weare, *Black Business in the New South*, 76–77; Turner interview.
4. Shaw, *What a Woman Ought to Be and to Do*, 14–42.
5. Faulk interview; Volkamenia Club Minutes, 1940s, JLP; Fisher, *Friends*; Shaw, *What a Woman Ought to Be and to Do*, 14–42, 83.
6. For a fine-grained study of the North Carolina Mutual Life Insurance Company and its social mission, see Weare, *Black Business in the New South*.
7. Spaulding, quoted in "They Call Him Co-Operation," article from unknown source, reprinted by North Carolina Mutual Life Insurance Company, 1945, box 1, CCSP; Higginbotham, *Righteous Discontent*, 14–15, 204–5; Shaw, *What a Woman Ought to Be and to Do*, 25.
8. "How Producers Produce," *The Mutual* (June 1923): 8, CCSP.
9. James B. Dudley to Booker T. Washington, 28 August 1903, in *BTWP*, 10:271–72. See also Brundage, *Lynching in the New South*; and Litwack, *Trouble in Mind*.
10. Locke, *The New Negro*, 7, 11.
11. Washington, "The Story of My Life and Work," in *BTWP*, 1:90.
12. Du Bois, "Of Mr. Booker T. Washington and Others" and "Of the Training of Black Men," in *Souls of Black Folk*, 55, 105.
13. Branson, *Directory of the Businesses and Citizens of Durham City*; Andrews, *John Merrick*, 41–45; E. Lewis Evans to Samuel Gompers, 8 November 1897, *Samuel Gompers and the American Federation of Labor*, collection 2, reel 5; Du Bois, *The College Bred Negro*, 85; Kennedy, *The North Carolina Mutual Story*, 4–6; Weare, *Black Business in the New South*, 29; Weare, "Charles Clinton Spaulding," 166–90; Holsey, "Pearson—The Brown Duke of Durham"; Brawley, "John Merrick: Pioneer in Business," in *Negro Builders and Heroes*, 477–80; Pearson interview; Goodwin interview, ca. 1992; Constance Merrick Moore Watts interview; *Durham Recorder*, 10 November, 18 December 1908, 16 March, 6 April, 8 July, 14 October 1909; Anderson, *Durham County*, 220–24, 256–57.
14. Charles C. Spaulding, "Life Insurance and Its Benefits," in *Report of the Sixteenth Annual Convention of the National Negro Business League, Boston, Mass., 1915*, 114–20, *NNBLR*, reel 3; *Durham Recorder*, 15 October 1896; *Durham Daily Sun*, 14 October 1896.
15. Washington, "Durham, North Carolina, a City of Negro Enterprise"; Weare, *Black Business in the New South*, 36.
16. Weare, *Black Business in the New South*, 22.
17. Powell, "Industrial Insurance," in *Report of the Eleventh Annual Convention of the National Negro Business League, New York City, 1910*, 96, *NNBLR*, reel 3; Weare, *Black Business in the New South*, 31, 69; Meier, *Negro Thought in America*, 139–43; *Private Laws of North Carolina* (1899), chap. 156, 375–76; *Durham Morning Herald*, 4 May 1925, 10 April 1926; Pearson interview; Turner interview.
18. *North Carolina Mutual*, January 1906, cited in Weare, *Black Business in the New South*, 64.

19. Williamson, *The Crucible of Race*, 224–25; "Join the Peoples Building and Loan Association," pamphlet, WGPP; Weare, "Black Business: A Reevaluation of the Functional Roles of Autonomous Black Institutions."

20. Weare, *Black Business in the New South*, 181–82.

21. "Important to You," 15 February 1906, folder 4, box 3, CNHP. This document, a stock offering, listed J. Hawkins, R. F. Fitzgerald, and J. E. Shepard as the "special committee" organizing the effort; Andrews, *John Merrick*, 52–56; Weare, *Black Business in the New South*, 81–82, 147–51; *Star of Zion*, 5 June 1924; *Durham Morning Herald*, 18 November 1924.

22. Du Bois, "The Upbuilding of Black Durham," 334–39; Durham Chamber of Commerce, *Durham: A Center of Industry and Education*, box 1920s, NCCC; *Durham Morning Herald*, 29 July 1908; Anderson, *Durham County*, 258.

23. "Greater Durham in 1904–05: A City of Many Industries."

24. Du Bois, "The Upbuilding of Black Durham," 334–38.

25. Moore, "Conducting a Hosiery Mill," in *Report of the Eleventh Annual Convention of the National Negro Business League, New York City, 1910*, 59–60, NNBLR, reel 2; *Norfolk Journal and Guide*, 26 February 1910, *African American Ledger*, 28 May 1910, PNCF.

26. *Norfolk Journal and Guide*, 4, 18 November, 2, 9 December 1916; *Durham Morning Herald*, 15 June 1918, 24 June 1919; Mary McLeod Bethune to Mrs. W. G. Pearson, 17 October 1917, Bethune Correspondence, 1927–28, NACWP; B. V. Lawson and J. W. Lewis to Fannie Rosser, 5 June 1935, Sadie Nurse to Fannie Rosser, 13 September 1937, FRP; Turner interview.

27. Frazier, "Durham: The Capital of the Black Middle Class," 333; Frazier, *Black Bourgeoisie*, 107–8. When Frazier spoke of Durham's black middle class, he used the term in comparative reference to the broader American class structure. At the same time, he recognized the Durham black elite as a step in class above the black bourgeoisie within the context of black life in America, as he explained to Spaulding in correspondence. E. Franklin Frazier to C. C. Spaulding, folder 18, box 131-15, EFFP.

28. Washington, "Durham, North Carolina, a City of Negro Enterprise," 642–50; *St. Luke Herald*, 7 January 1928, quoted in Weare, *Black Business in the New South*, 5.

29. Constance Merrick Moore Watts interview; Goodwin author interview; Andrews, *John Merrick*, frontispiece.

30. *Southern Ploughman*, 15 August 1908, Scrapbooks, box 14, C. C. Spaulding to C. N. Hunter, and Hunter to Spaulding, 12 April 1907, folder 2, box 3, CNHP; Weare, *Black Business in the New South*, 87.

31. Constance Merrick Moore Watts interview.

32. Ibid.; Goodwin author interview; Kennedy, *The North Carolina Mutual Story*, 12, 25; Lougee, *Durham: My Hometown*, 253; Gaines, *Uplifting the Race*, 4–5; Shaw, *What a Woman Ought to Be and to Do*, 14; Harley, "When Your Work Is Not Who You Are," 42–55.

33. "Join the Peoples Building and Loan Association," pamphlet, WGPP; *Private Laws of North Carolina*, chap. 156, 375–76.

34. Spaulding, "Life Insurance and Its Benefits," in *Report of the Sixteenth Annual Convention of the National Negro Business League, Boston, Mass., 1915*, 114–20, NNBLR, reel 3.

35. *North Carolina Mutual*, August 1903, clipping, folder 82, WJKP; "Observations from Conference," n.d., ca. 1920, box 1, CCSP.

36. *North Carolina Mutual*, January 1906, July 1912, cited in Weare, *Black Business in the New South*, 64, 95; *Durham Morning Herald*, 6 April 1924; Kennedy, *The North Carolina Mutual Story*, 62–64.

37. *North Carolina Mutual*, September 1904, quoted in Weare, *Black Business in the New South*, 65.

38. *Durham Negro Observer*, 7 July 1906, quoted in Weare, *Black Business in the New South*, 97.

39. Spaulding, "Life Insurance and Its Benefits," in *Report of the Sixteenth Annual Convention of the National Negro Business League, Boston, Mass., 1915*, 114–20, NNBLR, reel 3; *The North Carolina Mutual* (booklet), back piece.

40. *North Carolina Mutual*, September 1904, cited in Weare, *Black Business in the New South*, 65; Spaulding, "Life Insurance and Its Benefits," in *Report of the Sixteenth Annual Convention of the National Negro Business League, Boston, Mass., 1915*, 114–20, NNBLR, reel 3; *The North Carolina Mutual* (booklet), 15–16.

41. "Mechanics and Farmers Bank," in *North Carolina Mutual Life Insurance Company, Durham, North Carolina* (promotional booklet), 26–27.

42. Kennedy, *The North Carolina Mutual Story*, 12, 25, 72.

43. Sadie T. Mossell Alexander interview, in *Black Women Oral History Project*, 71–85; Weare, *Black Business in the New South*, 148B; Turner interview; *The North Carolina Mutual*, May 1906, in Kennedy, *The North Carolina Mutual Story*, 26.

44. Ethel Grice Demmons to Mrs. William J. Kennedy, 13 May 1936, Mrs. M. L. Kennedy to Mrs. Demmons, 28 May 1936, box 1, folder 1, WJKP; *Milestones along the Color Line*.

45. *Pittsburgh Courier*, 17, 24 December 1929; Turner interview; "In Memoriam: Mrs. Eva Whitted Goins," "Durham Obituaries," ADVC.

46. Hull, *Give Us Each Day*, 206–7.

47. Ethel Grice Demmons to Mrs. William J. Kennedy, 13 May 1936, Mrs. M. L. Kennedy to Mrs. Demmons, 28 May 1936, box 1, folder 1, WJKP; Turner interview.

48. *Pittsburgh Courier*, 17, 24 December 1929; Turner interview; "In Memoriam: Mrs. Eva Whitted Goins," "Durham Obituaries," ADVC.

49. "Orchids!" *Whetstone* 27 (1950), clipping in ADVC; "In Memoriam: For Mrs. Bessie Alberta Johnson Whitted," "Durham Obituaries," ADVC; Kennedy, *The North Carolina Mutual Story*, 28–29; Spaulding, "Life Insurance and Its Benefits," in *Report of the Sixteenth Annual Convention of the National Negro Business*

League, Boston, Mass., 1915, 114–20, *NNBLR,* reel 3; Turner interview; Murray interview; Lanier interview.

50. Kennedy, *The North Carolina Mutual Story,* 28–29, 85, 201; Turner interview.
51. Turner interview.
52. Goodwin author interview.
53. Weare, *Black Business in the New South,* 207; Kennedy, *The North Carolina Mutual Story,* 53–54, 214, 241–42, 258; Turner interview; Goodwin author interview.
54. Turner interview; *North Carolina Mutual,* 21.
55. Turner interview.
56. *Twenty-eighth Annual Report of the North Carolina Bureau of Labor Statistics,* 102; C. C. Spaulding to F. Rosser, 17 April 1914, FRP; Scott interview; Janiewski, *Sisterhood Denied,* 110–13; Thornhill Mercantile to F. B. Rosser, 3 December 1922, J. E. Shepard to Fannie Rosser, 21 December 1926, A. W. Grady to F. B. Rosser, 5 April 1927, Virginia Randolph to Fannie Rosser, 11 October 1929, copies of stock (including Durham Public Services Company) and bond certificates, and passim, FRP; Turner interview.
57. Weare, *Black Business in the New South,* 135–36; Turner interview.
58. Membership Lists, NAACP Durham Branch, ca. 1927, *NAACPP,* reel 18; *Durham Carolina Times,* 2 April 1938 and passim; Kennedy, *The North Carolina Mutual Story,* 136; Miscellaneous Programs Folder, CFSP; Turner interview; McLester interview; Lucas interview; Clement interview. The earliest membership lists available for the Durham branch of the NAACP date from 1919. The YWCA was established in 1922.
59. Clement interview; Constance Merrick Moore Watts interview; Turner interview; Hull, *Give Us Each Day,* 207.
60. Turner interview.
61. Turner interview; Lanier interview; Lyons interview.
62. "Strictly for the Girls," *Whetstone,* n.d., ca. 1945, WJKP.
63. More than one individual made this reference or a similar allusion. None would go on record. Anonymous author interview; Pearson interview; Weare, "Black Business: A Reevaluation of Functional Roles of Autonomous Institutions."
64. Anonymous author interview.
65. Turner interview.
66. Photograph of clerks' office, CCSP; Turner interview.
67. Washington, "Durham, North Carolina, a City of Negro Enterprise"; Du Bois, "The Upbuilding of Black Durham"; Weare, *Black Business in the New South,* 144–48; Department of Commerce, Bureau of the Census, *Negroes in the United States,* 279.
68. Brochures for the Royal Knights of King David, Peoples Building and Loan Association, and the Fraternal Bank and Trust, WGPP.
69. "The Servant in the South," *Crisis* 3 (April 1912): 245.

70. Murray, *Proud Shoes*, 234–36; Murray, *The Autobiography*, 60; Pauli Murray to Alma Louise Fitzgerald Biggers, 14 June 1975, folder 331, box 12, PMP.
71. Harley, "When Your Work Is Not Who You Are," 42; Higginbotham, "Beyond the Sounds of Silence," 58; Higginbotham, *Righteous Discontent*, 204–5.
72. Roberts, *Durham Architectural and Historical Inventory*, 117–18; McLester interview; Clement interview; Faulk interview; Turner interview.
73. Lanier interview.
74. Lyons interview.
75. Kennedy, *The North Carolina Mutual Story*, 72. Others later claimed that the issue of color and class was pervasive, among women in particular. Lucas interview; Lyons interview.
76. Constance Merrick Moore Watts interview.
77. Ibid.
78. Ibid.
79. Ibid.; Goodwin author interview.
80. Du Bois, "The Upbuilding of Black Durham"; Washington, "Durham, North Carolina, a City of Negro Enterprise"; Holsey, "Pearson — The Brown Duke of Durham"; Frazier, "Durham: The Capital of the Black Middle Class."
81. Du Bois, "The Upbuilding of Black Durham," 336.
82. Moore, "Conducting a Hosiery Mill," in *Report of the Eleventh Annual Convention of the National Negro Business League, New York City, 1910*, 59–60, NNBLR, reel 2.
83. "Last Tribute to Mrs. Cottie S. Moore," *Whetstone*, n.d., ca. 1950, clipping, box 5, CCSP.
84. Weare, "Charles C. Spaulding," 167–90.
85. Frazier, "Durham: The Capital of the Black Middle Class," 333–43; E. Franklin Frazier to C. C. Spaulding, 24 August 1925, folder 18, box 131-15, ser. B, EFFP.
86. On the Tulsa race riot, see Ellsworth, *Death in a Promised Land*; Kennedy, *The North Carolina Mutual Story*, 137; Weare, *Black Business in the New South*, 116–19; *Durham Morning Herald*, 21 December 1921; and unidentified clipping, 17 February 1921, cited in Weare, *Black Business in the South*, 119.
87. *Milestones along the Color Line*.

Chapter Five

1. Department of Commerce, Bureau of the Census, *Negro Population*, 331; Department of Commerce, Bureau of the Census, *Negroes in the United States*, 452; Department of Public Health, *Mortality among Negroes in the United States*, 30.
2. Gover, "Trend of Mortality among Southern Negroes since 1920," 276–88; Weare, *Black Business in the New South*, 83–84, 125–29.
3. Department of Commerce, Bureau of the Census, *Negro Population*, 363; Department of Commerce, Bureau of the Census, *Negroes in the United States*, 445; Woodbury, *Maternal Mortality*, 48–49; Guttentag and Secord, *Too Many Women*, 207–11.

4. Dula and Simpson, *Durham and Her People*, 9–12; Boyd, *The Story of Durham*, 209; Barbee interview.

5. Constance Merrick Moore Watts interview.

6. Department of Commerce, Bureau of the Census, *Negro Population*, 389; Durham County, *Annual Report of the Public Schools of Durham County Schools*, 1902–3, 1909–10.

7. Goodwin interview, ca. 1992.

8. Anderson, *Education of Blacks in the South*, 156–57.

9. Merrick speech, in Andrews, *John Merrick*, 161.

10. Weare, *Black Business in the New South*, 76n90, 118.

11. Holsey, "Pearson — The Brown Duke of Durham"; "Address to the Public," *Durham Morning Herald* and *Raleigh News and Observer*, 2 January 1907.

12. Merrick speech, in Andrews, *John Merrick*, 159–61.

13. Park, "The Bases of Race Prejudice," 11–20; Weare, "Charles Clinton Spaulding," 168. See also Doyle, *The Etiquette of Race Relations in the South*. Walter B. Weare refers to this practice as the "politics of no politics," meaning electoral politics. Because they kept the goal of reentering electoral politics as voters in view, the activities of black leaders were political by whatever definition might be employed.

14. Pearson interview; Holsey, "Pearson — The Brown Duke of Durham," 116. Regarding Duke's advice, some historians have written that the ideas for Merrick's investments came from Duke, in particular the concept of an insurance company. But, because Merrick began investing in the mid-1880s, it is unlikely that Duke significantly influenced Merrick's financial ventures. See Boyd, *The Story of Durham*, 286–87; and Weare, *Black Business in the New South*, 19–21. Weare refutes Boyd, based on his interview with Pearson and others. Part of the racial masquerade, it seems, was to allow whites to take partial credit for blacks' accomplishments.

15. Murray, *Proud Shoes*, 17.

16. Faulk interview.

17. Clement interview.

18. Shaw, *What a Woman Ought to Be and to Do*, 81–92.

19. Lincoln Hospital, *Thirty-eighth Annual Report*.

20. A. M. Moore to J. B. Duke, 16 October 1899, folder 1, box 1, JBDP; Pearson interview; Dr. Charles Watts interview; Moore, quoted in Andrews, *John Merrick*, 47–48.

21. Moore, quoted in Andrews, *John Merrick*, 47–48.

22. Rosenwald, quoted in Hine, *Black Women in White*, 10–22.

23. Andrews, *John Merrick*, 47–48; Goodwin author interview; Dr. Charles Watts interview; Weare, *Black Business in the New South*, 223. Dr. Charles Watts, who served on the medical staff of Lincoln Hospital in the 1940s, was not related to George W. Watts; he married Constance Merrick Moore Watts.

24. Lincoln Hospital, *Thirty-eighth Annual Report*.

25. Du Bois, "The Upbuilding of Black Durham," 338; Jenkins, *James B. Duke*, 244–45; Lincoln Hospital, *Thirty-eighth Annual Report*.

26. Williams, quoted in Hine, *Black Women in White*, 12; Lincoln Hospital, *Thirty-eighth Annual Report*.

27. Lincoln Hospital, *Bulletin of the School of Nursing*; Lincoln Hospital, *Thirty-eighth Annual Report*. On the ambivalent attitude both black women and men held about nursing, see Hine, *Black Women in White*, 11–16.

28. Lincoln Hospital, *Bulletin of the School of Nursing*; Lincoln Hospital, *Thirty-eighth Annual Report*; Boyd, *The Story of Durham*, 226; *Durham Morning Herald*, 5 January 1924.

29. *Durham Morning Herald*, 5 February 1918, 11 August 1924, 23 June, 15, 19 October, 18 November 1981; Boyd, *The Story of Durham*, 214, 222; Lincoln Hospital, *Thirty-eighth Annual Report*.

30. *Durham Morning Herald*, 23 June 1818, 5 January, 20 May 1924.

31. *Durham Morning Herald*, 7 May, 15, 23 June, 19 October, 18, 24 November 1918; Boyd, *The Story of Durham*, 214, 222; Lincoln Hospital, *Thirty-eighth Annual Report*.

32. Lincoln Hospital, *Thirty-eighth Annual Report*; Wesley, *A History of the National Association of Colored Women's Clubs*, 322; Vann, "Black Women United"; Hine, *Black Women in White*, 19–20.

33. Anderson, *Durham County*, 255; Gilmore, *Gender and Jim Crow*, 170–72; *Durham Morning Herald*, 5 February 1981. Although it is not clear in Moore's statement whether the Durham Civic League was a white women's or black women's organization, Jean Bradley Anderson distinguishes between the Durham Civic League (white) and the Negro Civic League. Because black women also would have raised funds, Moore might have used one term to refer to both. Most likely, given racial etiquette, which he certainly had mastered, he was recognizing only white women's work in this public setting.

34. *Durham Negro Observer*, 7 July 1906, cited in Weaver, "The Development of the Black Durham Community"; Fannie B. Rosser to Mrs. L. W. Wilhoite, 21 May 1934 (her emphasis), F. B. Rosser to West Durham Lumber Company, 13 July 1938, FRP; Lincoln Hospital, *Thirty-eighth Annual Report*.

35. Anderson, *Durham County*, 225; Gilmore, *Gender and Jim Crow*, 170–72; *Durham Morning Herald*, 5 February 1918, 18 August 1924, 19 April 1925.

36. *Durham Morning Herald*, 19 April 1925.

37. Lincoln Hospital, *Bulletin of the School of Nursing*.

38. Ibid.; Lincoln Hospital, *Thirty-eighth Annual Report*; Boyd, *The Story of Durham*, 226; *Durham Morning Herald*, 5 January 1924; Goodwin HHC interview; Goodwin author interview.

39. *Durham Morning Herald*, 4 May 1925, 10 April 1926.

40. Gover, "Trend of Mortality among Southern Negroes since 1920," 276.

41. Department of Commerce, Bureau of the Census, *Negroes in the United States*, 413, 445, 452; City and County of Durham, *Annual Report of the Department of Health, 1924*, 73; Gover, "Trend of Morality among Southern Negroes since 1920," 276. This decrease is all the more dramatic when one considers that reporting was more accurate in 1924 than in 1910.

42. "Letters from Farmers," in Bureau of Labor and Printing/Labor Statistics, *Annual Reports of the Bureau of North Carolina Labor and Printing/Labor Statistics*, Sixteenth Annual Report, 1902, 219–22. The compulsory school law was part of a series of child labor laws that the bureau recommended to the legislature.

43. Ibid., 226.

44. C. C. Spaulding, "Praises Pearson in Speech at Dedication of School," n.d., ca. 1932, clipping, *Durham Morning Herald*, Pearson Scrapbook, WGPP; "Obituary of William G. Pearson," miscellaneous clippings, WGPP; Pearson interview; Holsey, "Pearson — The Brown Duke of Durham," 116.

45. C. C. Spaulding, "Praises Pearson in Speech at Dedication of School," n.d., ca. 1932, clipping, *Durham Morning Herald*, Pearson Scrapbook, WGPP; Pearson interview; Holsey, "Pearson — The Brown Duke of Durham," 116; Anderson, *Durham County*, 258; Andrews, *John Merrick*; Weare, *Black Business in the New South*.

46. *Durham Morning Herald*, 1 June 1915.

47. "Letters from Farmers," in Bureau of Labor and Printing/Labor Statistics, *Annual Reports of the Bureau of North Carolina Labor and Printing/Labor Statistics*, Sixteenth Annual Report, 1902, 224.

48. Ibid., 225.

49. King, "Charles McIver Fights," 360–69.

50. Du Bois, *The Common School and The Negro American*, 45–50, especially 48.

51. Jones, *The Jeanes Teacher in the United States*, 4–5; Anderson, *Education of Blacks in the South*, 81. Anderson's extensive discussion of the intricate conflicts and alliances among African Americans and both northern white philanthropists and southern white reformers concludes that such conflicts impeded progress.

52. Ibid.

53. Anderson, *Education of Blacks in the South*, 117–32. Rosenwald supported the building of numerous black public schools in North Carolina. C. J. Calloway to Nathan C. Newbold, 28 December 1916, folder: "Rosenwald," box 3, DNE. Calloway wrote, "Mr. Rosenwald has made it possible for us to promise you money for at least five more schoolhouses in your state [North Carolina]."

54. Shepard, "National Training School and Chautauqua for the Colored Race"; Shepard, "National Training School . . . No Particular Creed, but Open to All Faiths"; addenda to letters from James Shepard to Wallace Buttrick, 5 February 1909, 19 September 1911, Records of General Education Board, ser. 1, Appropriations, sub series 1, The Early Southern Program.

55. Sage notes, 26 January 1910, "National Religious Training School and Chautau-

qua"; Jas. E. Shepard to Dr. Wallace Buttrick, 5 February 1909; Jackson Davis, [Report on Visit to] National Training School, Durham, N.C., 6 July 1921; "Graduates Engaged in Teaching," addenda to letter, James E. Shepard to E. C. Sage, 29 December 1916, all in *General Education Board Archives*. The correspondence between Shepard and the General Education Board illuminates the ideological conflict among independent white administrators. During the 1923–24 school year, Shepard convinced the state to engage in a cooperative teacher training program and to take over the school a year later.

56. Sage notes, 26 January 1910, "National Religious Training School and Chautauqua," in *General Education Board Archives*.

57. Jones, *Stanford L. Warren Branch Library*, 4; Shaw, *What a Woman Ought to Be and to Do*, 72–74.

58. Jones, *Stanford L. Warren Branch Library*, 5; Murray, *The Autobiography*, 20; Parker interview. The Colored Library moved to its present location on Fayetteville Street and was renamed for Dr. Stanford L. Warren.

59. James H. Dillard to N. C. Newbold, 14 August 1914, and N. C. Newbold to James H. Dillard, 17 August 1915, folder D, box 1, DNE; N. C. Newbold to C. W. Massey, 10 March 1916, A. M. Moore to N. C. McCrary, A. M. Moore, and C. H. Moore, 11 December 1916, folder M, box 3, DNE. The Anna T. Jeanes Funds for Rudimentary Schools for Southern Negroes "pledged money . . . for the furthering and fostering of rudimentary education in small Negro rural schools" (Jones, *The Jeanes Teacher in the United States*).

60. Jones, *The Jeanes Teacher in the United States*, 18–19; Newbold, "Jeanes Supervising Industrial Teachers in Negro Schools," Report to the Jeanes Fund, 1917, folder: "Jeanes," box 4, DNE.

61. Jones, *The Jeanes Teacher in the United States*, 18–19; Newbold, "Jeanes Supervising Industrial Teachers in Negro Schools," Report to the Jeanes Fund, 1917, folder: "Jeanes," box 4, DNE.

62. N. C. Newbold to C. W. Massey, 3 July 1915, folder M, box 2, DNE.

63. N. C. Newbold to S. H. Massey, 10 March 1916, folder M, box 3, Frank Husbands to N. C. Newbold, n.d., ca. 1916, folder H, box 3, DNE; *Durham Morning Herald*, 16 April 1916.

64. Wanamaker to N. C. Newbold, 6 August 1917, folder W, box 4, DNE.

65. C. H. Massey to N. C. Newbold, 8 July 1916, and Newbold to Massey, 17 July 1916, folder M, box 3, DNE; W. H. Wannamaker to N. C. Newbold, 6 August 1917, and Newbold to Wannamaker, 15 August 1917, folder W, box 4, DNE.

66. N. C. Newbold to Abraham Flexner, 17 May 1919, folder F, box 4, DNE; Anderson, *Education of Blacks in the South*, 153–56.

67. Anderson, *Education of Blacks in the South*, 153–56.

68. W. H. Wannamaker to N. C. Newbold, 5 March 1918, and N. C. Newbold to W. H. Wannamaker, 8 March 1919, folder W, box 3, DNE. Durham County never built a county training school.

69. Hill Directory Company, *Durham, N.C., Directory, 1911–1912*, 13–14; *Durham Morning Herald*, 8 June 1919.

70. Department of the Interior, Census Office, *Report on the Population of the United States at the Eleventh Census: 1890*, pt. 2, 592.

71. Department of Commerce, Bureau of the Census, *Negro Population*, 518–22; Durham City Schools, *Annual Report of the Superintendent of Public Instruction*, 1901–2; Durham City Schools, *Annual Report of the Superintendent of Public Instruction*, 1915–16, 111; *Durham Morning Herald*, 24 August 1919. Durham County also added a Jeanes supervisor in 1915. N. C. Newbold to C. W. Massey, 3 July 1915, box 1, Correspondence of the State Agent for Rural Education, Negro, 1907–15, and W. H. Wannamaker to N. C. Newbold, 6 August 1917, folder W, box 3, DNE.

72. *Durham Morning Herald*, 8 June 1919.

73. "Accounts with District School Committees," Book 5, 1903–6, Durham County Treasurer Collection, NCCC. Black teachers' salaries here seem high nonetheless, perhaps because, as Durham education officials bragged, the school year ran almost as long for black students as for white, eight months.

74. Durham City Schools, *Annual Report of the Superintendent: Rules and Regulations of the Board of Education, 1915*, 15.

75. Robert J. Tydall, statement before the Durham City Board of Education, Public School hearing, Morehead Elementary School, 4 November 1974, folder 272, box 11, PMP; Murray, *The Autobiography*, 17; Murray interview. Tydall was the principal of Lyon Park School in 1974, the year the city decided to close the facility. It has since reopened as a community center.

76. Murray, *Proud Shoes*, 270.

77. *Eighteenth Annual Report of the Bureau of Labor and Printing, 1904*, 42–43.

78. Pauline F. Dame, "Autobiography of My Life," typescript, folder 273, box 11, PMP.

79. It is unclear exactly how West End and East End might be considered city schools; in order to get Rosenwald funding to build them, they had to be classified as rural schools. They lay just outside of the city limits until the city boundaries extended to include those districts in 1925. Various city directories, newspaper articles, and superintendent reports, however, categorize the three institutions as colored schools in the City of Durham.

80. Westin, "A History of the Durham School System," 59.

81. *Durham Morning Herald*, 7 June 1913; Westin, "A History of the Durham School System," 81.

82. Jones, *Negro Education*, 390 (also known as the Phelps-Stokes Report).

83. "Some Suggestions for Summer School for Negro Teachers," n.d., ca. 1918, folder: "Summer School," box 3, DNE.

84. *Durham Morning Herald*, 27 July 1918.

85. Ibid., 12–18 July 1918.

86. Lyons interview.

87. "Number of Negro High Schools," folder: "Speeches, Reports, and Miscellaneous," box 3, DNE. Hillside High School opened in 1921 and went up to the eleventh grade; it did not offer twelfth grade until the 1950s.

88. *Durham Morning Herald*, 18 November 1918.

89. N. C. Newbold to J. E. Shepard, 1 July 1919, folder "R–T," box 4, DNE.

90. Ibid.

91. Murray, *The Autobiography*, 32. Murray wrote that in later years she mockingly quipped, "Be a credit to your space."

92. In 1925, the State Board of Charities and Public Welfare appointed Laurence O. Oxley to head the Division of Work among Negroes. Funded by Laura Spelman Rockefeller, Oxley's work focused on "an intelligent study of Negro life and its social problems" and on "developing cooperative self-help programs." *Biennial Report of the North Carolina Board of Charities and Public Welfare*, 1 July 1924–30 June 1926, 100.

93. Holland, "[North Carolina] School Attendance Report [in Response to] Questionnaire on Elementary School Attendance [for] Tuskegee Conference," n.d., ca. 1924, folder: "Speeches, Reports, and Miscellaneous," box 8, DNE.

94. Murray, *The Autobiography*, 15.

95. Faulk interview; Lucas interview.

96. Harris interview.

97. Holland, "School Attendance Report."

98. Lyons interview.

99. Steele interview. A teacher in Charlotte, Steele emphasized teachers' awareness of the class dynamic between themselves and parents.

100. Faulk interview.

101. Holland, "School Attendance Report."

102. Dame, "The Parent-Teacher Association: Its Relationship to the School and the Community," folder 278f+, box 11, PMP.

103. *Durham Morning Herald*, 19 July 1919.

104. Murray, *The Autobiography*, 59.

105. Ibid.

Chapter Six

1. *Durham Morning Herald*, 30, 31 March 1918; Murray, *The Autobiography*, 20.

2. *Durham Morning Herald*, 30, 31 March 1918.

3. Ibid., 6 November 1918; Du Bois, "Close Ranks," *Crisis*, July 1918. On the controversy over this essay, see Ellis, " 'Closing Ranks' and 'Seeking Honors,' " 96–114.

4. D. H. Hill to the County Chairman, 10 December 1917, folder: "Negroes," box 26, North Carolina Council on Defense, MC.

5. *Durham Morning Herald*, 6 November 1918; Du Bois, "Close Ranks," *Crisis*, July 1918.

6. Du Bois, "The Immediate Program of the American Negro," *Crisis*, April 1915.
7. Bickett, "Statement about Committee on Negro Economics," 16 June 1919, in House and Martin, *Public Letters and Papers of Thomas Walter Bickett, Governor of North Carolina, 1917–1921*, 287–91.
8. *Durham Morning Herald*, 16 March, 23 April, 20 September, 11 October 1918.
9. *Durham Morning Herald*, 26 May, 23 June 1918.
10. Quoted in Gilmore, *Gender and Jim Crow*, 195; *Durham Morning Herald*, 2 February, 28 March, 13 November 1918.
11. *Durham Morning Herald*, 29 May, 13 February 1918; *Durham Evening Sun*, 15 February 1918, clippings, n.d., ca. 1918, Scrapbooks, box 14, CNHP; *Durham Morning Herald*, 28 March 1918.
12. Murray, *Proud Shoes*, 5.
13. Department of Commerce, Bureau of the Census, *Stocks of Leaf Tobacco*, 35; Tilley, *The R. J. Reynolds Tobacco Company*, 189–284; Cox, *Competition in the American Tobacco Industry*, 40–59; North Carolina Department of Labor and Printing, *Biennial Reports*, 1911–23; Janiewski, *Sisterhood Denied*, 109; Scott interview; Miller interview; Barbee interview.
14. Scott interview.
15. Ibid.; Murray, *Proud Shoes*, 27.
16. Scott interview; "Minutes of the Membership Meeting," Minute Books, vol. 1, DCCP.
17. Mitchner interview.
18. Harris interview.
19. Scott interview.
20. Ibid.; Johnson, "The Tobacco Worker," 385–88, 391. Johnson studied Durham, Reidsville, and Winston-Salem, North Carolina; Danville and Richmond, Virginia; and Louisville, Kentucky; Trotter, *Black Milwaukee*.
21. Shields, "A Half-Century in the Tobacco Industry," 35–36; Manning and Byrne, *The Effects on Women of Changing Conditions in the Cigar and Cigarette Industries*; Janiewski, *Sisterhood Denied*; Jones, "Race, Sex and Class," 441–51.
22. Miller interview; Bailey interview; Brown interview; Cheatham interview.
23. Department of Labor, Women's Bureau, *Negro Women in Industry*, 18–21. In textiles, women averaged slightly longer hours per day; in tobacco, they worked more hours per week.
24. Shields, "A Half-Century in the Tobacco Industry," 420–21; Department of Labor, Women's Bureau, *Negro Women in Industry*, 24, 28–30, 58; Mebane, *Mary*, 165–70.
25. Miller interview; Scott interview; Barbee interview; Mebane, *Mary*, 173–76.
26. Barbee interview; Mack interview.
27. Barbee interview.
28. Department of Labor, Women's Bureau, *Negro Women in Industry*, 58.

29. Howerton (Whitted), "Remembering . . . 'The Meanderings of an Old Lady' [1900–1918]," HFP.

30. Bailey interview; Levine, *Black Culture and Black Consciousness*, 239–70, 300–320.

31. Bailey interview; Anderson, *Durham County*, 261; Shields, "A Half-Century in the Tobacco Industry," 420; Gavins, "North Carolina Black Folklore and Song in the Age of Segregation," 412–41; Levine, *Black Culture and Black Consciousness*, 239–70.

32. Barbee interview; Bailey interview.

33. Scott interview.

34. Department of Commerce, Bureau of the Census, *Fifteenth Census of the United States*, vol. 4, *Occupations*, 425; Mae, *Thursdays and Every Other Sunday Off*.

35. Brown interview.

36. Haynes, "Negroes in Domestic Service in the United States," 393–96. For first person accounts regarding domestic work, see Tucker, *Telling Memories among Southern Women*.

37. Miller interview; *Durham Morning Herald*, 18 September 1918.

38. Moore, "How to Keep Negro Labor," in Haynes, *The Negro at Work*, 102–3; Department of Labor, Women's Bureau, *Negro Women in Industry*, 41.

39. Williams, "Negro Exodus from the South," 94. A field agent representing Hampton Institute, Williams also worked for the General Education Board, the John F. Slater Fund, and the Anna T. Jeanes Fund.

40. Department of Commerce, Bureau of the Census, *Fourteenth Census of the United States Taken in the Year 1920*, 3:987; Department of Commerce, Bureau of the Census, *Negroes in the United States*, 307.

41. Haynes, "Negro Migration," 272; Hill, *Women in Gainful Occupations*, 9–21; Department of Commerce, Bureau of the Census, *Negro Population*, 522; Department of Commerce, Bureau of the Census, *Fourteenth Census of the United States Taken in the Year 1920*, 3:987; Department of Commerce, Bureau of the Census, *Negroes in the United States*, 307.

42. Hill, *Women in Gainful Occupations*, 17–21, 110–11.

43. Ibid., 110–17; Department of Commerce, Bureau of the Census, *Negro Population*, 522; Department of Commerce, Bureau of the Census, *Fourteenth Census of the United States Taken in the Year 1920*, vol. 3, *Occupations*, 987; Department of Commerce, Bureau of the Census, *Negroes in the United States*, 307.

44. Hill, *Women in Gainful Occupations*, 109–11, 119; Department of Commerce, Bureau of the Census, *Negro Population*, 522; Department of Commerce, Bureau of the Census, *Fourteenth Census of the United States Taken in the Year 1920*, vol. 3, *Occupations*, 987; Department of Commerce, Bureau of the Census, *Negroes in the United States*, 307.

45. Department of Commerce, Bureau of the Census, *Fifteenth Census of the United States*, 4:425.

46. Moore, "How to Keep Negro Labor," in Haynes, *The Negro at Work*, 99.

47. "Minutes of the Meeting of the Executive Committee," 13 July 1919, 19 July

1917, 7 February 1918, Durham Chamber of Commerce, Minute Books, vol. 1, DCCP; *Durham Morning Herald*, 14 June, 24 July, 1 September 1918.

48. White, "'Work or Fight' in the South," 144–46; *New York Age*, 28 September, 19 October, 2 November 1918; Hunter, "Domination and Resistance," 205–20; Hunter, *To 'Joy My Freedom*, 227–32; *Durham Morning Herald*, 15 June 1918.

49. *Durham Morning Herald*, 22 March, 24 July 1918, 18, 19 September 1919; Board of Public Charities, *Annual Reports of the Board of Public Charities of North Carolina*, 1907, 19, 178.

50. See Meyerowitz, *Women Adrift*.

51. Haynes, "Report of the Work in North Carolina," and Moore, "How to Keep Negro Labor," in Haynes, *The Negro at Work*, 97–98, 101–3; Minutes, 28 May 1917, Durham Chamber of Commerce, Minute Books, vol. 1, DCCP.

52. Moore, "How to Keep Negro Labor," in Haynes, *The Negro at Work*, 101.

53. Ibid., 102. One exception was the Tallahassee Power Company's "Model Village" in North Badin, North Carolina. Tallahassee, an aluminum manufacturer, offered good wages and set up housing, schools, a community center, a relief department, and first aid services for blacks. The "Black Town" included businesses, churches, a health department, and a women's club. It provided trained black welfare workers and a system of self-government. "Brief Study and Report of the Director of Negro Economics," 27 January 1920; *Black Workers in the Era of the Great Migration*, reel 14; Haynes, "Report of the Work in North Carolina," in Haynes, *The Negro at Work*, 100.

54. *Durham Morning Herald*, 13, 21 March, 6 August, 22, 24 September 1918; Foner and Lewis, *The Black Worker*, 5:428–79; *Norfolk Journal and Guide*, 15, 22, 29 September 1917; Department of Commerce, Bureau of the Census, *Negroes in the United States*, 85. See Lewis, *In Their Own Interests*.

55. *Durham Morning Herald*, 24 September 1918; Haynes, "Report of the Work in North Carolina," 97.

56. "Negroes and Organized Labor," *Survey* 39 (9 February 1918): 527–28. On blacks and unionization, see Reid, *Negro Membership in American Labor Unions*; Northrup, *Organized Labor and the Negro*; and Spero and Harris, *The Black Worker*.

57. "Calendar," box: "Picture and Volumes," AVCP; *Durham Morning Herald*, 19 September 1919; Arthur Vance Cole to E. Lewis Evans, 26 August 1919, folder 1, box: "Correspondence, 1912–1972," AVCP.

58. *Durham Morning Herald*, 27 June, 8, 14 August 1919; A. McAndrew to A. V. Cole, 29 September 1919, folder 1, box: "Correspondence," AVCP; Anderson, *Durham County*, 312; Tilley, *The R. J. Reynolds Tobacco Company*, 260–66. Union activity also occurred among white streetcar men and black construction workers. A textile union formed around this time, but it probably did not include any African Americans.

59. E. Lewis Evans to A. V. Cole, 13 October 1919, folder 1, box: "Correspondence, 1912–1972," AVCP.

60. E. Lewis Evans to A. V. Cole, 31 January, 21 March 1920, folder 1, box: "Correspondence, 1912–1972," AVCP.

61. Cora B. Hogan to A. V. Cole, n.d., ca. summer 1920, folder 1, box: "Correspondence, 1912–1972," AVCP.

62. E. Lewis Evans to A. V. Cole, 31 January 1920, A. V. Cole to F. W. Detlor, 7 February 1920, folder 1, box: "Correspondence, 1912–1972," AVCP.

63. *Durham Morning Herald*, 12 September, 19 September, 26 September, 30 September, 9, 10 October 1919.

64. *Star of Zion*, 21 February 1918; *Durham Morning Herald*, 7 April 1918; Gilmore, *Gender and Jim Crow*, 196; Breen, "Black Women and the Great War," 421–40; Hull, *Give Us Each Day*, 42–44.

65. "History of the Durham County Chapter of the American Red Cross," *Everywoman's Magazine*, 11–13, 16, SJFP. The "Extension Committee" organized auxiliaries among blacks and in West Durham among white mill workers. Although *Everywoman's Magazine* listed the officers of every other committee of the Durham chapter of the American Red Cross, it failed to note the names of the members of the Extension Committee. Thus it is unknown who among white women organized the black group, or perhaps the black group organized and presented itself to the Red Cross.

66. Ibid., 13–14; *Durham Morning Herald*, 11, 25 May 1918.

67. *Durham Morning Herald*, 19, 21 May, 19 February, 2 March, 6, 12 November 1918; "History of the Durham County Chapter," 14.

68. *Durham Morning Herald*, 11 October 1918; Murray, *The Autobiography*, 21.

69. Gilmore, *Gender and Jim Crow*, 196.

70. Minutes of the Executive Committee, 4 March 1919, Minute Books, vol. 1, DCCP.

71. "Order of Parade, 14 August 1917," Durham Civic Association Files, box 27, SJFP; "Official Program, Durham's Celebration in Honor of Her Soldiers and Sailors," 25 April 1919, folder: "Parades," box 1910s, NCCC.

72. A. M. Moore to Gov. T. W. Bickett, 24 June 1919, and attached newspaper clipping, n.d., n.p., folder 3, box: "May–June 1919," GPTWB; *Durham Morning Herald*, 17 June 1919.

73. *Durham Morning Herald*, 19, 20, 21 November 1918; *New York Age*, 23 November 1918; Miller, "Blacks in Winston-Salem, North Carolina," 196–225. According to Miller, as many as twenty-five African Americans were killed, with newspapers likely underreporting the severity of the riot.

Chapter Seven

1. Frazier, "Durham: The Capital of the Black Middle Class," 334.

2. *Milestones along the Color Line.*

3. McDougald, "Task of Negro Womanhood," 370.

4. Frazier, "Occupational Classes among Negroes in Cities."

5. *Milestones along the Color Line.*

6. Moore, "How to Keep Negro Labor," in Haynes, *The Negro at Work*, 102.

7. Patterson interview; Clark interview; Caesar interview; Carby, " 'It Jus' Be's Dat Way Sometime,' " 9–22; van Falkenburg and Dall, *Wild Women Don't Have the Blues.*

8. Ethel Waters, "No Man's Mama," in *Big Mamas*, re-released on Rosetta Records, 1982, quoted in Carby, " 'It Jus' Be's Dat Way Sometime.' "

9. *Durham Morning Herald*, 7 September, 19 October 1924.

10. McDougald, "Task of Negro Womanhood," 370.

11. Murray, *Proud Shoes*, 15; Murray interview.

12. "Spaulding Urges Business Men to Co-operate," *Tuskegee Messenger* 2 (28 August 1926): 1, 5, clipping, box 5, CCSP.

13. Frazier, "Family Disorganization among Negroes"; Brinton, "Negroes Who Run Afoul of the Law."

14. *Durham Morning Herald*, 8 June 1924; C. C. Spaulding, "The Negro's Contribution to the Development of Durham," 1921, box 12, CCSP.

15. Department of Commerce, Bureau of the Census, *Fifteenth Census of the United States*, vol. 3, *Population*, pt. 2, 351; Scarborough interview. 1930 was the first year that the Durham city population was large enough to warrant a statistical breakdown by sex and occupation.

16. Davis interview.

17. Mitchner interview.

18. Mack interview.

19. Ibid.

20. Barbee interview; Mack interview.

21. Mack interview; Jones, "Race, Sex, and Class."

22. Mack interview.

23. Barbee interview; Mack interview.

24. Barbee interview.

25. Ibid.

26. Lanier interview.

27. Ingram interview.

28. Clement interview; Faulk interview; Turner interview; Lanier interview.

29. *Star of Zion*, 11 December 1919.

30. Ibid.

31. "Hunton, Report, March 27 [1912]," and "Condensed Report of the Durham Conference (1912)," in *History of Colored Work, 1907–1920*, in YWCAP; *Records of the National YWCA*, microfilm, reel 278. *Bulletin of the National Training School* lists the YWCA as one of the extracurricular activities available to students. In her interview, Johnnie McLester—who headed the YWCA in the 1930s—distinguished the "College Y" chapter at North Carolina College for Negroes from the "Tubman Y" black city YWCA.

32. *History of Colored Work, 1907–1920*, in YWCAP.
33. Ibid.
34. Ibid.; "Minutes of the Board of Directors of the Durham Central YWCA," 3 July 1922, 19 February 1923, 17 November 1924, and "A Brief Historical Summary," YWCAP; Janiewski, *Sisterhood Denied*, 4, 85.
35. On the evolution of the YWCA programs, see Salem, *To Better Our World*; for another example of YWCA development and programming, see Rouse, *Lugenia Burns Hope*.
36. "Minutes of the Executive Committee," 27 January, 20 March, 16 March, 13 April, 27 April, 21 April, 30 November 1920, 21 October 1921, Chamber of Commerce Minute Books, vol. 1. North Carolina Mutual created a space similar to that of the white YWCA for the black women who worked in the businesses along its Parrish Street block.
37. Eva Bowles to Mrs. John Hope of Atlanta, Ga., 25 January 1920, Bowles, "What the Colored Women Are Asking of the YWCAs," and "Annual Reports by the Secretary for Colored Work, 1922," in Lerner, *Black Women in White America*, 477–85.
38. YWCA Minutes, 3 July 1922, YWCAP. The minutes referred to Marie Ruffin, but Adele Ruffin was the representative. YWCA Minutes, 19 February 1923, YWCAP.
39. YWCA Minutes, 22 February, 21 March 1924, YWCAP; Minutes, Durham Community Chest Federation, 1923–26, box 1920s, NCCC.
40. YWCA Minutes, 3 November 1925, YWCAP.
41. YWCA Minutes, 20 March, 20 November 1934, YWCAP.
42. Clipping, Scrapbooks, and YWCA Minutes, 17 May, 28 September 1938, 12 November 1939, YWCAP.
43. YWCA Minutes, 3 November 1925, YWCAP.
44. YWCA Minutes, 20 April 1937, *Nineteenth Annual Report of the YWCA, 1938–1939*, clipping, Scrapbooks, YWCAP.
45. *Durham Morning Herald*, 22 March 1928.
46. Brown, "Speaking Up for the Race," in Lerner, *Black Women in White America*, 467–72.
47. Charlotte Hawkins Brown, reading "The Colored Women's Statement to the Women's Missionary Council of the American Missionary Association," reprinted in Lerner, *Black Women in White America*, 461–67.
48. Brown interview.
49. *Durham Carolina Times*, 5 February 1938; *Durham Herald-Sun*, 24 April 1938.
50. *Durham Carolina Times*, 19 March 1938.
51. McLester interview; McDougald, "Task of Negro Womanhood," 369–82.
52. Wesley, *History of the National Association of Colored Women's Clubs*, 312.
53. C. Hawkins Brown to Mrs. Mary McLeod Bethune, 7 October 1924, *NACWCR*, reel 6.

54. Charlotte Hawkins Brown to Mrs. Sallie Stewart, 26 February 1929, *NACWCR*, reel 8.

55. Charlotte Hawkins Brown, "The Quest for Culture [speech to the Volkamenia Club, 1929]," CHBP, reel 2.

56. Wesley, *History of the National Association of Colored Women's Clubs*, 311; Vann, "Black Women United," 31–36; Gilmore, *Gender and Jim Crow*, 177–78.

57. "Southern Women Moving Right Direction," *Star of Zion*, 14 July 1921.

58. Ibid.

59. Ibid.

60. Charlotte Hawkins Brown to Nathan C. Newbold, 25 October 1919, folder B, box 5, DNE.

61. *Star of Zion*, 26 May 1921.

62. Board of Public Charities, *Annual Reports of the Board of Public Charities*, 1915, 7; Board of Public Charities, *Annual Reports of the Board of Public Charities*, 1917, 32–33; Harrison, "A School for Erring Boys—Why Not One for Girls?" box: "North Carolina Conference for Social Service," folder: "Publications," GWP. Rooted in the Progressive Era movements, the interest of the North Carolina Conference for Social Service overlapped with black and white women's clubs and efforts at interracial cooperation concerned with child care, welfare, and labor, the juvenile court system, community playgrounds, social responsibility of education, industrial welfare, local Associated Charities, Travelers' Aid, prohibition, and prison reform.

63. *Norfolk Journal and Guide*, 19 November 1927.

64. Charlotte Hawkins Brown to Nathan C. Newbold, 25 October 1919, folder B, box 5, DNE. The Stonewall Jackson School was for white boys. On Charlotte Hawkins Brown and her links to national, state, and local black and white women's clubs, see Gilmore, *Gender and Jim Crow*, 190–91, 199–202. Brown complained to Newbold, "The whole responsibility seems to lie on my shoulders."

65. Newbold to Brown, 28 October 1919, Brown to Newbold, 29 October 1919, Newbold to Brown, 4 November 1919, box B, folder 5, DNE.

66. *Biennial Report of the North Carolina School for Negro Girls, Efland*. The board of directors from Durham included Minnie Pearson, Julia Warren, William G. Pearson, and Cottie Moore.

67. "Minutes of the Meeting of the Negro Advisory Group," North Carolina Board of Corrections and Training, 25 March 1944, file: "NC Board of Corrections and Training"; copy, "Deed of Trust," 26 February 1926, satisfied on 31 January 1929, DWN; "Minutes of the Annual Meeting of the North Carolina Federation of Colored Women's Clubs," 8 May 1943, "NCFCWC," box 228, DWN; "Resolutions," "NCFWC, Report 1907–1957," box 68, GWP; clippings, n.p., n.d., ca. May 1925, *Tuskegee Institute News Clipping File*, microfiche 23; *Durham Daily Sun*, 17 April 1926; *Durham Morning Herald*, 21 March 1928; "North Carolina Federation of Colored Women's Clubs Raises $2000 for Home for Delinquent

Girls," National Association of Colored Women, *National Notes* 29 (August 1927): 5; Wesley, *History of the National Association of Colored Women's Clubs*, 312.

68. Board of Public Charities, *Second Biennial Report of the State Training School for Negro Girls* (at Dobbs Farms), 16. The Efland home formally closed in the late 1930s, but other facilities surviving on state and private funds continued to open, close, and relocate between 1937 and 1944.

69. John R. Larkins to C. C. Spaulding, 1 November 1937, box 227, file: "Efland," DWN. Larkins's efforts continued into the 1940s; see Larkins's Monthly Reports (1943–49), box 229, DWN.

70. John R. Larkins to Ruth Rush, 19 August 1946, Rush to Larkins, 20 May 1947, file: "NCFCWC," box 228, DWN.

71. John R. Larkins, Field Report, 20 April 1943, box 228, DWN.

72. Anniversary and graduation programs for Daisy E. Scarborough Nursery, CFSP.

73. Daisy E. Scarborough Nursery School was licensed by the North Carolina Welfare Department. *Durham Carolina Times*, 18 June 1938.

74. CFSP; Lucas interview. Julia Lucas, who owned a barbershop and pool hall, placed her daughter in Scarborough Nursery.

75. James Gray to A. M. Scales, 25 May 1920, Correspondence and Campaign Materials, ESAC.

76. Mattie Southgate Jones, "Speech" and "Petition to the Members of the General Assembly of North Carolina," box 29, and Minutes, Durham Civic Association, n.d., ca. 1918, box 33, SJFP; Gertrude Weil, "A Good Thing for Women," *Everywoman's Magazine*, Special Session Edition (July/August 1920): 8, Correspondence and Campaign Materials, Private Collections, ESAC; Gilmore, *Gender and Jim Crow*, 203–7.

77. Lanier interview.

78. On Shepard's liberal position on suffrage, see *Raleigh News and Observer*, 30 November 1918, republished in the *Washington Bee* and *Louisville News*, 11 January 1919, clippings, PNCF, frame 103. Although there are no extant records of the Volkamenia's programs for the 1920s, politics was always a point of discussion. Lucas interview; *Star of Zion*, 7 October 1920; Murray, *The Autobiography*, 30.

79. *Durham Morning Herald*, 15, 17 October 1920. The main thoroughfare of Hayti, Fayetteville Street, split the black community into two different wards.

80. Gilmore describes the plan to delay going to the polls and then appearing in groups, which was organized through the NACW and the NAACP and distributed through the NCFCWC by Charlotte Hawkins Brown. See Gilmore, *Gender and Jim Crow*, 220–21. No records of voter registration for Durham County from this period remain. At the state level, the records are spotty at best, and no files for Durham exist. In a conversation about the paucity of references to black women voters in Durham, Gilmore pointed out that Durham usually did not report voter registration figures to state officials precisely because white

Durham allowed enough blacks to vote that it might raise suspicions among other white politicians.

81. "Republican Ballot," FRP; Turner interview; Pearson interview. The papers of Mary Cowper (a suffragette and later head of the Durham League of Women Voters) contain no references to black women and voting (Rare Book, Manuscript, and Special Collections Library, Duke University, Durham), nor do the Equal Suffrage Amendment Collection in the North Carolina State Archives, the local newspapers, or the Charlotte Hawkins Brown Papers hint at any activity around the woman suffrage issue in Durham. Conrad O. Pearson, nephew of William G. Pearson, claimed that during the period when voting was severely restricted for blacks, Spaulding or Shepard had to accompany the registrant to the courthouse, and even their presence did not guarantee a successful attempt. Pearson interview.

82. Turner interview; Pearson interview.

83. Turner interview; Pearson interview.

84. Department of Commerce, Bureau of the Census, *Negroes in the United States*, 85; *Durham, N.C., City Directory, 1919–1920*; Kiser, "Occupational Changes among Negroes in Durham," 39, 50, 122b.

85. "Votes for Women: A Symposium by Leading Thinkers of Colored America"; Terborg-Penn, "Discontented Black Feminists," in Scharf and Jensen, *Decades of Discontent*, 261–78. See also Gordon et al., *African American Women and the Vote*.

86. For the debate on equal rights and economic rights, see Cott, *The Grounding of Modern Feminism*, 115–43; Muncy, *Creating a Female Dominion in American Reform*, especially 93–123 on the Sheppard-Towner Maternity and Infancy Act; and Berry, *The Politics of Parenthood*. Memo from Gertrude Weil to Adele Clark, n.d., ca. July 1924, and Adele Clark to Julia Lathrop, 1 August 1924, *League of Women Voters Papers, 1918–1974*, reel 8.

87. The *Durham Morning Herald* noted African American interest in the Democratic Party in 1921. *Durham Morning Herald*, 12 September 1921. Evelyn Brooks Higginbotham details the bipartisan nature of black politics, particularly among women activists, in Chicago and other northern cities, as black women seized on the migrating population to build a political base. Higginbotham, "In Politics to Stay"; Higginbotham, "Clubwomen and Electoral Politics in the 1920s."

88. *Durham Morning Herald*, 23 October 1922. Moore, Shepard, Pearson, and Spaulding all fit the description of "a leader not only known in Durham, but throughout the South," who could have written the letter published by the *Herald*. Merrick, a rare public speaker, had died in 1919; Spaulding and Pearson, while prominent, emerged as spokesmen for African Americans more often on race relations than on electoral politics. Moore wrote to individual whites and rarely wrote to the newspaper. Most likely Pearson or Shepard wrote the letter to the *Herald*; of the two, Shepard was an oft-rumored anonymous letter writer.

Pearson, a school administrator, would not have spoken publicly to the issue of voting. Pearson interview.

89. Wesley, *History of the National Association of Colored Women's Clubs*, 312. Minnie Pearson served as the president of the NCFCWC from 1936 to 1941. *Durham Morning Herald*, 18 January 1918; Murray, *The Autobiography*, 15.

Chapter Eight

1. *Durham Herald-Sun*, 31 December 1932, 1 January 1933; Clement interview.
2. *Biennial Report of the North Carolina State Board of Charities and Public Welfare*, 100–103.
3. *A History of the Unit Work among Negroes*, North Carolina State Board of Charities and Public Welfare, 1943, Pamphlet Collection, Duke University Library; *Biennial Report of the North Carolina State Board of Charities and Public Welfare*, 1 July 1930–30 June 1932, 97–98.
4. *Durham Herald-Sun*, 2 January 1933.
5. *Durham Sun*, 2, 3 January 1933.
6. C. C. Spaulding, "Praises Pearson in Speech at Dedication of School," n.d., ca. 1932, clipping, *Durham Morning Herald*, Pearson Scrapbook, WGPP; Pearson interview.
7. *Durham Morning Herald*, 14, 18, 28 December 1932, 11 February 1933.
8. Lorena Hickok to Harry L. Hopkins, 18 February 1934, Lorena Hickok Reports, 1934, box 68, LHP.
9. Secured Notes, 8 February, 8 April, 4 September 1933, box 2, FRP; F. Rosser to W. L. Wilhoit, 3 December 1934, box 1, FRP.
10. R. L. McDougal to William J. Kennedy, 10 November 1931, Ed Merrick to William J. Kennedy, 14 December 1931, Nola Dowell Jackson to Mr. William J. Kennedy, 14 September 1931, folder 1, WJKP.
11. Pauline F. Dame's Teacher Contracts, folder 269, box 11, PMP; Bueno et al., *Coming Together*, 15; *Durham Morning Herald*, 28 August, 5, 12 September 1933; Letters from "Mother" to "Lenie"/Pauli (Pauline Dame Fitzgerald to Pauli Murray), 21 October 1938, 15 September, 13 October 1940, box 10, folder 257, PMP. The teacher released from the industrial arts program became the attendance officer.
12. Clement interview.
13. Lorena Hickok to Harry L. Hopkins, 18 February 1934, Lorena Hickok Reports, 1934, box 68, LHP.
14. "Efficiency Ratings," 27 April 1934–22 July 1935, folder 68, WJKP.
15. Ross, "Mary McLeod Bethune and the National Youth Administration," 1–28.
16. Robert C. Weaver to C. C. Spaulding, 18, 25 October 1933, C. C. Spaulding to Clark H. Foreman, 7 November 1933, Clark Foreman to C. C. Spaulding, 8 November 1933, Clark Foreman to Robert C. Weaver, 23 October, 22 November 1933, C. C. Spaulding to Robert Weaver, 9 October 1933, RCWP, reel 2.

17. Sullivan, *Days of Hope*, 44–49; Williams, "Robert C. Weaver," 21; C. C. Spaulding to Robert Weaver, 28 September 1933, and C. C. Spaulding to Robert Weaver, 9 October 1933, RCWP, reel 2.

18. C. C. Spaulding to Clark H. Foreman, 7 November 1933, Clark Foreman to C. C. Spaulding, 8 November 1933, Clark Forman to Robert C. Weaver, 23 October, 22 November 1933, RCWP, reel 2; C. C. Spaulding to W. Arthur Mitchell, 11 February 1935, U.S. Congress, House, *To Create an Industrial Commission on Negro Affairs*, 21. Spaulding asked that this letter remain confidential, but it was published in the hearing's proceedings.

19. Sullivan, *Days of Hope*, 21–24.

20. Ibid.; *Durham Morning Herald*, 3 September 1933. On African Americans and the New Deal, see also Katznelson, *When Affirmative Action Was White*. Historians have sustained a rich debate on the positive and negative effects of the New Deal on African Americans. See also Sullivan, *Days of Hope*; Sitkoff, *A New Deal for Blacks*; Ferguson, *Black Politics in New Deal Atlanta*; Cohen, *Making a New Deal*; Weiss, *Farewell to the Party of Lincoln*; and Kessler-Harris, *In Pursuit of Equality*.

21. Williams, "Robert C. Weaver," 19.

22. *Durham Morning Herald*, 24 August 1933.

23. Robert R. Moton, *Atlanta World*, 3 September 1933, quoted in Chambliss, "What Negro Newspapers of Georgia Say about Some Social Problems."

24. Lyon, *The National Recovery Administration*, 332–33; Sullivan, *Days of Hope*, 45; Wolters, *Negroes and the Great Depression*, 124–35; Korstad, *Civil Rights Unionism*, 127–29; Williams, "Robert C. Weaver," 17–22.

25. Eugene Kinckle Jones to Franklin D. Roosevelt, "The Negro Working Population and National Recovery: A Special Memorandum Submitted to Franklin Delano Roosevelt," 4 January 1937, box 1, WJKP.

26. Ibid.; John P. Davis testimony, in U.S. Congress, Senate, Committee on Finance, *Investigation of the National Recovery Administration*, 2139–60.

27. Weaver interview by Hardin, 30 November 1973, and Weaver interview by Franz, 19 November 1968, folder 15, box 8, Lyndon B. Johnson Oral History Project (copy in folder 11, box 8, RCWP); Lyon, *The National Recovery Administration*, 319.

28. Johnson, "The Tobacco Worker," 394; Eugene Kinckle Jones to Franklin D. Roosevelt, "The Negro Working Population and National Recovery: A Special Memorandum Submitted to Franklin Delano Roosevelt," 4 January 1937, box 1, WJKP.

29. Lorena Hickok to Harry L. Hopkins, 18 February 1934, Lorena Hickock Reports, 1934, box 68, LHP.

30. Ibid.; Weaver, "The New Deal and the Negro," 200–220.

31. Lorena Hickok to Harry L. Hopkins, 18 February 1934, Lorena Hickock Reports, 1934, box 68, LHP.

32. U.S. Congress, Senate, Committee on Finance, *Investigation of the National Recovery Administration*, 2142–44.

33. Johnson, "The Tobacco Worker," 408–9.

34. Korstad, *Civil Rights Unionism*, 127–30.

35. W. B. Culbreth to Mr. Evans, 29 July 1933, box 7, ser. 3, Locals, TWIUA.

36. Johnson, "The Tobacco Worker," 407.

37. D. S. Upchurch to E. Lewis Evans, 22 March, 31 March, 7 April, 21 April, 5 May 1934, box 61, ser. 2, TWIUA.

38. D. S. Upchurch to E. Lewis Evans, 5 May, 11 May 1934, E. Lewis Evans to D. S. Upchurch, 23 May, 6 June 1934, Upchurch to Evans, 25 May, 8 June 1934, box 61, ser. 2, TWIUA.

39. H. A. McCrimmons to E. Lewis Evans, 28 January, 6 February 1935, box 42, ser. 2, TWIUA.

40. E. Lewis Evans to W. B. Culbreth, 6 June 1934, box 7, ser. 3, TWIUA.

41. E. Lewis Evans to D. S. Upchurch, 22 January 1934, box 42, TWIUA.

42. D. S. Upchurch to E. Lewis Evans, 21 July 1934, box 42, TWIUA.

43. Walker, "Changes in Race Accommodation," 199.

44. *Durham Morning Herald*, 1, 8 September 1934.

45. Johnson, "The Tobacco Worker," 414.

46. Ibid., 411–14.

47. Wilhelmina Jackson, "Memo-on-Winston Salem," folder 4, box 26, RBP.

48. H. A. McCrimmons to E. Lewis Evans, 26 March 1935, J. T. Newson and Arthur Stanley to E. Lewis Evans, n.d., ca. 1935, box 19, ser. 3, TWIUA.

49. E. Lewis Evans to C. V. Weaver, 2 June 1936, box 62, TWIUA.

50. H. A. McCrimmons to E. Lewis Evans, 23 February 1935, Daisy E. Jones to E. Lewis Evans, 10 October 1938, TWIUA; Lucas interview.

51. Radford G. Powell to E. Lewis Evans, n.d., ca. 1936, box 20, TWIUA.

52. R. G. Powell to E. Lewis Evans, 1 May 1937, 22 May, 6 June, 20 June, 11 September 1937, box 20, TWIUA.

53. Pearson interview; Lucas interview; Parker interview.

54. C. C. Spaulding, "For Release," February 1938, folder 2, box 1, CCSP.

55. Lucas interview; Turner interview.

56. Parker interview.

57. Pearson interview.

58. *Durham Morning Herald*, 28 May 1933, 29 May 1938.

59. Ibid.

60. *Durham Morning Herald*, 1 April 1932, 12 April 1933, 28 May 1938; Arthur Vance Cole to Charles D. Wildes, 31 May 1935, Minute Books, Durham County Republican Executive Committee, Campaign 1936, 4 March 1936, AVCP.

61. Walker, "Changes in Race Accommodation," 191–21.

62. Ibid., 193.

63. Robert R. Moton speech at the National Negro Business League Annual Meeting, Durham, 1933, reprinted in *Atlanta World*, 3 September 1933, reel 3, *NNBLR*.

Chapter Nine

1. McNeil, *Groundwork*, 133; Murray interview.
2. *Durham Morning Herald*, 14 February 1933.
3. Ibid., 21, 24 March 1933.
4. Kluger, *Simple Justice*, 154–58; Martin, *Brown v. Board of Education*, 11–14.
5. *Durham Morning Herald*, 22, 24, 25, 26 March 1933.
6. Pearson interview; Kluger, *Simple Justice*, 157.
7. Roy Wilkins to C. C. Spaulding, 18 September 1933, and George E. Nightengale to Walter F. White, 17 November 1933, Select Branch Files, box 146, North Carolina Conference, group 1, pt. 12, ser. A, *NAACPP*, 1912–33, reel 17.
8. Pearson interview.
9. George Streator to Walter White, n.d., ca. 1933, Select Branch Files, *NAACPP*, reel 17.
10. Taylor, in *North Carolina Teachers Record* (October 1932), reprinted in *Crisis* 40 (December 1933): 374–75.
11. Streator, "The Colored South Speaks for Itself," 374, clipping, and Miller, Nightengale, and Jones, "Negro Teachers' Salaries," 17 October 1933, Select Branch Files, *NAACPP*, reel 17.
12. Faulk interview.
13. Ibid.; Miller, Nightengale, and Jones, "Negro Teachers' Salaries," 17 October 1933, Select Branch Files, *NAACPP*, reel 17.
14. Lemert, "Durham, North Carolina: An Economic Survey," 1:8.
15. George W. Cox to Walter F. White, 10 October 1933, Branch Files, *NAACPP*; Pearson interview.
16. Miller, Nightengale, and Jones, "Negro Teachers' Salaries," 17 October 1933, Select Branch Files, *NAACPP*, reel 17; *Norfolk Journal and Guide*, 9 September 1933.
17. Pearson interview.
18. Rather, their younger assistants, William J. Kennedy Jr. and George W. Cox at the Mutual and James T. Taylor at North Carolina College, negotiated with Walter White to move the rally to Raleigh. George W. Cox to Walter F. White, 10 October 1933, Branch Files, *NAACPP*, reel 17; Pearson interview.
19. Streator, "The Colored South Speaks for Itself."
20. Walter White to George Nightengale, 30 October 1933, North Carolina Conference Files, *NAACPP*, reel 18.
21. Daisy E. Lampkin to Walter F. White, 27 November 1933, pt. 12, North Carolina Conference Files, *NAACPP*, reel 18.
22. W. J. Trent to Walter F. White, 17 November 1933, George Nightengale to Walter F. White, 17 November 1933, North Carolina Conference Files, *NAACPP*, reel 18; "National Negro Organization Feels It Must Go to Court over Negro Teachers' Salaries," *Greensboro Daily News*, 31 October 1933, clipping, and " 'Boogey Man' Cry by North Carolina Amuses NAACP," press release, 10 November 1933, North Carolina Conference Files, *NAACPP*, reel 18; *Norfolk Jour-*

nal and Guide, 17 November 1933; Daisy Lampkin to M. Hugh Thompson, 6 January 1934, Membership Lists, 15 January 1934, Durham Branch Files, pt. 12, *NAACPP*, reel 18; Daisy E. Lampkin to Walter F. White, 27 November 1933, North Carolina Conference Files, *NAACPP*, reel 18.

23. Streator, "The Colored South Speaks for Itself"; Taylor, quoted in *North Carolina Teachers Record* (October 1932).

24. W. J. Trent to Walter F. White, 17 November 1933, George Nightengale to Walter F. White, 17 November 1933, North Carolina Conference Files, *NAACPP*, reel 18; "National Negro Organization Feels It Must Go to Court over Negro Teachers' Salaries," 31 October 1933, *Greensboro Daily News*, clipping; "'Boogey Man' Cry by North Carolina Amuses NAACP," press release, 10 November 1933, North Carolina Conference Files, *NAACPP*, reel 18; *Norfolk Journal and Guide*, 17 November 1933; Daisy Lampkin to M. Hugh Thompson, 6 January 1934, Membership Lists, 15 January 1934, Durham Branch Files, pt. 12, *NAACPP*, reel 18.

25. Nightengale to White, 17 November 1933, North Carolina Conference Files, *NAACPP*.

26. W. J. Trent to Walter F. White, 17 November 1933, George Nightengale to White, 17 November 1933, White to Nightengale, 22 November 1933, North Carolina Conference Files, *NAACPP*, reel 18.

27. W. J. Trent to Walter F. White, 17 November 1933, George Nightengale to White, 17 November 1933, White to Nightengale, 22 November 1933, "North Carolina Factions Uniting behind Program," typescript copy of an article for a High Point newspaper, 24 November 1933 [George Nightengale to Walter White], North Carolina Conference Files, *NAACPP*, reel 18.

28. "'Boogey Man' Cry by North Carolina Amuses NAACP," press release, 10 November [1933], North Carolina State Conference Files, *NAACPP*, reel 18.

29. *Rocky Mount Evening Telegram*, 9 November 1933, typescript reproduction, addendum to letter, Nightengale to White, n.d., ca. 11 November 1933, North Carolina Conference Files, *NAACPP*, reel 18.

30. Pearson interview.

31. Ibid.; Rivera interview; Edmonds, *The Negro and Fusion Politics*, 168–69. See also Cecelski and Tyson, *Democracy Betrayed*.

32. Pearson interview.

33. Walker, "Changes in Race Accommodation," 178.

34. *Durham Carolina Times*, 7 November 1929, clipping, WJKP.

35. Smith, *The New Deal in the Urban South*; Ferguson, *Black Politics in New Deal Atlanta*.

36. Federal Emergency Administration of Public Works, Press Section, 18 February 1937, group 1, box 201, pt. 3A, Campaign for Educational Equality, Legal Department Central Office Records, 1913–50, *NAACPP*.

37. Membership Lists, 15 January 1934, Durham Branch Files, pt. 12, *NAACPP*, reel 18.

38. Membership Lists, 1919–40, Durham Branch Files, pt. 12, *NAACPP*, reel 18; William J. Kennedy Jr. to Professor James Taylor, 8 September 1931, folder 7, box 9, WJKP.
39. William J. Kennedy to James T. Taylor, 8 September 1931, folder 226, WJKP; Walter F. White to C. C. Spaulding, 28 May 1935, folder 51, WJKP.
40. North Carolina Teachers Association publications, passim.
41. L. E. Austin to Walter White, 4 March 1937, Durham Branch Files, pt. 12, *NAACPP*, reel 18.
42. Thurgood Marshall to L. E. Austin, 6 March 1937, ibid.
43. Thurgood Marshall to L. E. Austin, 19 March 1937, Charles Hamilton Houston to L. E. Austin, 29 April 1937, ibid.
44. Charles Hamilton Houston to Dr. J. M. Mills, 29 April 1937, CHH [Charles Hamilton Houston] to M. Hugh Thompson, 29 April 1937, ibid.
45. M. Hugh Thompson to Charles Hamilton Houston, 3 May 1937, ibid.
46. Charles Hamilton Houston to M. Hugh Thompson, 4 May 1937, ibid.
47. Curtis Cobb (Raleigh Branch) to Thurgood Marshall, 10 November 1937, ibid.
48. M. Hugh Thompson to Thurgood Marshall, 11 November 1937, ibid.
49. Lucas interview.
50. Turner interview; Pearson interview.
51. Minute Book, Durham Republican County Executive Committee, 4, 5 March 1936, box: "Pictures and Volumes," AVCP; "Cab Calloway and His Cotton Club Orchestra," ca. July 1930s, AVCP. This flyer, promoting a dance at the Bull Warehouse, contained ads for Republican candidates.
52. "Dean" to Walter White and Roy Wilkins, 8 December 1936, North Carolina Conference Files, *NAACPP*.
53. Madison Jones to Walter White, 10 December 1941, box A-583, group 2, National Staff Files, 1940–55, pt. 17, *NAACPP*.
54. Conrad O. Pearson to Charles H. Houston, 15 September 1936, *Washington Tribune*; 11 September 1936, reprint of story in the *Durham Carolina Times*, clippings, Select Branch Files, Durham, box G-147, ser. G, group 1, pt. 12, *NAACPP*.
55. Pearson to Houston, 15 September 1936, Durham Branch Files, pt. 12, reel 18, *NAACPP*.
56. Houston to Walter White and Roy Wilkins, memorandum, 1 October 1933, Durham Branch Files, *NAACPP*, reel 17.
57. Conrad O. Pearson to Charles H. Houston, 5 October 1936, Roy Wilkins to M. Hugh Thompson, 9 October 1936, Thompson to Roy Wilkins, 13 October 1936, Durham Branch Files, *NAACPP*, reel 17.
58. *Durham Carolina Times*, 8 January 1938.
59. Mother to Lenie, 11 June 1940, folder 257, box 10, PMP.
60. Pauli Murray to Thurgood Marshall, 13 April 1940, box 4, PMP.
61. Pauli Murray to Morris [Milgram], 9 April 1940, box 72, folder 1261, PMP.
62. Mother to Lenie, 18 May 1940, box 10, folder 257, PMP.

63. On the growth of the organizational activism of black women in Durham during the World War II era, see Greene, *Our Separate Ways*, 3–18.

64. "Basis for Interracial Cooperation and Development in the South." The Durham Manifesto has received only passing attention from historians. See Gavins, *Perils and Prospects of Southern Black Leadership*, 120–25; Crow et al., *A History of African Americans in North Carolina*, 150–52; Sullivan, *Days of Hope*, 165–67; Hall, *Revolt against Chivalry*, 258–59.

65. Murray, *Proud Shoes*, xiii–xv.

66. Murray, "The Liberation of Black Women," 186.

67. Pauline Fitzgerald Dame and Sarah A. Fitzgerald Small, "Role of Negro Teachers," editorial, *New York Times*, 30 May 1954.

68. Murray interview.

Conclusion

1. "Durham, North Carolina," promotional brochure, 1937, folder 191, WJKP.

2. Frazier, "Durham: The Capital of the Black Middle Class," 333–41; Holsey, "Pearson — The Brown Duke of Durham," 116–17; Weare, *Black Business in the New South*, 43–45; Washington, "Durham, North Carolina, a City of Negro Enterprise," 642–50; Du Bois, "The Upbuilding of Black Durham," 333–38; *Durham Morning Herald*, n.d., ca. 1920, cited in Boyd, *The Story of Durham*, 279.

3. See, for example, Will Alexander to C. C. Spaulding, 14 March 1928, Membership Lists, and other correspondence, folder 1, box 1, NCCICP.

4. "National Negro Organization Feels It Must Go to Court over Negro Teachers' Salaries," 31 October 1933, *Greensboro Daily News*, clipping; " 'Boogey Man' Cry by North Carolina Amuses NAACP," press release, 10 November 1933, North Carolina Conference Files, *NAACPP*, reel 18; *Norfolk Journal and Guide*, 17 November 1933; Daisy Lampkin to M. Hugh Thompson, 6 January 1934, Membership Lists, 15 January 1934, Durham Branch Files, pt. 12, *NAACPP*, reel 18.

5. Miller interview; Miller signed up workers for a TWIU local and was elected shop steward at Liggett and Myers. Radford G. Powell to E. Lewis Evans, folder: "Local 192," box 20, and Arthur Stanley to E. Lewis Evans, 13 November 1937, folder: "Local 204," box 27, TWIUA.

6. Dr. James E. Shepard, "A Message from Our President," *North Carolina Teachers Record* 9 (March 1938): 3.

7. Meeting with members of the Durham Committee on Negro Affairs, 24 October 1939, quoted in "Programs, Ideologies, Tactics, and Achievements for Negro Betterment and Interracial Organizations," 559, *Carnegie-Myrdal Study of the Negro in America*, reel 2.

8. Membership Lists, 1919–40, Durham Branch Files, pt. 12, *NAACPP*, reel 18; William J. Kennedy Jr. to Professor James Taylor, 8 September 1931, folder 7, box 9, WJKP.

9. Pearson interview.

10. Parker interview.
11. George Streator to Walter White, n.d., ca. 1933, Select Branch Files, Durham, pt. 12, *NAACPP*, reel 18.
12. Bunche, "Programs, Ideologies, Achievements for Negro Betterment and Interracial Organizations," "A Brief and Tentative Analysis of Negro Leadership," and "The Political Status of the Negro," all in *Carnegie-Myrdal Study of the Negro in America*, reel 2. Durham's black leadership, policy, and politics were of interest to a number of scholars. See Bunche, *The Political Status of the Negro*; Keech, *The Impact of Negro Voting*; Ladd, *Negro Political Leadership*; and Burgess, *Negro Political Leadership in a Southern City*.
13. Lucas interview; Turner interview.
14. *Durham Carolina Times*, 8 January 1938.
15. Turner interview.
16. The North Carolina Teachers Association had taken up the battle to equalize salaries in the state before the NAACP initiative began but put its effort into the NAACP program while continuing its own. See "Report of Committee on Teachers' Salaries," *North Carolina Teachers Record* 1 (March 1930): 8; Taylor, "Inequalities in Educational Opportunity," *North Carolina Teachers Record* 4 (October 1933): 62; and Harris, "Problems in the Education of Negroes: A Review of the Report of the Governor's Commission for the Study of Problems in the Education of Negroes in North Carolina," *North Carolina Teachers Record* 6 (October 1935): 61–71.
17. Greene, "Our Separate Ways" (dissertation), especially 1–49, on the extensive array of women's and female-dominated organizations evident in Durham in the 1940s and 1950s. See also Greene, *Our Separate Ways*, 7–32.
18. Greene, *Our Separate Ways*, 7–32.
19. *Durham Morning Herald*, 22 June 1941.
20. Daniel E. Byrd to Glouster B. Current, "Activity Report," Durham, 8–9 August 1949, National Staff Files, 1940–55, pt. 17, *NAACPP*, reel 7.
21. Ibid.

Epilogue

1. Pauline F. Dame, "Autobiography of My Life," typescript, folder 273, box 11, PMP.
2. Pauline Fitzgerald Dame and Sallie Fitzgerald Small, "Role of Negro Teachers," Letter to the Editor, *New York Times*, 30 May 1954, clipping, folder 266, box 11, PMP.
3. Ibid.

Bibliography

Manuscript Collections

Cambridge, Mass.
  Arthur and Elizabeth Schlesinger Library on the History of Women in America,
    Radcliffe Institute for Advanced Study, Harvard University
      Pauli Murray Papers
Chapel Hill, N.C.
  Southern Historical Collection, Manuscripts Department, Wilson Library,
    University of North Carolina
      Marion Butler Papers
      William Jesse Kennedy Jr. Papers
      North Carolina Commission on Interracial Cooperation Papers
      R. B. Russell Papers
College Park, Md.
  Special Collections, University of Maryland Libraries
      Archives of the Tobacco Workers' International Union
Durham, N.C.
  Julia Lucas Papers, privately held by Julia Lucas
  Johnnie Blount McLester Papers, privately held
  North Carolina Center for the Study of Black History, Hayti Heritage Center,
    North Carolina Central University
      William J. Kennedy Jr. Papers
  North Carolina Collection, Durham County Library
      Durham Historic Photographic Archives
  Rare Book, Manuscript, and Special Collections Library, Duke University
      Arthur Vance Cole Papers
      Mary O. Cowper Papers
      James Buchanan Duke Papers
      Washington Duke Papers
      W. Duke & Sons Tobacco Collection
      Durham Chamber of Commerce Papers
      Durham Community Chest Minutes
      Durham YWCA Papers
      Howerton Family Papers
      Charles N. Hunter Papers
      North Carolina Counties Collection: Durham County

W. K. Parrish Papers
William G. Pearson Papers
Fannie Rosser Papers
Clydie Fullwood Scarborough Papers
Southgate-Jones Family Papers
Asa T. Spaulding Papers
Charles C. Spaulding Papers
Andre D. Vann Collection of Durham Memorabilia, privately held by Andre D.
    Vann
Volkamenia Club Records, privately held by Julia Lucas
Hyde Park, N.Y.
    Franklin Delano Roosevelt Presidential Library and Museum
        Harry L. Hopkins Collection
New York, N.Y.
    Schomburg Center for Research in Black Culture, New York Public Library
        Ralph Bunche Papers
        Robert C. Weaver Papers
Raleigh, N.C.
    North Carolina State Archives, Archives and Records Section, North Carolina
        Division of Historical Resources
        Equal Suffrage Amendment Collection
        Governors' Papers: Thomas W. Bickett
        Military Collection
        North Carolina Conference for Social Service Papers
        North Carolina State Board of Charities and Public Welfare Records, Social
            Services Record Group, Division of Work among Negroes
        North Carolina State Department of Public Instruction Records, Division of
            Negro Education
        Gertrude Weil Papers
Washington, D.C.
    Mary McLeod Bethune Archives, National Council of Negro Women Office
        Papers of the National Association of Colored Women
    Moorland-Spingarn Research Center, Howard University
        John P. Davis Papers
        E. Franklin Frazier Papers
        Pauli Murray Papers
        Asa T. Spaulding Papers
        Edward E. Strong Papers
    National Archives
        Records of the National Recovery Administration, Division of Review, Indus-
            tries Studies Section (Record Group 9)
        Records of the Federal Works Agency, Works Projects Administration, Fed-
            eral Theater Project, 1935–39 (Record Group 69)

Records of the Women's Bureau, 1892–1971 (Record Group 86)
Records of the Bureau of Refugees, Freedmen, and Abandoned Lands (Record Group 105)

Microfilm Sources

Black Workers in the Era of the Great Migration, 1916–1925. Frederick, Md.: University Publications of America, 1985.

Carnegie-Myrdal Study of the Negro in America. Ann Arbor, Mich.: Microfilm International, 1972.

Charlotte Hawkins Brown Papers. Cambridge, Mass.: Schlesinger Library, Radcliffe College, 1992.

Congress of Industrial Organizations Papers of John L. Lewis. Frederick, Md.: University Publications of America, 1988.

General Education Board Archives, Series I, Appropriations, Early South Projects. New York: Rockefeller University; Wilmington, Del.: Scholarly Resources, 1993.

Hampton University Peabody Newspaper Clipping File. Alexandria, Va.: Chadwick-Healey, 1982.

League of Women Voters Papers, 1918–1974. Frederick, Md.: University Publications of America, 1985.

New Deal Agencies and Black America. Frederick, Md.: University Publications of America, 1984.

Papers of the NAACP. Frederick, Md.: University Publications of America, 1986–.

Papers of W. E. B. Du Bois. Sanford, N.C.: Microfilming Corporation of America, 1980.

Population Schedules of the Tenth Census of the United States, 1880, Orange County, Durham Township. Soundex series T-9, reels 975 and 976, National Archives.

Records of the National Association of Colored Women's Clubs, 1895–1992. Bethesda, Md.: University Publications of America, 1993.

Records of the National Negro Business League. Bethesda, Md.: University Publications of America, 1994.

Records of the National YWCA. New York: National Offices of the YWCA, 1976.

Samuel Gompers and the American Federation of Labor. Sanford, N.C.: Microfilming Corporation of America, 1983.

Tuskegee Institute News Clipping File. Tuskegee Institute, Ala.: Division of Behavioral Science Research, Carver Research Foundation, Tuskegee Institute, 1976.

Electronic Sources

Born in Slavery: Slave Narratives from the Federal Writers' Project, 1936–1938. North Carolina Narratives, vol. 11. Washington, D.C.: Library of Congress, American Memory. <http://memory.loc.gov/ammem/snhtml/snhome.html> (22 January 2006).

Documenting the American South. University Library, University of North Carolina at Chapel Hill. <http://docsouth.unc.edu> (20 January 2006).

Freedmen's Bureau Online, Bureau of Refugees, Freedmen, and Abandoned Lands. <http://www.freedmensbureau.com>.
Wilmington Race Riot Commission. *Draft Report on the Wilmington Riot, 15 December 2005*. Raleigh: N.C. Department of Cultural Resources, Office of Archives and History, 2005. *1898 Wilmington Race Riot, Final Report, 31 May 2006*. Raleigh: N.C. Department of Cultural Resources, Office of Archives and History, 2006. <http://www.ah.dcr.state.nc.us/1898-wrrc> (20 January 2006).

Interviews

Behind the Veil: Documenting African-American Life in the Jim Crow South Collection, Center for Documentary Studies, Rare Book, Manuscript, and Special Collections Library, Duke University, Durham, N.C.
Anonymous interview, 15 June 1994.
Garrett Sr., Dr. York D. Interview by Kara Miles, 3 June 1993.
Lucas, Julia. Interview by Leslie Brown, 21 September 1995.
Lyons, Theresa Jan Cameron. Interview by Leslie Brown, 16 August 1995.
Page, Mildred Oakley. Interview by Doris Dixon, 1 June 1995.
Parker, Florida Fisher. Interview by Tywanna Whorley, 10 August 1994.
Rivera, Alex. Interview by Mary Herbert and Felicia Woods, 2 June 1995.
Scarborough, George. Interview by Chris Stewart. May 1993.
Steele, Dorothy Fletcher. Interview by Leslie Brown, 15 June 1993.
Thorpe, Amelia Pride. Interview by Leslie Brown, 27 October 1995.
Watts, Dr. Charles. Interview by Delia Gamble, 25 June 1995.
Black Women Oral History Project, vol. 2, edited by Ruth Edmonds Hill (Westport, Conn.: Meckler, 1991), in Schlesinger Library, Radcliffe Institute, Cambridge, Mass.
Alexander, Sadie T. Mossell
Lyndon Baines Johnson Oral History Project, Lyndon Baines Johnson Library and Museum, Austin, Tex.
Weaver, Robert C. (transcript in Robert C. Weaver Papers, Schomburg Center for Research in Black Culture, New York Public Library, New York, N.Y.)
North Carolina Center for the Study of Black History, Hayti Heritage Center, North Carolina Central University, Durham
Davis, Rev. Julius, Jr. Interview by Dorothy Jones, n.d., ca. 1993.
Goodwin, Margaret Kennedy. Interview by Doris Terry Williams, n.d., ca. 1992.
Thorpe, Amelia Pride. Interview by Dorothy Jones, n.d., ca. 1992.
Southern Oral History Program, Southern Historical Collection, Manuscripts Department, Wilson Library, University of North Carolina at Chapel Hill
Bailey, Mary. Interview by Glenn Hinson, 26 January 1979. Interview H-189.
Barbee, Annie Mack. Interview by Beverly Jones, 28 May 1979. Interview H-190.
Brown, Maude. Interview by Beverly Jones, 3 August 1979. Interview H-192.
Caesar, Hallie. Interview by Glenn Hinson, 21 May 1979. Interview H-195.

Cheatham, Pansy M. Interview by Beverly Jones, 9 July 1979. Interview H-196.

Clark, Chester and Roxanna. Interview by Glenn Hinson, 5 January 1979. Interview H-197.

Mack, Charlie Neconda. Interview by Beverly Jones, 22 May 1979. Interview H-209.

Miller, Dora Scott. Interview by Beverly Jones, 6 June 1979. Interview H-211.

Mitchner, Reginald. Interview by Glenn Hinson, 15 November 1976. Interview H-212.

Murray, Pauli. Interview by Genna Rae MacNeil, 13 February 1976. Interview G-44.

Patterson, John. Interview by Glenn Hinson, 3 January 1979. Interview H-217.

Pearson, Conrad Odell. Interview by Walter B. Weare, 18 April 1979. Interviews H-218 and H-219.

Riley, Janie Cameron, and Lottie Phillips. Interview by George W. McDaniel, 6 June 1975. Interview B-64.

Scott, Blanche. Interview by Beverly Jones, 11 July 1979. Interview H-229.

Turner, Viola Richard. Interview by Walter B. Weare, 15 April 1979 and 17 April 1979. Interviews C-15 and C-16.

Interviews by author, in author's possession

Anonymous. 27 October 1995, Durham. Tape recording.

Clement, Josephine Dobbs. 15 February 1991, Durham. Tape recording.

Faulk, Addie Marie. 27 October 1995, Durham. Transcript.

Goodwin, Margaret Kennedy. 22 December 1995, Durham. Tape recording.

Harris, Mabel. 27 October 1995, Durham. Tape recording.

Ingram, Bernice. 14 November 1995, Durham. Tape recording.

Lanier, Thelma (Bailey). Summer and Fall 1995, Durham. Notes.

McLester, Johnnie Blount. 15 February 1991, Durham. Tape recording.

Watts, Constance Merrick Moore. 6 November 1995, Durham. Transcript.

Newspapers and Periodicals

Atlanta World
Charities and the Commons (New York)
Colored American (New York)
Crisis (New York)
Durham Carolina Times
Durham Morning Herald; *Durham Herald-Sun*
Durham Recorder
Durham Sun; *Durham Daily Sun*
Durham Tobacco Plant
Greensboro Daily News
Independent (New York)
Journal of Social Forces (Chapel Hill, N.C.)
New York Age
Norfolk Journal and Guide

North Carolina Teachers Record (Raleigh, N.C.)
Opportunity (New York)
Pittsburgh Courier
Southern Workman (Hampton, Va.)
Star of Zion (Salisbury and Charlotte, N.C.)
Voice of the Negro (Atlanta, Ga.)
Whetstone (Durham)

Pamphlets, Directories, and Miscellaneous Publications

Adams, Samuel L. *Directory of Greater Durham, North Carolina.* Vol. 5. Durham: Samuel L. Adams, 1902.

"A Basis for Interracial Cooperation and Development in the South: A Statement by Southern Negroes" (also known as Durham Manifesto or Durham Statement). Southern Conference on Race Relations, North Carolina College for Negroes, Durham, N.C., 20 October 1942.

Biennial Report of the North Carolina School for Negro Girls, Efland. 30 June 1932.

Biennial Report of the North Carolina State Board of Charities and Public Welfare. 1 July 1924–30 June 1926.

Branson, Levi, comp. *Directory of the Businesses and Citizens of Durham City for 1887.* Raleigh: Levi Branson, 1887.

Bulletin of the National Training School. 1920.

Centennial Year: Women's Baptist Home and Foreign Missionary Convention of North Carolina, 1884–1984.

Commencement Program, Durham State Normal School, 1924.

Duke Endowment. *Twelfth Annual Report of the Orphan Section, 1936.* Charlotte: Duke Endowment, 1937.

Durham Chamber of Commerce. *Durham: A Center of Industry and Education.* 1926.

——— . *Durham: Queen of the Golden Belt.* N.d., ca. 1895.

——— . *Map of East and West Durham, NC.* 1924.

Durham, N.C., City Directory, 1919–1920. N.p., 1920.

Fisher, Miles Mark. *Friends: A Pictorial History of Ten Years Pastorate (1933–1943).* Durham: White Rock Baptist Church, 1943.

Gray's New Map of Durham. 1881.

"Greater Durham in 1904–05: A City of Many Industries." 1905.

Hayden, Harry. *The Story of the Wilmington Rebellion.* 1936.

Hill Directory Company. *Durham, N.C., Directory, 1911–1912.* Durham and Richmond, Va.: Hill Directory Company, 1911.

——— . *Durham, N.C., Business Directory, 1915–16.* Richmond, Va.: Hill Directory Company, 1915.

——— . *Durham (N.C.) Directory, 1917.* Richmond, Va.: Hill Directory Company, 1917.

——— . *Hill's Durham Directory of Householders, Occupants of Office Buildings and Other Business Places.* Richmond, Va.: Hill Directory Company, 1936.

Hobson, E. C., and C. E. Hopkins. "A Report Concerning the Colored Women of the South." John F. Slater Fund Occasional Paper No. 9. Baltimore: Trustees of the John F. Slater Fund, 1896.

Jones, Beverly Washington. *The Stanford L. Warren Branch Library Celebrates Its 50th Anniversary at Historic Site (1940–1990).*

Jones, Beverly, and Claudia Eglehoff, eds. *Working in Tobacco: An Oral History of Durham's Tobacco Factory Workers.* Durham: History Department, North Carolina Central University, 1985.

Lincoln Hospital. *Bulletin of the School of Nursing,* 1931.

———. *Thirty-eighth Annual Report,* 1938.

Mangum, D. C. *Mangum's Directory of Durham and Suburbs.* Durham: Educator Company, 1897.

Manly, Alexander. "Mrs. Felton's Speech." *Wilmington Daily Record,* 18 August 1898, reprinted in Thomas Clawson, "Look at the Trio," *Wilmington Messenger,* 20 October 1898. Fragment, North Carolina Collection, University of North Carolina at Chapel Hill.

McLester, Johnnie Blount. *Brief History of the Woman's Auxiliary to the Lott-Carey Baptist Foreign Mission Convention.* N.p., n.d.

Milestones along the Color Line: A Souvenir of Durham, North Carolina, Showing the Progress of a Race. Durham: O. B. Quick, 1922.

North Carolina Mutual Life Insurance Company, Durham, North Carolina. November 1921.

Pearson, W. G., comp. *Rituals of the Lady Knights of King David.* Durham: Seeman Printery, 1920.

Proceedings of the Fortieth Annual Session of the Women's Home and Foreign Mission Convention of North Carolina, 1924.

Proceedings of the Forty-fourth Annual Session of the Women's Home and Foreign Mission Convention of North Carolina, 1928.

Ramsey, N. A. *Ramsey's Durham Directory for the Year 1892.* Durham: N. A. Ramsey, 1892.

Sanborn Fire Insurance Company. *Fire Insurance Maps of Durham (N.C.),* 1937.

Shepard, James E. "National Training School and Chautauqua for the Colored Race . . . Will You Not Help Us to Help Ourselves." N.d., ca. 1908.

———. "National Training School . . . No Particular Creed, but Open to All Faiths." N.d., ca. 1910.

Turner, E. F. *Turner's Durham City Directory, 1889–90.* Yonkers, N.Y.: E. F. Turner, 1890.

Twentieth Session of the Grand Supreme Chapter of the Eastern Star, North Carolina Jurisdiction, 1907.

Government Documents

Agricultural Experiment Station. *Rural-Urban Migration in North Carolina, 1920 to 1930.* Raleigh: North Carolina State College of Agriculture and Engineering, 1932.

Board of Public Charities (North Carolina). *Annual Reports of the (North Carolina) Board of Public Charities,* 1884–1925. Various publishers.

——. *Second Biennial Report of the State Training School for Negro Girls* (at Dobbs Farms). 30 June 1948.

Bureau of Labor and Printing/Labor Statistics. *Annual Reports of the Bureau of North Carolina Labor and Printing/Labor Statistics, 1876–1940.* Various publishers.

Byrne, Harriet A. *Child Labor in Representative Tobacco-Growing Areas.* Children's Bureau, U.S. Department of Labor, Bureau Publication No. 155. Washington, D.C.: Government Printing Office, 1926.

City and County of Durham. *Annual Report of the Department of Health, 1924.*

Department of Commerce, Bureau of the Census. *Thirteenth Census of the United States Taken in the Year 1910.* Vol. 3. Washington, D.C.: Government Printing Office, 1913.

——. *The Fourteenth Census of the U.S., 1919.* Vol. 8. Washington, D.C.: Government Printing Office, 1923.

——. *Fourteenth Census of the United States Taken in the Year 1920.* Vol. 3. Washington, D.C.: Government Printing Office, 1922.

——. *Fifteenth Census of the United States.* Vols. 3 and 4. Washington, D.C.: Government Printing Office, 1932.

——. *Sixteenth Census of the United States: 1940, Population.* Vol. 2. Washington, D.C.: Government Printing Office, 1943.

——. *Report of the Seventeenth Decennial Census of the United States, Census of the Population, 1950.* Washington, D.C.: Government Printing Office, 1952.

——. *U.S. Census of the Population: 1960.* Washington, D.C.: Government Printing Office: 1963.

——. *Final Report on Total and Partial Employment, 1937.* Vol. 3. Washington, D.C.: Government Printing Office, 1938.

——. *Historical Statistics of the United States, Colonial Times to 1970.* Vols. 1 and 2. Washington, D.C.: Government Printing Office, 1975.

——. *Negroes in the United States, 1920–32.* Washington, D.C.: Government Printing Office, 1935.

——. *Negro Population, 1790–1915.* Washington, D.C.: Government Printing Office, 1918.

——. *Stocks of Leaf Tobacco and the American Production, Import, Export, and Consumption of Tobacco and Tobacco Products.* Bulletin 151. Washington, D.C.: Government Printing Office, 1923.

Department of Commerce, Office of the National Recovery Administration, Division of Review. "The Tobacco Study." Typescript. Works Material Number 87, Industries Section, Tobacco Unit. March 1936.

Department of the Interior. *Manufactures of the United States in 1860, Compiled from Original Returns of the Eighth Census.* Washington, D.C.: Government Printing Office, 1865.

——. *Population of the United States in 1860, Compiled from the Original Returns of the Eighth Census.* Washington, D.C.: Government Printing Office, 1865.

——. *Statistics of Wealth of the United States.* Washington, D.C.: Government Printing Office, 1872.

Department of the Interior, Bureau of Education. *Survey of Negro Colleges and Universities.* Bulletin No. 7. Washington, D.C.: Government Printing Office, 1929. Reprint, New York: Negro Universities Press, 1969.

Department of the Interior, Census Office. *Ninth Census of the United States.* Washington, D.C.: Government Printing Office, 1873.

——. *Tenth Census of the United States: Statistics of the Population of the United States.* Vol. 2. Washington, D.C.: Government Printing Office, 1883.

——. *Tenth Census of the United States, Compendium.* Vol. 1. Washington, D.C.: Government Printing Office, 1883.

——. *Compendium of the Eleventh Census: 1890.* Washington, D.C.: Government Printing Office, 1895.

——. *Eleventh Census of the United States: 1890.* Washington, D.C.: Government Printing Office, 1895.

——. *Report on the Population of the United States at the Eleventh Census: 1890.* Washington, D.C.: Government Printing Office, 1897.

——. *Twelfth Census of the United States, Taken in the Year 1900.* Washington, D.C.: Government Printing Office, 1935.

——. *Twelfth Census of the United States: 1900, Special Reports.* Washington, D.C.: Government Printing Office, 1906.

Department of Labor, Children's Bureau. *The Promotion of the Welfare and Hygiene of Maternity and Infancy.* Bureau Publication No. 156. Washington, D.C.: Government Printing Office, 1926.

Department of Labor, Women's Bureau. *Negro Women in Industry.* Washington, D.C.: Government Printing Office, 1922.

Department of Public Health. *Mortality among Negroes in the United States.* Public Health Bulletin No. 174. Washington, D.C.: Government Printing Office, 1938.

Durham City Schools. *Annual Report of the Superintendent of Public Instruction, 1901–1916.* Various publishers.

——. *Annual Report of the Superintendent: Rules and Regulations of the Board of Education, 1915.*

——. *Directory of Officers and Teachers.* Various publishers, 1921–22, 1926–28, 1938–39.

Durham County. *Annual Report of the Public Schools of Durham County Schools, 1902–1917.* Various publishers.

Haynes, George E. *The Negro at Work during the World War and during Reconstruction: Statistics, Problems, and Policies Relating to the Greater Inclusion of Negro Wage Earners in American Industry and Agriculture.* Division of Negro Economics, Second Study on Negro Labor. Washington, D.C.: Government Printing Office, 1921. Reprint, New York: Negro Universities Press, 1969.

Hill, Joseph A. *Women in Gainful Occupations, 1870 to 1820.* Washington, D.C.: Government Printing Office, 1929.

Johnson, Charles S. "The Tobacco Worker: A Study of Tobacco Workers and Their Families." Typescript. Industries Section, Division of Review, 1935. Consolidated Reference Materials, Records of the National Recovery Administration, Record Group 69.

Jones, Thomas Jesse. *Negro Education: A Study of the Private and Higher Schools for Colored People in the United States.* Department of the Interior, Bureau of Education, Bulletin, 1916, No. 38–39. Prepared in cooperation with the Phelps-Stokes Fund. Washington, D.C.: Government Printing Office, 1917. Reprint, New York: Negro Universities Press, 1969.

Leavell, R. H., and J. H. Dillard. *Negro Migration in 1916–1917.* Department of Labor, Division of Negro Economics. Washington, D.C.: Government Printing Office, 1919.

Manning, Caroline, and Harriet Byrne. *The Effects on Women of Changing Conditions in the Cigar and Cigarette Industries.* Bulletin of the Women's Bureau No. 100. Department of Labor, Women's Bureau. Washington, D.C.: Government Printing Office, 1932.

Price, Daniel O. *Changing Characteristics of the Negro Population: A 1960 Census Monograph.* Washington, D.C.: Government Printing Office, 1969.

Private Laws of North Carolina. 1899.

Reid, Ira De A.(Department of the Interior). *The Urban Negro Worker in the United States, 1935–1936.* Reprint, New York: Negro Universities Press, 1970.

Thompson, Warren S. *Ratio of Children to Women, 1920: Census Monograph XI.* Washington, D.C.: Government Printing Office, 1931.

Upchurch, W. M., and M. B. Fowler. *Durham County Economic and Social: A Laboratory Study in the University of North Carolina Department of Rural Economics and Sociology.* Chapel Hill: University of North Carolina Department of Rural Economics and Sociology, n.d., ca. 1927.

U.S. Congress. House. *To Create an Industrial Commission on Negro Affairs.* 74th Cong., 1st sess., 18 June 1935.

U.S. Congress. Senate. Committee on Finance. *Investigation of the National Recovery Administration.* 74th Cong., 1st sess., 7 March 1935.

Williams, W. T. B. "The Negro Exodus from the South." In U.S. Department of Labor, *Negro Migration, 1916–1917.* Washington, D.C.: Government Printing Office, 1919.

Woodbury, Robert Morse. *Maternal Mortality: The Risk of Death in Childbirth and from All Diseases Caused by Pregnancy and Confinement.* Children's Bureau, U.S. Department of Labor, Bureau Publication No. 158. Washington, D.C.: Government Printing Office, 1926.

Yancy, Henry A. "Planning for the Future: A Capital Improvement Program of Durham, North Carolina, Prepared for the City Council and Citizens, April 1943." Exhibit 7, Growth of the City Area of Durham.

Books, Articles, and Films

Allen, James. *Without Sanctuary: Lynching Photography in America*. Santa Fe, N.M.: Twin Palms Publishers, 2000.

Allen, Robert L. *Black Awakening in Capitalist America*. New York: Anchor Books, 1970.

Anderson, Eric. "The Populists and Capitalist America: The Case of Edgecombe County, North Carolina." In *Race, Class, and Politics in Southern History: Essays in Honor of Robert F. Durden*, edited by Jeffery J. Crow, Paul D. Escott, and Charles L. Flynn Jr., 106–25. Baton Rouge: Louisiana State University Press, 1989.

———. *Race and Politics in North Carolina, 1872–1901: The Black Second*. Baton Rouge: Louisiana State University Press, 1981.

Anderson, James D. *The Education of Blacks in the South, 1860–1935*. Chapel Hill: University of North Carolina Press, 1988.

Anderson, Jean Bradley. *Durham County: A History of Durham County, North Carolina*. Durham: Duke University Press and the Historic Preservation Society of Durham, 1990.

Andrews, R. McCants. *John Merrick: A Biographical Sketch*. Durham: Seeman's Printery, 1920.

Atwan, Robert, Donald McQuade, and John W. Wright. *Edsels, Luckies, and Frigidaires: Advertising the American Way*. New York: Dell, 1979.

Ayers, Edward L. *The Promise of the New South: Life after Reconstruction*. New York: Oxford University Press, 1992.

Badger, Anthony J. *Prosperity Road: The New Deal, Tobacco, and North Carolina*. Chapel Hill: University of North Carolina Press, 1980.

Bailey, Snow, ed. *Dedication of the Ediam D. Markham Memorial Building and Parsonage*. Durham: St. Joseph AME Zion Church, 1953.

Barber, J. Max. "The Aggressiveness of Jim-Crowism." *Voice of the Negro*, 1 (June 1904): 216–217.

Bederman, Gail. *Manliness and Civilization: A Cultural History of Gender and Race in the United States, 1890–1917*. Chicago: University of Chicago Press, 1995.

Berry, Mary Frances. *The Politics of Parenthood: Child Care, Women's Rights, and the Myth of the Good Mother*. New York: Penguin Books, 1993.

Boyd, William K. *The Story of Durham: City of the New South*. Durham: Duke University Press, 1927.

Brant, Lillian. "The Make-Up of Negro City Groups." *Charities* 18 (7 October 1905): 7–11.

Brawley, Benjamin. *Negro Builders and Heroes*. Chapel Hill: University of North Carolina Press, 1937.

Breen, William J. "Black Women and the Great War: Mobilization and Reform in the South." *Journal of Southern History* 44 (August 1978): 421–40.

Brinton, Hugh Penn. "Negroes Who Run Afoul of the Law." *Social Forces* 11 (Fall 1935): 96–101.

Brown, Elsa Barkley. "Negotiating and Transforming Public Space: African American Political Life in the Transition from Slavery to Freedom." *Public Culture* 7 (Fall 1994): 107–46.

———. "To Catch the Vision of Freedom: Reconstructing Southern Black Women's Political History, 1865–1880." In *African American Women and the Vote*, edited by Ann Gordon et al., 134–55. Amherst: University of Massachusetts Press, 1996.

———. "What Has Happened Here": The Politics of Difference in Women's History and Feminist Politics." *Feminist Studies* 18, no. 2 (1992): 295–312.

———. "Womanist Consciousness: Maggie Lena Walker and the Independent Order of St. Luke." *Signs* 14 (Spring 1989): 610–33.

Brown, Leslie. " 'The Sisters and Mothers Are Called to the City': African American Women and an Even Greater Migration." In *Stepping Forward: Black Women in Africa and the Americas*, edited by Catherine Higgs, Barbara A. Moss, and Earline Rae Ferguson, 129–40. Athens: Ohio University Press, 2002.

Brown, Leslie, and Anne M. Valk. " 'Our Territory': Race, Place, Gender, Space, and African American Women in the Urban South." In *Her Past Around Us: Interpreting Sites for Women's History*, edited by Polly Welts Kaufman and Katharine T. Corbett, 207–34. Malabar, Fla.: Krieger, 2003.

Brownell, Blaine A., and David Goldfield, eds. *The City in Southern History: The Growth of Urban Civilization in the South*. Port Washington, N.Y.: Kennikat Press, 1977.

Bruce, Josephine D. "What Has Education Done for Colored Women?" *Voice of the Negro* 1 (July 1904): 294–98.

Brundage, W. Fitzhugh. *Lynching in the New South: Georgia and Virginia, 1880–1930*. Urbana: University of Illinois Press, 1993.

———. *Under Sentence of Death: Lynching in the South*. Chapel Hill: University of North Carolina Press, 1997.

Bueno, B., et al. *Coming Together: The Story of George Watts and Walltown Schools*. Durham, N.C.: Durham City Schools, 1989.

Bunche, Ralph J. *The Political Status of the Negro in the Age of F.D.R.* Edited by Dewey Grantham. Chicago: University of Chicago Press, 1973.

Burgess, Margaret Elaine. *Negro Political Leadership in a Southern City*. Chapel Hill: University of North Carolina Press, 1962.

Butler, John Sibley. *Entrepreneurship and Self-Help among Black Americans: A Reconsideration of Race and Economics*. Albany: State University of New York Press, 2005.

Bynum, Victoria E. *Unruly Women: The Politics of Social Control in the Old South*. Chapel Hill: University of North Carolina Press, 1992.

Carby, Hazel V. " 'It Jus' Be's Dat Way Sometime': The Sexual Politics of Women's Blues." *Radical America* 20 (1986): 9–22.

——. "Policing the Black Woman's Body in an Urban Context." *Critical Inquiry* 18 (Summer 1992): 738–57.

——. *Race Men*. Cambridge, Mass.: Harvard University Press, 1998.

——. *Reconstructing Womanhood: The Emergence of the Afro-American Woman Novelist*. New York: Oxford University Press, 1987.

Cecelski, David S., and Timothy B. Tyson. *Democracy Betrayed: The Wilmington Riot of 1898 and Its Legacy*. Chapel Hill: University of North Carolina Press, 1998.

Chafe, William H. *Civilities and Civil Rights: Greensboro, North Carolina, and the Black Struggle for Freedom*. New York: Oxford University Press, 1980.

——. "The Gods Bring Threads to Webs Begun." *Journal of American History* 86 (March 2000).

Chafe, William H., Raymond Gavins, and Robert Korstad, eds. *Remembering Jim Crow: African Americans Tell about Life in the Segregated South*. New York: New Press, 2001.

Cha-Jua, Sundiata Leita. *America's First Black Town: Brooklyn, Illinois, 1830–1929*. Urbana: University of Illinois Press, 2000.

Clark, Septima Poinsette. *Echo in My Soul*. New York: Dutton, 1962.

Clark-Lewis, Elizabeth. *Living In, Living Out: African American Women Domestics in Washington, 1910–1940*. Washington, D.C.: Smithsonian Institution Press, 1994.

Cohen, Lizabeth. *Making a New Deal: Industrial Workers in Chicago, 1919–1939*. New York: Cambridge University Press, 1990.

Cohen, William. *At Freedom's Edge: Black Mobility and the Southern White Quest for Racial Control, 1861–1915*. Baton Rouge: Louisiana State University Press, 1991.

Collins, Patricia Hill. *Black Feminist Thought: Knowledge, Consciousness, and the Politics of Empowerment*. Boston: Unwin Hyman, 1990.

Coon, Charles L. "The Beginning of the North Carolina City Schools, 1867–1887." *South Atlantic Quarterly* 12 (July 1913): 235–47.

Cooper, Anna Julia. *A Voice from the South*. Xenia, Ohio,: Aldine Print House, 1892. Reprint, edited with an introduction by Mary Helen Washington, New York: Oxford University Press, 1988.

Cott, Nancy. *The Grounding of Modern Feminism*. New Haven: Yale University Press, 1987.

Cox, Oliver Cromwell. *Caste, Class, and Race: A Study in Social Dynamics*. New York: Doubleday, 1948. Reprint, New York: Monthly Review Press, First Modern Reader Edition, 1970.

Cox, Reavis. *Competition in the American Tobacco Industry, 1911–1932*. New York: Columbia University Press, 1933. Reprint, New York: AMS Press, 1968.

Crow, Jeffrey J. "'Fusion, Confusion, and Negroism': Schisms among Negro Republicans in the North Carolina Election of 1896." *North Carolina Historical Review* 53 (October 1976): 364–84.

Crow, Jeffrey J., Paul D. Escott, and Flora J. Hatley. *A History of African Americans in North Carolina*. Raleigh: Division of Archives and History, Department of Cultural Resources, 1992.

Crow, Jeffrey J., Paul D. Escott, and Charles L. Flynn Jr., eds. *Race, Class, and Politics in Southern History: Essays in Honor of Robert F. Durden*. Baton Rouge: Louisiana State University Press, 1989.

Dailey, Jane. *Before Jim Crow: The Politics of Race in Postemancipation Virginia*. Chapel Hill: University of North Carolina Press, 2000.

Dailey, Jane, Glenda Elizabeth Gilmore, and Bryant Simon, eds. *Jumpin' Jim Crow: Southern Politics from Civil War to Civil Rights*. Princeton, N.J.: Princeton University Press, 2000.

Dancy, John C. *Sands against the Wind: The Memoirs of John C. Dancy*. Detroit: Wayne State University Press, 1966.

Daniel, Pete. *Breaking the Land: The Transformation of Cotton, Tobacco, and Rice Cultures since 1880*. Urbana: University of Illinois Press, 1985.

Davis, Allison B., Burleigh Gardner, and Mary R. Gardner. *Deep South: A Sociological Study of Caste and Class*. Chicago: University of Chicago Press, 1941.

Davis, Angela Y. *Blues Legacies and Black Feminism: Gertrude "Ma" Rainey, Bessie Smith, and Billie Holiday*. New York: Pantheon Press, 1998.

———. *Women, Race, and Class*. New York: Vintage Books, 1983.

Davis, Denoral. "Towards a Socio-Historical and Demographic Portrait of Twentieth Century African-Americans." In *Black Exodus: The Great Migration from the American South*, edited by Alferdteen Harrison, 1–19. Jackson: University Press of Mississippi, 1991.

Davis, George A., and O. Fred Donaldson. *Blacks in the United States: A Geographic Perspective*. Boston: Houghton Mifflin, 1975.

Demerath, Nicholas, and Harlan W. Gilmore. "The Ecology of Southern Cities." In *The Urban South*, edited by Rupert B. Vance, 135–64. Chapel Hill: University of North Carolina Press, 1954.

Deutsch, Sarah. *Women and the City: Gender, Space, and Power in Boston, 1870–1940*. New York: Oxford University Press, 2000.

Dill, Bonnie Thornton. "The Dialectics of Black Womanhood." *Signs* 4 (Spring 1979): 543–55.

Dowd, Jerome. "Negro Labor in Factories." *Southern Workman* 30 (November 1903): 588–90.

Doyle, Bertram Wilbur. *The Etiquette of Race Relations in the South: A Study in Social Control*. Chicago: University of Chicago Press, 1937. Reprint, Port Washington, N.Y.: Kennikat Press, 1968.

Du Bois, W. E. B. *Black Reconstruction in America*. Reprint, New York: Simon & Schuster, 1999.

———. *The College Bred Negro*. Atlanta University Publication No. 5. Atlanta: Atlanta University Press, 1900. Reprint, New York: Arno Press and *New York Times*, 1969.

———. *The Common School and the Negro American*. Atlanta University Publication No. 16. Atlanta: Atlanta University Press, 1912. Reprint, Arno Press and *New York Times*, 1969.

———. "The Damnation of Negro Women." Reprinted in *W. E. B. Du Bois: A Reader*, edited by David Levering Lewis, 309–10. New York: Henry Holt, 1995.

———. *Economic Cooperation among Negro Americans: Report of a Social Study Made by Atlanta University*. Atlanta: Atlanta University Press, 1907.

———. *The Gift of Black Folk*. Boston: Stratford Press, 1924.

———. *The Negro American Family*. Atlanta University Publication No. 13. Atlanta: Atlanta University Press, 1908. Reprint, New York: Arno Press and *New York Times*, 1969.

———. *The Negro Artisan*. Atlanta University Publication No. 7. Atlanta: Atlanta University Press, 1902. Reprint, New York: Arno Press and *New York Times*, 1969.

———. "The Servant in the South." *Crisis* 3 (April 1912): 245.

———. *Some Efforts of American Negroes for Their Own Social Betterment*. Atlanta University Publication No. 3. Atlanta: Atlanta University Press, 1898. Reprint, Arno Press and *New York Times*, 1969.

———. *The Souls of Black Folk*. Chicago: A. C. McClurg, 1903. Reprint, New York: Penguin, 1989.

———. "The Upbuilding of Black Durham: The Success of Negroes and Their Value to a Tolerant and Helpful Southern City." *World's Work* 3 (January 1912): 338–39.

Dula, W. C., and A. C. Simpson. *Durham and Her People: Combining History and Who's Who in Durham of 1949 and 1950*. Durham: Citizen's Press, 1951.

Dunbar, Paul Laurence. *The Complete Poems of Paul Laurence Dunbar*. New York: Dodd, Mead, 1905.

Durden, Robert F. *The Climax of Populism: The Election of 1896*. Lexington: University of Kentucky Press, 1978.

———. *The Dukes of Durham, 1865–1929*. Durham: Duke University Press, 1975.

Duster, Alfreda, ed. *Crusade against Justice: The Autobiography of Ida B. Wells*. Chicago: University of Chicago Press, 1970.

Edmonds, Helen G. *The Negro and Fusion Politics in North Carolina, 1894–1901*. Chapel Hill: University of North Carolina Press, 1951.

Edwards, Laura F. *Gendered Strife and Confusion: The Political Culture of Reconstruction*. Urbana: University of Illinois Press, 1997.

Ellis, Mark. " 'Closing Ranks' and 'Seeking Honors': W. E. B. Du Bois in World War I." *Journal of American History* 79 (June 1992): 96–114.

Escott, Paul D. *Many Excellent People: Power and Privilege in North Carolina, 1850–1900*. Chapel Hill: University of North Carolina Press, 1985.

———. *Slavery Remembered: A Record of Twentieth Century Slave Narratives*. Chapel Hill: University of North Carolina Press, 1979.

Fabre, Genevieve, and Robert O'Meally. "Introduction." In *Memory and History in African American Culture*, edited by Genevieve Fabre and Robert O'Meally, 3–17. New York: Oxford University Press, 1994.

Ferguson, Earline Rae. "African American Clubwomen and the Indianapolis NAACP, 1912–1914." In *Stepping Forward: Black Women in Africa and the Americas*, edited by

Catherine Higgs, Barbara A. Moss, and Earline Rae Ferguson, 73–85. Athens: Ohio University Press, 2002.

Ferguson, Karen. *Black Politics in New Deal Atlanta*. Chapel Hill: University of North Carolina Press, 2002.

Fields, Mamie Garvin, and Karen Fields. *Lemon Swamp and Other Places: A Carolina Memoir*. New York: Free Press, 1983.

Foner, Eric. *Reconstruction, America's Unfinished Journey*. New York: Harper and Row, 1988. Reprint, New York: Perennial Modern Classics, 2002.

——. *Story of American Freedom*. New York: W. W. Norton, 1998.

Foner, Philip S. *Organized Labor and the Black Worker, 1619–1974*. New York: International Publishers, 1974.

——. *Women and the American Labor Movement from Colonial Times to the Eve of World War I*. New York: Free Press, 1979.

Foner, Philip S., and Ronald L. Lewis, eds. *The Black Worker: A Documentary History from Colonial Times to the Present*. 8 vols. Philadelphia: Temple University Press, 1978.

Foxworth, Marilyn. *Aunt Jemima, Uncle Ben, and Rastus: Blacks in Advertising, Yesterday, Today, and Tomorrow*. Westport, Conn.: Greenwood Press, 1994.

Franklin, John Hope. *The Free Negro in North Carolina, 1790–1860*. Chapel Hill: University of North Carolina Press, 1943. Reprint, New York: W. W. Norton, 1971.

——. *Mirror to America: The Autobiography of John Hope Franklin*. New York: Farrar, Straus and Giroux, 2005.

Franklin, John Hope, and August Meier, eds. *Black Leaders of the Twentieth Century*. Urbana: University of Illinois Press, 1982.

Franklin, John Hope, and Albert A. Moss. *From Slavery to Freedom: A History of African Americans*. 8th ed. New York: Knopf, 2000.

Frazier, E. Franklin. "An Analysis of Statistics on Negro Illegitimacy in the United States." *Social Forces* 11 (December 1932): 249–57.

——. *Black Bourgeoisie*. New York: Free Press, 1957.

——. "Durham: The Capital of the Black Middle Class." In *The New Negro: An Interpretation*, edited by Alain Locke, 331–41. New York: Albert and Charles Boni, 1925. Reprint, New York: Antheneum/Macmillan, 1992.

——. "Family Disorganization among Negroes." *Opportunity* 9 (July 1931): 204–7.

——. *The Negro Family in the United States*. Rev. ed. New York: Citadel Press, 1948.

——. "Occupational Classes among Negroes in Cities." *American Journal of Sociology* 35 (March 1930): 718–38.

Gaines, Kevin K. *Uplifting the Race: Black Leadership, Politics, and Culture in the Twentieth Century*. Chapel Hill: University of North Carolina Press, 1996.

Gates, Henry Lewis, Jr. "The Face and Voice of Blackness." Introduction to Guy C. McElroy, *Facing History: The Black Image in American Art, 1710–1940*, iii–xx. New York: Bedford Arts Publishers, in association with the Corcoran Gallery of Art, 1993.

———. "The Trope of the New Negro and the Reconstruction of the Image of Black." *Representations* 24 (Fall 1988): 129–55.

Gatewood, Willard B. *Aristocrats of Color: The Black Elite, 1880–1920*. Bloomington: Indiana University Press, 1990.

Gavins, Raymond. *The Meaning of Freedom: A History of Black North Carolina, 1865–1965*. Chapel Hill: University of North Carolina Press, forthcoming.

———. "The Meaning of Freedom: Black North Carolina in the Nadir, 1880–1900." In *Race, Class, and Politics in Southern History: Essays in Honor of Robert F. Durden*, edited by Jeffrey J. Crow, Paul D. Escott, and Charles Flynn Jr., 175–215. Baton Rouge: Louisiana State University Press, 1989.

———. "The NAACP in North Carolina during the Age of Segregation." In *New Directions in Civil Rights Studies*, edited by Armstead L. Robinson and Patricia Sullivan, 105–25. Charlottesville: University Press of Virginia, 1991.

———. "North Carolina Black Folklore and Song in the Age of Segregation: Toward Another Meaning of Survival." *North Carolina Historical Review* 66 (October 1989): 412–41.

———. *The Perils and Prospects of Southern Black Leadership: Gordon Blaine Hancock, 1880–1960*. Durham: Duke University Press, 1993.

Giddings, Paula. *When and Where I Enter: The Impact of Black Women on Race and Sex in America*. New York: William Morrow, 1984.

Gilmore, Glenda Elizabeth. *Gender and Jim Crow: Women and the Politics of White Supremacy in North Carolina, 1896–1920*. Chapel Hill: University of North Carolina Press, 1996.

Glenn, Evelyn Nakano. *Unequal Freedom: How Race and Gender Shaped American Citizenship and Labor*. Cambridge, Mass.: Harvard University Press, 2004.

Glickman, Lawrence B. *A Living Wage: American Workers and the Making of Consumer Society*. Ithaca: Cornell University Press, 1997.

Goldin, Claudia. "Female Labor Force Participation: The Origin of Black and White Differences, 1870 and 1880." *Journal of Economic History* 37 (March 1977): 87–108.

Goodwyn, Lawrence. *Democratic Promise: The Populist Movement in America*. New York: Oxford University Press, 1976.

———. *The Populist Moment: A Short History of the Agrarian Revolt in America*. New York: Oxford University Press, 1978.

Gordon, Ann, et al., eds. *African American Women and the Vote*. Amherst: University of Massachusetts Press, 1996.

Gordon, Linda. *Pitied but Not Entitled: Single Mothers and the History of Welfare*. New York: Free Press, 1994.

Gover, Mary. "Trend of Mortality among Southern Negroes since 1920." *Journal of Negro Education* 6 (Summer 1937): 276–88.

Greene, Christina. *Our Separate Ways: Women and the Black Freedom Movement in Durham, North Carolina*. Chapel Hill: University of North Carolina Press, 2005.

Greene, Lorenzo, and Carter G. Woodson. *The Negro Wage Earner*. Washington, D.C.: Association for the Study of Negro Life and History, 1930.

Greenwood, Janette Thomas. *Bittersweet Legacy: The Black and White "Better Classes" in Charlotte, 1850–1910*. Chapel Hill: University of North Carolina Press, 1994.

Grossman, James R. *Land of Hope: Chicago, Black Southerners, and the Great Migration*. Chicago: University of Chicago Press, 1989.

Guldbrandsen, Thaddeus C. "Entrepreneurial Governance in the Transnational South: The Case of Durham, North Carolina." In *The American South in a Global World*, edited by James L. Peacock, Harry L. Watson, and Carrie R. Matthews, 83–98. Chapel Hill: University of North Carolina Press, 2005.

Gutman, Herbert G. *The Black Family in Slavery and Freedom, 1750–1925*. New York: Pantheon Books, 1976.

Guttentag, Marcia, and Paul F. Secord. *Too Many Women? The Sex Ratio Question*. Beverly Hills, Calif.: Sage Publications, 1983.

Guy-Sheftall, Beverly. *Daughters of Sorrow: Attitudes toward Black Women, 1880–1920*. Brooklyn, N.Y.: Carlson, 1990.

Hahn, Steven. *A Nation under Our Feet: Black Political Struggles in the Rural South from Slavery to the Great Migration*. Cambridge, Mass.: Belknap, Harvard University Press, 2003.

Haley, John H. *Charles N. Hunter and Race Relations in North Carolina*. Chapel Hill: University of North Carolina Press, 1987.

Hall, Jacquelyn Dowd. "Location, Location, Location." In *New Viewpoints in Women's History: Working Papers from the Schlesinger Library 50th Anniversary Conference*, edited by Susan Ware, 40–52. Cambridge, Mass.: Arthur and Elizabeth Schlesinger Library on the History of Women in America, 1994.

———. "The Long Civil Rights Movement and the Political Uses of the Past." *Journal of American History* 91 (March 2005).

———. " 'The Mind That Burns in Each Body': Women, Rape, and Sexual Violence." In *Powers of Desire: The Politics of Sexuality*, edited by Ann Snitow, Christine Stansell, and Sharon Thompson, 328–49. New York: Monthly Review Press, 1983.

———. *Revolt against Chivalry: Jessie Daniel Ames and the Women's Campaign against Lynching*. Rev. ed. New York: Columbia University Press, 1993.

Hall, Jacquelyn Dowd, James Leloudis, Robert Korstad, Mary Murphy, Lu Ann Jones, and Christopher B. Daley. *Like a Family: The Making of a Southern Cotton Mill World*. Chapel Hill: University of North Carolina Press, 1990.

Hamilton, C. Horace. "Recent Changes in the Social and Economic Status of North Carolina Farm Families." *American Sociological Review* 2 (October 1937): 786–87.

Harding, Vincent. *There Is a River: The Black Struggle for Freedom in America*. New York: Harcourt, Brace, Jovanovich, 1981.

Harlan, Louis R. *Booker T. Washington*. Vol. 2, *The Wizard of Tuskegee, 1901–1915*. New York: Oxford University Press, 1983.

———, ed. *The Booker T. Washington Papers*. 14 vols. Urbana: University of Illinois Press, 1972–89.

Harley, Sharon. "When Your Work Is Not Who You Are: The Development of

Working-Class Consciousness among African American Women." In *Gender, Class, Race, and Reform in the Progressive Era*, edited by Noralee Frankel and Nancy S. Dye, 42–55. Louisville: University of Kentucky Press, 1991.

———. "Working for Nothing but a Living." In *Sister Circle: Black Women and Work*, edited by Sharon Harley and Black Women and Work Collective, 48–66. New Brunswick, N.J.: Rutgers University Press, 2002.

Harley, Sharon, and Black Women and Work Collective, eds. *Sister Circle: Black Women and Work*. New Brunswick, N.J.: Rutgers University Press, 2002.

Harris, Joel Chandler, ed. *The Life of Henry W. Grady, Including His Writings and Speeches*. New York: Cassell, 1890.

Harris, Leslie M. *In the Shadow of Slavery: African Americans in New York City, 1626–1863*. Chicago: University of Chicago Press, 2003.

Harris, William H. *The Harder We Run: Black Workers since the Civil War*. New York: Oxford University Press, 1982.

Harrison, Mrs. T. B. "A School for Erring Boys — Why Not One for Girls?" *Social Service Quarterly* 2 (July–September 1915): 49–59.

Haynes, Elizabeth Ross. "Negroes in Domestic Service in the United States." *Journal of Negro History* 8 (October 1923): 384–442.

Haynes, George E. "Negro Migration: Its Effect on Family and Community Life in the North." *Opportunity* 2 (September 1924): 272–73.

Heberle, Rudolph. "The Mainsprings of Southern Urbanization." In *The New South*, edited by Rupert B. Vance and Nicholas Demerath, 6–24. Chapel Hill: University of North Carolina Press, 1954.

Henderson, Donald. "The Negro Migration of 1916–1918." *Journal of Negro History* 6 (October 1921): 383–499.

Henri, Florette. *Black Migration: Movement North, 1900–1920*. New York: Doubleday, 1975.

Hewitt, Nancy A. "Compounding Differences." *Feminist Studies* 18, no. 2 (1992): 313–26.

———. "In Pursuit of Power: The Political Economy of Women's Activism in Twentieth Century Tampa." In *Visible Women: New Essays on American Activism*, edited by Nancy A. Hewitt and Suzanne Lebsock, 199–222. Urbana: University of Illinois Press, 1993.

———. *Southern Discomfort: Women's Activism in Tampa, Florida, 1880s–1920s*. Urbana: University of Illinois Press, 2001.

Higginbotham, A. Leon. *Shades of Freedom: Racial Politics and Presumptions of the American Legal Process*. New York: Oxford University Press, 1996.

Higginbotham, Evelyn Brooks. "African-American Women's History and the Metalanguage of Race." *Signs* 17 (Winter 1992): 251–74.

———. "Beyond the Sounds of Silence: Afro-American Women in History." *Gender and History* 1 (February 1990): 50–67.

———. "Clubwomen and Electoral Politics in the 1920s." In *African American Women and the Vote, 1837–1965*, edited by Ann Gordon et al., 134–55. Amherst: University of Massachusetts Press, 1997.

———. "In Politics to Stay: Black Women Leaders and Party Politics in the 1920s." In *Women, Politics, and Change*, edited by Louise A. Tilley and Patricia Gurin, 199–220. New York: Russell Sage Foundation, 1990.

———. *Righteous Discontent: The Women's Movement in the Black Baptist Church, 1880–1920*. Cambridge, Mass.: Harvard University Press, 1993.

Hine, Darlene Clark. "Black Migration to the Middle West: The Gender Dimension, 1914–1945." In *The Great Migration in Historical Perspective: New Dimensions of Race, Class, and Gender*, edited by Joe William Trotter, 127–46. Bloomington: Indiana University Press, 1991.

———. *Black Women in White: Racial Conflict and Cooperation in the Nursing Profession, 1890–1950*. Bloomington: Indiana University Press, 1989.

———. "Rape and the Inner Lives of Black Women in the Middle West: Preliminary Thoughts on the Culture of Dissemblance." *Signs* 14 (Summer 1989): 912–20.

———, ed. *The State of Afro-American History: Past, Present, and Future*. Baton Rouge: Louisiana State University Press, 1986.

Hine, Darlene Clark, et al., eds. *Black Women in United States History*. 16 vols. Brooklyn, N.Y.: Carlson, 1990.

Hine, Darlene Clark, Linda Reed, and Wilma King, eds. *We Specialize in the Wholly Impossible: A Reader in Black Women's History*. Brooklyn, N.Y.: Carlson, 1996.

Hine, Darlene Clark, and Kathleen Thompson. *A Shining Thread of Hope: The History of Black Women in America*. New York: Broadway Books, 1998.

Holsey, Albon L. "Pearson — The Brown Duke of Durham." *Opportunity* 6 (April 1928): 116–17.

Holt, Sharon. *Making Freedom Pay: North Carolina Freedpeople Working for Themselves*. Athens: University of Georgia Press, 2000.

hooks, bell (Gloria Watkins). *"Ain't I a Woman": Black Women and Feminism*. Boston: South End Press, 1981.

House, R. G., ed., and Santford Martin, comp. *Public Letters and Papers of Thomas Walter Bickett, Governor of North Carolina, 1917–1921*. Raleigh: Edwards and Broughton, 1923.

Hughes, Langston. "Mother to Son." In *The Weary Blues*. New York: Knopf, 1926.

———. *Vintage Hughes*. New York: Vintage Books, 2004.

Hull, Gloria T. *Give Us Each Day: The Diary of Alice Dunbar-Nelson*. New York: W. W. Norton, 1984.

Hunter, Tera W. "Domination and Resistance: The Politics of Household Labor in New South Atlanta." *Labor History* 34 (Spring/Summer 1993): 205–20.

———. *"To 'Joy My Freedom": Southern Black Women's Lives and Labors after the Civil War*. Cambridge, Mass.: Harvard University Press, 1997.

Jacobs, Sylvia M. "Give a Thought to Africa: Black Women Missionaries in Southern Africa." In *Western Women and Imperialism*, edited by Nupur Chaudhuri and Margaret Strobel, 209–13. Bloomington: Indiana University Press, 1992.

Jacobson, Matthew Frye. *Whiteness of a Different Color: European Immigrants and the Alchemy of Race*. Cambridge, Mass.: Harvard University Press, 1998.

Janiewski, Dolores E. *Sisterhood Denied: Race, Gender, and Class in a New South Community*. Philadelphia: Temple University Press, 1985.

Jenkins, John Wilber. *James B. Duke: Master Builder*. New York: George H. Dornan, 1972.

Johnson, Charles Spurgeon. *Patterns of Negro Segregation*. New York: Harper and Brothers, 1943.

Johnson, Daniel M., and Rex R. Campbell. *Black Migration in America: A Social Demographic History*. Durham: Duke University Press, 1981.

Jones, Adrianne Lash. *Jane Edna Hunter: A Case Study of Black Leadership, 1910–1950*. Brooklyn, N.Y.: Carlson, 1990.

Jones, Beverly W. *Quest for Equality: The Life and Writings of Mary Eliza Church Terrell, 1863–1954*. Brooklyn, N.Y.: Carlson, 1990.

———. "Race, Sex, and Class: Black Female Tobacco Workers in Durham, North Carolina, 1920–1940, and the Development of Female Consciousness." *Feminist Studies* 10 (Fall 1984): 441–51.

Jones, Dorothy Phelps. *The End of an Era*. Durham: Brown Enterprises, 2001.

Jones, Jacqueline. *Labor of Love, Labor of Sorrow: Black Women, Work and the Family from Slavery to the Present*. New York: Basic Books, 1985.

Jones, Lance T. *The Jeanes Teacher in the United States, 1908–1933: An Account of Twenty-five Years' Experience in the Supervision of Negro Rural Schools*. Chapel Hill: University of North Carolina Press, 1937.

Katznelson, Ira. *When Affirmative Action Was White: An Untold History of Racial Inequality in Twentieth-Century America*. New York: W. W. Norton, 2005.

Keech, William R. *The Impact of Negro Voting: The Role of the Vote in the Quest for Equality*. Chicago: Rand McNally, 1968.

Kelley, Robin D. G. "The Black Poor and the Politics of Oppression in a New South City, 1929–1970." In *The "Underclass" Debate: Views from History*, edited by Michael B. Katz, 293–333. Princeton, N.J.: Princeton University Press, 1993.

———. *Freedom Dreams: The Black Radical Imagination*. Boston: Beacon Press, 2002.

———. *Hammer and Hoe: Alabama Communists in the Great Depression*. Chapel Hill: University of North Carolina Press, 1990.

———. *Race Rebels: Culture, Politics, and the Black Working Class*. New York: Free Press, 1996.

———. " 'We Are Not What We Seem': Rethinking Black Working Class Opposition in the Jim Crow South." *Journal of American History* 88 (June 1993): 75–112.

Kellogg, John. "Negro Urban Clusters in the Postbellum South." *Geographical Review* 67 (1977): 310–21.

Kellor, Francis A. "Assisted Emigration from the South: The Women." *Charities* 18 (7 October 1905): 6–8.

———. "Opportunities for Southern Girls in the North." *Voice of the Negro* 2 (July 1905): 472–73.

———. "Southern Colored Girls in the North: The Problem and Their Protection." *Charities* 7 (18 March 1905): 584–86.

Kennedy, Louise V. *The Negro Peasant Turns Cityward.* New York: Columbia University Press, 1930.

Kennedy, William J., Jr. *The North Carolina Mutual Story: A Symbol of Progress, 1898–1970.* Durham: North Carolina Mutual Life Insurance Company, 1973.

Kenzer, Robert C. *Enterprising Southerners: Black Economic Success in North Carolina, 1865–1915.* Charlottesville: University Press of Virginia, 1997.

———. *Kinship and Neighborhood in a Southern Community: Orange County, North Carolina, 1849–1881.* Knoxville: University of Tennessee Press, 1987.

Kern-Foxworth, Marilyn. *Aunt Jemima, Uncle Ben, and Rastus: Blacks in Advertising, Yesterday, Today, and Tomorrow.* Westport, Conn.: Greenwood Press, 1994.

Kessler-Harris, Alice. *In Pursuit of Equality: Women, Men, and the Quest for Economic Citizenship in Twentieth-Century America.* New York: Oxford University Press, 2001.

King, Deborah K. "Multiple Jeopardy, Multiple Consciousness: The Context of Black Feminist Ideology." *Signs* 14 (Autumn 1988): 42–72.

King, William E. "Charles McIver Fights for the Tarheel Negro's Right to an Education." *North Carolina Historical Review* 41 (July 1964): 360–69.

Kluger, Richard. *Simple Justice: The History of Brown v. Board of Education and the Black American Struggle for Equality.* New York: First Vintage Book Edition/Random House, 1975.

Korstad, Robert Rodgers. *Civil Rights Unionism: Tobacco Workers and the Struggle for Democracy in the Mid-Twentieth-Century South.* Chapel Hill: University of North Carolina Press, 2003.

Kousser, J. Morgan. *The Shaping of Southern Politics: Suffrage Restriction and the Establishment of the One-Party South, 1880–1910.* New Haven: Yale University Press, 1974.

Kunzel, Regina G. *Fallen Women, Problem Girls: Unmarried Mothers and the Professionalization of Social Work, 1890–1945.* New Haven: Yale University Press, 1993.

Kusmer, Kenneth, "The Black Urban Experience in American History." In *The State of Afro-American History: Past, Present, and Future,* edited by Darlene Clark Hine, 91–122. Baton Rouge: Louisiana State University Press, 1986.

Ladd, Everett Carll, Jr. *Negro Political Leadership in the South.* Ithaca, N.Y.: Cornell University Press, 1966.

Lebsock, Suzanne. *The Free Women of Petersburg: Status and Culture in a Southern Town, 1784–1860.* New York: W. W. Norton, 1984.

Lemke-Santangelo, Gretchen. *Abiding Courage: African American Migrant Women and the East Bay Community.* Chapel Hill: University of North Carolina Press, 1996.

Lerner, Gerda, ed. *Black Women in White America: A Documentary History.* New York: Vintage Books, 1973.

Levine, Lawrence W. *Black Culture and Black Consciousness: Afro-American Folk Thought from Slavery to Freedom*. New York: Oxford University Press, 1977.

Lewis, David Levering, ed. *W. E. B. Du Bois: A Reader*. New York: Henry Holt, 1995.

———. *W. E. B. Du Bois: Biography of a Race, 1868–1919*. New York: Henry Holt, 1993.

———. *W. E. B. Du Bois: The Fight for Equality and the American Century, 1919–1963*. New York: Henry Holt, 2000.

Lewis, Earl. "Expectations, Economic Opportunities, and Life in the Industrial Age." In *The Great Migration in Historical Perspective*, edited by Joe William Trotter, 28–42. Bloomington: Indiana University Press, 1991.

———. *In Their Own Interests: Race, Class, and Power in Twentieth-Century Norfolk, Virginia*. Berkeley: University of California Press, 1991.

Leyburn, James G. *The Way We Lived: Durham, 1900–1920*. Eliston, Va.: Northcross House, 1989.

Littlefield, Valinda. "Agency and Constructions of Professional Identity: African American Educators in the Rural South." In *Stepping Forward: Black Women in Africa and the Americas*, edited by Catherine Higgs, Barbara A. Moss, and Earline Rae Ferguson, 17–29. Athens: Ohio University Press, 2002.

Litwack, Leon F. *Been in the Storm So Long: The Aftermath of Slavery*. New York: Vintage Books, 1980.

———. *Trouble in Mind: Black Southerners in the Age of Jim Crow*. New York: Knopf, 1998.

Locke, Alain, ed. *The New Negro: Voices of the Harlem Renaissance*. New York: Albert and Charles Boni, 1925. Reprint, Antheneum/Macmillan, 1992.

Loewenberg, Bert James, and Ruth Bogin, eds. *Black Women in Nineteenth Century Life: Their Words, Their Thoughts, Their Actions*. University Park: Pennsylvania State University Press, 1976.

Logan, Frenise A. "The Economic Status of the Town Negro in Post-Reconstruction North Carolina." *North Carolina Historical Review* 35 (October 1958): 448–460.

———. "The Legal Status of Public School Education for Negroes in North Carolina, 1877–1894." *North Carolina Historical Review* 32 (July 1955): 346–357.

———. "The Movement in North Carolina to Establish a State Supported College for Negroes." *North Carolina Historical Review* 35 (April 1958): 167–180.

———. "The Movement of Negroes from North Carolina, 1876–1894." *North Carolina Historical Review* 33 (January 1956): 45–65.

———. *The Negro in North Carolina, 1876–1894*. Chapel Hill: University of North Carolina Press, 1964.

Lougee, George E., Jr. *Durham: My Hometown*. Durham: Carolina Academic Press, 1990.

Lynch, Mary C. "Social Status and the Needs of the Colored Woman." In *The United Negro: His Problems and His Progress, Addresses and Proceedings for the Negro Young People's Christian and Educational Congress, August 6–11, 1902*, edited by I. Garland

Penn and J. W. E. Bowen, 185–87. Atlanta: D. E. Luther Publishing Co., 1902. Reprint, New York: Negro Universities Press, 1969.

Lyon, Leverett S. *The National Recovery Administration: An Analysis and Appraisal.* New York: Da Capo Press, 1972.

Mabry, William A. *The Negro in North Carolina Politics since Reconstruction.* Durham: Duke University Press, 1940.

Mae, Verta. *Thursdays and Every Other Sunday Off: A Domestic Rap.* Garden City, N.Y.: Doubleday, 1972.

Marable, Manning. *How Capitalism Underdeveloped Black America.* Reprint, Cambridge, Mass.: South End Press, 2000.

Marks, Carole. *"Farewell — We're Good and Gone": The Great Black Migration.* Bloomington: Indiana University Press, 1989.

Martin, Waldo E. *Brown v. Board of Education: A Brief History with Documents.* Boston: Bedford/St. Martin's, 1998.

Massey, Douglas S., and Denton, Nancy A. *American Apartheid: Segregation and the Making of the Underclass.* Cambridge: Harvard University Press, 1993.

McDougald, Elise Johnson. "The Task of Negro Womanhood." In *The New Negro: An Interpretation*, edited by Alain Locke, 369–82. New York: Albert and Charles Boni, 1925. Reprint, New York: Antheneum/Macmillan, 1992.

McElroy, Guy C. *Facing History: The Black Image in American Art, 1710–1940.* New York: Bedford Arts Publishers, in association with the Corcoran Gallery of Art, 1993.

McMillen, Neil. *Dark Journey: Black Mississippians in the Age of Jim Crow.* Urbana: University of Illinois Press, 1989.

McNeil, Genna Rae. *Groundwork: Charles Hamilton Houston and the Struggle for Civil Rights.* Philadelphia: University of Pennsylvania Press, 1983.

Mebane, Mary. *Mary.* New York: Viking Press/Fawcett Juniper Books, 1981.

Meier, August. *Negro Thought in America, 1880–1915: Racial Ideologies in the Age of Booker T. Washington.* Ann Arbor: University of Michigan Press, 1988.

Meyerowitz, Joanne. *Women Adrift: Independent Wage Earners in Chicago, 1880–1930.* Chicago: University of Chicago Press, 1988.

Miller, Kelly. "The City Negro: Industrial Status (Part II)." *Southern Workman* 30 (June 1903): 340–45.

———. "Surplus Negro Women." In *Race Adjustment: Essays on the Negro in America.* New York: Neale Publishing, 1908. Reprinted as *Radicals and Conservatives: And Other Essays on the Negro in America*, 182–92. New York: Schocken Books, 1968.

Miller, Zane L. "Urban Blacks in the South, 1865–1920: The Richmond, Savannah, New Orleans, Louisville, and Birmingham Experience." In *The New Urban History: Quantitative Explorations by American Historians*, edited by Leo Schnore, 184–204. Princeton, N.J.: Princeton University Press, 1975.

Mitchell, Michele. "'The Black Man's Burden': African Americans, Imperialism, and Notions of Racial Manhood, 1890–1910." *International Review of Social History Supplement* 44 (1999).

——. *Righteous Propagation: African Americans and the Politics of Racial Destiny after Reconstruction.* Chapel Hill: University of North Carolina Press, 2004.

——. "Silences Broken, Silences Kept: Gender and Sexuality in African-American History." *Gender & History* (November 1999): 433–44.

Mobley, Joe A. *James City: A Black Community in North Carolina, 1863–1900.* Raleigh: Division of Archives and History, Department of Cultural Resources, 1981.

Mullane, Dierdre. *Crossing the Danger Water: Three Hundred Years of African-American Writing.* New York: Anchor Books, 1996.

Muncy, Robin. *Creating a Female Dominion in American Reform, 1890–1935.* New York: Oxford University Press, 1991.

Murray, Pauli. *The Autobiography of a Black Activist, Feminist, Lawyer, Priest, and Poet.* Knoxville: University of Tennessee Press, 1989. Previously published as *Song in a Weary Throat: An American Pilgrimage.* New York: Harper and Row, 1987.

——. "The Fourth Generation of Proud Shoes." *Southern Exposure* 4 (Winter 1977): 4–5.

——. "The Liberation of Black Women." In *Words of Fire: An Anthology of African-American Feminist Thought,* edited by Beverly Guy-Sheftall, 185–97. New York: New Press, 1995.

——. *Proud Shoes: The Story of an American Family.* New York: Harper and Row, 1956.

——. *States' Laws on Race and Color.* Cincinnati, Ohio: Women's Division of Christian Service, Board of Missions, and Church Extensions, Methodist Church, 1950.

Myrdal, Gunnar. *An American Dilemma.* 2 vols. New York: Harper and Row, 1944. Reprint, New York: McGraw-Hill, 1964.

NAACP. *Thirty Years of Lynching in the United States, 1889–1918.* New York: National Office of the Association for the Advancement of Colored People, 1919.

Nasstrom, Katherine. "Down to Now: Memory, Narrative, and Women's Leadership in the Civil Rights Movement in Atlanta, Georgia." *Gender & History* 11 (April 1999).

"Negroes and Organized Labor." *Survey* 39 (9 February 1918): 527–28.

Nelson, Bruce. *Divided We Stand: American Workers and the Struggle for Black Equality.* Princeton, N.J.: Princeton University Press, 2001.

Newby, I. A. *Jim Crow's Defense: Anti-Negro Thought in America, 1900–1930.* Baton Rouge: Louisiana State University Press, 1965.

Nora, Pierre. "Between Memory and History: *Les Lieux de Memoire.*" In *Memory and History in African American Culture,* edited by Genevieve Fabre and Robert O'Meally, 284–300. New York: Oxford University Press, 1994.

Northrup, Herbert R. *Organized Labor and the Negro.* New York: Harper and Brothers, 1944.

"Notes on a Trip with the Business Men's Party (Part I)." *Opportunity* 2 (June 1924): 186–88.

"Notes on a Trip with the Business Men's Party (Part II)." *Opportunity* 2 (July 1924): 221–22.

Odum, Howard. *Race and Rumors of Race: The American South in the Early Forties.* Baltimore: Johns Hopkins University Press, 1997.

Olson, Lynne. *Freedom's Daughters: The Unsung Heroines of the Civil Rights Movement, 1830–1970.* New York: Touchstone Books, 2001.

Ortiz, Paul. *Emancipation Betrayed: The Hidden History of Black Organizing and White Violence in Florida from Reconstruction to the Bloody Election of 1920.* Berkeley: University of California Press, 2005.

Packard, Jerrold M. *American Nightmare: The History of Jim Crow.* New York: St. Martin's, 2002.

Painter, Nell Irvin. *The Exodusters: Black Migration to Kansas after Reconstruction.* Reprint, New York: W. W. Norton, 1992.

———. *Southern History across the Color Line.* Chapel Hill: University of North Carolina Press, 2002.

Parisher, Don, and Harry Hennessey. "Negro Durham Marches On." Video reprint, Cary, N.C.: Media Consultants, ca. 1940s, 1989.

Park, Robert E. "The Bases of Race Prejudice." *Annals of the American Academy of Political and Social Sciences* 90 (November 1928): 11–20.

Paul, Hiram Voss. *The History of the Town of Durham.* Raleigh: Edwards, Broughton, 1884.

Payne, Charles M. *"I've Got the Light of Freedom": The Organizing Tradition and the Mississippi Freedom Struggle.* Berkeley: University of California Press, 1995.

Payne, Daniel A. *History of the African American Methodist Church.* Nashville, Tenn.: Publishing House of the A.M.E. Sunday-School Union, 1891. Reprint, New York: Arno Press and *New York Times*, 1969.

Pedraza, Silvia. "Women and Migration: The Consequences of Gender." *Annual Review of Sociology* 17 (Spring 1991): 303–25.

Penn, I. Garland, and J. W. E. Bowen, eds. *The United Negro: His Problems and Progress, Addresses and Proceedings from the Negro Young People's Christian and Educational Congress.* Atlanta: D. E. Luther, 1902. Reprint, New York: Negro Universities Press, 1969.

Penningroth, Dylan C. *Claims of Kinfolk: African American Property and Community in the Nineteenth-Century South.* Chapel Hill: University of North Carolina Press, 2003.

Prather, H. Leon. *We Have Taken a City: Wilmington Racial Massacre and Coup of 1898.* Rutherford, N.J.: Fairleigh Dickinson University Press, 1984.

Rabinowitz, Howard N. *Race Relations in the Urban South, 1865–1890.* New York: Oxford University Press, 1978.

Ransby, Barbara. *Ella Baker and the Black Freedom Movement: A Radical Democratic Vision.* Chapel Hill: University of North Carolina Press, 2003.

Ransom, Roger L., and Richard Sutch. *One Kind of Freedom: The Economic Consequences of Emancipation.* Reprint, London: Cambridge University Press, 2001.

Rawick, George P., ed. *The American Slave: A Composite Autobiography.* 19 vols. Westport, Conn.: Greenwood Press, 1972.

Reed, Ruth. *Negro Illegitimacy in New York City.* New York: Columbia University Press, 1926.

Reid, Ira De A. *Negro Membership in American Labor Unions.* Department of Research and Investigations of the National Urban League. New York: Alexander Press, 1930.

———. *The Urban Negro Worker in the United States, 1925–1936.* Westport, Conn.: Greenwood Press, 1970.

Reiff, Janice L., Michael R. Dahlin, and Daniel Scott Smith. "Rural Push and Urban Pull: Work and Family Experiences of Older Black Women in Southern Cities." *Journal of Social History* 15 (Summer 1983): 39–48.

Rice, Roger L. "Residential Segregation by Law, 1910–1917." *Journal of Southern History* 34 (May 1968): 179–99.

Roberts, Claudia Brown. *The Durham Architectural and Historical Inventory.* Durham: City of Durham and the Historical Preservation Society of Durham, 1982.

Robinson, Armstead L. "The Difference Freedom Made: The Emancipation of Afro-Americans." In *The State of Afro-American History: Past, Present, and Future*, edited by Darlene Clark Hine, 51–74. Baton Rouge: Louisiana State University Press, 1986.

———. " 'Plans Dat Comed from God': Institutional Building and the Emergence of Black Leadership in Reconstruction Memphis." In *Toward a New South? Studies in Post–Civil War Southern Communities*, edited by Orville Vernon Burton and Robert C. McMath Jr. Westport, Conn.: Greenwood Press, 1982.

Robinson, Armstead L., and Patricia Sullivan, eds. *New Directions in Civil Rights Studies.* Charlottesville: University Of Virginia Press, 1991.

Roediger, David R. *Wages of Whiteness: Race and the Making of the American Working Class.* New York: Verso Books, 1999.

Ross, Marlon B. *Manning the Race: Reforming Black Men in the Jim Crow Era.* New York: New York University Press, 2004.

Rouse, Jacqueline K. *Lugenia Burns Hope, Black Southern Reformer.* Athens: University of Illinois Press, 1989.

Salem, Dorothy. *To Better Our World: Black Women in Organized Reform, 1890–1920.* Brooklyn, N.Y.: Carlson, 1990.

Scharf, Lois, and Joan M. Jensen, eds. *Decades of Discontent: The Woman's Movement, 1920–1940.* Westport, Conn.: Greenwood Press, 1983.

Schnore, Leo F., ed. *The New Urban History: Quantitative Explorations by American Historians.* Princeton, N.J.: Princeton University Press, 1975.

Schnore, Leo F., and Philip C. Evenson. "Segregation in Southern Cities." *American Journal of Sociology* 72 (July 1966): 58–67.

Schwalm, Leslie A. *A Hard Fight for We: Women's Transition from Slavery to Freedom in South Carolina.* Urbana: University of Illinois Press, 1997.

Schweninger, Loren O. *Black Property Owners in the South, 1790–1915.* Urbana: University of Illinois Press, 1982.

Scott, Emmett J. *Negro Migration during the War.* New York: Oxford University Press, 1920. Reprint, New York: Arno Press and *New York Times*, 1969.

Scott, James C. *Domination and the Arts of Resistance: The Hidden Transcripts*. New Haven: Yale University Press, 1990.

Seeman, Ernest. *American Gold*. New York: Avon Books, 1978.

Sernett, Milton C. *Bound for the Promised Land: African American Religion and the Great Migration*. Durham: Duke University Press, 1997.

Shapiro, Herbert. *White Violence and Black Response: From Reconstruction to Montgomery*. Amherst: University of Massachusetts Press, 1988.

Shaw, Stephanie J. "Black Club Women and the Creation of the National Association of Colored Women." *Journal of Women's History* 3 (Fall 1991): 10–25.

———. *What a Woman Ought to Be and to Do: Black Professional Women Workers during the Jim Crow Era*. Chicago: University of Chicago Press, 1996.

Shields, Emma L. "A Half-Century in the Tobacco Industry." *Southern Workman* 51 (September 1922): 419–25.

Sidbury, James. *Ploughshares into Swords: Race, Rebellion, and Identity in Gabriel's Virginia, 1730–1810*. London: Cambridge University Press, 1997.

Sitkoff, Harvard. *A New Deal for Blacks: The Emergence of Civil Rights as a National Issue*. New York: Oxford University Press, 1981.

Smith, Betty. *Durham Station: A Play in One Act*. Raleigh: N.C. Confederate Centennial Commission, 1961.

Smith, Douglas L. *The New Deal in the Urban South*. Baton Rouge: Louisiana State University Press, 1988.

Smith, John David, ed. *Anti-Black Thought, 1863–1925: "The Negro Problem."* 11 vols. New York: Garland, 1993.

Smith, Susan L. *Sick and Tired of Being Sick and Tired: Black Women's Health Activism in America, 1895–1950*. Philadelphia: Temple University Press, 1995.

Smith, T. Lynn. "The Emergence of Cities." In *The New South*, edited by Rupert B. Vance and Nicholas J. Demerath, 24–37. Chapel Hill: University of North Carolina Press, 1954.

Snitow, Ann, Christine Stansell, and Sharon Thompson, eds. *Powers of Desire: The Politics of Sexuality*. New York: Monthly Review Press, 1983.

"A Sound Business Institution." *Opportunity* 2 (August 1924): 247.

A Southern Colored Woman. "The Race Problem—An Autobiography." *Independent* 56 (17 March 1904).

Spero, Sterling, and Abram L. Harris. *The Black Worker: The Negro Labor Movement*. New York: Antheneum Press, 1961.

Stack, Carol B. *All Our Kin: Strategies of Survival in Black Communities*. New York: Harper and Row, 1974.

———. *Call to Home: African Americans Reclaim the Rural South*. New York: Basic Books, 1996.

Stanley, Amy Dru. *From Bondage to Contract: Wage Labor, Marriage, and the Market in the Age of Slave Emancipation*. London: Cambridge University Press, 1998.

Stansell, Christine. *City of Women: Sex and Class in New York, 1789–1860*. Urbana: University of Illinois Press, 1986.

Sterling, Dorothy, ed. *We Are Your Sisters: Black Women in the Nineteenth Century.* New York: W. W. Norton, 1985.

Strom, Sharon Hartman. *Beyond the Typewriter: Gender, Class, and the Origins of Modern American Office Work, 1900–1930.* Urbana: University of Illinois Press, 1992.

Sullivan, Patricia. *Days of Hope: Race and Democracy in the New Deal Era.* Chapel Hill: University of North Carolina Press, 1996.

Summers, Martin Anthony. *Manliness and Its Discontents: The Middle Class and the Transformation of Masculinity, 1900–1930.* Chapel Hill: University of North Carolina Press, 2004.

Tayleur, Eleanor. "The Negro Woman: Social and Moral Decadence." *Outlook* 11 (30 January 1904): 266.

Taylor, Ula Yvette. *The Veiled Garvey: The Life and Times of Amy Jacques Garvey.* Chapel Hill: University of North Carolina Press, 2002.

Terborg-Penn, Roslyn. "Discontented Black Feminists: Prelude and Postscript to the Passage of the Nineteenth Amendment." In *Decades of Discontent: The Woman's Movement, 1920–1940,* edited by Lois Scharf and Joan M. Jensen, 261–78. Westport, Conn.: Greenwood Press, 1983.

Thompson, Lorin A. "Urbanization, Occupational Shift, and Economic Progress." In *The Urban South,* edited by Rupert B. Vance and Nicholas J. Demerath, 38–54. Chapel Hill: University of North Carolina Press, 1954.

Thompson, Mildred I. *Ida B. Wells-Barnett: An Exploratory Study of an American Black Woman, 1893–1930.* Brooklyn, N.Y.: Carlson, 1990.

Tilley, Nannie M. *The Bright-Tobacco Industry, 1860–1929.* Chapel Hill: University of North Carolina Press, 1948.

———. *The R. J. Reynolds Tobacco Company.* Chapel Hill: University of North Carolina Press, 1985.

Trotter, Joe William. *Black Milwaukee: The Making of an Industrial Proletariat, 1915–1945.* Urbana: University of Illinois Press, 1985.

———, ed. *The Great Migration in Historical Perspective.* Bloomington: Indiana University Press, 1991.

Tucker, Susan. *Telling Memories among Southern Women: Domestic Workers and Their Employers in the Segregated South.* Chapel Hill: University of North Carolina Press, 1988.

Vance, Rupert B. *All These People: The Nation's Human Resources in the South.* Chapel Hill: University of North Carolina Press, 1954.

———. *Human Geography of the South: A Study in Regional Resources and Human Adequacy.* Chapel Hill: University of North Carolina Press, 1932.

van Falkenburg, Carole, and Christine Dall, prod. *Wild Women Don't Have the Blues.* Documentary. 1989.

Vann, Andre D. "Black Women United: A Look at Black Club Women in Durham, North Carolina, 1917–1953." *Trading Path* 6 (Spring 1995): 31–36.

"Votes for Women: A Symposium by Leading Thinkers of Colored America." *Crisis* 10 (August 1915): 178–92.

Warner, W. Lloyd. "American Caste and Class." *American Journal of Sociology* 42 (September 1936): 234–37.
———. "Introduction." In *Deep South: A Sociological Study of Caste and Class*, edited by Allison B. Davis, Burleigh Gardner, and Mary R. Gardner. Chicago: University of Chicago Press, 1941.
Washington, Booker T. "Durham, North Carolina, a City of Negro Enterprise." *Independent* 70 (23 March 1911): 644–48.
———. *Up from Slavery: An Autobiography*. New York: Doubleday, Page, 1907.
Washington, Booker T., N. B. Wood, and Fannie Barrier Williams. *A New Negro for a New Century*. Chicago: American Publishing House, 1900. Reprint, New York: Arno Press and *New York Times*, 1969.
Washington, Mary Helen. "Introduction." In *Voice of the South*, by Anna Julia Cooper. Xenia, Ohio: Aldine Print House, 1892. Reprint, New York: Oxford University Press, 1988.
Weare, Walter B. *Black Business in the New South: A Social History of the North Carolina Mutual Life Insurance Company*. Urbana: University of Illinois Press, 1972. Reprint, Durham: Duke University Press, 1993.
———. "Charles Clinton Spaulding: Middle-Class Leadership in the Age of Segregation." In *Black Leaders of the Twentieth Century*, edited by John Hope Franklin and August Meier, 166–90. Urbana: University of Illinois Press, 1982.
Wells-Barnett, Ida B. *Selected Works of Ida B. Wells-Barnett*. Compiled by Trudier Harris. New York: Oxford University Press, 1991.
Wesley, Charles Harris. *A History of the National Association of Colored Women's Clubs: A Legacy of Service*. Washington, D.C.: National Association of Colored Women's Clubs, 1984.
———. *Negro Labor in the United States, 1850–1925: A Study in American Economic History*. New York: Vanguard Press, 1927.
White, Deborah Gray. *Ar'n't I a Woman: Female Slaves in the Plantation South*. New York: Norton, 1985.
———. "The Cost of Clubwork, the Price of Black Feminism." In *Visible Women: New Essays on American Activism*, edited by Nancy A. Hewitt and Suzanne Lebsock, 247–69. Urbana: University of Illinois Press, 1993.
———. "Private Lives, Public Personae: A Look at Early Twentieth-Century African American Club Women." In *Talking Gender: Public Images, Personal Journeys, and Political Critiques*, edited by Nancy Hewitt, Jean O'Barr, and Nancy Rosebaugh, 106–23. Chapel Hill: University of North Carolina Press, 1996.
———. "The Slippery Slope of Class in Black America: The National Council of Negro Women and the International Ladies' Auxiliary to the Brotherhood of Sleeping Car Porters, A Case Study." In *New Viewpoints in Women's History*, edited by Susan Ware, 180–95. Cambridge, Mass.: Arthur and Elizabeth Schlesinger Library on the History of Women in America, 1994.
———. *Too Heavy a Load: Race, Class, and Gender in Black Women's Associational History*. Urbana: University of Illinois Press, 1999.

White, Walter F. "'Work or Fight' in the South." *New Republic* 18 (1 March 1919): 144–46.

Whitted, James A. *A History of the Negro Baptists of North Carolina*. Raleigh: Edwards and Broughton, 1908.

Williams, Fannie Barrier. "The Club Movement among Colored Women of America." In *A New Negro for a New Century*, by Booker T. Washington, N. B. Wood, and Fannie Barrier Williams, 379–405. Chicago: American Publishing House, 1900. Reprint, New York: Arno Press and *New York Times*, 1969.

Williamson, Joel. *The Crucible of Race: Black-White Relations in the American South since Emancipation*. New York: Oxford University Press, 1984.

Winkler, John K. *Tobacco Tycoon: The Story of James Buchanan Duke*. New York: Random House, 1942.

Wolcott, Victoria W. *Remaking Respectability: African American Women in Interwar Detroit*. Chapel Hill: University of North Carolina Press, 2001.

Wolters, Raymond. *Negroes and the Great Depression: The Problem of Economic Recovery*. Westport, Conn.: Greenwood Press, 1970.

Woodson, Carter G. *A Century of Negro Migration*. New York: Russell and Russell, 1969.

Woodward, C. Vann. *Origins of the New South, 1877–1913*. Baton Rouge: Louisiana State University Press, 1971.

———. *The Strange Career of Jim Crow*. 3rd rev. ed. New York: Oxford University Press, 1974.

Woofter, Thomas J. "The Negro on a Strike." *Journal of Social Forces* 2 (1923–24): 84–88.

Wright, Gavin. *Old South, New South: Revolutions in the Southern Economy since the Civil War*. New York: Basic Books, 1986.

Dissertations, Theses, and Papers

Chambliss, Rollin. "What Negro Newspapers of Georgia Say about Some Social Problems." M.A. thesis, University of Georgia, 1933.

Gilmore, Glenda Elizabeth. "Gender and Jim Crow: Women and the Politics of White Supremacy in North Carolina, 1896–1922." Ph.D. diss., University of North Carolina, 1990.

Greene, Christina. "'Our Separate Ways': Women and the Black Freedom Movement in Durham, North Carolina, 1940s–1970." Ph.D. diss., Duke University, 1996.

Houck, Thomas. "A Newspaper History of Race Relations in Durham." M.A. thesis, Duke University, 1941.

Kiser, Vernon Benjamin. "Occupational Changes among Negroes in Durham." M.A. thesis, Duke University, 1942.

Lemert, Benjamin. "Durham, North Carolina: An Economic Survey." Vols. 1 and 2. Typescript. Durham: Durham Chamber of Commerce, 1939.

Maslowski, James Joseph. "North Carolina Migration, 1870–1915." Ph.D. diss., University of North Carolina, 1953.

Miller, Bertha Hampton. "Blacks in Winston-Salem, North Carolina, 1895–1920: Community Development in the Era of Benevolent Paternalism." Ph.D. diss., Duke University, 1981.

Walker, Harry J. "Changes in Race Accommodation in a Southern Community." Ph.D. diss., University of Chicago, 1945.

Weare, Walter B. "Black Business: A Reevaluation of the Functional Roles of Autonomous Black Institutions." Paper presented at Behind the Veil Research Conference, Center for Documentary Studies at Duke University and North Carolina Central University, 12 November 1990.

Weaver, Garrett. "The Development of the Black Durham Community, 1880–1915." Ph.D. diss., University of North Carolina, 1988.

.Westin, Richard Barry. "A History of the Durham School System, 1882–1933." M.A. thesis, Duke University, 1960.

Wilkerson, Edith. "Patterns of Negro Segregation in Durham, North Carolina." M.A. thesis, Duke University, 1950.

Williams, Alma Rene. "Robert C. Weaver: From the Black Cabinet to the President's Cabinet." Ph.D. diss., Washington University, 1978.

Index

Accommodation, 12, 19, 71, 74, 118, 251, 293

African Methodist Episcopal (AME) Zion Church, 66, 243, 261

Alexander, Sadie T. Mossell, 128, 131

Alpha Kappa Alpha, 162, 268–69, 328

American Federation of Labor (AFL), 93, 240, 241, 299, 303

American Tobacco Company, 41, 91, 223, 224, 255, 263, 298, 302, 304

Amey, C. C., 121–22

Anna T. Jeanes Fund, 170, 173, 374 (n. 59)

Armstrong, W. H., 156, 157

Aspiring class: and challenge to white supremacy, 8; and mid-range professionals, 21; and respectability, 22, 97, 355 (n. 26); development of, 37, 38; and capitalism, 46; and network of associations, 78; and black women, 84; and working-class blacks, 96, 107; and racial uplift, 97–100; and church-women, 102; and education, 142–43; and change in social structure, 353 (n. 41). *See also* Black middle class

Atkins, S. G., 222–23, 316, 317

Atlanta, Ga., 19, 70, 114, 121, 237

Atwater, Wash, 60–61, 63

Austin, Louis, 250, 303, 305, 307, 313, 318–19, 322–24, 326, 336–37

Autonomy from whites: and race relations, 4, 7, 8; and upbuilding, 14, 253; and respectability, 21; and Jim Crow, 24, 153; and emancipation, 30, 333; and black communities, 31; and black

neighborhoods, 32–33, 39; and black entrepreneurs, 37, 40; and political leadership, 48; and black migration, 52; and black elite, 110, 113, 114, 115, 123, 139, 143; and North Carolina Mutual, 118–19; and class, 139, 286; and institutions, 151; and education, 166, 174, 182, 183; and self-employment, 231; and "Work or Fight" laws, 237; and YWCA, 265; and household labor, 268; and black poverty, 277

Bankers Fire Insurance Company, 120, 266

Barbee, Annie Mack, 88, 149, 228–29, 230, 256–59, 268

Bethune, Mary McLeod, 128, 134, 269, 270, 291, 331

Bickett, Thomas W., 221, 222, 236

Biltmore Hotel, 128, 251

Black aristocracy, 5, 7, 37, 110, 140, 141, 155

Black business: and black women, 15, 16, 18, 124–25, 353 (n. 38); and black manhood, 19, 250; and Jim Crow, 19, 24, 121, 143, 145, 313; and segregation, 19, 111, 117; strengthening of, 21, 121, 251, 252, 263, 291, 333; and finances, 22; and race progress, 70; and black elite, 113, 119, 123, 139, 320; and upbuilding, 115, 117, 121; and self-help, 116, 143, 287, 333; and textile industry, 119, 121–22, 138; and buyouts, 126; and class, 141–42; symbolic meaning of success, 148, 338; and black middle class, 249. *See also* Black entrepreneurs

Black children: disputes over black childhood, 3; and migration, 32; labor of, 49, 83, 90, 165, 166, 184, 225–26, 227, 235, 295, 363 (n. 23); and black elite, 142–43; and infant mortality, 148, 149, 165; and compulsory education laws, 165, 166, 183, 373 (n. 42); and clubwomen, 271–75, 383 (n. 62); and Scarborough Nursery, 276–77. *See also* Black schools

Black churches: burning of, 11; and black migration, 17, 339; and black women, 20, 32, 33; and white beneficence, 69, 152; and race progress, 70; growth of, 78; and class, 102; and male ministers, 102–3; and education, 172; and black children, 272; and unions, 301, 304, 305, 337; and black elite, 319; and NAACP, 322. *See also* Churchwomen

Black disenfranchisement: and eligibility requirements, 47, 48; and obstructions at polls, 48, 51, 73; white discourse on, 56, 58, 63, 64, 73; and Wilmington Riot, 67, 84; and white supremacy, 73, 74; and literacy, 73, 166, 281; amendment for, 73, 361 (n. 48); and James E. Shepard, 76, 77, 152; and *Plessy v. Ferguson*, 79; and white portrayals of blacks, 86–87; and black manhood, 115; and public life, 151, 333; and suffrage amendment, 168, 169; and white registrars, 280; and Conrad Odell Pearson, 385 (n. 81)

Black doctors, 153, 156, 164

Black elite: and Jim Crow, 19, 106, 114, 118, 132, 144, 150–51, 335–36; and gender roles, 21, 110, 112, 113, 123, 124–25, 127–32, 139–40, 143, 220, 337, 339; emergence of, 21, 110, 147; and respectability, 21, 113, 132, 133, 135–36, 137, 138, 145, 253, 259, 262, 286, 338; and working-class blacks, 23, 110, 143, 258, 308, 326, 329, 334–35, 339; whites' tolerance of, 69, 71, 146; and electoral politics, 70; conceptions of, 96, 352 (n. 38); social world of, 105, 135–37, 141, 252–53; and wealth accumulation, 110, 114, 115, 123, 143, 144, 146, 254; and black manhood, 110, 115, 123, 250, 288, 332; and race progress, 110, 143, 252, 320, 335, 339; financial base of, 120, 139; and education, 123–24, 165, 166, 170; and sexual harassment of black women, 136–37, 369 (n. 63); and white beneficence, 150–51, 152; attitudes toward whites, 152, 313, 335, 341; and black teachers and nurses, 154; and Lincoln Hospital, 164; and intraracial tension, 219; and racial peace, 241, 335; and unions, 242–43; and black single women, 261; and New Deal, 289, 305; and Great Depression, 290; power of, 322; success of, 331; Frazier on, 367 (n. 27). *See also* North Carolina Mutual Life Insurance Company; Political leadership

Black elite women: and respectability, 20, 132, 135–36, 137, 138, 338; and gender roles, 21, 110, 112, 113, 123, 124–25, 127–32, 139–40, 143, 220, 252; and race relations, 21–22, 263–75; and NAACP, 134; and YWCA, 134, 263–68, 328, 369 (n. 58); and health care, 162; World War I efforts of, 220, 222, 244–46, 260, 261, 338–39; and woman suffrage, 220, 279, 280; and "Work or Fight" laws, 237;

and black womanhood, 250, 251, 262; and black children, 271–75

Black entrepreneurs: in Fitzgerald family, 3, 4, 8; and political leadership, 12, 36; and black women's role, 18; and upstarts, 22, 37; and class, 22, 38, 40; emergence of, 37, 333; and New South, 41; collaboration of, 116; whites doing business with, 120; and race progress, 252. *See also* Black business

Black labor: activism of, 23, 42–43; and upbuilding, 40; and tobacco factories, 43, 51, 52; and pay scale, 46; and industrialization, 50; demand for, 69, 71, 87, 92; and class, 95, 308; and Section 7a of NRA, 299–300. *See also* Working-class black men; Working-class blacks; Working-class black women

Black manhood: and black womanhood, 2, 11, 17, 86; role of, 7; upbuilding associated with, 18–19; models of, 42; and white supremacy, 59; redefinition of, 74; voting rights linked to, 76, 77, 85; and Jim Crow, 82; and aspiring class, 97; and black elite, 110, 115, 123, 250, 288, 332; ideologies of, 119; and North Carolina Mutual, 124, 125, 126, 144; and class, 140; and political economy, 250; and working-class blacks, 252

Black medical technicians, 153, 164

Black men: white women protected from, 4, 59, 60–61, 62, 63; protection of black women, 7, 17, 77, 85, 88, 110, 112, 115, 119, 124, 132–33, 136, 139–40, 142, 154, 159, 256, 258, 333, 338; and migration, 17, 255, 256; political leadership of, 18–19, 20, 55–57, 67–71, 72, 73–75, 107–8, 144, 220–21, 249–50, 272, 333–34; and electoral

politics, 65, 69–70; portrayals of, 86–87, 97; and morality, 101; and black business, 123; life expectancy of, 148, 149; and World War I service, 217–20; population shifts in, 233. *See also* Black manhood; Black patriarchs; Working-class black men

Black middle class: in Durham, 14, 18, 249, 332, 341; Frazier on, 14, 20, 21, 123, 145, 367 (n. 27); and intraracial relations, 16; values of, 19; and respectability, 20, 82, 275, 338; and upward mobility, 22; and Volkamenia Literary Club, 105; and black elite, 110; and identity, 139; and education, 142–43; and nurses, 155, 160; and teachers, 155, 315; World War I efforts of, 220, 244, 260; and gender roles, 252; success of, 254; and working-class blacks, 258; and Great Depression, 290–91; strengthening of, 308. *See also* Aspiring class

Black migration: and black women, 15, 16–17, 32, 45, 88–91, 106, 107, 109, 143, 220, 232–38, 240, 243, 254, 339; and black men, 17, 255, 256; and Durham's Station, 30; and black neighborhoods, 39, 78; patterns of, 51–53, 106, 223; and race relations, 69, 71; and churchwomen, 106; and Great Migration, 144, 232–33; and World War I, 222, 223, 233–34, 240; and working-class blacks, 232, 286; and political leadership, 233–34, 236, 238–39; and New Deal, 296

Black nationalism, 14, 114, 171, 250

Black neighborhoods: destruction of, 11, 67; demand for services, 17, 238–39, 307, 308, 328, 340; institutions in, 32–33, 251–52; growth of, 32–33, 339–40; and migration, 39, 78; and segregation, 39–40, 68–69; and class,

141; and Negro Civic League, 162; and electoral politics, 283

Black nurses, 21, 130, 148, 153–55, 159–60, 223, 235, 337

Black patriarchs: hegemony of, 17, 19; and race relations, 20; and black women, 21, 132, 133, 261; effectiveness of, 110, 186; and black elites, 125, 126, 133, 135, 138, 141, 320; political leadership of, 151–52; and gender roles, 250; and black poverty, 254; and working-class blacks, 257, 258, 259–60, 336; and New Deal era, 289; and masculinist vision of black achievement, 333

Black people: portrayals of, 11, 20, 85, 86–87, 94, 97, 98, 106, 113, 143, 170

Black poverty: perpetuation of, 11; and black women, 16, 44, 234, 253–54, 261, 263, 277, 338; black entrepreneurs escaping, 37; and black children, 49, 184, 272, 276; prevalence of, 70, 111, 147–48, 283, 333, 340; and political leadership, 75–76; and farming, 89–90; and churchwomen, 104; and black business, 139, 147; and life expectancy, 148–49; and black elite, 254–55; cause of, 293; and Great Depression, 331; and desegregation, 344

Black professionals: and aspiring class, 21; achievements of, 37, 331; and class, 40, 154–55; black women as, 46, 111–13, 124, 127–28, 130–34, 154–55, 159–60, 236, 281; and political leadership, 47; white opposition to, 79; and respectability, 112, 338; and black business, 143; and Lincoln Hospital, 164, 165; as New Deal advisers, 291–92, 293, 320–21, 333; and education, 311, 338

Black schools: freedmen's schools, 1, 2;

burning of, 11, 48, 49, 51, 68, 70, 72–73, 88, 166, 186–87, 258–59, 325; demand for services, 17; and white beneficence, 19, 49, 153–54; and churches, 33; municipal support of, 49, 50, 68; and black elite, 120, 166; and North Carolina Mutual, 123; and class, 142–43; attendance at, 150, 183, 307; Pauli Murray on, 178, 179, 180, 182, 183, 186; funding for, 290–91, 386 (n. 11). See also Education

Black teachers: and race relations, 21; salaries of, 22, 38, 177–78, 290, 308, 312–22, 323, 324, 328, 334, 335, 337, 375 (n. 73), 393 (n. 16); and women's employment, 32, 37, 82, 154–55, 177; and men's employment, 123, 177; and access to education, 153, 155; whites' attitudes toward, 154, 183; training for, 172, 178, 180–81, 185; contact with students' communities, 183–84; and parents, 184–85, 376 (n. 99); increase in, 235; recruitment of, 250; housing of, 261; from Efland Home, 274; and electoral politics, 283; and New Deal era, 289; and Great Depression, 290–91; and NAACP, 310, 313, 315, 320, 321, 322, 334, 337; respectability of, 314, 315; and certification standards, 315. See also Black middle class

Black towns: destruction of, 11, 14, 19

Black Wall Street, 14, 114, 145

Blackwell, Annie Walker, 102–3

Blackwell Tobacco, 43, 44, 240

Black womanhood: redefinition of, 2, 17, 20; slavery in past of, 5, 8; insults against, 11, 85, 86; models of, 82, 97, 110; and black elite, 110, 288, 332; and North Carolina Mutual, 129, 131, 132–33, 135, 144; and black elite women, 250, 251, 262; and working-

class black women, 252; and clubwomen, 264. *See also* North Carolina
Mutual Life Insurance Company
Black women: white men's sexual power
over, 2, 4, 5, 15, 20, 43, 45, 48, 62, 85,
231, 258–59, 262, 268, 271, 326; and
domesticity, 2, 20, 42, 88; hazards facing, 7, 8, 88, 149; black men's protection of, 7, 17, 77, 85, 88, 110, 112,
115, 119, 124, 132–33, 136, 139–40,
142, 154, 159, 256, 258, 333, 338; and
class, 7, 85, 139, 140, 155, 162, 277,
282–83; rape of, 11, 62, 74, 115, 325–
30; political leadership of, 12, 18, 56,
97–98, 101, 105, 106–8, 250, 263–70,
281, 307–8, 323–24, 328; respectability of, 12, 20, 82, 86, 110, 119, 127,
130, 259, 262, 263, 326; and migration, 15, 16–17, 32, 45, 88–91, 106,
107, 109, 143, 220, 232–38, 240, 243,
254, 339; and urbanization, 15, 88–
91, 261, 277, 350 (n. 21); and black
poverty, 16, 44, 234, 253–54, 261,
263, 277, 338; single women, 17, 127–
38, 155, 159, 250, 251, 261–64; and
demographics, 17, 233–35; institutions of, 33–34; sexual harassment of,
43, 136, 228, 258, 259; as professionals, 46, 111–13, 124, 127–28,
130–34, 154–55, 159–60, 236, 281;
and electoral politics, 65–67; portrayals of, 86, 87; resistance of, 87–88,
92–96, 101, 106–8, 220, 224, 229; as
widows, 91, 363 (n. 28); life expectancy of, 148–49, 165; as health care
providers, 149–50, 155; and library
support, 172–73; and New Deal, 289,
297, 298; and NAACP, 321; as wives
of black businessmen, 353 (n. 38). *See
also* Black elite women; Churchwomen; Clubwomen; Working-class
black women

Bottoms, the, 40, 225, 254
Bowles, Eva, 264, 265
Brown, Charlotte Hawkins, 98, 100,
143, 179, 267, 268, 269–73, 384
(n. 80)
Brown v. Board of Education (1954), 309,
312, 344
Bunche, Ralph J., 335, 336
Busy Women's Club, 100, 162
Byrd, Daniel, 341–42

Cameron, Paul, 27, 29
Capital: land as, 6; and respectability, 22;
building of, 29, 76; and tobacco
industry, 31; social capital, 31, 112,
117, 132, 139, 140, 153; and upbuilding, 108, 153; and black elite, 110,
114, 139, 143; and North Carolina
Mutual, 117, 119; and health care,
148, 150
Capitalism: and black sovereignty, 19;
and black business, 23, 123; and New
South, 41, 50; and unions, 43; and
employment, 45; and aspiring class,
46; and black elite, 114, 122, 123; and
black middle class, 294, 332
Carolina Times, 136, 250, 268, 303, 305,
318, 324, 325, 326, 336, 337
Carr, Julian S., Jr.: and white supremacy,
4, 60, 153; and O'Daniel, 29, 34, 37;
and textile industry, 41, 92, 93, 122;
on John Merrick, 42; on racial purity,
48; political leadership of, 56–57; and
electoral politics, 64–65; and black
schools, 68; and white beneficence,
69, 153; and William G. Pearson, 152,
288; and Lincoln Hospital, 158; and
education, 167
Carr, Julian S., III, 92–93, 303, 307–8
Carter, Patricia, 160, 244
Central Prohibition Club of Durham,
46–47

Charlotte, N.C., 32, 243, 317
Charlotte Observer, 92
Cheatham, Henry P., 64, 65
Child labor laws, 225, 281–82, 295, 373 (n. 42)
Children's Bureau, 148–49, 363 (n. 23)
Churchwomen, 18, 35, 100–106, 107, 140, 257
Citizenship rights: and Reconstruction, 40; and political organizations, 47; appreciation for, 56; and property rights, 69; and race relations, 72; and James E. Shepard, 77; and capital accumulation, 119, 143; and education, 166; and ending of World War I, 220; and Independent Voters League, 306–7. *See also* Civil rights; Voting rights
Civil rights: and black business, 19; and freedom's first generation, 24, 25, 342; and emancipation, 28; and political leadership, 57, 341, 342; and black women, 262, 340; and woman suffrage, 278; and Conrad Odell Pearson, 288, 289; and NAACP, 309–13, 326–27; and education, 310–13; and intraracial relations, 340. *See also* Citizenship rights
Civil Works Administration (CWA), 296, 297
Class: and social distance, 5; and black women, 7, 85, 139, 140, 155, 162, 277, 282–83; and challenges to white supremacy, 8; and upbuilding, 10, 108; and race progress, 12, 23; and racial unity, 13; and intraracial relations, 16, 23, 83, 87, 95–96, 98–99, 106, 107, 220, 254, 277, 307–8, 331, 336, 338, 339, 340–41, 343, 351 (n. 26); and respectability, 20–22, 82; fluid paradigm of, 22, 37; and education, 22, 38, 97, 142–43, 155; catego-
ries of, 22, 99, 140, 141, 143, 352–53 (n. 38); and marriage, 22, 110–11, 135–36; and upward mobility, 22, 134, 141–42, 224, 259, 269; and status designations, 37–38; and gender, 85, 154, 314, 352 (n. 38); and church-women, 102, 106, 140; and color consciousness, 141–42, 370 (n. 75); and institutions, 154; and hospital work, 163; and Red Cross, 245. *See also* Aspiring class; Black elite; Black middle class; Working-class blacks
Clement, Josephine, 24, 155, 286
Clerks' Home, 133, 261
Clubwomen: and gender relations, 12; and women's spaces, 18; and respectability, 20, 82, 98, 99; and Jim Crow, 24; and racial uplift, 97–100, 101, 106, 107, 251, 257–58, 269–70, 338; and health care, 162, 163, 165; and education, 183; World War I efforts of, 220, 244, 260; and working-class blacks, 257–60, 263, 272; on black men's leadership, 260, 275; and black poverty, 261; and gender roles, 262, 272; and black womanhood, 264; training for household labor, 267–69; and black children, 271–75, 383 (n. 62); and Scarborough Nursery, 276–77; and woman suffrage, 278, 280, 283; and NAACP, 321
Cole, Arthur Vance, 241, 242
Coleman Cotton Mill, 36, 72
Color consciousness, 1, 78, 141–42
Colored Orphan's Asylum, 34, 272
Colored School, 48, 50
Colored Voters League, 282
Color line. *See* Veil of color
Commission on Interracial Cooperation, 313, 315–16, 317, 333
Committee on Colored Work, 265, 266
Community Chest, 265, 303–4

Community dynamics, 16–18, 351 (n. 26), 353 (n. 41)

Compulsory education law, 165, 168, 183, 373 (n. 42)

Cooper, Anna Julia, 20, 65

Cowper, Mary, 385 (n. 81)

Cox, George, 315, 389 (n. 18)

Crime, 17, 254–55, 307

Crisis, 139, 223, 279, 313, 316–17, 322

Dame, Charles Morton, 78–80, 81, 82, 83, 97, 330, 344

Dame, Mary Pauline Fitzgerald: and freedom's first generation, 5, 288; as teacher, 7–8, 14, 35–36, 38, 39, 49, 80, 82, 83, 150, 154, 155, 174, 177, 178–79, 183, 185, 186, 224, 283, 290–91, 315, 329–30, 343–44; and St. Titus Chapel, 33; education of, 38–39, 81; and segregation, 53, 329; and electoral politics, 66; marriage of, 78, 79; and Jim Crow, 81; and literary clubs, 112; and class, 140, 343; World War I efforts of, 244; and woman suffrage, 279; and voting rights, 281; and NAACP, 322; and Pauli Murray, 327, 330

Dancy, John C., 35, 58–59, 64, 65, 66, 116

Daughters of Dorcas, 100, 162, 163, 260, 270

Davis, John P., 292, 294, 295, 298, 301

Day, William, 36, 37

Daye, Mattie, 175, 176, 185, 186

Death rates, 148–49, 165, 333

Debro, Sarah, 27, 28

Delta Sigma Theta, 328

Democracy: and Jim Crow, 11; ideology of, 25; and Reconstruction, 40; and industrialization, 50; and racial violence, 79; and education, 166; rhetoric of, 185, 219, 282; and NAACP civil

rights campaign, 309; and racial caste system, 328–29

Democratic Party: and white supremacy, 47–48, 60, 64, 293, 307; and black schools, 49; and Julian S. Carr Jr., 56–57, 153; and race relations, 59, 60, 64, 385 (n. 87); and black disenfranchisement, 73; and clubwomen, 283, 306; and black support, 324

Division for Negro Youth, 269

Division of Negro Economics, 221, 232, 333

Division of Work among Negroes, 183, 286, 376 (n. 92)

Dodson, J. A., 78, 116, 244

Dodson, Lillian Fitzgerald, 78, 244

Donnell, Martha Merrick, 129, 135

Dowd, Jerome, 84, 92

Du Bois, W. E. B.: on veil of color, 9–10; on upbuilding, 10, 12, 18; on Durham, 12, 14, 18, 121, 262, 263, 332; and Booker T. Washington, 13–14; assertiveness of, 56, 144; on Trinity College, 69; on Negro Problem, 84–85; on black women, 88–89; and black elite, 110, 115, 129, 333; and North Carolina Mutual, 117; and education, 122; on black business, 138; on capital, 143; and James E. Shepard, 172; on World War I service, 218, 219, 339; on equality, 220

Duke, Benjamin N., 159, 163

Duke, Brodie, 162

Duke, James B., 156, 163, 164, 172

Duke, Washington: and tobacco industry, 41; and New South, 42, 153; and political leadership, 57; and race relations, 69; and John Merrick, 116, 120, 152, 156, 157–58, 371 (n. 14); and health care, 157–58

Duke Endowment, 164

Duke Tobacco Company, 156

Dunbar-Nelson, Alice, 129, 135, 243
Durham, Exter, 29, 30
Durham, N.C.: blacks' opportunities in, 6, 14, 45; Du Bois on, 12, 14, 18, 121, 262, 263, 332; and New South, 13, 31, 41, 50, 68, 332; industrial racism of, 15; demographics of, 16–17, 381 (n. 15); population growth of, 31–32; black population of, 32, 89, 91, 94; residential segregation in, 39; tobacco industry in, 41, 45; race relations in, 42, 69–70; and myth of racial peace, 70–71
Durham, Tempie Herndon, 29
Durham Business and Professional League, 146
Durham Chamber of Commerce, 246
Durham Civic Club, 278
Durham Civic League, 162, 372 (n. 33)
Durham Colored Graded School, 68, 72–73, 78, 105, 150
Durham Colored Library, 172–73
Durham Commercial Security Company, 120
Durham Committee on Negro Affairs (DCNA), 323–24, 325, 335, 336, 340, 342
Durham County Public Library, 172
Durham County School Board, 174, 175, 176, 186
Durham Daily Sun, 55, 57, 60, 64, 65, 67, 68, 73
Durham Group, 12–13, 310, 317, 332
Durham Herald-Sun, 268
Durham Manifesto, 328–29
Durham Ministerial Alliance, 301
Durham Morning Herald: on household labor, 94; on black women, 109–10, 238; and North Carolina Mutual, 121, 126, 145; on Lincoln Hospital, 164; on William G. Pearson, 167, 180; and education, 181–82, 310, 311, 312; and

World War I service of blacks, 217–18; on unions, 240; on racial violence, 247, 380 (n. 73); and woman suffrage, 280; and Colored Voters League, 282; on Oscar King, 325; on upbuilding, 332–33
Durham Negro Observer, 126, 163, 279
Durham Negro Youth Federation, 328
Durham Recorder, 48, 51
Durham Red Cross, 221, 244
Durham's Station, N.C., 3, 6, 30–31
Durham Tobacco Plant, 48, 51, 52

East End, 32
East End Betterment Society, 340
East End Mission, 100
East End School, 150, 179, 186, 287, 315, 375 (n. 79)
Education: blacks' desire for, 9–10, 28, 49, 50, 165–66, 169; and class, 22, 38, 97, 142–43, 155; equality in, 23, 168, 177, 341, 344; black women's support of, 34, 150, 155, 176–77, 182–84, 269; and black colleges, 34–35; as instrument of liberation, 40; and race relations, 51; and political leadership, 56, 58, 75, 77, 153, 186, 310–13, 315; and gendered professional opportunities, 82; and black migration, 91; and churchwomen, 104; and North Carolina Mutual, 119; and black elite, 123–24, 165, 166, 170; of black women, 128, 130, 131, 132, 141, 155; and double tax burden on blacks, 151, 169, 175–76; for black nurses, 159–61; and Negro Civic League, 162; whites' attitudes toward, 165–66, 167, 168, 169–70, 171, 172, 176, 178, 182–83, 186, 311, 374 (n. 55); Hampton-Tuskegee model of, 169, 170, 171; and white beneficence, 169, 170–71, 172, 174, 176, 373 (n. 51); industrial

education, 169, 170–71, 172, 176;
Jeanes Supervising Industrial Teacher
program, 170, 173–75, 176, 181, 182,
223, 272; high school education, 179–
80, 186, 310, 322, 341, 376 (n. 87);
funding for, 290–91; and NAACP,
310, 311–12, 322–23; and Conrad
Odell Pearson, 310–11, 312; limited
options in, 333. *See also* Black schools
Efland Home, 271–74, 275, 282, 384
(n. 68)
Electoral politics: and black business,
23; and Aaron M. Moore, 35, 47, 55,
56, 57, 58, 66, 69; and William G.
Pearson, 47, 48, 55, 56, 57, 66, 69;
and black disenfranchisement, 48, 73;
and race relations, 51, 55, 59, 60–61,
63–70, 152, 371 (n. 13); and white
supremacy, 51, 55–56, 57, 59, 60, 61,
63, 64, 67, 70; blacks' withdrawal
from, 75–76; and working-class
blacks, 283, 307–8. *See also* Political
leadership
Emancipation, 4, 8, 9–10, 27–31, 53,
118, 332, 333. *See also* Freedom;
Slavery
Emancipation Day celebrations, 76,
152, 285–88
Employment: and industrialization, 31,
32, 44, 71, 75, 253; and political economy, 32, 40, 87, 88–89, 253, 295–96;
and race relations, 38, 44, 45, 50–51;
race hierarchy in, 42, 44, 45, 46, 52,
64, 231; gender hierarchy in, 45, 46,
83–84, 132, 224, 294–95; and subordination of blacks, 45–46, 170, 228,
295; instability in, 226, 253, 290, 296,
333
Equality: in education, 23, 168, 177,
328, 341, 344; in political leadership,
47–48, 56, 59; and white supremacy,
71; education leading to, 166; and

World War I service, 219–20; obstacles to, 247; and New Deal, 298; in
wages, 301, 302, 328; and NAACP,
316, 318; and Durham Manifesto,
328–29
Evans, Addie, 156, 157
Evans, E. Lewis, 241, 242, 300, 301,
302, 304
Everywoman's Magazine, 245, 279

Faulk, Marie, 141, 154, 183, 184, 185,
250, 314, 322
Federal government, 79, 84, 293, 297
Federal Theater Project, 298, 321
Fisk University, 7, 35, 78, 170
Fitzgerald, Cornelia Smith, 1–7, 8, 29,
254
Fitzgerald, Mary Pauline. *See* Dame,
Mary Pauline Fitzgerald
Fitzgerald, Richard: brick business of, 3,
41, 68, 115–16; property of, 6, 42; status of, 7; and black entrepreneurs, 8,
37; as political leader, 12, 41–42, 69;
and Mechanics and Farmers Bank, 14,
36, 120; and Emmanuel AME Zion
Church, 33; mansion of, 40; and black
suffrage, 47; and education, 50, 78;
wealth of, 71; and Coleman Cotton
Mill, 72; death of, 144, 249
Fitzgerald, Robert George: marriage of,
1–2, 3, 4–7; and education, 1–2, 8,
38–39, 49, 330; and black manhood,
7; home of, 40, 225; and electoral politics, 66; and racial uplift, 79, 82, 330;
financial position of, 140
Fitzgerald, Sallie. *See* Small, Sallie
Fitzgerald
Fitzgerald, Sarah Ann, 3, 4, 5
Fitzgerald, Thomas, 3, 4, 5, 348 (n. 9)
Fitzgerald Drug Company, 121
Foreign Missionary Convention of
North Carolina, 34, 35, 36, 103–5

Foulk's Reformatory for Negro Youth, 272
Fourteenth Amendment, 327
Franklin, John Hope, 14
Fraternal Bank and Trust Company, 120, 167
Frazier, E. Franklin, 14, 20, 21, 122, 123, 144–45, 249, 254, 332, 333, 367 (n. 27)
Freedmen's Bureau, 28
Freedom: ideologies of, 8, 219, 286, 336; sense of entitlement to, 9; attacks on, 10; meaning of, 13, 24, 28, 29, 43–44, 332, 338, 339; masculinist perspective on, 19; celebrations of, 76; multiple strategies for attaining, 87
Freedpeople, 1, 2, 4, 13, 27, 28, 37, 43–44, 110, 130
Fusion politics, 57, 67, 264, 278

Gambling, 16, 22, 286
Gender: and intraracial relations, 11–12, 16, 17, 23, 85, 87, 102, 321, 336, 339, 340–41, 351 (n. 26); and Jim Crow, 11–12, 83–84, 85, 88; and respectability, 21, 82, 127; ideologies of, 23, 24; and New South, 40; and race relations, 59, 60–61; and education, 82; and class, 85, 154, 308, 314, 352 (n. 38); and racial uplift, 97–98; and black poverty, 253–54
Gender hierarchy: in employment, 45, 46, 83–84, 131–32, 224, 294–95
Gender roles: and freedpeople's aspirations, 2; and black women's work, 7, 17, 89–90, 104; and ideologies of freedom, 8; and upbuilding, 10; and internal community dynamics, 16–18, 351 (n. 26); and gender relations, 17, 20; and respectability, 20; and black elite, 21, 110, 112, 113, 123, 124–25, 127–32, 139–40, 143, 220, 337; and

black entrepreneurs, 37, 42; and farming, 89–91; and class, 99, 139–40; and churchwomen, 105; and black nurses, 159–60; and working-class blacks, 252, 256, 259–60; and clubwomen, 262, 272
General Education Board (GEB), 169–70, 171, 175, 374 (n. 55)
Generations: freedom's first generation, 5, 24, 25, 35, 38, 53, 59, 78, 79, 81, 84, 110, 114, 150, 288, 316, 342; and intraracial relations, 16, 220–21, 249, 250, 288, 310, 313, 319–21, 322, 324, 328–29, 330, 336; and slavery, 23, 24, 38; challenges to memory, 72, 319; and education, 75; Charles N. Hunter on, 77–79; and black women, 134; Jim Crow generation, 150, 254, 310; and change in political leadership, 220–21, 249, 250, 288, 310, 313, 319–21, 322, 324, 328–29, 330, 336–37, 342; and black professionals, 289; and New Deal, 293; and unions, 305
Gille, Susie V. See Norfleet, Susie V. Gille
Gilmore, Glenda Elizabeth, 384–85 (n. 80)
Goins, Eva Whitted, 130
Gompers, Samuel, 93
Goodwin, Margaret Kennedy, 131, 150, 164
Grady, Henry, 42
Great Depression: and working-class blacks, 259, 290; Oxley on, 286; unstable economy of, 289; and black middle class, 290–91; and blacks on relief, 295–97; and racism, 308, 331; and black teachers, 314–15
Great Migration, 144, 232–33
Green, Caleb, 48
Green, John R., 31
Greene, Christina, 351 (n. 26)

Greensboro, N.C., 70, 317
Greenwood, Okla., 14, 114, 145
Guy, Cy, 4, 28

Hampton Institute, 35, 50, 78
Hampton-Tuskegee model, 169, 170, 171
Harlem, N.Y., 122–23, 144–45
Harris, Mabel, 91, 184, 226
Hart, Cy, 29
Haskins, Luetta, 245
Hastie, William, 312
Hawkins, John R., 101
Haynes, George E., 221, 234, 235, 240, 241
Hayti: central business district of, 14, 68, 110, 128, 167, 251, 257; as black community, 31, 32–33, 39–40; and temperance groups, 47; and black elite, 140; living conditions in, 149; crime in, 254–55; demand for services in, 307
Health care: and white beneficence, 19, 150, 153–54, 156; and black business, 119; and capital, 148, 150; black women providing, 149–50, 155; and Jim Crow, 150–51, 153, 156–57, 164; for black women, 155, 158–59; and race relations, 155–57, 267; public health care work, 160, 161, 162, 181, 239, 260, 264; and Scarborough Nursery, 276–77; need for, 333. See also Lincoln Hospital
Hickok, Lorena, 296–98
Hickstown, 32
Hickstown School, 290–91
Higginbotham, Evelyn Brooks, 385 (n. 87)
Hill, Joseph A., 234–35
Hillside High School, 14, 250, 252, 287, 288, 291, 376 (n. 87)
Hocutt, Thomas, 311–12, 319, 326

Holland, Annie W., 183, 184–85
Household labor: and working-class black women, 15, 16, 18, 21, 32, 43, 44, 46, 52, 83, 86, 88, 90, 91–92, 94, 112, 231, 236, 267, 353 (n. 38); and respectability, 20; and unions, 43, 94; demand for, 44, 94, 95, 226, 237; and black women's acquiring information, 66; and black children, 90, 225, 235; and aspiring class, 107; and class, 139; and black employers, 140, 269; and Jim Crow, 143; and health care needs, 157; and subordination of blacks, 170; working conditions of, 231, 239, 268, 271, 274, 329; instability of work in, 253, 290, 296; training programs for, 267–69, 274, 275, 282, 288, 297, 298, 321; and New Deal, 295
Household of Ruth, 105, 270
Houston, Charles Hamilton, 322–23, 326
Howard University, 35, 78, 79, 170
Hughes, Langston, 24
Hunter, Charles N., 50, 77–79, 93–96, 107, 123–24, 222
Hunter, Tera, 350 (n. 21)
Hunter College, 180
Hunton, Addie, 84, 85, 107, 227, 262–63
Hurston, Zora Neal, 14
Husband, Sadie, 177
Husbands, Frank, 174–75

Identity, 10, 16, 139
Immigrants, 42
Imperial Tobacco, 224, 225, 237
Income: and class, 22; of black teachers, 22, 38, 177–78, 290, 308, 312–22, 323, 324, 328, 334, 335, 337, 375 (n. 73), 393 (n. 16); wages, 43, 69, 92, 93, 94, 133, 224, 241, 243, 295, 299–305, 314, 324, 328, 329, 334, 338; and race hierarchy, 46, 300, 301; and black

migration, 88, 90; and black elite women, 132, 133; rise in, 253; and New Deal, 305

Independent Voters League, 306–7

Industrial Commission on Negro Affairs, 292–93

Industrial education, 169, 170–71, 172, 176, 288

Industrialization: and working-class black women, 15, 16; and employment, 31, 32, 44, 71, 75, 253; and Durham's power structure, 41, 50; and life expectancy, 149; and World War I, 234; and wage structure, 295; and black middle class, 332

Infant mortality, 148, 149, 165

Institutions: and upbuilding, 10; effect of black women's migration on, 17; white beneficence toward, 19, 74, 151–52; and respectability, 20; quality of life, 32; in black neighborhoods, 32–33, 251–52; and churchwomen, 107; and black elite, 110, 119, 150, 167, 320; and antiapartheid activism, 153; and race relations, 154; and intraracial relations, 319, 320; and black business, 333; and unified action, 334, 349 (n. 9)

Interracial Committee, 266, 267

Interracial sexual relations, 48, 60, 61, 62, 63

Intraracial relations: and gender, 11–12, 16, 17, 23, 85, 87, 102, 321, 336, 339, 340–41, 351 (n. 26); tensions in, 12, 13, 15, 23, 95–96, 98–99, 107, 334, 339–40, 349 (n. 9); and protests, 12, 219, 331–32; and resistance, 12, 331–32, 336; and class, 16, 23, 83, 87, 95–96, 98–99, 106, 107, 220, 254, 277, 307–8, 331, 336, 338, 339, 340–41, 343, 351 (n. 26); and generational differences, 16, 220–21, 249, 250, 288,

310, 313, 319–21, 322, 324, 328–29, 330, 336; and race relations, 20, 23, 289, 351 (n. 26); and respectability, 20–21; and racial ties, 37; and Emancipation Day celebrations, 287; and New Deal, 292–93; and NAACP, 313, 321–22

Iota Phi Lambda, 134, 162

Janiewski, Dolores, 350 (n. 26)

Jeanes Supervising Industrial Teacher program, 170, 173–75, 176, 181, 182, 223, 272

Jeffries, William L., 360 (n. 21)

Jim Crow: and veil of color, 10, 53; and white southerners, 10–11; as American apartheid, 11, 24, 84, 87–88, 114, 153, 289, 308, 332; and race relations, 11, 24, 152; and subordination of blacks, 11, 56; duplicity of, 11, 153, 219; gendered aspects of, 11–12, 83–84, 85, 88; and black business, 19, 24, 121, 143, 145, 313; and respectability, 20, 84; and working-class blacks, 22, 143, 232, 259, 329; and intraracial relations, 24, 87, 332, 340; and railroad, 57, 73, 109; solidification of, 79; and black manhood, 82; resistance to, 84, 101, 108, 137–38, 289, 319, 321, 332, 335–36, 338; and black elite, 91, 106, 114, 118, 132, 144, 150–51, 335–36; and black achievements, 114, 334; and black poverty, 148, 254; and health care, 150–51, 153, 156–57, 164; and proposed segregated hospital ward, 156–57; paradox of, 161–62; and tobacco factories, 224; and YWCA, 266; NAACP civil rights campaign against, 309; status of, 311, 324. See also Segregation

Johnson, Charles S., 298, 303, 328–29, 352–53 (n. 38)

Johnson, James Weldon, 134, 287
Jones, Beverly Washington, 350–51 (n. 26)
Jones, Eugene Kinckle, 295
Jones, Fannie, 124, 127
Jones, Mattie Southgate, 278–79
Jordan, J. F., 165–66
Journal of United Labor, 43
Julius Rosenwald Fund, 164, 170, 171, 174, 175, 375 (n. 79)
Junior Lady Board, 162, 163
Juvenile delinquency, 276

Kellor, Frances, 95
Kennedy, William J., Jr., 131, 290, 389 (n. 18)
King, Oscar, 325–26
Knights of Labor, 42–43, 48
Ku Klux Klan, 4, 28, 138, 247

Lampkin, Daisy, 317, 318, 321
Landlord Tenant Act of 1877, 29
Larkins, John R., 274, 275
Latta, Julia, 160, 161, 244, 281
League of Women Voters, 281–82
Lennon, Maggie Moore, 162, 163
Liberia, 51, 104
Liberty Bonds, 223, 244, 245, 260
Liberty Loan, 222, 264
Library services, 172–73, 174, 176
Life expectancy, 148–49, 165, 267
Liggett and Myers, 91, 178, 223–25, 230, 255, 257, 259, 263, 298, 301–2
Lincoln, Abraham, 158, 285, 306
Lincoln Hospital: black women's support of, 134, 159, 162–63, 164, 165, 260, 270; movement for building of, 155–58; and white beneficence, 158–59, 163; black women as employees of, 159; nursing school of, 159, 160–61, 164; black women as patients of, 159, 165; and Aaron M. Moore, 160,

162, 164, 249, 372 (n. 33); and flu pandemic of 1918, 161–62, 260; and fire of 1924, 163; funding for, 163–64, 222; and William G. Pearson, 167; and Red Cross, 244, 245; and Charles Shepard, 249
Literacy: and black disenfranchisement, 73, 166, 281; and churchwomen, 101; and Volkamenia Literary Club, 105, 173, 283; black population's rate of, 150; and education, 168, 176; and white beneficence, 174, 176; and clubwomen, 275, 276
Literary Digest, 93
Locke, Alain, 114, 122, 144
Lucas, Julia, 24, 305, 323–24
Lynchings, 4, 11, 28, 60–62, 64, 72, 74, 85–87, 114, 271
Lyon Park, 32, 40
Lyon Park Elementary School, 287, 291, 343
Lyons, Theresa Jan Cameron, 29, 30, 91, 141, 181, 184, 186, 187

Mack, Annie Miller, 256–57
Mack, Charlie Neconda, 88, 229, 256–60
Manly, Alexander, 61–64, 67
Marshall, Thurgood, 322–23, 327
Mason, Lucy Randolph, 299
Masonic Lodge, 36, 173, 221–22
Massey, C. W., 180, 185
McAndrew, Anthony, 241, 242
McCauley, Manley, 60–61, 63, 64, 65, 70, 72, 318
McCoy, Cecil, 310, 312, 313, 319
McDougal, Richard L., 120, 139
McDougald, Elise Johnson, 251, 254, 352–53 (n. 38)
McIver, Charles D., 168–69
McLester, Johnnie Blount, 141, 269, 275–76, 381 (n. 31)

Mechanics and Farmers Bank, 14, 36, 120–21, 127, 139, 141, 167, 257, 291, 319

Memory: of slavery, 15, 23, 37, 38, 130, 287, 331; of Wilmington Riot, 72, 74, 114, 115, 117, 145, 282, 319, 335; of racial violence, 72, 316, 319, 325, 335; generations' challenge to, 72, 319

Memphis, Tenn., 62, 237

Merrick, Ed, 120

Merrick, Geneva, 124

Merrick, John: barbershops of, 36, 37, 40, 66, 76, 116, 127; as political leader, 41–42, 52–53, 56, 69, 75–76, 152, 187, 219; and black suffrage, 47; and electoral politics, 76; and black manhood, 76, 123; and black elite, 110, 139, 163; and North Carolina Mutual, 116, 118, 119, 125, 127; and Washington Duke, 116, 120, 152, 156, 157–58, 371 (n. 14); death of, 144, 220, 249, 250, 260; and health care, 156, 157–58; and library, 172; World War I efforts of, 222, 244

Merrick, Lyda Moore, 124, 162

Merrick, Mabel, 124

Merrick, Martha, 163, 222, 245, 250

Merrick-McDougal-Wilson Company, 120

Merrick-Moore-Spaulding Land Company, 120, 355 (n. 24)

Miller, Dora Scott, 228, 232

Miller, Kelly, 17, 95, 122, 351 (n. 30)

Missionary societies, 33, 100, 102, 104, 106, 107, 183, 245

Missionary work, 82, 101, 103, 167

Missouri ex rel. Gaines v. Canada, 322, 327

Mitchell, Michele, 349 (n. 9), 353 (n. 41), 355 (n. 26)

Mitchell, Rhoden, 93–94

Mitchner, Reginald, 91, 225–26, 255

Moore, Aaron M.: and electoral politics, 35, 47, 55, 56, 57, 58, 66, 69; and black business, 37, 122, 144; as black professional, 40; and political leadership, 58–59, 219, 221, 238–39, 246, 333; wealth of, 71; and black elite, 110; and White Rock Baptist Church, 112; and North Carolina Mutual, 116, 118, 125, 127; death of, 144, 162, 220, 249, 260; and proposed segregated hospital ward, 156–57; and Lincoln Hospital, 160, 162, 164, 249, 372 (n. 33); and education, 167–68, 173, 174, 175, 186; and working-class blacks, 236, 252; and black migration, 238–39, 246; and unions, 240, 246; and Charlotte Hawkins Brown, 272

Moore, Sarah McCotta "Cottie" Dancy, 35, 66, 100, 144, 162, 163, 250

Morality: and respectability, 20, 35, 82; and interracial organizations, 46–47; of poor white women, 61; and Manly, 62; and political leadership, 77; of black women, 84, 92, 93, 94, 97, 98, 99, 253, 261–62; and aspiring class, 96, 97; and clubwomen, 98, 99; and churchwomen, 101, 104; and black business, 113; and black teachers, 155; and black nurses, 155, 160; and working-class blacks, 258; of black children, 271–72

Moton, Robert R., 120, 294, 308

Murray, Pauli: on Cornelia Fitzgerald, 5–6; on Fitzgerald family, 7, 348 (n. 9); on segregation, 11, 329, 330; feminist insights of, 25; and institutions, 33; on Mary Pauline Dame, 82; and black aristocracy, 140; on black teachers, 154; on black schools, 178, 179, 180, 182, 183, 186; on World War I, 218; World War I efforts of, 223, 245; and class, 254, 343; education of, 288, 327, 329, 330

Mutual aid societies, 36, 257, 260, 287, 333

Myrdal, Gunnar, 87

National Association for the Advancement of Colored People (NAACP): and political leadership, 23, 310, 311–13, 316–22, 325, 326–27, 334, 336; and black elite women, 134; and Charles C. Spaulding, 292, 309, 313, 316, 317, 319, 321–22, 323, 326–27; civil rights campaign of, 309–13, 326–27; and black teachers' salaries, 312–22, 334, 335; and Durham Committee on Negro Affairs, 323–24, 325, 341–42; Durham membership list for, 369 (n. 58); and voter registration, 384 (n. 80)

National Association of Colored Women (NACW), 97, 98–99, 100, 260, 269–70, 284 (n. 80)

National Council of Negro Women, 328

National Defense Council, 243

National Federation of Afro-American Women, 98

National Industrial Recovery Act, 292

National Negro Business League (NNBL), 116, 117, 122, 125, 128, 130, 144, 254, 294, 308

National Negro Finance Corporation (NNFC), 120, 138

National Negro Financy Company, 14, 138

National Negro Housewives' League, 294

National Recovery Administration (NRA), 292, 294, 295, 296, 298, 299, 305, 316

National Religious Training School and Chautauqua for the Colored Race, 35, 122, 171–72, 222, 250, 263, 381

(n. 31). See also North Carolina College for Negroes

National Urban League, 292, 295

National War Savings Committee, 222–23

National Youth Administration, 269, 291, 298, 321

Negro Advisory Committee, 221, 239–40

Negro Civic League, 162, 372 (n. 33)

Negro Democratic Convention, 307

Negro Industrial League, 292

Negro Problem, 53, 73, 84–87, 96, 97, 106, 115, 118, 233

Negro Young People's Christian and Educational Congress, 99

New Bern, N.C., 32, 59, 69–70

Newbold, Nathan C., 169, 173–74, 175, 176, 180, 182, 272–73, 315, 317

New Deal: and black elite, 289, 305; and black professionals as advisers, 291–92, 293, 320–21, 333; and tobacco industry, 296, 298–99; and working-class blacks, 307

New Negro, 13–14, 74, 114–15, 138, 144–45, 249, 250–51

New Negro Renaissance, 25, 122

New South: Durham's role in, 13, 31, 41, 50, 68, 332; political economy of, 13, 250; and residential segregation, 39; and labor needs, 40, 52, 53; and Washington Duke, 42, 153; and black business, 114; and New Negro, 115; black women's role in development of, 350 (n. 21)

Nightengale, George E., 317, 318

Nineteenth Amendment, 278, 279, 280, 283

Norfleet, Susie V. Gille, 109–15, 119, 127, 128, 130, 134–36, 279, 281

Norfolk Journal and Guide, 122, 223

North Carolina Bureau of Labor, 165, 166, 168

North Carolina Central University, 14, 35, 122, 171

North Carolina College for Negroes, 14, 35, 122, 128, 171, 250, 310, 320, 321, 327, 328

North Carolina Federation of Colored Women's Clubs (NCFCWC), 100, 163, 167, 269–73, 275, 279, 306, 324, 328, 384 (n. 80)

North Carolina Federation of Women's Clubs, 272, 273, 278

North Carolina Industrial Home for Colored Girls, 271–72

North Carolina Mutual, 126

North Carolina Mutual Life Insurance Company (North Carolina Mutual and Provident Association): and black business, 14, 114–15, 119–20, 122; women employees of, 109, 110–11, 113, 127–38, 155, 159, 250, 251, 261, 274, 278, 321, 382 (n. 36); and respectability, 113, 119, 127–28, 130, 132–36, 138; and New South, 114–15; founding of, 115–16; goals of, 117–18; and political leadership, 118, 119, 336; and autonomy from whites, 118–19; white clients of, 120–21; agents of, 123–24, 125; and black manhood, 124, 125, 126, 144; women customers of, 125, 126–27, 138; and black womanhood, 129, 131, 132–33, 135, 144; public health program of, 130, 148; and white visitors, 133, 137–38; and sexual harassment of black women, 136–37, 369 (n. 63); subsidiaries of, 139, 144; and black elite, 140, 147; and color conscious-ness, 142, 370 (n. 75); growth of, 143–46, 147; success of, 148, 254, 291; and Negro Health Week, 165; World War I efforts of, 223; and YWCA, 266; and Efland Home, 273; and voting rights, 281; and Emancipation Day celebra-tions, 287; and New Deal, 297; sup-port of Radical Young Negroes, 319, 337; and NAACP, 325; as public institution, 333; reputation of, 335; Weare on, 350 (n. 26)

North Carolina Supreme Court, 50, 322

North Carolina Teachers Association, 173, 273, 317, 321, 322, 334, 335, 337, 393 (n. 16)

O'Daniel, John, 29, 31, 34, 36, 37, 71

Old South, 13, 40, 41, 44, 45, 153, 332

Order of the Eastern Star, 34, 66, 105, 260, 270

Oxley, Lawrence O., 274, 286, 290, 292, 376 (n. 92)

Palmer Memorial Institute, 143, 179, 269

Parent-Teacher Association (PTA), 185, 290

Parker, Florida Fisher, 306, 335

Paternalism, 69, 153

Pearson, Conrad Odell: on William G. Pearson, 72, 288; law practice of, 250; and voting rights, 281, 385 (n. 81); and civil rights, 288, 289; and New Deal, 297; and unions, 306; and edu-cation, 310–11, 312; and NAACP, 313, 318, 319; and Oscar King case, 326; and black elite, 335

Pearson, Minnie Sumner: and Order of the Eastern Star, 34, 35; marriage of, 35, 167; and political leadership, 66, 250, 270, 273, 281, 321; and club-women, 100, 163; World War I efforts of, 222, 244, 245; and YWCA, 263–65; and woman suffrage, 279, 280; and voting rights, 283, 324

Pearson, William G.: and education, 35, 36, 68, 166–67, 179, 180, 182, 183,

186, 250, 261, 287, 288; and black elite, 37, 167; and electoral politics, 47, 48, 55, 56, 57, 66, 69; and political leadership, 58, 66, 72, 166–67, 219, 288, 320, 328; and Carolina Mutual Life Insurance Company, 116; on black entrepreneurship, 119; and Mechanics and Farmers Bank, 120; and racial uplift, 124; on black women, 125; and Southern Fidelity and Surety Company, 139; education of, 152; World War I efforts of, 222; and Efland Home, 273; and woman suffrage, 279; and NAACP, 313, 316, 318–19, 321, 323, 326–27; and black teachers, 315, 316, 317

Pearson Elementary School, 287

People's Benevolent and Relief Association, 126, 130

Peterson, Annie, 302–3, 307–8

Plessy, Homer, 57

Plessy v. Ferguson (1896), 79, 311–12, 344

Political economy, 13, 15, 32, 40, 87–89, 250, 253, 289, 295–96

Political leadership: of black women, 12, 18, 56, 97–98, 101, 105, 106–8, 250, 263–70, 281, 307–8, 323–24, 328; of black men, 12, 18–19, 20, 55–57, 67–71, 72, 73–75, 107–8, 144, 220–21, 249–50, 272, 333–34; and black entrepreneurs, 12, 36; and demographics, 17, 233–34; and NAACP, 23, 310, 311–13, 316–22, 325, 326–27, 334, 336; and free blacks, 28; and voting rights, 47, 336; and race relations, 47–49, 56–60, 152, 220–21, 239, 243, 247, 326, 328–29, 333, 335, 371 (n. 13); and education, 56, 58, 75, 77, 153, 186, 310–13, 315; and Wilmington Riot, 72, 335; and North Carolina Mutual, 118, 119, 336; and

World War I service, 218–19; generational change in, 220–21, 249, 250, 288, 310, 313, 319–21, 322, 324, 328–29, 330, 336–37, 342; and black migration, 233–34, 236, 238–39; and unions, 240–43, 301, 302, 305–6, 334, 336, 337; and class, 307–8, 335. *See also* Black elite

Property ownership: and class, 38; and John Merrick, 42, 76; and political leadership, 47; and citizenship rights, 69; and James E. Shepard, 77; and churchwomen, 104; and racial violence, 114; and Richard L. McDougal, 120, 139; and black women, 133–34; and Negro Civic League, 162; increase in, 252

Prostitutes and prostitution, 16, 18, 22, 85, 238, 254

Quality of life, 32, 148, 181, 254, 337, 338

Race hierarchy, 42, 44–46, 49, 52, 59, 64, 231

Race pride: and black communities, 31; and teachers, 80; and North Carolina Mutual, 124, 125, 135, 138, 147; and Lincoln Hospital, 164; and education, 182, 252; and World War I service, 218; and working-class blacks, 257; merits of, 334

Race progress: collective and separate efforts toward, 12, 23, 340–41, 342; and black women, 15, 20; assessment of, 15–16; and generations, 35, 78; models of, 42, 83, 128, 129; and black business, 70; Du Bois on, 85; and aspiring class, 97; and clubwomen, 99; and black elite, 110, 143, 252, 320, 335, 339; symbols of, 148, 338

Race relations: and autonomy from

whites, 4, 7, 8; and Jim Crow, 11, 24,
152; and black nationalism, 14, 171;
and intraracial relations, 20, 23, 289,
351 (n. 26); and black elite women,
21–22, 263–75; and employment, 38,
44, 45, 50–51; and residential segregation, 40; and unions, 42–43, 241,
299–305, 327; and moral reform, 46–
47; and political leadership, 47–49,
56–60, 152, 220–21, 239, 243, 247,
326, 328–29, 333, 335, 371 (n. 13);
and electoral politics, 51, 55, 59, 60–
61, 63–70, 152, 371 (n. 13); and black
migration, 69, 71; and myth of racial
peace, 70–71; Myrdal on, 87; and
black achievement, 114; and World
War I efforts, 244–45, 246, 338–39;
and veil of color, 251–52; and respectability, 262; and woman suffrage,
278–79, 280; and New Deal, 294–95
Racial caste system, 39, 49, 71, 148, 295,
325, 328–29
Racial etiquette, 133, 137–38, 152–53,
156–57, 231, 266, 330, 372 (n. 33)
Racial peace: maintenance of, 20, 23, 56,
70–71, 114, 241, 335, 342
Racial purity, 4, 48, 60, 61, 62, 329
Racial uplift: and respectability, 20, 80,
82; and Robert Fitzgerald, 80, 82,
330; and aspiring class, 97–100; and
clubwomen, 97–100, 101, 106, 107,
251, 257–58, 269–70, 338; and
churchwomen, 100–106, 107; and
black elite, 110, 120, 125–26, 129,
130; and professional women, 112,
155; and economics, 119; and black
nurses, 160; and black elite women,
220, 250, 262, 269, 338; and black
children, 272; and black middle class,
275, 338; and training programs, 297.
See also Upbuilding
Racial violence: freedpeople's vul-

nerability to, 2; blacks' arming
against, 4; and voting rights, 5, 8; and
Jim Crow, 11, 114; and emancipation,
28; and blacks' assertive activity, 51,
78, 97; and electoral politics, 55, 57,
58, 60–61, 64, 67–68, 70; threats of,
68, 72, 319, 335–36; and racial order,
71; memory of, 72, 316, 319, 325,
335; prevalence of, 74; and white
supremacy, 79, 307; and property
ownership, 114; James E. Shepard on,
152; in post–World War I era, 247,
380 (n. 73)
Racism: and working-class black
women, 8, 15, 16, 224, 339; thriving
in face of, 10; and Jim Crow, 11; and
gender roles, 18; and respectability,
20, 80, 106, 334; and aspiring class,
21; and black elite, 113, 114–15, 118;
and unions, 240–41; lack of accommodation of, 251; and veil of color,
252; and New Deal, 297; and Great
Depression, 308, 331
Radical Young Negroes, 289, 318, 319,
336–37, 341
Raleigh, N.C., 32, 41
Raleigh Blade, 77
Raleigh Morning Post, 95
Raleigh News and Observer, 13, 63, 64,
66, 96
Randolph, A. Philip, 134, 341
Rape: of black women, 11, 62, 74, 115,
325–30; of white women, 61, 72, 74
Reconstruction, 49, 59, 60, 70, 287
Red Cross, 221, 244, 245–46, 260, 264,
272, 380 (n. 65)
Reidsville, N.C., 242, 304
Republican Party: and Washington
Duke, 41, 57, 153; and interracial
cooperation, 46, 47; and black leaders,
55, 56–59, 65, 68, 73–77, 166, 167,
168, 324; and race relations, 57–58,

64; black women's support of, 66, 67, 306

Resistance: and intraracial relations, 12, 331–32, 340; upbuilding as tactic of, 19; education as means of, 49; variety of tactics of, 79, 107, 340, 341; to Jim Crow, 84, 101, 108, 137–38, 289, 319, 321, 332, 335–36, 338; of black women, 87–88, 92–96, 101, 106–8, 220, 224, 229; and World War I, 222

Respectability: of black women, 12, 20, 21, 82, 86, 110, 127, 130, 259, 262, 263, 326; hegemony of, 20, 35, 333, 334, 339; as weapon against racism, 20, 80, 106, 334; and clubwomen, 20, 82, 98, 99; and black middle class, 20, 82, 275, 338; and Jim Crow, 20, 84; and class, 20–22, 82; and black elite, 21, 113, 132, 133, 135–36, 137, 138, 145, 253, 259, 262, 286, 338; and upper-class blacks, 21, 253; and aspiring class, 22, 97, 355 (n. 26); and churchwomen, 35, 106; and black professionals, 112, 338; and black business, 147; and black nurses, 160; and household labor, 267, 268; and voting rights, 281; of black teachers, 314, 315

Rockefeller Foundation, 159, 169–70

Roosevelt, Eleanor, 134

Roosevelt, Franklin D., 128, 283, 291, 293, 294, 295, 298, 306, 341

Rosenwald, Julius, 157, 159

Rosenwald School, 258–59, 343

Rosser, Fannie, 134, 163, 280, 281, 290

Royal Knights of King David, 36, 119, 167, 217, 266, 287

Rush, Ruth, 274–75

St. Augustine's College, 7, 35, 36, 38

St. Joseph AME Zion Church, 33, 66, 69, 78, 111, 167, 230, 240, 279

St. Luke Herald, 123

St. Mark AME Zion Church, 279

St. Titus Chapel, 33, 183

Scarborough, Clydie Fullwood, 129, 135, 250, 276–77

Scarborough, John, 129, 141, 276

Scarborough Nursery, 276–77, 282, 298

Schubert Shakespeare Club, 105, 279

Scott, Blanche, 224–25, 228, 231, 235

Scott, Minnie, 224, 225

Scott, Richard, 224, 225

Scottsboro Boys, 266

Searchlight, 67

Segregation: Pauli Murray on, 11, 329, 330; and black business, 19, 111, 117; and black neighborhoods, 39–40, 68–69; and blacks' negotiations with whites, 40, 117, 118, 120, 151, 171, 310, 327; escalation of, 53, 73; Plessy's challenge to, 57; of railroad cars, 57, 73, 109; and white support of black institutions, 74, 152; in education, 75, 253, 310–11; codification of, 79, 253; and black elite, 114, 118; and health care, 164; and World War I service, 219; in employment, 224, 295; and unions, 241, 301, 302, 327; and Red Cross, 244; and YWCA, 263; in churches, 266; and New Deal, 292, 293–94; and Great Depression, 331; as retreat from white animosity, 338; in industry, 341. *See also* Jim Crow

Self-help, 20, 31, 33, 40, 116, 143, 286–87, 289–90, 333

Self-protection, 28, 75, 332

Separate but equal doctrine, 79, 344

Sharecropping system, 29–30, 37, 91, 184, 187, 296

Shaw University, 34–35, 76, 104

Shepard, Annie D., 101, 105, 279

Shepard, Augustus, 33, 34, 318

Shepard, Charles, 249, 321

Shepard, Hattie E., 33–34, 35, 66, 100, 103, 112

Shepard, James E.: and education, 35, 122, 171, 180, 249–50, 312, 320, 374 (n. 55); and black entrepreneurs, 37; and political leadership, 58, 72, 74, 76–77, 219, 306, 310, 319, 320, 328; on Manly, 63–64; and electoral politics, 66, 69; and voting rights, 76, 77, 152, 281, 385 (n. 81), 385–86 (n. 88); and literary clubs, 105; and Carolina Mutual Life Insurance Company, 116; and institutions, 119; and Mechanics and Farmers Bank, 120; and black elite, 139; and white beneficence, 152; World War I efforts of, 222; and black children, 275; and woman suffrage, 279; and unions, 305; and NAACP, 313, 316, 318, 321, 323, 325, 326–27; and black teachers' salaries, 315–18, 335

Shepard, Pattie G., 34, 101, 103

Slater Industrial and Normal School, 169

Slavery: memory of, 15, 23, 37, 38, 130, 287, 331; and black manhood, 19; and respectability, 21; and working-class black women, 22; sharecropping compared to, 30; black fears of, 75; distance from, 97, 99, 252; and church-women, 104; tobacco factory work compared to, 228; and Emancipation Day celebrations, 287. *See also* Emancipation

Small, Sallie Fitzgerald: as teacher, 7–8, 14, 39, 154, 155, 177, 183, 343; and St. Titus Chapel, 33; and education, 38; and electoral politics, 66; and literary clubs, 78, 105, 112; World War I efforts of, 244, 245; and woman suffrage, 279; and segregation, 329

Smith, Harriet, 4

Smith, Mary Ruffin, 2, 5, 6, 29

Smith, Sidney, 2, 5

Social capital, 31, 112, 117, 132, 139, 140, 153

Southern Education Board, 168–69

Spaulding, Charles C.: education of, 36; as black business leader, 37, 40, 120, 144, 249; and political leadership, 58, 119, 249, 281, 306, 307, 310, 320–21, 328, 335, 336, 337, 341, 342; and respectability, 113; as manager of North Carolina Mutual, 116, 118, 125, 127–28, 133, 135, 147; and Du Bois, 117; marriage of, 124; on education, 130–31, 181–82; on William G. Pearson, 166, 288; World War I efforts of, 218, 222; and black migration, 238, 254; and race relations, 247; and black poverty, 254–55; and black children, 274; and voting rights, 280–81, 385 (n. 81); and NAACP, 292, 309, 313, 316, 317, 319, 321–22, 323, 326–27; and New Deal, 292–93, 297, 333, 387 (n. 18); and state of race, 295; and unions, 305–6; and Democratic Party, 306; and racial violence, 316

Spaulding, Janie, 263–65

Spaulding, Lula, 98

Spaulding & Merrick, 36

Stanton, Elizabeth Cady, 278–79

Star of Zion, 66, 243, 261–62, 279

State Industrial Home for Colored Girls, 275

State Training School for Negro Girls, 274, 275

Stonewall Jackson Training School, 272, 383 (n. 64)

Streator, George, 313, 316–18

Strikes, 23, 43, 93, 302, 303, 328

Subordination of blacks: and Jim Crow, 11, 56; and workers defined by race

and gender, 13; and racial order, 39;
and employment, 45–46, 170, 228,
295; and New Negro, 114; and industrial education, 170–71; and household labor, 268; and working-class
black women, 268, 338

Talented Tenth, 110, 115, 170
Taylor, James T., 306, 318, 319, 389
(n. 18)
Temperance, 34, 35, 46–47, 77, 135
Terrell, Mary Church, 98, 110, 172
Textile industry: and Julian S. Carr Jr.,
41, 92, 93, 122; employment in, 44;
and working-class white women, 44,
45, 84, 92; and working-class black
men, 45, 255, 295; and working-class
black women, 92–93, 94, 95–96, 119,
138, 236–37, 263, 295, 302–3; and
black business, 119, 121–22, 138;
growth in, 223, 253; working conditions in, 377 (n. 23)
Thirteenth Amendment, 5
Thompson, M. Hugh, 319, 323, 326
Thrift, 35, 76, 77, 113, 138
Tobacco factories: and working-class
black women, 15, 16, 18, 21, 22, 43–
46, 88, 90–92, 94, 107, 112, 133, 220,
224–28, 236–37, 259, 282, 289–90,
296, 298–301, 353 (n. 38); instability
of work in, 16, 226, 253; and respectability, 20; and black labor, 43, 51, 52;
and working-class white women, 44,
224; and working-class black men, 45,
226, 255, 256–60; wages in, 94, 224,
243, 299–305, 314, 324, 334; and
black child labor, 225–27, 259
Tobacco industry: growth of, 31, 32, 41,
44, 45, 51, 223–24, 225, 242, 243,
253, 296; and immigrant labor, 42;
working conditions in, 43, 227–32,
239, 243, 263, 290, 329, 334, 377

(n. 23); and unions, 240–43, 299–305,
319, 324, 327; and New Deal, 296,
298–99
Tobacco Workers International Union
(TWIU), 240–43, 299–304, 327, 328,
334
Training: for black teachers, 172, 178,
180–81, 185
Training programs: blacks' access to,
153; for nurses, 159, 164; for midwives, 165, 267; for household labor,
267–69, 274, 275, 282, 288, 297, 298,
321
Trinity College, 69, 84, 180
Tulsa, Okla., 14, 19, 114, 145, 146
Turner, Viola, 131–38, 141, 160, 250,
280–81, 337
Twentieth Century Club, 105, 272, 279

Underground economy, 16, 22, 238
Union Bethel African Methodist Episcopal (AME) Zion Church, 33
Union Insurance and Realty Company,
120
Union League, 1, 28
Unions: value of, 23, 93; and working-
class blacks, 23, 220, 224, 241–42,
299–306, 319, 334, 337–38, 379
(n. 58); and race relations, 42–43, 241,
299–305, 327; and household labor,
43, 94; and labor supply, 69; and
working-class whites, 240, 241–43,
299–301, 337, 379 (n. 58); and
working-class black women, 240, 242,
300–301, 302, 304, 328, 334; and
labor activism, 240–43, 246; and
political leadership, 240–43, 301, 302,
305–6, 334, 336, 337; and New Deal,
299. See also Knights of Labor
University of Maryland v. Murray, 322
University of North Carolina at Chapel
Hill, 310–11, 319, 327, 330

Upbuilding: Du Bois on, 10, 12, 18; and
    class, 10, 108; black women's role in,
    15, 32, 132, 260; black manhood asso-
    ciated with, 18–19; as resistance tac-
    tic, 19; groundwork for, 31; and labor,
    40; and John Merrick, 42; and politi-
    cal leadership, 56; and racial peace,
    56; multiple forms of, 107; and capi-
    tal, 108, 153; and black business, 115,
    117, 121; and black elite, 118, 288–
    89; and public spaces, 253; whites'
    attitudes toward, 332–33. See also
    Racial uplift; Social capital
Urbanization, 15, 88–91, 149, 261, 277,
    332, 350 (n. 21)
U.S. Congress, 58, 59, 278
U.S. Department of Labor, 221, 227
U.S. Supreme Court, 57, 79, 169, 296,
    309, 327, 344

Veil of color, 9–10, 13, 40, 53, 119, 129,
    251–52, 338, 339
Voice of the Negro, 73
Volkamenia Literary Club: and racial
    progress, 78; and literacy, 105, 173,
    283; and voting rights, 105, 306, 324;
    and black professionals, 112; and sup-
    port of black schools, 183–84; and
    clubwomen, 260; and Charlotte
    Hawkins Brown, 270; and woman suf-
    frage, 279; and political discussion,
    384 (n. 78)
Voting rights: and racial violence, 5, 8;
    as instrument of liberation, 40; and
    political leadership, 47, 336; blacks'
    appreciation of, 56; and race relations,
    69, 70, 72–73, 74; and James E.
    Shepard, 76, 77, 152, 281, 385 (n. 81),
    385–86 (n. 88); and black women, 99,
    281, 282, 307–8, 324, 328; and liter-
    acy, 101, 166, 168, 173; and educa-
    tion, 104, 166; and World War I, 277,
    278, 306; and Independent Voters
    League, 306–7; confrontation over,
    329. See also Black disenfranchise-
    ment; Woman suffrage

Wade, Eula Lee, 129, 134, 250
Walltown Community Council, 328,
    340
Walltown School, 290
Wannamaker, W. H., 175, 176
Warren, Julia McCauley, 78, 105, 244,
    250, 261, 263–65, 273, 281
Warren, Stanford L., 158, 173, 244
Warren, Selena, 173
Warren Library, 173, 174, 304
Washington, Booker T.: and Du Bois,
    13–14; conservatism of, 56; and elec-
    toral politics, 56, 63; on Manly, 63; on
    race relations, 69; on prejudice, 71; on
    New Negro, 74, 115; nationalist
    agenda of, 75; and black elite, 110,
    333; and James B. Dudley, 114; and
    North Carolina Mutual, 116, 117,
    144; and Moore, 122; and black men,
    123; and education, 170, 171; death
    of, 220; and accommodation, 293; on
    upbuilding, 332, 333
Watts, Charles, 371 (n. 23)
Watts, Constance Merrick Moore, 124,
    142, 143, 149, 371 (n. 23)
Watts, George W., 155–56, 371 (n. 23)
Watts Hospital, 156–57
Weare, Walter B., 350 (n. 26), 371
    (n. 13)
Weaver, Robert C., 291–93
Weil, Gertrude, 273, 279, 281–82
Wells-Barnett, Ida B., 62, 85
West End, 32, 140
West End School, 80, 150, 178–79,
    185, 186, 224, 314, 315, 343, 375
    (n. 79)
Wheeler, J. H., 341–42

Whetstone, 136
White, George H., 58
White, George W., 57
White, Walter, 313, 316, 317, 318, 326, 389 (n. 18)
White beneficence: and black schools, 19, 49, 153–54; toward black institutions, 19, 74, 151–52; and health care, 19, 150, 153–54, 156; and black churches, 69, 152; and black elite, 150–51, 152; and education, 169, 170–71, 172, 174, 176, 373 (n. 51); and black children, 272
White children, 168, 178
White manhood, 4
White men: and sexual power over black women, 2, 4, 5, 15, 20, 43, 45, 48, 62, 85, 228, 231, 258–59, 262, 268, 271, 326; and protection of white women, 48, 61–62; elite men, 147, 241; life expectancy of, 149; World War I service of, 218; working-class black women's conflicts with, 220, 224, 226, 227–30, 233
White middle class, 147
White poverty, 48, 61, 178
White power, 11, 48, 278, 334, 335
White Rock Baptist Church, 33–35, 76, 78, 100, 111, 112, 135, 172, 305
White southerners: and racial purity, 4; animosity of, 8, 21, 28, 50, 59, 68, 95, 121, 145, 338; and Jim Crow, 10–11; and black achievements, 13, 114; and color line, 19; attacks on black liberation, 56; and portrayals of blacks, 86–87; attitudes toward education, 165–66, 167, 168, 169–70, 171, 172, 176, 178, 182–83, 186, 311, 374 (n. 55); and woman suffrage, 278; and New Deal, 293, 298; and Durham Manifesto, 329; and race relations, 333
White supremacy: and sexualized

assaults, 4; challenges to, 8, 24, 62, 316; and Jim Crow, 10–11, 19, 84; protection of, 13; and shared struggle, 38; and Democratic Party, 47–48, 60, 64, 293, 307; and electoral politics, 51, 55–56, 57, 59, 60, 61, 63, 64, 67, 70; strengthening of, 53; discourse of, 68; blacks' accommodation of, 71, 74; and black disenfranchisement, 73, 74; and racial violence, 79, 307; Washington on, 116; and compulsory education for whites, 168; and patriotic duty, 219
White teachers, 177–78, 180–81, 312–15, 334, 335
White women: southern womanhood, 2; and racial purity, 4, 48, 62; protection from black men, 4, 59, 60–61, 62, 63; working-class women, 44, 45, 50, 84, 92, 224, 227; and morality of poor whites, 61; and electoral politics, 65; life expectancy of, 149; elite women, 156–57, 220, 244–46, 261, 264–75, 279, 338–39; and cross-racial/cross-class concerns, 162; and YWCA, 263, 264, 265; and woman suffrage, 277, 278–79, 281
Whitted, Bess Johnson, 130, 131, 134, 135–36, 138, 142, 286
Whitted, Dore, 127
Whitted, James A., 34, 36, 47, 48, 49, 50, 69, 103–4
Whitted, Orin Amey, 135
Whitted, Tempie, 34
Whitted School, 36, 150, 166, 179, 181, 186, 187, 226, 245
Wilkins, Roy, 313, 326
Williams, Fannie Barrier, 97, 99, 100
Williams, W. T. B., 233, 378 (n. 39)
Williamson, W. C., 287
Wilmington, N.C., 19, 32, 39, 60, 61–62, 66, 67–70

Wilmington Daily Record, 61–62, 63, 67, 360 (n. 21)

Wilmington Messenger, 63, 64

Wilmington Riot: and black disenfranchisement, 67, 84; news of, 67–68; and race relations, 71–72; memory of, 72, 74, 114, 115, 117, 145, 282, 319, 335; and self-protection, 75; and electoral politics, 78, 119; and democracy, 79

Wilson, Thomas, 311, 312

Wilson, Woodrow, 278

Winston-Salem, N.C., 70, 93, 240, 242, 247, 303, 317, 380 (n. 73)

Woman's Convention, 34, 35, 36, 103–5

Woman suffrage, 20, 220, 277–80, 283, 384–85 (n. 80)

Women's Bureau, 227, 228, 232

Women's Defense Committee, 264

Women's Home and Foreign Missionary Society (WHFMS), 102–3, 105, 270, 273

Women's Home and Foreign Mission Convention, 100, 101

Women's Training School, 104

Wonderland Theater, 251, 253, 304, 305

Wooten, Hattie, 172–73, 244

Working-class black men: and tobacco factories, 45, 226, 255, 256–60; and Jim Crow, 83; and "Work or Fight" laws, 237

Working-class blacks: and respectability, 20, 21, 22; and Jim Crow, 22, 143, 232, 259, 329; leadership of, 22, 352 (n. 38); and black elite, 23, 110, 143, 258, 308, 326, 329, 334–35, 339; and unions, 23, 220, 223, 224, 225, 241–42, 299–306, 319, 334, 337–38, 379 (n. 58); portrayals of, 85, 95; and aspiring class, 96, 107; and North

Carolina Mutual, 118; and identity, 139; and church and civic work, 140; professionals compared to, 154; as parents, 184–85; World War I efforts of, 222; working conditions of, 229, 239–40, 304, 379 (n. 53); migration of, 232, 286; and gender roles, 252, 256, 259–60; and music, 253; and Great Depression, 259, 290; and black elite women, 271; and electoral politics, 283, 307–8; and political leadership, 333. *See also* Black labor

Working-class black women: and racism, 8, 15, 16, 224, 339; and tobacco factories, 15, 16, 18, 21, 22, 43–46, 88, 90–92, 94, 107, 112, 133, 220, 224–28, 236–37, 259, 282, 289–90, 296, 298–301, 353 (n. 38); and household labor, 15, 16, 18, 21, 32, 43, 44, 46, 52, 83, 86, 88, 90, 91–92, 94, 112, 231, 236, 267, 353 (n. 38); and respectability, 20, 259, 326; and economic conditions, 44, 253; and race hierarchy, 46, 231; and Jim Crow, 83, 143; and textile industry, 92–93, 94, 95–96, 119, 138, 236–37, 263, 295, 302–3; portrayals of, 95–96, 267; resistance of, 106–8; as teachers, 155; education of, 226; working conditions of, 227–32, 242, 254, 262, 263, 274, 334, 337; and unions, 240, 242, 300–301, 302, 304, 328, 334; and black womanhood, 252; subordination of, 268, 338; needs of, 269

Working-class whites, 240, 241–43, 299–301, 337, 379 (n. 58)

Working-class white women, 44, 45, 50, 84, 92, 224, 227

World War I: black men's service in, 217–20; home front efforts in, 218, 220, 222–23, 243–46, 260–61, 278,

338–39; resistance of black men to service in, 221; black migration during, 222, 223, 233–34, 240; and tobacco production, 225; and labor demands, 232; and population shifts of black women, 233; and race relations, 244–45, 246, 338–39; parade supporting, 246–47; and voting rights, 277, 278, 306; and unions, 299

World War II, 233, 328

Wright, John, 36

YWCA, 18, 134, 227, 262, 263–69, 275–76, 303–4, 328, 369 (n. 58), 381 (n. 31)

www.ingramcontent.com/pod-product-compliance
Lightning Source LLC
Chambersburg PA
CBHW031822270326
41932CB00008B/515